Entrepreneurship

A SOUTH AFRICAN PERSPECTIVE

Gideon **Nieman**

Johan **Hough**

Cecile **Nieuwenhuizen**

(Editors)

Van Schaik
PUBLISHERS

Published by Van Schaik Publishers
1064 Arcadia Street, Hatfield, Pretoria
All rights reserved
Copyright © 2003 Van Schaik Publishers

First edition 2003
Second impression 2004

ISBN 0 627 02544 7

Commissioning editor Leanne Martini
Production manager Ernst Schlatter
Editorial coordinator Daleen Venter
Copy editor Aïda Thorne
Proofreader Wendy Priilaid
Cover design by Andrew Ford
Typeset in 9.5 on 11 pt ITC Century Book by Pace-Setting & Graphics, Pretoria
Printed and bound by Paarl Print, Oosterland Street, Daljosafat, Paarl, South Africa

Overview of contents

Table of contents

Van Schaik
Publishers

Part C: Alternative routes to entrepreneurship

Part D: Post-start-up challenges

Part F: Case studies

Editors and contributors

Editors

Prof. G.H. Nieman – BCom (Acc), MBA (UP), PhD (Vista), is an associate professor and coordinator of the Chair in Entrepreneurship at the University of Pretoria.

Prof. Johan Hough – MSc Agric (UP), DCom (Unisa), is a professor of business management, and chairman of entrepreneurship and innovation management at the University of Stellenbosch.

Prof. Cecile Nieuwenhuizen – MBL (Unisa), PhD (PU for CHE), is a professor in the MTech Business Administration and entrepreneurship programmes at Technikon SA.

Contributors

Ms M.N. Adams – MCom (UWC), is a lecturer in entrepreneurship in the Department of Business Management at the University of Stellenbosch.

Mr A.J. Antonites – BCom (cum laude), BCom (Hons), MCom (Pret), is a senior lecturer in entrepreneurship in the Entrepreneurship Section of the Department of Business Management at the University of South Africa.

Prof. L.E.R. de Vries – BCom (Hons) and HED (UWC), MBA (US), is an associate professor and Head of the Department of Management at the University of the Western Cape.

Ms H. Jacobs – MCom (RAU), is a senior lecturer in entrepreneurship and international business and head of the Strategic Management Honours Programme at the Rand Afrikaans University.

Mr M.W. Ladzani – BCom (Unizul), BCom (Hons) (Unisa), MBA (Pret), is a senior lecturer in entrepreneurship and small business at Technikon SA.

Prof. J.A.A. Lazenby – BCom (Hons), MA, MBA, DPhil (UFS) is an associate professor in business management and the programme director of Private Sector Management at the University of the Free State.

Prof. G. Maas – PhD (US), holds the International Chair in Entrepreneurship at the PE Technikon and Rhodes University.

Mr P.E. Mayhew – BCom (Hons) (Business Management) is a student at the University of Pretoria.

Mr J. Nel – MCom (UFS) is a lecturer in business management at the University of the Free State.

Ms B. Nhlengethwa – BCom, BCom (Hons) (Pret), M Phil (Pret), is a junior lecturer in entrepreneurship at the University of Pretoria.

Dr M. Pretorius – BSc Agric (UP), MSc Agric (University of the North), MBL (Unisa) and DTech (Pretoria), is a senior lecturer in entrepreneurship in the Department of Business Management at the University of Pretoria.

Prof. F.W. Struwig – MCom (UPE), HED (UPE), PhD (Vista), is an associate professor and Head of the Department of Business Management at Vista University (Port Elizabeth campus).

Ms M. van der Merwe – BCom (Tourism), MPhil in entrepreneurship (UP), is a lecturer in entrepreneurship at the University of Pretoria.

Preface

Entrepreneurship education has experienced remarkable growth in the last three decades. Entrepreneurship became the buzzword of the 1990s in South Africa and the need for a major work on entrepreneurship for universities and technikons soon became apparent. The editors of and contributors to this book are all involved in entrepreneurship teaching at the major universities and technikons in South Africa. Through these different contributions we were able to get a wonderful osmosis of new thoughts and approaches to the subject matter.

This book was written with the intention of filling a number of gaps in the South African academic market. It provides an original text that comprehensively describes and illustrates entrepreneurship and new venture creation within a South African context. It is also aimed at both graduate and undergraduate students in particular, through a reader-friendly text, exercises and activities, and case studies.

In this book we have followed basically two points of departure. The first is the entrepreneurial process for new venture creation. Parts B to D of the book take the reader through this process, as well as the post-start-up challenges that the entrepreneur will have to face once the business is in operation. Part A of the book looks at entrepreneurship and entrepreneurs, and is a guide as to what is required to become a successful entrepreneur.

The second point of departure was the aspects that are critical to the entrepreneur during the venture life cycle. Part B covers the start-up process, Part C the growth stages while Part D looks at the challenges in the maturity phase of the business. Corporate venturing is discussed in Part E, and Part F presents several South African case studies.

We wish to thank the contributors to the book, as well as our project manager, Leanne Martini, and other staff of Van Schaik Publishers who worked behind the scenes to bring this book to fruition.

Please feel free to share your experiences of, and problems with, the use of this book. We welcome any recommendations for future editions. You can direct your comments to us by email at: ghnieman@hakuna.up.ac.za.

This book is dedicated to Anton Rupert, one of the great entrepreneurs of this country and honorary professor for many years at the Department of Business Management at the University of Pretoria.

Gideon Nieman (Editor-in-Chief)
Johan Hough (Co-editor)
Cecile Nieuwenhuizen (Co-editor)

January 2003

Ⓒ Van Schaik Publishers

PART **A**

Entrepreneurship and entrepreneurs

1

The nature and development of entrepreneurship

Cecile Nieuwenhuizen

1.1 Introduction

Economic development can be directly attributed to the level of entrepreneurial activity in a country (Schumpeter 1934; Bird 1989). Entrepreneurial businesses ensure growth in the economy. Large corporations retrench, automate, downsize, unbundle, outsource and become smaller. Entrepreneurs intend to grow their businesses and are responsible for growth and job creation in the economy. Although entrepreneurs mostly own their own businesses, they can also be part of a team owning a business, or in large corporations or firms, or even in the public sector.

Most entrepreneurial activity takes place in small, medium and micro-enterprises (SMMEs). According to the Ntsika Annual Review, SMMEs form 97,5 per cent of all businesses in South Africa. They generate 34,8 per cent of the gross domestic product (GDP), contribute to 42,7 per cent of the total value of salaries and wages paid in South Africa, and employ 54,5 per cent of all formal private sector employees (Diederichs 2001: 64).

As an introduction to entrepreneurship as a field of study, this chapter describes the entrepreneur, the orientation of the entrepreneur and how this person differs from a small business owner. The entrepreneurial process – including the identification of opportunities, development of a business plan, identification and application of resources and the start-up and management of the business – is introduced and forms the basis of this book. The entrepreneurial and managerial success factors of successful entrepreneurs are discussed to give insight into what entrepreneurs do in the establishment and management of their businesses. To conclude, the development of entrepreneurship as a science and the impetus entrepreneurship gives to the economy is addressed.

Learning outcomes

After completion of this chapter, you should be able to:

- Identify the contribution of entrepreneurs to the economy
- Describe the development of entrepreneurship theory
- Identify the research trends in entrepreneurship
- Determine what is involved in the orientation of entrepreneurs
- Discuss and define the concept of entrepreneurship
- Differentiate between entrepreneurial and small business ventures
- Describe the entrepreneurial process
- Explain the domains of entrepreneurship, leadership and management
- Distinguish between the entrepreneurial and managerial functions of an entrepreneur
- Analyse the entrepreneurial and managerial success factors that contribute to successful entrepreneurship
- Evaluate the impetus of entrepreneurship in the economy

1.2 The economic impetus of entrepreneurship

It is important to note that the combination of all businesses, namely small, micro- and medium-sized enterprises as well as large national and international businesses, determines the state of the economy. The South African economy has declined over the past twenty years. The gross domestic product (GDP) is the total final production within a country's geographic boundaries and is used to determine the growth or decline of a country's economy. The year-on-year change in the value of real GDP determines the economic growth rate of a country. In the 1960s, South Africa's GDP averaged nearly 6 per cent per year. This means that the economy of the country improved with 6 per cent per year. During the 1980s, the GDP decreased to 2,2 per cent, with no growth in the 1990s.

Employment is closely linked to the state of the economy. When there is no growth in the economy, there are fewer employment opportunities available. The availability of employment in our country is at an all-time low, with an approximate unemployment rate of 30 per cent.

The success of other leading countries in the world, such as the United States of America, Japan and England, has proven that the only growth sector in the economy is the SMME sector, driven by entrepreneurs. This means that SMMEs are being established and grow. In contrast, employees of large businesses are often laid off or become self-employed. They also become employed by new SMMEs that are formed as some of the activities of large businesses are contracted out. In addition, some of the sections of these large businesses are closed down or sold off to function as SMMEs.

Once again, entrepreneurs play an important role. They are responsible for the formation of new businesses to which non-core functions are outsourced, to take over or buy the sections that would have been closed down. An example is three employees of a large mining group who decided to buy two mines that would have been closed down. They had experience in the field and developed a plan, took some risks, started off with a loan, took over the operations, restructured and made some crucial changes. They have been extremely profitable, are growing and are considering buying additional mines to provide employment to many. The importance of entrepreneurs is therefore crucial for the improvement of the South African economy and is also regarded as the best employment opportunity that exists.

Think, for example, what the entrepreneur Mark Shuttleworth, who started an Internet-related business, means to our country. He filled a much-needed gap by issuing Internet companies with a certificate to verify that they are properly registered businesses and therefore safe for the public to do business with. His biggest competitor, an American company, bought him out for R3,5 billion – this is money that at least partially comes to South Africa. Although Mr Shuttleworth is an exceptional example of the value of an entrepreneur to the economy of the country, other successful entrepreneurs – albeit not to such an extent – also contribute positively to the economy of the country.

1.3 The development of entrepreneurship theory

The progress in entrepreneurship research and our understanding of entrepreneurs can be divided into five periods, according to Fillion (1991). In a study of the trends in entrepreneurship, Fillion coined the development as a movement from entrepreneurship to *entreprenology* and the emergence of a new discipline. Although the periods and development of the theory are not clearly defined, Fillion's work provides what is probably the best perspective on the field. The remainder of this section is, to a great extent, a summary of Fillion's paper. (All the references to authors cited in this section can be sourced from the original article.)

People working in the field of entrepreneurship are convinced that there is a remarkable level of confusion surrounding the definition of an entrepreneur. We prefer the term "difference". Researchers tend to perceive and define entrepreneurs using the premises of their own disciplines. Taken from this standpoint, the confusion is perhaps not as great as people would have us believe, because similarities in the perception of the entrepreneur emerge within each discipline. For example, the economists have associated entrepreneurs with innovation, whereas the behaviourists have concentrated on the creative and intuitive characteristics of entrepreneurs. We will look more closely at these two standpoints in the following subsections.

1.3.1 The economists

First, we must qualify the popular belief that entrepreneurship originated from the science of economics alone. A careful reading of the first two authors usually identified as the pioneers in the field, Cantillon (1755) and Say (1803, 1815, 1816, 1839), reveals that they were interested not only in the economy but also in the managerial aspects of enterprises, business development and business management. Cantillon was a banker who would be described as a venture capitalist today. His writings reveal a man seeking business opportunities, with a concern for shrewd, economic management and obtaining optimal yields on invested capital.

Venn (1982) examined the origin and development of the term "entrepreneur", revealing that it acquired its current meaning in the 17th century. Although the term was used before Cantillon, it is clear, as Schumpeter (1954) pointed out, that Cantillon was the first to offer a clear conception of the entrepreneurial function as a whole.

Jean-Baptiste Say was the second author to take an interest in entrepreneurs. He regarded economic development as the result of venture creation, and hoped that the English Industrial Revolution would spread to France (Say 1815, 1816) Cantillon and Say regarded entrepreneurs as risk takers, basically because they invested their own money. In Cantillon's view, entrepreneurs bought raw material – often a farm product – at a certain price, in order to process it and resell it at an uncertain price. Entrepreneurs were therefore people who seized opportunities with a view to making profits, and who assumed the inherent risks. Say drew a distinction between the entrepreneur and the capitalist, and between their profits (Say 1803, 1827, 1815, 1816; Schumpeter 1954). In doing so, he associated entrepreneurs with innovation and viewed them as change agents. He himself was an entrepreneur and became the first to define the boundaries of what an entrepreneur, in the modern sense of the term, actually is. Schumpeter (1954) admitted that a major part of his own contribution was to tell the Anglo-Saxon community about the world of the entrepreneur, as described in the writings of Jean-Baptiste Say. As Say was the first to lay a foundation for the field, he has been described as the father of entrepreneurship.

It is, perhaps, interesting to note that Say basically drew together two major trends of thought of his time: that of the physiocrats and that of the Industrial Revolution in Great Britain. He was a great admirer of Adam Smith (1776), whose ideas he brought to France, and of the English Industrial Revolution (Say 1816). In fact, he tried to establish a framework of thought that would enable the Industrial Revolution to move across the Channel to France. He applied to entrepreneurship the liberal thinking proposed by Quesnay, Mercier de La Rivière, Mirabeau, Condorced, Turgot and other physiocrats as a means of developing farming.

However, it was Schumpeter (1928) who really launched the field of entrepreneurship, by associating it clearly with innovation:

> The essence of entrepreneurship lies in the perception and exploration of new opportunities in the realm of business... it always has to do with bringing about a different use of national resources in that they are withdrawn from their traditional employ and subjected to new combinations.

Not only did Schumpeter associate entrepreneurs with innovation, but his imposing work also shows the importance of entrepreneurs in explaining economic development.

In fact, he was not the only one to associate entrepreneurship with innovation. Clark (1899) had done so quite clearly some time before, and Higgins (1959), Baumol (1968), Schloss (1968), Leibstein (1978) and most of the economists who took an interest in entrepreneurship after him also did the same. The economists were mainly interested in understanding the role played by the entrepreneur as the motor of the economic system (Smith 1776; Mill 1848; Knight 1921; Innis 1930, 1956; Baumol 1968; Broehl 1978; Leff 1978, 1979; Kent et al. 1982). From this standpoint, the economists viewed entrepreneurs as "detectors" of business opportunities (Higgins 1959; Penrose 1959; Kirzner

1976), creators of enterprises (Ely & Hess 1893; Oxenfeldt 1943; Schloss 1968) and risk takers (Leibenstein 1968; Kihlstom & Lafont, 1979; Buchanan & Di Pierro 1980). Hayek (1937, 1959) pointed out that the role of entrepreneurs was to inform the market of new elements. Knight (1921) showed that entrepreneurs assumed a risk because of the state of uncertainty in which they worked and that they were rewarded accordingly by profits they made from the activities they initiated. Hoselitz (1952, 1968) spoke of a higher level of tolerance that enabled entrepreneurs to work in conditions of ambiguity and uncertainty. Casson (1982) made an interesting attempt to develop a theory linking entrepreneurs with economic development. He emphasised the aspect of resource coordination and decision making. Leibenstein (1979) had already established a model for measuring the level of efficiency and inefficiency in the use of resources by entrepreneurs.

Entrepreneurs are mentioned in economics, but they appear very seldom – and sometimes not at all – in the classical models of economic development. Where they are present, they are represented by a function. The economists who took an interest in entrepreneurs were usually marginals, as was the case in other disciplines. If we were to summarise the main economic trends of thought on entrepreneurship, we would probably accept the standpoint of Baumol (1993), who proposed two categories of entrepreneurs: the entrepreneur-business organiser and the entrepreneur-innovator. The former includes the classical entrepreneur described by Say (1803), Knight (1921) and Kirzner (1983), and the latter the entrepreneur described by Schumpeter (1934).

It is never easy to introduce elements of nationality into the complex behaviour of entrepreneurs. One of the criticisms that can be levelled at the economists is that they have not been able to make economic science evolve. They have also been unable to create a science of the economic behaviour of entrepreneurs. Casson (1982) went as far as he could go in terms of what is quantifiable and acceptable in economic science. The economists' refusal to accept non-quantifiable models clearly demonstrates the limits of this science in entrepreneurship. In fact, it was one of the elements that led the world of entrepreneurship to turn

to behaviourists for more in-depth knowledge of the entrepreneur's behaviour.

1.3.2 The behaviourists

For the purpose of this chapter, the term "behaviourists" includes the psychologists, psychoanalysts, sociologists and other specialists of human behaviour. One of the first authors from this group to show an interest in entrepreneurs was Max Weber (1930). He identified the value system as a fundamental element in explaining entrepreneurial behaviour. He viewed entrepreneurs as innovators, independent people whose role as business leaders conveyed a source of formal authority. However, the author who really launched the contribution of the behavioural sciences to entrepreneurship was undoubtedly David C. McClelland.

McClelland (1961, 1971) did not define entrepreneurs in the same way as the rest of the literature. His definition was as follows:

> An entrepreneur is someone who exercises control over production that is not just for his personal consumption. According to my definition, for example, an executive in a steel-producing unit in the USSR is an entrepreneur.

In fact, McClelland's (1971) work concentrated on managers of large organisations. Although he is strongly associated with the field of entrepreneurship, a careful reading of his writings shows that he never made a connection between the need for achievement and the decision to launch, own or even manage a business. McClelland also identified the need for power, but he paid less attention to this aspect in his later work, and it is less well known. A number of researchers have related it to entrepreneurial success (Durand & Shea 1974; Hundall 1971; Shagne 1965; Singh & Singh 1972).

After McClelland, the behaviourists dominated the field of entrepreneurship for 20 years, until the early 1980s. Their goal was to define entrepreneurs and their characteristics. The behavioural sciences were expanding rapidly, and there was more consensus on the most valid and reliable research methodologies than in other disciplines. The movement was reflected in research on a number of subjects, including entrepreneurs. Thousands of publications described a whole series of entrepreneurial characteristics.

In reality, one of the conclusions to be drawn with respect to the characteristics of entrepreneurs can be summarised as the social being. Human beings are products of their environment. A number of authors have shown that entrepreneurs reflect the characteristics of the period and the place in which they live (Ellis 1983; Fillion 1991; Gibb & Ritchie 1981; Julien & Marchesnay 1996; McGuire 1964, 1976; Newman 1981; Toulouse 1979). Seen from the viewpoint of entrepreneurial behaviour, entrepreneurship seems first and foremost to be a regional phenomenon.

To conclude, it is clear that we have not yet established a scientific profile that allows us to identify potential entrepreneurs with any certainty. However, we know enough about entrepreneurial characteristics to enable would-be entrepreneurs to situate themselves. In fact, the scope of the term "behaviour" has been extended, and it is no longer the exclusive province of the behaviourists. Research is tending to move towards other spheres, such as the skills and competencies required for a person to function well in the activities related to the entrepreneurial trade.

1.3.3 The explosion of the field of entrepreneurship

In the 1980s the field of entrepreneurship exploded and spilled over into almost all the soft sciences and management sciences. The transition was marked by two events: the publication of the first-ever encyclopaedia containing the state of the art in the field (Kent et al. 1982), and the first major annual conference (The Babson Conference) dedicated to research in the new field.

It is interesting to note that the development of entrepreneurship as a discipline did not follow the same pattern as other disciplines. In fact, large numbers of researchers, each using a culture, logic and methodology established to varying degrees in their own fields, began to take an interest in the field of entrepreneurship.

The first doctoral graduates in entrepreneurship and small business appeared in the 1980s. Nevertheless, the vast majority of those interested in the field were from disciplines other than entrepreneurship, and the study of entrepreneurship was not their main field of activity. Now, however, more people are devoting time and effort exclusively to entrepreneurship. The number of venture creations is growing, and the share of gross national product attributable to small business in all countries is increasing every year. To follow the development and needs of their students and clients, many professors are having to learn more about entrepreneurship and small business. Thus, the assimilation and integration of entrepreneurship into the other disciplines, especially the soft sciences and management sciences, are unique as a phenomenon, and has never before occurred to such an extent in the paradigmatic construction of a soft science discipline.

Progress in research and in our understanding of entrepreneurs can be divided into five periods, as shown in Table 1.1.

The thinking about entrepreneurs first established by Cantillon (1755) began from a venture capital and economic perspective around 1700. This viewpoint is still progressing, although it lost its leadership to the behaviourist perspective in the 1950s. The behaviourists led the field for several decades. Their approach to the study of entrepreneurs, while still progressing, has been less dominant since the 1980s, when management scientists of all kinds were working to identify more appropriate support systems for entrepreneurs. The 1990s, on the other hand, have produced more research that can be applied to help the practice of entrepreneurial action, in particular regarding entrepreneurial activities and the related competencies.

It is interesting to observe that the emergence of a research perspective in the field of entrepreneurship is limited by, and has not generally led to an evolution in the original discipline. For instance, the proliferation of behavioural studies of entrepreneurs was a consequence of the emergence of the behavioural science itself, not vice versa, and the limits of that science were clearly revealed in the limited understanding of entrepreneurial behaviour that it produced. Thus, the science of entrepreneurship is, to some extent, fettered by the limitations of source paradigms that have evolved as a result of their application to entrepreneurship, and by its own inability to generate new paradigms with existing tools.

Table 1.1 Research trends in entrepreneurship

Period	Topics	Authors and researchers
1. What entrepreneurs do 1700– (1950)	From an economic perspective	Cantillon, Say, Schumpeter
2. Who entrepreneurs are 1960–(1980)	From a behaviourist perspective	Weber, McClelland, Rotter, De Vries
3. What entrepreneurs do 1980–	From a management science perspective (finance, marketing, operations, human resources)	Drucker, Mintzberg
4. What support is needed by entrepreneurs 1985–	From a social perspective, including economists, geographers and sociologists	Gartner, Welsh, Bygrave, Reynold
5. What entrepreneurial activities are, and what competencies are required to perform them 1990–	From an entrepreneurship perspective	Timmons, Vesper, Brockhaus

Source: Adapted from Fillion (1991).

1.3.4 The development of entreprenology

Why do we need entreprenology? In our own case, we have been using terms such as entrepreneurology – the study of entrepreneurial behaviour in a broad sense – and entreprenology – the study of the overall entrepreneurial process – in the classroom for the last decade. Scott and Anderson (1994) also used the term "entreprenology", associating it with the creation and extraction of value. Others have used it in verbal presentations. The meanings given to the term by the various users clearly show the diversity of definitions of an entrepreneur and entrepreneurship, which generally reflect the core disciplines used as a basis for the studies in question.

However, we now seem to have reached a point where we need a more integrated, more comprehensive understanding of the entrepreneurial process, covering not only individual entrepreneurial behaviour but also the more complex forces of entrepreneurship (Fillion, 1997b.) In other words, the term "entreprenology" could be used to designate a comprehen-

sive, multidisciplinary understanding of the entire entrepreneurial process.

The field of entrepreneurship can be defined as one that studies the practices of entrepreneurs. It examines their activities, characteristics, economic and social effects and the support methods used to facilitate the expression of entrepreneurial activity. However, to create a theory of the entrepreneur, it will be necessary to separate applied research from studies of entrepreneurs by entreprenologists in the various disciplines. Entrepreneurship itself would continue as an applied research field, producing results of interest to practising and potential entrepreneurs. However, several thousand more publications will be published, and perhaps a few more decades will have elapsed, before we finally reach this point.

1.4 Defining entrepreneurship, the entrepreneur, small businesses and entrepreneurial ventures

It is often said that confusion reigns in the field of entrepreneurship because there is no consensus on the definition of an entrepreneur and the boundaries of the paradigm. However, the reverse may also be true – entrepreneurship is one of the rare subjects that attracts specialists from such a wide range of disciplines, leading them to discuss and observe what others are doing in related disciplines, and to question how they are doing it. In fact, the confusion seems greatest if we compare the definitions of an entrepreneur between disciplines (Fillion 1991).

On the other hand, if we compare the definitions produced by specialists within the same field, we find a quite astonishing consensus. The economists tend to agree that entrepreneurs are associated with innovation and are seen as the driving forces of development. The behaviourists ascribe to the characteristics of mainly the flexible interpretative models. Any theory of entrepreneurship must be flexible and multidimensional to reflect its multidisciplinary roots.

1.4.1 Entrepreneur and entrepreneurship

Entrepreneurship is the emergence and growth of new businesses. The motivation for entrepreneurial activities is to make profits. Entrepreneurship is also the process that causes changes in the economic system through innovations of individuals who respond to opportunities in the market. In the process, entrepreneurs create value for themselves and society. Defining an entrepreneur remains a problem, as academics and researchers never seem to come to an agreement on the definition. Some definitions of entrepreneurship are given below.

An entrepreneur is an individual who establishes and manages a business for the main purposes of profit and growth. The entrepreneur is characterised principally by innovative behaviour and will employ strategic management practices in the business (Carland et al. 1984: 358). The distinguishing factors of entrepreneurs are most strongly innovation, and then opportunity recognition and growth in a business (Watson 2001: 50). An entrepreneurial venture is one that engages in at least one of Schumpeter's four categories of behaviour.

Hisrich and Peters (1998) see the entrepreneur as someone creating something new with value by devoting time and effort, assuming the accompanying financial, physical and social risks, and receiving the resulting rewards of monetary and personal satisfaction and independence.

Timmons (2000) believes entrepreneurship is the process of creating or seizing an opportunity and pursuing it, regardless of the resources currently controlled.

For the purpose of this book the following definition has been developed:

> An entrepreneur is a person who sees an opportunity in the market, gathers resources and creates and grows a business venture to meet these needs. He or she bears the risk of the venture and is rewarded with profit if it succeeds.

Taking key concepts from a number of definitions, including the ones above, one can identify some important aspects of entrepreneurship and the entrepreneur (Nieman & Bennett 2002: 58):

- *Identifying an opportunity:* This means that there must be a real business opportunity.
- *Innovation and creativity:* Something new and different is required.
- *Getting resources:* Capital labour and operating equipment must be found.
- *Creating and growing a venture:* This refers to the starting of a new business venture or the conversion of an existing business.
- *Taking risk:* This means that there will be personal and financial risk involved for the person who embarks on the entrepreneurial process.
- *Being rewarded:* Reward is an essential element of the free market system. It can be in the form of profit or an increase in the value of the business.
- *Managing the business:* This means that there must be planning, organisation, leadership and control of all the functions in the business venture.

Entrepreneurs prefer to be in control of their own businesses, but can also be found in large corporations where they have the freedom to build their own organisation in their own way with profit motives. They are then referred to as intrapreneurs or corporate entrepreneurs.

1.4.2 Small business

It is important to distinguish between entrepreneurial ventures and small businesses. Both are critical to the performance of the economy but serve different economic functions. Wickham (2001) believes that they pursue and create new opportunities differently, they fulfil the ambitions of their founders and managers in different ways, and they present different challenges to economic policy makers. Both need entrepreneurial action for start-up, but the small business venture will tend to stabilise at a certain stage and only grow with inflation.

Small business owners are individuals who establish and manage their businesses for the principal purpose of furthering personal goals and ensuring security. The activities of artisan/craftsman, administration/manager and security/family are indicated as characteristics of small business ownership (Watson 2001: 50). Therefore, a small business is any business that is independently owned and operated, but is not dominant in its field and does not engage in any new marketing or innovative practices (Carland et al. 1984: 358).

This definition is not much different from the criteria listed in the National Small Business Act, Act 102 of 1996. The Act offers an official definition of small business in South Africa. This definition covers all sectors of the economy, as well as all types of enterprises, and consists of two parts – qualitative and quantitative criteria.

In terms of the qualitative criteria, which relate to the ownership structure of the business, it must:

- Be a separate and distinct business entity
- Not be part of a group of companies
- Include any subsidiaries and branches when measuring the size
- Be managed by its owners
- Be a natural person, sole proprietorship, partnership or a legal person, such as a close corporation or company

The quantitative criteria are presented in the Schedule to the Act and classify businesses into micro-, very small, small and medium, using the following guidelines in respect of different sectors of the economy:

- Total full-time paid employees
- Total annual turnover
- Total gross asset value (excluding fixed property)

Owners of small businesses are not necessarily interested in growth as an objective. They see themselves as successful when their businesses are profitable. Autonomy and security are the primary objectives of some owners of small businesses. They consider themselves successful even if they earn a smaller income than they would have as employees. Quite often the small business only supports a certain lifestyle of the owner.

1.4.3 Entrepreneurial ventures

Entrepreneurial ventures are businesses where the principal objectives are profitability and growth. Three characteristics distinguish the entrepreneurial venture from the small business (Wickham 2001):

- *Innovation:* Entrepreneurial ventures thrive on innovation, be it a technological innovation, a new product or a new way of producing, offering a service, marketing or distributing, or even the way in which an organisation is structured or managed. Small business is usually only involved in delivering an established product or service.

- *Potential for growth:* Due to its innovative approach, an entrepreneurial venture has a great deal more potential for growth than a small business. It is in a position to create its own market. The small business operates in an established industry and is unique only in terms of its locality. It operates within a given market.

- *Strategic objectives:* The entrepreneurial venture will usually set itself strategic objectives in relation to:
  - Market targets
  - Market development
  - Market share
  - Market position

The small business rarely cares about these aspects. Its objectives seldom go beyond survival, sales and profit targets.

Entrepreneurial ventures are the ones that create employment. Although small businesses and entrepreneurial ventures both need entrepreneurial action for start-up, the small business will tend to stabilise at a certain stage and only grow with inflation.

1.5 A model for entrepreneurial development

Our model for entrepreneurship in countries attempts to demonstrate in their relative context the external variables that affect entrepreneurship in any given country. Such a model must therefore evaluate the influence of the business environment. The important elements that play a role in the development of a model for entrepreneurship are depicted in Figure 1.1 and discussed in the rest of this section (Maasdorp & Van Vuuren 1998: 720).

1.5.1 Entrepreneurial orientation

Entrepreneurial orientation is critical to the survival and growth of firms, as well as the eco-

nomic prosperity of nations. Entrepreneurial orientation is crucial for the process of entrepreneurial development at the societal level of countries. Entrepreneurial orientation is fostered by a unique blend of factors, such as culture, family and role models, education, work experience and personal orientation.

■ Culture

Policy makers in the government need to take heed of the influence of culture on entrepreneurial orientation. In some cultures, for example the United States, entrepreneurs are recognised and celebrated, there is no stigma attached to failure of a business, and role models are visible and not only distant celebrities. Entrepreneurship is seen as a desirable career choice and very often the career of first choice. In societies with entrepreneurial cultures, people have a high need for achievement and there is a proliferation of entrepreneurial ventures.

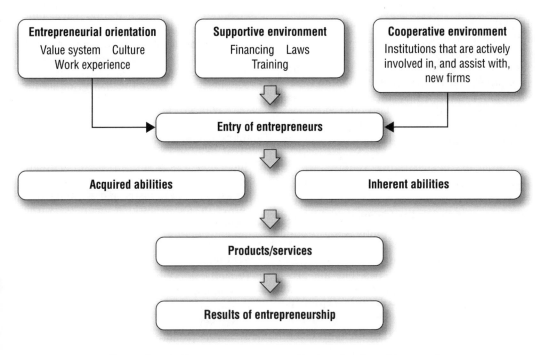

Figure 1.1 A model for entrepreneurship

Compare, for instance, the entrepreneurial culture of the United States with that of Russia, where communism ruled. Everything in the USSR was owned and managed by the state and business ownership was not allowed. Only recently, with the fall of communism, could private businesses be established. This caused a serious backlog with regard to private enterprise and the development of an entrepreneurial culture. Very few role models exist in Russian and similar societies, and experiences, education and skills are not oriented towards private enterprise.

The research by Hofstede on cultural differences and cultural similarities between nations is generally regarded as the best source. Kanungo concluded that four sociocultural dimensions distinguished developing countries from developed countries (as cited in Themba et al. 1999). According to Kanungo, developing nations (in particular, in sub-Saharan Africa) are relatively high on power distance and avoidance of uncertainty, and low on individualism and "masculinity". In societies with high power distance, social institutions such as the family, school and organisations believe strongly in the hierarchy of authority. In tradition-bound societies, authority and control are based largely on factors such as age and kinship. This denies people the opportunity to develop decision-making skills and the self-confidence to run a business, and has inhibited entrepreneurship in African countries.

High avoidance of uncertainty implies a tendency to shy away from uncertain situations or an inherent unwillingness to take risks. Also associated with this behaviour is the fear of failure. Low individualism implies a greater predisposition towards family or group interests than individual interests (collectivism). The pursuit of collective interests, which characterises most African societies, has not promoted the spirit of independence and self-reliance that individuals need to be more enterprising. A society that is characterised by low "masculinity" has a low drive for achievement. This may be the reason why people in developing nations tend to be so heavily dependent on the government to provide for their needs, instead of seeking their own solutions. High-need achievers tend to stimulate the economic growth and prosperity of a nation (Themba et al. 1999).

■ Family and role models

The extent to which individuals are exposed to entrepreneurial activities in their direct circumstances, such as the activities of family members and other role models, also increases the propensity towards entrepreneurship. Children who grow up in families where family members are entrepreneurs are more inclined to start their own businesses or become involved in the family businesses.

■ Education

Successful entrepreneurship has also been directly linked to education. Tertiary education can provide valuable additional entrepreneurial capacity, particularly for high-potential entrepreneurs (Driver et al. 2001: 57). These findings indicate that entrepreneurship can be developed by education and can be learned. In addition, a focus on teaching learners to become employers rather than employees will contribute to increased levels of entrepreneurship in a society.

■ Work experience

The type of work and skills gained in the workplace contributes to an individual's entrepreneurial orientation. Entrepreneurs often gain experience as employees and then apply the knowledge, skills and experience gained in employment in their own businesses.

■ Personal orientation

Personal entrepreneurial orientation is based on a number of dimensions:

- Creativity and innovation (experimentation)
- Autonomy (independence)
- Risk taking
- Proactiveness (taking initiative, and pursuing and anticipating opportunities)
- Competitive aggressiveness (achievement oriented)

These characteristics and traits are discussed in detail in Chapter 2.

1.5.2 The supportive environment

In modern society the environment should create a climate favourable to the entry of entrepreneurs. Some decisive factors in a supportive environment are the possibility of financing for small businesses, the training and development of entrepreneurs, the available infrastructure, and the legal restrictions in the economic sphere. The positive attitude of the entrepreneur's family is also seen as an important supportive source.

- Finance is an important resource in new venture creation. Financing must be available and is mostly supplied by ordinary financial institutions such as banks. However, there also have to be institutions that are prepared to make a certain amount of venture capital (risk capital) available. Government institutions should be actively involved in assisting the development of entrepreneurship by financing schemes and other means.

- Training and development programmes should include views on, and encourage entrepreneurship. Positive attitudes to taking calculated risk should be cultivated and information about the management process should be given. The criticism is sometimes expressed that the education and training system in South Africa prepares people to be job seekers instead of job providers.

- Other infrastructure facilities such as roads, bridges and telecommunications networks must exist before there can be any economic activity at an advanced level.

- Deregulation of certain economic activities enables the private sector to engage in activities that were not previously open to it. Restrictions of free trade areas, other trading restrictions and an overabundance of legal regulations and rules may discourage entrepreneurs from exploiting business opportunities.

1.5.3 The cooperative environment

Besides the support and approval of society in general, there should be institutions that are actively involved in promoting entrepreneurship. Universities, technikons and other educational institutions play an important role here. They should do research in order to improve the body of knowledge in this new science, and should build capacity in the supportive environment through formal programmes. School and educational programmes need to encourage and develop entrepreneurs and entrepreneurial orientation.

Large firms and non-governmental organisations also have an important role to play. Through their social responsibility programmes and funds they could help tertiary and other institutions to develop programmes and encourage research. They could also fund and sponsor specific entrepreneurship interventions in previously disadvantaged communities.

1.6 The domains of entrepreneurship, management and leadership

One academic recently posed the question at a conference in South Africa whether there was any difference between entrepreneurship, management and leadership. The answer is rather elementary. All entrepreneurs are not good leaders or managers, but leadership and management skills are critical success factors. All managers and leaders are not necessarily entrepreneurs or entrepreneurially oriented, as one can witness from the fact that many firms go into decline or failure and that many political and social leaders have no entrepreneurial inclination at all. Figure 1.2 below illustrates the domains of entrepreneurship, management and leadership more clearly.

The entrepreneurial process culminates in the last phase of the entrepreneurial process where the business is started and the entrepreneur has to start managing it. There are important differences between the entrepreneurial and managerial functions, as well as the expertise and competence with regard to each.

Entrepreneurial functions include innovative thinking and the identification of opportunities, planning and establishment and/or growth of the business, and application of resources.

After establishing the business, the entrepreneur has to start managing it. The efforts of everyone involved in the business have to be integrated and the different business and managerial functions have to be tied together. Management of the business involves the managerial functions of planning, organising, leading and control. The entrepreneur also has to manage the various business functions, such as finance, marketing, production, purchasing, administration, human resources and public relations.

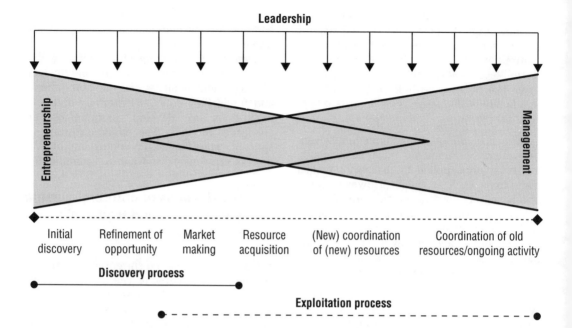

Figure 1.2 The domains of entrepreneurship, management and leadership

There are major differences between these important roles to be played by the entrepreneur, and not all entrepreneurs are equipped to perform all the roles of establishing and managing the business. They often have the natural ability to identify opportunities and establish the business, but need some training, employees or the assistance of specialists to manage the business successfully.

Some academics have also questioned whether entrepreneurship education and courses are not simply traditional management courses with a new label. Traditional business management programmes have a functional or generalist approach that integrates and combines a variety of functional skills and knowledge. They present the functional format as if it were equally applicable to ventures of different sizes and at all levels of development, and as though no differentiation by stage of development is required. While there is general consensus that the core management courses offered in traditional business programmes are essential for success in any business career, there are fundamental differences between business principles applied to new ventures and those applied to large corporations (Solomon et al. 2002).

The core objective of entrepreneurship education is to generate a greater variety of ideas, to show how to exploit a business opportunity and to cover the extensive sequence of actions for entering a business or creating a new venture. Business entry is fundamentally a different activity than managing a business, and entrepreneurship education must address the equivocal nature of business entry. The integrated and applied nature, specific skills and business life cycle issues inherent in new ventures differentiate entrepreneurial education from traditional business education.

The following section addresses the entrepreneurial and managerial success factors of entrepreneurs.

1.7 Success factors of entrepreneurs

Successful entrepreneurs have certain entrepreneurial success factors or personal characteristics, as well as managerial success factors or skills. It is important for entrepreneurs to analyse themselves to know exactly what their strengths and weaknesses are. They can then capitalise on their strengths and concentrate on improving their weak points.

1.7.1 Entrepreneurial success factors

■ Creativity and innovation

Creativity can involve the adjustment or refinement of existing procedures or products, the identification of opportunities and the identification of solutions to problems. Basically it involves new ideas. Any application of new ideas is based on innovation. Although entrepreneurs understand the importance of innovation, they often view the risk and the high investment that the development of innovative products or services require as out of proportion to the profit potential. This explains why owners of small businesses often creatively adapt innovations of competitors by, for example, adjustments to products, marketing and client service.

Although not all entrepreneurs find new products or services or discover new resources, every person who establishes an enterprise, who adds value and who sets out to ensure that an enterprise continues to exist and thereby develops job opportunities, is involved in economic creation. Creativity is used to refine ideas, identify problems and find the accompanying solutions (Bird 1989: 56).

Schein's (1977: 55) study included 44 graduates before they obtained their qualifications and then again three to five years later. He identified career anchors that are associated with various roles, namely those of the entrepreneur, the manager and the professor. The career anchor of entrepreneurs is creativity and innovation; that of the manager competence and effectiveness; and professors choose autonomy in the control of their own time.

Creativity is the generation of new and useable ideas to solve any problem or use any opportunity (Amabile 1996: 36). In the long term, an enterprise's success is determined by the degree to which good ideas are generated, developed and implemented. Creativity consists of people being open to new ideas and new approaches to the business, and focusing on what can be done differently to ensure success in the enterprise. In other words, effective entrepreneurs take the initiative to solve problems in a unique manner.

Creativity underlies innovation and leads to innovation, which then brings about change in the enterprise. Individual creativity is a precursor of the initiation of innovation in enterprises (Glynn 1996: 1098). An individual's ability to think creatively points to creativity, and innovation is the utilisation of creative abilities when establishing something. This can be a new product, service, method, technique or enterprise. The joint creativity of joint attempts by entrepreneurs and staff often also contributes to the development of unique products and services.

■ Risk orientation

Readiness to take risks involves a preparedness to make use of opportunities that are identified, even if there is a possibility of financial loss. Successful owners of small businesses are prepared to take calculated risks and evaluate innovation and risk critically. There is a clear relationship between innovation and readiness to take risks, and a hesitation to take risks hampers innovation.

Successful entrepreneurs do not take chances, but sometimes feel it is necessary to take calculated risks. Unsuccessful entrepreneurs, on the other hand, do not take any risks, or take expensive, impulsive decisions that they do not think through (Boeyens 1989: 80).

Entrepreneurs evaluate themselves positively with regard to their ability to solve problems, their tolerance for conflict and stress, the fact that they take calculated risks and the fact that they can function despite insecurity (Crous et al. 1995: 55). Entrepreneurs investigate the situation and calculate the probable results before they take decisions (Cox & Jennings 1995: 7). Successful entrepreneurs avoid opportunities where there is a high probability that they will be unsuccessful, regardless of the reward involved (Osborne 1995: 5).

Entrepreneurs manage the risk of their enterprise by accepting control and being involved in the basic aspects of the enterprise. They control their enterprise by gaining access to information. They reduce their exposure to financial loss by involving investors, often with the risk of losing control. They shorten the period between the conceptualisation of an idea and making the product or service available in the market. In this way they often limit the risk of competition. Hasty actions often also involve risk, and can be harmful because the incubation period of the idea is insufficient and the time calculation poor (Bird 1989: 88).

■ Leadership

To be comfortable with people and have good personal interactions, to confront problems, to be amenable to differences in opinion, to trust people and to give recognition where it is deserved, is behaviour that is linked to leadership. These are aspects that are taken into account in the success factors of "good human relations" and "involvement in an enterprise".

Leadership in an SME is unique and different to that in a large organisation, and focuses on different forms of interpersonal behaviour. The character, vision and contributions of the business have a direct impact, because the owner is involved in all of these. Team effort and cross-functional approaches are required, because the entrepreneur is often responsible for all or most of the organisational functions. They are multidimensional, with a broad foundation of interests in various disciplines. The influence of decisions is larger in SMEs and they spend less time giving direction and more time bringing out the best in people (Kinni 1995: 2).

Leadership in an enterprise can be compared with a conductor's task. The conductor must select the right music to play for the audience. His hearing must be well developed to identify the best musicians for each instrument and then it is his job to get all the players to play together so that the music sounds as if it comes from one single entity. The aim is to determine how willing the audience is to stand in a queue in order to pay to listen to their music (Pendley 1995: 4).

■ Good human relations

Successful entrepreneurs are team builders and let people feel worthy by giving them responsibility and giving them credit for what they have achieved. They know how to work with people and motivate them, how to build a comprehensive network of contacts which they know will possibly be useful in the future.

Successful entrepreneurs realise the importance of business relationships. They have good relations with clients, see human relations as an important source of the enterprise and regard long-term goodwill as more important than short-term benefits. This success factor has been identified as more typical of successful than average entrepreneurs in developing countries (McClelland 1986: 225).

Four types of human processes that are important for the successful management of people are motivation, team building, communication skills and conflict management (Vega 1996: 56). A study involving 200 owners of small businesses showed that interpersonal communication, intrapersonal communication and motivation were rated as critical skills by all respondents (Eggers & Leahy 1995: 72).

The motivation of employees takes place in various ways. Employees are developed by changing them from people who merely work together to a highly motivated team that understands the vision of the enterprise, supports it and wishes to put it into practice. The team is developed by creating and inspiring loyalty and belief in every team member. The efforts of employees and what they want to achieve are prized and supported. Formal programmes that reward team efforts but also recognise individual contributions are in place. Success is rewarded in a tangible way, and this inspires and motivates action and strengthens trust in, and loyalty to, the leader and the enterprise (Eggers & Leahy 1995: 72).

Most entrepreneurs also regard the motivation of others as more important than self-motivation. Through the collective efforts of others they achieve their own biggest goals (Eggers & Leahy 1995: 72). Self-motivation is more important in the forming phase of the business, while motivation of employees is of critical importance during the growth phase (Barrier 1995: 42).

Research findings show that owners of SMEs realise the importance of business relations. They develop networks, make ownership available to those involved in the enterprise, and display important types of interpersonal behaviour like motivation, persuasion, team building and conflict management. Successful entrepreneurs ensure employee performance by instituting various performance appraisal methods. They realise that they themselves must focus on developing human relations.

■ Positive attitude

Entrepreneurs who have a positive attitude regarding their business will ensure that people will feel positive towards them and will enjoy doing business with them. No one likes doing business with a negative person, and entrepre-

16 ©Van Schaik Publishers

neurs who are unsure of themselves or of their business cannot expect others to believe in them (Zeelie 1998: 15). Self-confidence thus forms the basis for a positive attitude and approach, just like perseverance. A positive attitude and approach are closely related to human relations, and are important qualities that contribute to leadership and successful entrepreneurship.

The cognitive processes of entrepreneurs and others were tested by Palich and Bagby (1995: 425), by reading to both groups a series of imaginary business scenarios. Entrepreneurs observed more strengths than weaknesses, more opportunities than threats, and more potential for positive performance than non-entrepreneurs did.

■ Perseverance

Perseverance in the enterprise is linked to the positive approach of entrepreneurs to their enterprise. Entrepreneurs who have a positive attitude towards their enterprise believe in their business despite setbacks, and are prepared to persevere in their efforts to ensure success. Perseverance is synonymous with drive.

All enterprises start off as small businesses. Ford Motor Company started in Henry Ford's garage and General Motors is a collection of erstwhile small motor manufacturers (Brady 1995: 46). Ford persevered despite many setbacks and problems, and because he believed in his product and his enterprise, he finally achieved success.

Perseverance is the ability of entrepreneurs to strive after their business ideals despite problems, obstacles and setbacks. True entrepreneurs are born with the skill of intuition that makes it possible for them to persevere. It is overcoming the challenge of the unknown that motivates entrepreneurs.

Determination and energy are part of perseverance. Despite physical or psychological obstacles or problems and setbacks, entrepreneurs are set on reaching their goals. The term "determination" is often used in the literature instead of perseverance. Self-confidence is probably one of the most important characteristics of entrepreneurs, because they must believe that things will work out for them despite any setbacks.

Perseverance is an indicator of the entrepreneur's ability to take repeated or different actions to solve a problem or overcome obstacles (McClelland 1986: 227). Often the entrepreneur is successful only after a number of attempts. It is possible that successful entrepreneurs persevere through every challenge, while unsuccessful entrepreneurs are people who try once, fail and then do not try again.

■ Commitment

The success factor "commitment to business" refers to the willingness of entrepreneurs to commit their personal resources to the business. It is an indication of the level of confidence that entrepreneurs have in their business.

A high-potential enterprise cannot be established and developed part-time. It requires total commitment and involvement. Commitment means that entrepreneurs make personal sacrifices or extraordinary efforts to deal with a task. They work together, or in the place of employees, to accomplish the task (McClelland 1986: 225).

1.7.2 Managerial success factors

■ Planning

Successful entrepreneurs go to work systematically, for example by taking decisions about the products that they are going to supply, the location of the enterprise, the organisation of each division and target markets. They plan by formally budgeting and by thoroughly calculating turnover, stock, gross and net profit and cash flows in advance. They determine objectives with regard to their financial statements and calculations. They realise the value of accurate, timely and practical management information. Their financial statements are analysed by themselves or by experts, and the information is used to manage their businesses better and to make adjustments where necessary (Moolman 1996: 5).

A good business plan ensures that entrepreneurs can establish the business with confidence because the required research and planning have been done. This does not mean that entrepreneurs who have not drawn up a business plan in writing (either because they do not know how or because they do not have the time) are unsuccessful. Entrepreneurs who do their planning in an informal manner are also successful. Successful planning does not necessarily imply a business plan in writing (Nieuwenhuizen 1997: 15).

Up to 80 per cent of successful enterprises have a strategic plan with a planning period of one to two years (Reuber & Fischer 1998: 36).

The ability to plan ahead is a characteristic of leaders, and planning is critical to growth. In SMEs, the owners are often totally involved in the operational functions of the enterprise, but successful entrepreneurs have the ability to distance themselves from immediate pressure and to focus on the needs of the future.

■ Knowledge of competitors

Knowledge of competitors means that entrepreneurs know who their competitors are, what the competitors are doing and what the position of their own business is compared with that of competitors. Only once they have this knowledge can they determine the competitive advantage of their business in order to differentiate it from other businesses. Knowledge of one's competitors is important for the successful establishment, continued existence and growth of a business. By constantly evaluating and monitoring their competitors, successful entrepreneurs can take informed decisions, act proactively, plan strategically and make adjustments where necessary.

Entrepreneurs determine their competitive advantage by finding out why clients prefer their products or services. To ensure a competitive advantage, successful entrepreneurs ensure that they offer something better and/or different to their competitors.

■ Mainly market oriented

Successful entrepreneurs are market oriented. They know who their target market is, what the target market's requirements and needs are and how to meet these profitably. The products and services of a market-oriented entrepreneur are developed to meet the needs of the clients. The market-oriented entrepreneur also positions the business in such a way as to differentiate it from competitors in order to ensure profitability and a competitive advantage. The consumer is the focus of the enterprise, and products and/or services are developed and adapted to

meet the client's needs. Product-oriented entrepreneurs often experience problems because they are more interested in the product than in the client and therefore do not know how to market their products successfully.

Winner entrepreneurs know their markets. They know what the market segment and target market is, what the market wants, what the demographics of the market are and how to communicate effectively in the market. They use the right media to achieve their objectives. They provide the highest quality at the best price and develop a competitive advantage (Moolman 1996: 5).

According to Appiah-Adu (1997: 1), the relationship between market orientation and performance in large enterprises also applies to small businesses. Market orientation thus has a positive influence on the performance of SMEs.

Luk's (1996: 71) study found that although quite a number of entrepreneurs started in the industrial sector, they attributed their success mainly to their marketing management abilities. Production and general management factors were not indicated as being that important. Good personal sales techniques were identified as the second most important functional ability of successful entrepreneurs. An effective niche market strategy is also an important factor that contributes to success in SMEs.

■ Client service

Client service is a key success factor because it fits in with so many other success factors. It is behaviour over which people have reasonable control and is linked to good human relations. To ensure good client services, entrepreneurs usually have good relations with their employees and their clients. This is closely related to the quality of their products and service. By meeting the clients' expectations, entrepreneurs ensure client satisfaction, which is closely connected to marketing. Satisfied clients will use the enterprise's products and/or service again and will recommend the business to prospective new clients.

Administrative and technical factors are also important for good client service. Record keeping and filing systems for reference purposes and stock control, a diary for planning and making appointments, contract planning and target dates for completing work, contracts and work charts for information about clients are a few examples of methods that can help ensure an effective client service.

The clients of winner entrepreneurs get special service because these entrepreneurs are client and market oriented. The ultimate goal of policy with regard to purchases, administration, production and personnel is client satisfaction. Good service involves everything that influences the client positively: friendliness and politeness, delivery, credit facilities, the standard and availability of products, layout, appearance inside and outside, effectiveness of administration, location of enterprise and parking facilities (Moolman 1996: 5).

■ High-quality work enjoys priority

Successful entrepreneurs realise the importance of quality products and service. Quality products are not necessarily expensive. The client expects that the quality of the product must be in line with the price asked. Value for money is important. The successful entrepreneur is ready to supply the client with a quality product and still make a profit. To make this possible, costs must be controlled without affecting the quality of the products. Quality products and services contribute to the marketing of the enterprise, because this ensures new clients through personal recommendations from existing, satisfied clients.

Successful entrepreneurs want to be the best in their business. Their goal is to manage the best security company, be the best supplier of equipment for mines, run the best retail chain, etc. They want to provide the best products to their clients.

■ Financial insight and management

Insight into financial concepts, knowledge of what financial management is, how important it is and how it must be applied in the SME, and a bookkeeping system are important factors that can contribute to success. To achieve the objectives of the enterprise and the entrepreneur, sound financial principles must be applied.

Merely by looking at their profit and loss statements one can identify good entrepreneurs. Successful entrepreneurs are often not responsible themselves for the bookkeeping

system of their enterprise – they use experts for this – but they ensure that the bookkeeping is done and that they can interpret it. It is crucial that owners of small businesses understand their bookkeeping system. Business decisions are based on financial analysis and if entrepreneurs do not have clarity on the meaning of specific information, they get expert advice.

Cost control contributes to the success of an enterprise to a great extent (Brady 1995: 46). The successful entrepreneur is conscientious and realises the importance of effective financial planning and control.

Financial expertise, systems and insight do not guarantee a successful enterprise by themselves – other factors also play an important role. This conclusion concurs with Farrell's (1997: 6) findings that management skills alone do not ensure success in an enterprise. He adds the need for expertise in specific products or services that are in demand and for which people are prepared to pay, and this is regarded as entrepreneurship.

■ Knowledge and skills with regard to the business

Successful entrepreneurs usually have sufficient knowledge and skills regarding their enterprise to ensure reasonable success. They are also thoroughly aware of their own limitations and make use of experts to provide them with advice and assistance, and in this way improve their performance.

Sufficient relevant experience that has been gained before starting one's own business is one of the most important determinants of success. A significant number of successful entrepreneurs started their own businesses in the same industry in which they worked for a few years (Luk 1996: 70).

Highly successful entrepreneurs depend on their own strengths. They keep core competencies in the enterprise, but non-core activities are contracted out.

■ The use of experts

Successful entrepreneurs make use of experts inside and outside their enterprise to carry out some of the functions in the business, and also attend seminars and training sessions.

Interviews with successful and unsuccessful entrepreneurs revealed that the successful group emphasised the importance of obtaining information from experts. This group repeatedly said that they critically analyse advice and suggestions and experiment with new methods. This is an indication of the creative attitude of successful entrepreneurs (Boeyens 1989: 79).

Entrepreneurs make use of advisers – probably in the sequence of lawyers, accountants, bankers and business consultants. The importance of consultants to smaller businesses and entrepreneurs, what they do for the enterprise or the value that their service adds is not known and requires further research (Bird 1989: 288).

Two important aspects that may contribute to the failure of an SME are the way in which business advice is given and the limited financial nature of the advice. Entrepreneurs must be helped to implement the advice because they may not necessarily be able or knowledgeable enough to do this themselves. Some 50 to 60 per cent of enterprises fail within the first three years as a result of mismanagement or incompetence. Entrepreneurs need to be given help with the implementation of advice (Leslie et al. 1985: 22).

1.8 The entrepreneurial process

The entrepreneurial process is one through which a new venture is created by an entrepreneur. This process results from the actions of the entrepreneur in bringing the resources together to form the organisation in order to pursue the opportunity. There are four distinct phases in this process (Nieman & Bennett 2002):

- Identify and evaluate the opportunity
- Develop the business plan
- Determine the resources required
- Start and manage the enterprise

1.8.1 Identifying and evaluating the opportunity

An opportunity is a gap left in the market by those who currently serve it. Good ideas are not necessarily good opportunities. Timmons (2000) states that a good opportunity is attractive, durable and timely, and is anchored in a product or service that creates or adds value for its buyer or end-user.

Identifying and evaluating an opportunity is a most difficult task. An entrepreneur must deliberately look for creative ideas that can be converted into a business opportunity. A number of techniques can be used to generate ideas from:

- The entrepreneur's skills, expertise or aptitude
- Common needs
- Existing unsolved problems
- Everyday activities
- Other reference sources

Converting ideas into opportunities requires that one must evaluate each idea. This is done through a feasibility study and a viability study. The former is a general examination of the potential of the idea to be converted into a new business venture. The focus is primarily on the ability of the entrepreneur to pursue the idea and to match his or her skills with what is required. The viability study is an in-depth investigation into the potential of the idea to be converted into a new business venture. The focus is largely on the market and profit potential of the idea.

The market size and length of the window of opportunity are important for determining risks and rewards. The window of opportunity refers to the time period available for creating the new venture. As a market grows, more and more opportunities become possible (the window opens), but as it matures the window starts to close and there are fewer opportunities in that market.

1.8.2 Developing the business plan

A good business plan must be developed to exploit the opportunity identified. It is important not only in developing the opportunity, but also in determining the resources required, obtaining those resources and successfully managing the resulting venture. A business plan is essential if one will be needing funding (finance) from any financial institution or venture capitalist.

One of the greatest benefits of the business plan is that it helps to reduce the risk of the venture. In writing and developing the business plan, the entrepreneur is forced to think about the various aspects of the enterprise. This, in itself, means that information needs to be collected on all aspects of the opportunity and the business venture. Chapter 5 provides detailed information on the business plan.

1.8.3 Determining the resources required

Resources comprise the capital available for investment in the venture, people who need to be employed, and physical assets such as equipment, machinery, buildings and vehicles. Intangible assets such as trademarks and patents will also require an outlay of capital.

This process starts with determining one's own resources and how much investment or loans one will need to attract or obtain to start operating. Resources cannot be determined without a cash flow projection, which is done simultaneously with the development of the business plan.

1.8.4 Starting and managing the enterprise

After the minimum capital for start-up has been acquired, the entrepreneur must utilise it by implementing the business plan. Initially, the business might be small with only one or two employees besides the entrepreneur. Once the business starts to grow, the management style and key variables for success will need to be determined. Some entrepreneurs have difficulty managing and growing the business they created.

1.9 Conclusion

The contribution of entrepreneurs to the economy can be attributed to their special qualities. Over the centuries they have been responsible for growth and development, and they are key role-players in the economy of every country. Their role in the successful economies of the world has become even more important in recent years, as the growth of large corporations has slowed down and innovative businesses have created additional needs and new markets. Countries in which an entrepreneurial culture is prominent benefit more and are doing better on the economic front. It therefore becomes crucial to identify what entrepreneurs do, to teach and expose more people to that, and to assist more people in developing their own entrepreneurial ventures.

Looking back

1. What do high-potential entrepreneurs do?
   - They establish and grow their businesses.
   - They create jobs.

2. Describe what entrepreneurs do.
   - They identify opportunities in the market.
   - They are willing to take calculated risks.
   - They gather and apply resources appropriately to make profit.
   - They establish and grow their own businesses, alone or with a team.
   - Their motive is to make profits.
   - They create value for themselves and society.
   - They are creative and innovative in various ways.

3. Distinguish small business owners from entrepreneurs.
   They also own their businesses and are of critical importance to the economy, but they:
   - Are not engaged in any new or innovative practices
   - Stabilise at a certain stage
   - Only grow with inflation
   - See their principal purpose as being to further their personal goals, e.g. to be autonomous and to ensure security

4. What determines an entrepreneurial orientation?
   - A person's entrepreneurial orientation is determined by personal characteristics,

the culture of the society, education, work experience and the entrepreneurial inclination of the family.

5. Name the four distinct phases of the entrepreneurial process.
   - Identify and evaluate the opportunity.
   - Develop the business plan.
   - Determine the resources required.
   - Start and manage the enterprise.

6. Distinguish between the entrepreneurial and managerial functions of the entrepreneur.
   - Entrepreneurial functions include innovative thinking and identifying opportunities, planning and establishing and/or growing the business and applying resources.
   - Managerial functions involve planning, organising, leading and control. They also include management of the various business functions, such as finance, marketing, production, purchasing, administration, human resources and public relations.

7. Distinguish between the entrepreneurial and managerial success factors of entrepreneurs.
   Entrepreneurial success factors:
   - Creativity and innovation .
   - Risk orientation
   - Leadership
   - Good human relations
   - Positive attitude
   - Perseverance

- Commitment
Managerial success factors:
   - Planning
   - Knowledge of competitors
   - Mainly market oriented
   - Client service
   - High-quality work enjoys priority
   - Financial insight and management
   - Knowledge and skills with regard to the business
   - The use of experts

8. Name the five perspectives of entrepreneurship research.
   - Economic
   - Behaviourist
   - Management science
   - Social Science
   - Entrepreneurship

9. Describe the impetus entrepreneurship gives to the economy.
   - SMMEs are the only growth sector in the economies of all leading countries.
   - SMMEs contribute to the economies of the country in various ways, such as economic growth, wealth generation, creation of employment opportunities and an increased flow of capital.

10. List the main components of the model for entrepreneurship development.
   - Entrepreneurial orientation
   - Supportive environment
   - Cooperative environment

Key terms

Business plan
Commitment
Creativity and innovation
Economic impetus
Entrepreneur
Entrepreneurial orientation
Entrepreneurial process
Entrepreneurial success factors
Feasibility study
Good human relations
Gross domestic product (GDP)
High-potential entrepreneurs

Independent ownership
Innovation
Leadership
Perseverance
Positive attitude
Recognition of opportunities
Resources
Risk orientation
Small business owner
Small, medium and micro-enterprises (SMMEs)
Viability study

Discussion questions

1. Read the case study below and decide whether these two men are entrepreneurs or small business owners. Substantiate your answer.

2. Identify the success factors evident from what they have done and are still doing to ensure the success of the business.

3. Discuss what their contribution is to the economies of South Africa and other countries.

Case studies

Case study 1: Nando's – Robert Brozin and Fernando Duarte

Robert Brozin and Fernando Duarte, Nando's namesake, started the business. Brozin worked at Sanyo and knew nothing about the food industry, while Fernando Duarte was the food specialist.

Nando's started as a fast-food shop selling spicy, grilled chicken meals in the south of Johannesburg in 1995. It was mainly an area where Portuguese people resided and was a typical Portuguese style of food. Business grew fast and it was often difficult to enter the shop due to its popularity. Shortly afterwards, another outlet was opened in the northern and more affluent part of Johannesburg.

Today, there are 343 Nando's worldwide. Of this total, 184 are franchises while 70 are owned by Nando's and 159 are international, mainly in Britain and Australia. Shops in the Middle East are still problematic.

Nando's is well known and popular for its quirky, fun and cheeky advertising. Although the perception is that Nando's spends large amounts on advertising, due to its high visibility and exceptional character, the annual amount spent is only R17 million, which is much lower than the advertising budgets of the big players. This means that the company has to be, and certainly is, innovative. Brozin describes himself as a people-oriented marketer.

The international operations already afford Nando's 57 per cent of its earnings and the goal is to grow it to 70 per cent. However, the South African market is close to becoming saturated.

Brozin acknowledges that the process of internationalisation is difficult. They have had quite a number of serious setbacks and he acknowledges that they have not always acted correctly and probably went international too soon. The learning curve in Australia was very steep and they realised that the business climate could not be dictated to, but had to be adapted to. Today they are proud of their results in Australia.

The most controversial aspect, apart from their advertisements, is probably their loan position. The extensive international expansion created a loan-to-equity ratio of more than 100 per cent. Over the last six months to 31 August 2000 it was brought down to 69 per cent. Brozin attributes this to the success with internationalisation. In Britain, the profit for this period of six months was R2,6 million and R7 million in Australia. Nando's is now experienced and known in those markets and Brozin is determined to extend the international expansion.

Source: Adapted from *Beeld* (2001).

Questions

1. What entrepreneurial orientation does Brozin exhibit?
2. List Brozin's entrepreneurial, leadership and managerial characteristics.

Case study 2: Impact – Eric du Plessis

Eric du Plessis studied BCom at the University of Stellenbosch, after which he started working at Stellenbosch Farmers' Winery. He also completed two BCom Honours degrees while working at a marketing research company. Here he first became the media director and then research director.

When the company planned to expand, Eric was assigned to start up and manage the new division. He realised that somebody else, his employer, was selling his skills. Eric decided that if it was a good idea to start a new division, it would be an even better idea to do so for himself rather than for an employer. Although he realised the risk involved, he reasoned that the only thing he could lose was his overdraft, bond and other debts that he had. He started Impact in 1984. Today Eric fills all the following posi-

tions in businesses he has started: CEO: Impact Information; Managing Director: Impact Information; CEO: Millward Brown Impact Africa; Director: Division 7; Director: In-Perspective; Deputy Managing Director: Media Performance Management; Director: Observision.

Impact is an advertising research company. The major objective is to measure the impact that specific advertisements have. Various methods are employed, for example telephonic questionnaires and an innovative method used in movie theatres. Approximately 900 000 respondents answer advertisement-related questions to 300 fieldworkers per annum. Apart from the fieldworkers, Impact employs 20 specialists ranging from market researchers, information technology specialists, bookkeepers to administrative workers. Each has their own responsibilities. Sixteen years later the team has expanded and the employees remain loyal.

Eric experienced some really hard times when he won large contracts but had difficulty in carrying them out due to the high associated financial needs and cash flow problems. On occasion, Impact was on the verge of bankruptcy.

Eric's marketing strategy for his company included a variety of methods. He marketed Impact by selling the concepts directly to big organisations that have an interest in determining the success of their advertising campaigns. In addition, he does extensive research in his field of business and regularly presents papers at international and national marketing conferences. He is the winner of three international best paper awards and the author of a book published in the United Kingdom and the Netherlands.

The international presence and visibility of Impact caught the attention of international companies and on various occasions offers were made to Eric to purchase Impact. During 2001 he accepted an offer from Millward Brown, and Impact is now part of the Millward Brown group, with Eric as CEO. He says that by becoming a part of the international network of Millward Brown he has gained easier access to even more lucrative contracts.

Question

1. What lessons can be learned from Eric's story?

Experiential exercises

1. Identify a successful business that you can analyse. Interview the owner of the business or read as much as possible about the owner and the business. Determine whether it is a small business or an entrepreneurial venture, and motivate your decision.

2. Evaluate yourself and determine whether you are an entrepreneur. Write a description of yourself relating to entrepreneurship.

3. Identify your strengths and weaknesses regarding the entrepreneurial and managerial success factors.

Exploring the Web

Visit the following websites for information on entrepreneurs and the supportive environment:

- Business Referral and Information Network (BRAIN): www.brain.org.za
- Central Statistical Services: www.statssa.pwv.gov.za
- Department of Trade and Industry: www.dti.gov.za
- International Council for Small Business (ICSB): www.ICSB.org

References and recommended reading

Amabile, T.M. 1996. Unlimited genius. *Success*, 43(7): 36-37.

Appiah-Adu, K. 1997. Market orientation and performance: do the findings established in large firms hold in the small business sector? *Journal of Euromarketing*, 6(3): 1-26.

Barrier, M. 1995. The changing face of leadership. *Nations Business*, 83(1): 41-42.

Beeld. 2001. Die hoender kom hier beslis eerste. *Sakebeeld*, Maandag 12 November, 2.

Bird, B.J. 1989. *Entrepreneurial behavior*. Glenview, IL: Scott, Foresman & Company.

Boeyens, J. 1989. Identifying entrepreneurs by means of a simulation game. *Suid-Afrikaanse Tydskrif vir Wetenskap*, 85: 79-80.

Brady, A. 1995. Small is as small does. *Journal of Business Strategy*, 16(2): 44-46.

Carland, J.W., Hoy, F., Boulton, W.F. & Carland, J.C. 1984. Differentiating entrepreneurs from small business owners: a conceptualization. *Academy of Management Review*, 9(2): 354-359.

Cox, C. & Jennings, R. 1995. The foundations of success: the development and characteristics of British entrepreneurs and intrapreneurs. *Leadership and Organisation Development Journal*, 16(7): 4-9.

Crous, M.J., Nortjé, J.D. & Van der Merwe, R.B. 1995. 'n Profiel van suksesvolle kleinsake-entrepreneurs in die Republiek van Suid-Afrika: 'n verkenningstudie. *South African Journal for Entrepreneurship and Small Business*, November: 52-62.

Diederichs, A.W. 2002. *Whirlpool of change*. Cape Town: Old Mutual.

Driver, A., Wood, E. Segal, N. & Herrington, M. 2001. *Global Entrepreneurship Monitor: 2001 South African executive report*. Graduate School of Business. Cape Town: University of Cape Town.

Eggers, J.H. & Leahy, K.T. 1995. Entrepreneurial leadership. *Business Quarterly*, 59(4): 71-76.

Farrell L.C. 1997. The missing management link. In: Budman, M., Do universities stifle entrepreneurship? *Across the Board*, 34(7): 32-38.

Fillion, L.J. 1991. From entrepreneurship to entreprenology: the emergence of a new discipline. *Journal of Enterprising Culture*, 6(1): 1-24.

Gibb, A.A. 1997. Small firms' training and competitiveness: building upon the small business as a learning organisation. *International Small Business Journal*, 15(3): 13-29.

Glynn, M.A. 1996. Innovative genius: a framework for relating individual and organizational intelligences to innovation. *Academy of Management Review*, 21(4): 1081-1111.

Hisrich, R.D. & Peters, M.P. 1998. *Entrepreneurship*, 4th ed. Boston: Irwin McGraw Hill.

Kinni, T.B. 1994. The credible leader. *Industry Week*, 243(12): 25-26.

Kinni, T.B. 1995. Leadership up close. *Tapping the Network Journal*, 5(3): 2-4.

Leslie, M., Magdulskie, G. & Champion, N. 1985. The role of the accountant in the survival of small business. *Australian Accountant*, 55(1): 22-30.

Luk, T.K. 1996. Success in Hong Kong: factors self-reported by successful small business owners. *Journal of Small Business Management*, 34(3): 68-74.

Maasdorp, E.F. de V. & Van Vuuren, J.J. 1998. Entrepreneurship. In: Marx, S., Van Rooyen, D.C., Bosch, J.K. & Reynders, H.J.J. (Eds), *Business management*, 2nd ed. Pretoria: Van Schaik.

Marsh, R. 1992. *Business success in South Africa*. Cape Town: Struik.

McClelland, D.C. 1986. Characteristics of successful entrepreneurs. *Journal of Creative Behavior*, 21(3): 219-233.

Merz, G.R., Weber, P.B. & Laetz, V.B. 1994. Linking small business management with entrepreneurial growth. *Journal of Small Business Management*, 32(4): 48-60.

Moolman, P.L. 1996. The "win" characteristics of the successful entrepreneur. *Entrepreneur*, 96(6): 4-6.

Nieman, G. & Bennett, A. (Eds). 2002. *Business management: a value chain approach*. Pretoria: Van Schaik.

Nieuwenhuizen, C. 1997. Key success factors of entrepreneurs. *Success Magazine*, January: 34.

Nieuwenhuizen, C. 2001. Entrepreneurship and small business management in perspective. In:

Strydom, J.W. (Ed.), *Entrepreneurship and how to establish your own business*. Kenwyn: Juta, 15.

Osborne, R.L. 1995. The essence of entrepreneurial success. *Management Decision*, 33(7): 4-9.

Palich, L.E. & Bagby, D.R. 1995. Using cognitive theory to explain entrepreneurial risk-taking: challenging conventional wisdom. *Journal of Business Venturing*, 10(6): 425-438.

Pendley, C. 1995. In: Kinni, T.B., Leadership up close. *Tapping the Network Journal*, 5(3): 2-4.

Reuber, B. & Fischer, E. 1998. Small successes. *CA Magazine*, 131(1): 36-37.

Schein, E.H. 1977. Career anchors and career paths: a panel study of management school graduates. In: Van Manne, J. (Ed.), *Organizational careers: some new perspectives*. New York: Wiley.

Schein, E.H. 1985. *Career anchors: discovering your real values*. San Diego, CA: University Associates.

Schumpeter, J.A. 1934. *The theory of economic development*. Translated by R. Opic. Cambridge, MA: Harvard University Press.

Solomon, G.T., Duffy, S. & Tarabishy, A. 2002. The state of entrepreneurship education in the United States: a nationwide survey and analysis. *International Journal of Entrepreneurship Education*, 1(1): 1-22.

Themba, G., Chamme, M., Phambuka, C.A. & Makgosa, R. 1999. Impact of macro-environmental factors on entrepreneurship development in developing countries. In: Kinunda-Rutashobya, L. & Olomi, D.R., *African entrepreneurship and small business development*. Dar es Salaam: DUP.

Timmons, J.A. 2000. *New venture creation: entrepreneurship for the 21st century*, 5th ed. Burr Ridge: Irwin.

Vega, G. 1996. When growing businesses self-destruct. *Small Business Forum*, 14(2): 56-66.

Watson, C.H. 2001. Small business versus entrepreneurship revisited. In: Brockhaus, R.H. (Ed.), *Entrepreneurship education: a global view*. Burlington: Ashgate.

Wickham, P. 2001. *Strategic entrepreneurship: a decision-making approach to new venture creation and management*, 2nd ed. Harlow: *Financial Times*/Prentice Hall.

Zeelie, J. 1998. Self-confidence and a positive attitude. In: Nieuwenhuizen, C. (Ed.), *Entrepreneurial skills*. Kenwyn: Juta, 15-32.

2

The entrepreneur

Melodi van der Merwe

2.1 Introduction

Entrepreneurs have a fundamental effect on the economy by establishing new businesses that provide not only goods and services to customers, but also job opportunities for individuals in various industries. Nieman and Bennett (2002: 57) describe the entrepreneur as a catalyst for business. This chapter provides an overview of the role played by the entrepreneur in the economy, entrepreneurs at various levels of entrepreneurial sophistication, the background and characteristics of entrepreneurs, role models and support systems, and push and pull factors. We discuss different kinds of entrepreneurs, such as women and minority entrepreneurs, and distinguish the entrepreneur from the inventor. When an entrepreneur starts a business he or she is faced with numerous barriers during the entrepreneurial process. In this chapter some of the most important barriers are discussed and possible solutions are given. Further insight into entrepreneurship is provided by focusing on the informal sector in South Africa, emphasising survivalist and emerging entrepreneurs.

2.2 The entrepreneur as a catalyst for economic activity

In the South African economy, entrepreneurs are seen as the primary creators and drivers of new businesses and therefore they are clearly distinguished as economic actors. Entrepreneurship plays a vital role in the survival and growth of any emerging economy. Due to low economic growth, high unemployment and an unsatisfactory level of poverty in South Africa, entrepreneurship becomes a critical solution. More people are either choosing entrepreneurship as their career path or they are forced to create their own employment – even women and youth are exploring this phenomenon. Entrepreneurship plays an important role in the informal sector in South Africa, where there is a greater direct link between the entrepreneur's

Learning outcomes

After completion of this chapter, you should be able to:

- Understand the effects of entrepreneurship on the economy
- Appreciate that entrepreneurs can conduct business at various levels based on their entrepreneurial activities
- Understand that entrepreneurs have unique characteristics that distinguish them from other individuals
- Know that certain types of networks and support systems are available to entrepreneurs
- Understand that there are challenges that entrepreneurs and SMMEs must overcome
- Acknowledge women and emerging entrepreneurs and the role they play in the economy
- Understand the relationship between entrepreneurship and other upcoming industries
- Understand that entrepreneurship must be initiated in schools and universities to make the youth more aware of entrepreneurship as a career option

standard of living and the customer: if the customer does not buy, the entrepreneur does not survive. While the relationship between entrepreneurship and economic growth is multifaceted and complex, entrepreneurial capability is a necessary ingredient of a country's capacity to sustain economic growth (Driver et al. 2001: 6). The informal sector in South Africa has grown enormously over the past ten years, illustrating why entrepreneurship is seen as an important career option for both men and women.

It is universally accepted that a well-functioning small business sector contributes to the economic and social growth of a country. It exerts a positive influence on the economies of all countries, particularly in the fast-changing and increasingly competitive global market. Small, medium and micro-enterprises (SMMEs) are recognised as playing a fundamental role in the advancement of prosperity in our communities. In a study conducted by Driver et al. (2001: 3), it was found that one in 18 South African adults are entrepreneurs, as measured by the Total Entrepreneurial Activity (TEA) index. This is a relatively low figure when compared with countries such as Germany and Japan. To ensure economic prosperity in our country, the number of entrepreneurs who successfully establish and develop small and micro-enterprises needs to increase significantly. A relevant question at this stage could be: If one in 18 adults in South Africa are entrepreneurs, does it mean that the other 17 are not entrepreneurial at all, or do they carry out some form of entrepreneurial activity? The next section illustrates the various levels of entrepreneurial activities in South Africa.

2.3 Entrepreneurs at various levels of entrepreneurial sophistication

Entrepreneurs can be found at different levels of entrepreneurial sophistication based on the nature of their entrepreneurial activities. These levels are discussed below (adapted from Adhikary et al. 1997: 7).

2.3.1 Basic survivalists

No economic independence, little involvement with other entrepreneurs within their social network (individualism).

Entrepreneurial activities: Isolated from markets, unaware of their own potential, illiterate, few income-generating activities. A practical example could be a person standing on a street corner and holding a sign stating that he will wash cars in exchange for R10.

2.3.2 Pre-entrepreneurs

Follow the group's initiative (collectivism).

Entrepreneurial activities: Welfare-oriented approach, not expected to be self-sustaining, training needed in entrepreneurial competency. A practical example could be a person selling crafts next to the road with ten other pre-entrepreneurs selling exactly the same products at exactly the same price.

2.3.3 Subsistence entrepreneurs

Self-employed, independent income generation, temporary market stall or stand.

Entrepreneurial activities: Inexperienced in business management and still needs general support and training in technical and management skills. Street vendors are an example at this level.

2.3.4 Micro-entrepreneurs

Zero to nine employees, operating licence from local authority, fixed workshop.

Entrepreneurial activities: Difficulty in getting loans from banks. Assistance projects focus on credit rather than training and technical assistance. A practical example is an entrepreneur who runs a home-based business such as a hairdressing salon from his or her dwelling.

2.3.5 Small-scale entrepreneurs

Ten to 49 employees.

Entrepreneurial activities: Qualifies for a loan from a bank. Well-educated and has adequate collateral to apply for a loan. An entrepreneur who operates a small accounting or law firm is an example at this level.

2.4 The background and characteristics of entrepreneurs

Entrepreneurs also need to adopt and internalise entrepreneurial attitudes and characteristics. These characteristics can contribute to the background of the entrepreneur, for instance whether he or she was brought up in an entrepreneurial family environment. Other qualities are that of being hardworking, honest, ambitious and persistent in overcoming numerous failures, and to ever strive for excellence and constant self-improvement.

2.4.1 The background of entrepreneurs

South Africa is a very diverse country with many different cultures, and it is therefore a difficult task to summarise the background of South African entrepreneurs. There are, however, certain commonalities, as set out below.

■ Childhood family environment

Frequently, entrepreneurs have at least one parent who also was (or still is) an entrepreneur. Entrepreneurship is best learnt through experience and teachers may be far less likely to be able to teach what is required of an entrepreneur than, for example, entrepreneurial parents. Informal learning opportunities, for example through contact with family members who are entrepreneurs, can play a key role in developing entrepreneurial capacity. However, South Africa is lacking in these, partly because of the lack of entrepreneurial experience amongst the majority of the population.

■ Education

Education is seen as one of the most significant barriers to entrepreneurial activity. General basic education is poor for a large proportion of the population. Higher levels of education are associated with significantly higher levels of entrepreneurial activity. Driver et al. (2001: 22) stress the importance of education and two findings are suggested: firstly, that matriculation increases one's capacity to pursue entrepreneurial activities and, secondly, that tertiary education increases the durability of entrepreneurial activity.

■ Age

According to a study done by Driver et al. (2001: 42), the highest number of entrepreneurs is found in the 35 to 54 age category. Many

of these people will have worked for someone else before embarking on their own venture.

■ Work experience

Entrepreneurs will most likely succeed where they have gone from school to training, combined with work experience. They have therefore seen entrepreneurial opportunities from an employment base.

2.4.2 Characteristics of entrepreneurs

The definition of entrepreneurship in Chapter 1 indicated that there are certain characteristics that a person must have in order to differentiate him or her as an entrepreneur. Entrepreneurs are not necessarily born with these characteristics – they can be acquired through life experience and even through the entrepreneurial process itself. What does it take to become an entrepreneur? Much research has gone into trying to determine what type of people make good entrepreneurs. Because of diverse business opportunities, diverse societies and diverse individual histories, entrepreneurs are at least as different from each other as they are similar! Nevertheless, certain characteristics stand out, and these are summarised below.

■ Passion

If people start a business, they must preferably pursue business activities for which they have a passion. Entrepreneurs sometimes turn their love for sports and hobbies into a business venture. It is often said that entrepreneurs are go-getters – if they pursue a business activity that they find interesting and fascinating, they are much more likely to succeed in that business.

■ Locus of control

Individuals like to be in charge of their own lives, and one way of ensuring this is by being in control of one's own venture and business activities. Entrepreneurs are typically people who like to be in control and have good delegating skills. They have a high degree of autonomy and do not want to be told what to do by somebody else.

■ Need for independence

To be one's own boss is one of the biggest reasons why people become entrepreneurs. Many individuals leave their traditional jobs to become entrepreneurs. They are tired of working for somebody else and therefore establish their own ventures. Entrepreneurs do not like to be tied down to rules and regulations.

■ Need for achievement

The need for achievement is closely linked to the entrepreneurial motivation to excel. McClelland (1961) states that entrepreneurs have a very high need for achievement when compared with other individuals who are not entrepreneurially inclined. Nieman and Bennett (2002: 59) agree that entrepreneurs are self-starters who appear driven internally by a strong desire to compete against self-imposed standards and to pursue and attain challenging goals.

■ Risk taking and uncertainty

Risk taking involves much more than just financial resources that will be lost when the venture fails; it can also include social and personal risks. All entrepreneurs face personal risks because they might lose valuable time with their families. Entrepreneurs do not really have 9 to 5 jobs but rather 24-hour jobs, especially when their businesses are still in the start-up phase. Entrepreneurs are no more protected from business failure than their employees and investors are. Liquidation can result in financial ruin. Moreover, they will have to face the social stigma associated with failure, as well as the personal distress of letting down investors, employees, clients and their families.

■ Creativity and innovation

It is believed that everybody is capable of being creative; it is just a matter of how individuals develop that creativity within them to produce the most favourable results. There is currently a great deal of pressure on both small and big organisations to establish a sustainable competitive advantage within their firms. Creativity and innovation are seen as the key ingredients needed to establish a niche market.

■ Determination and persistence

Well-known South African entrepreneur, Jenna Clifford, once said: "I've learnt that no one is immune to change and it takes single-minded focus to be able to ride out the rough times. Just when you think you have the game plan worked out, the rules change. If you really want to succeed, you must know there is always a price to pay, but also that you must not lose yourself in the process" (Smith 2000: 10). Being a true entrepreneur means never giving up and learning from previous failures and mistakes.

2.5 Role models and support systems

People need role models in their everyday lives – a living role model (such as Herman Mashaba or Pam Golding) in one's community is a more powerful example than a distant media icon. Businesspeople may often say that they do not trust anyone except themselves, but for entrepreneurship to flourish entrepreneurs must have the ability to build partnerships, relationships and trust between people with whom they come into direct contact. One example of this is the Business Women's Association, the largest association of business and entrepreneurial women in the country, with branches in Johannesburg, Cape Town, Durban, East London, Port Elizabeth and Richards Bay. This is an association that goes beyond networking and socialising.

Entrepreneurial networking can be seen as an active process of setting up and maintaining a win–win and cooperative relationship with other persons or businesses that can offer critical support for the development and growth of a business. As Chapter 9 focuses more on networking for entrepreneurs, this section will only include an overview of the types of networks:

- *Social networks:* These include communication and the exchange of information, for example two entrepreneurs exchanging business cards at a kitchen tea or social event.

- *Personal networks:* These include those people with whom the entrepreneur has day-to-day direct contact, for example a satisfied customer will bring in more customers by means of word-of-mouth advertising.

- *Extended networks:* These networks are focused on a network of organisations rather than on an individual. Members of the Business Women's Association, which is sponsored by Nedbank, meet on a regular basis to improve their current relationship. The South African Women Entrepreneurs Network (SAWEN), Fabcos, Nafcoc, Afrikaanse Handelsinstituut (AHI) and the Johannesburg Chamber of Industries, are also examples of an extended network.

- Other networks include:
  - The Internet   – Lawyers
  - Suppliers   – Government policy
  - Investors   – Competitors
  - Bankers   – Role models

Networks, particularly networks of entrepreneurs, have a number of benefits that they can offer their members. These benefits include:
- Group or joint marketing of products
- Group or joint buying of input materials and services
- Joint tendering or bidding on contracts
- Sharing of information on new markets and opportunities

- Sharing of containers when exporting
- Using members of the network as suppliers or distributors
- Getting advice and information from members of the network who can play a mentoring or supportive role to newer businesses

Any entrepreneur or SMME needs support to succeed. This is a critical issue, which in most cases is ignored or forgotten. Only when a business is motivated can one truly say that a successful SMME has been created.

2.6 Push and pull factors

Entrepreneurship is not always seen as a legitimate or desirable career choice. Many South Africans are forced to become entrepreneurs due to retrenchment, job frustration and job losses. This section of the chapter focuses on the main reasons or forces that cause individuals to become entrepreneurs. They can be classified as either opportunity (pull factors) or necessity (push factors) of entrepreneurship. Most people face a combination of push and pull factors, as indicated in Figure 2.1.

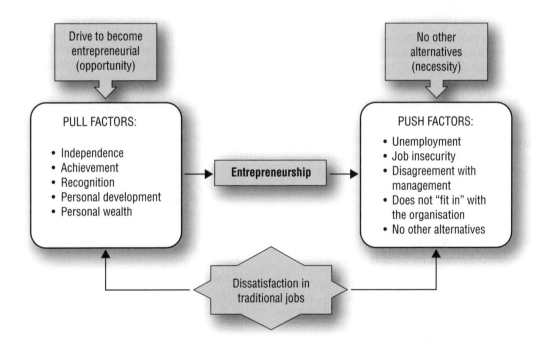

Figure 2.1 The push and pull factors of entrepreneurship

Push factors are those that encourage entrepreneurship due to traditional jobs being less attractive because an individual does not have any other career choice or option. They include:

- Unemployment – a person who does not have a job in the established economy
- Job insecurity, for example if a person is appointed on a contract basis for a short-term period
- Disagreement with management, career limitations and setbacks in a conventional job
- Not fitting in with the organisation, or the inability to pursue a personal innovation in a conventional job
- The limitations of financial rewards from conventional jobs
- Having no other alternatives

Pull factors are those factors that encourage people in traditional positions to leave their current jobs to become entrepreneurs. They include:

- Independence: the freedom to work for oneself
- Achievement: a sense of acknowledgement to be gained from managing one's own venture
- Recognition: a desire to gain the social standing achieved by entrepreneurs
- Personal development: the freedom to pursue personal innovation
- Personal wealth: the financial rewards of entrepreneurship

Wickham (1998: 63) is of the opinion that the number of entrepreneurs operating at any one time will depend on the strength of the push and pull forces. If they are strong, then a large number of entrepreneurs will emerge.

2.7 Challenges facing entrepreneurs and SMMEs in South Africa

In South Africa an unacceptable and disappointingly high number of small and micro-enterprises fail during their early years of operation. They face myriad challenges. According to Nieman (1999: 8), the largest percentage of small businesses fail during the first two years of their existence due to cash flow problems

that arise because they could not manage growth. Taking into account the high failure rate of new small enterprises, and their importance to the national economy, it is critical to look at how challenges facing entrepreneurs and SMMEs could be overcome. These challenges include:

- Access to start-up and expansion finance
- Access to markets
- Access to appropriate technology
- Access to resources (especially human resources)

2.7.1 Access to start-up and expansion finance

Raising money in capital markets, including for bank loans, is a minefield for start-ups, and they often launch their businesses using their own money or occasionally their family's money. More than 80 per cent of these start-ups have been financed through founders' personal savings (Mokoena 1998: 16). They have relied on debt or retained earnings to grow.

Access to appropriate finance is a major constraint on the successful development of SMMEs in South Africa. Too many creative ideas are not developed into viable new ventures due to the lack of finance. In the last few years the government, through the Department of Trade and Industry and Khula Enterprise Finance, has designed and put in place incentives, subsidies and schemes that have improved SMMEs' access to finance. However, a significant number of SMMEs are still not able to access affordable start-up and expansion finance. The reasons for this lack of access to finance include:

- Risk aversion of the banking sector towards SMMEs. SMMEs are traditionally seen as "high-risk" borrowers. The high number of SMME business failures exacerbates this view.
- There is a decline in strong alternative financial institutions. A large percentage of micro finance institutions (MFIs) have gone under. Very few MFIs are actively providing finance to SMMEs.
- Inadequate funding proposals and business plans. Although financial institutions are willing to finance SMMEs, the business proposals submitted by the SMMEs are not re-

searched and presented properly. If entrepreneurs have adequate business plans and collateral and they are still denied finance from financial institutions, the entrepreneurs have the right to know why the loan application was rejected.

The above challenges could be overcome by:

- *Business success:* The business success and profitability of SMMEs need to be improved. As most entrepreneurs lack sound business understanding, experience and exposure, effective training, counselling, mentorship and coaching are critical before and after accessing finance. Improved and enhanced business performance of small and micro-businesses will make them more attractive to financiers.

- *Financial products:* Financial institutions and MFIs should provide SMMEs with appropriate financial products. These include bridging and contract finance, equity and venture capital. Information on the sources of this type of finance should be made available to SMMEs.

- *Training:* SMMEs need to be trained and coached in conducting research on and presenting funding proposals, feasibility studies and business plans. They will be able to achieve this by accessing effective business development services.

- *Financial guidance:* Financial institutions must provide guidance and direction to SMMEs that were denied finance, as well as give them viable reasons why their loans were rejected.

2.7.2 Access to markets

Another major challenge facing SMMEs is the lack of sustainable markets for their products and services. They tend to produce and offer services that do not have a ready market.

Few entrepreneurs, especially the previously disadvantaged ones, start with an original concept or plan to achieve a sustainable competitive advantage through proprietary technology or a product. These entrepreneurs tend to follow "the group", hoping that whatever has worked for the others in the past will work for the entrepreneur as well. A major cause for this

constraint is that SMMEs do not give priority to marketing in their overall business approach. Most of them do not probe and segment their markets, analyse customer demand, know their competition or interpret trends.

The above could be addressed by the following:

- *Marketing training:* SMMEs need to be provided with effective marketing training. It is imperative that SMMEs constantly upgrade their marketing appeals and competencies, by putting more effort and a greater part of their budget into marketing training. They should also be able to identify business development service (BDS) agencies, which will provide quality training and coaching.

- *Commitment to marketing:* SMME entrepreneurs need to appreciate that to be successful they must demonstrate an early awareness of, and commitment to, marketing. Most SMMEs emphasise the production and finance functions and do not have a clearly defined marketing function.

- *Commitment to the market:* SMMEs need to place the needs of markets at the forefront of their business concerns. This will lead to the necessary behaviour for developing superior value for customers and constant superior business performance. It is imperative for entrepreneurs to stay close to their customers. If an entrepreneur thinks that he or she has created a brilliant new product but there is no market for it, product as well as business failure would result.

- *Market-oriented products:* SMMEs should only produce and offer services that are demanded by the market. Entrepreneurs must do market research before they start a business to measure the products or service they can supply to customers against the demand (need) that exists in the market.

- *Networking:* BDS agencies should assist SMMEs in gaining access to markets by facilitating vertical and horizontal (networking) business linkages.

2.7.3 Access to appropriate technology

The lack of technology is another constraint facing SMMEs. The use of appropriate technology is one of the most important factors behind a successful SMME's competitive advantage. Successful SMMEs constantly upgrade their operational and production equipment and techniques. The use of up-to-date and new technology leads to:

- Better and more competitive products and services
- Improved efficiency
- Reduced operational and production costs
- Improved quality of products and services

SMMEs can access appropriate technology by availing themselves of services offered by organisations such as the National Research Foundation, the South African Bureau of Standards and the South African Quality Institute. These organisations have active SMME development programmes.

2.7.4 Access to human resources

It is the entrepreneur who has to gather and mobilise the other production resources (land, capital and labour) to create a new business venture or to change the direction of an existing firm (Nieman & Bennett, 2002: 57). Another important constraint facing SMMEs in South Africa is the way they deal with people-related issues. Human resources are widely acknowledged as being the "most precious asset" of a business. Issues involved in human resource management include addressing the skills, attitudes and expectations of employees and of the entrepreneurs themselves.

Entrepreneurs might have excellent ideas but they quite often do not know how to manage those ideas or the people within their businesses. This contributes to the statement that not all managers are good leaders or entrepreneurs, and that not all entrepreneurs are good managers or leaders. However, it is necessary for entrepreneurs to have both managerial and leadership skills.

Entrepreneurs, as the drivers of their businesses, need to address the attitudes and expectations of their employees. They can do this by:

- Building team spirit amongst the employees, for example going away together for a weekend once every two months
- Nurturing life-long learning in themselves and their employees

- Ensuring that their employees regard meeting customer needs as their responsibility
- Initiating an intrapreneurial climate within the organisation to allow employees more freedom of choice
- Being role models for their employees
- Practising a code of ethics to ensure an ethical foundation in the business

If employees are loyal to the entrepreneur and his or her business, they will confer their loyalty on the customers they serve.

2.8 Women and emerging entrepreneurs

Maharaj (1998: 16) estimates that between 40 and 80 per cent of the urban workforces of developing nations are in the informal sector. Street vendors constitute a significant share of this workforce. In Africa especially, women represent the majority of these vendors because they often lack the necessary technical skills to do much else in the informal sector. A vast number of households in South Africa are dependent on the woman's financial support. Adhikary et al. (1999: 59) defines a successful woman entrepreneur as follows: she has been in business for longer than two years, operates an enterprise with more than five employees and less than 30, makes a profit and has expanded in terms of infrastructure and growth.

Traditionally, a woman's role has been that of mother and wife, but the economic role of women has emerged in South Africa. Women were always seen to be in the kitchen; nowadays they are represented in large numbers in boardrooms. Women entrepreneurs seem to be the most disadvantaged group because until recently they could not pursue a business activity without taking their husband or a male family member along. Although the woman entrepreneur has made her mark in the self-employment sector, one cannot help but to ask how a woman can be a successful entrepreneur if she is overworked in the home, or uneducated or untrained, or unexposed to markets, or cut off from financial resources, or just generally discriminated against in a male-dominated society.

2.8.1 Types of women entrepreneurs

Goffee and Scase (1985: 24) designed a typology that distinguishes women entrepreneurs on the basis of two criteria:

- Attachment to entrepreneurial ideas refers to the presence of entrepreneurial attitudes as originally defined by McClelland (1961), such as achievement motivation, independence, risk-taking propensity, self-esteem and the internal locus of control.

- Acceptance of traditional gender roles refers to the extent to which women conform to culturally presumed roles.

Traditional women business owners are highly committed to entrepreneurial ideas, as well as to conventional gender roles. They are motivated to start a business due to economic pressure at home, which contributes to the push factor in the economy. Their primary concern is to maintain profits by keeping overheads, wages and costs low.

Innovative women business owners are highly committed to entrepreneurial ideas but not to traditional gender roles. They start their business because of limited career prospects in large organisations, they are ambitious and their business has high priority. Most of the South African women business owners can be found in this category.

Domestic women business owners are not committed to entrepreneurial ideas but have a high attachment to traditional gender roles. They usually give up work to have children. Their motives are self-fulfilment, the exercise of creative skills and a search for personal autonomy. Most of their businesses are run from the home and are often geared to the low-volume production of high-quality goods and services.

Radical women business owners have little commitment to entrepreneurial ideas or to traditional gender roles; these women cannot be seen as entrepreneurial venture seekers. They are usually young, without children and well educated, but have limited work experience.

2.8.2 Barriers facing women entrepreneurs

Starting and operating a business involves considerable risks and effort for entrepreneurs, particularly in view of the high failure rate. Perhaps the risk is even greater for a woman entrepreneur, who not only has to contend with the problems associated with operating in a traditionally male-dominated area but also due to the lack of education and training in this specific field. Although both men and women face difficulties in establishing an enterprise,

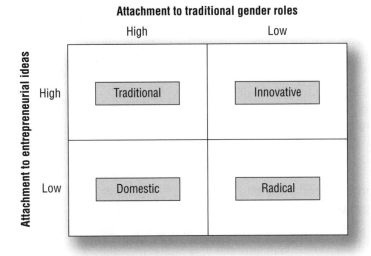

Figure 2.2 Types of women entrepreneurs

Source: Adapted from Goffee and Scase (1985: 25).

women experience specific barriers. Among these barriers are:

- Limited access to financial resources
- Lack of support
- Negative prevailing sociocultural attitudes
- Gender discrimination or bias
- Personal difficulties

Women often also suffer from low credibility when dealing with the various stakeholders associated with their firm, such as suppliers, bankers or customers. In a study conducted in South Africa, Allie and Human (1997: 8) found that although 72 per cent of micro-enterprises were owned by women, both internal and external barriers impacted on the success of these businesses. These barriers ranged from basic life skills of women entrepreneurs (self-confidence, assertiveness, self-motivation, achievement orientation, reliability and communication skills) to the virtual absence of mentorship opportunities and marketing and basic holistic management training (Allie & Human 1997: 8).

Ntsika Enterprise Promotion Agency held some workshops for women entrepreneurs where problems or barriers facing women were highlighted. Some of these barriers were the following (Adhikary et al. 1999: 30):

- There is limited networking for women within specific industries.
- Women entrepreneurs lack start-up funds.
- Banks/financial institutions readily criticise women's business plans without giving directions and guidance.
- Exposure to the media is very expensive.
- No database of women entrepreneurs by sector is available.
- There is replication and duplication of too many craft centres or groups in an area.
- Courses offered by training institutions focus on training the traditional manager and not the entrepreneur.

2.8.3 Comparison between male and female entrepreneurs in South Africa

It is necessary to draw a comparison between male and female entrepreneurs to highlight the most important differences between them. Table 2.1 indicates the differences between

these entrepreneurs based on their characteristics and needs.

2.9 Some new "labels" for entrepreneurship

2.9.1 Emerging entrepreneurs

"Emerging entrepreneurs" is a term used when referring to the previously disadvantaged groups who, since 1994, have been given preference by the government as a group to enable them to become entrepreneurs. The Preferential Procurement Act of 2001 is part of the government's effort to use public sector procurement to give preference to these entrepreneurs in the tendering system. Mokoena (1998: 16) states that entrepreneurship has long been celebrated and studied and is now more desirable than ever, and that the previously disadvantaged entrepreneurs in the townships have not received the attention they deserve. Black economic empowerment and the upliftment of the previously disadvantaged groups have seen a number of new and emerging entrepreneurs come into the limelight since 1994.

2.9.2 Survivalist and micro-enterprises (the informal sector)

Researchers' interest in the informal sector had its beginnings in the 1970s after the publication of the International Labour Office/United Nations Development Programme (ILO/UNDP) report on Kenya. In this report, the positive role in economic development of petty traders, street hawkers, "shoeshine boys", the working poor and other groups was recognised for the first time. Although most academics do not believe that these participants in the informal sector are entrepreneurs, they do meet most of the criteria contained in our definition. They do have entrepreneurial characteristics, but most of them end up as small and micro-enterprises bordering on mere survival. Their propensity to create employment or grow is limited by a lack of skills, knowledge and resources.

The ILO/UNDP report considered informal activities as those not merely confined to the periphery of large towns but as a way of doing things, characterised by:

- Ease of entry
- Reliance on indigenous sources

Table 2.1 A comparison between male and female entrepreneurs

Characteristic/ need	Male entrepreneurs	Women (female) entrepreneurs
Starting a business	Male entrepreneurs have set the foundation in the business environment for women entre-preneurs to follow.	Latecomers to the entrepreneurial game – some women are unaware of the fact that they can conduct business activities on their own.
Type of business started	Manufacturing or construction.	Service related – examples include guest houses, coffee shops and even a business that teaches women how to repair their own cars (a woman entrepreneur started a business called "Spanner and Wrench").
Relationship building	More short-term orientated. Male entrepreneurs search for the best way to get the job or deal done.	Women tend to build strong relationships with service providers, especially lenders such as bankers.
Access to finance	Can be a barrier if the male entrepreneur does not have adequate collateral.	This is seen as women entrepreneurs' most severe barrier, as well as discrimina-tion when applying for finance. They must take their husband or a male member of the family along to the bank when applying for financial assistance.
Support groups	Friends, professional acquain-tances, colleges, business partners and spouse.	Spouse, network group or association, e.g. the Business Women's Association and family members.

- Family ownership of the enterprise
- Small scale of operation
- Labour-intensive and adapted technology
- Skills acquired outside the formal school system
- Unregulated and competitive markets

According to Qua-Enoo (2001: 3), informal entrepreneurs are not recognised by the mainstream business enterprises and in all cases are denied the basic inputs they desperately need to develop their business enterprises. They come from the very poorest of poor areas of the economy. They have no formal training and very little educational background. They are denied banking facilities by the established banks and the government only pays lip service to solving their problems. An informal business enterprise is one that requires no formality to establish such a business and can be operated from the entrepreneur's own home. Depending on the nature of the business enterprise, the capital is very little, a day's wages being enough to start the venture. Most entrepreneurs only start these businesses to bring food to the table at the end of the day.

Maharaj (1998: 16) emphasises that street vendors are the most visible aspect of the informal economy. They are often regarded as a nuisance, obstructing the flow of commerce, and are an unwelcome proof of the country's underdevelopment. Yet street vendors contribute positively to the economy by distributing a significant share of goods and services at low prices, thus helping consumers in the low- to medium-income brackets.

To fully understand the informal and survivalist enterprises, it is expedient to know the characteristics of the environment from which they come and in which they operate (Qua-Enoo 2001: 7).

- The informal and survivalist entrepreneurs mostly come from the rural areas. The only vehicle in the area leaves at dawn for the big towns and returns late in the evening. If one misses the return trip, one has to find a place to lodge for the night in the town.

- There is no tap water or electricity. People have to rely on pools and running water for daily use and on paraffin for lighting.

- It is the most diversified sector of the economy, and includes trading, retailing, handcrafts, farming, food vendors (fruit and vegetables), hairdressing, phone services, typing, sewing, brick making, construction and manufacturing.

- The level of formal education is very low; most reach Standard 7 (Grade 9) and then drop out. As a result, most people cannot understand, let alone comprehend, the legalistic legislation placed before them. Every written document has to be interpreted for them.

- Economic activities are very low. Where the economy is vibrant, people engaged in economic activities could have easy access to either working capital or investment capital, thus enhancing their livelihood. However, this is not the case in the informal and survivalist environment; as a result, they are among the most economically deprived in society.

- Demographically, it is the most impoverished environment. The majority of the economically active labour force has left, leaving the young and the old to take care of each other. Most of the elderly who are left behind are women who support "the family", the size of which is usually fairly large.

- Most informal and survivalist entrepreneurs live in shacks, and if affluent enough, build mud houses with weeds as roofing material.

2.9.3 Youth entrepreneurship

Youth entrepreneurship has become a major focus in South Africa in recent years, especially after the formation of the Umsombomvu Youth Fund. This fund was created with the finance generated by the government from the demutualisation of Sanlam and Old Mutual. The objective of the fund is to encourage young people to become entrepreneurs and to give them access to finance and markets.

Some schools in South Africa have introduced entrepreneurship as a subject in their syllabi. The reason why they do this is not only to foster and celebrate the new successes achieved by young entrepreneurs, but also to creatively market entrepreneurship as a viable option for even younger persons still at school. By joining up successful youth with potential clients, investors and strategic partners, the youth can make up a proud piece of South Africa's economic development initiatives. An example of minority or youth entrepreneurship is evident at the University of Pretoria, where the South African Student Entrepreneurship Club (SASEC) was formed to promote entrepreneurship among the youth.

Another example of youth entrepreneurship is present at the University of Cape Town (UCT) Bookstore – it has heralded the latest chapter in the growth of student entrepreneurship on campus. The bookshop is owned by University of Cape Town Student Enterprises (UCT has a minority stake), which in turn forms part of the newly registered Student Enterprises Trust. According to Mojapelo (2002: 1), the primary vision of Student Enterprises Trust is to encourage entrepreneurship among students within the tertiary sector in South Africa. If entrepreneurship has to do with turning ideas into viable companies or operations, it follows logically that the one place we would expect to find entrepreneurial human resources is at a university or technikon. The Trust will encourage student entrepreneurship through four programmes:

- Innovative educational programmes
- Business development
- Special projects
- Student businesses

2.10 Entrepreneurship and certain industries

Nowadays, it has become more popular for individuals in other upcoming industries or

© Van Schaik Publishers

markets to merge with entrepreneurship to create growing new entrepreneurs. These entrepreneurs include technology entrepreneurs (technopreneurs), social entrepreneurs and tourism entrepreneurs.

2.10.1 Technology entrepreneurs (technopreneurs)

Wickham's (1998: 21) definition of technology-based entrepreneurs states that technopreneurs are especially important in modern business. It is they who are taking advantage of new scientific developments, especially in the areas of information technology, biotechnology and engineering science, and offering their benefits to the wider world.

Ntsika Enterprise Promotion Agency (1999: 4) in South Africa provides technological programmes that aim to create sustainable enterprises through quality training and support services. These programmes provide the technopreneur with knowledge of:

- Opportunity analysis
- Skills audit
- Holistic development of the SMME sector
- A support network for potential entrepreneurs in the development process

2.10.2 Social entrepreneurs

In the United Kingdom it is estimated that social entrepreneurs create ten times more jobs than business entrepreneurs (Mojapelo 2002: 2). A social entrepreneur is someone who runs a non-governmental organisation. For business entrepreneurs and social entrepreneurs alike, finding start-up capital remains a major problem. It is actually more an entrepreneurial orientation than true entrepreneurship that is present in these instances.

2.10.3 Tourism entrepreneurs

Tourism is currently the fastest growing industry in South Africa, the largest industry in the world and also the biggest employer. Saayman and Saayman (1998: 3) report that the South African tourism market has changed and accepted a new paradigm by creating new products. Visits to townships and cultural villages, viewing of traditional dancing and expe-

riencing a shebeen, to name but a few examples, have gained popularity. The new tourist's different approach creates a demand for new products. Entrepreneurs in SMMEs within the tourism industry are dependent on major tourism developments.

Koh (1996: 30) defines tourism entrepreneurship as activities related to creating and operating a legal tourist enterprise. Legal enterprises refer to those businesses that operate on a profitable basis and seek to meet the needs of tourists and visitors. These enterprises include hotels, guest houses, travel agencies and tour operators. Entrepreneurship and tourism can be seen as complementing each other in striving towards the mutual goal of generating employment opportunities in South Africa.

Many opportunities are available for entrepreneurs within the tourism industry in South Africa:

- The accommodation sector of the industry is vibrant, especially the development and operation of camping grounds, caravan parks, game parks, holiday camps, hotels, motels, chalets, bed-and-breakfast establishments and guest houses. The guest house sector, as part of the hospitality trade in South Africa, has grown considerably over the past five years and indications are that this growth will be maintained in the near future.

- The transport industry also holds many opportunities for potential entrepreneurs. In becoming a tour operator, the entrepreneur can package tours and then make use of other entrepreneurs for rendering support services such as transporting people.

- Man-made attractions, for example monuments, theme parks, waterfront developments, zoos, parks, game reserves and wedding and conference venues, have also become a popular entrepreneurial activity.

2.11 Entrepreneurs vs inventors

It is common misconception that entrepreneurs and inventors are the same or interrelated and that they undertake the same activities. The role of entrepreneurs is distinctive from that of other business actors, including employees and silent partners. For example, investors are not involved in day-to-day activities. Rather, there is an ongoing process between the entrepreneur and the inventor – if the inventor creates something new for the first time but lacks the skills to sell the product, the entrepreneur will take over and start a business venture.

According to Wickham (1998: 48), the inventor is someone who has developed an innovation and who has decided to make a career out of presenting that innovation to the market. It may be a new product or an idea for a new service. The entrepreneur takes over where the inventor stops, by selling the new product or service to customers and by selling the venture to investors. The inventor may have high creativity but relatively few management skills. A good inventor prefers to investigate and to discover. The typical entrepreneur needs a relatively high level of creativity, combined with considerable management skills.

2.12 Conclusion

From this chapter it is evident that entrepreneurship is the key driver of economic growth and development in South Africa. This chapter outlines the current thinking and research related to identifying the unique characteristics of a person who successfully launches a new venture. SMMEs will prosper if they can find the proper time for action, utilising the right BDS agencies and constantly updating their management and human assets. In addition, by establishing good networking with suppliers, customers and other relevant parties, they will succeed in creating an environment in which their businesses will thrive. Effective internal people management will result in harmonious employee relations. This chapter has also focused on the challenges facing entrepreneurs in the informal sector, with specific reference to the previously disadvantaged groups. Women entrepreneurs are seen as the most disadvantaged entrepreneurs and face numerous barriers when starting a business.

There is a Chinese saying: "Success depends on good timing, a proper environment, and people in harmony" (Qua-Enoo 2001: 17). In sum, successful South African entrepreneurs try to create a future for themselves by responding to the changes in the environment.

Looking back

1. List various reasons why entrepreneurship can be seen as a catalyst for economic activity.
   - Creates and drives new businesses
   - Survival and growth of the economy
   - Creates employment
   - Improves level of poverty
   - Direct link between the entrepreneur and the customer
   - Sustains economic growth and development
   - Career option for women and youth

2. Name the various levels of entrepreneurial sophistication.
   - Basic survivalist
   - Pre-entrepreneur
   - Subsistence entrepreneur
   - Micro-entrepreneur
   - Small-scale entrepreneur

3. Name the dominant characteristics that are found in successful entrepreneurs.
   - Passion
   - Locus of control
   - Need for independence
   - Need for achievement
   - Risk taking and uncertainty
   - Creativity and innovation
   - Determination and persistence

4. Briefly discuss the types of networks and support systems available to entrepreneurs.
   - Social networks
   - Personal networks
   - Extended networks
   - Other networks, including the Internet, suppliers and investors

5. Indicate the difference between the push and pull factors of entrepreneurship by referring to their definitions.

- Push factors are those factors that encourage entrepreneurship due to traditional jobs being less attractive or because an individual does not have any other career choice or option.
- Pull factors are those factors that encourage people in traditional jobs to leave their current positions to become entrepreneurs.

6. Briefly discuss the challenges facing entrepreneurs and SMMEs in South Africa.
   - Access to start-up and expansion finance
   - Access to markets
   - Access to appropriate technology
   - Access to resources (especially human resources)

7. List and discuss the types of women entrepreneurs.
   - Traditional
   - Innovative
   - Domestic
   - Radical

8. Name the most significant barriers or problems that women entrepreneurs face.
   - There is limited networking for women within specific industries.

- Women entrepreneurs lack start-up funds.
- Banks/financial institutions readily criticise business plans without giving directions or guidance.
- Exposure to the media is very expensive.
- No database of women entrepreneurs by sector is available.
- There is replication and duplication of too many craft centres or groups in an area.
- Courses offered by training institutions focus on training the traditional manager and not the entrepreneur.

9. Explain the characteristics of the informal and survivalist environment.
   - It is mostly in a rural area.
   - There is no tap water or electricity.
   - The level of formal education is low.
   - Economic activity is low.
   - These entrepreneurs live in shacks.

10. Briefly explain how student entrepreneurship can be encouraged.
    - Innovative educational programmes
    - Business development
    - Special projects
    - Student businesses

Key terms

Background of entrepreneurs
Catalyst for economic activity
Emerging entrepreneurs
Entrepreneurial sophistication
Informal and survivalist environment
Investors
Networking
Pull factors
Push factors

Role models
Small, medium and micro-enterprises (SMMEs)
Social entrepreneurs
Support systems
Technopreneurs
Tourism entrepreneurs
Women (female) entrepreneurs
Youth entrepreneurship

Discussion questions

1. In your own opinion, why do you think entrepreneurship is an important driver for economic growth and development in South Africa?

2. Explain the different levels of entrepreneurial sophistication by making use of your own practical examples.

3. What is entrepreneurial networking? How can it support upcoming and emerging entrepreneurs?

4. Make use of a diagram to illustrate the difference between the push and pull factors of entrepreneurship.

5. Explain the major challenges that entrepreneurs and SMMEs face, as well as possible solutions to these problems.

6. Make use of a diagram to draw a comparison between male and female (women) entrepreneurs in South Africa. Do you think that there are significant differences between them?

7. Use practical examples to describe the opportunities for entrepreneurs within the tourism industry in South Africa. Why do you think the relationship between the tourism industry and entrepreneurship is so important?

8. Use examples to make a significant distinction between entrepreneurs and investors.

Experiential exercises

1. Analyse your own education, experience and characteristics as qualifications for entrepreneurship. Identify your greatest strengths and weaknesses.

2. Visit an entrepreneur and summarise his or her background: childhood environment, age, education and work experience.

3. Identify a person whom you consider a good entrepreneurial role model. Write a short case study on that person's accomplishments, challenges and successes as an entrepreneur.

4. Interview a previously disadvantaged entrepreneur in the informal sector and establish the most severe barriers that he or she faces in his or her everyday business operations.

5. Identify a successful woman entrepreneur. Evaluate her background and career against the definition of a successful woman entrepreneur as provided in this chapter.

Exploring the Web

1. If you wish to find out more about the Business Women's Association in South Africa, go to www.bwasa.co.za to examine the support systems available to women entrepreneurs.

2. Visit www.gemconsortium.org to find out more about the *International Executive Report on Entrepreneurship.* It compares South Africa's entrepreneurial activities to those of 28 other countries.

3. To learn more about minority entrepreneurship, visit www.utc.ac.za/general/monpaper.

4. To find out more about opportunities for women and other previously disadvantaged entrepreneurs, go to the Department of Trade and Industry's website at www.dti.gov.za/newsarticles2002.

Case study

"Boss Lady"

She sits on a bright red stool behind her stall, fanning herself as the sun climbs higher in the sky. It is the end of the month and people have money to spend – it's going to be a hectic day! Elsie Matonsele, or Sis Elsie as everyone calls her – stands up as a woman approaches her stall, a wailing baby on her back. Beads of sweat run down the woman's face as she pulls a handful of coins from her purse and gives them to Elsie. She buys some sweets and gives one to the baby, who stops crying instantly. As the mother moves away, Elsie sits down again and records the sale in a notebook. She has been doing it for the past eight years – every sale, no matter how small, is written down. It is the only way she can keep track of everything she sells. She has sold plenty since she opened her stall in downtown Johannesburg in 1990. So much, in fact, that she has paid off her house and extended it, and bought her own car, a BMW, which she operates as a metered taxi. This 32-year-old mother of two is probably more committed than most street vendors – and her customers know that. They know she will always be at her stall on the corner of Bree and Quartz Streets, come rain or shine. They know they will be able to buy just about anything from her – fruit and vegetables, underwear and nappies, sweets and biscuits, ballpoint pens and mothballs, health and beauty products, cleaning aids and safety pins.

Her stall is like a mobile general dealer, and her customers know everything they buy there is of top quality. Elsie knows that keeping her customers satisfied over the years has been the key to her success. "I take care of my customers the way a doctor takes care of patients," she says, as a rust-coloured BMW comes to a halt in front of her stall. It is the second-hand one she bought for R7 500 and uses as a taxi. It is driven by Johannes Masuku and operates between the city centre and Hillbrow, Yeoville and Berea. A street vendor with a metered taxi and a driver to operate it is not something you come across every day, let alone one who has paid off her home. Elsie deserves everything she has – she has worked her fingers to the bone to achieve a lifestyle most vendors can

only dream of ... Armed with just R160, she went to the City Deep market and bought her first supply of fresh fruit and vegetables. "And that," she smiles, "was my first step towards financial independence". Back then, R160's worth of fruit and vegetables went quite a long way and usually lasted her a couple of days. Slowly but steadily, people started buying from her stall and before long she was making a profit of about R80 a day. But times – and the economy – have changed and Elsie now has to pay about R500 for her stock every time she goes to the market. But her profits have also increased. "On good days I take home about R300," she says.

Elsie saved every cent she could, because owning her own home has always been her dream. It did not matter if it was a shack or a mud hut – she wanted to own every bit of it. It is a five-roomed house in Alexandra Township, a stone's throw away from Sandton, north of Johannesburg. But the house did not look the way it does today when she bought it – it was an ordinary two-roomed structure on the market for R20 000. She and the owners reached an agreement that the house would be hers as soon as she had paid off the amount, as Elsie did not want to move in until then. She still remembers the day in 1996 when she made the last instalment and the house was well and truly hers. "Then came the extensions," she says. "The house had just a kitchen and a bedroom, but I knew I'd be able to convert it to suit my and my children's needs." She built on three extra rooms at a cost of R15 000 and the family lives there comfortably now.

Hard work is Elsie's recipe for success. She rises at 5 a.m. every morning, has a hot bath and a light breakfast, and is at the market by 6 a.m. on the days she has to stock up. "You have to get there early to get the best produce," she says. Laden with her stock she gets to her stall, which consists of four tables pushed together and covered with spotlessly clean cloths. Everything is set out by 8 a.m. and she's ready for business. Elsie keeps going all day, sometimes only packing up shop at 7 p.m. She claims she is happiest when she knows her customers are satisfied. Elsie says she does not have a special skill or talent, but what she does have in large doses is determination and a strong spirit. And it has proved to be a winning combination. She has some advice to share with other would-be businesspeople. "Set yourself long- and short-term goals," she says. "Don't be satisfied with less than the best. Learn to convert stumbling blocks into stepping stones by moving on to more worthwhile and profitable ventures. Always learn from your own mistakes. Put your money in trust, not your trust in money – in other words, save whenever you can and put luxuries on hold until you can really afford them." Elsie should know what she is talking about – after all, these are words she has lived by. And look at her now.

Source: Adapted from *Drum,* 15 October 1998.

Questions

1. Briefly discuss Elsie's success story with reference to the barriers that women (female) entrepreneurs experience in general.

2. The informal sector is characterised by women who start and operate small (micro-) businesses to survive.
   - Do you think Elsie can break out of this sector? Substantiate your answer.
   - What entrepreneurial characteristics does Elsie possess?

3. Is Elsie perceived as a role model in her community? Explain.

References and recommended reading

Adhikary, D., Rai, A. & Rajaratnam, B. 1999. *Successful women entrepreneurs in South Africa.* Pretoria: Ntsika Enterprise Promotion Agency.

Allie, F. & Human, L. 1997. Networking/support systems for female entrepreneurs in South Africa. In: *Proceedings of the FCEM 45th International Congress of Women Business Owners.* Cape Town, 14-16 October.

Driver, A., Wood, E., Segal, N. & Herrington, M. 2001. *Global Entrepreneurship Monitor: 2001 South African executive report.* Graduate School of Business. Cape Town: University of Cape Town.

Goffee, R. & Scase, R. 1985. *Women in charge.* London: Allen & Unwin.

Koh, K.Y. 1996. The tourism entrepreneurial process: a conceptualisation and implications for research and development. *The Tourism Revue,* 4: 24-39.

Maharaj, Z. 1998. Recognising women's role in informal economies. *Pretoria News: Business Report.* 28 July, 16.

McClelland, D.C. 1961. *The achieving society.* Princeton: Von Nostrand.

Mojapelo, M. 2002. New chapter for student enterprises. *Monday: Weekly newspaper of the University of Cape Town.* Department of Communication and Marketing. Cape Town: University of Cape Town.

Mokoena, M. 1998. Endangered township entrepreneurs need survival plan. *Pretoria News: Business Report.* 21 July, 16.

Nieman, G.H. 1999. Cash is the lifeblood of small business enterprises. *Accounting and Financial Update.* April: 8-9.

Nieman, G.H. & Bennett, A. (Eds). 2002. *Business management: a value chain approach.* Pretoria: Van Schaik.

Ntsika Enterprise Promotion Agency. 1999. *State of small business in South Africa.* Review 1998. Pretoria: Ntsika.

Qua-Enoo, G.A. 2001. *Uplifting the informal entrepreneurs to mainstream business enterprises.* In the proceedings of the South African Entrepreneurship and Small Business Conference, Caesars, Gauteng, August.

Saayman, M. & Saayman, A. 1998. Tourism and the South African economy: growing opportunities for entrepreneurs. *African Journal for Health, Physical Education, Recreation and Dance,* 5(1): 1-26.

Smith, L. 2000. Jenna Clifford, one of South Africa's top women entrepreneurs. *The Entrepreneur,* March/April: 9-11.

Wickham, P.A. 1998. *Strategic entrepreneurship: a decision-making approach to new venture creation and management,* 2nd ed. London: Prentice Hall.

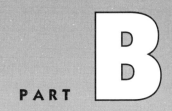

PART **B**

The entrepreneurial process

Creativity and business opportunity

Alex Antonites

3.1 Introduction

To be an entrepreneur and act entrepreneurially is not merely a forced action due to unforeseen conditions and circumstances. It is a challenge from day one, and the moment you do not experience the unique challenge anymore, look for a salaried job! Entrepreneurship yields various awards and spontaneous failures, on a daily basis. Not one day will be the same. The routine is different, you manage it by yourself, and you need to find time not based on the conventional eight to five slot. The new venture you start up and establish will compete with one or the other corporate giant's products or services. Various other obstacles will also hamper immediate growth and expansion.

How do entrepreneurs manage to succeed? How do these individuals cope and overcome both foreseen and unforeseen obstacles? One of the primary driving forces is found in creative behaviour. Creative behaviour and thinking lead to innovative actions and even processes. Consider the most successful entrepreneurs on a global level. They have all discovered, invented or innovated new products, services or processes. Some of them only changed the existing or conventional into the new. All of these actions are the result of intense creativity, a differentiating entrepreneurial skill.

This section of the book will equip you, the potential entrepreneur, with the essential skill of thinking and acting creatively. It will furthermore create a platform for effective problem solving and the identification of opportunities. Creativity is also the fundamental cornerstone of all marketing tasks, based on the effective introduction of your new product, service or process to the primary target market.

A question you are probably asking yourself now is: Am I creative? Our first exercise is a short creativity assessment, before we embark on the exciting route of creativity development. Complete the questionnaire in Question 1 under "Experiential exercises" at the end of the chapter in order to determine your level of cre-

Learning outcomes

After completion of this chapter, you should be able to:

- Understand the basic theory behind creativity and innovation
- Create an awareness of your current creative abilities
- Remove all the possible obstacles to creative thinking
- Develop and improve creativity within yourself to excel in the expected fields of entrepreneurial venturing and small business management
- Generate new ideas
- Create new feasible products, services or processes, thus innovate
- Assess the likely commercial success of your new innovation

ativity. The scoring and interpretation of the questionnaire are also given. The result of your questionnaire is only a vague indication of your level of creativity at this stage. A low score does not mean that this is the end of all your entrepreneurial endeavours. Likewise, a high score (e.g. above 100) does not mean that there will be a million rand in your pocket within the next few days! Creativity is something that can be developed and the result of creative thinking is only a small, but important part of the high road to success.

3.2 The theory of creativity

Creativity is a result of brain-driven actions. The brain is a powerful weapon and contemporary research shows that human beings only utilise 2 per cent of this organ! It is furthermore interesting to note that the fastest and strongest computer has one four-millionth of the brain's capacity! To manufacture a computer with the brain's capacity will cost in the region of R200 trillion. One's brain is a tool that can transform various complex problems into attractive opportunities.

It is currently estimated that 80 per cent of problems in life are solved by creative thinking skills – so much more in the entrepreneurial environment. Think about the fact that you are considering starting your own business or you are forced by economic conditions to do so. Firstly, you have to identify a viable opportunity. You need a product or service and a feasible business model. The whole process is creatively driven. This section will enlighten you on the theoretical concept of creativity and innovation.

There are more than 450 definitions of creativity, which have been developed over the last hundred years. Couger (1995) defined creativity extensively and formulated it in the sense of solving definite problems. His generally accepted definition contains the following conditions:

- The product of creativity is firstly a product or result of a thinking process. This product or idea should have novelty as a result and should create value (i.e. the brain is uniquely utilised in the thinking process and the result is supposed to create a useful item).

- This thinking process is usually unconventional, meaning that previously accepted ideas or concepts are normally rejected or modified.

- The thinking process is supported by performance motivation and is mostly time and energy consuming.

- The initial problem is normally vague and not structured. The problem definition is thus integrated in the thinking process.

Creativity is furthermore:
- Unusual; uncommon; unique; something with surprise value
- Practical; functional; feasible
- Understandable and also able to be used by others

Glassman (1993) expands this view and sees creativity as the ability to:
- Associate remote stimuli in the environment with elements in the mind, and to combine them into new and unusual ideas (we will apply this statement practically)
- Keep an open mind and see new perspectives
- Generate many ideas
- Generate a variety of really different ideas
- Develop ideas
- Generate infrequent and uncommon ideas
- Hang in there when going against consensus and be persistent in the face of criticism (especially when developing a new product)

The word "creativity" is derived from the Latin root *creare*, which means to produce – thus *creating* something new. Creativity is the catalyst for all new creations, from the invention until the final innovation and implementation process. It is significant to assess the entrepreneurial process and see that all entrepreneurs, whether successful or unsuccessful, enter the business environment with a creative intervention. The following section will elaborate on how potential entrepreneurs and even existing small businesses can utilise creativity as a fundamental tool in business venturing. However, it is very important to understand the supporting theory and process behind creative and innovative actions.

3.3 The creativity model

Few models exist that explain the creative process in a simplistic way. The nature of creativity, its role in entrepreneurship and its benefits in the growth of a successful business are still being debated. An accepted model of creativity elucidates the concept in a simplistic way. This model – *the 4 P model of creativity* – serves as a basis for entrepreneurial creativity.

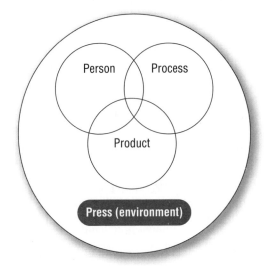

Figure 3.1 The 4P model of creativity

Source: From *Creative Problem Solving and Opportunity Finding*, 1st edition by Couger. © 1995. Reprinted with permission of South-Western, a division of Thomson Learning: www.thomsonrights.com. Fax (091) 800 730-2215.

This is an interactive model, which implies that creativity can be improved by giving special attention to each variable individually and in an interdependent context. The following subsections are based on the above model.

3.3.1 The person

The most important variable in the creativity model is the person, in this case the entrepreneur. It is a common fact that creativity is a fundamental entrepreneurial skill and, more importantly, a learnable or acquired skill. As mentioned before, the brain is the main factory in the creative result. Research has been conducted over the ages to determine the role of the brain in creativity and, likewise, to establish which parts of the brain are the major supporting functions in creativity. The last two to three decades indicated a definite split between left- and right-brain orientations. The left hemisphere of the brain orientates itself towards

factual, logical, rational, theoretical, mathematical, ordered, detailed, sequential, controlled and conservative matters. The right hemisphere orientates itself towards musical, spiritual, talkative, emotional, empathetic, artistic, holistic, flexible, imaginative and synthesising matters. Creativity is predominantly a right-brain activity, but in the entrepreneurship environment a process of whole brain activity is utilised.

It is firstly important to consider what it takes to develop creativity in a person. How does a creative person look and is it possible to develop creativity? Amabile (1999) analysed three components of creativity as seen in the context of the person: expertise, motivation and creative thinking skills.

■ Expertise

Expertise includes all the knowledge, experience and talent a person can use to apply in a certain situation. Some employees have extensive experience gained over years in, for example, marketing, production purchasing or general management. This expertise could be acquired through the person's educational background, training interventions, experience and even his or her daily interaction with others.

■ Motivation

The motivation component of creative people determines what they will do and also whether they will do it. It does not matter in what position or level of work they find themselves, new ideas and their development are fuelled by a certain level of motivation. Think for yourself, the reward and success of a new product that you have developed would also motivate you to develop another and yet another! In a certain sense, therefore, the level of motivation could determine your performance or success in the long run.

■ Creative thinking skills

Creative thinking skills play an enormous role in the way the person will deal with a problem or idea. He or she could associate unrelated components and combine them in a new or unique format. Managers of a restaurant could, for instance, combine music and atmosphere, or music and aroma, or the type of meal and atmosphere. Thus, creative thinking skills are used to combine rather unrelated elements to develop a new idea for the restaurant.

What prevents the entrepreneur from acting creatively? Thus, what are the myths about, and stumbling blocks to being creative?

3.3.2 The creative myth

Various myths and misconceptions surround creativity. The following quotes indicate just some of the earlier myths:

Everything that can be invented has been invented.
(Director of Patent Office, 1899)

Television won't be able to hold on to any market it captures after the first six months. People will soon get tired of staring at a plywood box every night.
(Daryl F. Zanuck, CEO 20th Century Fox, 1946)

We will never release our cartoons and movies on videotape. There's too great a danger of illegal copying.
(Ronald Miller, CEO President Disney Corporation, son-in-law of Walt Disney)

Sensible and responsible women do not want the right to vote.
(Grove Cleveland, when running for presidency a second time – he lost)

Heavier-than-air flying machines are impossible.
(Lord Kelvin, famous scientist)

Man will never find a practical use for the atom.
(Lord Ernest Rutherford, famous scientist)

Who the hell wants to hear actors talk?
(Jack Warner, Warner Bros studios, 1927)

The general myths surrounding creativity are as follows:

■ Creativity is an innate skill and cannot be acquired by means of training

It is definitely possible to train someone to improve his or her level of creativity. Not all individuals are designing unique and award-winning products all the time, but we can improve our level of creative ability by means of specific creative techniques. This chapter offers you an opportunity to do so.

■ You need to be a rebel to be seen as creative

This fact is especially present on a secondary school level. Rebels are the individuals who "creatively" surpassed general rules and regulations. Nowadays we can teach people of any kind to think and act more creatively.

■ Artists are the only creative beings

The work of artists is indeed creative. However, only a small percentage of artists sell their products profitably to their markets. Some artists can even reach a point where their art stagnates and therefore always looks the same (think about the whole Claerhout debacle where the artist's work was copied and sold, mainly because his style did not change much over many years). You don't have to be an artist to think creatively and solve problematic business issues!

■ You need to be "crazy" before creativity will kick in

To be crazy, in the sense of being funny and different, could certainly encourage unconventional thinking. However, some product development processes take place under quite serious conditions and procedures. These new products are also part of the creative process and require huge amounts of creative thinking that is not related to "crazy" roots.

■ Intelligence and creativity

A well-known study shows that creativity and IQ go together up until the 120 mark, whereafter creativity decreases. This study is not necessarily conclusive, but think for yourself, do you have to be highly intelligent to think and act creatively?

■ Group vs individual

Are you more creative in a group situation or when operating individually? Various studies have been conducted in this regard. The results say an individual's decision making and personal experience will tell. There will be opportunities in this chapter that will indicate to you which format induces creative thinking and actions.

■ **All new products were accidental discoveries**

The majority of all new products are the result of in-depth research and a development process. This may sound as though it is applicable only to corporate set-ups, but small ventures can hedge serious risks by doing proper research.

There are, furthermore, certain obstacles in the way of thinking creatively. These blocks need to be removed in order to "create" effectively.

3.3.3 Blocks to creativity

The following barriers are normally obstacles to thinking and acting creatively. These blockages are based on the individual and will influence many tasks in the business and workplace.

■ **Environmental barriers**

In this context we look at the social, economic and physical environments.

The **social** environment in itself creates certain barriers:

- There is a lack of understanding of, and support for, new ideas in the community, among friends and family.
- Risk taking is not allowed
- Many families have an autocratic decision-making structure, which does not allow children to think for themselves.
- Cultural barriers as such form part of the social environment.

The **economic** environment may create barriers:

- The economy in general is not conducive to the development of new ideas and products.
- There are no growth prospects in the economy.
- No financial support is available for the development of new products.
- Risk taking is seen as a negative element of the economy.
- No rewards for new and feasible ideas exist.

The **physical** environment could be restrictive:

- Distractions, for example sounds, the climate and a lack of energy

- Conventional venues in the education and training environment (even rows, and grey or dull colours)
- Routine – you have to eat, work, study and sleep as part of a specific timetable and routine
- Work routine – always conducting the same tasks at the same time and in the same way

■ **Cultural barriers**

There are more than 12 different cultural groups in South Africa. Each one of them has characteristics that will, at some point in time, influence creative development negatively. It is, however, important not to stereotype in this regard due to the sensitivity and pride involved in cultural beliefs. The following barriers are reckoned to be generic cultural barriers or mindsets:

- You have to go to school, after that study at a university or college, and after that you will find a job at a government institution.
- The unknown is unsafe.
- You always have to be practical and think economically before you generate ideas.
- To ask a question, or to question an issue, is out of bounds and not permitted.
- Stereotyping – assumptions are made about certain issues without proper knowledge of the background or particulars of the matter.
- The policy of the company is to follow strict orders and procedures, and stay in line with the organisational structure.

■ **Perceptual barriers**

Perceptual blocks are barriers in the way we see or perceive objects and/or abstract things clearly and correctly. The following perceptions are potential blocks to creativity:

- Using a narrow mindset to analyse problems. An example in this regard is "idea anxiety" – one has an idea and focuses on the "great" idea without analysing the relevant facts supporting it.
- Making assumptions about a problem or idea without getting the bigger picture – or, on the other hand, being unable to structure the problem and evaluate the smaller elements.
- Assuming that something will work without doing proper marketing research or feasibili-

ty studies. Relying on the "gut feeling" only may lead to a premature idea.

- Different perceptions of the characteristics and even utilities of the new product by the owner and the potential customer. For many new products, this perceptual block has had failure in the marketplace as a result.

There are various barriers that affect the creative process negatively, for example intellectual, emotional and time barriers. It is, therefore, advisable to try to remove these barriers before embarking on any means of creativity.

> What lies behind us and what lies before us are tiny matters compared to what lies within us.
>
> William Morrow

3.3.4 The process

Creativity forms part of a continuous process. Creative thinking is the fundamental basis for, or facilitator in, the development of new initiatives, products or services. Figure 3.2 indicates how the whole process flows.

- The first step in the creative process is **idea generation**. This is a process on its own whereby a multitude of ideas is generated. Emphasis is placed on quantity and not necessarily quality. This is predominantly a process of discovery. (A practical exercise will be conducted later).

- The second step leads to developing the most suitable and/or feasible idea. This is a process of **invention**. More research is being done on the selected idea to determine its viability, for instance in the marketplace.

Certain functionality tests are also undertaken.

- The most suitable idea or invention is then transformed into an **innovation**, thus a new product, service or process.

Creativity is the fuel for the first three steps of the process. The creativity process in Table 3.1 shows what specific steps one can take in order to facilitate new inventions.

There are various creative techniques that will facilitate creative behaviour and also induce the development of new ideas.

3.3.5 Creative techniques

There are hundreds of creativity techniques that will assist you to think more creatively, act more creatively, generate ideas and even analyse opportunities in the marketplace. The techniques below form an integral part of the creative process.

■ Random input

Random inputs are based on the development of words, pictures or images. You can use any random method available, for example:

- Write 20 words on small pieces of paper, throw them in a hat and choose one with your eyes closed. Take the word and think of all related elements.

- Open a magazine or newspaper, take every second or third word and analyse the meaning or related elements.

- Take the first 20 photos in your family album and use colours, images and situations to develop new ideas from them.

This technique is normally used to stimulate the creative thinking process.

Figure 3.2 The process of creative thinking

Source: From *Creative Problem Solving and Opportunity Finding*, 1st edition by Couger. © 1995. Reprinted with permission of South-Western, a division of Thomson Learning: www.thomsonrights.com. Fax (091) 800 730-2215.

Table 3.1 Stages of the creative process

Stages	Requirements
1. Awareness and interest	• Recognition of a problem or situation • Curiosity
2. Preparation	• Openness to experience • Analysis of how the task might be approached • Tolerance of ambiguity • Willingness to redefine concepts • Divergent thought processes (explore many possibilities) • Intuitive ability
3. Incubation	• Imagination • Absorption • Seeking ideas, possible answers and solutions • Independence • Psychological freedom
4. Illumination (insight)	• Ability to switch from intuitive to analytical patterns of thought • Eureka! • A-ha!
5. Verification	• Critical attitude • Analytical ability • Testing

Source: Adapted and integrated from Williams (1999: 7) and Nystrom (1979: 39).

■ **Problem reversal**

Almost all ideas, arguments or attributes have an opposite. This method forces you to see things backwards, inside out and upside down, thus enabling you to analyse the whole concept or problem. The following procedure can be followed:

1. See your problem in the reverse form. Change a negative form into the positive, or the other way around.
2. Define what something is "not", or the opposite thereof.
3. Analyse what everybody else is not doing, or the opposite thereof.
4. Use the "what if" question.
5. Change the direction of your perspective.
6. Evaluate all results.
7. Turn defeat into victory, and the other way around.

■ **5Ws & H technique**

This technique is also called the "questioning technique". It embraces the following questions: "Who; What; Where; When; Why; and How". Apply all the questions to every idea you have in mind. Take the advantages of your idea and ask these questions; do the same with the potential disadvantages of your idea.

■ **Association technique**

The linkages or associations among unrelated or related concepts, ideas or objects have led to many new and unique products. Take a problem and make use of unrelated elements in, for example, nature to develop a solution to the problem. Alfred does not know what colour to use in his restaurant, and colour plays an enormous role in the ambience and atmosphere of a place. How could nature possibly assist him?

■ Discontinuity principle

The more we get caught in a routine or fixed environment, the less stimulating it is for our creative thinking. This method implies that we intervene in our daily routine or programme by means of unusual interruptions, such as:

- Change the way or route to work, class or a friend's house.
- Listen to a different radio station.
- Read newspapers, magazines or books but totally outside your frame of reference.
- Start talking to strange individuals.
- Use a different approach during your lunch break, for example lie on your back on the grass and concentrate on nothing at all.

With this method we force ourselves to think "out-of-the-box" and possibly see problems in a different light. It can also develop a new routine of idea generation.

3.3.6 Idea vs opportunity

In most cases, the idea generation phase of the creative process is neglected. Individuals normally identify a problem or an opportunity (that may seem like an opportunity, but it is just an idea), and then develop a new product in line with the assumed idea or opportunity. It is, therefore, important to distinguish between an idea and an opportunity. Resources may be wasted when a mere idea is incorrectly perceived to be an opportunity.

This dilemma reminds one of the question, "Which came first, the chicken or the egg?". There is, however, a critical difference between the two constructs. Think about the following: Is it an idea or an opportunity to develop a high-speed train between two major cities that are not far from each other? Some people would say it is a great idea, but when you need to pay R100 a day to make use of it, it is just not an opportunity. Only a few individuals would make use of the service and would therefore affect the size of the market negatively. If it is possible to transport people between the cities at a cost of R20, it would already appear to be a more feasible opportunity.

The question now arises is: How do I differentiate between an idea and an opportunity? Table 3.2 shows the different industries in South Africa and the level of entrepreneurial activity.

This study – the Global Entrepreneurship Monitor – specifically identified the entrepreneurial activity in the various industries of our country. It can be generalised that an industry with a high level of entrepreneurial activity yields more business opportunities (e.g. manufacturing; retail, hotel, restaurant; and business services), while one with a low level would indicate fewer opportunities (e.g. agriculture, forestry, hunting, fishing; finance, insurance, real estate; and health, education and social services). If we analyse just one "high opportunity" industry, for instance manufacturing, it might be an opportunity today to manufacture a final product and export it to an international market. A "low opportunity" industry, for instance insurance (especially in the market entry phase), might be negative in the sense that we have an extremely high crime rate and insurance companies need to pay out claims at an alarming rate. It is also evident that low opportunity industries may create feasible opportunities. The agricultural industry shows a very low level of entrepreneurial activity (1,6 per cent), but was the fastest growing industry (6 per cent) in the local economy in 2002, due to its exporting potential. An entrepreneur should therefore be wary of following a fad and just exploiting assumed opportunities in a "popular" industry. For example, the cash loan environment seemed to be an extremely profitable industry in the mid-1990s, but is this still the case?

What is an opportunity and how does an entrepreneur exploit a feasible opportunity?

An opportunity is defined by Hisrich and Peters (2002) as the process whereby the entrepreneur assesses whether a certain product, service or process has the necessary earnings based on the resource inputs that are required to manufacture and market it (e.g. the entrepreneur can make a T-shirt for under R10 and sell it for R35).

The causal nature of opportunities needs to be assessed – thus, what leads to the existence of an opportunity? The following factors may result in an opportunity:

- General and specific problems faced by consumers (e.g. ineffective public transport)
- Technological changes (e.g. home shopping via the Internet)

Table 3.2 The percentage of entrepreneurs in the different industries in South Africa

	% of entrepreneurs		
ISIC category	Start-ups	New firms	Total
Agriculture, forestry, hunting, fishing	1,3	2,6	1,6
Mining, construction	9,7	5,0	4,1
Manufacturing	14,3	19,1	13,8
Transport, communications, utilities	9,8	0,7	8,0
Wholesale, motor vehicle sales, repairs	6,0	6,5	6,3
Retail, hotel, restaurant	40,8	47,9	43,5
Finance, insurance, real estate	0,3	5,2	1,4
Business services	10,1	7,9	9,4
Health, education, social services	2,6	0,7	2,3
Consumer services	11,0	3,5	9,7

Source: Driver et al. (2001).

- Market shifts (e.g. people making use of SMS communication on their cellphones instead of phoning, thus creating marketing opportunities)
- Government regulations (e.g. procurement policies of local governments create immense opportunities for previously disadvantaged entrepreneurs)
- Competition (e.g. a high level of competition creates an opportunity for new product development)

There are two building bricks in the assessment of an opportunity. Firstly, the size of the market (e.g. will the number of customers reward the input and energy required to create and deliver the product?) and, secondly, the length in terms of the time frame of the opportunity, also called the window of opportunity. For example, is the need for this product only a short fashionable phenomenon or is it based on sustainable business or, how long will it take

before someone else (a competitor) grabs the opportunity? These two aspects should also link directly with the personal skills and competence of the entrepreneur. For example, entrepreneurs with no skills or interest in the information technology environment will not necessarily achieve their personal goals than when they venture into an opportunity that fits their experience and skills make-up.

Table 3.3 shows how the development of a business plan links to the identification and evaluation of opportunities, the determination of the resources required and the eventual management of the enterprise. All of these factors play a significant role in the correct assessment of the business opportunity.

3.3.7 The product

The new innovation or product is the direct result of the process described above. We have generated a multitude of ideas that are in line

Table 3.3 How the development of a business plan links to the identification and evaluation of opportunities, the determination of the resources required and the eventual management of the enterprise

Identify and evaluate the opportunity	Develop the business plan	Determine the resources	Manage the enterprise
Creation and length of opportunity	Title page Table of contents	Existing resources of entrepreneur	Management style
Real and perceived value of opportunity	Executive summary	Resource gap and available supplies	Key variables for success
Risk and returns of opportunity	1.0 Description of business	Access to needed resources	Identification of problems and potential problems
Opportunity versus personal skills and goals	2.0 Description of industry 3.0 Marketing plan		Implementation of control systems
Competitive situation	4.0 Financial plan 5.0 Production plan 6.0 Organisational plan 7.0 Operational plan 8.0 Summary		
	Appendices (exhibits)		

Source: Hisrich, R.D. and Peters, M.P. 2002: 40. *Entrepreneurship.* Boston: Irwin/McGraw-Hill. The material is reproduced with permission of The McGraw-Hill Companies.

with the problem to be solved. The problem can be the need for an improvement of an existing product, an opportunity in the market or the development of a unique discovery. The ideas are a result of the creative thinking process. All the ideas are then evaluated and the most suitable one is subjected to the product development process. Take the case of Nando's, and how this highly successful restaurant and take-away was invented. The founder, Robert Brozin, bought a very small existing Portuguese take-away shop, just for the chicken recipe. He developed that recipe into its now internationally renowned form. At present, Nando's owns 140 stores worldwide! All of this is the result of a creative thinking process.

There are many examples that illustrate this process:

- *Fundamental changes:* Here one finds a radical new solution to a problem, e.g. the development of a vaccine that will solve the Aids issue or an efficient method that will replace normal motor car fuel.

- *Incremental changes:* Here changes take place incrementally, e.g. the regular update of *Windows* software and applications.

Wickham (2001) identifies critical areas where innovations might be made:

- *New products:* The most evident examples of innovation are found in tangible products. Customers are literally flooded with new products on a daily basis. *Verimark,* for example, focuses on selling new products in line with specific or latent customer needs.

- *New services:* The services industry in South Africa is growing at an immense rate. Think about the entrepreneur Mark Shuttleworth who created an innovative new service on the Internet, generating millions of rands annually!

- *New production techniques:* Innovation is also present in the way products are created or manufactured, whether by applying new technological methods and machines or by replacing the old totally. Consider, for example, the way the print media has changed over time. More or less 90 per cent of all daily newspapers can be partly accessed on the Internet.

- *New operating practices:* The way in which services are rendered creates an array of opportunities for entrepreneurs. The new economy is based on speed and innovation. The smaller entity (entrepreneur) is by definition more flexible to adapt to these changes and therefore more equipped to identify opportunities concerning service quality. The cellular phone has become one of the most effective customer service tools. A small restaurant can, for instance, easily and quickly send important information (e.g. specials) to its direct target market by means of Short Message Sending (SMS).

- *New ways of delivering the product or service to the customer:* Technology has changed the way in which various products are distributed to customers. The Internet plays a pivotal role in this process. Modern customers prefer the comfort of ordering their basic and specialised goods via the Internet. Pick 'n Pay has recently introduced an innovative home shopping strategy, where the customer can order normal groceries for delivery at home at a nominal fee. The entrepreneur should, however, be aware of all the pitfalls of such a process before introducing this distribution strategy. Problems like delivering the wrong product or customers' general reluctance to provide credit card details on the Internet, can easily hinder business progress.

- *New means of informing the customer about the product:* The Internet, again, has transformed the way in which customers are informed about new features of a product. The emphasis is on comfort, where the customers can easily access detailed product information on the company's website. See how Kalahari.net provides comprehensive product information (e.g. in the case of a book, a summary of the content of the book is provided).

- *New ways of managing relationships within the organisation:* Technological innovation has fundamentally changed the way

employees communicate within the work environment. In the majority of larger companies, the "paper war" is replaced by efficient electronic methods of communication (e.g. an Intranet system).

It is evident that we find different examples of change and uniqueness in products. Some innovations are totally new and novel. Others are not that new, but have unique characteristics added and developed over time. All these new products, and also functions, are the result of creative thinking and innovative actions.

The **p**roduct part of the model is the final outcome of the creative **p**rocess and forms an integral part of the creative **p**eople who created it. Generating ideas and transforming the most suitable one into a prototype product is only part of a very intense and complex product development process. The phases in the development of a product depend on the nature of the product and also the branch of industry. A general product development process is illustrated in Table 3.4.

3.3.8 Legal protection of the product

Any new product can easily be copied. A legal form of protection is therefore needed (e.g. a patent or copyright). The following options are available to protect a new product or intellectual property in South Africa (as provided by John & Kernick Patent Attorneys and Trademark Agents).

■ Patents

Patents are granted for inventions that have not been previously known and that differ adequately from what was previously done along the same line. Any invention in the form of an apparatus, an article, device, method or process is patentable. The following are not patentable:

- Mathematical methods
- Aesthetic creations (e.g. fashion designs, motor vehicle designs)
- Architectural designs
- Schemes (e.g. investment or insurance schemes)
- Business methods (e.g. credit or stock control)

Table 3.4 General product development process

1. Observe and identify a problem or opportunity	
	FOUNDATION PHASE (1-2)
2. Analyse and diagnose the situation	
3. Generate ideas (creative techniques)	
4. Develop feasible ideas	
	PLANNING AND ORGANISING (3-5)
5. Decide on the most suitable or feasible idea	
6. Develop designs, specifications and drawings	
7. Test	
	TECHNICAL DEVELOPMENT (6-11)
8. Retest, modify and evaluate	
9. Retest, modify and improve	
10. Build and test a working model	
11. Build a prototype	
12. Test the marketing	
13. Produce the product	
14. Launch the new product	
	MARKETING (12-16)
15. Monitor sales performance	
16. Conduct ongoing monitoring and feedback	

- Rules for playing games, although the games equipment may be patented
- Computer programs
- Scientific programmes (e.g. Einstein's theory of relativity)

New inventions should comply with the following requirements before patentability can be determined:
- Novelty
- Utility
- Inventiveness (e.g. non-obvious and not a lack of the inventive step)

▪ Know-how

Secret technology, which may or may not be of a patentable nature and which usually relates to processes, can be licensed to others in return for payment.

▪ Trademarks

The name or logo (device) in association with which an article is marketed, or a service is rendered, or even the shape of a special container, can be registered as a trademark. Trademarks must be sufficiently different from prior trademarks in order to be registrable. A trademark is indicated with the written word "Trademark" or the symbol ™.

▪ Registered designs

The visual, or as it is generally termed, aesthetic, appearance of an article may be protected by means of one form of registered design, provided that it is new in comparison with that previously known for articles of a similar nature. Such designs are termed aesthetic designs and are judged solely on their visual appearance. Functional aspects, and more particularly the shape of an article, cannot be covered by an aesthetic design but the Designs Act does provide for the separate registration of functional designs that cover these aspects of an article.

▪ Unlawful competition

This category of the law enables a person or company to prevent others from marketing products, or carrying out a service, in a manner that confuses them with those of the person or company having established rights (generally termed "passing off"); to prevent an employee from using a former employer's secret information; or generally to prevent competition in an unlawful manner with another.

▪ Copyright

Artistic works and other works containing intellectual content, such as literary works, music, cinematography films, sound recordings, drawings (including engineering drawings), plans, computer programs, pictures of all forms, and numerous other two-dimensional and three-dimensional articles having intellectual content are covered by copyright. Copyright means right not to be copied. Copyright exists automatically and no steps need to be taken in South Africa to register it, although in the exclusive case of video recordings and cinematographic films, the copyright can be registered. Copyright is indicated with the following symbol: ©.

▪ Plants

Protection is available for new varieties of plants. These can be protected in terms of the Plant Breeders' Rights Act and are excluded from being made the subject of a patent. All new varieties are subject to an evaluation and examination period that can take three to five years. The plants may not be sold commercially during this period.

▪ Licences

All forms of intellectual property mentioned can be licensed to others. The following forms of licences are available: a non-exclusive licence, a sole licence, an exclusive licence and an implied licence. Remuneration in terms of a licence contract can take place in the form of money or indirect remuneration other than money.

3.4 Conclusion

If you know how to look and learn, then the door is there and the key is in your hand. Nobody on earth can give you either the key or the door open, except yourself.

J. Krishnamuri

The true entrepreneur uses his or her creative and innovative skills to overcome many obstacles in almost every phase of the business cycle. To think and act creatively spells an intense input for removing the blocks to creativity, all the time. The application of the following variables will assist you in this process:

- Fluency: Strive towards having many ideas
- Flexibility: Focus on different types of ideas
- Elaboration: Concentrate on adding details
- Originality: Strive for uniqueness
- Openness: Resist instant answers

- Unusual viewpoint: Try the baby's view!
- Combination of ideas and facts: Combine ideas
- Internal perspective: Climb "inside" and look around
- Feelings and emotions: Focus on your feelings and those of others
- Fantasy: Imagine/pretend
- Future orientation: Go into the future, look back from the future

As Krishnamuri stated, open the door, the key is in your hand. Enjoy life creatively.

Looking back

1. Define creativity and include all the variables of a possible definition.
   - The product of creativity is firstly a product or result of a thinking process.
   - This product or idea should have novelty as a result and should create value.
   - It should involve unconventional thinking.
   - The thinking process is supported by performance motivation.
   - The initial problem is normally vague and unstructured.

2. Graphically illustrate the creativity model and explain its contents.
   See Figure 3.1.

3. List the myths of creativity.
   - Creativity is an innate skill and cannot be acquired by means of training.
   - You need to be a rebel to be seen as creative.
   - Artists are the only creative beings.
   - You need to be "crazy" before creativity will kick in.
   - High intelligence and creativity go hand in hand.
   - The group is always right.
   - All new products were accidental discoveries.

4. List and discuss the potential blocks to creativity.
   - Environmental barriers:
     - Social environment
     - Economic environment
     - Physical environment
   - Cultural barriers
   - Perceptual barriers

5. Graphically illustrate the creativity process.
   See Figure 3.2 in combination with Table 3.1.

Key terms

5Ws & H technique	Cultural barriers	Incremental change	Perceptual barriers
Association technique	Discontinuity principle	Innovation	Physical blocks
Copyright	Discovery	Invention	Problem reversal
Creative myths	Economic blocks	Licences	Random input
Creative process	Environmental blocks	Opportunity	Registered design
Creative thinking skills	Fundamental change	Patents	Trademarks
Creativity	Idea		

Discussion questions

1. What is meant by creativity? Formulate your own definition within an entrepreneurship context.

2. To what extent can creativity as an entrepreneurial skill assist the entrepreneur in establishing and growing a business?

3. Apply the creativity model of Couger in assessing the creative entrepreneur. What environmental factors in South Africa will affect his or her business opportunity negatively?

4. Assess the basic barriers to creativity for the entrepreneur in your immediate environment. To what extent will these factors hinder growth?

5. Explain the difference between an idea and an opportunity. Make use of suitable examples in this regard.

Case study

Bright spark is "best invention"

Jan-Jan Joubert

Read the following case study. Then assess the likely commercial success of this new venture with the *Innovator*©, which follows the case study.

The saying that one spark can lead to a flame was proved again this week when a South African-made braai oven, which offers a cheaper, safer and healthier way of cooking for the poor, was named as one of the best new inventions in the world. *Time* magazine found the "best new idea" in Wynberg, an industrial area close to where Sandton meets the Alexandra township.

The Cobb, a genuine South African product, has the potential to end the tragedies caused by paraffin stoves falling over and setting fire to shacks. It is an oven-type cooking apparatus not unlike the Weber, but able to cook a whole meal using only six pieces of charcoal. That means up to 20 meals can be prepared with just 5 kg of charcoal. A cylindrical shell of plastic and stainless steel provides the covering in which the food can be cooked. Inside is enough space to arrange the charcoal, with a grill on which to braai meat, fish, prawns or the food of your choice.

Another grill is also provided on which you can rest a pot. There is a circular depression on the outside perimeter of this grill for cooking vegetables. Everything can be taken off to make cleaning easy. Seventy per cent of the fuel energy is absorbed during the heating process and very little smoke escapes – a welcome development in informal settlements where dark columns of smoke usually cloud the sky at sunset. The finishing on the outside of the Cobb prevents heat from being relayed, making it safe for children. You have to hold your hand against the Cobb for quite some time before being burnt.

Inventor Ken Hall says the idea was developed out of need and is as South African as "pap and wors". He used to work in the construction business but says the government's new policy on housing subsidies led to his retrenchment. Hall says he was forced to find an alternative source of income. He says during his many years as building supplier, he was shocked to see the burns suffered in the townships, especially by children tipping over paraffin stoves.

Hall claims the Cobb, which costs R199, is very difficult to tip over and because smouldering coals rather than open flames are used as a heat source, the possibility of starting a fire is very small. A more luxurious model is being marketed overseas for anyone in the mood for a barbecue in a confined space. More than 10 000 of the small ovens have already been sold in the United Kingdom, the Netherlands, Australia and Mexico over the past four months.

Source: Adapted from Joubert, Jan-Jan. 2001. SA kooktoestel bekroon as voorste uitvindsel. *Die Burger*, 6 December.

Innovator© (Williams 1999): Developing the feasibility of a new product

Although the success of a new product will be influenced by an array of factors, it is possible to assess its likely success. Make use of the following questionnaire to determine the potential commercial success of the new product in the case study above.

Group A: Effects on society

1. Legality

In terms of relevant laws, regulations and industry standards (particularly relating to product safety and risk), this invention will:

adequately meet all legal requirements	5
meet most legal requirements	4
need further legality and/or safety checks	3
need some major modifications	2
fail to meet the legal requirements	1

2. Safety

This invention, process or product will probably be:

quite safe if used under normal operating conditions	5
safe if used properly and according to instructions	4
safe if the user is properly trained/qualified	3
unsafe unless modifications are made	2
quite dangerous in its present form	1

3. Environmental impact

In terms of its effects on the environment (e.g. through excessive energy usage, pollution, misuse and/or waste of vital resources, etc.) this invention:

should contribute to an improved quality of life	5
may result in some environmental improvements	4
should have little or no adverse effect	3
could create some minor environmental "damage"	2
may seriously damage the environment	1

4. Societal impact

In terms of its impact on the welfare of society at large (or on some identifiable part of it), this invention:

will have considerable benefits for society generally	5
should benefit some sections of the community	4
may be of some benefit to society	3
should have little or no effect on society	2
may have some detrimental effects	1

Group B: Business risk

5. Technical/functional feasibility

Thorough testing, to assess whether or not the invention will work as it is intended to do, shows that it:

works reliably under all normal operating conditions	5
works satisfactorily if used according to instructions	4
will work if used with care by an expert	3
has some technical problems that need to be solved	2
does not work properly yet	1

6. Production feasibility

In terms of availability of materials, equipment and other resources, and know-how of the technical processes needed, production of this invention has:

no problems and can start immediately	5
minor problems that may lead to brief delays	4
minor problems, and delays of several months are likely	3

a serious problem, leading to delays of at least six months	2
many serious problems, and cannot start for at least a year	1

7. Stage of development

This invention, at least in the form of a fully working prototype, has:

no technical problems, and is complete or almost complete	5
some problems but should be completed within three months	4
some problems but should be completed within six months	3
some major problems, and may be completed in nine months	2
an uncertain completion date, but is at least a year away	1

8. Development cost

Total funding needed to cover all likely development costs, and to bring the invention to the point of being ready to market or use, is estimated to be:

minimal, available, and will not cause any cash flow problems	5
light, probably available, with minor cash flow problems	4
moderate, probably available, but with debt servicing problems	3
fairly heavy, not easy to get and hard to service	2
substantial, and fairly difficult to get and to service	1

9. Payback period

The period needed to recover the overall investment in developing the invention is likely to be:

under one year	5
one to three years	4
four to six years	3
seven to nine years	2
ten years or more	1

10. Profitability

Expected revenue from selling this invention should cover all relevant direct and indirect costs, and earn average annual pre-tax profits:

in excess of 30%	5
of between 25 and 30%	4
of between 20 and 25%	3
of between average bank interest and 20%	2
below the current bank interest rate	1

11. Marketing research

The research needed to make the invention "market ready", and to properly and accurately assess its likely success in the market, will probably be:

no problem and therefore inexpensive	5
fairly straightforward and at a reasonable cost	4
moderately difficult and expensive	3
rather difficult and expensive	2
very difficult and therefore very costly	1

12. Research and development

The technical research and development needed to bring the invention to the stage of being ready to produce are expected to:

be quite easy	5
be reasonably straightforward	4
show up some problems	3
prove rather complicated	2
be very difficult	1

Group C: Analysis of demand
13. Potential market

The total market for this type of invention or product would appear to be:

very large	5
quite large enough to ensure success	4
adequate to give a viable market share	3

just adequate (and will need some aggressive marketing)	2
very limited (very much specialised and/or local)	1

14. Product life cycle

The life cycle of this invention or product is expected to be:

at least ten years	5
between six and ten years	4
three to six years	3
one to three years	2
under one year	1

15. Potential sales

Expected total sales revenue from this product or invention during its expected life cycle is likely to be:

very large (over R15 million)	5
quite substantial (between R5 and R10 million)	4
most satisfactory (between R1 and R5 million)	3
adequate (between R250 000 and R1 million)	2
small (probably under R250 000)	1

16. Likely trend in market

The market demand for this type of invention or product seems to be:

growing rapidly	5
growing at a moderate speed	4
growing, but slowly	3
fairly stable	2
falling	1

17. Stability of demand

Fluctuations in market demand for this invention or product are expected to be:

minor and easily predicted	5

minor to moderate, and fairly easy to predict	4
moderate and usually predictable	3
moderate to large, and difficult to predict	2
fairly large and quite unpredictable	1

18. Potential product line expansion

The potential for additional products, models, lines, styles, qualities, price ranges and other variations is:

excellent	5
quite good	4
uncertain	3
limited to minor modifications only	2
virtually nil	1

Group D: Market acceptance

19. Learning

The amount of learning and practice needed for the correct and safe use of the invention or product is:

very little – minimal instructions are needed	5
quite manageable	4
moderate	3
quite considerable	2
extensive and quite demanding – instructions are detailed	1

20. Need

The "level of need" filled by this invention or product (i.e. its level of usefulness) is:

very high	5
high	4
moderate	3
low	2
very low	1

21. Dependence

The extent to which the sale or use of this product or invention depends on its linkage(s) with other products or processes is expected to be:

very low – it is quite independent	5
low – it is fairly independent	4
moderate – depends somewhat on other products or processes	3
high – depends heavily on other products or processes	2
very high – can only work with other products or processes	1

22. Visibility

The advantages or benefits of this invention or product to likely users are:

highly visible	5
fairly obvious to most	4
moderately obvious – some users may need help	3
barely visible – most users will need help	2
not obvious – all users will need a detailed demonstration	1

23. Promotion

The costs and effort needed to promote the major features, advantages and benefits of this invention or product are likely to be ... compared with expected sales:

very low	5
fairly low	4
moderate	3
somewhat high	2
very high	1

24. Distribution

The costs and difficulty of setting up effective distribution channels for this product or invention will probably be ... compared with expected sales:

very low	5
fairly low	4
moderate	3
somewhat high	2
very high	1

25. Aftersales service

The cost and difficulty associated with providing good aftersales service for this product is likely to be ... compared with expected sales:

very low	5
fairly low	4
moderate	3
somewhat high	2
very high	1

Group E: Competitive advantage

26. Appearance

In comparison with its competition and/or substitutes, this product's appearance will be:

highly attractive	5
reasonably attractive	4
of average appearance	3
rather lacking in visual appeal	2
inferior, with little customer appeal	1

27. Function

Compared with its competitors and/or substitutes, the performance of this product, invention or process will be:

much superior	5
somewhat superior	4
similar	3
somewhat inferior	2
much inferior	1

28. Durability

Compared with its competitors and/or substitutes, the durability and reliability of this invention or product are likely to be:

much superior	5
somewhat superior	4
similar	3
somewhat inferior	2
much inferior	1

29. Price

Compared with its competition and/or substitute products, the selling price of this product or invention will probably be:

considerably low	5
somewhat lower	4
about the same	3
somewhat higher	2
considerably higher	1

30. Existing competition

Competition from existing firms, products, processes or inventions is expected to be:

virtually non-existent	5
weak at present, but needs careful monitoring	4
moderately strong – need to be alert to potential threat	3
strong enough to be a potentially serious threat	2
very severe, making a viable market share hard to achieve	1

31. New competition

Competitive reaction from new entrants to the industry (i.e. new firms, products, etc.) is likely to be:

slow and weak – no threat to competitive position	5
slow but fairly strong – strategic action needed in the future	4
moderately quick and moderately strong – must be watched closely	3
fast and fairly threatening	2
fast and posing a serious threat to competitive position	1

32. Protection

An appropriate form of protection (through patent, design registration, trademark, copyright, licence, etc.):

has already been successfully taken out	5
is currently being investigated or applied for	4
may be (or will be) investigated in the future	3
has not yet been considered	2
was applied for, but unsuccessfully	1

Question

1. Do you assess the product as being feasible in terms of the criteria listed in the questionnaire? If not, please indicate why and suggest how you would develop a more feasible innovation.

Experiential exercises

The experiential exercises are based on the creativity process set out in the text. Complete each exercise only if you understand the theory.

1. Complete the following questionnaire in pencil in order to determine your level of creativity (mark with an X):

Statement	Strongly agree	Agree	Unsure	Disagree	Strongly disagree
1 I really hate to be given a job I don't fully understand					
2 I find that daydreaming often helps me solve problems					
3 For me, success is often the result of good old hard work					
4 I find that change can be exciting and rewarding					
5 I tend to look past my failures and focus on my successes					
6 Most people I know seem to be more creative than I am					
7 It's more rewarding to work alone					
8 Sometimes I say things that turn other people off					
9 I enjoy using unconventional thinking to develop ideas					
10 I resent having to put everything in its "proper place"					
11 I often rely on hunches and gut feeling in making decisions					
12 I prefer hard facts to work with, not fuzzy theories					
13 I have no problem working in situations that are unpredictable					
14 I prefer problems for which there is no precise solution					
15 I sometimes tend to get overenthusiastic about things					
16 It's always better to do what is right than to win					
17 I would rather be an explorer than an accountant					
18 It's better to have flexible instructions than very specific ones					
19 Sometimes I get great ideas when I'm just relaxing or doing nothing in particular					

Statement	Strongly agree	Agree	Unsure	Disagree	Strongly disagree
20 When a solution to a problem can't readily be found, I tend to get discouraged and give up on it					
21 I tend to see problems as challenges and opportunities					
22 I have a good sense of humour in all situations					
23 Sometimes it's good for employees to fool around and have fun					
24 Conventions and rules were meant to be broken					
25 I am confident of my ability to solve tricky problems					
26 Usually I'm tolerant of creative people and their ideas					
27 It's best to approach problems in a logical sense					
28 I really enjoy kicking ideas around in my head					
29 I'm not comfortable working with people who are always rational and objective in their thinking					
30 I don't have a need to achieve power and status in life					
31 It's better to be an expert in one field than a "Jack of all trades"					

Source: Williams (1999).

Scoring of creativity questionnaire:

For items 1, 6, 12, 20 and 27, score your responses as follows:

Strongly agree = 1; Agree = 2; Unsure = 3; Disagree = 4; Strongly disagree = 5

For all other items, score as follows:

Strongly agree = 5; Agree = 4; Unsure = 3; Disagree = 2; Strongly disagree = 1

Carry your answers over to the table below:

Item	Score	Item	Score	Item	Score	Item	Score
1		9		17		25	
2		10		18		26	
3		11		19		27	
4		12		20		28	
5		13		21		29	
6		14		22		30	
7		15		23		31	
8		16		24		**Total**	

Interpretation

Scores	Creativity quotient	Approx. % of population
131–155	Very high	5
106–130	High	20
81–105	Moderate	50
56–80	Low	20
31–55	Very low	5

2. Listen to any piece of music and draw a picture of any feeling you get while listening to the music.

3. Listen to a next song or piece of music and draw a picture of any place in the world that the song reminds you of.

4. Listen to another song and draw a picture of any person that the song reminds you of.

5. Listen to a next song and write a poem consisting of only one paragraph (approximately five lines). The poem should relate to the specific song.

   Title: _____

6. Listen to the next song and write a poem consisting of only one paragraph (approximately five lines). The poem should relate to the specific song AND should link to the previous poem!

   Title: _____

7. This exercise is normally more effective in a group format, but you could complete it individually as well.

Develop as many uses or ideas for the following objects. It must be useful!

(Time: 20 minutes)

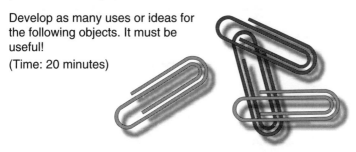

8. You have now gone through a quick idea-generation process. Now, choose the most feasible idea in Exercise 7 (based on a class assessment). Take the idea and apply the following association and imaging technique.

Step 1: Draw a picture of the most suitable paper clip idea.

Step 2: Take a characteristic from the drawings in Exercises 2–4, and add it to the beneficial development of your new idea or concept (illustrate the process).

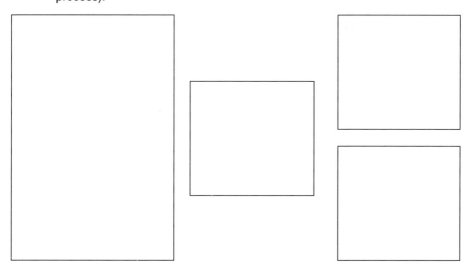

Step 3: Develop a physical example of the concept. Make notes on the process you follow.

Step 4: Add any attribute to your product with a distinctive uniqueness impetus. This attribute should be based on the critique offered by the co-entrepreneurs in your group. Remember to make notes of how you came upon the unique nature of the new product.

Step 5: Develop a brand name for the product.

```
┌────────────────────────────────────────────────────────┐
│                                                          │
│                                                          │
└────────────────────────────────────────────────────────┘
```

(Make notes on how you formulate the brand name. State how the name comple-
ments the product and why.)

```
┌────────────────────────────────────────────────────────┐
│                                                          │
├────────────────────────────────────────────────────────┤
│                                                          │
├────────────────────────────────────────────────────────┤
│                                                          │
├────────────────────────────────────────────────────────┤
│                                                          │
└────────────────────────────────────────────────────────┘
```

Step 6: Design a television advertisement of at least two minutes for your new product and present it to the class. Remember we are focusing on creativity,
which implies: UNIQUENESS, ORIGINALITY and EXCITEMENT!

```
┌────────────────────────────┬─────────────────────────────┐
│                            │                             │
│                            │                             │
│                            │                             │
│                            │                             │
│                            │                             │
│                            │                             │
│                            │                             │
├────────────────────────────┼─────────────────────────────┤
│                            │                             │
│                            │                             │
│                            │                             │
│                            │                             │
│                            │                             │
│                            │                             │
│                            │                             │
└────────────────────────────┴─────────────────────────────┘
```

Exploring the Web

http://www.cbi.cgey.com/journal/Issue8/Demysti
fying.html
http://www.futureshock.co.za/ecotbusiness.htm
http://www.network-marketing.co.za/bizops.htm
http://www.schoolbuyersonline.com/bizsolu-
tion/Home.asp

http://www.siyanqoba.co.za/business.html
http://www.visualthinking.co.za/products/pks/ind
ex.html

References and recommended reading

Amabile, T.M. 1999. *How to kill creativity*. Breakthrough Thinking. *Harvard Business Review*.
Boston, MA: Harvard Business School Press.

Couger, J.D. 1995. *Creative problem solving and
opportunity finding*. London: International Thomson.

De Bono, E. 1996. *Serious creativity*. London:
HarperCollins Business.

Driver, A., Wood, E., Segal, N. & Herrington, M.
2001. *Global Entrepreneurship Monitor: 2001 South
African executive report*. Graduate School of
Business. Cape Town: University of Cape Town.

Glassman, E. 1993. *Creativity handbook: a practical
guide to shift paradigms and improve creative thinking at work*. Chapel Hill: LCS Press.

Hisrich, R.D. & Peters, M.P. 2002.
Entrepreneurship. Boston: Irwin/McGraw-Hill.

Nieman, G.H. & Bennett, A. (Eds). 2002. *Business
management: a value chain approach*. Pretoria: Van
Schaik.

Nystrom, H. 1979. *Creativity and innovation*. New
York: John Wiley.

Wickham, P.A. 2001. *Strategic entrepreneurship: a
decision-making approach to new venture creation
and management,* 2nd ed. London: Prentice Hall.

Williams, A. 1999. *Creativity, invention and innovation: a guide to building your business future*. St
Leonards, N.S.W.: Allen & Unwin.

The window of opportunity

Baphicile Nhlengethwa

4.1 Introduction

The aim of this chapter is to look at opportunity evaluation and utilisation from the perspective of an entrepreneurial start-up. The chapter walks the entrepreneur through the different phases of a window of opportunity, and highlights the different issues that the entrepreneur has to face and overcome in order to successfully start and grow a venture.

A window of opportunity is divided into five phases: seeing, locating, measuring, opening and closing the window. The generation of ideas is also touched upon, as are the important issues that an entrepreneur has to consider when evaluating an opportunity so as to make the most of it, or to be able to determine when an opportunity is not as lucrative as it may initially have seemed to be.

4.2 The opportunity

According to Nieman and Bennett (2002), an opportunity is a gap left in the market by those who currently serve it. Timmons (1999) states that an opportunity has the qualities of being attractive, durable and timely. A good idea is not necessarily a feasible and viable opportunity. In order for an idea to be a lucrative one, besides being attractive, durable and timely, it must create and/or add value for the purchaser or end-user (in terms of the product or service offering). There is no sense in reinventing the wheel; among other characteristics, entrepreneurs should therefore be creative and innovative.

Entrepreneurs are generally seen as the drivers of economic growth in most countries. Their contribution to the economy is commonly seen in the creation, establishment and growth of new businesses. In order for these new businesses to be created, entrepreneurs need to identify new business opportunities, new products and new ways to meet customer needs (Nieman & Bennett 2002). It is not an easy task to identify and evaluate opportunities. This process demands that the entrepre-

Learning outcomes

After completion of this chapter, you should be able to:

- Differentiate between an idea and an opportunity
- Understand why large organisations leave gaps in the market
- Define and understand the concept of a window of opportunity
- Identify and differentiate between the five stages of a window of opportunity
- Understand the issues pertaining to the different stages of opportunity evaluation
- Identify the facets of idea generation
- Identify and understand the criteria used to evaluate an opportunity
- Understand the integrated approach to opportunity evaluation

neur should search for ideas to be converted into a business opportunity in a creative and innovative manner.

4.3 The role of ideas

Finding a good idea is the first step in the task of converting an entrepreneur's creativity into an opportunity. A good idea does not always automatically translate into an opportunity. More often than not, potential entrepreneurs put too much emphasis on their ideas. This can result in myopia on the entrepreneur's behalf concerning the assessment and evaluation of the value the product or service can add.

In 1996, Peggy Mokhonto was involved in making clay pots. Unfortunately, the demand and scope for this type of product were limited, which forced her to look for a better opportunity. In her search, she made the acquaintance of Flora Mathebula and together, these two dynamic African ladies approached the Department of Health and Welfare for financial assistance.

A grant of R10 000 was given to Peggy and Flora with which they were able to purchase equipment necessary to manufacture fencing products. A sound business practice and the production of high-quality fencing ensured that these two ladies were given a second grant worth R100 000 by the Department of Health and Welfare. They invested in more equipment and expanded their product range to incorporate the manufacturing of bricks. Flora and Peggy are now the employers of 23 mothers in their community. In order to further uplift and provide assistance to the less privileged, labourers from amongst the impoverished sector of their community are employed as casual workers on a part-time basis (NEPA 2001).

The first part of this example proves that a good idea does not necessarily translate into a brilliant opportunity. However, these ladies were able to realise this at an early stage and could find another idea that translated into an opportunity. The next logical question to ask, then, is: When is an idea an opportunity?

4.4 When is an idea an opportunity?

According to Timmons (1999), in order for an idea to be an opportunity, it must be attractive, durable and timely, as well as be anchored in a product or service, which creates or adds value for its purchaser or end-user. Essentially, this means that the idea must have the power to please the consumer's mind or eye and arouse his or her interest, thus drawing the consumer to purchase the goods or service. In order for the idea to be durable, it must have the inherent ability to continue in a particular condition and not wear out soon. Finally, in order for the idea to be timely, it must be presented to the market at an opportune time – a time when the market is ready for it. It must be an idea whose time has come. If an entrepreneur takes these factors into serious consideration, he or she is effectively en route to establishing a sustainable business.

For example, fewer than 12 years ago, commercial use of the Internet was considered improper. From 1969 to the early 1990s, the Internet was restricted to military, academic and a few corporate research users. The National Science Foundation (NSF) of the United States maintained the main long distance backbone of the Internet. The NSF had a use policy that prohibited all but the most indirect commerce online.

Despite these restrictions, the Internet grew rapidly because many universities and laboratories found it to be an effective way to communicate. The researchers, seeing the benefits of sharing academic information, started arguing that the rest of society would benefit from this type of technology transfer. A fundamental breakthrough occurred. Suddenly there was the World Wide Web, which had web browsers and web servers. They provided key innovation in the ease of use and the use of multimedia. It became much easier for individuals to use the Internet, because obscure and complicated commands were eliminated and replaced with a simpler way to navigate – clicking on links and typing in web addresses.

Firms and organisations found themselves in a position where they were able to create marketing material that had global reach at a very low cost. Small firms could compete on a much more even footing with the largest companies in the world. Customers found that they could use the Web to communicate very effectively with each other. The new Web, combined with the power of the earlier email technology, created an entirely new and effective mechanism for relating to customers. Between January

1994 and January 1999, Internet hosts grew from 2,2 million to over 43 million worldwide. The growth rate in 1998 was 46 per cent.

The Internet user base has grown rapidly as well. In 1999, the number of worldwide Internet users was estimated at over 160 million people. Much more growth is possible, as this constitutes less than 4 per cent of the world's adult population. The Internet with its limitless potential is an idea that has translated into an extremely viable opportunity in a plethora of different ways (Ward 2000).

4.5 Sources and drivers of ideas and opportunities

There are countless sources of business opportunities and the entrepreneur, especially in a rapidly developing and changing society such as South Africa, has numerous places to find these. However, a good opportunity seldom falls out of the sky. Finding good ideas and converting them into opportunities is a conscious, deliberate, creative process.

Nieuwenhuizen et al. (2001) state that certain techniques can be made use of when searching for a business idea. These can be divided into five broad approaches: the generation of ideas from skills, expertise and aptitude, from common needs, from existing problems, from everyday problems and from other sources. This is illustrated in Figure 4.1 and discussed in the following paragraphs.

Business opportunities can arise when entrepreneurs use their skills, expertise or aptitude to provide a product or service to the market. Common needs among organisations or individuals for a particular product or service can

be met by entrepreneurs. Solving existing problems, i.e. things that irritate, annoy or rile the general public, can become the source of a thriving business opportunity.

Instead of getting caught up in a routine with firmly entrenched day-to-day activities, the desire and ability of an entrepreneur to produce goods or services that enable people to do things differently in a better or faster way, can be another source or driver of opportunities.

Other sources from which entrepreneurs commonly obtain the inspiration for business opportunities are, according to Nieuwenhuizen et al. (2001), business publications, inventors' associations, expired patents, advertisements, trade shows, overseas products and the *Yellow Pages*.

4.6 Opportunity evaluation

In order to determine whether or not a business idea will translate into a lucrative opportunity, which possesses the qualities of being timely, attractive and durable, the entrepreneur must follow a strategy of evaluating or screening the revealed opportunity.

By screening potential opportunities, important issues and aspects that might be overlooked or underemphasised to the detriment of the venture are brought to light. The process of screening and evaluating opportunities helps the entrepreneur to see clearly whether his or her venture will be a high or low potential one. Once this has been determined, the entrepreneur can decide whether or not the opportunity is worth pursuing.

The criteria used to screen opportunities can be summarised as follows:

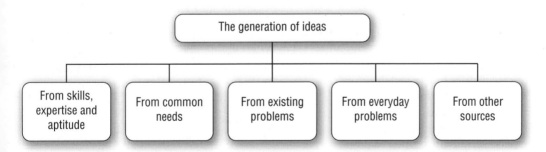

Figure 4.1 The generation of ideas

Source: Nieuwenhuizen et al. (2001).

- Industry and market issues
- Economics
- Harvest issues
- Management team
- Fatal flaw issues
- Personal criteria
- Strategic differentiation

4.6.1 Industry and market issues

The market for higher-potential ventures usually comprises a niche market that caters for needs that certain customers deem to be important, and is therefore sustainable. These products and services must add and/or create great value to the customers.

The customers that make up the niche market tend to be accessible, as well as willing to purchase the product or service. They also tend not to display brand loyalty to other products or services. An attractive market to enter into is one where the life of the product or service extends far beyond the time period required to recover the investment in the venture, as well as make a profit. With regard to customer need, lower-potential opportunities tend to be fragmented in focus and customers are not easily accessible. More often than not, customers are brand loyal, making it rather difficult to entice them to try new and/or different products. The attractiveness of a market is determined by the following factors:

- Market structure
- Market size
- Market capacity
- Market share
- Cost structure.

▪ Market structure

When speaking of market structure, reference is made to:

- The number of sellers present in a market
- The size distribution of sellers
- Product differentiation
- Entry/exit conditions
- The number of buyers present
- Demand sensitivity to price changes

Market conditions that make it possible for higher-potential ventures to thrive are ones where unfulfilled market niches are involved, i.e. there are not very many sellers present in the market and differentiated products and services are prevalent. The entry conditions should be rather difficult. This aids in eliminating competition, as not everybody has the ability to enter the market and provide the same service or product. Ideal exit conditions, on the other hand, are ones where it is easier for the entrepreneur to leave the market should the need or desire to do so arise. Ideally, an abundance of buyers is present and they have substantial buying power. Further ideal market conditions for a higher-potential venture would be the presence of information or knowledge gaps, and profitable – but not overwhelming – competition.

An unattractive market, or that which promotes low-growth potential for entrepreneurial ventures, is one in which there is a high concentration of buyers and sellers, mature or declining industries and perfect competition. Demand sensitivity to price changes by the consumers is not an ideal situation for the entrepreneur, as are facile entry conditions and difficult exit conditions. Where there is low product differentiation, the entrepreneur may be faced with a scenario of extreme brand loyalty by consumers that are unwilling to try out new or different products or services.

▪ Market size

A large and growing market is the type of market a high-potential venture seeks to engage in and, more often than not, thrives in. A large and growing market refers to one in which competitors do not perceive capturing a portion of the market to be a threat to them and where a small portion of the market share can still translate into substantial and increasing sales volumes.

A small and stagnant market is not an attractive one to enter. This type of market stifles ventures, leading to unrealised potential of both the venture and the entrepreneur.

▪ Market capacity

A market at full capacity in a growth situation – where demand outweighs possible current supply – is a very attractive one to enter. By virtue of its nature, this type of market encourages ventures to reach their highest potential.

■ Market share

The potential and ability of a venture to become a market leader and capture a substantial portion of the overall market are significant contributing factors to the firm becoming a high-growth venture. A firm that is unable to become a market leader by capturing a substantial portion of the overall market is a low-growth potential venture.

■ Cost structure

Generally, a firm that can provide low cost goods and services while providing value for money is attractive. However, a firm that faces declining cost conditions on a continual basis ceases to be attractive or exhibit great growth potential.

4.6.2 Economics

Businesses that possess high and durable gross margins usually have high and durable profits (after tax). A venture that achieves a positive cash flow quickly, i.e. within three years, is attractive. Once the time to reach break-even and a positive cash flow takes longer than three years, the potential for the venture to be attractive is substantially reduced. Ventures that require low start-up funds and little or no initial capital equipment are attractive. Should a venture require too much money for start-up or too much initial capital outlay, it ceases to be a proposition. This is because the possibility of recovering returns on the investment and making a profit within a reasonable time frame diminishes greatly.

4.6.3 Harvest issues

The eventuality that a venture will be sold is a reality most entrepreneurs should bear in mind. Some entrepreneurs start and grow their businesses with the aim of selling them some time in the future. This is referred to as an exit strategy. Attractive ventures in attractive markets tend to have the harvest objective in mind. Unattractive ventures in not so attractive markets tend to postpone drawing up a contingency plan of harvesting. Should the need then arise to dispose of the venture by selling it, buyers are not willing to purchase the business due

to the unattractiveness of both the venture and the industry it is operating in.

4.6.4 Management team issues

It is both important and beneficial for a venture to have an entrepreneurial team that possesses proven experience within the chosen industry. A team that possesses a complementary and compatible skills base contributes to the attractiveness of the venture. Usually, when an unattractive, low-potential venture is examined, it is found that it does not have such teams.

The members of the team should ideally exhibit qualities such as industry and technical experience, integrity and intellectual honesty, commitment to excellence, tolerance of ambiguity, opportunity obsession, creativity and innovativeness, internal locus of control, as well as determination and perseverance.

4.6.5 Fatal flaw issues

The presence of one or more fatal flaws renders an opportunity unattractive. It would then go without saying that attractive ventures do not have any fatal flaws.

Fatal flaws in the venture can be caused by:
• Markets that are too small
• Markets with overwhelming competition
• Markets where the cost of entry is too high
• Markets where entrants are unable to produce a sustainable competitive advantage

Other fatal flaws include the lack of an entrepreneurial team, non-existent industry and/or technical experience, and the lack of or compromised intellectual honesty and integrity on behalf of the owner or the management team.

4.6.6 Personal criteria

Successful entrepreneurs have a good fit between what they wish to derive from the venture and what the venture requires of them. An attractive opportunity does not have excessive downside risks attached to it. An attractive opportunity is both desirable and good for the entrepreneur to pursue. A successful entrepreneur takes calculated risks and has relatively high stress tolerance levels, in addition to being opportunity obsessed, committed to excellence, exhibiting the need to achieve, being creative and innovative, tolerant of ambiguity and uncertainty, and possessing an internal locus of control.

4.6.7 Strategic differentiation

Strategic differentiation refers to how a venture positions itself to take advantage of the given market conditions to its benefit, while at the same time differing from the competitors in terms of the value added to consumers.

A high-potential venture tends to have an entrepreneurial team of the highest calibre, exhibits excellent service management and is perceived by the customers to be a good service provider. The timing of the product or service offering is opportune and the technology ground breaking or exclusive. The venture management is very flexible and can make decisions on its feet, as well as de-commit equally fast, should circumstances deem it necessary to do so.

A high-potential venture is always searching for new opportunities and the pricing strategy enables it to be the industry leader, or be positioned very near that prime position. A venture that is conducive to high growth has distribution channels that are accessible, as well as networks that are firmly in place. The culture of a high-potential growth venture has an integral strategy of forgiveness, which allows for mistakes to be made and learned from by the owners, management team and staff members.

4.7 The pursuit of opportunities

Generally, established businesses have a stronger position than smaller entrepreneurs in terms of market entry and share. This is because established businesses have more experience; they have a strong and secure network with suppliers, customers and intermediaries; and their costs are lower due to their development of experience curve economies.

Larger organisations also attain positions of strength due to their possession of economy of scale cost advantages. All of this said, entrepreneurs can (and do) take on the larger players successfully. They manage to identify opportunities in the market and turn them into viable business ventures regardless of the presence of the more established organisations.

There are numerous reasons for this. The most common ones can be attributed to:
- Organisational inertia
- Organisational complacence
- Bureaucracy

Organisational inertia occurs when an organisation refuses to adapt in a responsive manner to changes that occur in the marketplace. Organisational complacence refers to the organisation resting on its laurels due to past successes and adopting the "we have made it" mentality. This can result in the organisation not exploiting opportunities as effectively and as efficiently as it could, and as it used to in the past.

Once businesses grow and become larger and more successful, the levels in the hierarchy expand due to increased financial, operational and human resources. Communication between the different functions and departments becomes slow and cumbersome. Thus, these organisations become bureaucratic. This can result in opportunity-seeking mechanisms and techniques used by the organisation becoming rigid and inadequate for the needs of the market.

Wickham (2001) states that gaps left open due to the technological inertia, cultural inertia, internal politics and economic inefficiency of large organisations enable smaller entrepreneurs to take advantage of presented opportunities that these larger organisations have failed to grab and exploit to their benefit.

4.8 Why bigger businesses leave gaps in the market

Bigger or established businesses tend to leave gaps in the market for numerous reasons. Once these gaps (however small) are left open, it makes it very easy for smaller organisations to spot the opportunity and make the most of it. Timmons (1999) states that a good opportunity may sometimes not look too attractive at first, but has the potential to blossom into one that is bigger than the venture itself, even after the venture grows to a substantial size.

The most common reasons for bigger or more established businesses leaving gaps in the market are the following:
- Failure to see new opportunities
- Underestimation of new opportunities

- Technological inertia
- Cultural inertia
- Politics and internal fighting
- Government intervention to support new and (smaller) entrants

4.8.1 Failure to see new opportunities

As said earlier, opportunities must be consciously and actively sought by the entrepreneur. Large organisations must, in order to grow and not fall prey to the trap of rigidity, bureaucracy and stagnation, also actively search for new opportunities. Large businesses should scan the environment for opportunities that they can make the most of by utilising their strengths. Failure to do this may result in organisational inertia, which means the failure or inability to respond to environmental changes as they occur. This quite often leads to the loss of the organisation's competitive edge. Once a large organisation exhibits this type of apathetic or lethargic behaviour, it leaves a wide open gap that smaller entrepreneurs can, and usually do, take advantage of.

4.8.2 Underestimation of new opportunities

Most firms view opportunities in terms of monetary value. This means that the value of the opportunity is analysed in relation to the size of the business that will potentially pursue it. Large organisations with substantial turnovers tend not to regard opportunities that only represent a fraction of their turnover as being lucrative.

Alternatively, smaller firms will pursue opportunities that a larger firm would not, because to the smaller firm these opportunities are ones with value and are thus attractive. For example, for a business with an annual turnover of R25 million, an opportunity worth R250 000 may not be viewed as substantial in monetary terms. However, to a smaller firm with a turnover of R2,5 million, the same opportunity of R250 000 would be attractive as it would add value to the firm.

This attitude exhibited by larger organisations has been instrumental in providing gaps for small firms. What may seem to be an insubstantial opportunity on the surface to the myopic larger firm, could actually turn into an extremely durable and profitable one for the smaller firm. The smaller firm taking advantage of the opportunity could end up making a lot of business and money.

4.8.3 Technological inertia

According to Wickham (2001: 206), opportunities are pursued by innovation. Innovation involves doing something different in a radical or incremental manner. Radical innovation refers to unprecedented breakthroughs, while incremental innovation can be defined as a systematic evolution of a product or service into newer or larger markets (Pinchot 2000). An innovation is founded on some technological approach.

Technology simply refers to the methods and mannerisms used to do certain things or to achieve certain objectives or goals. Needless to say, the world today is one of an extremely technologically dynamic nature. Larger organisations that were the technological pioneers and trailblazers of yesteryear tend to rest on their laurels and feel that they do not need to conform to the technological changes that occur in the marketplace. This type of mindset could prove to be very detrimental to big businesses in the medium to long term. Due to the agility and flexibility of small businesses and their need to survive, they tend to be very quick to spot new technologies and run with them. This often leaves big businesses in a very precarious position.

4.8.4 Cultural inertia

Organisational culture refers to the beliefs, norms and values that an organisation upholds and lives or operates by. Organisational culture and technology are very closely linked. This is an organisation's culture and its use of technology to a great extent determine how the firm responds to changes within the environment in which it operates.

Once again, larger businesses tend not to be too keen to change the way they do things in order to meet or surpass the challenges that the market environment may throw at them. Their unwillingness to change puts them in a position of not being able to pursue new opportunities. This leaves wide open gaps for technologically and culturally nimble smaller firms to take advantage of the opportunities and cash in substantially.

4.8.5 Politics and internal fighting

Most organisations have some form of political scenario, whether subtle or blatant. The more established an organisation becomes, the more entrenched political infighting and bickering become. In order for there to be a healthy amount of harmony within an organisation, employees should feel and exhibit a certain affiliation to, and alignment with, the organisation's goals and objectives. In turn, the organisation must also ensure that it does the same to the employees.

Once individual employees start feeling that their best interests are not being taken into consideration by the organisation, infighting begins. If the firm does not work as a cohesive whole from an internal perspective, then it becomes extremely difficult, if not impossible, to pursue valuable opportunities because no general consensus has been gained. This may result in the loss of a great opportunity that may never present again. The more focused and less politically obsessed smaller firms will take advantage of these opportunities.

4.8.6 Government intervention to support new (and smaller) entrants

Most governments the world over recognise the important role that small and growing businesses play in national economies. Small, medium and micro-enterprises (SMMEs) are responsible for many new innovations and for job creation. The situation is no different in South Africa. At the moment, the government is seriously involved in efforts to bolster and support SMMEs in numerous ways.

This means that the smaller businesses tend to get more support and attention than big businesses do. This support takes the form of skills training, financing, access to government tenders, assistance with market access, as well as the development and implementation of SMME-friendly legislation. This support clearly favours smaller businesses, which enables them to grab opportunities that have been proverbially placed in their lap, while bigger firms are forced to fend for themselves.

4.9 The window of opportunity

What is the window of opportunity? Nieman and Bennett (2002) state that the window of opportunity refers to the time period available for creating new ventures. As a market grows, more and more opportunities are revealed, in other words, the window opens. However, as the market matures, the window begins to close and the available opportunities in the market begin to dwindle and eventually peter out.

Wickham (2001) suggests that in order to effectively visualise the window of opportunity, it is helpful use a metaphor. Picture a solid wall. This wall is representative of the competitive nature of the environment that the entrepreneur endeavours to penetrate. The solidity of the wall represents competition from established businesses.

Going back to our earlier definition of an opportunity, these businesses have left certain gaps in the market by not completely servicing all the needs of consumers. These gaps represent the window that the entrepreneur can look and move through, thus enabling him or her to create a new and better product or service for the buyer or end-user. Here the entrepreneur must emphasise value addition, as this provides him or her with the ability to achieve a sustainable competitive advantage. Sustainable competitive advantage allows the opportunity to be a durable one, as opposed to becoming a momentary fad.

For an opportunity to possess the qualities of being attractive, durable and timely, the window of opportunity must be opening. This is illustrated in Figure 4.2.

The window must remain open long enough for the entrepreneur to be able to take advantage of the business opportunities it may provide. In order for the entrepreneur to take proper advantage of the window of opportunity, he or she should enter the market with the right characteristics, as well as have a management team or the personal skills and resources that make it feasible to do so.

The size of the market and the length of the window of opportunity are important determinants of the risk and reward involved in

Van Schaik
Publishers

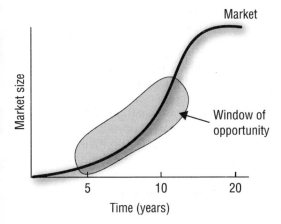

Figure 4.2 The window of opportunity

Source: Timmons, J.A. 1999. *New venture creation: entrepreneurship for the 21st century*, 5th ed. McGraw-Hill. The material is reproduced with permission of The McGraw-Hill Companies.

exploiting the presented opportunity. This is because different markets grow at different rates over time. The quicker it takes for a market to grow, the sooner more and more opportunities become available for entrepreneurs to take advantage of. As the market becomes larger with more players in it, the opportunity is no longer as lucrative as it initially was, thus resulting in less favourable conditions. The market becomes more structured and competition becomes stiffer. This is when the window of opportunity begins to close, although it may take some time before it does so completely.

The length of time that the window remains open is also of great importance. The longer it remains open, the more time it allows the entrepreneur to determine whether or not the venture will be a success, as well as providing the entrepreneur with adequate time to reap the sweet fruits of his or her labours in exploiting the opportunity if the venture is indeed successful.

4.10 Seeing, locating, measuring and opening the window of opportunity

Once the entrepreneur has spotted and located the window of opportunity, he or she must measure, open and close it. This process is illustrated in Figure 4.3, and each stage is discussed in this section.

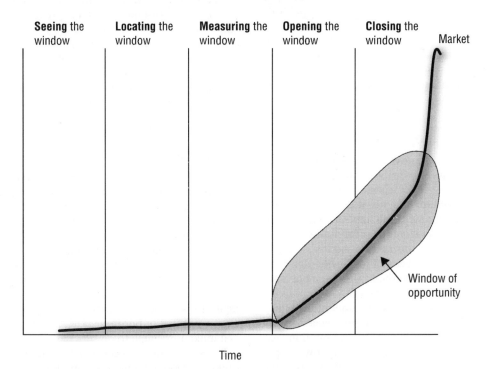

Figure 4.3 A holistic view of the window of opportunity

4.10.1 Seeing the window

It is important to return to the metaphor of the window of opportunity discussed earlier. Seeing the window of opportunity involves an active approach to searching the solid wall for gaps that have been left open by competitors, which the entrepreneur can proactively and productively take advantage of in a manner that will be beneficial for him or her while simultaneously adding value to the consumer or buyer for a prolonged period of time. This means that the entrepreneur must identify ways in which he or she can serve customer needs in the market while providing and benefiting from a sustainable competitive advantage. The entrepreneur does this by being creative and innovative, i.e. identifying and outlining how he or she can provide a better and/or different product or service.

4.10.2 Locating the window

Once the window has been spotted, it is important to understand the location of this window. The entrepreneur is then required to fully comprehend the positioning of the novel product or service offering in relation to competitors' products and services that already exist in the market. This will enable the entrepreneur to take the fullest advantage of the product or service offering in order to gain a sustainable competitive advantage over existing competitors and prospective entrants to the market.

4.10.3 Measuring the window

Measuring the window involves ensuring that the opportunity is feasible and viable. This is done by means of a feasibility and viability study. A feasibility study is a general examination of the potential of the idea to be converted into a new business venture. The issues primarily focused on are the entrepreneur's ability to pursue the idea in terms of his or her skills and abilities, and to match these with the necessary requirements of the venture.

A viability study is conducted by critically determining whether or not the idea has the potential to be converted into a new business venture. The entrepreneur must, as it were, put a finger on the pulse of the market to determine its response to an innovation, i.e. is the market

likely to respond to innovative changes in a negative or positive manner? This is usually done by means of market research, whereby the entrepreneur becomes in tune with market trends. Other important demands placed on the entrepreneur at this stage of opportunity evaluation are to determine how many consumers or end-users will be willing to pay for the products provided or services rendered, as well as the risk that is to be incurred by embarking on the venture.

4.10.4 Opening the window

The next logical step for the entrepreneur to take after seeing, locating and measuring the window of opportunity is to open the window. This is a very important step for the entrepreneur to take, as it represents entry to the market and the beginning of business activity. Revisiting the window metaphor, this is the point at which the entrepreneur moves through the window and starts the journey in terms of actively taking advantage of the opportunity presented or revealed.

This step involves the entrepreneur obtaining the commitment of the venture's stakeholders, as well as coordinating their activities. These stakeholders are financiers, employees, suppliers, customers and intermediaries, depending on the type of venture. This relationship and network building that takes place between the entrepreneur and the stakeholders is imperative to the existence and success of the venture.

4.10.5 Closing the window

On opening the window of opportunity, it is critical that the entrepreneur should promptly close it afterwards. If he or she does not, the venture is left open to competitors who, more often than not, are most willing to exploit the very same opportunity and capitalise on late mover advantages. The competitors may not have had to face the challenges that the pioneering entrepreneur had, and may take advantage of his or her pioneering moves. They may even usurp his or her innovatively and creatively gained position.

Failure by the entrepreneur to close the window of opportunity effectively could reduce his or her potential market share and business activity and, at worst, could render the venture obsolete. The window can be closed by the entrepreneur creating and maintaining a sustainable competitive advantage. The bases of competitive advantage are illustrated in Figure 4.4.

A competitive advantage exists when a firm offers a product or service that the customers perceive to be superior to those of competitors. The bases for competitive advantage are unique service features, value for money, customer convenience, customer experience and notable product attributes. A sustainable competitive advantage is one that the competitors find very difficult or even impossible to imitate, for example excellent customer service and ambience in a restaurant, or patented products such as the Colonel's eleven secret herbs and spices at KFC.

If an entrepreneur takes these factors into serious consideration, he or she is effectively en route to establishing a sustainable business.

4.11 The real-time window of opportunity – a holistic approach

It must be noted clearly that opportunities do not occur at a leisurely pace and wait for the entrepreneur to grab them before they cease to exist. Mark Twain said: "I was seldom able to see an opportunity until it ceased to exist." The process of seeing, locating, measuring, opening and closing the window of opportunity described previously gives the impression that the process of identifying and utilising oppor-

tunities is a systematic one. The process can also involve very dynamic and ad hoc occurrences in the market that the entrepreneur must evaluate and take advantage of in a timely manner.

The process is best seen as a combination of opportunity evaluation and actual activity by the entrepreneur in order to make the most of the different stages of the presented window.

4.12 Continuous opportunity evaluation and utilisation

Once entrepreneurs have successfully moved through the different stages and motions of opportunity evaluation, it is not good for them to rest on their laurels, thinking that they will maintain their position forever. Competitors will continue to evaluate their situation and conduct competitive analyses in order to become the market leader. Business opportunities will always continue to exist for those who can produce products and services that the market desires. Furthermore, as more and more entrepreneurs enter a particular industry, the market becomes smaller, because the number of entrepreneurs selling a particular product or service is increasing but the number of consumers may not be increasing. This results in market saturation and eventual stagnation of the industry.

In order to have a durable and sustainable venture, it is critical for the entrepreneur to be on the constant lookout for other opportunities

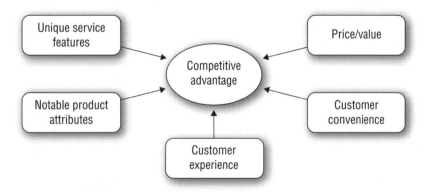

Figure 4.4 The bases of competitive advantage

Source: From *Small Business Management, an Entrepreneurial Emphasis* with CD-ROM, 12th edition by Longenecker/Moore/Petty. © 2003. Reprinted with permission of South-Western, a division of Thomson Learning: www.thomsonrights.com. Fax (091) 800 730-2215.

that he or she can successfully take advantage of. However, once entrepreneurs are used to the process of opportunity evaluation, it becomes second nature to them, and they begin to see opportunities in almost every action and occurrence in their everyday experience.

4.13 Conclusion

The aim of this chapter was to introduce the entrepreneur to the concept of the window of opportunity, and to draw a distinction between an idea and a viable business opportunity. The process of opportunity evaluation was elaborated on, as well as the stages of seeing, locating, measuring, opening and closing the window of opportunity. Opportunity evaluation from the perspective of the right time and right market was discussed, as were idea generation and the criteria used to evaluate opportunities. The chapter also touched on the common reasons why big businesses leave gaps in the market that small businesses can successfully exploit. Factors that lead to the achievement of a sustainable competitive advantage by the entrepreneur were highlighted, as well as the importance of constantly searching for and evaluating opportunities.

The process of opportunity evaluation is not always a clear-cut, straightforward one; it is usually fraught with ambiguity and uncertainty. The aspects mentioned above are the issues that the entrepreneur must be aware of, and take action to take advantage of or resolve in order to make the most of the presented opportunity. He or she will then be able to start and grow a venture that has all the qualities and potential for becoming a high-growth venture.

Looking back

1. What is the window of opportunity?

   The window of opportunity is the time period available for creating new ventures.

2. When pursuing opportunities, what factors make it easy for smaller entrepreneurs to effectively take advantage of opportunities overlooked by larger companies?

   Larger organisations'
   - Organisational inertia
   - Organisational complacence
   - Bureaucracy

3. For what reasons do larger organisations leave gaps in the market that smaller firms can effectively take advantage of?
   - Failure to take advantage of new opportunities
   - Underestimation of opportunities
   - Technological inertia
   - Cultural inertia
   - Politics and internal fighting
   - Government intervention to support SMMEs

4. What is the difference between an idea and an opportunity?
   - An idea does not necessarily automatically translate into an opportunity.
   - An opportunity is an idea that is attractive, durable and timely and anchored in a product or service that creates and/or adds value for the end-user.

5. What are the common generators of business ideas and opportunities in southern Africa?
   - Skills, expertise and aptitude
   - Common needs
   - Existing problems
   - Everyday problems
   - Other sources

6. What criteria are used to screen opportunities?
   - Industry and market issues
   - Economics
   - Harvest issues
   - Management team
   - Fatal flaw issues

- Personal criteria
- Strategic differentiation

7. What actions are required of the entrepreneur when "seeing" the window of opportunity?
    - Actively searching the market for gaps that have been left open by competitors
    - Identifying ways that customer needs can be served while providing and making use of a sustainable competitive advantage
    - Creativity and innovation

8. What actions are required of the entrepreneur when "locating" the window of opportunity?
    - Understanding the location of the window of opportunity
    - Positioning the product or service favourably in relation to competitors' products and services

9. What actions are required of the entrepreneur when "measuring" the window of opportunity?
    - Ensuring that the opportunity is feasible and viable through carrying out feasibility and viability studies
    - Performing market research in order to be in tune with market trends

10. What actions are required of the entrepreneur when "opening" the window of opportunity?

- Starting the business activity
- Obtaining the commitment of the venture's stakeholders
- Relationship and networking building between the entrepreneur and stakeholders

11. What actions are required of the entrepreneur when "closing" the window of opportunity?
    - Creating and maintaining a sustainable competitive advantage
    - Ensuring that the product or service offers unique service features, value for money, customer convenience, customer experience and notable product attributes

12. What is a sustainable competitive advantage and what are the bases of competitive advantage?
    - Sustainable competitive advantage exists when a firm offers a product or service that customers perceive to be superior to those of the competitors and one that the competitors find very difficult or impossible to imitate.
    - The bases of competitive advantage are:
      - Unique service features
      - Value for money
      - Customer convenience
      - Customer experience
      - Notable product attributes

Key terms

Ambiguity
Closing the window
Entrepreneur
Fatal flaw issues
Idea
Idea generation
Locating the window
Market
Market capacity
Market conditions
Market share
Market size

Measuring the window
Opening the window
Opportunity
Opportunity evaluation
Seeing the window
Stakeholders
Sustainable competitive advantage
Uncertainty
Value addition
Venture
Window of opportunity

Discussion questions

1. Why is ongoing evaluation and utilisation of opportunities important to the entrepreneur?

2. Discuss why it is necessary for the entrepreneur to screen opportunities.

Case studies

Case study 1

Mr Richard Richman inherited R5 billion after his father's death. He had abundant financial resources to work with and vast freedom to experiment in terms of finding business ideas and turning them into business opportunities. He decided to venture into the rapid delivery business and established a company called Quantum Leap Mail. This venture used satellite hook-ups to connect faxes in Quantum Leap offices throughout southern Africa. Drivers collected customer documents from their local office and then faxed the documents via satellite to another Quantum Leap Mail site. Quantum Leap employees then drove the reproduction to the ultimate destination – all within a period of two hours. For three-and-a-half years, Quantum Leap Mail continued to encounter serious technological problems and home and office fax machines began to appear everywhere. Finally, after losing R90 million, Mr Richman is wondering whether or not he should terminate his venture.

Questions

1. Did Mr Richman perform his opportunity evaluation and analysis well? What should he have done initially?

2. Is there any hope for Mr Richman's venture? What should he do to save his venture? Substantiate your answer.

Case study 2

Vusi Dlamini and Tshepo Molefe are fashion design and entrepreneurship graduates respectively. The two young men had not been able to find formal employment for nine months after they graduated. The situation was initially frustrating until they started toying with the idea of starting and managing their own business. Their dream business was to establish a fashion house that would manufacture and retail clothes that would have an urban youth culture feel to them, but still be distinctively South African.

The two young men believed that although they met the requirements of being funky and fashionable, the clothes available on the market at the time possessed too much of an overseas influence. They performed a competitor analysis and found that there was a proliferation of fashion houses and labels on the market that were designing and producing urban Afro-hip clothes for women, but none of them had in mind the young male target market.

These findings represented a gaping and potentially highly profitable niche market for Vusi and Tshepo, which was currently not being served by anyone. They then decided to interview a number of hip, trendy, young, professional males who had substantial buying power. They asked them how they would respond to the presence of such a fashion range in the market. The response was overwhelmingly positive and encouraging to Vusi and Tshepo. The pair then decided to take their savings – which was all they had between them and poverty – and bought fabric. They designed and manufactured their version of what young, hip and trendy South African men should be wearing in summer. From there on they were able to secure trial contracts with leading upmarket department stores for their range of clothing. The stipulations of the trial contracts state that if their clothing line reaches and maintains a certain sales volume within a certain period, then the contracts will be extended for 24 more months. Vusi and Tshepo are more than certain that they will be able to achieve and surpass the stipulated levels. They are also working on ways and means of opening up their own outlet, so that they have more control over their retailing to the public.

Questions
1. Is Vusi and Tshepo's business a good idea or a viable opportunity?
2. Vusi and Tshepo have seen the window of opportunity. Advise them on how to exploit the opportunity to their best advantage.

Experiential exercises

1. Identify two entrepreneurs, one within the service industry and one within the retail industry. Interview them to find out how they managed to turn their ideas into profitable business opportunities. How did they go about evaluating their opportunities?

2. Think of a business you have always wanted to start or the one you have started already. What criteria would you use to determine whether or not the opportunity you identified is a viable endeavour?

Exploring the Web

1. Visit www.entrepreneurmag.com/startup where you can read more about opportunity evaluation and business start-up.

2. Go to www.enterprisezone.co.za where you will find information on what South African entrepreneurs are doing in terms of turning their ideas into valuable opportunities. You will also find information on what business opportunities are currently available for entrepreneurs to exploit.

3. At www.dti.gov.za you will find out more about what the South African government is doing to support South African small businesspeople and entrepreneurs, and how you can benefit from such initiatives.

4. You have performed your opportunity evaluation and are quite certain that your idea can be turned into a potential business opportunity. Go to www.khula.org.za to find out how you can obtain financing for your venture.

References and recommended reading

Hisrich, R.D. & Peters, M.P. 2002. *Entrepreneurship,* 5th ed. Boston: McGraw Hill.

Longenecker, J.G., Moore, C.W. & Petty, J.W. 2003. *Small business management: an entrepreneurial emphasis,* 12th ed. Mason, OH: Thomson.

Nieman, G.H. & Bennett A. (Eds). 2002. *Business management: a value chain approach.* Pretoria: Van Schaik.

Nieuwenhuizen, C., Le Roux, E.E. & Jacobs, H.E. 2001. *Entrepreneurship and how to establish your own business.* Small Business Management Series. Cape Town: Juta.

Ntsika Enterprise Promotion Agency (NEPA). 2001. *Success stories.* Pretoria: Ntsika.

Pinchot III, G. 2000. *Intrapreneuring: why you don't have to leave the corporation to become an entrepreneur.* New York: Harper Row.

Timmons, J.A. 1999. *New venture creation: entrepreneurship for the 21st century,* 5th ed. Boston: McGraw Hill.

Ward, H. 2000. *Principles of Internet marketing.* Cincinnati: South Western.

Wickham, P.A. 2001. *Strategic entrepreneurship: a decision-making approach to new venture creation and management,* 2nd ed. London: Prentice Hall.

5

The business plan

Miemie Struwig

Learning outcomes

After completion of this chapter, you should be able to:
- Define a business plan
- Explain the reasons why a business plan is needed
- Use a standard layout to draw up a business plan
- Differentiate between a business plan for obtaining a loan and a business plan for strategic planning
- Discuss how the Internet can be used as a tool in drawing up a business plan

5.1 Introduction

In Chapters 3 and 4 generating new ideas and identifying opportunities were discussed. Once the entrepreneur has identified a viable opportunity, he or she should then pursue it. To be effective, the entrepreneur must plan how he or she will go about doing this. This planning of the potential business will be discussed in this chapter.

5.2 A definition of a business plan

It has been said: "If you don't know where you are going, any road will take you there." This statement applies not only to the individual who lacks direction or an objective, but to a business as well.

The business plan is a written document that spells out where the business is heading and explains in detail how it is going to reach that destination. The business plan helps the business to focus all its activities in an organised manner on reaching that destination or objective.

The business plan is a written presentation that carefully explains the business, its management team, its products or services and its goals, together with strategies for reaching the goals.

From this definition it is clear that the business plan involves:
- A process of planning – *what* the businessperson would like to achieve, i.e. his or her goals
- Strategies and action plans for achieving the goals – *how* the businessperson will achieve them.

5.3 Reasons for drawing up business plans

There are three primary reasons for compiling a business plan, as set out below.

5.3.1 To obtain funding

Any business needs capital. The business plan can be considered a vital sales tool for approaching and capturing financial sources, be they investors or lenders. Any investor or lender wants to know that the business it is lending money to, or is investing money in, has been carefully planned.

Given the limited resources most entrepreneurs have at their disposal in the start-up stage, few can afford to waste these resources. Without a business plan, the entrepreneur could easily waste the resources without even realising it before it is too late. For existing and even large businesses, stakeholders such as shareholders, investors and creditors demand a high return on their capital. This will require optimal utilisation of capital and the other factors of production. Without the assistance or guidance of a business plan, this is most unlikely.

5.3.2 To serve an inside purpose

The business plan has the potential to provide the businessperson with:

- A focus – a coordinated effort towards a clearly defined objective
- An objective – everybody will know where they are heading or what they are working for
- A tool for measuring performance against – to know whether performance is satisfactory, unsatisfactory or outstanding
- A marketing tool for obtaining finance or selling the business – outsiders will form a clear picture of what the business is doing or hoping to achieve
- A road map to direct the business
- A systematic evaluation of the chances of success in the market
- A method for determining the risks facing the business, product or idea

5.3.3 To be used as a tool for reducing the risk

The business plan helps the prospective entrepreneur to reduce the risk in starting the new venture. The process of drawing up the business plan forces the entrepreneur to think carefully and consider each aspect of the new

business venture. In doing so, the entrepreneur quite often has to consider alternatives and new directions. It also helps the businessperson to focus all his or her efforts on achieving a specific objective. The business plan serves as a yardstick for comparing actual and budgeted results in order to provide feedback on the success rate or failure rate of the business activities and effort.

It is important that the business plan be regarded as a tool that can assist the businessperson to clarify and direct the activities in the business. The business plan should be seen as something businesspeople are doing for themselves and not for outsiders.

5.4 Standard format and layout of a business plan

There are many specifics that should be included in a successful business plan. A general outline or standard format and layout of a business plan is given in Table 5.1. This outline should only be used as a preliminary planning guide. The components outlined in the table are discussed in more detail in the paragraphs below.

5.4.1 Cover sheet

The cover sheet should contain the following information:
- The full name of the business
- Ownership status
- Full street address
- Address, if different from the street address
- Phone, fax, email and website information
- Contact name and title
- Date of the plan

5.4.2 Table of contents

- Categorise the contents. List main headings (e.g. 1.1, 1.2) or give detailed (sub-) categories (e.g. 1.1.1).
- Remember also to list all charts, tables or graphs in your table of contents.

5.4.3 Summary

The summary briefly sets out the contents of the business plan. It normally contains key sentences from each section of the plan to give an

Table 5.1 An outline of a business plan

Cover sheet • Full name of business • Full street address • Mail address • Phone, fax and email • Contact name and title • Date of plan
Table of contents • Lists main headings • Includes graphs, charts and tables
Summary Highlights important aspects of the plan
Products and/or services plan • The business • The products • The industry
Marketing plan • Outline the 4 Ps (product, price, promotion and place) • Competitive advantage • Customers, market size, competition and market evaluation
Operations plan • Focus on facilities, manufacturing, capability and equipment • The steps and time taken to bring the business up to full speed
Management plan The management team. List all directors, consultants, advisers and key professionals who will be involved in the business. Attach detailed CVs as appendices.
Financial plan • Start-up capital • Projected income • Projected balance sheet • Projected cash flow statement • Projected capital equipment
Appendices All pieces of evidence, such as CVs, product brochures, testimonials and news articles.

overview of the project to the reader. Limit the summary to two or three pages.

Remember, the summary of a business plan should highlight the important features and opportunities, which will allow the reader a quick overview of whether or not the business described in it is of interest. The summary is normally written after the business plan has been drawn up.

5.4.4 Products and/or services plan

This section should briefly describe the product or service, to whom it is sold, the current status of the industry and where the new business fits in. This will give the reader a chance to establish a basis for detailed understanding.

To succeed, entrepreneurs must know their products or services. To obtain finance, potential investors or lenders should be provided with the following information of the business's products and services:

• *Description of the products and service to be sold:* Describe the primary end-use, as well as any significant secondary applications. Emphasise any unique features and how the products or services on offer will account for market penetration.

• *Proprietary position:* Describe any patents, trade secrets or other features.

• *Potential:* Describe any features of the product or service that will give it an advantage over the competition. Discuss opportunities for expansion of the product line and how to take advantage of them. Also, discuss any product disadvantage or technological changes or marketing fads, if applicable.

5.4.5 Marketing plan

This is a critical section that should clearly specify the business's marketing goals, how they are to be achieved and who will have the responsibility for achieving them. Attention should be paid to the 4 Ps, namely product, price, place and promotion. Make sure to describe these in detail.

This section also focuses on customers, industry and competition:

• *Customers:* Discuss who the customers of the product or service are. Briefly describe the basis of the purchase decisions, for example price, quality, service, personal contacts or political pressure.

- *Industry:* Describe the size of the current total market for the product or service offered. This market size should be determined from available market data sources. Also discuss potential distributors and dealers.
- *Competition:* Make a realistic assessment of the strengths and weaknesses of competitive products and services, and name the businesses that supply them. Compare the competing products and services on the basis of price, performance, service, warranties and other pertinent features.

Do not take any guesses in this section. Check all facts and note all sources. These will surely be checked. It is also important to indicate whether the business has a competitive advantage over similar businesses.

5.4.6 Operations plan

This section focuses on facilities, manufacturing capability and equipment. If the business is in manufacturing, it will help to include floor plans as well as future space plans.

The length of this section will depend on whether it is a service or product business. If the latter, it will depend on how technical the product is. The following aspects need attention:

- *Capacity:* Capacity includes, amongst other things, how many products can be produced by the business.
- *Scheduling of production:* Scheduling refers to the timing and steps that will be taken to bring the business up to full speed. Graphs and charts can help to show interrelationships between events. It is advisable to show the progress on a month-by-month basis for the first year. Thereafter, showing progress on a quarterly basis is acceptable.
- *Quality management:* This concerns what the business will do to ensure quality and control of inventory.

5.4.7 Management plan

The quality of the management team often determines the potential success of the business. List all directors, consultants, advisers and other key professionals who will be involved in the business. Indicate whether the team has worked together in the past. Detailed résumés of the key management should be included in the appendix. The management plan therefore details the organisational structure of the business. Also, present current and proposed salary structures for those on board and for those still to come on board.

5.4.8 Financial plan

The financial part of the business plan has to prove above all reasonable doubt that the business has the potential to be operated profitably. It will also explain how much money is needed to start and operate the business, how the business will be financed and the additional funds required. Issues such as break-even point, pricing policy and the cash flow position have to be addressed. Supporting projected income statements, balance sheets and cash flow statements for a three-year period will have to be provided.

■ A. Establishment costs

In the first instance, the establishment costs will be calculated. Examples of typical establishment costs are:

- Product development costs (including research and development costs of the product idea)
- Legal costs (e.g. registration of the company, the patent and the trademark)
- Product testing costs (e.g. testing of the prototype)
- Market research costs
- Cost of purchasing business premises if not rented
- Cost of machinery and equipment
- Cost of installing machinery and equipment
- Office equipment and modifications
- Provision for operating costs – for at least six months for factories and three months for retailers – for expenses such as salaries and wages, rental, interest, advertising, replacement costs and sundries
- Provision for unforeseen expenses
- Current assets such as stock

Although operating costs are a subsection of the total financial need and were consequently mentioned above, they are of a repetitive nature and not one-off expenses normally incurred during establishment, such as the purchase of land and buildings.

Operating costs may be grouped into the following categories (O'Neill et al. 1997: 170-172):

PEOPLE

- Salaries and wages
- Owner compensation
- Unemployment Insurance Fund contributions
- Pension fund contributions
- Registration of workers
- Bonuses
- Medical fund contributions
- Secretarial services
- Auditors' fees

FACILITIES

- Rental of buildings, machinery and equipment
- Equipment
- Water and electricity services
- Insurance
- Maintenance of building, machinery and equipment

MONEY

- Interest on loans
- Bank charges

PROMOTION

As a rule of thumb, depending on the type of business, promotion costs normally vary between 0,5 and 1 per cent of sales turnover. Promotion costs may be for the following:

- Advertisements in the print media, such as newspapers and magazines
- Pamphlets
- Demonstrations of products
- Outdoor advertising
- Sponsorships
- Competitions
- Advertisements on television or radio
- Promotion campaigns for specific products
- Free samples to potential customers

ADMINISTRATION

- Postage
- Telephone and faxes
- Stationery and printing
- Local taxes
- Trade licences
- Legal expenses and collection costs

REPLACEMENT COSTS

These include depreciation on furniture and equipment, manufacturing, machinery and vehicles.

SUNDRY COSTS

These entail all costs not included under one of the above subsections.

■ B. Break-even analysis

After the operating costs have been estimated for a specific period, the next step is to calculate the break-even point. The break-even point refers to the level of turnover where the gross profit is equal to the estimated operating costs. Break-even turnover is an important guideline for the prospective entrepreneur, as he or she should know the minimum turnover necessary for covering all costs. It is essential, of course, that the turnover be higher than the required level for breaking even in order to realise a profit.

EXAMPLE

An entrepreneur sees an advertisement for a supermarket that is offered for sale. After calculating the operating costs, the annual operating costs are estimated at R100 000. The gross profit percentage for supermarkets in the area is 20 per cent. What will the break-even turnover be?

Solution:	
To break even, gross profit	= Operating costs
Gross profit	= 20%
Therefore, 20%	= R100 000
And 100%	= $\dfrac{R100\ 000 \times 100}{20 \quad 1}$
Therefore, break-even turnover	= R500 000

Test:

Sales turnover	R500 000 (100%)
Cost of sales	R400 000 (80%)
Gross profit	R100 000 (20%)
Operating costs	R100 000
Net profit	R0

Formulae to remember:

$$\text{Mark-up (\%)} = \frac{\text{Gross profit}}{\text{Cost of sales}} \times \frac{100}{1}$$

$$\text{Gross profit (\%)} = \frac{\text{Gross profit}}{\text{Sales}} \times \frac{100}{1}$$

In the example:

$$\text{Mark-up (\%)} = \frac{100\,000}{400\,000} \times \frac{100}{1} = 25\%$$

$$\text{Gross profit (\%)} = \frac{100\,000}{500\,000} \times \frac{100}{1} = 20\%$$

EXAMPLE

If the entrepreneur wants to make a net profit of R50 000 in the same supermarket, what would the sales turnover have to be?

Solution:

In order to break even, budgeted operating cost = budgeted gross profit.

$$\begin{aligned}
\text{Budgeted operating costs} &= \text{R100 000} = \text{Budgeted gross profit} \\
\text{Required gross profit} &= \text{R100 000 + R50 000, in order to realise a R50 000 net profit} \\
\text{Gross profit (\%)} &= 20\% \\
\text{Required turnover} &= \frac{\text{R150 000}}{1} \times \frac{100}{20} \\
&= \text{R750 000}
\end{aligned}$$

Test:

Sales turnover	R750 000
Cost of sales	R600 000
Gross profit	R150 000
Operating costs	R100 000
Net profit	R 50 000

Source: O'Neill et al. (1997: 172-173).

At this stage, the entrepreneur should be able to determine the total amount of capital needed to start the business. Once this figure is known,

he or she has to decide how financing will take place. It is important to remember that most financial institutions will require the owners to provide at least 35 per cent of the start-up capital themselves before they will consider lending them the balance. In the business plan the contribution by owners will have to be clearly pointed out as a percentage of total capital needed.

■ C. Budgeted financial statements

The following budgeted financial statements, known as pro forma financial statements, need to be drawn up for a two-year period:
• Pro forma cash flow statement
• Pro forma income statement
• Pro forma balance sheet

PRO FORMA CASH FLOW STATEMENT

This should be done on a monthly basis for at least two years. It will imply that the turnover budget and the purchasing and operating cost budgets will also need to be projected on a monthly basis for two years.

An example of cash flow budget for a three-month period is given below.

	Jan	Feb	March
Opening balance	10 000	11 000	10 000
Cash receipts:			
Cash sales	30 000	29 000	32 000
Receipt from credit sales	20 000	18 000	22 000
Interest	2 000	1 500	2 000
Sundries	1 000	500	1 000
Total cash receipts	53 000	49 000	57 000
Cash purchases:			
Stock purchases	30 000	25 000	35 000
Trade creditors	10 000	10 000	8 000
Other creditors	2 000	4 000	3 000
Operating costs	8 000	8 000	8 000
Capital	1 000	2 000	2 000
Other	1 000	1 000	1 000
Total cash disbursements	52 000	50 000	57 000
Cash increase/decrease	1 000	(1 000)	0
Closing balance*	11 000	10 000	10 000

Note: *Closing balance = Opening balance + cash increase or minus cash decrease.

Source: O'Neill et al. (1997: 175).

PROJECTED INCOME STATEMENT

Based on the results of the market research, a provisional projected income statement should be compiled as demonstrated in the following example.

Projected income statement	
	Calculation method
1. Potential unit sales	
2. Average price per unit	
3. Potential sales (turnover)	$(1) \times (2)$
4. Unit costs (manufacturing)	
5. Cost of sales	$(1) \times (4)$
6. Gross profit	$(3) \times (5)$
7. Operating costs	
8. Net profit before tax	$(6) \times (7)$

PROJECTED BALANCE SHEET

The projected balance sheet will include the following components:

ASSETS

Current assets

Cash
Inventory
Accounts receivable
Provision for income tax

Fixed assets

Machine
Equipment
Vehicle
Trademark
Goodwill
TOTAL ASSETS

LIABILITIES AND EQUITY

Current liabilities

Accounts payable (income tax)

Long-term liabilities

Bank loan
Vehicle

Equity

Mr X
Dr Y
Mrs Z
Retained earnings
TOTAL LIABILITIES AND EQUITY

Note: Depreciation on fixed assets was not brought into consideration.

■ **Risks and problems**

The development of a business entails risks and problems, and the business plan invariably contains implicit assumptions about these. Among the risks that may require discussion are:

• Potential price cutting by competitors
• Any unfavourable industry-wide trends
• Design or manufacturing costs in excess of estimates
• Sales projections not achieved
• Product development schedule not met
• Difficulties or long lead times encountered in the purchase of raw materials
• Difficulties to obtain needed bank credit
• Larger than expected innovation and development costs

5.4.9 Appendix

Include all essential pieces of evidence such as résumés, product brochures, customer listings, testimonials and news articles.

Please note that the case study at the end of this chapter provides an example of a business plan that was drawn up according to the above components

5.5 How to select the most appropriate business plan

It is not an easy process to select the most appropriate business plan for a specific business, as the wrong choice could defeat the whole object.

The following guidelines could assist the entrepreneur in selecting the most appropriate business plan and to identify the need to adapt it according to the unique requirements of the specific business:

- Understand exactly how the new or existing business is going to operate.
- Understand the exact purpose(s) of the specific business plan.
- Study and understand the different types of business plans from which you can choose.

Try to find examples of business plans designed for similar situations as the intended business. It is unlikely that an exact replica of the intended business will be found, but a close example may exist. Obtain expert opinion on your choice prior to attempting the tedious task of finalising the business plan preparation.

5.6 Types of business plans and their functions

All business plans are not the same, because business plans are written for different reasons. There are different situations that may require different types of business plans, as explained below.

5.6.1 To plan a new business

This business plan will have to concentrate on:

- A clear description of the product or service to be offered
- A clear stipulation and definition of the target market
- Scientific market research on a representative sample of that target market
- Proof that sufficient demand exists in the stipulated target market to run a profitable business
- An organisational flow chart to explain how the business will be implemented, managed and controlled
- Condensed résumés (curriculum vitaes) of the management team, with special emphasis on their experience, qualifications and ability to manage the new business
- Realistic estimates of the financial needs of the new business with regard to establishment costs, initial marketing expenses and provision for operating costs during the first few months (normally three to six months for a retail business and one to three years for a manufacturing business)

- A breakdown of where the finance will come from, for example what percentage of the start-up capital the owner will provide and exactly how much money will have to be borrowed
- Proof to financing institutions that the business has the potential to make loan repayments as required

5.6.2 To transform or expand an existing business

This business plan will require specific emphasis on:

- Why transformation is taking place
- Why expansion is taking place
- What the profit and growth implications of the transformation or expansion could be
- What the cost of the transformation or expansion could be
- How the transformation or expansion will be financed by means of loan capital and equity (owners') capital
- What the return on investment in the transformation or expansion would be, compared with previous business actions or alternative options
- Whether the business has the capacity (capital, labour, entrepreneurial acumen and management) to successfully implement the transformation or expansion

5.6.3 To create a strategic document for an existing or a new business

As mentioned earlier, the business plan should serve as a road map to coordinate and lead the business towards a clearly identified objective. This applies to both existing and new businesses. To perform the function of a strategic document, the business plan should, among other things, contain the following:

- A vision and mission statement
- Clearly stated objectives for achieving the mission
- Competitive analysis
- Statement of competitive advantage
- Strategy for reaching objectives
- Action plan for implementing the strategy
- Controls to monitor performance

- Plan to implement corrective action, if necessary

Except if the business plan was specifically designed for obtaining a loan, for example, there should be no need to have two separate documents, such as a business plan on the one hand and a strategic plan on the other. A well-prepared business plan should equally well be used as a strategic plan.

In order to avoid the need for a separate strategic plan, the business plan should have the following qualities:

- It must be flexible in order to allow for changes in the environment.
- It must be realistic with regard to quantifiable projections, otherwise the staff will discard it as a pipe dream.
- It must include precise objectives and time schedules.
- It must include all the implementation and control elements of the normal strategic plan.
- Top management must endorse it.

As explained, the standard business plan could, subject to certain provisions, be used as a strategic planning tool. It is, however, unlikely that a business plan specifically designed to obtain a loan will lend itself in a not-amended form to be used as a strategic planning tool, as the owners might be hesitant to give all managers access to its financial gearing position. This does not mean that even business plans designed for specific purposes cannot be adapted for use in strategic planning. Management has to assess each situation on merit and then decide whether the business plan can be adapted for strategic planning purposes.

The ideal would be to design a business plan that could serve both as a business plan and as a strategic planning tool. This would not only save time, energy and costs, but also force management to start considering the business plan as the serious planning tool it ought to be and not merely as a fund-raising document. Good planning and a thorough knowledge of the design of both a business plan and a strategic plan can ensure that this ideal becomes a reality.

5.6.4 To obtain a loan

Ideally, the business plan specially designed for obtaining a loan should not differ from the business plan that is used as a strategic document. In practice, however, financial institutions are very conservative in their evaluations of loan applications and have to be convinced that the business will be able to meet the repayment requirements timeously.

Important aspects of the business plan that financial institutions will carefully consider prior to granting loans include:

- Evidence of the customers' acceptance of the venture's product or service (proof of scientific market research and "realistic" findings and forecasts is needed)
- An appreciation of the policy of banks with regard to risk and collateral
- Evidence of focus and concentration on only a limited number of products and/or services
- Realistic financial projections
- Realistic growth projections
- Avoidance of infatuation with the product or service, rather than familiarity with real marketplace needs
- Identification and consideration of potential risks
- Avoidance of exaggeration of own and management's credentials and abilities

The prospective entrepreneur should attempt to be realistic, thorough and objective with his or her business plan, as any perceived attempt to mislead the experienced bank manager will simply lead to the request for a loan being turned down and the image of the entrepreneur being tarnished.

A business plan for obtaining a loan has to pay attention to aspects other than those included in a business plan designed for strategic purposes. First, establish who the potential creditors will be and which criteria they apply to assess a loan application. Second, determine whether the business plan will have credibility among potential creditors. In order to reach an acceptable credibility level, be precise about:

- The niche you plan to serve in the market
- Whether the niche will be sufficient to meet profit objectives (explain and document the market research conducted)
- Whether the target market has been correctly defined and selected
- How large the target market is

- In what stage of the product life cycle the target market is and what its growth potential is
- How to attract, maintain and increase market share
- Any environmental factors such as legal, political or social factors that may pose a threat to the business
- How the products and services compare with those of competitors
- Whether the business has a competitive advantage
- Proving to potential creditors that the business will realise sufficient profits to repay the loan
- Justifying the suitability of the proposed location with regard to market needs and accessibility to customers
- Explaining the goals and strategy with regard to the promotional plan
- Explaining how much money will be needed to start the business and where it will be obtained (creditors would like to see that the owners are also committed to take a substantial share of the risk)
- Motivating why the present management team has been chosen and why they will be able to manage the business successfully
- What security can be given to creditors if things go wrong
- Presenting the business plan in a format that will be interesting to potential creditors
- Differentiating the business plan from the stereotypical business plan normally submitted to financial institutions

■ **Requirements of financial institutions**

Financial institutions will expect a business plan that is submitted to obtain a loan to address the following questions:
- Does the proposed business venture have a good chance to develop into a successful business?
- Will the product or service sell?
- How committed are the targeted customers?
- Was thorough market research conducted among a representative sample of the target market to determine whether there is a need for the product or service at a profitable price?

- Does the business have a competent management team that works well together?
- Will the business make a large enough profit to be able to meet interest and capital repayments on the proposed loan on time?
- What security is available if things go wrong?
- Has provision been made in the cash flow forecast for loan repayments?
- What percentage of the start-up capital has the owner provided?
- How realistic are the forecasts presented in the business plan?
- Does the business plan address the perspective of creditors?

When applying for a loan from a financial institution, the application may be one among many others for relatively limited available funds. In order to improve one's chances of success, it only makes sense to differentiate the application from those of other businesses. Likewise, do the same to build up a competitive advantage with products or services in the real market. Try to establish a competitive advantage with the business plan among all the other applicants. This is no easy task, as the business plans of the other applicants will be unknown. Fortunately, many loan applicants do not stick to the basic requirements for a good business plan and do not address the concerns of financial institutions mentioned. Differentiate your business plan by attending to these basics.

5.6.5 To attract shareholders or partners

Unlike the business plan that is specifically designed to obtain a loan, the business plan to attract shareholders or partners does not have to concentrate on proving its ability that loan repayments will be made on time. Instead, it has to concentrate on proving that the business has:
- Growth potential
- Profit potential
- Solid management
- A comprehensive strategy for achieving its profit and growth projections
- Realistic projections based on solid market assessment and research

5.6.6 To sell the business

The business plan designed to sell the business is in many ways similar to both the one for obtaining a loan and the one for attracting shareholders or partners. The business plan that is designed to sell a business should allay the fears of a prospective buyer, such as:

- What are the reasons for selling?
- What is the position of the business in relation to competitors?
- Are there any laws or regulations in the pipeline that could change the future of the business?
- What is the position with regard to the continuation of the lease if the property is rented?
- Can the business licence be taken over or a new one obtained (e.g. a liquor licence)?
- How competent is the staff and should they be retained?
- What is the credit rating of the business?
- Is the business profitable?
- Has the business been growing over the past few years or months?
- What are the growth prospects of the business?
- What is the condition of the equipment and machinery?
- What do present customers think of the business?
- What are the reasons for asking the specific selling price and how can the price be justified?

5.6.7 To provide direction for management and staff in a new or existing business

A clearly defined business plan provides management with direction and focus in their efforts. This applies to both new and existing businesses. To perform the function as direction provider, the business plan should contain the following elements and qualities:

- A comprehensive and clear description of the business
- All the steps of the standard business plan, in chronological order
- Realistic objectives
- Quantifiable objectives
- Built-in adaptability to allow for change in a dynamic environment
- Precise stipulation and description of the organisational structure for accomplishing the objectives

5.6.8 To prepare the business for a merger with another business

The type of business plan that is designed to prepare a business for a merger with another business has a dual function: first, to explain the current operations and future plans of the business and, second, the competitive advantage and growth prospects. Special attention will have to be paid to these aspects:

- A clear explanation of what exactly the business is all about and what its major activities entail
- An independent valuation of the business done by a professional valuator
- Audited financial statements of past performance
- A situational analysis (SWOT analysis)
- A competitive analysis
- An explanation of the competitive advantage(s)
- An explanation of the future plans of the business

It is not suggested that the reasons for seeking a partner to merge with be included in the business plan, as the reasons will depend on the type of business the merger is planned with. These reasons should be predetermined and logically listed prior to negotiating a merger and therefore form part of the negotiations and not part of the business plan.

5.6.9 To prepare the business for the takeover (acquisition) of another business

Contrary to the business plan preceding a merger that is prepared to attract outsiders, the business plan to prepare the business for the takeover of another business is prepared for insiders or the business itself. The business plan to prepare the business for taking over another business should pay special attention to the following:

© Van Schaik Publishers

- The main reasons why the takeover is planned
- The impact of the takeover on the business with regard to:
  - Profit
  - Growth
  - Cash flow
  - Staff
  - Competitive advantage
  - Market share
  - Management
- The opportunity cost of not taking over the other business
- How the takeover will be financed
- Whether the takeover will be in accordance with laws and regulations
- Whether the takeover is in accordance with the vision and mission of the business

5.6.10 To help position the business in the market

Positioning refers to the perception of the business in the mind of the customer. The business plan designed to position the business in the market may have the function of helping all the workers in the business to focus their efforts on positioning the firm in the market. If the positioning is successful, it will clarify the positioning of the business in the minds of the customers.

Specific emphasis in the business plan to help position the business in the market should be placed on:

- Thorough and scientific market research to identify opportunities in the market with profit potential
- Whether the business has the necessary resources available to position itself in the desired position in the market
- An analysis of the profit and growth potential of different positioning options in the market
- The reasons for selecting a specific positioning strategy
- The potential impact of the selected positioning strategy on the operations, profit and long-term growth of the business

Apart from the situations described above, which require specific business plans, more variations are possible such as:

- Businesses that need to borrow money, as well as to use it as a strategic document
- Owners who want to transform or expand an existing business but also need a strategic document to direct their efforts
- New businesses that want to attract both loan and equity capital
- Owners who want to sell the business or prepare it for a merger with another business
- Businesses that want to take over another business and need loan or equity capital to make it possible

5.7 Problems when drawing up a business plan

When conceiving a business plan, the entrepreneur has to be aware of possible problems in order to avoid them. A business plan is usually not a private document. In most instances it will be carefully scrutinised by other people, which will reveal any flaws in it. If such flaws are seen as the result of obvious problems, the image of the entrepreneur will be severely tarnished. Would-be creditors would then be most hesitant to finance the business and potential partners and investors would almost definitely reconsider their options.

Table 5.2 outlines the most obvious problems when drawing up a business plan and also what should be done to avoid them.

As a selling document to potential investors and creditors, the business plan should do better than merely avoiding the problems listed in Table 5.2.

5.8 Using the Internet as a tool for drawing up a business plan

The changing world of technology offers new opportunities for entrepreneurs to use the Internet as a tool when drawing up a business plan. The Internet can serve as an important source of information on such components as the industry analysis, competitor analysis and measurement of market potential.

The Internet can also be used as a valuable resource in later planning and decision-making stages. A website or home page typically describes a business's history, existing products or services, the background of the

Table 5.2 Problems when drawing up a business plan and how to avoid them

Problem	Avoidance measure
1. Lack of proven market demand	• Do thorough, scientifically based market research to support claims.
2. Lack of objectivity	• Let an independent consultant critically assess the business plan. • Base projections on research. • Be conservative with projections. • Try to look at the business plan from the point of view of a potential investor.
3. Ignoring competition	• Make a list of all existing and potential competitors. • Conduct a SWOT analysis on each competitor. • Determine the competitive advantage. • Consider both direct and indirect competition. • Consider the possibility of introducing substitutes for the product or service. • Determine the chances of success should competition be considered.
4. Inappropriate market research	• Define the problem to be researched. • Define the target market. • Select a representative sample of the target market. • Collect the data. • Analyse and interpret the data. • Draw conclusions. • Make projections.
5. Inability to produce according to quantity and quality required	• Determine the quantity required (based on market research). • Determine the capacity to produce the quantity required (machines, capital and trained labour). • Determine the quality specifications. • Determine the capacity to meet the quality specifications.
6. Underestimating financial requirements	• Determine the total capital needed to get started. • Provide for at least three months' operating costs in a retail business and 6–12 months in a manufacturing business. • Determine the additional capital needed if selling on credit. • Determine the loan required and the ability to repay it.
7. Insufficient proof that loan repayments will be made timeously	• Start with realistic financial requirements (as explained in No. 6). • Use realistic sales projections. • Do a thorough but realistic projected cash flow budget on a monthly basis for three years. • Indicate clearly on the cash flow budget how loan repayments will be made.

Table 5.2 Continued

Problem	Avoidance measure
8. Lack of a unique product or service	• Ensure that the product possesses a competitive advantage. • Test the product concept or a prototype in the target market to determine whether customers regard it as unique and are willing to purchase it.
9. Disregard for legal requirements	• Determine the legal and regulatory requirements by consulting provincial, regional and municipal authorities. • Determine whether patent or trade name registration is required. (Consult an attorney or a patent attorney if necessary.) • Ask an attorney to double-check all attempts to meet the legal requirements.
10. Ignoring potential influence of the external environment	• Establish the potential influence of the physical, institutional, technological, economic, political and social environments on the proposed business. • Develop strategies for coping with these influences.
11. Lack of sufficient financial commitment by the founders	• Determine what minimum percentage contribution banks require from the founders of a business before they will grant a loan. • Ensure that the founders of the business meet at least that minimum amount prior to approaching the bank for a loan.
12. Lack of appropriate business experience by management and staff	• Management should try to gain appropriate business experience by working in a similar type of business prior to start-up. • If this is not possible, appoint experienced and well-trained staff. • Get training and experience in the aspects in which staff are lacking the knowledge.
13. Failure to anticipate obstacles	• Make a list of all obstacles most likely to prevent success. • Design strategies for dealing with such obstacles, should they occur.
14. Lack of a logical sequence	• Have a critical outsider comment on the logical sequence of the business plan. • Design a flow chart for the business plan in order to determine whether it is done in a logical sequence.
15. Failure to indicate the stage in the product life cycle at market entry	• Determine the product life cycle by summarising historical sales in the branch of industry. • Draw a product life cycle. • Determine the present stage in the product life cycle.
16. Understatement of expenses	• Check expenses with an accountant and/or the actual trial balance of an existing business to ensure all potential cost items are covered. • Ensure that all marketing plans (e.g. advertising) are converted into financial terms. Most entrepreneurs underestimate these costs or forget to include them in the expense forecast.

founders or management team, and other information that might create a favourable image.

The Internet is therefore a very good marketing tool for any business, be it advertising or direct selling. Besides being a marketing tool, the Internet also provides valuable information on competitors.

In addition to websites, the entrepreneur can also gather valuable information through news groups and other online groups on the Internet.

Software used to draw up business plans is also readily available on the Internet and it can assist potential entrepreneurs in their task. See "Exploring the Web" later in this chapter for some useful Internet addresses in this regard.

5.9 Conclusion

In this chapter we have defined the business plan as a written presentation that carefully explains the business, its management team, its products or services and its goals, together with strategies for reaching these goals. There are primarily three reasons why business plans are drawn up: to obtain funding, to serve an inside purpose and to be used as a tool for reducing risks.

A standard layout of a business plan was provided to serve as a preliminary planning guide. Guidelines on how to select the most appropriate business plan were given. This will assist the entrepreneur in selecting the most useful business plan for his or her business.

Business plans are written for different reasons. The different situations that will require different business plans were outlined, as well as what components the selected business plan should contain.

When drawing up a business plan, the entrepreneur should also be aware of potential problems in order to avoid them. Problems and avoidance measures in this regard were outlined. Tips on how to do better than merely avoid the potential problems when drawing up a business plan were also given.

The adaptations necessary to draw up a business plan for obtaining a loan or for strategic planning were also discussed. To conclude, use of the Internet as a tool for drawing up a business plan was briefly explained.

Looking back

1. Define a business plan.

   The business plan is a written presentation that carefully explains the business, its management team, its products or services and its goals, together with strategies for reaching the goals.

2. List the reasons for compiling a business plan.
   - To obtain funding
   - To serve an inside purpose
   - To be used as a tool for reducing risks

3. Name the components to be included in a standard format or layout of a business plan.
   - Cover sheet
   - Table of contents
   - Summary
   - Products and/or services plan
   - Marketing plan
   - Operations plan
   - Management plan
   - Financial plan
   - Appendix

4. Briefly explain how one should select the most appropriate business plan.

   Select a business plan according to the unique requirements of the specific business:
   - Know how the new or existing business is going to operate.
   - Consider the exact purpose(s) of the specific business plan.
   - Study and understand the different types of business plans from which to choose.

5. List the different situations that will require a different type of business plan.
   - To obtain a loan
   - To attract shareholders or partners
   - To sell the business

- To provide direction for management and staff in a new or existing business
- To prepare the business for a merger with another business
- To prepare the business for the takeover (acquisition) of another business
- To help position the business in the market

6. Briefly explain the problems experienced when drawing up a business plan.
   - Lack of proven market demand
   - Lack of objectivity
   - Ignoring competition
   - Inappropriate market research
   - Inability to produce according to quantity and quality required
   - Underestimating financial requirements
   - Insufficient proof that loan repayments will be made timeously
   - Lack of a unique product or service
   - Disregard for legal requirements
   - Ignoring the potential influence of the external environment
   - Lack of sufficient financial commitment by the founders
   - Lack of appropriate business experience by management and staff
   - Failure to anticipate obstacles
   - Lack of a logical sequence
   - Failure to indicate the stage in the product life cycle at market entry

7. Briefly describe the two main aspects to consider when drawing up a business plan for obtaining a loan.
   - Establish who the potential creditors will be and which criteria they apply to assess a loan application.
   - Determine whether the business plan will have credibility among potential creditors.

8. Explain how to adapt the standard business plan to be used as a strategic document.

   A well-prepared business plan should equally well be used as a strategic plan. In order to avoid the need for a separate strategic plan, the business plan should have the following qualities:
   - It must be flexible in order to allow for changes in the environment.
   - It must be realistic with regard to quantifiable projections, otherwise the staff will discard it as a pipe dream.
   - It must include precise objectives and time schedules.
   - It must include all the implementation and control elements of the normal strategic plan.
   - Top management must endorse it.

9. Briefly describe how the Internet can be used as a tool for drawing up a business plan.

   The Internet can serve as:
   - An important source of information in the preparation of the business plan for such components as the industry analysis, competitor analysis and measurement of market potential
   - A valuable resource in planning and decision making at a later stage
   - A very good marketing tool for any business, be it advertising or direct selling
   - A valuable source of information on competitors
   - A means of gathering valuable information through news groups and other online groups

   Software that can assist entrepreneurs in their task to write a business plan, is also readily available on the Internet.

Key terms

Business plan
Executive summary
Internet
Market description and analysis

Marketing strategy
Operations plan
Strategic document

Discussion questions

1. Define the term "business plan" and explain the components contained in this definition.
2. Explain how a business plan can be used to serve an inside purpose for a business.
3. Describe the components contained in a business plan.
4. Why is the summary important?
5. Explain how to go about selecting the most appropriate business plan for a business.
6. List the situations that may require different types of business plans.
7. Discuss how to avoid potential problems when compiling a business plan.
8. Why should a business plan do better than merely avoiding problems?
9. Distinguish between a business plan for obtaining a loan and a business plan as a strategic tool.
10. How can the Internet be used as a tool for drawing up a business plan?

Case study

Cover sheet

ADVENTURE TRAVEL EASTERN CAPE

Sole proprietor

31 Govan Mbeki Avenue
PORT ELIZABETH
6001

PO Box 320
PORT ELIZABETH
6000

Tel. 041-585 5000
Fax 041-585 6700
Email: ThaboKele@magicnet.co.za

October 2003

Table of contents

1. Summary
2. Products and/or services plan
3. Marketing plan
4. Operations plan
5. Management plan
6. Financial plan
7. Appendix

1. Summary

Adventure Travel Eastern Cape (ATEC) will begin operations in October 2004 and provide adventure, sport/travel packages to people in the Eastern Cape, specifically the Port Eliza-beth area. The founder and employees of ATEC are experienced travel industry professionals and are passionate about the activities ATEC will promote and offer. An opportunity for ATEC's success exists because the national tourism and travel industry is growing by 4 per cent and adventure travel by 10 per cent, annu-ally. Furthermore, the Port Elizabeth adventure travel market is growing by at least 12 per cent annually and there are no providers that spe-cialise solely in adventure travel in the greater Port Elizabeth area. ATEC is poised to take advantage of this growth and lack of competi-tion with an experienced staff, excellent loca-tion, and effective management and marketing. The Port Elizabeth area, like much of the East-ern Cape, has a large concentration of outdoor recreation enthusiasts. These health-conscious individuals, couples and groups interested in popular adventure sports, such as skiing, kayaking, trekking, etc., are ATEC's primary customers. ATEC's target market is an exploitable niche, and ATEC will provide a spe-cialised and thus differentiated service. Prices will be competitive with the remainder of the market. The company's estimated sales for the first year of operations is R534 000, increasing by 10 per cent annually over the next two years.

The main objectives of ATEC are to:

• Achieve sales of R6 500 000 by year three.

- Maintain margins of 10 per cent on all airline travel.
- Achieve 15 per cent of sales from the Internet.
- Develop strategic alliances with service providers nationally, internationally, and in the Port Elizabeth area.

ATEC is a sole proprietorship owned and operated by Thabo Kele in Port Elizabeth, Eastern Cape, South Africa. ATEC's owner is researching the possibility of establishing ATEC as a close corporation. This may occur within 18 months of operation.

2. Products and/or services plan

Adventure Travel Eastern Cape (ATEC) is a travel agency that specialises in adventure tourism and travel. It will provide consulting and custom travel arrangements and packages. ATEC's mission is to become the foremost provider of adventure travel to the people of the Eastern Cape. ATEC's employees and owner are outdoor adventure and travel enthusiasts, as well as seasoned travel industry professionals. ATEC seeks to connect adventure travel newcomers and veterans with service providers, adventure activities and accommodation that fit the clients' desires, budget and skill level.

ATEC is a full service travel agency that specialises in adventure travel and provides recreational and business travellers with professional service and consultation. ATEC will position itself as a specialist in the field of adventure travel and will generate the majority of its income from this segment.

ATEC sells standard travel agency goods and services, including airfare and travel packages. Additional services include assistance with passports, providing access to top-of-the-line equipment and supplies, and a superior offering that includes access to better-than-average terrain and activities, accommodation and entertainment. The value added of ATEC's offering is its knowledge and expertise, competitive rates and specialty focus on adventure travel, which translates into increased satisfaction for the customer.

The travel agency market is competitive, and technology – the Internet and Computerised Reservation Systems (CRS) – has changed the way travel agencies operate. ATEC has positioned itself as an adventure travel specialist. ATEC has not identified a direct competitor in the greater Port Elizabeth area. However, a travel agency does not have to be an adventure travel specialist to book an adventure travel trip. Therefore, ATEC will compete with other travel agencies in the Port Elizabeth area, as they offer alternatives to adventure travel, have the ability to arrange adventure travel themselves, and have the advantage of established relationships with clients.

ATEC may in the future open agencies at additional locations. In addition, as the adventure travel market reaches maturity, ATEC may participate in additional segments of the travel market.

3. Marketing plan

ATEC plans to focus its initial efforts on the adventure travel market in the greater Port Elizabeth area. Adventure travel falls primarily into the leisure travel category. Revenues from leisure travel earned by South African travel agencies exceed R50 billion annually. Adventure travel is a subcategory of leisure travel and can be further broken down into hard and soft adventure travel. Annual expenditures in the South African market are estimated at R40-50 million for soft and R12-15 million for hard adventure travellers.

ATEC is located in the heart of the Eastern Cape. The natural beauty and abundance of outdoor activities attract many fitness-oriented individuals. Per capita, the area has more people than any other in the country who actively participate in mountain and water sports such as skiing, climbing, kayaking, white water rafting, mountain biking, etc. These are the people of ATEC's target market. ATEC will focus on the sale and promotion of adventure travel primarily to individuals, but also to corporate clients in the Port Elizabeth area.

ATEC offers people the ability to get away and remember how much they love the challenge and excitement of an athletic endeavour. ATEC will promote the benefits of adventure travel. These benefits include better health, excitement, personal growth, ear-to-ear grins, and a whole lot of fun.

Much of ATEC's pricing is determined by market standards. During ATEC's first year of operation it will hold a grand opening and will organise and sponsor several athletic events. Events will include an offroad triathlon, a 10 km road race and a 5 km fun run, and a mountain bike race.

ATEC's distribution strategy will focus on the target market in the Port Elizabeth area, to whom it will sell directly. Secondarily, ATEC seeks to establish distribution capability on the World Wide Web. Doing so will improve ATEC's ability to establish a national reputation.

• Customers

ATEC's target customers are health-conscious couples and individuals, with median household incomes of approximately R50 000. They are interested in popular adventure activities such as skiing, white water sports, and mountain biking. Major purchasers are located in urban areas within South Africa.

Adventure travellers are slightly more likely to be men between the ages of 18 and 34. Men on average spend more than women on their adventure travels. ATEC's primary customers, however, are married couples, aged 25 to 35, with children, and household incomes over R50 000.

• Competition

The travel industry is similar to many others. There are large national chains, small home-based businesses, consolidators on the Internet, etc. ATEC has approximately 30 immediate competitors in the greater Port Elizabeth area, including two agencies that are branches of national travel agency chains.

4. Operations plan

ATEC will sell the benefits of the services it offers and the activities it promotes. ATEC sells the freedom that is part of a healthy and balanced lifestyle. The benefits of that lifestyle are many. People need to be reminded occasionally that there is more to life than just work. ATEC can provide clients with all the arrangements they can think of and many they possibly would not have thought of.

ATEC has identified three potential locations for office space. All three are in the city of Port Elizabeth. Once successfully established, ATEC will be one of approximately 30 travel

agencies in the greater Port Elizabeth area. ATEC will be the only adventure travel specialist in the immediate area.

There are many activities and types of travel available to people contemplating an adventure vacation. These substitute products and services are one type of competition. Theme parks, motor-home trips, and cruises are just a few. Other substitutes include less expensive, self-planned or traditional vacations. In addition, potential customers do not have to take a vacation. Instead, they may elect to spend elsewhere, or invest the money they would otherwise have spent.

Strategic alliances for promotion have been developed with Body Works Health Club, Port Elizabeth Whitewater, The Great Wall climbing gym, and several area retailers. Alliances with adventure trip providers in South Africa and foreign countries have also been established.

5. Management plan

Thabo Kele will act as the general manager. However, ATEC is a small organisation and its employees will share in management duties and decision making. It will be important for each member of the team to be capable in all aspects of the business. Prerequisites for all ATEC employees include at least five years' travel industry experience, knowledge and ability in the types of activities ATEC will promote, and Certified Travel Counsellor (CTC) certification for applicable positions. The CTC designation can be obtained through the Institute of Certified Travel Agents (ICTA). See the appendix for CVs of key personnel.

6. Financial plan

Preliminary estimates suggest that ATEC will experience slow growth in the first two quarters of operation. This is partly due to ATEC's status as a start-up business, as well as seasonal factors. ATEC has sufficient cash to endure the negative cash flow situation that it may encounter initially. ATEC also anticipates an increase in gross margin and sales volume.

ATEC's total start-up capital requirement is approximately R402 500. Start-up will be financed through the owner's personal investment and a long-term loan secured from the Port Elizabeth First National Bank. Start-up details are:

- *Expenses:* These will be for rent, office supplies, consultants' fees, insurance, utilities, etc. The largest start-up expense will be for computers.
- *Assets:* Primarily cash and computers.
- *Investment:* The bulk of the investment will come from a loan from Port Elizabeth First National Bank. The remainder will come from Thabo Kele's personal savings.
- *Loans:* A loan of R306 063 has been secured from Port Elizabeth First National Bank.

PROJECTED INCOME STATEMENT FOR YEAR 1

Total sales (after VAT, in Rand)		2 900 000
Minus cost of sales (including manufacturing, labour, packaging and transport)		1 353 331
Gross profit		1 546 669
Minus operating costs	Rand	
Advertising	150 000	
Sales promotion	140 000	
Insurance	30 000	
Telephone	60 000	
Factory rental	90 000	
Water and electricity	60 000	
Interest on loan	69 430	
Repairs and maintenance	60 000	
Indirect labour	60 000	
Repayments on vehicle	19 055	
Office supplies	10 000	
Petrol and transport (general)	10 000	
Computer costs	10 000	
Manager's salary	100 000	
Accounting fees	10 000	
Registration fees	5 000	
Research and development	20 000	
Bank charges	10 000	
Sundries	5 000	
Legal fees	5 000	
Total operating costs		923 485
Income before tax		623 184
Minus interest on loan		69 430
Net profit after interest and before tax		553 754
Minus income tax (45%)		249 189
Net profit after income tax		304 565

PROJECTED BALANCE SHEET AS ON 31 DECEMBER 2005

ASSETS	Rand	
Current assets:		**594 931**
Cash	84 068	
Inventory	20 000	
Accounts receivable	241 674	
Provision for income tax	249 189	
Fixed assets:		**776 000**
Machine	600 000	
Equipment and modifications	65 000	
Vehicle	60 000	
Trademark	10 000	
Goodwill	41 000	
Total assets		**1 370 931**

LIABILITIES and EQUITY		
Current liabilities:		249 189
Accounts payable (income tax)	249 189	
Long-term liabilities:		306 063
Bank loan	306 063	
Equity:		780 679
Own capital	600 000	
Retained earnings	180 679	
Total liabilities and equity		1 370 931

7. Appendix

Abbreviated CV of owner:

Thabo Kele, age 37, BA Marketing Management, University of XYZ. Thabo has 12 years of experience in the travel industry, including five years' experience as manager of the Transworld travel agency. As manager at Transworld, Thabo increased revenues by R1,5 million and established the adventure travel division that, in its first 18 months, generated an additional R400 000 in revenues. His background in adventure sports includes four years on the South African pro kayaking tour, two years as a sponsored cross-country mountain bike racer, 25 years of surfing, including three years as an amateur competitor. He has also participated in many other adventure and organised sports such as snowboarding, beach volleyball, and track and field events.

Note that the information used in this case study is for illustration purposes only and is not factually correct. The business plan is also presented in a much shorter format than would be needed in real life.

Questions

1. As a bank manager who must approve a loan to ATEC, explain whether or not this application will be considered.

2. As part of the management team of ATEC, indicate whether the business plan can be used for strategic planning. Explain.

Experiential exercises

1. Identify an entrepreneur who wants to start a business. Then draw up a business plan for the entrepreneur that will enable him or her to obtain a loan from a bank.

2. Take the same business plan and adapt it so that the entrepreneur can use it as a strategic document for his or her business.

Exploring the Web

1. Go to www.Bplans.com for exploring ways in which the Internet can be used to draw up business plans and for many sample business plans. It also provides software to assist in writing business plans, and contains personalised industry news and "how to start" business kits.

2. Visit www.businessplans.org for more sample business plans. It also provides links to software used for business plans.

3. At www.morebusiness.com you will find more sample business plans, as well as sample contracts and marketing plans.

4. Go to www.Bpiplans.com for over 200 business plans.

5. Visit www.online-business-plans.com for online services in designing business plans and doing financial projections.

References and recommended reading

Longenecker, J.G., Moore, C.W. & Petty, J.W. 2003. *Small business management: an entrepreneurial emphasis,* 12th ed. Mason, OH: Thomson South Western.

O'Neill, R.C., Terblanche, N.S. & Keyter, L. 1997. *Creative entrepreneurship.* Pretoria: Kagiso Tertiary.

Timmons, J.A. 1999. *New venture creation: entrepreneurship for the 21st century.* Boston: Irwin.

Vista University. 2001. *Designing a business plan.* Unpublished module for BMA 5008. Pretoria: Vista University.

6

Resource requirements and legal and related aspects

Hannelize Jacobs

Learning outcomes

After completion of this chapter, you should be able to:

- Determine the various resources you will need to start an own small business and indicate how you would acquire it
- Examine the different legal forms a small business can take and identify a suitable form for a new small business
- Describe the registration process when starting a particular type of business
- Illustrate the different ways prospective entrepreneurs can protect their intellectual property
- Explain how the law on counterfeit goods can influence a prospective small business owner
- Indicate the taxation requirements that apply to each type of business
- Describe the process and conditions for registering with the Receiver of Revenue
- Explain the requirement of registering with the Department of Labour when starting an own business
- Discuss the requirements that exist for obtaining trade licences and for having to pay Regional Services levies
- Demonstrate your understanding of the importance of taking care when concluding contracts
- Explain how entrepreneurs can use licensing to their advantage
- Explore the major labour legislations governing employment in South Africa
- Explain how entrepreneurs should handle product liability
- Appreciate the regulations pertaining to standards when starting a small business
- Understand how competition policies can influence the establishment of a small business
- Appreciate and explain the environmental regulations pertaining to starting an own business
- Give your opinion on the Promotion of Access to Information Act

6.1 Introduction

In order to pursue business opportunities, entrepreneurs need resources. Resources are the fuel needed to start and operate a business, just as petrol or diesel is the fuel for vehicles. If a business has insufficient resources or an inappropriate mix of resources, it cannot start or will operate just as poorly as the car with not enough or the wrong kind of fuel. Businesses rely on four major kinds of "fuel": financial, human, physical and information resources. Acquiring these resources can be a challenging task for any prospective entrepreneur.

Entrepreneurs also have to comply with many legal regulations when starting and operating their own businesses. Understanding the legal aspects pertaining to a small business can be just as challenging. Entrepreneurs do not have to possess the knowledge and expertise of a lawyer, but they should be sufficiently knowledgeable about certain legal aspects that have implications for their prospective businesses. These legal aspects can be divided into two groups: those that relate to the establishment of the business, and those that relate to the normal flow of the business.

In this chapter the focus will be on the main resources requirements, and the legal and related aspects when starting a new business venture in South Africa.

6.2 Resource requirements in establishing a new business venture

6.2.1 The nature of resources

Resources are the things that an entrepreneur uses to pursue a business opportunity. They include the money that is invested in the business; the people who contribute their efforts, knowledge and skills to it; the physical assets such as equipment and machinery, buildings and vehicles; and the information used to make decisions. All these can be subject to investment. One of the key functions of the entrepreneur is to attract investment to the business and to use it to build up a set of assets that allow the business to supply its product and/or service. As the business grows, it develops its own processes and systems and the people within it adopt distinct roles. During this process, the responsibility of obtaining resources is taken over by specialist functions in the business.

Resources are limited to the entrepreneur. Using funds to acquire one resource can mean that there are less funds for acquiring other resources. It is therefore important that the entrepreneur makes the right choice as to which resources to invest in. To take this decision, the entrepreneur must decide which contributes the greater value for the business to pursue its goals and strategies. Then again, one resource is sometimes needed for another resource to be used. The entrepreneur therefore also needs to consider the right mix of resources.

6.2.2 Major types of resources

In broad terms, there are four types of resources that prospective entrepreneurs will combine to build a business: financial, human, physical and information.

■ **Financial resources**

Financial resources are those resources that take the form of, or can be readily converted into, cash. Financial resources are valuable in that they do not have a single purpose but can be used to acquire other resources. Therefore, the acquisition and use of this type of resource are very important.

Finance can be obtained from different sources. A first source is the entrepreneur. Money invested by the entrepreneur is called *equity financing*. Entrepreneurs may put some of their personal funds into the business, raise money by taking in a partner or through selling shares to investors. These shareholders become part owners of the business in exchange for the money invested.

The second source of funds is money loaned to the business by outsiders, such as individuals, banks or other lending institutions. Loaned cash is called *debt financing*. There are also two significant differences between debt financing and equity financing. First, debt financing requires the borrower to pay interest on loans to the business. The loan contract is a legally binding agreement that the business will pay back the loan plus interest. Equity financing does not require paying back the investment. Second, the providers of the debt financing are called lenders. These lenders do not become owners.

As soon as the business is operational, the most critical source of finance will be revenue. Revenue is cash that is generated from the sale of goods or services to customers. As customers purchase goods or services from the firm, they pay for those purchases with either cash or credit that is later turned into cash. Revenue is the most critical source of funding because it is a continual source of new funds. Revenue-generated funds may not be enough to keep the business running at the time of start-up, during seasonal fluctuations, or when the firm is growing rapidly. In these cases, either additional debt or equity financing may be required.

Other sources of obtaining finance are government support programmes (such as Ntsika Enterprise Promotion and Khula Enterprise Finance Ltd), venture capital funds (e.g. Horizon Equity), companies (such as Business Partners, the Industrial Development Corporation of South Africa), mortgages for financing business property and long-term investments in operating assets (machinery, etc.) and leasing for machinery, equipment, vehicles, etc.

© Van Schaik Publishers

Human resources

Human resources are all the people and the efforts, skills, knowledge and insights they contribute to the success of the business. Human resources consist of four groups: top management, middle management and professional staff, supervisory management and non-managerial workers. It is important that each position be staffed with the best people possible, given the financial constraints of the new business.

Building up a business is a task that requires a wide variety of talents, which are hardly ever to be found in a single person. A group of people with complementary skills will always solve problems better than individuals ever could. Simply by working as a team, many typical mistakes that occur in the early stages of a business can be avoided. Involving other people in the business as co-founders or partners is therefore not only a financial decision, but also one that can improve the chances of success in starting or growing a new business. Another way of obtaining the needed expertise is to employ people.

A prospective entrepreneur is mainly concerned with the following challenges in employing people:

* Accurately forecasting human resource needs
* Recruiting candidates and selecting the best person for the job

As soon as the business is running, the entrepreneur will also have to pay attention to training and developing, and encouraging high performance from employees.

The following steps can be taken to accurately forecast, recruit and select employees for the new business:

1. List all the tasks that must be performed in the business.

2. Group together those tasks that can logically be done by one person (the description of these tasks is known as a job description). This step will give you an indication of the number of people you need to employ.

3. Determine what qualifications and skills the person must have to perform the tasks (this is the job specification).

4. Recruit people who are willing and able to do the tasks in the job description and who meet the job specification by:
   * Advertising the positions
   * Using recruitment agencies
   * Approaching training organisations, such as schools, technical colleges or tertiary institutions

5. Interview candidates

6. Appoint the best person for the job and conclude a contract with the person.

Physical resources

Physical resources include:
* Fixed assets, such as buildings and equipment
* Raw materials that will be used to create the business's products
* General supplies used in the operation of the business

Planning is important in acquiring all four types of resources, but especially physical resources. This is because a large amount of capital is required to acquire fixed assets, i.e. building facilities, vehicles and production equipment. Careful planning is also important because of the need for scheduling. The production process can only move if raw materials are available. Too much raw material at one time, however, means excessive inventory, which must be paid for, counted, stored, insured, protected and moved around. This represents a major cost for a business.

Because fixed assets usually are the most expensive resource a new business has to acquire, the decision on where to locate the business is crucial. An entrepreneur can decide to purchase or renovate existing facilities, or to build new facilities. In each case the location decision can have a major impact on the success of the new business. The location decision also applies to service-related businesses.

The factors that need to be taken into consideration when deciding on a suitable location include:
* Accessibility to the market
* Availability of raw materials
* Availability of labour and skills
* Infrastructure – transport, water supply, electricity supply, existing business environment
* Climate

There are many sources of raw materials and general supplies. Each has its own benefits and requires a different type of coordination and arrangement. Suppliers of raw materials include independent contractors, regional producers, national or international producers, speciality goods producers and foreign producers.

■ **Information resources**

The "Information Age" necessitates a fourth resource, namely information. This resource is just as crucial as the other three. Without information, the entrepreneur cannot make appropriate decisions.

An entrepreneur mainly needs two categories of information, namely information about his or her prospective business's external environment, and information that bears on the internal working of the business:

• The former includes information about the prospective business's competitors, customers and other external uncontrollable variables that may impact the new business, such as politics, the economy, technology and legal concerns (the focus of the second part of this chapter).

• The latter includes information that will ensure that the business will run efficiently when it starts to operate. This information includes marketing information, manufacturing information, accounting and financial information, quality control information and human resources information.

There are many sources of information, including the Internet, government departments (the Department of Trade and Industry, South African Revenue Services, SABS, Stats SA), chambers of commerce, trade associations, financial institutions, science councils, educational institutions, independent organisations, professional societies and venture capital fund organisations.

6.3 Legal requirements for establishing a business

An entrepreneur who wishes to establish a new business has to adhere to certain legal aspects. These depend on various factors, including the legal form of the new business, the type of service or product that it wants to provide, and the way it wants to organises its business.

In addition to registering the business (depending on the legal form the entrepreneur chooses), a business generally has to register its intellectual property (if it has any) and register with the Receiver of Revenue (for VAT, if the income of the business is big enough, and for income tax for self and employees), with the Department of Labour (for the Unemployment Insurance and Compensation for Occupational Injuries and Diseases Funds), with the Regional Services for a monthly payment for services, and for special licences when trading in food, for example.

In the next section, these legal aspects relating to the establishment of a new business will be discussed.

6.3.1 Legal forms a business can take in South Africa

One of the most important decisions an entrepreneur must make after deciding on which business opportunity to utilise, is what legal form the business must take. A small business in South Africa can take one of four legal forms: a sole proprietorship, a partnership, a close corporation or a private company. Each one has its own legal implications and the prospective entrepreneur must take these into consideration when choosing an appropriate option for his or her situation.

■ **Sole proprietorship**

A sole proprietorship has only one owner. The owner conducts business in his or her own personal capacity and therefore does not have to register the business as a legal entity. This also means that the owner is taxed on his or her individual share of the income generated by the business and does not have the protection of limited liability. The owner is therefore personally liable for all his actions. Thus, the risks of the business extend to all his assets, both business and personal.

The statutory requirements for a sole proprietorship are limited. This person is, for example, not required to prepare financial statements for auditing. However, he or she has to register for tax, pay Regional Services levies, obtain licences (depending on the product or service) and contribute to the Compensation and the Unemployment Insurance Funds.

A sole proprietorship therefore offers the advantage that it is fairly easy to start, since there are hardly any legal statutory requirements other than those that apply in the normal flow of a business. The biggest disadvantage is, however, the fact that the owner is personally liable for all debts and liabilities of the business and can in the process lose personal assets, such as a house. This includes not only money owed to, for example, creditors but also costs associated with employees' claims (e.g. injuries not covered by the Compensation Fund or claims due to non-compliance with labour legislation) or claims from a third person or a client (e.g. for injuries sustained due to the carelessness of employees).

■ Partnership

A partnership comes into existence when a minimum of two and a maximum of 20 people conclude an agreement. No major formalities are necessary to establish a partnership; it does not have to be registered and the agreement can be by word of mouth or behaviour. However, for a partnership agreement to be valid it must meet three requirements: the partners must share a common purpose of financial gain (a partnership therefore cannot be established if the purpose is not to make a profit, e.g. in the case of promoting art and culture or charity); the business of the partnership must be handled to the common advantage of all its partners; and each partner has to contribute (financially or otherwise) to the partnership. A written partnership agreement drawn up by an attorney is recommended, as it can help prevent misunderstandings and disputes. The agreement should contain the names of the partners, the name and nature of the business, the contributions and remuneration of the partners, the division of profits and other aspects.

In a partnership, partners do not have the protection of limited liability and bear joint and several responsibility for any action taken by individual members. That is, each partner may be held personally liable for all the debts of the business. Partners are taxed on their individual share of the income generated by the business.

If one owner leaves the partnership, the whole partnership is dissolved and a new partnership agreement has to be concluded.

Except for the other requirements that a partnership has to meet in the normal flow of business, the partnership also has to adhere to Sections 3, 4 and 5 of the Act on Business Names (Act 27 of 1960). According to these sections of the Act, a partnership may not issue catalogues, letters, orders or statements without the following detail written on it: the name of the business, the place of business, the name of each partner, and his or her nationality if he or she is not a South African citizen. Not complying with these requirements is a criminal violation and is punishable by law.

■ Close corporation

A close corporation must have at least one member, with the total number of members not exceeding ten, and the members must be natural persons, for example not companies, societies and clubs.

A close corporation is a legal entity and, as such, it has to be registered with the Registrar of Close Corporations and its members enjoy limited liability. Members must adhere to the Act on Close Corporations (Act 69 of 1984), which, for example, stipulates that the name of the business may not be used without the abbreviation "CC" in English and "BK" in Afrikaans at the end of the name.

An association agreement between the members of a close corporation must be drawn up in writing, signed by each member and kept in safe keeping, where it is available only to members. The rules governing the internal relations of a close corporation may be changed if the association agreement permits this.

The close corporation does not have a separate board of directors. However, the members can share the management of the business. The equivalent of company dividends can only be paid to the members of a close corporation if the company is both solvent and liquid. Payments can, therefore, only be made if the corporation's assets will still exceed its liabilities after the payments have been made, and if the corporation can still pay its business debts when they fall due. Dividends to its members are tax free. A close corporation is taxed as if it were a company.

The most important advantage of forming a close corporation is that there is a minimal amount of formation and administrative requirements. While a close corporation is obliged to keep proper accounting records and prepare an annual financial statement, it is not necessary to conduct an audit unless its members want to do so. Another advantage is that, unlike for companies, there are only a limited number of punishable offences applicable to close corporations. The benefit of perpetual succession also applies to close corporations.

■ Private company

A company is an association of people incorporated in terms of the Companies Act (Act 61 of 1973). It may have share capital, or if it is not a profit-making business, be without share capital. Profit-making companies may take one of two forms – public or private. A private company is usually used to form a small business and differs from a public company in that capital cannot be acquired by the selling of shares to the general public.

A private company must be registered with the Registrar of Companies and is identified by the words "(Proprietary) Limited" or the abbreviation "(Pty) Ltd" after its name. It restricts the transfer of its shares and is limited to a minimum of one shareholder and one director and a maximum of 50 shareholders. The registration process is more complex than that of a close corporation and also more expensive. When all the registration requirements are met, the Registrar of Companies will issue a Certificate of Incorporation.

The biggest advantages of a private company are that it is a legal entity, separate from its shareholders; members have limited liability; and there is perpetual succession (i.e. the legal personality of the company lives on beyond the lives of its shareholders). A private company is not obliged to disclose certain information to the public. It must prepare financial statements but does not have to publish them.

■ The registration process

The Companies and Intellectual Property Registration Office (CIPRO) is a subdirectorate of the Department of Trade and Industry, and is responsible for matters relating to the registration of new businesses (close corporations and companies).

SOLE PROPRIETORSHIPS AND PARTNERSHIPS

There are no formal procedures relating to the formation of partnerships and sole proprietorships.

CLOSE CORPORATIONS

All South African close corporations are governed by the Close Corporations Act (Act 69 of 1984). The purpose of the Act is to provide for the formation, registration, incorporation, management, control and liquidation of close corporations, and for related matters.

For the incorporation of a close corporation, the following documents have to be lodged with the Registrar of Close Corporations at CIPRO:

- CK7 – Reservation of the business's name for a period of two months (completing a CK9 document lengthens one's reserved name for another month)

- CK1 (in duplicate) – Founding statement

- Letter by an accounting officer – Consent of the person named as accounting officer of the close corporation to act as such. This person must be a member of one of the following recognised professions: The Institute of Administration and Commerce of Southern Africa, accountants and auditors registered in terms of the Public Accountants' and Auditors' Act (Act 51 of 1951), The Chartered Institute of Management Accountants, The Institute of Commercial and Financial Accountants of Southern Africa, The South African Institute of Chartered Accountants, The South African Institute of Secretaries and Administrators, The Chartered Association of Certified Accountants, or The South African Institute for Business Accountants.

The reservation of the name on form CK7 must be done before lodging form CK1 for registration. The approved CK7 and the letter by the accounting officer must accompany the CK1. The referred documents can be obtained at Waltons or Hortons Stationery, or online from CIPRO's site at http://www.cipro.gov.za. Note that certain prescribed fees apply when lodging the documents.

CIPRO can be contacted at Zanza Building, 116 Proes Street, Pretoria or P.O. Box 429, Pretoria, 0001. The public counter hours are 08:30 to 12:30, and 13:15 to 15:00.

PRIVATE COMPANIES

All South African companies are governed by the Companies Act (Act 61 of 1973), which is administered by the Department of Trade and Industry. The Act prescribes the procedures to be followed to form a private or public company. Incorporating a company entails the following main steps:

- Reserving a company name
- Filing the memorandum and articles
- Filing the written consent of auditors to act for the company

A company name must be reserved with, and approved, by the Registrar of Companies at CIPRO. It is advisable to suggest alternative names in case the first name is deemed unsuitable by the Registrar.

The memorandum and articles must also be filed with the Registrar of Companies at CIPRO. The memorandum must indicate, among other things:

- The name of the company
- The company's main object, although there may be any number of objects
- The amount of authorised share capital – there is no minimum capital requirement

Registering a private company is a much more complex process than registering a close corporation. The following are the documents to be completed and lodged when registering a private company:

- CM5 (in duplicate) – Application for reservation of the name (to lengthen the reservation of the name for a further period, a CM7 document should be completed)
- Power of Attorney – Authorisation to act on behalf of promoters
- CM22 (in duplicate) – Notification of situation of registered and postal address
- CM29 – Return containing particulars of directors
- CM1 – Certificate of incorporation
- CM46 – Application for a certificate to commence business
- CM47 (by each director) – Statement by directors regarding adequacy of share capital
- CM31 (in duplicate) – Consent to act as auditor
- CM44B, 44C – Articles of Association

A private company that meets the requirements of a close corporation may convert to a close corporation, and a close corporation may convert to a private company. Upon conversion of another legal form of business into a private company, all documents listed above have to be lodged, except CM5 if the name does not change.

Information on obtaining the referred documents was given in the section discussing the registration of a close corporation. Note that certain prescribed fees apply when lodging the documents.

Due to the relative complexity in the compilation of the memorandum of articles of a company, and the fact that these documents to a greater extent have to be adjusted to fit the specific circumstances and needs of each individual company, it is wise to obtain the services of a legal practitioner. The memorandum and articles also have to be certified by a notary public, who in any event, will have to be a member of the legal profession.

6.3.2 Intellectual property rights

Intellectual property refers to all creations or products of the human mind that can be used for commercial gain. Many small businesses are started with original business or product ideas. To ensure that these entrepreneurs or creators of the intellectual property (or their employers) will derive the full commercial benefit of it and not an unauthorised user or infringer using the intellectual property, it is essential that legal protection be obtained.

Intellectual property can be protected by means of copyright, the registering of a patent, a trademark or a design. The Companies and Intellectual Property Registration Office (CIPRO) registers intellectual property. Its registers of patents, trademarks, designs and copyright in film and videos are updated daily. These registers contain information about the specific forms of intellectual property. They also indicate the owners of the different forms of intellectual property.

The different ways of protecting intellectual property will be discussed next.

■ Copyright

The Berne Copyright Convention covers most countries of the world, including South Africa, and lays down basic principles of copyright law that all member countries have to comply with. These principles are included in South Africa's Copyright Act (Act 98 of 1978).

Copyright protects the author of original works from others making a reproduction (or copy) of the copyright work. Works that qualify for copyright are literary works, musical works, artistic works, cinematographic films, sound recordings, broadcasts, programme-carrying signals, published editions and computer programs. It is important to remember that the copyright does not protect the underlying concept of the work, only the particular rendition of it, which the creator has reduced to a material form (including in a computer).

The author or creator of the work is the owner, unless employed in a contract of service or apprenticeship, in which the employer becomes the owner. Certain exceptions apply, which can be changed by agreement between the parties concerned. Copyright can be transferred or licensed, but has to be in writing.

Copyright law protects the reputation and identity of the creator, by giving a right of action against unauthorised distortion or mutilation of the work in a way that is to the detriment of the honour or reputation of the creator.

Copyright is automatically obtained by law (a ground principle of the Berne Convention). No prior registration or any other formality is required. Registration with CIPRO does, however, offer certain advantages, e.g. a public record is created and if registration took place within three months of the publication of the work, a court will award full compensation to the creator if the copyright was infringed, and not only partly as would be the case if it was not done.

Copyright endures for the entire lifetime of the author and for a period of 50 years after his or her death. It is advisable to put your name, the date and a copyright statement (e.g. "Copyright reserved") on the original copy and to authenticate it by a notary or commissioner of oaths. It is also preferable to use the copyright warning notice on all copies. The abbreviated form is the year of first publication of the work followed by the sign ©, and the name of the copyright owner. Very often the words "All Rights Reserved" are added to the notice.

■ Designs

Registration is essential before one has the right to a design. The design must be new for it to be registered. The Paris Convention allows one to register in further countries up to six months after the basic registration in one's home country (or a first registration anywhere).

Whereas original and innovative design may be protected under the copyright, patent and trademark laws, South Africa has a specialised law for design protection. Although good design usually inherently blends both aesthetic (eye appeal) design and functional (e.g. ergonomic) design in the product, the law in South Africa (Design Act No. 195 of 1993) grants separate protection and different protection periods to aesthetic and functional features of design, and requires different conditions to be met before protection is given.

An aesthetic design registration protects the features of appearance of an article, for example the features of shape or configuration or pattern or ornamentation (or any combination of these), which appeal to and are judged by the eye, as shown in drawings or photographs of the registration. A functional design registration protects the features of an article, which are necessitated by the function that the article has to perform. These features are pattern, shape and configurations.

An application for registration of a design must be filed with the Registrar of Designs at CIPRO. In South Africa, the register of designs has two parts: part A for protection of aesthetic designs and part B for protection of functional designs. Many designs are accordingly registered in both parts A and B. A design must also be registered in one or more specified classes listed in the Designs Classification of Goods. The protection afforded by the registration is restricted to the nominated class or classes in which the design has been registered.

Design registration gives the owner the right to prevent others from making, importing, using or disposing of in South Africa an article that falls within the class in which a design is registered, incorporating the design or a design not substantially different. It is not necessary for the owner of the design to prove that the infringer had actually copied the design.

A South African-registered design has effect only in the territorial area of South Africa. To obtain protection in other countries, applications have to be filed in such countries. In South Africa, maximum duration of protection for an aesthetic design is 15 years, whereas the duration for a functional design is ten years from registration or from the release date, whichever is the earlier. Annual renewal fees must be paid after the third year.

Once the design is registered, it should be marked with the words "Registered Design" and the registration number; otherwise one may find that infringement damages are not recoverable. It is a criminal offence to indicate that a design is registered if it is not.

■ Patents

A patent is the registered exclusive right of an inventor to make, use or sell an invention. An invention can be a new non-obvious product, process or device applicable to trade, industry or agriculture or an improvement on any of the above. It must, however, be unique and meet special requirements relating to novelty, utility and inventiveness.

There are two types of patents:
- A design patent covers the appearance of a product and everything that is an inseparable part of the product.
- A utility patent covers a new process, or protects the function of a product.

According to the Department of Trade and Industry, the following apply:

1. It is advisable not to tell anyone about your invention before you have applied for a patent because you could risk losing the right to the patent.

2. The person who created the invention can apply for a patent. The inventor can also nominate a company or a patent attorney to apply to the Registrar of Patents (at CIPRO of the Department of Trade and Industry).

3. The inventor must make sure that the invention is new and original. To do this, the procedure is as follows:

- Do a search in the patent office registers to ensure that any existing patents are not being infringed.
- Complete the application forms and pay the registration fees in revenue stamps. (Note that filing a provisional patent yourself is much cheaper than it would be if a patent attorney files the patent.)
- Attach a clear, detailed description of the invention, supported by a drawing (if applicable).
- A provisional patent is valid for one year and must be followed by a completed patent within that year (the complete patent filing must be done by a patent attorney or agent).

4. The provisional patent will protect the inventor for 12 months (to give him or her time to develop the invention into a tangible product whereby the novelty, technical merit and commercial prospects can be further investigated). It can be filed relatively quickly and secures a filing date, but it does not guarantee that the inventor's claim will be legitimate.

5. The complete application will protect the inventor for 20 years (from date of filing), but it has to be renewed from the fourth year at a cost.

6. The South African patent is national and does not extend to other countries.

7. The protection of patents is governed by the Patents Act (Act 57 of 1978).

8. South Africa is one of 100 countries that have acceded to the Patent Corporation Treaty (PCT). The treaty enables individual inventors to file an international patent (instead of a national one), but the inventor designates the countries where the patent should be registered.

9. The inventor who applies for a patent will be protected, but can assign someone else to be protected by the patent.

10. Certain inventions are excluded from patent protection:
- Traditional copyright works
- Aesthetic creations
- Methods, schemes or rules of doing business or playing a game

- Scientific theories or mathematical methods
- Presentation of information
- Computer programs
- Methods of medical treatment

11. A South African patent application can serve as a basis for the inventor to claim "convention priority" in respect of foreign applications in most of the other industrialised countries. The foreign application must be filed within 12 months of the first application in South Africa.

Inventions and supporting literature should all be marked with "Patent Applied For" or "Patent", with the relevant patent number, to ensure that infringement damages can be recovered. Falsely claiming that patent rights exist is a criminal offence.

■ Trademarks

A trademark is any work, phrase, symbol, design, sound, smell, colour, product configuration, group of letters or numbers, or combination of these, adapted and used by a company to identify its product or service, and to distinguish it from products and services made, sold or provided by others.

The primary purpose of marks is to prevent consumers from becoming confused about the source of origin of a product or service. Marks help consumers answer the question: "Who makes the product?" and "Who provides the service?" As consumers become familiar with particular marks and the goods or services they represent, marks can acquire a "secondary meaning", as indicators of quality. Thus, established marks help consumers answer another question: "Is this product or service a good one to purchase?" For this reason, the well-known marks of reputable companies are valuable business assets, worthy of nurturing and protection.

Although trademarks can be devised and used without having to register them, their main benefits accrue through registration. A trademark registration entails numerous advantages. For example, it affords the owner the right to prevent the unauthorised use by another party of an identical or confusingly similar trademark in relation to goods or services that are covered by the registration, as well as similar goods and services; it can also form the basis of an objection to an application by another enterprise or person to register a confusingly similar trademark.

Unlike in the case of patents and designs, novelty is not a requirement for a valid filing. Generally speaking, the person who is using or intends to use the trademark may file the application. Thus an intention to use is a requirement.

The owner of a trademark may allow a licensee to use his or her mark, but must ensure that no public deception or confusion will arise as a result. Registration as a "Registered User" is advisable.

A trademark may become non-distinctive where everyone uses it as the accepted description of a product or service. If it becomes customary in current language, it will no longer be validly registered.

A trademark is an adjective and is not used as a noun or verb. It should, therefore, be followed by the generic name of the product. Trademarks should be made to look distinctive in their colour, typeface or background or any combination of these. If they are registered, "Registered Trademark" should be indicated, or an abbreviation, namely ® given.

The procedure to register a trademark is as follows:

1. Any person with a bona fide intent to use a mark as a trademark, either personally or through any person permitted by him or her to use the mark (i.e. a licensee), may file an application for its registration.

2. After filing of an application, an official acknowledgement of receipt is issued.

3. The application is then examined by CIPRO to determine inherent registrability, as well as possible conflict with prior registrations or applications.

4. After examination, CIPRO takes action on the application, either accepting it or refusing it or indicating the conditions subject to which it may be accepted.

5. Once a trademark application has been accepted, it is advertised in the *Patent Journal.*

6. In the absence of objections by third parties within three months of the advertisement

Van Schaik Publishers

date, the application will proceed and a certificate of registration will be issued.

A trademark is registered for a period of ten years, calculated from the date of the original application. It may be renewed in perpetuity for like periods on application in the prescribed manner and on payment of the renewal fees.

■ Counterfeit goods

Counterfeiting is defined as manufacturing, producing or making any goods, whether in South Africa or elsewhere, without the authority of the owner of the intellectual property rights in the protected goods, or applying to such goods the subject matter of that intellectual property right, or a colourable imitation thereof, so that the goods are calculated to be confused with or to be taken as being the protected goods of the owner of the right.

The Counterfeit Goods Act was introduced on 1 January 1998. It gives the owners of trademarks, copyright works and certain merchandise marks more effective ways to prevent piracy of their rights. Examples of counterfeit goods include:

- Designer-labelled clothing, sportswear and equipment; watches; perfume and cosmetics; belts and pens
- Chart-topping film and music on video and audio tapes, blank video and audio tapes
- Artistic works, such as pictures, photographs and posters, china figures and models
- Computer software, such as games and business programs

Dealing in counterfeit goods is prohibited, for example:

- The possession or control of such goods in the course of business
- The manufacture of such goods, except for private and domestic use
- The sale, hire, barter or exchange of such goods, and the offer or exposure of such goods for sale
- The exhibition of such goods in public for purposes of trade
- The distribution of such goods for purposes of trade or for any other purpose, resulting in the owner of the intellectual property right suffering prejudice

- The importation or export of such goods, except for private and domestic use
- The disposition of such goods in any other manner in the course of trade

The Act empowers inspectors and police, who have a warrant, to enter premises; stop a vehicle (if necessary by force); seize, remove and detain counterfeit goods; collect evidence; search and terminate counterfeit activities. The Commissioner for Customs and Excise and customs staff have the power to seize and detain counterfeit goods imported into the country.

6.3.3 Taxation

Most taxes in South Africa are levied by the central government and administered by the South African Revenue Services (SARS). The Constitution gives some taxing powers to the provinces. These mainly involve assessment rates and other taxes based on immovable property.

The South African government imposes two main types of taxes, namely direct and indirect taxes. Direct taxes include:

- Individual income tax – an annual tax on the income of individuals (also owners of sole proprietorships) and partnerships
- Company tax – an annual tax on the income of companies and close corporations
- Secondary tax on companies – a tax imposed on dividends declared by companies and distributions made by close corporations, payable and borne by the companies and close corporations
- A tax on dividends from foreign registered or incorporated companies, including retirement funds and insurers.

Indirect taxes include:

- Value-added tax – an invoice-based value-added tax levied on supplies of goods and services
- Excise and customs duties – duties on the local production of certain commodities, such as automobiles, jewellery, beer and wine, without regard to their sale (clothing, basic foods, medicine, rent, certain utilities and professional services are exempt from excise duties)

- Stamp duties – charges levied on a number of documents in South Africa (tax is on the document itself, not the transaction, and the tax may be imposed in the case of a written agreement even though a similar agreement made orally would not be subject to tax)

■ The Receiver of Revenue

The local Receiver of Revenue ensures that tax laws are complied with and collects from each taxpayer the correct amount of the tax due.

As discussed earlier, owners of sole proprietorships and partnerships do not have separate legal personalities, as is the case with close corporations and companies. They must, therefore, include the income from the business in their own gross income, as they are responsible for the payment of taxes in their individual capacity. They must register as provisional taxpayers with their local Receiver of Revenue.

Close corporations and private companies must register as taxpayers in their own right. Unlike natural persons, a company or close corporation pays tax at a flat rate on its taxable income for the year of assessment. A company is required by law to appoint an auditor to audit its financial statements, while a close corporation is required to appoint an accounting officer. Normally, the auditor or accounting officer will assist the small business owner in determining the taxable income and the amount of tax to be paid.

■ PAYE and SITE

Pay As You Earn (PAYE) and Standard Income Tax on Employees (SITE) are systems of tax collection whereby employers are obliged by law to deduct tax from their employees' remuneration and to pay such amounts over to the Receiver of Revenue on behalf of their employees on a monthly basis.

It is the duty of an employer to register with the local Receiver of Revenue as soon as people are employed. To register as an employer, an IRP1 form must be completed. Upon registration, the Receiver of Revenue will provide a set of tables according to which tax must be deducted. This tax is known as employee's tax. An employer, however, requires certain information from employees to enable him or her to determine according to which deduction table employee's tax should be deducted. Employees

provide their particulars on an IRP2 form. When completing their annual income tax returns, the employees will require proof that tax was in fact deducted from their salaries and wages. Employers must issue employees with a IRP5 certificate for this. On termination of an employee's service, the employer must immediately issue him or her with an IRP5 reflecting the amount of tax deducted for the employment period during the year of assessment.

■ Value-added tax

VAT is tax (currently 14 per cent) applied at each point where value is added to goods or services from primary production to final consumption. When a vendor is supplied with goods or services by another vendor, VAT will be levied by the supplier of those goods or services. This VAT is referred to as the input tax of the vendor who receives the goods or services. When that vendor in turn supplies goods or services to other persons or vendors, VAT must be included in the price charged for those goods or services. This is referred to as the output tax of the vendor.

If you start a business and your turnover has exceeded R20 000 per year you may voluntarily register for VAT. If it is likely that your turnover could exceed R300 000, you must inform SARS and register within 21 days. If you can prove that your turnover will exceed R300 000, then you may register before you start trading. Failure to register will result in liability for VAT, even if you have not charged your customers VAT. In addition, interest and penalties may be imposed and you may be prosecuted. If your business has branched and each branch maintains separate bookkeeping systems and is located separately, you can apply for separate VAT registrations. Application for registration must be completed on the VAT101 form, "Application for Registration", which is obtainable from your local Receiver of Revenue.

6.3.4 Registration with the Department of Labour

The owner of a new business that will employ people, must register as an employer with the Department of Labour to contribute to the Unemployment Insurance and Compensation Funds.

■ Unemployment Insurance Fund

The Unemployment Insurance Fund provides benefits to unemployed people and to the dependants of deceased contributors. Tax-free benefits are distributed at the rate of 45 per cent of previous earnings, provided certain criteria are met. Illness, maternity, adoption and dependant's benefits are also paid.

Contributions are compulsory for all staff whose annual income is less than a certain limit. An employer is obliged by the Unemployment Insurance Act 30 of 1966 to pay contributions to the UIF for each qualifying employee for each month (exceptions exist). The amount is 2 per cent of the employee's earnings (1 per cent paid out of the employee's salary and 1 per cent paid by the employer).

To register for UIF, an employer must get a UF1 form from the Department of Labour. The form must be completed and returned to the Department within 14 days of employing an employee.

Every employee who qualifies must have a blue UIF card, which is a record of the employee's employment and UIF contributions. This must be given to the new employer. If the new employee does not have a blue card, the employer must apply for one on a UF85 form.

When leaving the business, the employer must give back the employee's blue card, which must be signed by both the employer and the employee.

Payment is made by sending a cheque, together with a completed UF3 form, to the Department of Labour within ten days after the end of each month. For example, the UIF for January must reach the Department by 10 February.

■ Compensation Fund

The Compensation for Occupational Injuries and Diseases Act (Act 61 of 1997) requires employers to insure their employees (including temporary staff) against accidents or illness that could result in death or disability by making contributions to the Compensation Fund. All persons who employ one or more employees are required to register and to make annual payments to the Compensation Fund. These amounts may not be recovered from employees.

The rate at which compensation is paid varies from industry to industry, based on the principle that each industry should carry the cost of its own accidents. At the end of January, workmen's forms are sent to all registered employers and these have to be returned and the amounts paid by the end of March.

The benefits to the employer are that the Compensation Fund will compensate the employee on sustaining an injury on duty, as well as protecting the employer from any civil claims resulting from his or her potential negligence.

Within 14 days after gaining knowledge of an alleged occupational disease or injury, an employer must complete an "Employer's Report of an Occupational Disease", form W.C1.1 in the case of a disease and an "Employer's Report of an Occupational Injury" form W.C1.2, in the case of an occupational injury. It is forwarded to the Compensation Commissioner, P.O. Box 955, Pretoria, 0001.

6.3.5 Trade licences

Local authorities issue trading licences. Such a licence is not required in all instances. The prospective entrepreneur should contact the local authority in his or her town or city.

Trading licences are governed by the Business Act 71 of 1991, which states that businesses that perform the following activities require a trading licence:

- Sale or supply of meals or perishable foodstuffs (as declared by an Administrator by notice in the Official Gazette)

- Provision of certain types of health facilities or entertainment (e.g. Turkish baths, saunas or other health baths; massage or infrared treatment; providing the services of an escort; keeping three or more mechanical, electronic or electrical contrivances, instruments, apparatus or devices)

- Hawking in meals or perishable foodstuffs, including any foodstuffs that are conveyed from place to place, whether by vehicle or otherwise; on a public road or at any other place accessible to the public; in, on or from a movable structure or stationary vehicle

To obtain a trading licence, an L1 form must be completed and submitted, together with a one-off fee to the local municipality's licensing department. The normal processing time is approximately 21 working days. An L2 form is the actual licence issued by the municipality.

6.3.6 Regional Services levies

A businessperson who has started a small business within a region must register with the council of that region within 30 days of having commenced business. There are two types of levies" a service levy and an establishment levy. The service levy is based on a percentage of the net remuneration of all the employees employed by the business, while the establishment levy is based on a percentage of the turnover of the business.

The levies are allowable income tax deductions and are due within 20 days of the end of each month. The board is empowered to estimate the amount upon which the levies are payable if a levy payer fails to submit a return in respect of a period. Interest accrues on overdue payments.

6.4 Legal aspects in the normal flow of business

An entrepreneur's legal commitments do not stop after the establishment of the business, but continue throughout its existence. In the next section we will discuss some of the major legal aspects an entrepreneur will have to consider in the normal flow of the business.

6.4.1 Concluding contracts

A small business owner may have to conclude several contracts throughout the starting and running of his or her business, for example to acquire business premises, to arrange for finance at a bank or to repay loans for assets bought. Many small business owners do not, however, consider these contractual arrangements with the necessary seriousness. They fail to make and use contracts, even for purchases or sales that are large enough to warrant them.

In general, a small businessperson in the process of concluding an arrangement must do the following:

- Check the small print because it contains many stipulations and terms of an agreement.

- Make sure that the other contracting party is indeed the contracting party and not a front company or a representative of the real company.

- Make sure that the arrangement contains all the pages and that it is completed in full before signing it. This will ensure that changes are not made after signing.

- Always request a copy of the signed agreement and keep it in a safe place.

- Get legal advice if the arrangement is difficult or contains many Latin or incomprehensible terms.

The different types of agreements a small business owner can expect to sign include agreements for hiring premises, leasing, hire purchase and pay-off, sponsors, goods and/or service trade, employment and franchising.

Each type of arrangement involves many considerations, possibilities and requirements. Legal assistance is recommended for advice on the dangers and possible problems that may occur. It is important to take time to investigate and negotiate the terms of an agreement to ensure that it reflects the true intentions of the parties, that the rights of the small businessperson are protected and that it conforms to all possible statutory requirements.

6.4.2 Licensing

A licensing arrangement revolves around a contractual agreement in which one partner makes intangible assets such as technology, skills and knowledge available to another partner in exchange for some remuneration, such as royalties. The licensor usually has little or no control over the licensee beyond the terms of the agreement.

A patent licence agreement specifies how the licensee would have access to the patent. For example, the licensor may still manufacture the product but give the licensee the rights to market it under the licensor's label in a non-competitive market (i.e. a foreign market). In other instances, the licensee may actually manufacture and market the patented product under its own label.

Licensing a trademark generally involves a franchising agreement. The entrepreneur operates a business using the trademark and agrees to pay a fixed sum for the use of the trademark, pay a royalty based on sales volume, buy supplies from the franchisor (examples include Coca Cola and Shell), or any combination of these.

Copyright is another popular licensed property. It involves the right to use or copy books, software, music, photographs and plays, to name a few. The right to use the name, likeness or image of a celebrity in a product (i.e. Mickey Mouse clothes and Elvis Presley memorabilia) is often licensed.

6.4.3 Labour legislation governing employment in South Africa

Employment in South Africa is regulated by the following Acts: the Labour Relations Act (LRA), the Basic Conditions of Employment Act (BCEA), the Occupational Health and Safety Act, the Skills Development and Skills Development Levies Acts, and the Employment Equity Act.

The LRA deals with procedures for the termination of any employee's employment and grants employees remedies against unfair dismissal. In terms of the BCEA, employees are entitled to certain periods of annual leave and sick leave, additional pay for overtime, and daily and weekly maximum working hours. In addition, the Skills Development and Skills Development Levies Acts are aimed at improving the working skills of workers, while the Employment Equity Act provides for affirmative action for historically disadvantaged people by private business.

As employers, entrepreneurs should familiarise themselves with the provisions of these Acts. It is also advisable to become a member of an employers' organisation, such as the Confederation of Employers of Southern Africa (COFESA). COFESA protects employers' rights and provides a service to them by translating legal jargon into user-friendly practice. COFESA's services include:

- A practical manual covering Acts, contracts, disciplinary procedures and procedures for fair labour relations
- A 24-hour hotline to prevent expensive litigation
- Consultants

■ Labour Relations Act

In 1979, major reforms in the area of labour legislation, including the removal of discriminatory legislation restricting trade union activities, opened the way for all commercial and industrial workers to participate in organised labour. A powerful trade union movement has since developed and, in addition, employers have developed an increased awareness of the need for sound labour relations.

Until late in 1996, labour relations were regulated by the 1979 Labour Relations Act (the old LRA). However, the Labour Relations Act of 1995 (the new LRA), which came into force on 11 November 1996, has fundamentally altered the legal framework in which labour relations are now conducted.

The old LRA dealt extensively with the termination of an employee's employment and introduced the broad concept of the "unfair labour practice". It also brought into being an Industrial Court, which was essentially a tribunal applying principles of equity and fairness, primarily in interpreting the concept of unfair labour practice in relation to dismissals. All non-voluntary terminations of employment on the part of the employer had to be fair, both substantively and procedurally.

The new LRA restricts the concept of unfair labour practice to specific acts on the part of the employer, and has codified the principles established by the Industrial Court relating to the requirements that dismissals be substantively and procedurally fair.

The main features of the new LRA are the following:

- The Act recognises collective bargaining as the most acceptable means of resolving disputes of mutual interest, and encourages and provides the means to reach agreement.
- The Act recognises that strikes and lockouts are an intrinsic part of the process of collective bargaining and therefore simplifies the procedure to be followed before embarking on such action.
- As part of the process of encouraging collective bargaining, and in order to make bargaining more meaningful, the Act imposes an obligation on employers to disclose information that may be required for bargaining and negotiations. This obligation is subject to lim-

itation and is designed to assist the parties in reaching agreement.

- The Act has simplified the previous dispute-resolving procedures by replacing the Industrial Court with the Commission for Conciliation, Mediation and Arbitration (CCMA) in the hope of processing disputes more efficiently and at less cost to the parties.

- The introduction of the workplace forum is perhaps the most radical innovation of the Act. Workplace forums are organisations consisting of elected employees who have the right to consult with management and to reach joint agreement with management over matters defined in the Act. Such matters are relevant to the interests of the parties in a particular workplace.

- The Act has been extended in its scope and now includes employees who were previously excluded from the previous Act. For example farm workers, domestic workers, state employees, and teachers and tertiary lecturers are specifically included in the Act. In other words, all employees and employers have the same rights and obligations.

■ Basic Conditions of Employment Act

The purpose of the Basic Conditions of Employment Act 75 of 1997 is to implement and enforce basic conditions, as well as making provision for sectoral and ministerial determination of basic conditions for some sectors pertaining to, for example:

- Working time (ordinary hours of work, overtime, meal breaks and rest periods, Sunday work, night work, public holidays)
- Leave (annual, sick, maternity and family responsibility leave)
- Job information and payment (job information, keeping records, payment, payslip information, approved deductions, adding up wages)
- Termination of employment (notice, severance pay, certificate of service)
- Child labour and forced labour

The Basic Conditions of Employment Act provides, inter alia, for a maximum working week of 45 hours and increases the minimum annual leave entitlement. The Wage Act establishes minimum wages and conditions of service for particular industries and trades.

■ Occupational Health and Safety Act

The Occupational Health and Safety Act (Act 85 of 1993) is administered by the Chief Directorate of Occupational Health and Safety of the Department of Labour.

The main purpose of the Occupational Health and Safety Act is the protection of the health and safety of workers, as well as persons other than workers, from hazards arising from activities at a workplace. To this end, occupational health and safety inspectors from the provincial offices carry out inspections and investigations at workplaces.

The main objects of the Act are as follows:

- To keep abreast of, and to adjust to, the developments in the fields of occupational safety in other countries, as well as local developments
- To endorse the rights of employees to be informed regarding dangers in their work environment and to receive training in order to handle such dangers

General requirements relating to this Act include:

- An employer with more than 50 employees has to prepare and maintain a written policy regarding the protection of his or her employees at work, which the chief executive officer has to sign.

- The employer has to designate in writing one or more full-time employees who are acquainted with the conditions at the workplace, as safety representatives for that workplace or different sections of that workplace.

- All incidents that result in death, unconsciousness or loss of a limb or part of a limb, or where a substance was spilled or any substance under pressure was released uncontrolled, must be reported. Any incident that incapacitates the affected person(s) so that they cannot work or are in any way limited in the type of work they can do for a period of 14 days or more, must also be reported.

■ Skills Development Act

The aim of the Skills Development Act (Act 97 of 1998) is to improve the working skills of South Africans so that the economy can grow and all citizens can lead a better life. Whereas the South African Qualifications Authority (SAQA) Act is about the quality of learning, the Skills Development Act is about the relevance of that learning to existing jobs and new jobs, and to the country's economic and employment growth and social development. The Skills Development Act fits into, and builds on, the basis of the SAQA Act. It creates the structures and framework for the National Skills Development Strategy. To carry out the objectives of this strategy, the Department of Labour set up 25 Sector Education and Training Authorities (SETAs).

The steps below can be followed to adhere to this Act:

1. Register with a SETA by filling in the SDL101 form that can be obtained from the Receiver of Revenue's offices. The Receiver's office will refer you to the relevant SETA.

2. Appoint a skills development facilitator – either internal or external.

3. Work with the skills development facilitator to complete the Workplace Skills Plan for your business.

4. Submit your Workplace Skills Plan to the SETA.

5. Engage in learnerships that are offered by the SETA.

6. At the end of the year, at dates stipulated by the SETA, submit your Annual Training Report. Your skills development facilitator can assist you with this report.

7. Claim your grants from the SETA.

■ Skills Development Levies Act

One of the reasons for poor skills development in the past was that not enough money was being spent on training. The Skills Development Act lays down regulations stating how the skills development strategy will be funded. The Skills Development Levies Act (1999) describes how money will be collected through levies (taxes) paid by employers.

Employers were obliged to pay a skill development levy of 0,5 per cent of payroll from 1 April 2000. The levy increased to 1 per cent of payroll with effect from 1 April 2001.

From 1 March 2002, all companies had to deduct and withhold Pay As You Earn (PAYE) and skills development levies (SDL) from all amounts or remuneration paid by a company to its directors, and also by close corporations to its members. Persons who ignore these regulations will be subject to penalties and interest.

■ Employment Equity Act

The purpose of the Employment Equity Act is to eliminate unfair discrimination by providing equal opportunities, fair treatment in employment and affirmative action in appointments and promotion.

The Act prohibits discrimination against employees and job applicants on the basis of race, gender, pregnancy, marital responsibility, ethnic or social origin, sexual orientation, age, disability, HIV status, religion, conscious belief, political opinion, culture, language and birth.

6.4.4 Product liability

This is the liability of any parties along the manufacturing chain of any product for damage caused by the product. This includes the manufacturer of components (at the top of the chain), an assembling manufacturer, the wholesaler, and the retail store owner (at the bottom of the chain).

Products containing inherent defects that cause harm to the consumer of the product are subject to product liability suits. The liability is based either on a breach of warranty (express or tacit) that the product will be suitable for its purpose, or on the warranty (tacit) of a seller against latent or hidden defects in the product.

Liability can be excluded by way of a suitable indemnity clause. Such a clause will be enforceable, provided that it has been brought to the notice of the other contracting party, and provided that it is reasonable and not against public policy. If the product involves inherent dangers or risks, it is essential that suitable warnings be given.

6.4.5 Standards

The South African Bureau of Standards (SABS) is a government agency appointed to carry out the regulatory functions of the Department of Trade and Industry. The SABS is governed by Act 29 of 1993 and administers approximately 70 legal compulsory specifications across a wide spectrum of fields. These compulsory specifications are legal measures and requirements for ensuring that products locally manufactured or imported into or exported from South Africa meet the minimum requirements for health and safety as set out in the relevant national standards. Examples would be the processing and canning of fish products or the importation of motor vehicles. These two products must be tested against specified technical health standards and then certified that they are suitable and ready for use.

6.4.6 Fair trade, competition and consumer protection

The Competition Commission has a range of functions in terms of the Competition Act (Act 89 of 1998). These include investigating anti-competitive conduct, assessing the impact of mergers and acquisitions on competition and taking appropriate action, monitoring competition levels and market transparency in the economy, identifying impediments to competition and playing an advocacy role in addressing these impediments.

The Competition Commission is independent but its decisions may be appealed through a Competition Tribunal and the Competition Appeal Court. More information on the Competition Commission can be obtained from its website at http://www.compcom.co.za.

6.4.7 Environmental legislation

Environmental legislation is receiving increasing attention in South Africa, with severe penalties under discussion in a proposed Environmental Bill for those found guilty of damaging the environment. The penalties could extend even to those who were directors of a company at the time the environmental damage was caused.

The main legislation affecting environmental issues are the Atmospheric Pollution Prevention Act, the Health Act and the Water Act. The Bill of Rights of the South African Constitution stipulates that everyone has the right to an environment that is not harmful to health or well-being.

6.4.8 Promotion of Access to Information Act

The Promotion of Access to Information Act enables individuals to get information or records in the possession or under the control of a public institution (e.g. a government department or municipality) or a private body, when complying with certain requirements. This Act gives effect to the open access to information guarantee in terms of the Constitution. The Act (excluding certain sections) came into effect on 9 March 2001.

A section of the Promotion of Access to Information Act came into effect on Thursday, 15 August 2002, requiring all government departments and private companies to compile company manuals of various records. The information required to be disclosed by companies in the manuals includes their incorporation documents and documents relating to their taxation, employee contracts, share option schemes and banking details. The purpose of the Act is to foster a culture of transparency and accountability in public and private bodies. The manuals had to be published in the *Government Gazette* on 15 August 2002.

6.4.9 Usury Act

The Usury Act 73 of 1968 aims to protect the interests of persons entering into leasing, credit and money-lending transactions. Its purpose is to prevent their exploitation with regard to repayment schedules and finance charges. It applies to both natural and juristic persons, who enter into money-lending and credit and lease transactions. The most notable regulations of the Act are the maximum finance charges and amount recoverable, as well as the disclosure of information with regard to the transaction to the borrower or debtor.

6.5 Conclusion

This chapter explored the major resource requirements for a prospective new business. The human resources of a business are seen by many as the key to their success. One of the major issues involved in appointing the best people is forecasting the human resource needs of the business. One important determinant of employee productivity is the nature of the physical resources used by workers. The right plant, equipment, raw materials, etc. will enable workers to achieve peak performance. Inadequate or inappropriate physical resources will prevent even dedicated workers from doing their best. Information resources enable the entrepreneur to make informed decisions. Human, physical and information resources have to be purchased with financial resources.

Acquiring financial resources is one of the major challenges facing prospective entrepreneurs.

The legal aspects in establishing a new business venture and those in the normal flow of business were also explored. It is important for the entrepreneur to seek legal advice in making legal decisions. Resources were identified in this chapter that should be considered before hiring a legal practitioner. Some of this information can save time and money for the entrepreneur.

Looking back

1. What are some major characteristics of the acquisition and use of financial resources?
   - Financial resources are cash or can be readily converted into cash.
   - Financial resources can be used to acquire other resources.
   - Finance can be obtained from different sources:
     - Money invested by the entrepreneur, called equity financing
     - A loan from outsiders such as individuals, banks and lending institutions, called debt financing
     - Revenue generated from the sale of goods and/or services
     - Other: government support programmes, venture capital funds, companies, mortgages, long-term investments, leasing, etc.

2. What are the major concerns of an entrepreneur when employing people? What steps can he or she take to address these concerns?
   - Major concerns:
     - Accurately forecasting human resource needs
     - Recruiting candidates
     - Selecting the best person for the job
   - Steps to alleviate concerns:
     - List the tasks to be performed.

   - Group each person's tasks and describe them (job description).
   - Determine the qualifications and skills needed to perform the tasks (job specification).
   - Recruit people who can perform the tasks in the job description and meet the job specification.
   - Interview candidates.
   - Appoint the best person for the job.

3. What are some of the major issues related to the acquisition of physical resources?
   - It is important to plan the acquisition of resources carefully because it can be an expensive exercise (e.g. in the case of fixed assets) and its timing can be crucial (e.g. in the case of raw materials).
   - The location decision is important when acquiring fixed assets.
   - The different benefits offered and types of coordination required should be considered when deciding between the many sources of raw materials and general supplies.

4. Identify the legal forms a small business can take in South Africa.
   - Sole proprietorship
   - Partnership
   - Close corporation
   - Company (private, public and limited by guarantee)

5. Define each of the following terms: sole proprietorship, partnership, close corporation and private company.
   - In a sole proprietorship, one owner conducts business in his or her personal capacity with limited statutory requirements.
   - In a partnership, a minimum of two and a maximum of 20 people conclude an agreement to do business together in their personal capacities, with limited statutory requirements and with a common purpose of financial gain.
   - A close corporation is a legal entity separate from its members (at least one and not more than 10) and has to be registered with the Registrar of Close Corporations.
   - A private company is a legal entity that issues shares to a minimum of one and a maximum of 50 shareholders and has to register with the Registrar of Companies, which is a more complex and expensive process than that for a close corporation.

6. Compare the major tax considerations of a partnership with those of a close corporation.

   In a partnership, each partner is taxed on his or her individual share of the income generated by the business, while the dividends paid to members of a close corporation are tax-free.

7. What is intellectual property, and why is it considered an asset to a business?

   Intellectual property refers to all creations or products of the human mind. It is considered an asset to a business because it can be used for commercial gain.

8. Patents are often imitated. What can an entrepreneur do to protect his or her product? What procedures must be followed to file for a patent?
   - The entrepreneur should not tell anyone about the product invention before applying for a patent.
   - Imitating a patent is a criminal offence.
   - To apply for a patent an entrepreneur must do the following:
     - Search the patent office registers to make sure that the patent does not already exist.
     - Apply for a patent at the Registrar of Patents by completing the application forms and paying the registration fees.

9. What are the benefits of a trademark to an entrepreneur?

   It prevents consumers from becoming confused about the source or origin of an entrepreneur's product or service.

10. Differentiate between the need for an Unemployment Insurance Fund and a Compensation Fund.
    - Both funds are to the benefit of employees.
    - Contributions to both funds are enforced by law.
    - Employers are obliged to contribute to the Compensation Fund irrespective of the employee's annual earnings, while they only have to contribute to the UIF if the employee's annual income is less than a certain amount.
    - Both the employer and the employee contribute equally to UIF, while employer contributions to the Compensation Fund may not be recovered from employees.
    - The UIF provides benefits to employees when they become unemployed or deceased, while the Compensation Fund compensates an employee who sustains an injury while on duty.

11. Explain the conditions for obtaining a trade licence and having to pay Regional Services levies.
    - Trade licences:
      - Sale or supply of meals or perishable foodstuffs
      - Provision of certain types of health facilities or entertainment
      - Hawking in meals or perishable foodstuffs
    - Regional Services levies:
      - Any business that is started within a region

12. What are the essential ingredients of an acceptable written contract?
    - The small print containing many stipula-

tions and terms of the agreement is acceptable.

- The contracting party is not a front company or a representative of the real company.
- Legal advice is obtained for the wording of difficult arrangements and for understanding incomprehensible terms.
- All pages are completed in full and signed by both parties.
- A copy of the signed agreement is provided for safe keeping.

13. List the conditions legislated by the Basic Conditions of Employment Act.
- Working time
- Leave
- Job information and payment
- Termination of employment
- Child labour and forced labour

14. Explain the steps an entrepreneur should follow to adhere to the Skills Development Act and the Skills Development Levies Act.
- Skills Development Act:
  - Register with a SETA.
  - Appoint a skills development facilitator.
  - Complete a Workplace Skills Plan.
  - Submit the Workplace Skills Plan to the SETA.
  - Engage in learnerships.
  - Submit annual training reports.
  - Claim grants from the SETA.
- Skills Development Levies Act:
  One per cent of the remuneration paid to directors of a company and members of a close corporation must be deducted and paid to the government as a Skills Development Levy at the end of each financial year.

Key terms

Basic Conditions of Employment Act	Pay As You Earn
Close corporation	Physical resource
Compensation Fund	Private company
Contract	Product liability
Copyright	Promotion of Access to Information Act
Counterfeit goods	Receiver of Revenue
Debt financing	Regional Services levies
Employment Equity Act	Resources
Environmental legislation	Revenue
Equity financing	Skills Development Act
Financial resources	Skills Development Levies Act
Human resources	Sole proprietorship
Information resource	Standard Income Tax on Employees
Intellectual property rights	Standards
Labour Relations Act	Trade licence
Licensing	Trademark
Occupational health and safety	Unemployment Insurance Fund
Partnership	Usury Act
Patent	Value-added tax

Discussion questions

1. Why would investors tend to favour a new business led by a management team over one headed by a lone entrepreneur? Is this preference justified?

2. Suppose a partnership is set up and operated without formally registering it as a partnership. What problems might arise? Explain.

3. How much protection does copyright afford an owner? Can any of the individual's work be copied without paying a fee? Explain in detail. If an infringement of the copyright occurs, what legal recourse does the owner have?

4. South Africa probably has one of the most advanced labour relations Acts, the LRA. What was good about the old LRA and what is good about the new LRA?

Case study

As a small child, Dianne's artistic talent was evident in everything she did. Her love for flowers, the fact that her husband owned a flower farm and her artistic talent led to her decision to start her own florist shop. Her husband supported this idea and indicated his willingness to actively become part of the business. To finance the business, Dianne considered several possibilities. She also approached her bank manager, who suggested that she take out a loan. She needed the money, among other things, to employ two full-time workers.

Questions

1. What resources, except financial, does Dianne need to start her business?

2. What are the benefits of the business becoming a private company? It is a better idea than the banker's proposal of taking out a loan? Explain.

3. How does a close corporation work? Would this be an appropriate legal form for this business? Why or why not?

4. What legal form of business would you recommend to Dianne? Explain in detail.

5. As an employer, Dianne would have to comply with various legal requirements. Explain these.

Experiential exercises

1. Entrepreneurs need to know how to protect their intellectual property legally. The most effective way to gain legal protection is to obtain a copyright or to register a patent, a trademark or design. On the following list, indicate next to each item whether it can be protected as a copyright, a patent, a trademark or a design.

Photographs   _____

Functional milk jar   _____

Logo   _____

Technical drawing   _____

Computer program   _____

Breakthrough diet pill _____

Symbol _____

Best-selling novel _____

A business's initials, _____
e.g. SANLAM,
ISCOR, SASOL

Designer earrings _____

Motion picture _____

A name, e.g. Defy _____

2. Interview a director of a small private company. Ask the following questions: What value
does he or she add to the management of the
business? What qualifications are essential
for a director? Is ownership of shares in the
business a prerequisite for being a director?

Exploring the Web

Conduct a search on the Internet for sites that provide support and advice on developing
a business plan.

References and recommended reading

Companies and Intellectual Property Registration
Office (CIPRO). At http://www.cipro.gov.za.

Competition Commission. At
http://www.compcom.co.za.

Confederation of Employers of Southern Africa
(COFESA). At http://www.cofesa.co.za.

Department of Labour. At http://www.labour.gov.za.

Department of Trade and Industry. At
http://www.dti.gov.za.

Design Institute of the SABS. At
www.sabs.co.za/design.htm.

Fry, F.L., Stoner, C.R. & Hattwick, R.E. 1998. *Business: an integrative framework.* Boston:
Irwin/McGraw-Hill.

Nieuwenhuizen, C., Le Roux, E.E. & Jacobs, H.
2001. *Entrepreneurship and how to establish your
own business.* Cape Town: Juta.

South African Bureau of Standards (SABS). At
www.sabs.co.za.

Wickham, P.A. 2001. *Strategic entrepreneurship: a
decision-making approach to new venture creation
and management,* 2nd ed. Cornwall: *Financial
Times*/Prentice Hall.

7

Getting started

Linda de Vries & Gideon Nieman

Learning outcomes

After completion of this chapter, you should be able to:

- Demonstrate an understanding of the countdown to the start-up of a new business venture
- Meet the various requirements necessary for starting up any business
- Consider the various factors involved in locating a new business venture
- Continually evaluate the risks attached to managing and starting a business
- Design work structures to ensure that total quality management is maintained
- Consider and provide overall ethical leadership linked to the specific enterprise
- Understand the necessity of record keeping, accounting systems and internal control

7.1 Introduction

The preceding chapters covered the process of idea generation, the conversion of ideas into opportunities and the preparation of the business plan. The previous chapter also explored the major resource requirements for new business ventures and the legal aspects involved in establishing the business opportunity.

This chapter will focus on things that need to be done before starting up, as well as important matters that the entrepreneur must attend to. It also focuses on the management of the new venture and important aspects that must be in place from the start to ensure a successful venture. The evaluation and management of the risks involved will be evaluated, and attention given to total quality management. Lastly, any entrepreneur needs to focus on the ethical considerations that are involved in starting a business.

7.2 Countdown to start-up and gradual start-up

Most new businesses start out as small businesses. Many new entrants to the job market and also new job seekers start their first jobs with small businesses or start-ups.

From the preceding chapters, it is clear that to start up any business would need skills, preparation and proper planning through an effective business plan to ensure success. Most new businesses are very vulnerable at the beginning of the venture life cycle. It is also important that risk management, quality and ethics be established very soon after start-up, as part of the planning for future growth. The choice of a location for the business is a critical decision when planning the start-up.

The process of starting up is based on the fundamentals of management: planning, organising, leading and control.

■ Planning

Planning the venture largely takes place during the idea generation and opportunity recognition process that culminates in the business plan. The business plan (Chapter 5) forces the entrepreneur to think about and plan the marketing, production, operations, management and finances of the new business venture. The business plan helps to reduce the risk. To get started, the business plan must be converted into a number of action plans, with time frames (deadlines) and resources required in respect of each plan (people, money and/or assets) linked to each action plan.

■ Organising

Organising the venture requires the gathering of resources, meeting legal requirements (Chapter 6), finding a site for the business and deciding on a legal form of business. It also requires the development of policy and procedures in respect of employment, ethics and quality assurance.

■ Leading

Leading starts when the venture is awarded business aspects and also when staff members are appointed. These people need to be motivated, coordinated and controlled. The various functions (marketing, finance, production, purchasing, communication and information) in the business need to be structured.

■ Control

Control requires that record keeping, risk management, quality, ethics and internal control systems to be set up to ensure the smooth running of the business and the protection of the assets.

There is a general misconception that one must start big and in the best venue possible. Start-up and growth can be an evolutionary process that can take a number of years. An excellent example is Protea Bookshop in Pretoria. Today, it is a flourishing business in its own premises in Hatfield. The owner started a number of years ago by selling second-hand books at a flea market, and only after this proved to be a lucrative business opportunity, moved into a small shop in a small business centre. Growth forced him to move the business into a house across the street. Eventually, the house was demolished and a new building built on the same premises to accommodate this growing business.

The checklist set out in Table 7.1 outlines the matters to be resolved before a business can start trading.

The logistics of the processes for starting a new venture are essential. The start-up must be treated as a project and managed accordingly.

The various processes must be linked to a flow chart of activities and essential times when tasks must be performed before others can commence, such as environmental clearance before a building project can start or health clearance before a restaurant can operate, or even registration before a tender will be considered. The bare minimum that would be needed to start the business would be contact details, an answering machine, fax or computer support, as well as a physical location or site. Be clear when the starting date is and work backwards with a time schedule to prepare for all the logistics.

7.3 Locating the business

Location is one of the aspects that must be investigated as part of the business plan. "Location, location, location" is one of the well-known sayings in marketing. This quite true but, in reality, the perfect location might not be available to an entrepreneur. For example, there might not be industrial sites available near the entrepreneur, or shopping centres and suburban retail centres might be fully occupied with a long waiting list.

Location is not a one-time decision. An entrepreneur must occasionally consider relocating the business to reduce costs, get closer to customers or gain other advantages. As a business grows, it sometimes is desirable to expand to other locations.

Location plays an important role in the establishment of the business. Formal businesses that rent office, trading or manufacturing space are required to pay closer attention to location factors than informal businesses because of the permanency of their decisions. Informal businesses, on the other hand, tend to move along with the shift in traffic or demographic patterns.

It is very easy for an entrepreneur who makes hamburgers and hot dogs in a converted caravan to move from one location to a more promising one. However, a manufacturer of exhaust pipes cannot move that easily, because this kind of business is likely to be tied up in some form of long-term factory rental. Secondly, it may be very costly to disconnect,

Table 7.1 Checklist for a business start-up

1. Prepare a business plan.

2. Review the form of business. If applicable, form a close corporation or private company or draw up a partnership agreement.

3. Select a business name. Apply for registration. If working from home, contact the local municipality with regard to by-laws that may affect the business.

4. Find and cost premises. Determine fixtures, fittings and equipment costs. Also, decide what alterations or sign writing are required.

5. Complete the business plan. Ensure that it includes sufficient cash available to cover the requirements of the first 12 months.

6. Make a formal application for a loan.

7. Obtain from the bank written confirmation of the loan or overdraft facilities. Seek to understand how arrangement fees, bank charges and interest will be charged. Open the bank account.

8. Determine what licences, certificates, etc. will be necessary to permit you to trade. Apply for these. Investigate patent, registered design, trade market and copyright protection. Apply for protection if justifiable.

9. For business premises, take professional advice on leases, purchase and licences.

10. Establish management controls.

11. Inform the South African Revenue Service that you are starting a business. Register as a provisional taxpayer. Obtain a VAT registration certificate.

12. Inform the Department of Labour and take necessary steps with regard to the Unemployment Insurance Fund and Compensation for Occupational Injuries and Diseases.

13. Contact the Regional Services Council. Register.

14. Review all your responsibilities as an employer to ensure you comply with legal requirements.

15. Contact the relevant Bargaining Council, if applicable, to learn of requirements.

16. Finalise arrangements with the landlord, if not done already. Attend to any special requirements, i.e. hygienic conditions if a butchery.

17. Refurbish premises if required. Ensure all mains services are connected to your premises: electricity/water.

18. Confirm postal and telephone links with the post office. The latest date for advertising in the *Yellow Pages* is November.

19. Plan a detailed activity schedule for communicating and selling your product or service to the market. Make sure appropriate insurance cover is taken out.

20. Draw up job descriptions and establish terms and conditions of employment. Note the requirement to maintain existing terms and conditions where an existing business is being taken over.

21. Find, recruit and train staff.

22. Take delivery of all business stationery and promotional materials.

23. For sales on credit, be aware of legal requirements relating to finance charges.

24. Prepare the launch of the business with press/media support.

25. Take out bank and credit references for major new, unknown credit customers. For credit information, contact your bank or check with Information Trust Corporation, Consumer or Kredit-inform.

26. Consider joining the Chamber of Commerce and other organisations that can help you.

27. Advise your bank manager of your plans. Investigate leasing options, insurance and other financial options. Investigate loan possibilities.

28. Appoint your attorney and accountant or bookkeeper; agree on a service and fee. Establish the business records system to be used.

29. Locate key suppliers; confirm their prices, terms and deliveries.

30. Establish minimum inventory requirements and distribution methods. Establish your prices and discounts.

Source: Adapted from Clarke (1997: 25–27).

move and reconnect very expensive and heavy machinery.

There is also a trend to work from home. The home office is closely related to the concept of a virtual office. The modern trend is for many entrepreneurs, especially professionals such as psychiatrists and attorneys, to establish an office at home.

7.3.1 Factors to consider in the physical establishment of a business

The factors that impact on the physical establishment of a business are closely related to the business plan, especially the marketing plan, and will differ from business to business. For instance, as a rule a restaurant should be established in an area with high customer traffic. However, some very successful restaurants are based outside cities and towns in the countryside and their patrons prefer the secluded location.

The entrepreneur should able to determine the specific success factors impacting on the chosen business. Some general factors to be considered are listed below.

■ Access to the target market

For some businesses it is important to be near the target market. For instance, if the business is a convenience store, such as Spar or Rite Value, it is important that the store be established in or near a residential area, because most of its potential customers would be persons based nearby who require convenience goods such as milk, bread or the odd grocery item.

■ Availability of raw materials

Some businesses are dependent on area-based raw materials. A good example is floor tiles, which are manufactured from very specialised clay. It would make economical sense to base the factory near the clay deposits, instead of transporting the clay to a far-off factory. The transport cost of the clay may otherwise render the factory uneconomical.

■ Support and technical infrastructure

In certain cases a business uses complicated equipment. If a complicated piece of equipment breaks down, it would be important to have the support of repair technicians and spare parts available without losing productive time.

■ Transport infrastructure

Transport infrastructure refers to aspects such as roads, trains and public transport. There are cases where the road infrastructure is not important for a business, but usually road, rail and water links are essential to transport staff, products and customers to and from the business. Likewise, the availability of buses, taxis, and so on is important to ensure that your staff is able to reach your business.

■ Availability of labour and skills

In most cases, the availability of skilled labour and administrative staff is an important factor. If such people are not available to the organisation, certain key areas of the business may suffer. For instance, the unavailability of a skilled electrician to maintain equipment could render a factory helpless.

■ Climatic conditions

In certain businesses, climate conditions play a crucial role in their success. For instance, certain products cannot be produced in very cold or very hot conditions, or in very dry or humid conditions. Climate also plays a role in the attraction of skilled staff to your business. An unpleasant climate may make it unattractive for key staff to join the business.

■ Political and social stability

In most cases, it is important that the business be based in a stable political climate in order to enjoy maximum productivity within a stable environment. However, certain businesses thrive on instability. For instance, a security business is more likely to profit from political instability because there will be a greater demand for the organisation's services.

7.3.2 Home-based businesses

A home-based business is located in the residence of the entrepreneur. This type of location is appropriate to a business where space requirements are modest.

Establishing a business from home has particular pitfalls. It is important that spatial and non-spatial boundaries between business and home are established to prevent the one from interfering with the other. This includes physical space, as well as office hours. Other considerations include:

- It must be accessible to clients (it may be difficult to reach the premises or parking is insufficient).
- Zoning ordinances of the local authority may not allow the business to operate from a residence.
- Space restriction in phases of rapid growth may have a negative impact on the business.

7.3.3 Residential area-based businesses

There is a trend in South African cities for businesses to be established in residential areas. Such businesses are distinct from, for instance, those that are operated from an office block, shopping mall or factory mall. When an entrepreneur acquires the use of a residential property for business purposes, the rationale usually ranges from access to the target market, to convenience and affordability. Most of these businesses are situated along the main roads through cities and suburbs, and the residential homes are converted into office space and parking. This particular trend has been exploited mostly by service industries, professional services and medical practitioners.

7.3.4 Shopping centres

Businesses dealing in fast-moving consumer goods (FMCG) generally need to find shopping or suburban retail centres in which to open a shop. It is important to note that the space in most of these centres or malls is rented out even long before they start building. When allocating space, landlords prefer national chains and franchises. In general, they do not like the "mom and pop stores", as they believe these businesses do not contribute to the image of the centre. Most landlords "bully" smaller businesses in shopping centres into accepting a one-sided lease agreement and agreeing to conditions on trading hours, shopfittings and sale of business.

In selecting a shopping centre, the following factors must be considered:

- *Feet count:* This refers to the number of consumers visiting the centre on a weekly and monthly basis. Most shopping centres have electronic counters at all the main entrances to the centre. They should be able to give the figures if asked for them. Keep in mind that you will be competing for the disposable income of consumers in that particular passage or mall.
- *Parking:* Consumers want easy and accessible parking. Things such as the first hour being free also add to the attractiveness of a centre.
- *Maintenance:* The regular cleaning and maintenance of the centre and upkeep of appearance ensure that consumers will keep visiting the centre.
- *Conditions of lease agreement:* This is probably the most critical factor. Most lease agreements have one-sided clauses covering the trading hours, sale of business, shopfittings and appearance of the shop, access to sales figures and escalation in excess of inflation. These conditions are difficult to negotiate for a new and small business. Landlords tend to adopt a "take-it-or-leave-it" attitude.
- *Security:* The crime situation in South Africa always makes this a factor for consideration. Shops and shopping centres in most South African cities have been robbed. Access to the centre, as well as the presence of security guards, needs to be looked at.
- *Attitude of centre management:* Most centres are managed by property management firms. Their attitude and actions are deciding factors in whether one will have a happy experience as a tenant. Talk to other small tenants in the shopping centre.
- *Location within the centre:* There are areas in all shopping centres that are not prime spots. Consider a number of options and find out why particular shops have not been rented out before. Quite often the shop is available because a previous tenant could not survive there and had to move or close down.

7.4 Risk management

Quite often new business ventures pay insufficient attention to risk management or even to the exposure of the firm. Risk is involved because valuable resources must be committed to a venture. Uncertainty is uncontrollable and unpredictable, and is an inextricable part of a business. Risk management consists of all efforts to prepare the assets and earning power of a business (Longenecker et al. 2000: 544).

7.4.1 Types of risk

Business risk arises from operating in the macro-, market and micro-economic environments. In the macro-economic environment business cycles, technology and politics can cause problems. In the market environment, consumer preferences, price changes and competition require constant managing. In most cases these changes are beyond the control of

management. Figure 7.1 illustrates a number of risks in the micro-economic environment, which can befall any enterprise. This is referred to as the "wheel of misfortune" (Longenecker et al. 2000: 547).

Financial risk arises from the financial structure of the business. Profitability, liquidity and debt play important roles. It is therefore important to evaluate the financial position of the business at regular intervals and to take corrective action if necessary.

Personal risk is the loss of stature and income that the entrepreneur faces should the business fail. In South Africa, bankruptcy carries a certain stigma and may even result in the entrepreneur ending up in the "financial wilderness".

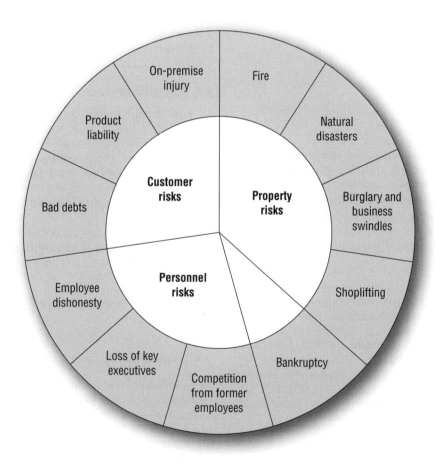

Figure 7.1 The wheel of misfortune

Source: Adapted from Longenecker et al. (2000: 547).

7.4.2 Management of risk

Risk needs to be managed actively by the entrepreneur. There are a few possible strategies to be considered, as discussed below.

■ Retention

In certain circumstances, it might be a strategy to bear the risk or to accept it as part of the business. This normally happens where the potential loss is small or insignificant, and also where the cost of transferring the risk to a third party such as an insurance company is too high. Some risks are retained because they are not identified, or no decision has been made as yet how to handle them.

The following conditions must be prevalent for one to consider a strategy of retention:
• There is no practical means of avoidance.
• The risk is unknown.
• The consequences are not serious.
• The consequences of avoiding the risk are unacceptable.
• Risk is actively desired.

■ Reduction

This strategy is considered if the possibility of a loss cannot be eliminated completely, but its impact can be reduced. The entrepreneur can do the following to reduce risks:
• Revise the business plan regularly.
• Implement management control systems.
• Implement safety programmes.

■ Avoidance

Risk is an integral part of being in business. To avoid risk may mean that nothing will be done or explored. Risk avoidance may mean not investing in the new venture in the first instance and, in an existing business, to avoid doing something at all. The principle of risk and return applies to all business ventures: the higher the risk, the higher the return. If the chances of loss and severity are high, avoidance of risk is the best strategy.

■ Transfer

To transfer risk or a part of it to another party is one of the most popular strategies followed by businesspeople. There are a number of ways in which this can be done, e.g. through underwriting and insurance.

Taking out insurance is a sound business practice for a start-up entrepreneur. Many new business ventures operate without any insurance and, consequently, any disaster can impact heavily on their continued existence. The basic principle to follow when considering insurance is:
• Identify the business risks to be insured.
• Limit cover to major potential losses.
• Relate premium costs to the probability of the loss.

The process of risk management basically comprises the following five steps:
1. Identify risks.
2. Evaluate risks.
3. Select methods to manage risks.
4. Implement the decision.
5. Evaluate and review at regular intervals.

7.5 Quality systems and management

All new firms have an operations process or production activities that produce goods and services for customers. In a service business, it begins with the first contact with the customer. In a manufacturing process, it begins with the purchase of raw material and includes all the steps required to create the products desired by customers.

To ensure quality and particularly if the firm wishes to expand globally in future, it is important to have a quality system in place. Most countries require ISO 9000 and ISO 14000 certification by a national certification body, which in South Africa is the South African Bureau of Standards (SABS).

7.5.1 What are quality systems?

All businesses, large and small, already have an established way or system of doing business. In a small business, the likelihood is that the system is quite effective, but informal and probably not documented. Quality system standards identify those features that can help a business to consistently meet its customers' requirements. They are not about imposing something totally new on the business.

7.5.2 Why have a quality system?

Some customers in both the private and public sectors are looking for the confidence that can be given by a business having a quality system. While meeting these expectations is one reason for having a quality system, there may be others, which could include the following:

- Improvement of performance, coordination and productivity
- Greater focus on the business objectives and on customers' expectations
- Achievement and maintenance of the quality of the product to meet the customers' stated and implied needs
- Management confidence that the intended quality is being achieved and maintained
- Evidence to customers and potential customers of the organisation's capabilities
- Opening up new market opportunities or maintaining market share
- For certification/registration
- The opportunity to compete on the same basis as larger organisations (e.g. the ability to tender or submit price quotations)

While a quality system can help in meeting these expectations, it is only a means and cannot take the place of the goals set for the business. The entrepreneur should regularly review and upgrade the quality system to ensure that worthwhile and economically viable improvements are made.

7.5.3 Putting a quality system in place

Most businesses have some problems in putting a quality system in place. In a new business these problems are potentially greater due to the following:

- Minimal available resources
- Difficulty in understanding and applying the standards
- Costs involved in setting up and maintaining a quality system

For new and small businesses, implementing a quality system costs time and money and should be looked at in the same way as any other investment. For such a system to be viable, one has to achieve a return for one's time and effort, through improvements in marketability and/or internal efficiency. The decisions at the early stages of introducing or developing the quality system will have a major influence in these areas. The SABS will assist new and existing businesses in setting up quality systems. It has a number of excellent procedures for helping and guiding those businesses.

To ensure standardisation of service delivery, it is important to have in place a system of service delivery that has specific tasks and monitoring systems. The philosophy of total quality management has as much to do with the people skills involved as the system in place to support the process. Both of these are equally important when considering the start-up process.

Many business owners are occupied seven days a week, 24 hours a day. Even though they care about the business, normal fatigue also sets in and can influence service delivery. Ensuring that tasks are well planned and that responsibilities are assigned will ensure greater compliance with the quality standards of products and processes, as well as actual service delivery.

7.6 Ethics

The challenges that face businesspeople during the business operation are immense. Many are ethical by nature, i.e. they involve questions of right and wrong. The business needs to have an ethical charter and a statement of personal values to ensure that everybody (even the owners) understands the values that underpin the business.

Unless the owner is clear about these values during the start-up phase (e.g. that no milk will diluted to create the idea of cream milk), and service deliveries are very poor and inconsistent, the business will soon be exposed to ethical pitfalls. Clients who are not clear on the ethics that govern the business will generally become mistrustful of the owners, which will impact negatively on the business in the long term.

The entrepreneur will face many ethical challenges throughout his or her career. New and small growing firms are especially vulnerable to extortion and bribery, and can be under extreme pressure to compromise ethical standards. Such unethical behaviour includes:

- Skimming – concealing income to avoid taxes, or even claiming excessive expenses
- Deception of consumers through advertisements or claims
- Inaccurate reporting of financial information and state of affairs

It is therefore important to build an ethical business from the start, through thorough leadership, culture and instruction that support ethical behaviour. As the business grows, a code of ethics setting out the principles to be followed will become necessary.

The limited resources of small firms make them especially vulnerable to allowing, or becoming involved in, unethical practices. The most troublesome issues for new businesses involve:

- Relationships with customers, clients and competitors
- Management processes and relationships
- Employees' obligations to their employers

The inherent values of business leaders and the examples they set by their actions are powerful factors affecting ethical performances. An organisational culture that supports ethical performance must be actively developed.

7.7 Record keeping and internal control

Entrepreneurs must have accurate, meaningful and timely information in order to manage their business well and to make good decisions. The accounting system for a business should accomplish the following objectives:

- To maintain source documents and provide an audit trail
- To provide an accurate, thorough picture of operating results
- To permit a quick overview of present and past operating results
- To facilitate prompt filing of reports and tax returns to all government agencies
- To offer financial statements for use by management and other stakeholders

The ability to maintain records will in the long term be an advantage for the small business owner. Record keeping begins before the start-up, with systems and mechanisms being put in place to ensure proper functioning and accounting and maintenance of all the records.

The challenge to set up the system with files, ordering books and computer system, as well as the process of determining the costs, cost of sales and cash flow position, is essential when planning for success. The start-up business could secure the services of a small accounting business that understands the recording requirements from a tax perspective, accounting perspective and a process flow perspective. Finding an accountant or bookkeeper is relatively easy, as they advertise in the smalls section of the daily newspapers in the country. The record keeping and accounting function can easily be outsourced. In general, this is a time-consuming function and the entrepreneur can use the time better by focusing on marketing, for example.

The entrepreneur who can manage the record system from the beginning will be able to make sense and learn from the business, and assist with the correcting of decisions. Accounting records can be kept in just about any form, as long as they provide users with the needed date and meet legal requirements. Some form of record keeping must be set up from the first day of operation. This requires filing of all source documents and the recording of sales and expenditure.

The quality of a firm's accounting system is, however, dependent on the effectiveness of the controls that exist within the firm. Internal control is a system of checks and balances that plays a key role in safeguarding a firm's assets and in enhancing the accuracy and reliability of its financial statements.

The importance of internal control has long been recognised in large corporations. Some owners of smaller firms, who may be concerned about the cost or appropriateness of a system of internal control for a small firm, do not always appreciate its value, although they should (Longenecker et al. 2000: 486).

Building internal controls may be difficult in a small company, but it is no less important than for a large company. The absence of internal controls significantly increases the chances not only of fraud and theft, but also of bad decisions based on inaccurate and untimely accounting information. Effective internal controls are also necessary for an audit by independent accountants. Chartered accountants are unwilling to express an opinion about a firm's financial statements if it lacks adequate internal controls. The entrepreneur should consult an accountant, who will be able to assist in managing the problems that may result from the absence of internal control.

7.8 Conclusion

The start-up phase demands that entrepreneurs have in place the following key elements in order to ensure that growth will result. In this chapter, a checklist was supplied and a number of key issues were discussed. The business needs to ensure that all these aspects are in place:

- Legal requirements of the business
- Regulatory requirements linked to the specific business concept or business plan
- Licensing of the business premises
- Building of relations with suppliers (these relationships must be formalised to ensure ongoing provision of materials, products and services)

- The physical location of the business (e.g. will it be virtual or physical?)
- An implementable business plan
- A management team or employees with expertise linked to the specific type of business
- The required finances to start up and run the business
- Effective products and materials to run the business for the first period (the most economic quantities)
- Employees who understand the business and its ethos, as well as the skills of salesmanship
- Technical knowledge skills
- Accurate estimation of the cash flow needs from start-up until the business becomes self-sufficient
- Willingness to be involved as an owner or an employee who will not merely work from 8 a.m. to 5 p.m. but who is willing to spend enough time to evaluate, monitor and adjust the business as the needs arise
- Media support of the business
- Ethical code of conduct

Looking back

1. Discuss the process of business start-up.
   - Planning the venture through the business plan
   - Organising the venture through the gathering of resources and various registrations
   - Leading by managing the functions in the enterprise
   - Controlling the business through record keeping, internal control, ethics, quality and risk management

2. List the factors to consider in the physical establishment of a business.
   - Access to target market
   - Availability of raw materials
   - Support and technical infrastructure
   - Transport infrastructure
   - Labour and skills accessibility
   - Climatic conditions

3. List the factors to consider in selecting a shopping centre as a location for a business.
   - Feet count
   - Parking
   - Maintenance
   - Conditions of lease agreements
   - Security
   - Attitude of centre management
   - Location within the centre

4. Which strategies can be followed in the management of risk?
   - Retention
   - Reduction
   - Avoidance
   - Transfer

5. Why does a firm need a quality system?
   - Improvement of performance, coordination and productivity

- Greater focus on the business objectives and on customers' expectations
- Achievement and maintenance of the quality of the product to meet the customers' stated and implied needs
- Management confidence that the intended quality is being achieved and maintained
- Evidence to customers and potential customers of the organisation's capabilities
- Opening up new market opportunities or maintaining market share
- Certification/registration
- Opportunity to compete on the same basis as larger organisations (e.g. ability to tender or submit price quotations)

6. List some of the unethical behaviour found in firms.
    - Skimming – concealing income to avoid taxes or even claiming excessive expenses
    - Deception of consumers through advertisements or claims
    - Inaccurate reporting of financial information and state of affairs

7. Why are accounting, record keeping and internal control necessary?
    - To maintain source documents and provide an audit trail
    - To provide an accurate, thorough picture of operating results
    - To permit a quick overview of present and past operating results
    - To facilitate prompt filing of reports and tax returns to all government agencies
    - To offer financial statements for use by management and other stakeholders

Key terms

Accounting systems	Organising
Avoidance	Planning
Control	Quality systems
Ethics	Record keeping
Feet count	Reduction
Home-based businesses	Residential-based businesses
Internal control	Retention
Leading	Risk management
Location factors	Transfer

Discussion questions

1. What are the key attributes of a good business location?
2. How would you ensure that pilferage and theft do not take place in a store?
3. Give some suggestions for the record-keeping process and how this can assist with the decision-making process on new stock and purchases.
4. How would you ensure that your staff is ethical in their dealings with customers?
5. Should entrepreneurs have an outside specialist set up an accounting system for their new venture or should they do it themselves? Why?

Case studies

Case study 1: Vicky's Bed and Breakfast

The growth in the tourism sector in South Africa in particular, and in the world in general, provides many opportunities for small businesses to start up and to flourish. The needs of the tourist and the tourism sector are diverse and very people orientated. The growth in tourist destinations, ecotourism and heritage tourism enables new entrepreneurs to focus on niche markets and to exploit the opportunities. In South Africa, township tourism is a novel idea and one that allows entry to the tourism market. Many visitors to South Africa seek to experience an authentic South African experience and they often plan to stay in a township for a number of days to study the lifestyles, the community spirit, the way people live, and to hear the stories from the community itself.

Vicky's Bed and Breakfast started within this context. She had a baby, no business experience and no formal training in running a business, but she had a great idea. She recognised the need for the community to benefit from the many tourists to South Africa and also her opportunity to provide a link between tourists and the township.

How did she begin? Vicky did market research. She visited many homes in her community and shared her idea with them. She also pointed out that no tourist would visit the township unless they would feel safe and be safe within the Khayelitsha community in Cape Town. She also had community meetings with the local shebeen, as well as the crafters in the community. She explained to them that if she has visitors, they would be able to benefit from her business.

With the support of the community in her area, she started bringing visitors to her home. She marketed her bed and breakfast venture through printed flyers at the Cape Town information centre. Currently, her visitors' book boasts tourists from the Netherlands, Germany and around the world. She has an email address through which individuals and tourists can make bookings. Vicky goes to Cape Town once week to respond to her emails and to confirm her bookings. Her cellphone is a very important item, as most bookings come from the contact telephone number. Her neighbours assist with accommodation when her guests are more than her two-roomed home can accommodate.

A specific speciality is her breakfast, which represents good "soul food". Items on the menu include "mieliepap", "smoortjie" and "potbrood", as well as a number of other unique township specialities. She spends time with guests around the breakfast and supper table and walks with them through her community.
Source: Adapted from Harvey et al. (2002).

Questions

1. What do you think were the key success factors behind Vicky's bed and breakfast?
2. What would be key considerations in setting up a bed and breakfast venture?

Case study 2: Bite Curio – an experience in community development

The Bite Curio shop initially was a huge success. On opening day and opening week, all the items relating to the sea, the ocean and birds were sold but the ethnic items with a high capital outlay did not sell. The owner did not have any more funds to replenish the stock that moved fast. Regular visitors became quite disenchanted with the limited product lines and the lack of constant innovation. The shop lost its curiosity appeal. Yet, tourists liked practical gifts such as peaked caps for the sun, T-shirts with a logo, as well as large items with significance.

After three months, the owner considered complementing the stock with many small curios and items under R10,00 to cater for the growing school population that visited her curio shop. She also managed to arrange with a supplier to carry stock but not purchase it, and to be rewarded with commission only for the more expensive items. She discovered that postcards have a huge appeal and visitors would always leave the store with at least a postcard.

She started to make items linked to the area and of which the cost was minimal. By balancing the cost of her stock between handmade, locally manufactured, commissioned items as well as purchased curio items in large volumes, she started having a better product assortment mix.

After three years her business is still in existence and she is considering a total new layout of the store. Having learnt some hard lessons, she will implement a mixed product assortment strategy. She also commissions a local professional photographer to capture various scenes from around the town to ensure a representative collection of photographs for purchase. As a start-up entrepreneur she has discovered the importance of product selection and the cost of carrying wrong stock the hard way.

Source: Adapted from Graham (2002).

Questions

1. Do you think this business owner did proper start-up planning? Substantiate your answer.
2. How would you have determined the needs of the customers of a curio shop?
3. How would you monitor sales and other costs?

Experiential exercises

1. Interview an entrepreneur about the strengths and weaknesses of his or her business location.
2. Visit a number of new or small businesses and report on the level of sophistication of their accounting systems.
3. Contact a new or small business and obtain permission to conduct a risk analysis of the business. Prepare a report for the owner.
4. Contact the SABS about the requirements for ISO 9000 certification.
5. Examine recent newspapers and business journals and report briefly on some ethical problem in the news.

Exploring the Web

Go to www.sabs.co.za for information on ISO 9000 certification.

References and recommended reading

Clarke, A.G. 1997. *The small business action kit for South Africa.* Cape Town: Francolin.

Espelund, G. 2001. Welkom in Khayelitsha. *Zuidelijk Afrika.* Winter No. 4.

Graham, S. 2002. It's boomtime for the craft industry. *Sunday Times,* 13 October, 6.

Harvey, K., Hilton-Barber, B. & Tukwelani, T. 2002. Moving to the beat. *Sawubona,* October.

Longenecker, J.G., Moore, C.W. & Petty, J.W. 2000. *Small business management: an entrepreneurial emphasis,* 11th ed. Cincinnati: South Western.

Malan, J. & Lessing, N. 2002. Establishing a business. In: Nieman, G. & Bennett, A. (Eds), *Business management: a value chain approach.* Pretoria: Van Schaik.

Financing an entrepreneurial venture

Gideon Nieman

8.1 Introduction

Finding finance, or gaining financial support for any new venture, is one of the difficulties experienced by entrepreneurs. It is important to know what sources of finance are available and what is required from the various financial institutions like banks, development agencies and investors.

This chapter is divided into five sections:
- Determining the financial requirements of the business venture
- Sources of finance: short, medium and long term
- Suppliers of finance
- The venture capital market
- Preparing the application and preparing for the interview

8.2 Determining the financial requirements of the business venture

A successful business cannot be established or managed without setting realistic goals and planning towards these. The business plan is generally used for this purpose. Amongst other things, the financial requirements of the business must be set out in this plan. Although a business plan helps to reduce uncertainty, it cannot accurately forecast the future. More than half of all new venture and small business loan applications are rejected at an early stage, because many entrepreneurs simply do not do their homework and put their plans together *before* applying for loans.

Many small businesspeople will immediately say that they have "managed up to now", simply by relying on a "gut feel". This approach has indeed worked for some people, but they are few and have managed to do so only in very special circumstances. The business plan, and in particular the financial plan, is a tool for determining one's financial requirements. The business plan is more than just a financial plan. It is a comprehensive analysis of your business, the market you are active in, your products, and what finance will be required. The process and content of the business plan are explained in depth in Chapter 5. The main purpose of this plan is to attract money to finance the business, as most financial institutions and lenders will require it as part of the application.

The financial plan forms an important part of the total business plan. This is generally referred to as "budgeting". A budget is simply a forecast of future events. Financial forecasts are put to use in constructing a financial plan. These plans culminate in the preparation of a cash budget and a set of pro forma statements for a future period in the business's operations.

Determining the firm's financial requirements will require forecasting of the future. The basic steps involved in predicting these financing needs include the following:

1. Project the firm's sales, revenues and expenses over the planning period.

2. Estimate the levels of investment in current and fixed assets that are necessary to support the projected sales.

3. Determine the firm's financing needs throughout the planning period.

Budgets and financial plans are estimates and are only as good as the person who makes them. Incorrect information and unreasonable estimates will carry through the entire financial plan and result in unduly high or low performance targets and potentially harmful financing and investment decisions. Incorrect performance targets will frustrate the entrepreneur and the staff, and harmful financing and investment decisions can bankrupt the firm.

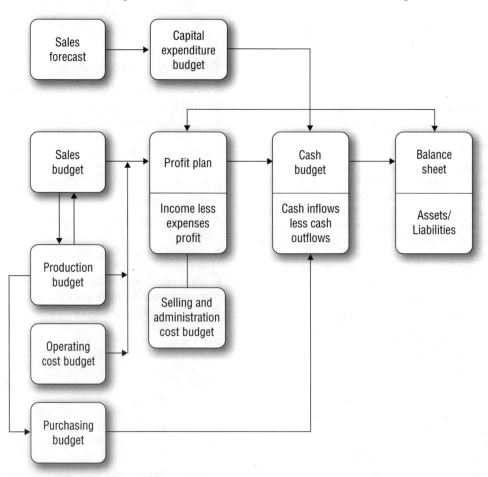

Figure 8.1 The financial planning process

8.3 Sources of short-term finance

Short-term finance refers to finance that is normally repayable or reviewed within 12 months. In accounting terms, short-term finance refers to debt repayable within 12 months from the balance sheet date.

8.3.1 Trade credit

It is common practice in South Africa that businesses buy their stock or inventory on credit from other firms. Credit means that the buyer is not expected to pay cash for the goods or services. Such credit extended by one firm to another in the normal course of business is referred to as "trade credit".

To obtain credit from a supplier one normally has to complete the supplier's credit application form. The seller or supplier will then verify the creditworthiness of the buying firm and obtain a credit check on the bank account and other trade credit accounts. The overall picture will decide whether the credit will be granted.

If the credit is granted, there will be certain credit limits and certain credit terms. The credit limit will be a certain maximum amount that will be allowed for purchases on credit. As the business grows and proves to be an honest and regular payer, the limit may be increased. Late or failed payments will result in the limit being reduced or cancelled. Credit terms vary from one field of business activity to another and are strongly influenced by the economic nature of the product. Goods that are perishable or have a high sales turnover are likely to be sold on relatively short credit terms, as in the case of the meat trade where settlement (payment) is normally required within seven days. Motor vehicles, on the other hand, usually take much longer to sell and manufacturers may offer terms of 90 days or more to their dealers.

When buying on credit, the seller will invoice the goods to the buyer and becomes a creditor in the financial statements. The invoice will normally reflect the payment terms, such as "30 days". This means that one has 30 days after the date of the statement to pay the creditor. Should you not make payment on due dates, the supplier will be free to cancel the credit facility and to institute legal action to recover the money due. This can lead to a bad credit record, resulting in the firm not being able to buy on credit again. This source of finance is very important for small businesses, which often experience difficulty in obtaining finance from other, more formal sources.

8.3.2 Bank credit

Bank credit in the form of an overdraft facility is a very common method of short-term finance. It is normally associated with a cheque account facility. Cheques are financial instruments that are used to transfer funds from one person to another without using bank notes and coins. The cheque system operated by commercial banks is an important mechanism in business in South Africa. To open a cheque account with a bank, one will have to complete an application form at a bank and have some funds (money) available to deposit into the account. The bank will consider one's character and obtain certain credit references before approving the account. It is definitely not so easy or quick as portrayed in the television commercials!

Once the account is approved, you will receive a cheque book and a deposit book. By depositing money or cheques received in a current account, the business is able to make payments by issuing cheques against this sum of money. As you issue cheques, the balance will become smaller. Your bank account will therefore fluctuate as you deposit money or issue cheques. The bank, however, will dishonour your cheques if you exceed your balance. These cheques will be returned marked "R/D" (Refer to Drawer) and will create a bad credit record for you and your business.

Short-term financing by banks usually takes the form of an overdraft. It is regarded as short term as it is normally a facility granted for a short period, and needs to be renewed at least once a year. The bank manager will consider your application after a personal interview and after your credit record has been checked. Any application for an overdraft facility will be considered more favourably when it is supported by a business plan.

What will the bank manager want to know? Most of it will be stated in your business plan, but basically the bank will want to know:
- Who the applicant is
- What the managerial abilities of the applicant are

- What the overdraft is required for
- How, when and from which sources it will be repaid (cash projection)
- What security is offered to ensure repayment to protect the lender
- Financial statements of the business

In granting the overdraft facility, the bank agrees to allow the business to issue cheques in excess of the funds held in the current account. There will be an agreed limit (facility) up to which the account can be overdrawn. As cheques are issued the overdraft is steadily increased, possibly up to the agreed limit. Deposits can create a positive balance again.

The overdraft is useful to a business in meeting temporary financial needs and is normally granted to finance transactions that will generate cash flows in the near future.

Interest can be high but is calculated only on the daily balance actually outstanding and not on the full sum that can be utilised. The rate of interest will depend on the ruling interest rates and the credit status of the borrower. There will be charges for various services on the bank statement. These vary from ledger fees to individual charges for each cheque. There is also a tax levy on every cheque issued or debit against the account.

8.3.3 Short-term funds from other sources

Trade credit and bank overdrafts are the main short-term sources of finance for small and other businesses. It might, however, be difficult to come up with the security sometimes required for these sources. There are numerous other lesser-known sources that may be used, but these might not be readily available to the smaller business.

■ Bills of exchange

Bills of exchange in the form of bills payable and promissory notes are negotiable instruments and are used in practice mostly in the process of paying or replacing trade credit. By signing a bill ("acceptance") the buyer undertakes to pay the debt (plus interest) at some agreed future date. This arrangement has the following benefits to the buyer and seller of the goods:

- The buyer is given credit for the period stipulated in the bill (normally 60, 90 or 120 days).
- The seller possesses a negotiable instrument. This means that he or she may obtain cash for the bill by selling ("discounting") it to a financial institution such as a bank.

■ Acceptance credits

Acceptance credits, or banker's acceptances, simply mean financing by means of bills of exchange. This is a facility made available by merchant banks, whereby "first-class" client borrowers are issued a "letter of credit" permitting them to draw bills to a specified limit. The bill is then accepted by the bank and subsequently discounted in the money market.

By accepting the bill, the bank assumes responsibility for payment on maturity – normally 90 days later – on the understanding that the client will repay the bank by the due date. As an alternative to repayment, the bank may agree to "roll over" the old bill. In practice, acceptance credits are mainly used to finance the movement of goods, where the transaction is completed within the life of the bill, i.e. the transaction is self-liquidating. Generally, the total cost of this method is less than that for bank overdrafts.

■ Factoring

Factoring is a term referring to the raising of funds by the sale or assignment of book debts to a third person, i.e. a factor. The sale may be with or without recourse for bad or doubtful debts; it may include all or some of the debts sold; it may require the debtor to pay directly to the factor or via the original creditor or agent for the factor, or the transaction can be structured so that at the time of sale of goods to the debtor, the "seller" sells the goods to the factor and completes the transaction as an agent of the factor. This latter method has the advantage of maintaining the confidentiality of the arrangement between the seller and the factor.

Factoring is a very convenient method of financing increases in working capital, provided that gross income margins can satisfactorily absorb the strain of the discount imposed by the factor. An additional advantage accrues to the seller by the reduction in staff and paperwork associated with maintaining accounts and monitoring debtors. Furthermore, cash is received immediately and the seller is not obliged to include a discount for prompt payment.

■ **Customer advance payments**

This source of funds is peculiar to the construction and engineering industries, and consists of progress payments upon the completion of defined stages of a project. It is rare, however, that such a source of finance would be considered for short-term projects.

■ **Shipper's finance**

Shipper's finance pertains to a specific financial institution that provides finances necessary to cover the movement of goods from supplier to purchaser – generally for the importation of goods.

The cost of shipper's finance is high. For this reason it is normally used only when alternative sources are not available.

8.4 Sources of medium-term finance

The boundary between short- and medium-term finance is often blurred and it is for this reason that the two sources are sometimes considered together. Medium-term finance refers to finance that is repayable between one and three years.

8.4.1 Instalment sale transaction (hire purchase)

Hire purchase and leasing are the most popular methods of financing fixed assets such as machinery, equipment, furniture and motor vehicles. This form of financing is available from most commercial banks. Hire purchase, or an instalment sale transaction as it is officially named, is a credit sale in which it is agreed that the purchase price of the item will be paid in instalments. Although the buyer takes possession of the item, the ownership of the item sold will not pass to the buyer until the last instalment has been paid.

An initial payment deposit, which is a portion of the cash price, is usually payable by the buyer of the item. Deposits differ for different items, as they are prescribed by the Minister of

Finance in terms of the Credit Agreement Act, Act 7 of 1980 (as amended). The balance of the purchase price after deducting the deposit is normally paid with interest over a certain period of time. The Minister has prescribed maximum periods within which the full price must be paid. It is important to note that although interest rates are limited by regulation, interest must be negotiated for each transaction separately.

The Credit Agreement Act protects both the buyer and the seller. Some of the most important legal requirements for a hire purchase or credit sale agreement are the following:
- It must be in writing and signed by the parties.
- It must state the amount of the initial payment (deposit).
- It must contain a description of the goods that are being purchased.
- It must state the names and addresses of the credit grantor and credit receiver.

Most suppliers of machinery, furniture, equipment or motor vehicles have an arrangement with some or other financial institution to finance the goods on a credit sale agreement. Many major businesses have their own finance company for this purpose. If the supplier has no arrangement with a bank, obtain a specified quotation for the goods and approach your bank or any bank for a hire purchase approval. The bank will give precise instructions on how to proceed to collect the goods from the supplier.

8.4.2 Leasing finance

Leasing finance is also regulated by the Credit Agreement Act, Act 7 of 1980 (as amended) and offers the buyer and the credit supplier similar protection. It has become common practice for businesses to lease, rather than purchase, such items as motor vehicles, office equipment, plant and machinery, and buildings.

A leasing transaction is a transaction in which goods are leased at a stated sum of money at certain dates or a future date, in whole or in instalments. In other words, it is a contractual arrangement in which the owner of an asset (the lessor) grants the use of hire property to another person (the lessee) under certain conditions for a certain period. The lessee is therefore expected to make a payment or series of payments for the use of an asset.

In a leasing agreement, the lessor (usually a bank or financial institution) becomes the owner of the asset because it pays the supplier the total cost. The user or lessee has complete use of the asset but never actually owns it and does not have to find funds to purchase it. The most important principle of leasing is that the asset is being paid for as it is used in the production of income. One is, for example, more concerned about having the "use" of a certain piece of equipment and not necessarily "ownership".

A financial lease involves a commitment to make certain payments over a specified period. These payments will exceed the purchase price of the asset, as they include an interest portion. The lease is non-cancellable. The period is normally between 12 and 60 months, and is geared to the useful life of the asset. Operating leases are basically the same as financial leases, the main difference being that the lease can be cancelled by giving an appropriate period of notice to the lessor. This "cancellation" is, however, mostly conditional upon a "trade-in" or upgrade to a new model.

Operating leases are popular in circumstances where the asset is subject to constant technological changes. Computers are often leased under these terms. Operating leases mostly include maintenance or service agreements.

Sale-and-leaseback is actually a long-term source of finance, but is discussed in this section as part of leasing. This source of funding is quite popular where a business owns a valuable asset and requires an injection of funds. The property is then sold (normally to an insurance company, pension fund or property portfolio company) and simultaneously the business enters into an agreement with the buyer to lease it back. The lease period is normally between five and ten years. The procedure for entering into a financial lease agreement or to apply for a leasing facility is exactly the same as for a hire purchase agreement.

The supplier, after doing a credit check on the buyer, usually arranges the operating lease. Again, many of these businesses have a separate finance company or discount the lease agreement at a financial institution.

Sale-and-leaseback will entail negotiations with the financial and other institutions involved in these transactions. The property must be prime property, and the business entering into the leaseback agreement must be a well-established business.

8.4.3 Medium-term loans

Many commercial banks have a medium-term loan facility for clients. These loans are normally repayable over a 24 to 36 month period and are granted to finance working capital, providing bridging finance until long-term sources of finance can be obtained, or for the acquisition of fixed assets. The lender will require security for the loan, and will seek to entrench the safety of the loan by imposing certain restrictions on the borrower, such as maximum permissible equity to debt and working capital ratios, and limitations on the sale or pledge of assets and payments of dividends. Interest rates are generally higher than the prime overdraft rate and are dependent on the ruling interest rates.

Some banks have a "revolving credit" facility that can be classified as medium-term finance. A client will be granted a facility of, say, R50 000 which must then be repaid in monthly instalments over 24 months. Once a certain percentage (e.g. 25 per cent) has been repaid, a further drawing may be made. The instalments only change if interest rates change. These loans might not be available to new businesses, as they will not have a proven track record or security.

8.5 Sources of long-term finance

Long-term funding means that capital is provided for anything up to the entire lifespan of your business. As the owner you usually provide only long-term capital in the form of shares, capital or loans. Most of the sources of long-term finance are available mostly to public companies (listed and non-listed), although an established small- or medium-sized business could consider these sources.

8.5.1 Equity capital

The initial capital that you contribute to the business to get it started is often referred to as equity capital. Equity capital is capital is invested in the business with no obligation to repay the principal amount, or to pay interest on it, to another party. Equity capital takes different forms different form depending on the form of organisation that you have selected for your business (Table 8.1).

It is not within the scope of this chapter to discuss the merits of each form of business or the aspects that should be taken into consideration when selecting a form of business. The different forms of business do, however, have different abilities to attract finance.

■ Sole proprietorship

The sole proprietor cannot attract equity capital as a source of long-term finance. The availability of outside capital and financing will be limited to the proprietor's personal assets and creditworthiness. It will therefore have to depend on outside borrowing. The business and the personal assets of the proprietor (owner) in such a form of business are regarded as one entity, and the owner is personally responsible for debts incurred by the business.

■ Partnerships – capital accounts

A partnership is formed when two or more people (a maximum of 20) decide to conduct business together. It does not necessarily mean that each partner will contribute money to the partnership; skills or assets can also be part of the contribution. These contributions by the partners (owners) are referred to as the "capital accounts" and are normally not repayable during the lifespan of the partnership. It is recommended that when you enter into a partnership,

all partners consult an attorney and a written partnership agreement is drawn up based on aspects agreed mutually by the partners.

A partnership is not regarded as a separate legal entity and the entrepreneur should carefully consider the advantages and disadvantages of entering into one. It can be a negative factor if the business does not perform according to plan. Despite all the cautions mentioned, raising capital often necessitates taking one or more partners into the business. If more than one manager is not needed, the new partners may not be employed in the firm but may hold full partner status as a result of their investment in the firm. Inducement can be offered to such a finance partner, but the duties, responsibilities and authority of each partner must be clearly understood and defined.

Should any partner supply capital on a loan basis, the period of the loan, interest payable and repayment terms should be clearly set out in a loan agreement or in the partnership agreement. The availability of outside capital or financing is therefore limited to the resources of partners and to outside borrowing.

■ Close corporations – members' contribution

A close corporation is in essence a business with a separate legal status from its members. Only individuals may be members and the number of members is limited to ten. The original purpose of the Close Corporation Act was to make it easier for small businesses to operate as close corporations rather than companies.

Table 8.1 Form of business and the applicable equity capital

Form of business	Name of equity capital	Legal requirements
Sole proprietorship	Capital	None
Partnership	Capital accounts	Written agreement between partners is recommended
Close corporation (CC)	Members' contribution	Close Corporations Act, 1984 (as amended)
Company • Public • Private	Share capital	Companies Act, 1973 (as amended)

They are cheaper to establish, cheaper to maintain than a company, have fewer legal requirements and also provide their members limited liability on condition that the provisions of the Act are observed.

The initial capital contributed by members is referred to as members' contribution and becomes permanent capital to the corporation. For tax purposes it is recommended that the members' contribution be kept to a minimum, with other contributions rather being loan capital bearing interest. The requirements of the Act concerning solvency must be kept in mind. This type of "borrowed" capital implies an obligation to repay the capital plus interest. By setting a definite time for repayment and by deferring interest payments until the business can afford it at some future date, it becomes a form of permanent capital to the close corporation. At the same time, it can also be tax effective.

The availability of outside capital or financing is limited to members' contributions and outside borrowing. If you are the only member (or one of fewer than ten people) in the corporation, additional members can be taken in but the same considerations as for partnerships will apply.

■ Companies – share capital

In companies the members are referred to as shareholders and their contributions convert to share capital. The statutory requirements for establishing and maintaining a company are fairly onerous and relatively expensive. The advantages are that shareholders are not personally liable for the company's debts and the company has an indefinite lifespan. The company does not cease to exist when a shareholder or shareholders die or sell their shares.

Public companies must have seven or more members. The number of members will only be limited to the number of authorised shares in the Memorandum of Association.

In a public company, a share certificate is issued for capital introduced, and this certificate is fully negotiable and transferable to third parties. A public company can attract outside capital by selling shares to the public, provided its offer to the public is supported by a prospectus as required by the Companies Act. This form of business, however, is seldom used for a small business starting out. Once you have an established profitability record and reputation, it can be considered.

Companies have two main types of shares that can be used to attract long-term finance: ordinary and preference shares.

ORDINARY SHARES

This form of finance plays a central role in the life of a company. Not only do ordinary shares, or "equities" as they are commonly known, generally constitute the first source of funds for a new company, but it can also be said that "equity capital forms the foundation of the entire capital structure of a business enterprise".

Since ordinary shares have no rights to a fixed return and rank last in order of priority with regard to both dividends and capital, they do not impose any onerous obligations on management. Moreover, even though ordinary shares carry votes, the separation of ownership and control in most large companies usually means that management has little to fear from making further issues of equities and may, in fact, simply entrench its position even more!

In theory, the ordinary shareholder receives large dividends when profits are high and small dividends, or no dividends at all, when they are low.

PREFERENCE SHARES

These are so called because they have priority over ordinary shares as to the payment of dividends and/or the return of capital in the event of liquidation. They do not, however, have priority over creditors, such as debenture holders. Preference shares may be recognised by the fact that they contain a percentage in their title, which indicates the dividend payable, e.g. a 9 per cent R1,00 preference share. Once again, there are several types of preference shares in use, although some are extremely rare.

Over the years, preference shares have become increasingly neglected as a source of finance. Today, the indications are that they account for not even 5 per cent of total company funds. In part, this is no doubt due to the general preference that investors have displayed for ordinary shares at the expense of fixed interest-bearing securities.

In effect, preference shares may bring with them obligations that are similar to those of a loan, but, since they represent ownership, the fixed payment to shareholders is defined as a dividend and not interest. Consequently, it is not deductible from profits before calculating tax, as is normally the case with interest. Thus the cost of financing by means of preference shares may be higher than that of using some form of debt.

8.5.2 Debentures

Debentures are another form of loan capital that can be attracted by companies as a form of long-term funding. Money is borrowed from outside sources by issuing debentures. Debentures are normally printed documents that are fully negotiable and transferable. The principal sum of the loan is normally repayable at some future date, while interest payments at stipulated times (usually annually) are guaranteed.

This form of finance is, however, mostly used by public companies. An established track record in profitability and credit will be a prerequisite for this type of finance.

8.5.3 Retained earnings: internal financing

For many businesses an important source of long-term finance takes the form of profits that are retained in the firm as "reserves" instead of being distributed as dividends. In South Africa, statistical evidence indicates that share capital and reserves comprise about 50 per cent of total company finance.

The popularity of internal finance is undoubtedly due to the fact that management has almost complete control over this source of funds. Once prior charges have been met, it is for management to decide what, if any, dividends will be paid to the ordinary shareholders, bearing in mind the desirability of a stable dividend policy. Given the reality of company control, it is unlikely that disgruntled shareholders will be able to challenge this decision.

It should be noted that depreciation allowances constitute a significant form of internal financing. While it is true that depreciation is the setting aside of funds to replace existing assets, it has the effect of reusing those funds for other uses during the lives of the assets in question. Depreciation allowances do not simply lie idle until some future date when they are needed. In the interim, they are likely to be used for the purchase of other assets.

For the new venture and small business this form of "self" finance is virtually the only type of finance available until it has established itself. It is therefore important to keep expenses to a minimum in the initial stages of the business.

Some of the larger sources of capital from within the average small business are likely to be available through more effective expense control. Three aspects are of special importance:

- Owner withdrawals should be consistent with the needs of the business and can often be cut drastically when capital is needed.
- Certain operations performed in traditional ways may be done according to less expensive methods, for instance changing personal service to self-service.
- Closer control over payroll, rent, publicity and other major expenses may be possible.

This does not necessarily mean reduction of the rand-and-cents expenditures but, rather, securing maximum profitable returns from every expenditure. These procedures also greatly strengthen the firm's borrowing position if outside financing is still needed.

8.5.4 Long-term loans/mortgage bonds

This form of finance can only be considered if the company owns immovable property that is not encumbered or only partly encumbered by a mortgage bond. As repayment periods on mortgage bonds are normally 20 to 30 years, this is an easy source of finance. It can be used for bridging purposes or to finance a specific long-term project. You will need the funds to pay the fees of registering the bond upfront.

8.6 Institutions that support small and new business ventures

There are a number of government, non-governmental and private enterprises involved in financing new and existing ventures. In Chapter 9 on networking and support, the institutions involved are discussed in more detail. As the products and services change regularly, these are not discussed in detail. Entrepreneurs can approach any or all of the following institutions for finance of some sort:

- Commercial banks
- Merchant banks
- Business Partners
- Khula Enterprise Finance Agency (mostly through a commercial bank)
- Industrial Development Corporation
- Ithala Finance Corporation
- Local business support centres (a list is obtainable from Ntsika Enterprise Promotion Agency)

8.7 Informal sources of finance

Most small and micro-enterprises start with finance obtained from informal sources. This is often referred to as the three "Fs", namely Family, Fools and Friends. It is quite often the only and last resort of start-up entrepreneurs. The other source of finance is the so-called "grey market", although this has to a great extent been formalised in the microlending industry.

Many new business owners are encouraged in their enterprise by parents, relatives or friends who offer to supply loans to the firm to get it started. Quite often, no other sources are available after normal trade credit and supplier contracts have been utilised. It is unfortunate that many otherwise successful firms have been fraught with troubles because relatives or friends interfered with the operations. Mixing family or social relationships with business can be problematic. Many situations of this kind might have been averted if the terms of the loans had been more clearly specified, including the rights of the lenders to insist on making operational policy.

The best way to avoid subsequent problems is to make sure that loans are made on a businesslike basis. They should be viewed as business dealings. The right of the owner to make decisions should be respected by all parties involved. Arrangements for retiring such loans, including any options for early payment and the procedure if loans become delinquent, should be clearly understood. The owner should make sure that such loans are properly presented on the balance sheet – payments due

in one year are current liabilities; the others are fixed liabilities.

8.8 The venture capital and private equity market

Venture capital is the funding that is supplied to a firm during its earliest stages of development. The growth stage is where entrepreneurs can consider approaching venture capital firms for finance. Waiting until this stage is advantageous, because using venture capital in the start-up stage can mean giving away significant control of the new venture. The venture capital market focuses primarily on growth financing. Private venture capital firms seldom finance start-ups unless they are in the high-technological arena. Figure 8.2 illustrates the spectrum of venture capital and private equity finance in South Africa.

To put themselves in a better position to negotiate a deal, some entrepreneurs use mezzanine financing. This is a layer of subordinated debt between long-term debt and equity. Through subordination of the debt, creditors and financial institutions gain a "preference" claim in cases of liquidation or sequestration.

The venture capital firm invests in a growing business through the use of debt and equity instruments to gain long-term term appreciation on the investment within a specified period of time, typically five years. The venture capitalist also seeks varying rates of return, depending on the risk involved. Seed and start-up capital (early stage investment) will typically command a higher interest rate than finance in the later growth stages of a firm. Older, more established firms have a track record and financial history on which forecasts can be based. Normal business cycles and income patterns have been identified and the firm is usually in a better position to respond through experience to a dynamic environment (Allen 1999: 498).

What do venture capitalists look for? Usually, the first thing they rate highly is a management team with a good track record and the ability to take the firm to the next level of growth. The business opportunity must be substantial and profitable and the product innovative. The potential for significant growth, feasible exit options and a strategic fit with their fund or portfolio will also be important factors

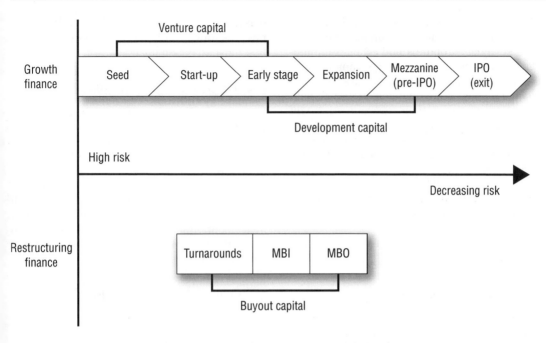

(Abbreviations used in the figure refer to initial public offering (IPO),
management buy-ins (MBIs) and management buyouts (MBO).)

Figure 8.2 The spectrum of venture capital and private equity finance in South Africa
Source: Adapted from Dyer (2001).

in their consideration. Table 8.2 sets out what venture capitalists look for in an investment.

When negotiating with venture capitalists, the entrepreneur should have a good sense of the value of his or her business and be properly prepared, as set out in the section on preparing and presenting applications for venture capitalists and private equity funding.

8.9 Attracting investors and the private placement of shares

Investment is a buying and selling process. The entrepreneur is trying to sell the venture as an investment opportunity, and the investor is looking to buy opportunities that offer a good return. Entrepreneurs need to understand the process of deal structuring, as well as the marketing-buying behaviour behind investment deals to manage it more effectively.

Venture capitalists reject the vast majority (over 95 per cent) of proposals made to them (Wickham 2001: 295). Though banks may back a higher proportion of proposals, rejections

Table 8.2 What venture capitalists look for

Attractive business opportunity
- Feasible business concept
- Profitability
- Large operating margins
- Large, sustainable growing markets

Competitive business venture
- Experienced and balanced management team
- Unique and competitive product or service

Feasible exit options
- Three to five years' harvest potential
- Global growth potential

Strategic fit with fund or portfolio
- Stage of the firm in the venture life cycle
- Size and terms of the investment
- Industry sector
- Skills and experience required for the industry sector

still greatly outnumber acceptances. Even if the business idea is sound, entrepreneurs need to make sure that proposals and other communications to financial backers are sympathetic to their information needs, that they are well constructed as pieces of communication, will help the investors make their decision and will reflect positively on the professionalism of the entrepreneur. This will ensure that the investment in time and money in preparing the proposal is well spent.

Wickham (2001: 289) gives a model of the process of attracting investors and/or seeking private placement of shares. The model is outlined in Figure 8.3.

The five key stages in the investment process are set out below.

8.9.1 Stage 1: Making contact

The entrepreneur and the investor have to become aware of each other and make contact. This is also referred to as deal origination. It results mostly from a promotional activity by the entrepreneur, as few venture capitalists actually search for new opportunities. They wait for the entrepreneur, or more often a third party, to approach them. Commercial banks place the onus on the entrepreneur to make the first move to obtain finance.

8.9.2 Stage 2: Deal screening

Investors will do an initial evaluation of the proposal to see whether it fits in with the profile of their activities and/or their investment profile. Important criteria include the amount of investment being sought, the type of technology on which the venture is based, the industry sector of the venture and the stage of growth the venture is in. Before investors will make an investment, they need certain information about the venture. Thus the entrepreneur will need to answer questions such as:

- Is the venture of the right type?
- How much investment is required?
- What return is likely?
- What is the growth stage of the venture?
- What projects will the capital be used for?
- What is the potential of the venture?
- What are the risks for the venture?
- How does the investor get in?
- How does the investor get out?

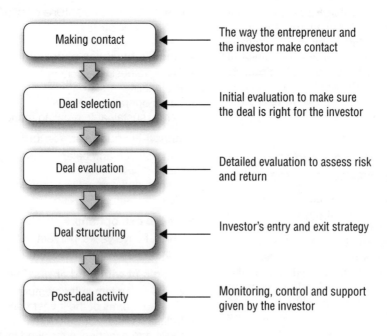

Figure 8.3 The process of attracting investors

Source: Adapted from Wickham (2001: 289).

- What post-investment monitoring procedures will be in place?
- What control mechanisms will be available?

8.9.3 Stage 3: Deal evaluation

The next stage will be a more detailed evaluation of the proposal. The objective of this exercise is to compare the returns offered by the venture to the risk that it faces. The key factors to be considered in this evaluation will be the potential for the venture in terms of the innovation it is offering, the conditions in the market it aims to develop, and the competitive pressures it will face. The ability of the management team behind the venture to actually deliver will also be a major consideration.

8.9.4 Stage 4: Deal structuring

Deal structuring refers to how the initial investment will be made and how the investor will see that investment bear fruit. The critical issues are how much the entrepreneur is seeking and over what period the investment is to be made. Critical aspects will be the actual return offered, how long the investor must wait before that return is seen, and the form it will take.

8.9.5 Stage 5: Post-investment activity

Investors usually prefer to retain a degree of involvement. There are two broad areas of post-investment activity: monitoring and control. Monitoring relates to the procedures that are put in place to enable the investors to evaluate the performance of the business so they can keep track of their investment. Investors may demand more frequent and detailed information going beyond purely financial data. Control mechanisms give the investor an active role in the venture and the power to influence the management's decision making. One common control mechanism is for the investor to be represented on the firm's management team, perhaps as a board member or director.

Entrepreneurs and investors meet through a process of communication. Communication is a human process involving not only the passage of information, but also an attempt to influence behaviour. Entrepreneurs communicate with investors not just because they wish to tell them about their ventures, but also because they want the investors to support them.

The process of communication between an entrepreneur and an investor is not just a matter of *what* of but also *how*. The entrepreneur can exert a positive influence on investors by understanding the questions they are asking, by ensuring that the answers to those questions have been explored and, where appropriate, by having hard evidence to back up the answers given.

8.10 The cost of raising finance

Raising finance for a new and growing business venture is a timely and costly process. For this reason many entrepreneurs prefer to grow slowly by using internal cash flow to fund growth. Some have a fear of debt and of giving up control of the firm to investors. The costs of funding are more than the interest rate on the funds obtained.

The costs of seeking funding for the business can be significant, as seen in Figure 8.4.

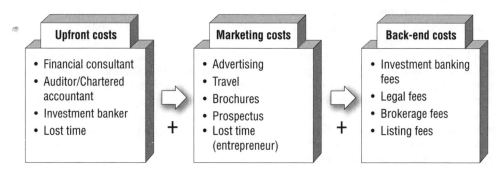

Figure 8.4 The cost of raising finance

Source: Adapted from Allen (1999).

The upfront costs refer to the preparation of the proposal, which will require inputs from specialists such as chartered accountants, financial consultants, the entrepreneur and possibly an investment banker. Experts in preparing loan and investment proposals understand the dynamics of potential funding sources and know exactly how to structure proposals. The maintenance of current financial statements is essential in the process of raising capital. If the entrepreneur is seeking equity capital, he or she might need a prospectus or an offering document that will require legal expertise and often has significant printing costs.

In addition to the upfront costs, there are also costs involved in marketing the offering, namely advertising, travelling and brochures. The cost to the entrepreneur in terms of time away from the business while preparing and marketing the proposal is difficult to quantify. There can also be certain back-end costs in situations where the entrepreneur seeks capital by selling securities. It will depend largely on the financial intermediary or institution used in raising the finance. Back-end costs can include investment banking fees, legal fees, brokerage fees and various other fees.

8.11 Initial public offering

"Going public", or the initial public offering (IPO), is quite often the ultimate way of raising growth capital. Allen (1999: 506) says it has an aura of prestige and represents an exciting time in the life of a rapidly growing business. The decision whether or not to go public is difficult at best. Once taken, it sets a series of events in motion that will change the business and the entrepreneur's relationship to it forever.

There is no "rule of thumb" as to when the firm must go public. It will need to meet the Johannesburg Securities Exchange's requirements for listing, in particular that of profit history for a specified number of years. In general, most firms consider it as an option once their need for growth capital has exceeded their debt capacity. The main advantage of a public offering is that it provides the venture with a great source of interest-free capital for growth and expansion, reducing debt, and for product and market development. A listed company has more prestige and clout in the marketplace. It is easier to form alliances and negotiate deals

with suppliers, customers, commercial banks and creditors. Founding members can harvest the rewards of their efforts by selling off a portion of their ordinary or preference shares. It is also a way of rewarding existing employees through share options.

The major disadvantage of listing is that everything the company does or has becomes public information subject to the scrutiny of anyone interested in the company. Public companies face intense pressure to perform financially in the short term. Investors expect immediate gains in earnings, revenues and share prices. The reporting requirements of public companies on the JSE are very strict and costly.

The public offering process is a very time-consuming and expensive process, which can take anything from four to 12 months and sometimes even longer. This is mainly because private companies seldom keep proper records or keep them in the format as required for public companies. The cost of going public (see also Figure 8.4) will exceed R10 million in most instances. Most of this will not need to be paid upfront, as it will be financed through the listing and issuing of shares in lieu of payment. In preparing for listing, it is suggested that entrepreneurs study the requirements of the JSE and set a long-term plan in motion to get financial and other information in place. It will help to spend the year or two prior to listing preparing for it by talking to others who have gone through the process, and reading and putting a team together that will see the firm through the offering.

8.12 Conclusion

Finding finance for a new and growing business venture is one of the difficulties experienced by entrepreneurs. Access to finance is acknowledged worldwide as being a barrier to entrepreneurship. Before embarking on the venture, the entrepreneur needs to determine the financial needs of the enterprise. It is important that the term of finance be matched with the expected lifespan of the asset or project that is being financed, so that the venture will not land up in a capital crunch. It is therefore important to take note of the various sources of finance available over the short, medium and long term.

The fast-growing firm will need access to finance to support the business growth. This will quite often require venture capital funding or an injection of private equity. In this chapter, the entrepreneur can find out what venture capital is, how investments are evaluated, as well as the process of attracting investors. Going public is quite often the ultimate way of raising growth capital and harvesting. This process has a number of advantages and disadvantages which one must be aware of.

Looking back

1. Describe the steps in predicting the financial needs of the venture.
   - Step 1: Project the firm's sales, revenues and expenses over the planning period.
   - Step 2: Estimate the levels of investment in current and fixed assets that are necessary to support the projected sales.
   - Step 3: Determine the firm's financing needs throughout the planning period.

2. List the sources of short-term finance available.
   - Trade credit
   - Bank credit
   - Bills of exchange
   - Acceptance credits
   - Factoring
   - Customer advance payments
   - Shipper's finance

3. List the sources of medium-term finance available.
   - Instalment sale
   - Leasing finance
   - Medium-term loans

4. List the sources of long-term finance available.
   - Equity capital
   - Debentures
   - Retained earnings
   - Long-term loans

5. Briefly describe what venture capitalists look for in an investment.

   An attractive business opportunity
   - Feasible business concept
   - Profitability
   - Large operating margins
   - Large, sustainable growing markets

   Competitive business venture
   - Experienced and balanced management team
   - Unique and competitive product or service

   Feasible exit options
   - Harvest potential within three to five years
   - Global growth potential

   Strategic fit with fund or portfolio
   - Stage of the firm in the venture life cycle
   - Size and terms of investment
   - Industry sector
   - Skills and experience required for the industry sector

6. List the five key factors in the process of attracting an investment.
   - Making contact
   - Deal screening
   - Deal evaluation
   - Deal structuring
   - Post-investment activity

Key terms

Acceptance credits
Bank credit
Bills of exchange
Customer advance payments
Deal evaluation
Deal origination
Deal screening
Deal structuring
Debentures
Equity capital

Factoring
Financial requirements
Going public
Initial public offering
Instalment sale transaction
Leasing finance
Long-term finance
Medium-term finance
Mortgage bonds
Ordinary shares

Overdraft facility
Preference shares
Private equity market
Private placement
Retained earnings
Shipper's finance
Short-term finance
Trade credit
Venture capital

Discussion questions

1. Discuss the different ways in which new and existing ventures can finance their businesses with debt.

2. Discuss whether commercial banks are prepared to finance new venture start-ups.

3. Discuss the ways in which fast-growing business ventures can finance their growth.

4. Discuss the advantages and disadvantages of listing on the Johannesburg Securities Exchange.

Case study

Shabangu Nursery

Frans Shabangu wants to open a citrus nursery near Tzaneen in the Limpopo province. Frans, who holds a B.Sc. degree in Agriculture, says Tzaneen and the lowveld region of Mpumalanga currently lack sufficient nurseries producing the exceptionally high quality of trees demanded by growers. The aim is to produce high-quality, disease-free, horticulturally superior plant material and to offer supporting services that would include a consultancy on technical matters.

The following portion of land, infrastructure and equipment are required for the production operations:

• 5 ha of land with permanent water and electrical supplies

• 2 x 2 m brick-built incubation room with heating and humidification facilities
• 12 x 6 m plastic-covered greenhouse
• 500 m² structure covered with insect-proof netting
• Water purification and liquid fertilisation plants
• Irrigation system
• Spray machine for pesticides
• Tractor and trailer

Frans has purchased a piece of land about 5 km from Tzaneen with an adjoining river. It also has an existing residence. The nearest competition is about 120 km away from this site. The start-up requirements for this new venture are as follows:

		Rand
Land and buildings		600 000
Vehicles:		385 000
A tractor	180 000	
A light delivery vehicle	180 000	
A trailer	25 000	
Furniture and fittings		20 000
Equipment		160 000
Irrigation system	45 000	
Greenhouse	25 000	
Insect-proof house	75 000	
Spray machine	15 000	
Stock		
R3,00 per tree for 50 000 trees		150 000
Overheads for the first year		300 000
Cash		25 000
Total estimated start-up cost		**1 640 000**

After buying the farm, Frans still has about R100 000 in cash available, but that is clearly not enough. He has prepared a comprehensive business plan and estimates a turnover in excess of R750 000 per annum, with a net profit of R450 000 per annum over the first two years. Thereafter the annual growth in profits will exceed 30 per cent per year. The problem, however, is that the production cycle of the nursery means that the first batch of trees will only be available for sale after 12 months.

Source: Adapted from SBDC (1994: 13.2–13.20).

Questions

1. Discuss the different options of finance available to Frans and whom he could approach.
2. Will this venture qualify for private venture and equity finance? Explain.

Experiential exercises

1. Visit a bank and learn at first hand what is required to obtain a loan for a new business venture.
2. Investigate the possibilities of funding a small business in your community and advise on the basis of a recommended priority which sources are best.
3. Visit a venture capital and/or private equity firm and determine the requirements it sets for funding business ventures.

Exploring the Web

1. Go to Khula Enterprise Finance Ltd at www.khula.org.za to find out about its guarantee schemes, as well as other financial assistance it offers new and small business ventures.

2. Visit Business Partners at www.business-partners.co.za to find out about the financial products.

3. Go to the following websites to find out what these firms offer in respect of venture capital and private equity funding:

- Viking at www.viam.co.za
- AMB Private Equity Partners at www.ambpartners.co.za
- Southern Africa Enterprise Development Fund at www.saefd.org.za
- Ethos Private Equity at www.ethos.org.za

4. Visit the Johannesburg Securities Exchange at www.jse.co.za and click on "Information" to get the guidelines for listing on the JSE.

References and recommended reading

Allen, K.R. 1999. *Growing and managing an entrepreneurial business.* Boston: Houghton Mifflin.

Bloom, J.Z. & Boessenkool, A.L. 2002. Financial management. In: Nieman, G. & Bennett, A. (Eds), *Business management: a value chain approach.* Pretoria: Van Schaik.

Dyer, T. 2001. *Introductory overview of venture capital in South Africa.* Lecture given at the South African Students Entrepreneurship Club (SASEC) at the University of Pretoria, Pretoria, November.

Small Business Development Corporation (SBDC). 1994. *How to start your own small business,* 4th ed. Johannesburg: SBDC.

Wickham, P.A. 2001. *Strategic entrepreneurship: a decision-making approach to new venture creation and management,* 2nd ed. Harlow: *Financial Times*/Prentice Hall.

Van Schaik Publishers

Networking and support

Menisha Adams

9.1 Introduction

Making a decision to start one's own business may seem quite adventurous at first, until one is struck by the harsh realities of the business world. In the previous chapters it was highlighted that the prospective entrepreneur has to consider a number of key concerns, such as resource requirements, legal aspects, financing and being able to get the business started. If one has no previous business experience, this may be too much to handle at one time.

Small, medium and micro-enterprises (SMMEs) are recognised as one of the key mechanisms for job creation globally. One of the first priorities of the new South African government was to begin a process of changing the environment in which small and medium businesses could operate. Prior to 1994, there was no strategy for the development and promotion of the small business sector in the country. It was only after the President's Conference on Small Business in 1995 that a new and innovative framework was put into place to support the development of this important sector of our economy (Van der Westhuizen et al. 2002).

The chapter attempts to identify the key role-players who have the task of establishing or creating an enabling small business environment, and to what extent emerging entrepreneurs may be able to benefit from it. Different forms of business support, such as counselling, mentoring, networking and incubation, are also highlighted.

9.2 The role of the government in developing an enabling small business environment

According to Nieman (2001), the National Small Business Act of 1996 paved the way for the Department of Trade and Industry to address SMME development in South Africa. The Act was developed after the publication of the *White Paper on the national strategy for the development and promotion of small business*

Learning outcomes

After completion of this chapter, you should be able to:
- Define an enabling small business environment
- Identify the objectives of the White Paper on the national strategy for the development and promotion of small business in South Africa
- Understand the National Small Business Enabling Act
- Understand business counselling and mentoring
- Understand business networking
- Understand business incubation
- Understand the different roles and functions of key players in developing small business, e.g. Khula, Ntsika, Business Partners and commercial banks

in South Africa and the first President's Conference on Small Business in March 1995.

The National Small Business Enabling Act, as its name indicates, intended to create a positive enabling environment for emerging and expanding SMMEs, with particular emphasis on the impediments faced by black entrepreneurs and others disadvantaged in the past.

The key objectives of the White Paper – the basis of SMME development in South Africa – are to:

- Create an enabling environment for small enterprises (refer to Figure 9.1)
- Facilitate greater equalisation of income, wealth and earning opportunities
- Strengthen the cohesion between small enterprises

- Prepare small businesses to comply with the challenges of an internationally competitive economy
- Address the legacy of apartheid-based disempowerment of black business
- Support the advancement of women in all business sectors
- Create long-term jobs
- Stimulate sector-focused economic growth
- Level the playing fields between bigger and small business, as well as between rural and urban businesses

It is the task of different role-players and organisations to accomplish these objectives. In the next section we discuss what an enabling small business environment means.

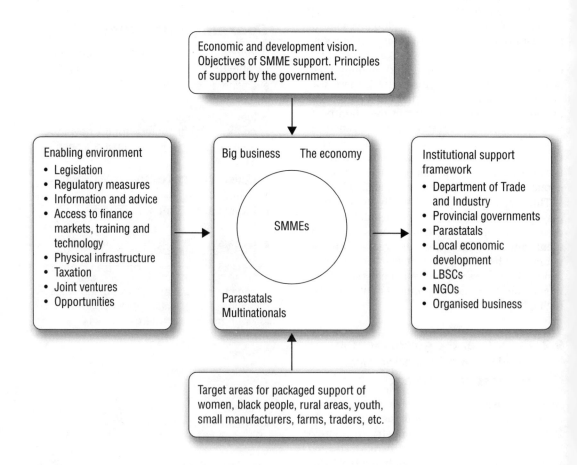

Figure 9.1 The South African national SMME support strategy

9.3 Defining an enabling small business environment

An enabling small business environment refers to a supportive environment in which emerging entrepreneurs can function. The government should help to establish this environment by means of legislation and policies. The environment should create a climate favourable to the entry of entrepreneurs by means of the following:

- Financing by ordinary financial institutions such as banks
- Venture capital access
- Training and development programmes to encourage entrepreneurship
- Infrastructural development – a prerequisite for any economic activity at an advanced level
- Deregulation with regard to economic activities, as well as legal regulations

In addition, a cooperative environment must be fostered in which other institutions also actively promote entrepreneurship, such as:

- Tertiary institutions for education and training
- Institutions giving business support, finance and/or training
- Involvement through SMME development units
- Non-governmental organisations (NGOs)
- International aid agencies

According to Kinunda-Rutashobya (1996), it is not the entrepreneur or the environment that matters, but rather the strategic actions of the entrepreneur or the firm, which outweigh the other elements. It is the ability of the entrepreneurs or the firms to modify the environments to their advantage rather than being subjected to predetermined situations and seeking to obtain a strategic fit with the environment.

Other interesting contextual perspectives of entrepreneurship by Kinunda-Rutashobya (1996) are that entrepreneurial activities and outcomes vary from one socio-economic context to another. These differences are due to differences in economic, political, historical and social circumstances, laws and the regulatory frameworks, policies and levels of state involvement, formal and informal socio-eco-

nomic institutions, the type and distribution of resources, sociocultural settings, etc. (Baume 1996). This view is further amplified by Morris and Lewis (1991), who argue that entrepreneurial motivations and behaviour are influenced by the political and economic systems (the infrastructure), rapid and threatening environmental change (turbulence) and one's life experience. Some contexts are considered to be conducive and others hostile to entrepreneurial outcomes and activities. Knowledge of the contextual factors should create more confidence in entrepreneurs and engender policy reform. Public policy reforms should, in turn, be able to provide the right infrastructure and institutions to stimulate the development and growth of businesses.

Themba and Chamme (1997) highlight that the sociocultural, economic, technological, political and legal environments have enduring influences on the development of personality attributes such as entrepreneurship. These environments can either facilitate or hinder the development of entrepreneurship in developing nations.

The cultivation of entrepreneurship in developing countries has met numerous obstacles. With proper planning and support from those in power, entrepreneurs can occupy their rightful place in the development of their countries. Entrepreneurs have an important contribution to make to the development process of developing countries, and with proper nurturing they can play a leading role.

9.4 Business support required by emerging entrepreneurs

Different entrepreneurs are faced with different challenges, but business support such as business counselling, mentoring, networking and incubation should be rewarding to all entrepreneurs.

9.4.1 Business counselling

By definition, business counselling is a process whereby business problems are diagnosed and resolved in such a way that the clients learn not only how to overcome their current difficulties, or exploit their opportunities, but also how to tackle similar situations in future (Stone 1999).

The aim of counselling is to boost individual and firm performance, and this is an ongoing process for development. One-on-one meetings should take place between the new venture owner and the experienced entrepreneur.

The counselling objectives should include the following:

- To identify problems and their source
- To evaluate actual performance against expected performance
- To develop action plans to bring performance up to minimum expectations

The need for new business counselling is to provide expert help in the start-up and growth process, a guiding hand, an anchor to hold onto in crises, to fill the skills deficiency gap and to avoid crisis management.

Business mentoring is an ongoing, long-term business counselling relationship between an experienced business adviser (or corporate executive) and a client, which covers a diverse range of topics as a business develops over time towards an agreed set of objectives.

9.4.2 Networking and networks for entrepreneurs

Networking is a useful tool in terms of "know-how" and "know-who", as critical external relationships contribute to business success. The information, knowledge and data gathered via networking are important resources for the entrepreneur. He or she is not expected to know everything from the start; however, it is important to know about networking and to develop networking skills.

■ What are networks?

Networks are patterned, beneficial relationships between individuals, groups or organisations that are used to secure critical economic and non-economic resources needed to start and manage a business. (Refer to Figure 9.2.)

■ Types of networks

Social networks refer to communication between different parties. An exchange of information usually takes place. It also refers to an exchange of goods and services, as well as normative exchanges based on social expectations.

Personal networks refer to those persons with whom one has a direct relationship and the focus is on the individual. These networks include direct ties linking the entrepreneur and those with whom he or she does direct business. The areas in which an entrepreneur would need to develop contacts are called a role set. Role sets might include partners, customers, suppliers, bankers, distributors, professional associations and family members. A direct tie is someone you know or whom you may have face-to-face communication with. It can either be strong or weak. A casual acquaintance would be a weak tie. A solid acquaintance is someone you could count on. An indirect tie would be someone you could contact through a direct relationship.

Extended networks focus on a network of firms and/or organisations rather than on an individual. Examples are the Afrikaanse Handelsinstituut (AHI), Nafcoc, etc.

■ Entrepreneurial networking

Entrepreneurial networking is the active process of setting up and maintaining mutually rewarding and cooperative relationships with other persons or businesses that can offer critical support for the development and growth of a business.

■ Networking principles

The first principle is reciprocity, and it refers to "give and take". The second principle highlights the importance of networking that should be built on friendship, good humour and sharing interests and activities. The third principle emphasises the need for networks to be constantly maintained. They are very hard to repair if broken by confrontation or neglect.

■ How to develop an effective network

- Identify people and organisations among existing connections who are close to potential shareholders.
- Seek criticism, advice and suggestions on the new venture from these people.
- Ask them for advice about contacts.
- Ask them what preparations are necessary.
- Tell existing contacts later how they have helped.

■ Functions of a network in the growth of a business venture

- It ensures that goals for growth and the vision of the entrepreneur are realistic.
- It increases the entrepreneur's level of aspiration.
- It helps to identify opportunities.
- It provides practical assistance.
- It provides emotional support.
- It provides a sounding board for ideas.

■ Other networks

Other networks can include the following:

- Internal networks such as formal and informal structures
- The Internet
- Using outside people resources such as a board of directors, attorneys, bankers and other lenders, accountants, consultants, advisers, etc.

9.4.3 Business incubation

Business incubation is a new and innovative system of support designed to nurture start-up and early stage enterprises in a managed workspace (Cassim 2001). A business incubator is a facility and set of activities through which entrepreneurs can receive the following:

- Essential information and assistance
- Value-added shared services and equipment

These may have been otherwise unaffordable, inaccessible or unknown to the entrepreneur. The business incubator provides an entrepreneurial and learning environment, ready access to mentors and investors, as well as visibility in the marketplace. Incubation is a fascinating concept and one in which a great deal of research needs to be undertaken. In South Africa it is still in the very early stages as a development modality. State support is still being witnessed. South Africa can benefit from the world experience in incubation.

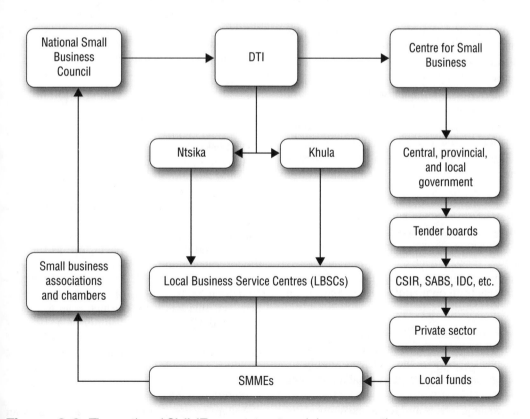

Figure 9.2 The national SMME support network in perspective

9.5 The role of the Department of Trade and Industry

The Department of Trade and Industry (DTI) has been set up to facilitate the most critical function of economic growth, which includes wealth and job creation. The DTI had to establish an implementation strategy for the delivery of programmes that would contribute to economic growth. This has resulted in the establishment of the institutional framework for supporting SMMEs. The institutions established for SMME development are Ntsika Enterprise Promotion Agency, Khula Enterprise Finance, and the National Small Business Council (now defunct). Thus far they have made some progress in delivering to the sector, but there are still shortcomings that need to be overcome.

9.5.1 The role and functions of Ntsika

The objectives of Ntsika are set out in the National Small Business Act of 1996. It states that Ntsika shall:

- Formulate and coordinate a national programme of policy research
- Collect and disseminate information concerning small business
- Facilitate the strengthening of small business service providers
- Channel finance to small business service providers to deliver accredited services
- Facilitate increased demand-side interventions

Ntsika promotes mainly business support centres and the government's three major efforts in getting out into the market:
- Local business service centres (LBSCs)
- Manufacturing advice centres
- Techno-entrepreneur programmes designed to concentrate on manufacturing support for SMMEs

In summary, Ntsika provides non-financial support to SMMEs. It does not give out loans or grants. Ntsika provides the following services:
- Management and entrepreneurial skills training
- Counselling, advice and technical support
- Service provider network development

- Institutional funding
- Research and the provision of information
- Programme design services
- Market access and business linkages
- Advice on tendering

9.5.2 The role and functions of Khula Enterprise Finance Limited

Khula Enterprise Finance Limited was established in 1996 in terms of a DTI initiative and operated as an independent, "limited liability" company. The importance of a body such as Khula to promote economic liberalisation and to provide support and incentives to both small and large enterprises cannot be overemphasised. It is imperative for aspiring and established businesses alike to be acquainted with both the roles envisaged and the various products offered by this institution.

Khula is a wholesale agency, which provides financial support for small businesses through intermediaries. Its financial products include loans, a national credit guarantee scheme, grants and institutional capacity building. The roles and functions of Khula are categorised into support for financial intermediaries as retail distribution networks, and direct services to SMMEs. In September 1998, a microlending scheme, Khula Start, was launched to meet the needs of SMMEs, mainly in the rural areas of the country. It provides loans of up to R3 000 to survivalist entrepreneurs.

According to Khula's website it is stated that it would guarantee loans, but does not provide the funding. Khula has other institutions or organisations that are responsible for the actual funding. Banks dealing with Khula have welcomed the enterprise's improved marketing strategy and it is already paying off, as seen by the increased numbers of loan applications and approvals (Bogopa 2002). Previously there was confusion as to how to access Khula's products, but this has been clarified. The first stop for an SMME to apply for support is a commercial bank, which has the responsibility of checking the application and recommending approval of an SMME loan in principle. Khula generally accepts the recommendations of the commercial banks.

According to Terblanche (2002), bank loan guarantees constitute Khula's most stable project, but the progress is slow and fraught with conflict. The project has assisted about 2 000 entrepreneurs to date. Khula is prepared to guarantee up to 80 per cent of a bank loan to an entrepreneur with little security, and expects banks to avail themselves sufficiently of the scheme. Khula's latest project, the Land Reform Credit Fund, is apparently making impressive progress. The fund grants soft loans to farmers willing to give disadvantaged communities a share of their land. Interest on the loans is usually 2 to 3 per cent below prime, depending on the extent of empowerment.

Despite the many challenges, Khula has accomplished a great deal since its inception, but much remains to be done.

9.5.3 The LBSC programme

The local business service centre (LBSC) programme is both a vehicle for local partnerships in development and a mechanism for encompassing and directing SMME development activities within a national development framework. This is achieved through practical programme partnerships between all three levels of government, local communities and the private sector.

At the national level, the LBSC programme contributes to a number of national development priorities. These include:

• Job creation
• Wealth creation
• Transformation and empowerment

At local level, the LBSC programme has been established to perform a number of important functions within local economies. These functions include:

• Increasing the access of local people to SMME support services
• Increasing opportunities for participation in local development efforts by local communities
• Providing a focal point for the expansion and development of local economic, employment and enterprise opportunities
• Increasing the flow of resources (e.g. money and expertise) into the local community

The core services of the LBSC programme are set out below.

■ Information

The provision of information to entrepreneurs is extremely useful. It can include technical publications on specific aspects of production; source books and guides on assessing viability; viable business opportunities; manuals or guides on market research and business planning; contact information of local enterprise development agencies and services.

■ Training

Training is usually provided to entrepreneurs to improve their competence in running an enterprise or its production processes. It may include technical training to improve technical skills and capacities of the enterprise; entrepreneurial training to improve entrepreneurship and management skills within the enterprise; organisational training to enhance the capacity of organisations such as LBSCs or small business membership organisations to represent their members or provide services to entrepreneurs.

■ Counselling and advisory services

Counselling or consultancy, like training, is provided to entrepreneurs to improve their competencies in running an enterprise. In contrast to training, counselling is a specifically tailored service provided to an individual enterprise or to small groups of enterprises, and usually addresses a particular problem.

■ Networking and linkages

Networking and linkages refer to the formulation of contracts, collaboration, clustering or twinning arrangements between and across firms. These can involve vertical (i.e. small firm to large) and horizontal linkages (e.g. small firms collaborating together), and can exist within a country or region or amongst firms in different countries. Networks and linkages are an important instrument for SMME development. They can be formed within specific industry sectors or regions, or by particular types of entrepreneurs to learn from each other rather than from people working outside the entrepreneurial setting.

The effectiveness or the results of the LBSC programme will only be determinable in the long run. Problems cited by Ntsika at present include incomplete or too little knowledge of the LBSC programme by people, and wrong or lacklustre approaches taken by LBSCs to achieve their objectives.

9.6 The role of the Industrial Development Corporation

Established in 1940, the Industrial Development Corporation of South Africa Limited (IDC) is a self-financing, state-owned national development finance institution. The core business of the IDC is to provide finance to entrepreneurs for the development of competitive industries. Even though the IDC is state-owned, it functions as an ordinary business, following normal company policy and procedures in its operations, paying income tax at corporate rates and dividends to its shareholders, while reporting on a fully consolidated basis.

The vision of the IDC is to be the primary force of commercially sustainable industrial development and innovation to the benefit of South Africa and the rest of the African continent. The primary objectives of the IDC are to contribute to the generation of balanced, sustainable economic growth in Africa and to the economic empowerment of the South African population, thereby promoting the economic prosperity of all citizens. The IDC achieves this by promoting entrepreneurship through the building of competitive industries and enterprises based on sound business principles.

The core strategies of the IDC are as follows:
- Maintaining financial independence
- Providing risk capital to the widest range of industrial projects
- Identifying and supporting opportunities not yet addressed by the market
- Empowering emerging entrepreneurs
- Promoting medium-sized manufacturing
- Establishing local and global involvement and partnerships in projects that are rooted in or benefit South Africa, the Southern African Development Community (SADC) and the rest of Africa
- Investing in human capital in ways that systematically and increasingly reflect the diversity of the African continent

The operations (Projects and Sector Divisions) of IDC are streamlined into strategic business units (SBUs) to ensure an industry-specific focus and the delivery of high-quality, innovative services to both traditional and new customer bases.

The Projects Division SBUs include the following:
- The Agri-Projects SBU that provides expertise and finance to promote development in the agriculture, aquaculture, fishing and related value-added industries
- The Mining and Beneficiation SBU that provides financial and technical assistance for the development of mining and metal projects in South Africa
- The Oil, Gas and Chemicals SBU focuses on the chemicals sector in South Africa, specifically empowerment opportunities within the chemicals sector, and on exploiting the considerable opportunities for developing the oil and gas sector in the rest of Africa.
- The Public–Private Partnership SBU supports projects involving private sector participants in e-business, energy, oil and gas, privatisation initiatives, transportation, information technology and telecommunications.

The Industrial Sectors Division SBUs include:
- Agro-industries
- Chemicals and allied industries
- Entrepreneurial mining and beneficiation
- Metal, transport and machinery products
- Textiles, clothing, leather and footwear
- Wood, paper and other industries

The Services Sectors Division SBUs include:
- Empowerment
- Media and motion pictures
- Techno-industries
- Tourism
- Wholesale and bridging finance

The IDC provides numerous financial products (see www.idc.co.za), each of which is discussed under the following headings:
- Who it is aimed at
- How it works
- Who should apply
- Whom to contact

It is the aim of the IDC to match its financing packages to the needs of the project. Its financing instruments include equity, quasi-equity, limited recourse finance, commercial loans, wholesale finance, share warehousing, export/import finance, short-term trade finance, and guarantees. Selecting the IDC as an investment partner makes sound business sense.

9.7 The role of Business Partners

Business Partners is an unlisted public company with an asset base of more than R1,2 billion. Business Partners currently has a network of offices located in all major cities and towns in South Africa.

Business Partners invests in viable small and medium enterprises (SMEs) in the commercial, manufacturing and service sectors of the economy, with no particular preference. There are, however, a few exceptions such as on-lending, non-profit-oriented organisations and farming operations, which will not be considered.

Business Partners finances the following:

- Start-ups
- Expansions
- Take-overs
- Management buyouts (MBOs)
- Management buy-ins (MBIs)
- Leveraged buyouts (LBOs)

The entry level is normally more than R150 000 but will not exceed R15 million. The decisive criteria for assessing whether to, or how much to invest, are based on viability. Although security offered forms part of the risk assessment, a lack of adequate security does not necessarily disqualify an application. Business Partners offers the following:

- A flexible approach to doing business
- A business opportunity – it is prepared to make investments when other institutions are not
- Peace of mind – viability is evaluated by an independent party
- Investment decisions based on sound business and investment principles
- Information, advice and guidance on business-related issues
- Regular aftercare – business advisers and mentors visit the business to offer advice and

guidance, or merely act as a sounding board – for a fee
- Broad industry knowledge, expertise and networks
- Fair and equitable rates, terms and conditions, even in times when the business is under pressure
- Access to further finance
- Personal service – each client is allocated to a portfolio manager who will ensure personal professional service
- A credible company with a proven track record

9.8 The role of commercial banks

There has been criticism that banks do not help new business ventures with finance. Banks, however, are business ventures like any other and have to minimise and manage their risk. In recent years, there have been welcome signs that commercial banks are paying increasing attention to the needs of SMMEs. Many innovative financing schemes have been introduced to assist particular types of SMME clients. It is not within the scope of this chapter to explore all the products and services offered by all the banks. We will briefly look at what the major banking groups are offering. Bear in mind that these products and services change on a regular basis.

9.8.1 Standard Bank

Standard Bank's research and experience with small businesses have shown that small businesses seek a bank that provides effective, efficient and safe transactional methods more than provision of start-up capital or credit. To address this need, SBSA developed the following products to assist its clients:

- A package on planning and financing an SME
- A booklet on SMEs entitled, "A business of your own"
- SME Business Plan and Loan Application
- SME Call Line
- Public Liability and Personal Accident Insurance for SMEs
- Business deposits via the ATM
- SME AutoBank card
- Owner Loan Protection Plan

The product range offered by SBSA for start-up businesses is not user-friendly for the average person with no business background. Emerging entrepreneurs who are seeking finance are therefore being faced with their first obstacle, namely to understand these documents. SBSA does not offer the "hand-holding service" that these entrepreneurs need and they are left to themselves to prepare the documents in the format prescribed by SBSA. This problem applies to most banks.

9.8.2 First National Bank

First National Bank (FNB) offers the following financing specifically related to new and small businesses:

- The SME Investments (SMEI) programme could be classified as a form of early stage venture capital. It is run in partnership with the Small Business Project (SBP). The fund has been structured to take advantage of the many opportunities opening up for the sector while simultaneously addressing the key obstacles confronting emerging business. SME Investments provides financing in the region of R250 000 to R1 million to companies that meet the criteria.

- FNB's small business support, specifically financing, takes place through its SME segment. This division offers finance primarily to franchisees, but also makes smaller amounts available to non-franchised start-up businesses. There are also certain criteria that must be met.

- The Export Finance Scheme was introduced by the Department of Trade and Industry to help promote exports by underwriting finance made available to approved exporters. The advantage of this scheme is that exporters are provided with the required working capital in order to manufacture and/or produce the goods for export without affecting their normal bank credit facilities. Interest is charged at FNB's prime overdraft rate.

Other banking products include:
- Business plan guidelines
- Business/technical assistance
- Specialised trade services

9.8.3 NedEnterprise

NedEnterprise is a specialised small and medium business finance unit within Reconstruction and Corporate Affairs of Nedcor Bank Ltd. It offers a one-stop, full-service relationship banking via skilled, professional business development managers. NedEnterprise offers assistance to SMEs on the basis of sound and acceptable business principles, but adopts a slightly unconventional and flexible approach when assessing an application for finance.

According to NedEnterprise's website, different financial institutions cater for various amounts and types of finance. It is therefore the objective of NedEnterprise to make an expert contribution to the SME sector – thus helping to create vitally needed jobs, improve the level of skills and generate wealth.

NedEnterprise can finance loans between R50 000 and R1,5 million. The bank requires a contribution from the entrepreneur of at least 25 per cent, which can consist of either income-generating assets or cash. Various types of collateral are considered as security for loans, for example business assets, investments, mortgage bonds and insurance policies. However, people who are not in a position to provide adequate or acceptable security can approach Khula for a guarantee.

NedEnterprise does not finance all types of business, especially businesses whose main activities relate to the agriculture, transportation or construction industry. Its interest rates are competitive, linked to the prime lending rate, and are negotiable, depending on the risk associated with the entrepreneur's business.

Applications for finance are usually processed within ten working days. There are underlying charges involved, such as a 1 per cent administration fee on approved loans, legal fees such as bond registration fees where applicable, 3 per cent Khula fees, revenue stamps and valuation fees.

9.8.4 ABSA

The ABSA Banking Group realises that the South African banking sector is very competitive and thus, in order for it to succeed, there is a need to offer products and services aimed at adding value to the SME sector and facilitating business growth that will boost the economy.

The ABSA Bank Group offers a number of tailored-made products for providing support to the SME sector:

- ABSA has designed an innovative business support tool targeting SMEs, known as the ABSA Business Banking Toolbox, which offers a complete business guide with 14 brochures. These cover various aspects of starting and managing a business but, most importantly, how the bank can help the entrepreneur to achieve success.

- ABSA, as one of the leading banks in South Africa, has gained substantial ground in the SME sector and has proven that it is serious about having a good presence in the market. It does this by offering tailor-made products to businesses and making sure that it is innovative in its approach as far as possible. In fact, ABSA has shown a remarkable understanding of the vital pillars of entrepreneurial ventures, which are innovation, strategic objectives and growth potential, despite any challenges that exist in the market.

Emerging entrepreneurs should close the gap between themselves and banks by conducting proper research on the types of funding available, before approaching a commercial bank for assistance.

9.9 Conclusion

Samli (2002) maintains that entrepreneurship cannot be developed all by itself. It is critical to develop an entrepreneurship-friendly atmosphere. This chapter attempted to explore the support available to emerging entrepreneurs to enable them to make a success of their business ventures. Business support such as counselling, mentoring, networking and incubation was highlighted and discussed.

The small business enabling environment was discussed, and the roles and functions of key players such as the Department of Trade and Industry, Khula, Ntsika, Business Partners and the commercial banks identified. Despite the government's commitment to the creation of a supportive SMME environment, its efforts have been met with mixed results (Viviers 2001). In the end, the entrepreneur must realise, as well as feel, that he or she is not alone in the challenging business world.

Looking back

1. Describe how an enabling business environment can be created.
   - Financing should be made available by ordinary financial institutions such as banks
   - There should be adequate access to venture capital.
   - Training and development programmes should encourage entrepreneurship.
   - Infrastructural development is a prerequisite for any economic activity at an advanced level.
   - Deregulation with regard to economic activities, as well as legal regulations, is necessary.

2. List the institutions that can help to create a cooperative business environment.
   - Tertiary institutions for education and training

   - Institutions giving business support, finance and/or training
   - Involvement through SMME development units
   - NGOs
   - International aid agencies

3. Briefly discuss the different types of business networks.
   - Social networks refer to communication between different parties. An exchange of information, goods and services usually takes place.
   - Personal networks refer to those persons with whom one has a direct relationship, and the focus is on the individual.
   - Extended networks focus on a network of firms and/or organisations rather than on an individual. Examples are AHI, Nafcoc, etc.

4. List the support services provided by Ntsika.
   - Management and entrepreneurial skills training
   - Counselling, advice and technical support
   - Service provider network development
   - Institutional funding
   - Research and the provision of information
   - Programme design services
   - Market access and business linkages
   - Advice on tendering.

5. Identify at least five reasons why an entrepreneur should consider doing business with Business Partners.
   - The organisation has a flexible approach to doing business.
   - It offers a business opportunity and is pre-pared to make investments when other institutions are not.
   - It offers peace of mind – viability is evaluated by an independent party.
   - It offers investment decisions based on sound business and investment principles.
   - It offers information, advice and guidance on business-related issues.

6. Briefly describe what counselling objectives should entail.
   Counselling objectives should:
   - Identify problems and their source
   - Evaluate actual performance against expected performance
   - Develop action plans for bringing performance up to minimum expectations

Key terms

Business counselling
Business incubation
Business mentoring
Business Partners
Business support
Contextual perspectives
Department of Trade and Industry
Emerging entrepreneurs
Enabling small business environment
Entrepreneurial motivations
Entrepreneurial networking

Environmental change
Export Finance Scheme
Industrial Development Corporation
Khula
LBSC programme
Linkages
National Small Business Act
Networking
Ntsika
SME Investments

Discussion questions

1. What is the aim of business counselling?
2. Explain the term "entrepreneurial networking".
3. How can an entrepreneur develop effective networks?
4. Identify the advantages of business incubation.

5. What role does the Department of Trade and Industry play in creating an enabling small business environment?
6. Briefly discuss the core services provided by the LBSC programme.
7. Commercial banks can play a key role in assisting entrepreneurs. Discuss.

Case studies

Case study 1: Bitline SA

Ms Vivian Mhaga and Gladys Tyapholwana were previously involved in community development projects. During their work they discovered a huge need for providing employment opportunities for their communities, but did not know how to go about doing this. They were also not certain whom to approach for advice on how to start a business and how to register a company.

Source: Adapted from the BRAIN website.

Questions:
1. Whom do you think they should approach first to acquire business advice?
2. How could the LBSC programme be of help to them?

Case study 2: Baatile Printers, Gauteng

Baatile Printers is a woman-owned, silk screen printing company. The owner, Ms Baatile Ramokwoane, is a product of the incubation programme of the Mamelodi Technical College. Since her days at the incubation programme, Ms Ramokwoane has been using the BRAIN website extensively. She has used it for the business plan for her business, for tendering information, for obtaining a list of financial institutions and for acquiring premises for her expanding business, which now employs two people.

Source: Adapted from the BRAIN website.

Questions
1. Describe business incubation in your own words.
2. Identify the advantages of business incubation.

Experiential exercises

1. Visit three commercial banks in your area and find out what services (if any) they provide to emerging entrepreneurs.
2. Contact the head office of Business Partners to find out what kind of services or support they can offer to persons who wish to expand their business.
3. You would like to establish business networks for your business. How would you go about doing it?

Exploring the Web

Visit the following websites to obtain the latest information on what these organisations have to offer in new business venture support:
- The government at www.parliament.gov.za/na/index/asp
- Ntsika at www.ntsika.org.za
- Khula at www.khula.org.za
- Department of Trade and Industry at www.dti.gov.za
- FNB at www.fnbinvest.co.za/trade/expfinance.htm
- IDC at www.idc.co.za
- BRAIN at www.brain.org.za
- NedEnterprise at www.nedenterprise.co.za

References and recommended reading

Aldrich, H. & Zimmer, C. 1986. Entrepreneurship through social networks. In: Sexton, D. & Smiler, R. (Eds), *The art and science of entrepreneurship*. New York: Ballinger.

Baume, S.K. 1996. Entrepreneurship: a contextual perspective, discourses and praxis of entrepreneurial activities within the institutional context of Ghana. *Lund Studies in Economics and Management,* 28. Lund: Lund University Press.

Bogopa, K. 2002. *The role and functions of Khula Enterprise Finance.* Unpublished MPhil assignment. Pretoria: University of Pretoria.

Cassim, S. 2001. *The South African business incubation experience: an exploratory study.* Paper presented at the Internationalising Entrepreneurship Education (IntEnt) Conference, Kruger Park. 2-4 July.

Dubini, P. & Aldrich, H. 1991. Personal and extended networks are central to the entrepreneurial process. *Journal of Business Venturing,* 6(5): 305-314.

Industrial Development Corporation of South Africa Limited (IDC). 2002. Generic brochure. Johannesburg: IDC.

Khula Enterprise Finance Limited. 2001. *Annual report.* Johannesburg: Khula.

Kinunda-Rutashobya, L. 1996. African entrepreneurship and small business development: a conceptual framework. In: Kinunda-Rutashobya, L. & Olomi, D.R. (Eds), *African entrepreneurship and small business development.* Dar es Salaam: DUP.

Molefe, O. 2002. *The role of the Department of Trade and Industry and the national and provincial small business councils (or SMME desks) in South Africa.* Unpublished MPhil assignment. Pretoria: University of Pretoria.

Morris, M.H. & Lewis, P.S. 1991. The determinants of societal entrepreneurship: an environmental per-

spective. *American Marketing Association (AMA) Educators' Proceedings.* Enhancing knowledge development in marketing, 2 (Summer): 583-591.

Nieman, G. 2001. Training entrepreneurs and small business enterprises in South Africa: a situational analysis. *Education and Training,* 43(8/9): 445-450.

Ntsika Enterprise Promotion Agency. 2001. *Annual report.* Pretoria: Ntsika.

Samli, A.C. 2002. *Entrepreneurship and small business development: the necessary ingredient for economic progress.* Paper presented at the International Management Development Association Conference, Turkey, 10-14 July.

South Africa. 1995. *White Paper on the national strategy for the development and promotion of small business in South Africa.* Cape Town: Government Printer.

Stone, F.M. 1999. *Coaching counseling and mentoring: how to choose and use the right technique to boost employee performance.* New York: American Management Association.

Terblanche, B. 2002. Khula: some business speed bumps. *Finance Week,* 2 October: 53-54.

Themba, G. & Chamme, M. 1997. *Impact of macro-environmental factors on entrepreneurship development in developing countries.* Revised version of a paper presented at an International Conference on African Entrepreneurship and Small Business Management, Dar es Salaam, 23-24 October.

Van der Westhuizen, J. 2002. *The roles and functions of Ntsika Enterprise Promotion Agency.* Unpublished MPhil assignment. Pretoria: University of Pretoria.

Viviers, S. 2001. *Identifying small business problems in the South African context for proactive entrepreneurial education.* Paper presented at the Internationalising Entrepreneurship Education (IntEnt) Conference, Kruger Park, 2-4 July.

Alternative routes to entrepreneurship

10

Entering the family business

Gideon Maas

10.1 Introduction

Joining the family business is one route to entrepreneurship. It is an option for those people who have parents or grandparents who have an operating business venture. The limited job opportunities in South Africa after school or even university have made this option far more attractive in recent years.

The importance of family businesses is recognised throughout the world and enjoys growing support in developing and developed economies. In Western Europe, for example, it is estimated that family businesses contribute between 45 and 65 per cent of the gross national product and that they represent between 75 and 95 per cent of registered companies. In America, 95 per cent of all corporations are family controlled (Chicago Family Business Centre n.d.: 3). In these cases, family businesses are mainly small to medium sized, and are regarded as the most important job creation mechanism. Against this backdrop, it can be assumed that family businesses can also make an important contribution to the development and growth of South Africa's socio-economic environment.

A family business is not a normal business because of the involvement of family issues that are, by nature, more emotional. In addition to the problematic nature of family businesses is the fact that their contribution to socio-economic growth has never really received sufficient attention in South Africa. Objections like, "Who wants to do business with family?", or "Stay away from family in business!", or "It is difficult enough to accept him as a family member and now you expect me to go into business with him?" have aggravated the situation. These are all too familiar phrases in the South African environment and may be a reason why family businesses have not received adequate attention until now.

This chapter will provide an overview of family businesses and offer selective guidelines for the successful management of such a business. This is done to facilitate a positive attitude towards the concept of a family business.

Learning outcomes

After completion of this chapter, you should be able to:

- Understand the nature of family businesses
- Have a positive mindset towards family businesses
- Apply selective principles in the South African family businesses environment

10.2 Defining family businesses

There are numerous and varied definitions of family businesses, based on aspects such as percentage of ownership, voting rights, power with regard to strategic directions, and active management by family members. However, a simplified and practical definition for a family business can be formulated as follows:

> A family business is one that is influenced by family ties in order to achieve the vision of the family over, potentially, several generations.

With the above definition in mind, the following general remarks can be made to aid our understanding of what constitutes a family business:
- The family (or a part thereof) is actively involved in that particular business.
- Family members have a definite input into the strategic direction of the business.
- There is more than one family member involved in the business.
- The intention is to continue the family business over time.

There is an observable trend in South Africa that more husband and wife teams are joining hands in business. Within the above framework, however, these cannot be regarded as family businesses as such. If they are getting more family members involved and/or their children, and they want to continue with the business into the next generation, then it becomes a family business. Husband and wife teams without the intention to create a family business will be regarded as "co-preneurs".

In terms of influencing the strategic direction of a family business, the family should own the majority of shares and/or the members of the family should hold a significant number of the top management positions. Therefore, the shares might be less than 50 per cent but can still be the majority shareholding, or the number of family members on a board will ensure that strategic decisions are taken that are in line with family values.

10.3 Systems in family businesses

Essentially, there are two broad systems in a family business: the family and the business (Figure 10.1). The family system is a social system that focuses on caring for its members and can therefore be regarded as more emotional. Questions like, "What is good for the family?" could lead to actions becoming more conservative, which in turn could result in changes not being readily accepted. The protection of the family's name and reputation could become more important than the exploitation of new ideas. Entrepreneurship is therefore negatively influenced, which may cause the stagnation of the business.

The main characteristic of business in general is that it is task orientated. In order to survive in a rapidly changing environment, new ideas are continually being identified and turned into opportunities. Change is therefore a way of living. In order to maintain a balance with change, the focus falls on productive action. Relations between employer and employee are therefore of a contractual nature and are aimed particularly at productivity or the exploitation of new opportunities.

Success in a family business can only be ensured if the two broad systems (family and business) are balanced. If one system dominates the other, negative conflict can be expected, which could destroy the family business. These two systems can, however, be further divided into subsystems. The family system can

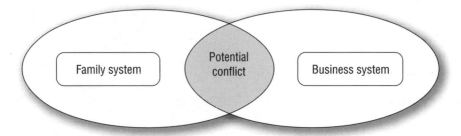

Figure 10.1 The two broad systems of a family business

comprise the family, family by marriage, parents, brothers and sisters, family inside and outside the business. Every member of the family system should know exactly where they fit into the total system and what their rights and privileges are. Even the business system consists of various subsystems such as managers, owners, employees and external networks.

The above model can be expanded to give a truer reflection of the complexity of a family business (Figure 10.2).

The different roles are as follows:

1. Family members
2. Non-family investors
3. Non-family employees
4. Family shareholders
5. Non-family working owners
6. Working family members
7. Working family owners
8. Family owners and business leaders

From the figure it is quite clear that all these different roles must be managed in such a way that conflict is minimised. Role clarification is therefore a critical activity within the family business. Add to this the life cycle theories (different stages in one's life), and a true challenge exists for the members of a family business! One finds that the owner of a family business, who is approaching his sixties, is more concerned with retirement than his 30-year-old child, who still wants to pursue new opportunities. These conflicting expectations can be a cause of contention if not managed carefully.

10.4 Problems in family businesses

It stands to reason that if the systems of family businesses are not in harmony, then conflict might have a detrimental effect on the long-term survival and growth of the business. These problems are clear from the following facts:

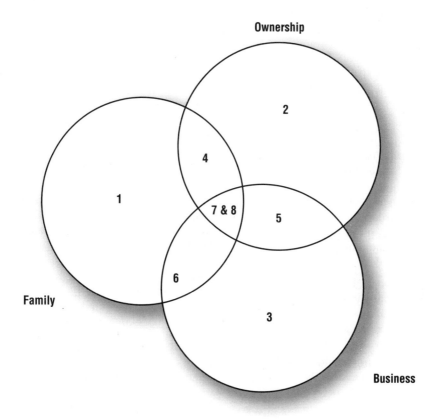

Figure 10.2 The three-circle model

Source: Murray, B. 2001. Travelers in time. *Families in Business*, Autumn, 37.

- Only 30 per cent of family businesses are successful into the second generation.
- Only 10 per cent of family businesses are successful into the third generation.
- The average lifespan of a family business is 24 years – the average time that the founder-manager stays in business.
- Family businesses become less entrepreneurial when the family system dominates.

Lank (2000: 195) adds the following list of specific problems of family businesses:

- Failure to find capital for growth without diluting the family's equity
- Inability to balance optimally the family's needs for liquidity and the business's need for cash
- Poor estate planning and the inability of the next generation to pay inheritance taxes
- Lack of willingness of the older generation to "let go" of ownership and management power at an appropriate moment
- Inability to attract and retain competent and motivated family successors
- Unchecked sibling rivalries with no consensus having been reached on the chosen successor
- Inability to attract and retain competent senior non-family professional managers
- Unmanaged conflict between the cultures of the family, the board and the business

The following are typical South African problems that can be added to the above list:

- Favouritism can result in nepotism, i.e. family members are appointed without real concern for expertise.
- Expectations were not clarified among members (e.g. a father bought a business with the intention to hand it over to his children in future but neglected to ask them whether they wanted to be involved in that business).
- Family conflicts were never addressed before commencing with the family business because "the business will sort it out".
- There is a lack of entrepreneurial initiatives because they were not needed in a stable environment or members were not trained according to that mindset.

- Divorce can lead to the destruction of a family business.
- Members of the family business emigrate to other countries, thus destroying the dream of a family business.

All these hindrances could create the impression that a family business should be avoided at all costs! However, that is not the case at all. The above problems illustrate the uniqueness of family businesses. One must therefore be aware of them before starting such a business, and manage them properly whilst in the business.

There are various reasons why a family business is really a good place to be, apart from the macro-indicators (e.g. employment, contribution to gross domestic product) already discussed. Some of the positive aspects of a family business are:

- A strong family culture can ensure that the business will survive over generations.
- Greater sensitivity will exist for the business and its stakeholders, thus minimising clinical business decisions.
- A better sense of community will exist between the various members, which is necessary for growing the business.
- Jobs are created and ensured, which can lead to greater social stability, especially in South Africa where unemployment is currently quite high.
- Specialist knowledge and experience of the business are created. This is transferred to the younger generations over breakfast table discussions. In a global economy, specialists in given fields are needed to maintain a successful business.
- More freedom exists to develop one's creative potential because family businesses are mostly small and medium sized. Decisions are also made and implemented faster.

The question is, how can one go about creating and maintaining a highly successful family business? Although various strategies can be identified, three vital aspects are succession, family councils and advisory boards. These issues will be discussed in the following sections. Due to its relative newness in South Africa, statistics for this important sector are still very scarce.

However, information that will be used to highlight the South African situation was obtained from observations and from 266 respondents who participated in family business workshops presented by the author during 1998.

10.5 Succession

One of the main aspects ensuring the survival of a family business is succession. Succession is the process through which the leadership of the business is transferred from the existing leader to a subsequent family member or non-family member (a professional manager).

However, the following obstacles to succession could result in few family businesses being transferred successfully to a second and third generation:

- The founder is autocratic and does not want to transfer leadership.
- The existing leader acts as though he will never die.
- A child-stays-child scenario ("How can my child tell me what to do?")
- The existing leader misinterprets environmental trends and does not implement changes in time.
- The leader does not want to make a choice with regard to a possible successor.
- The leader selects a successor who can be his or her "slave".

Even the management style of the leader can influence succession. According to Lank (2000: 199), the different styles are as follows:

- *Monarchs:* They do not leave office until they are decisively forced out through death or an internal "palace revolt".
- *Generals:* They are forced out of office, but plot their return, and quickly come back out of retirement to "save" the business.
- *Ambassadors:* They leave office gracefully and frequently serve as post-retirement mentors.
- *Governors:* They rule for a limited term of office, retire, and switch to other vocational outlets.

Succession is not always a natural process in a family business. It remains one that should be carefully managed. In order to help the leader with the matter of succession, the following critical questions identified by Aronoff and Ward (1992: 14) should be answered:

- Am I committed to family succession?
- Is it a viable dream that I have?
- Is it really a dream that I have?
- Will my spouse and I be financially independent if I retire?
- Have I selected a successor?
- Is there life after retirement?
- Do I trust key personnel in the business?
- Do I have the ability to delegate?
- Am I prepared to take risks?

If the leader has decided to go ahead with succession, the following options are open to him or her:

- Appoint a family member.
- Appoint a caretaker manager if the family manager is still too young to take over.
- Appoint a professional manager if no family manager wants to take over the management of the business.
- Liquidate the business.
- Sell the business, in whole or in part.
- Do nothing, i.e. adopt a wait-and-see approach.

However, if a parent is still young and does not want to retire yet, other strategies can be followed, for instance:

- The child(ren) can first gain wider experience in other industries or organisations and/or countries. This is also called a delayed entry into the family business and has the advantage that the child first gains experience elsewhere before entering the family business. The child-stays-child problem can be overcome in such a manner.
- The child(ren) can be employed as normal employees where justified. They then learn the business from shop-floor level and gain detailed knowledge and experience. A negative result might be inbreeding, which can be detrimental to entrepreneurship.
- New projects can be started in which the children are interested and where they can be given an opportunity to express themselves in these projects. This can be inside or outside the business. To a certain extent this is a combination of the first two strategies.

From the above it might appear as if the leader of the business is the sole factor in determining the success of succession. This is only partly true, as the successor and the rest of the family have an equally important role to play. Social harmony, which is essential for successful succession, can only be created if all the stakeholders are satisfied with the total process. Involvement in, and transparency of, the whole process of succession are therefore critical elements.

It is also true that no two successions will be the same due to, inter alia, different family cultures, the age differences between the children and the parents, and the industry involved. A family could have an open relationship where successions will be openly discussed. If the parents are still young, then they will probably not see the urgency in discussing succession. If it is a stable industry, then the need for succession plans is also not foreseen because it is business as usual! The truth of the matter is, however, that no one can really predict when succession is necessary and, therefore, one needs to start with the procedure sooner rather than later. Otherwise it might come down to a forced decision, which could derail the whole process.

Succession planning in South African business is not well supported. Probable reasons for this are:

- The family business is still in the first generation and therefore not established yet.
- The business is not big enough for its owners to worry about succession.
- The children are not interested in joining the business.
- The parents may be afraid of family conflict if a successor is selected.

Where a succession plan does exist, it may not always be clear to other stakeholders who the successor is going to be; the successor is not always accepted by everybody; a development plan does not exist for the successor; and in half the cases he or she will be a family member.

It can therefore be deduced that a formal succession process, which culminates in formal written statements, seems not to be the order of the day in South Africa. Certainly a reason for this is the fact that the new founders do not possess managerial skills that will enable them to deal with critical family business issues such as succession planning.

Family business owners also seem to be cautious when selecting a successor and announcing it publicly. The most important reason seems to be the avoidance of conflict. In some cases, they tend to select a joint management team where two or more of the children are active in the business and have different skills that complement each other.

The most disturbing issue is the lack of financial planning for life after retirement. A large percentage of owners still think that the business must look after their needs after retirement. In certain cases, the financial burden of looking after the retired parents and still managing a profitable business becomes too heavy and impacts negatively on the organisation's cash flow. This situation (where the business is the retirement scheme) also leads to unnecessary involvement of the parents, who are watching every decision to make sure that it will not affect their retirement plans. It is usually better to cut the "umbilical cord" and to make sure that the parents' financial planning is in order before taking over office.

Senior family members in the business are steadily becoming more involved in succession planning – a trend that may be linked to information being available on how to conduct succession planning. In the case of less developed family businesses, tradition can still be regarded as a stumbling block – children must be seen, not heard! Therefore, a business ethos of the founder being the one and only "chief in charge" is still in place in many family businesses.

In "mature" family businesses, key employees other than family members are involved in succession planning, especially if the successor is still too young to take over the business. In this regard, key personnel play a mentoring and supportive role. In one particular situation, the workers agreed to mentor the potential new leader in terms of specific business issues.

More developed family businesses tend to expose their children to the business from a young age. In certain business environments (e.g. farms) and culture groups (e.g. Indians), exposure to the family business is a natural process.

Exposure of the children to the business and larger business environment is currently becoming more important, because of the threat of unemployment and the implications of certain legislation in South Africa.

In order to help family businesses with the matter of succession, Bieneman (1997) has identified five critical steps:

1. Define what the owners and family want to happen, now and in the future. This step comes down to discussing everyone's individual visions and a collective vision for the family as a whole. When discussing a vision, it would be natural to consider life after retirement, career goals, leisure activities and finances.

2. Evaluate and test the succession goals to confirm that they are feasible and compatible. Issues to address are what it would cost if the parents retire, what kind of leadership skills are needed for the next phase of the business, and who would be on the management teams.

3. Develop a preliminary succession plan. A formal plan must be developed on the basis of the previous discussions. Time frames should be included in the plan, together with financial plans, a plan for the selection and training of the future leader, and a plan for current and future wealth distribution.

4. Communicate, modify and improve the plan while striving for acceptance from all family members. The plan should be openly discussed with all parties concerned. In this case, the family council and the advisory board can be of great help. Refinements should be made where needed.

5. Implementation. All that remains is to start implementing the plan. However, one knows that in reality not everything always goes according to plan. Therefore, the plan should remain flexible and be refined whenever needed.

Again, the above steps are easier said than done because of various perceived problems. The parents may have the following concerns:

- When is the right time?
- What will I as an owner do after handing over the business?
- How will the other children accept my decision?
- What about the children outside the business? I must ensure equality.

From the successor's point of view, the following problems might exist:

- Will my parents accept that I am the new owner and that I will make my own decisions?
- Will the workers accept me as the new boss?
- Will the old boys' network of the family accept me as the new leader?
- Will the family accept me as the new leader?

As there are no easy answers to these perceived problems, one needs to start quite early with the succession process. In one family's case it was decided to have a five-year period to complete succession. However, the process did not get off to a good start. Various reasons for the slow start were identified and resolved, but still the process was quite slow in getting off the ground. Two years after the process had started, the successor admitted that his biggest concern was whether his father would have something to do with the business after the succession process and whether his father's financial position would be such that he could enjoy a relaxed and carefree retirement. After his fears were addressed through open discussion, the whole process was on track for the first time and was completed well within the five years set aside for this. The lesson from this is that it is not always the visible and big issues that are creating stumbling blocks but the small ones, which, fortunately, can be solved fast once detected. In order for them to be detected, open communication over time is needed.

10.6 Advisory board

The role of the family advisory board is mainly focused on the business/management-related aspects. The board should ensure that the business is strategically aligned to major environmental trends; that the business stays entrepreneurial by constantly exploiting opportunities; that conflicts within the business are managed timeously; that decisions are taken based on facts and not emotions; and that decisions are in line with the family value system. In the past, family businesses were not always in favour of advisory boards because of the "secret" nature of the business – to protect the family name, no outsider was permitted in the business.

Therefore, it is critical that:

- The board consists of family members, non-family members and external specialists (not necessarily from the same industry).
- Regular meetings are held during a year.
- Board meetings should be seen as a formal occasion.
- Service providers (e.g. bankers, auditors, consultants) are not necessarily part of an advisory board because they are already involved in one way or another.

In South Africa the use of advisory boards is not common. Where such boards exist, mostly family members are board members, formal meetings are not always held, and board members are not necessarily remunerated for their service. Board members are mainly approached for their advice, and they also play a role in averting conflict.

The above corresponds with other observations that family businesses in South Africa are still very secretive. Various reasons can be given for this, but one is certainly linked to society and culture. People fear failure, and bankruptcy is punished severely in a social sense – one is identified as a loser and will lose friends. That bankruptcy is actually a learning experience is not appreciated. The idea of bringing in somebody from the outside is therefore unthinkable.

The lack of knowledge of, and experience in managing a family business can be regarded as a further important factor. The idea to bring in outsiders to stimulate growth and development in a family business is steadily being seen as an important strategy, but we have a long way to go before this will be a natural process.

10.7 Family council

The role of the family council is to oversee family-specific matters, such as the family's philosophy, succession planning, employment criteria, involvement in the business and response to the external environment. The family council must consist of selected members of the family organised in such a way that there is a good balance between different age groups and genders.

The biggest challenge for the family council is to draw up a family protocol or creed. This protocol should reflect what the family stands for and should be supported by all family members.

Family businesses that are exposed to knowledge of family business management have a family creed. Those without this background (i.e. the majority of small and medium family businesses) usually do not have one. Conflict in the latter businesses may be above normal because the ground rules regarding issues such as shares, compensation, employment of in-laws, management philosophy and remuneration, have not been spelled out.

In order to facilitate a conversation around the creation of a family creed, the following process questions can be used:

- Management philosophy and objectives
  - In whose interests are we acting?
  - What are our ethical standards?
  - Which is more important: business principles or family issues?
  - What is our aim for the business?
  - What influence can family members exercise over management policies and objectives?

- Jobs for family members and remuneration
  - Should family members possess relevant experience to join the business?
  - Is a job in the business a right or an opportunity?
  - What commitment is expected of family members?
  - Can family members be asked to quit the business if they cannot maintain standards?
  - Will family by marriage be allowed in the business?
  - On which basis will family members be remunerated?

- Leadership
  - On what basis will the next managing director be selected?
  - What support must the new managing director have?
  - What criteria must the managing director satisfy?
  - What type of leadership style must exist in the business?
  - What type of training must leaders in this business have?

- Shareholding
  - Who may own shares in the business?
  - Who may vote in the business?
  - May shares be sold to other family members?
  - May non-family members own shares?
  - Who determines the value of shares and at what moment?
  - What happens to a person's shares if he or she leaves the business?
- Board of directors or advisory board
  - Which family members may serve on the board of directors?
  - Will directors from outside the business be appointed?
  - Will the board accept suggestions from non-board members?
  - What are the functions and powers of the board?
  - What are the guidelines for appointing directors?
- Communication
  - How many times in a year must the family council meet?
  - What will happen in the case of disputes?
  - Who may serve on the family council?
  - What are the procedures to be followed in terms of new projects?
- Employees
  - What is the role of employees in the business?
  - How will employees be managed?
  - What are the skills and experience expected of employees?
- Changes in the family constitution
  - How can the constitution be changed?

- What is the binding power of the constitution?
- Who may vote to change the constitution?
- What percentage constitutes a majority vote?

The best way to go about formulating a family creed is to appoint a facilitator who is trusted by all family members, and then to organise a retreat during which all the above questions can be discussed. The retreat must be organised at a neutral place – which excludes the parents' house!

10.8 Conclusion

The family business sector is still characterised to a certain extent by a traditional mindset – from father to son, and the mother is there to look after the children. Fortunately, this trend seems to be changing, with more females entering business.

The biggest concern regarding family businesses in South Africa is the level of family business management skills. The majority of family businesses are simply not trained to manage their business successfully – either business- and/or family-wise. This also influences their ability to manage risk in a fast-changing environment where one needs to stay entrepreneurial in order to survive and grow.

It may be concluded that family businesses in South Africa are a growing sector, but that there are certain deficiencies that block their accelerated growth and expansion, such as a lack of management skills. Decisions are still taken on an ad hoc basis without regard for balancing the relationships among all subsystems.

Looking back

1. List the key concepts that you can identify from the definition of a family business.
   - Influenced by family ties
   - Achieves the vision of the family
   - More than one generation

2. Name the two dominant systems in a family business.
   - Family system
   - Business system

3. List the subsystems of a family system.
   - Family
   - Family by marriage
   - Parents
   - Brothers and sisters
   - Family inside and outside the business

4. List the subsystems of a business system.
   - Managers
   - Owners
   - Employees
   - External networks

5. What problems exist in family businesses?
   - Failure to raise capital for growth
   - Inability to balance family and business needs
   - Poor estate planning
   - Reluctance to let go
   - Inability to attract the right successor
   - Sibling rivalry
   - Inability to retain non-family members
   - Favouritism
   - Unclear expectations
   - Lack of entrepreneurial drive
   - Emigration

6. Why can a family business be a good place to be?
   - Strong family culture
   - Greater sensitivity
   - Job creation
   - Specialist knowledge
   - Freedom to express creativity

7. What options are open during succession?
   - Appoint a family member.
   - Appoint a caretaker manager if the family member is still too young to take over.
   - Appoint a professional manager if no family member wants to take over the management of the business.
   - Liquidate the business.
   - Sell the business, in whole or in part.
   - Do nothing, i.e. adopt a wait-and-see approach.

8. Identify five critical steps to succession.
   - Define what the owners and family want to happen.
   - Evaluate and test the succession goals.
   - Develop a preliminary succession plan.
   - Communicate and adapt the plan.
   - Implement the plan.

9. What category questions can be asked to formulate a family creed?
   - Management philosophy and objectives
   - Jobs and remuneration
   - Leadership
   - Shareholding
   - Board of directors
   - Communication
   - Employees
   - Changes in creed

Key terms

Advisory boards
Business system
Family business

Family council
Family system
Succession

Discussion questions

1. Explain the term "family business" and its significance for South Africa.
2. What can one do to ensure that a family business will be successful?

3. What can one do to ensure that family values are in line with business activities?
4. If you had a family business, what would your family creed look like?

Case study

Will Venter stay in the centre?

Trying to keep the business in the family is a tough challenge, writes STUART GRAHAM.

Altron founder and chairman Bill Venter and his two sons are trying to turn the group into a global giant. But their biggest challenge is still to come: how to keep the business in the family.

Venter's eldest son Robbie, 42, Altron's CEO, has reported excellent results since the board decided last year to split the roles of chairman and CEO, moving him into the top operating position. Altron has profits of R763 million and annual sales of more than R10 billion. Younger son Craig, 40, CEO of Altron's largest subsidiary, Altech, has also reported excellent results. Altech has sales of R4 billion and generates an operating profit of R357 million a year.

But if history is anything to go by, there is only a small chance of Altron being passed down successfully to the third generation of Venters. Research in the US shows that only one in three family businesses survive into the second generation and only one in ten survive into the third. It also shows that more than 35 per cent of the Fortune 500 companies are family controlled, create the most jobs and have an average lifespan of 24 years. By 2040, $10,4 trillion will have been generated via family businesses.

South African business is dotted with companies controlled by families such as the Ackermans, Kroks, Gordons, Wieses, Frankels, Blooms and Spitzs, many of which never passed on to successive generations.

Venter says the biggest reason is because parents generally bring their children straight into the top of the company, instead of working them through the ranks, where they have to earn respect. He says Robbie and Craig both worked their way up in the company on merit. "If there were people who were more suitable and better qualified for the jobs, I assure you they would be in these positions," Venter says of his sons.

Much has been written about a rift between the brothers, but Robbie says nothing could be further from the truth. "Having my father and brother so close to me at Altron often makes doing business easier. It makes for a very transparent environment with open communication and trust, which is often absent in other businesses. We also get to spend time with each other."

Craig says he finds being part of a family business inspiring but tough. In his formative years in business, he says, he had to prove himself by a margin of 200 per cent. "My father did not achieve his icon status by not paying attention to detail or by overlooking the mistakes of others," Craig adds. "You see, if I did not perform it would not have been some outsider that I was letting down, it would have been my father – and which son would willingly do that?"

Venter was 33, married, and Robbie and Craig were boys when he decided that his managerial job at STC, a telecoms and engineering company, was going nowhere and that he would risk everything to start his own technology business. "I started the business, Allied Electric, on 1 April 1965 so that I could say it was an April Fool's joke if it failed," Venter quips. "I also decided to compete with my previous employers in the electronics technology field, since this was the industry I knew best."

Altron now employs about 12 000 people, but at one stage Venter was forced to sell his wife's car to pay the wages of his two employees. Whatever "meagre savings" he had, he says, he ploughed back into the business in the form of working capital. Venter slowly built Altron into a technological pioneer. It became the first technology company to lay fibre optic telecommunications cables in Africa, and was also the first to negotiate and assist with the fibre optic undersea cable to Europe.

Venter says much of his success came from sticking to Altron's technological core businesses and choosing the right people. He says a reason why many businesses fail is that they diversify too rapidly into areas where they have little expertise. Altron has never failed to declare a dividend to its shareholders, which Venter says is largely due to its healthy cash flow. Altron has also never stretched itself financially, and this has given the group financial independence. Venter says many companies fail because they commit to unrealistic borrowings,

take loans and literally run before they know how to walk. "These companies usually take on too many contracts at low margins and are then unable to deliver on them." Altron's exports have grown to R2,3 billion over the past ten years or 23 per cent of turnover in the recent financial year.

Venter says the company has a solid asset base, which is why it was not hit by the crash in the IT sector. "Many of those dotcom companies were built up by the markets when there was no real substance to them. Altron, on the other hand, is backed up by assets and cash." Critics say Venter has always been quick to use the politicians of the day to build his company, but he brushes these remarks aside. "I still have to meet someone who can sustain a business for 37 years through political contacts alone. Politicians don't last forever. Market conditions and governments change."

Venter is sure to have drummed all his life's lessons into his sons, who are bound to do the same for their children. "In family businesses, the third generation is always far removed from the first in terms of values and principles because they were not raised with the grandparent," says Robbie. "It is up to the second generation to make sure the values and principles that were used to make business successful are passed on to their children."

Source: Sunday Times, Business Times, 1 September 2002, p. 6.

Questions

1. Discuss the problem of family succession in the above-mentioned family business.
2. Make use of a model to indicate how Venter can prepare the third generation of his family business for succession.

Experiential exercises

1. Interview a family business owner. In your report, identify the characteristics of the business, the motivation for start-up, and the reasons for success.
2. Interview the siblings in a family business to

establish why they are involved in the business and what problems they experience.
3. Identify a family business that has an advisory board and a family creed. What can you deduce from this?

Exploring the Web

Visit the website of the Family Firm Institute:
www.ffi.org to read more about family businesses.

References and recommended reading

Aronoff, C.E. & Ward, J.L. 1992. *Family business succession: the final test of greatness*. Marietta, GA: Business Owner Resources.

Bieneman, J.N. 1997. *The Howarth international guide to total planning in the family and owner-managed business*. New York: Howarth International.

Chicago Family Business Centre. No date. *Global perspectives on family business*. Chicago: Loyola University.

De Vries, M.K. 1996. *Family business: human dilemmas in the family firm*. London: International Thomson Business Press.

Donckels, R. 1996. The fascinating world of family business: about old challenges in a future-orientated perspective. *Southern African Journal for Entrepreneurship and Small Business,* 8(2): 1-13.

Handler, W.C. 1994. Succession in family business: a review of the research. *Family Business Review,* 7(2): 133-155.

Hoover, E. & Hoover, C.L. 1999. *Getting along in family business*. London: Routledge.

James, E.W. & James, J. 1997. *Couples at work.* Denver: Boomer House Books.

Kaye, K. 1994. *Workplace wars and how to end them.* New York: American Management Association.

Lank, A. 2000. Making sure the dynasty does not become a Dallas. In Birley, S. & Muzyka, D.F., *Mastering entrepreneurship*. London: Prentice Hall, 193-199.

Leach, P. 1994. *The Stoy Hayward guide to the family business,* 2nd ed. London: Stoy Hayward.

Maas, G. 1996. Family businesses in South Africa. *Family Business Newsletter* No. 16, December.

Maas, G.J.P. 1997. *Enhancing the creative potential of owners in family businesses.* Proceedings of the 10th Annual Conference, SAESBA Conference, 27-29 April. Edited by Ahwireng-Obeng, F., Havenga, K., Viviers, W. and Saayman, A.

Maas, G.J.P. 1999. *Family business in South Africa: a development model.* The 12th Annual Southern African Small Business Association Conference. Johannesburg, 30 July 1999 to 1 August 1999.

Murray, B. 2001. Travelers in time. *Families in Business*, Autumn, 36-39.

Sharna, P., Chrisman, J.J. & Chua, F.H. 1997. Strategic management of the family business: past research and future challenges. *Family Business Review,* 10(1): 1-35.

11

Buying a franchise

Johan Hough

Learning outcomes

After completion of this chapter, you should be able to:

- Know the different concepts in franchising
- Understand the structure of the franchise industry in South Africa
- Identify the various types of franchising
- Elaborate on the advantages and disadvantages of franchising
- Evaluate franchise opportunities
- Select a franchise system
- Understand the relationship(s) between the franchisor and franchisee
- Give your opinion on the potential of franchising in the emerging entrepreneurial sector of South Africa

11.1 Introduction

The franchise concept gives an entrepreneur the opportunity to start a business that has been proven in the marketplace. The entrepreneur then becomes a franchisee. The franchisor gives the franchisee the right to operate a business using the franchise company's name, products and systems. In return, the franchisee pays the franchise firm for this right on an ongoing basis.

There are many different and new franchise systems in operation and there are more of them every year. Names like Mugg & Bean, Steers, Spur, Debonair, PG Autoglass, 7-Eleven and Spar are household names in South Africa (and some of them even internationally), and we all buy from them from time to time. Franchising systems have grown at a very high rate from 1994 and the expectation is that growth will be sustained until 2004/2005. Figure 11.1 depicts this growth in the franchising systems in South Africa from 1994.

11.2 Definition and characteristics of the franchise concept

Franchising offers someone who has developed a certain business system and who owns certain intellectual property (such as trademarks, copyright and patents) used in connection with it, the opportunity to make the system and the use of the intellectual property available to others in exchange for payment. Such a person is known as the franchisor; the person who obtains the rights to operate the franchisor's business system and the licence to use the intellectual property is known as the franchisee. In principle, franchising is suitable for any kind of business system. Today, some of the most important franchises are connected with motor products and services, cleaning services, building and home services, business services and fast printing, education and training, entertainment and recreation, food, health and beauty care, and property services.

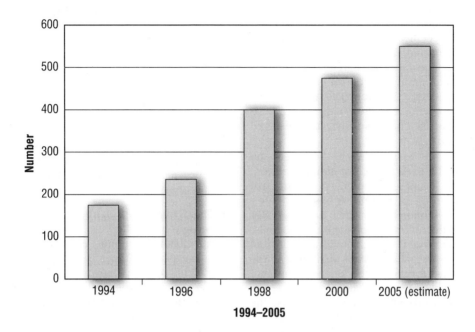

Figure 11.1 The growth of franchising systems in South Africa

A franchise operation is a contractual relationship between the franchisor and the franchisee in which the franchisor offers, or is obliged, to maintain a continuing interest in the business of the franchisee in such areas as know-how and training. The franchisee operates under a common trade name, format and/or procedure owned or controlled by the franchisor. The franchisee has made, or will make, a substantial capital investment in the business from his or her own resources.

A functional definition of franchising is also given by the Franchise Association of Southern Africa (FASA 2002):

A franchise is a grant by the franchisor to the franchisee entitling the latter to the use of a complete business package containing all the elements necessary to establish a previously untrained person in the franchise business, to enable him or her to run it on an ongoing basis according to guidelines supplied efficiently and profitably.

It is clear from these definitions that franchising involves an ongoing activity, which is unlike the situation in, for example, a contract of sale. Franchisors are obliged continuously to allow franchisees to operate the business system and to use the intellectual property that is part of the business system. Usually, franchisors are also obliged, on a continuing basis, to provide support services, market the business system and develop it to adapt to new and changing market conditions. Apart from the initial amount that franchisees must pay when the contract is concluded, they are also obliged to pay royalties to the franchisor for the duration of the franchising agreement.

Although the franchisee becomes the owner of the franchise outlet and makes a substantial investment from own funds, it remains a characteristic of franchising that the franchisor constantly exercises a measure of control over the business system that has been made available to the franchisee. The franchisee must operate the business system under the trade name or trademark of the franchisor. The franchisee is also provided with an operating manual that forms part of the franchising agreement, and is obliged to operate the franchise strictly according to the prescriptions, methods and standards contained in the operating manual. Usually, the franchisee undertakes to comply strictly with all written specifications and instructions that the franchisor may from time to time lay down after the conclusion of the agreement. The purpose of such continuing control is to maintain uniformity within the franchise network, so that the goodwill associated with the name or trademark of the franchisor may be preserved and enlarged.

Goodwill may be described as the benefit and advantage of a good name, reputation, and connection of a business. Goodwill is the attractive force that brings in custom. A business enterprise is an economic unit that has a greater value than that of its independent components. This greater value is represented by intellectual property; its formation can be attributed to the organisational forging of the independent components of the enterprise. The aim of the entrepreneur is to attract customers and keep the suppliers, creditors and employees satisfied. Through the forging of the independent components of the enterprise, the entrepreneur strives to create a favourable attitude on the part of the suppliers, creditors and employees, and to create an attracting force or goodwill. If he or she is successful, the economic unit of the enterprise will acquire a greater value than the sum of the value of its independent components. The enterprise will then comprise goodwill in addition to the independent components. Goodwill can be regarded as a dependent component of the enterprise in that it can enjoy a more or less permanent existence only within the context of the enterprise. Factors that contribute to the formation of goodwill include the location of the business, the entrepreneur's personality and the reputation of the business. It is not, however, determined by any one of these factors alone. Instead, goodwill originates by their functioning within the context of the enterprise according to a specific scheme.

Another characteristic of franchising is the fact that the intellectual property of the franchisor is made available to the franchisee. The intellectual property may include designs, know-how, copyright, goodwill, trademarks, trade secrets and patents. The franchisor grants the franchisee a licence to use such intellectual property, while he or she remains its rightful owner.

11.3 Important concepts of franchising

The following are important concepts:

- The **franchisor** is the firm that owns the business concept. The franchisor must have been in existence for some time and be operating a few stores of its own before it can franchise. This allows the franchisor to sort out any problem areas before other people invest in the system. The Steers holding company and Mica hardware holdings are examples of franchisors.

- The **franchisee**, on the other hand, is the entrepreneur who buys a franchise from the franchisor and in most cases will operate the business. The franchisee is the person who puts his or her money at risk, and it is therefore of the utmost importance that franchisees should ensure that the franchise system they choose belongs to a quality company.

- One of the most important elements of the franchise concept is the **franchise contract**, which is also called the **franchise agreement**. This contract specifies all the terms on which the relationship between the franchisor and the franchisee is based. It also specifies all the rights and obligations of the two parties and how the franchise is to be operated. Spur, for instance, might include in its franchise agreements that franchisees must buy all the sauces and burger patties from the Spur central factory, that all the staff will wear the Spur T-shirt, and that franchisees must pay a royalty of say 5 per cent per month based on turnover and an advertising fee of say 3 per cent. This contract helps both parties to know what the terms of the relationship are and serves as a legal document if any disputes should arise. Franchising involves duplicating or copying the business over and over again, and establishing the concept and quality standards and also brand loyalty in the minds of the customers. The customers will then know when they see a Spur outlet (for example) what quality they can expect, what the prices are and what types of products they can buy.

- **Royalties** are generally also called **management services fees** in South Africa. Royalties are the monthly fee that the franchisee has to pay the franchisor for the right to operate the franchise. This can be either a fixed amount, say R2 000 per month, or a percentage of the franchisee's turnover, say 5 per cent. The percentage is calculated monthly by multiplying the turnover by the percentage. If the turnover is R500 000 in April, then the royalties for April will be R500 000 times 5 per cent or R25 000. This is the franchisor's primary income. It uses this monthly income to finance the support services of the franchise system, namely staff salaries, administrative systems and operating costs, and the difference between these costs and the income from the royalties is its profit.

- The **advertising fee** that the franchisee has to pay can also be a fixed amount or a percentage of turnover. It is used to finance the advertising campaigns of the franchise company. This allows a company like Spur to advertise on television and on the radio, something which an individual business would be unable to do. This is one of the advantages of the franchise concept if it is properly implemented. In the marketplace, however, the advertising fee is one of the main sources of conflict between franchisees and franchisors.

- Another cost for the franchisee, which forms part of the franchise concept, is the **franchise fee**. This fee is a lump sum payment that the franchisee pays to the franchisor when they sign the franchise contract. The franchisor uses this money to finance the opening of the new franchisee's business. The franchisor might also pay the expenses of searching for a site, legal fees for the franchise contract, and so forth, out of this fee.

11.4 The structure of the industry in South Africa

Franchisors and franchisees are the two main parties in the franchise industry. A franchisor may be a manufacturer or any other channel member who has an attractive business concept worthy of duplication. A franchisor can sell a franchise directly to individual franchisees or market it through master licensees or area developers. Most franchisors also own one or more outlets that are not franchised.

These outlets are referred to as company-owned stores or corporate stores.

In addition to these parties, the franchising industry comprises other important groups. These groups, called facilitators, include industry associations, governmental agencies and private businesses.

The International Franchise Association (IFA), for example, is an industry association that serves franchise members by attempting to safeguard and enhance the business and regulatory environment of the industry. It has over 30 000 members – franchisors, franchisees and suppliers – that operate in more than 100 countries.

The IFA is, nevertheless, highly selective, and not all applications for membership are accepted. Referring to itself as "The Voice of Franchising", the IFA sponsors legal and government affairs symposiums, franchise management workshops, seminars on franchisor/franchisee relations, and trade shows. The IFA also champions the causes of minority business groups. For example, the Women's Franchise Committee (WFC), formed in 1996, represents women in the franchising industry. The WFC provides leadership conferences, mentoring programmes, a network of professionals, and other services to women franchisees.

Numerous state agencies are involved in the franchise industry in South Africa. Agencies such as the Industrial Development Corporation (IDC), Franchise Advice and Information Network (FRAIN) and Business Referral and Information Network (BRAIN) provide information on franchise opportunities and enforce franchising laws and regulations. Pre-sale franchise disclosure practices are subject to special scrutiny by these agencies.

A third category of facilitators includes private businesses providing franchise information and consulting services to franchisors and franchisees. For example, FASA, Franchise Directions and Franchising Plus are three businesses that assist with franchising evaluation and offer development services. Figure 11.2 shows the different franchise parties and facilitators in South Africa.

11.5 Types of franchising

There are three available types of franchises available, according to Hisrich and Peters

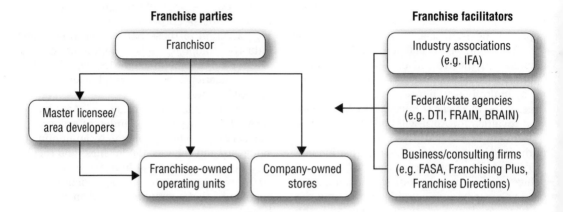

Figure 11.2 The structure of franchising in South Africa

(2002). The first type is the dealership, a form commonly found in the car industry. The manufacturers use franchises to distribute their product lines. In essence, they act as the retail store for the manufacturer and may be required to meet quotas established by the manufacturer. They also benefit from the advertising, service and management support provided by the manufacturer.

The most common type of franchise is the type that offers a name, image and method of doing business, such as McDonald's, KFC, Nando's, Spec-Savers and Supa Quick. There are many of these types of franchisors and their listings can be found in various resources. This is referred to as business format franchising, the most popular type.

A third type of franchise offers services. These include personnel agencies, estate agencies and personal services. These franchises have established names and reputations and methods of doing business. Examples are Aida, ERA, Pam Golding, Realty1-Elk, RE/MAX of Southern Africa, Martin's Funerals and PostNet (FASA, 2002).

11.6 Advantages and limitations of franchising

11.6.1 Introduction

Over the past decades, franchising has assumed ever-increasing importance in the creation of new small businesses. This phenomenon can be observed throughout the world, and South Africa is certainly no exception. On the contrary, name recognition and skills transfer, two of the cornerstones of business format franchising, hold special attraction for our country, where a levelling of the playing field is imperative to the advancement of the formerly disadvantaged sector of the population. Franchising holds many advantages, but like most things in life, there are disadvantages as well. Prospective franchisees must be aware of this, so that they can weigh up the pros and cons and arrive at an informed decision. It is the objective of this section to help you do just that.

11.6.2 Advantages from the franchisee's viewpoint

- *A proven system:* Unlike a truly independent entrepreneur, a franchisee need not prove the viability of the concept. This has been done for him or her by the franchisor, who will have tested the concept in his own stores. This would extend to the product or service, the marketing thereof and the systems and procedures necessary for the profitable operation of the business.

- *Start-up assistance:* The franchisor will take every new franchisee under his wing and provide them with initial training, assist with site selection, fitting out and stocking up of the store, help with staff selection and training, and also with pre-opening and opening publicity. There will be no need for the new entrepreneur to "reinvent the wheel", and this is obviously a big advantage.

- *Ongoing assistance:* The franchisor will provide the franchisee with ongoing assistance in all aspects of operations. This will be linked to quality control and appropriate feedback, aimed at helping the franchisee to improve all-round performance of his or her business in accordance with group norms.

- *Advertising and purchasing:* The franchisor will operate an effective marketing programme from which all franchisees benefit. Moreover, local advertising undertaken by franchisees will often be developed centrally, resulting in increased effectiveness and substantial cost savings. The same would apply to joint purchasing schemes – the franchisor either supplies goods to members of the network, or negotiates favourable terms on their behalf.

- *Easier to obtain finance:* For a long time now, bankers have been well aware that the odds for business success are far more favourable for franchised operations than for their independent counterparts. This is taken into account when a loan application is being considered.

11.6.3 Disadvantages from the franchisee's viewpoint

- *Increased set-up costs:* Established franchisors will insist on certain minimum standards of furnishings, fittings and equipment to be maintained. This may increase the initial cost of setting up shop. It could be held, however, that this initial investment aids the franchisee in establishing the business more quickly and shortens the period until breakeven is reached.

- *Rigid operating procedures:* The success of the franchised network depends on replication of the proven formula. For individuals who thrive on experimentation and innovation, this may be a bitter pill to swallow.

- *Bad decisions by the franchisor:* If the franchisor makes mistakes, for example in reading market trends, then this could have serious consequences for franchisees in the network. This is but one reason why it is imperative to investigate the track record of

a franchise before deciding to operate an outlet.

11.6.4 Advantages from the franchisor's viewpoint

- *Rapid expansion:* With franchisees providing the start-up capital and assuming responsibility for day-to-day operations, franchisors can grow their business much faster via the franchise route than if they had set up a network of branches.

- *Dedicated owner-operators:* Seeing that franchisees invest their own money, they are usually far more committed to the long-term success of the business than could be expected from a salaried branch manager. This, in turn, tends to lead to increased customer satisfaction and accelerated growth of the individual outlets. It also results in enhanced feedback on market trends and competitor activity at local level, further enhancing the entire network's chances for accelerated growth.

11.6.5 Disadvantages from the franchisor's viewpoint

- *High operating costs:* To set up and operate an effective head office structure – a vital component in the long-term success of any franchise – is costly. This is especially true in the early stages, when income from management service fees tends to be significantly lower than the cost of providing support to a small number of inexperienced franchisees.

- *Reduced income per unit:* The franchisor's income is usually limited to a percentage of franchisees' sales. This factor must be weighed against the potential for rapid growth and increased contributions from more outlets.

- *Restrictions on freedom to act:* Unlike entrepreneurs who go it alone, franchisors accept money from others and promise them a blueprint for success in return. This places them under a moral obligation to ensure ongoing successful operation. Moreover, given the fact that franchisees are the owners of their businesses, the franchisor can no longer dictate changes in business policies. To secure the cooperation of franchisees, the franchisor will have to convince them of the merits of every proposal.

11.7 Evaluating franchise opportunities

The evaluation of a franchise opportunity is very much the same as when buying an existing business. The following additional aspects and questions need to be considered (FRAIN 2002):

- What is the company's financial position?
- Is it possible to obtain trade or bank references?
- What is the background of the directors?
- How long had the company been in existence before it started franchising, or was it specifically set up to franchise?
- What evidence is there that the franchise format has been sufficiently piloted in a number of locations?
- How many franchised units are currently open? Are there any company-owned units in operation?
- What has been the company's rate of expansion? (A steady rate is preferable to extremely rapid expansion.)
- Have any franchised units failed or ceased trading in the past 12 months? If so, what were the reasons?
- Is the franchisor a member of FASA? Have they ever been members or refused membership?
- Is there an ongoing demand for the product or service? Is there much competition in the marketplace?
- If appropriate, is the geographical location of the business suitable? (Go and have a look!)
- What are the initial and ongoing fees? Are there any other costs? (Any request for a non-refundable deposit prior to signature should set alarm bells ringing!)
- Will there be sufficient profit left once you have paid all your expenses?
- How does the franchisor calculate the financial projections, and what happens if these projections, are not met?
- How long will it take you to obtain a full return on your investment?

- Are any bank financing arrangements provided by the franchisor?
- Is it possible to talk freely to existing franchisees? (If not, beware!)
- On what criteria are franchisees selected?
- Can the franchisor demonstrate his or her capacity to provide the necessary initial and ongoing support services? What precisely will this support involve?
- Can you have a copy of the franchise agreement?
- Is the franchisor happy for you to take independent advice on the agreement prior to signature?
- What are your obligations as a franchisee? (This should include any operational restrictions, e.g. on pricing or the use of suppliers.)
- What are the nature and extent of the rights granted to you, including territorial rights?
- What is the length of the agreement?
- Does the agreement permit you to sell the franchise and, if so, are there any restrictions?
- What happens in the event of a dispute with the franchisor?
- What is the procedure for terminating the agreement, and what are the consequences of doing so?
- Is there open ongoing communication between the franchisor and franchisees?
- What are the franchisor's long-term plans for the future of the business?

After you have identified suitable industries, you will be ready to begin your evaluation of each franchise opportunity. You will now have to contact each of the organisations and make your interest known. Many of these franchise organisations will forward information packs to you containing application forms and additional information about the organisation. In order to be able to assess each of these opportunities based on their individual strengths and weaknesses, you will need to do the following:

1. Carefully scrutinise each organisation's "disclosure document". This document should answer many of your questions and provide you with a great deal of details about the organisation, such as its financial status,

how many franchisees it has, when it got started, etc.

2. Be sure to speak to current franchisees within the system and even go as far as to speak with those who are no longer a part of the network to enquire why not. If you are planning to open your outlet a long distance from the city or base of the franchisor, it is always a good idea to speak with other franchisees who too are based a long distance from head office. This will give you a good understanding of how much and what type of support those franchisees are currently getting from the organisation. You will then know exactly what to expect.

11.8 Complying with ethical requirements

The offer and sale of franchises are not strictly regulated in South Africa as is the case in most other countries. Many unscrupulous business-people and confidence tricksters have used the word "franchise" in advertisements in recent years to add some credibility to their business proposals. Many unsuspecting consumers (or would-be franchisees) have lost their life savings as a result of falling for these scams. It is therefore imperative that any prospective franchisor take note of the ethical requirements associated with franchising. These are basically the Consumer Code for Franchising (issued by the Business Practices Committee; see section 11.8.1 below), FASA's disclosure document (see section 11.8.3) and membership of FASA.

There is nothing to be gained, and much that can be lost, from a negative attitude towards the Consumer Code and disclosure requirements emanating from the Code. One should rather regard compliance with these regulations as marketing tools.

11.8.1 Consumer Code for Franchising

The unethical behaviour of many businesspeople prompted the Business Practices Committee to draw up and publish a Consumer Code for franchising in September 1995 to protect consumers and prospective franchisees. This Committee also worked with FASA to amend its Code of Ethics in order to provide for a disclosure document.

The Business Practices Committee administers the Harmful Business Practices Act No. 71 of 1988. The purpose of this Act is, simply, to prohibit harmful business practices. A harmful business practice is any practice that harms the relationship between consumers and businesses and unreasonably prejudices and deceives any consumer.

The Code is intended to govern the conduct of franchising operations. A consumer who is dissatisfied with the treatment received from a franchisee or a franchisor can complain to FASA. This also applies to a prospective franchisee who is dissatisfied with the treatment received from a franchisor. A consumer or franchisee who is also not satisfied with FASA's handling of the complaint has further recourse to the Business Practices Committee. The Committee may after investigation declare a certain activity to be a harmful business practice.

11.8.2 FASA Code of Ethics

The South African Franchise Association (SAFA) was established in Johannesburg in 1979 under the auspices of the Johannesburg Chamber of Commerce. SAFA changed its name to the Franchise Association of Southern Africa (FASA) during 1993. The main objectives of FASA are as follows:

- To promote the concept of franchising and to ensure that franchising as an industry is above reproach
- To issue guidelines according to which sound franchising schemes should operate; to apply a Code of Ethics to the industry; and to act against those who transgress the Code
- To represent the industry vis-à-vis the government, the media and the general public as the need arises

Prospective members are carefully screened before admittance and all must subscribe to the FASA Code of Ethics and Business Practices.

11.8.3 Disclosure document

FASA's disclosure document requirements are aimed at a full and complete disclosure by a franchisor to a prospective franchisee. One of the most important requirements of the Code is that a prospective franchisee should not be permitted to part with any money or to sign a franchise agreement less than seven days after receiving the disclosure document.

Franchisors should not have any difficulty in complying with the requirements. The requirements should be regarded as minimum disclosure requirements and franchisors should have no objection to providing significantly more information. Franchisors can use the document as a mechanism for promoting their businesses.

11.8.4 Advertising practice

Because of the popularity of franchising, advertisements that include words such as "franchise" attract immediate attention. As a result, unscrupulous businesspeople and confidence tricksters have inserted the word "franchise" into advertisements to attract respondents.

It was greatly due to the intervention and pressure from FASA that the Advertising Standards Authority of South Africa has inserted into its Code of Advertising Practice the following section:

Franchise schemes

- Franchise scheme means a scheme where a company, firm or individual, known as the "franchisor", gives to a person, known as a "franchisee", the right, often exclusive, to sell specified products or other specified services in return for an initial payment, a percentage of the profits (or a royalty), or any other consideration.

- Advertisements by franchisors seeking franchisees are not acceptable unless the franchisor has provided the information required by media in advance of publication. Such advertisement should not mislead, directly or by implication, as to the support available or the likely reward for the investment and work required. For the franchisor or the franchisor's agent (if any) the advertisement must state:

- the name of the senior executive

- the full title of the company; and

- the street address of the company.

These requirements apply to both display and "smalls" advertisements.

The following is an example of an unacceptable advertisement:

FRANCHISE!

Publishing Business. No stock/equipment req'd. Instant start-up. Operate from home. Full/part time. No royalties. Profit of R10 000 p.m. A once-off investment of R150. People from all areas welcome.

Further info: Franchise Officer, Box 3059, Dbn 4000

Source: Nieman (1998).

11.8.5 Competition Board

In 1993 the Competition Board undertook an investigation into a specific franchise operation. Although the operation in question became defunct during the period of investigation, the Board decided to complete the investigation and extend it to franchising in general.

The Board's findings were published in its Report No. 45. This report opened the door to disgruntled franchisees wishing to lodge complaints against their franchisors. It is suggested that franchisors should confer with their legal advisers from time to time to ensure the continued validity of their franchise agreements.

11.9 Selecting franchise opportunities

The prospective franchisee should put pertinent questions to the franchisor and existing franchisees. Their answers and comments will assist the potential franchisee in deciding which of the franchise companies are most compatible with his or her own personality, desires, ethics and goals (FRAIN 2002).

11.9.1 Questions to ask the franchisor

The following are some of the most important questions:

- When did your company begin and what has been its history?
- How long have you been franchising?
- Why did you decide to franchise your business?

- What are your plans for the next few years?
- How many franchised locations do you have? How many were opened last year?
- What do you look for in a prospective franchisee and why?
- What is the franchise fee? What do I get for this money? How and when do you require payment of the fee?
- Do you require a deposit? If so, is this deposit refundable?
- Is there a management service fee or royalty? How much is it?
- Do you charge any other fees (e.g. advertising fees, training fees, etc.)?
- How much initial investment is required to open the franchise?
- What is the working capital requirement? How many months does this amount cover?
- How long will it take from the moment I sign an application form before I am able to open the doors for business?
- How long does it usually take for this type of business to start covering the bills? How long before it makes a profit?
- What are the average profit margins?
- Do you assist me in finding the proper site for my franchise?
- Do you assist me with the design and construction of the business?
- Do you train my staff?
- What type of training do I get?
- How long is the initial training?
- What is the organisational structure of your company? Who is responsible for providing ongoing support to me as a franchisee?
- What type of advertising, operational and accounting assistance do you provide to your franchisees?

11.9.2 Questions to ask existing franchisees

The following questions will assist you in your selection process:
- How long have you been a franchisee?
- How do you feel about your franchisor and his or her employees? What kind of people are they?
- Does your franchise business make money?

- Have you made the profit you expected to make?
- How competitive do you find the cost for products purchased from the franchisor compared with similar products from other suppliers?
- How would you describe the quality of the products supplied by the franchisor? How timely are the deliveries?
- How do you feel about the initial support provided to you by the franchisor? Was it sufficient? Did the franchisor deliver on his promises, and how?
- How effective do you feel the training you received in the beginning was, and what type of ongoing training is provided?
- In your opinion, how fair and how easy to deal with is the franchisor?
- Do you feel that the franchisor and the staff listen to your concerns? Do they take action when they promise? How receptive is the franchisor to your comments?
- Have you had any disagreements with your franchisor and if so, how were they resolved?
- Do you know any franchisees that have left the organisation and why they left?
- How do you feel about the advertising and marketing support provided by your franchisor?
- If there is a monthly advertising fee, how is this money spent?
- How does your franchisor communicate with you? Are there monthly newsletters, regular meetings or annual conventions or conferences?
- Does the franchisor or one of his employees visit your offices regularly; and, do you find their visits worthwhile? Could you describe to me the process of this visit?
- If you were in my shoes, would you purchase a franchise from this company?

11.10 Understanding the relationships set out in the franchise contract

Although the contracts of the various franchise networks may differ, many of them have certain terms in common. On the whole, franchise contracts are standard form contracts that leave little room for negotiation. The reason for this is that successful franchise networks require internal uniformity and the maintenance of set standards. The franchise contract is used as a tool to "regulate" the franchisor/franchisee relationship and to enforce uniformity and the maintenance of standards within the franchise network. It places obligations on both parties to their mutual advantage.

It must also be remembered that in most cases the franchise contract provides merely a framework. The conclusion of other contracts will be necessary for the execution of the contract. If, for example, the franchise contract provides for the training of personnel and the supply of products and services, such training and supply will take place in terms of further contracts signed after the conclusion of the franchise contract. The parties are obliged to the conclusion of such contracts in terms of the franchise contract which, in part, regulates the content of such contracts.

11.10.1 The duties of the franchisor

The franchisee needs to be successfully assimilated into the franchise network. The franchisor is not only obliged to disclose the business system to the franchisee and to make available the intellectual property licensed to the franchisee in terms of the franchise agreement. He or she should also advise the franchisee on matters relating to the establishment of the franchised business on the premises, such as the design and decor of the premises; suitable building, shopfitting, electrical, signwriting and other such contractors; sources of supply for equipment and furnishings; and other requirements specifically related to the particular franchise. In support of the establishment of the franchise, the franchisor will also assist the franchisee in the buying of stock and in acquiring services and equipment necessary for the operation of the franchise.

Of course, the franchisor provides the franchisee with training. He or she determines, in consultation with the franchisee, which of the franchisee's employees will undergo training in the business system. The franchisor must provide or supply the franchisee with the same services and facilities as the other franchisees.

The franchise contract obliges the franchisor to provide continuous support services after the conclusion of the contract. These services include marketing, development of the business system to adapt to the changing demands of commerce, advice and training. The franchisor is also obliged to disclose all improvements and developments in the business system to the franchisee and, as a result, to provide such further training to the franchisee and other persons engaged in the conduct of the franchised business. Where improvements and developments in the business system involve improvements and additions to intellectual property, they must be disclosed to the franchisee and will form part of the intellectual property that was licensed to the franchisee in terms of the franchise agreement.

11.10.2 The duties of the franchisee

Usually, the franchisee is obliged to conduct the franchised business strictly in accordance with the operations manual. All the terms of the operations manual and any amendments to, or revision of, the manual form part of the agreement between the franchisor and the franchisee. The manual contains instructions on all aspects of the franchise. The franchisee also undertakes to adhere strictly to any written specifications and directions as may be laid down or given by the franchisor from time to time.

As explained earlier, uniformity within the franchise network is necessary for the success of such a network. The franchisee must ensure that the franchised business conforms with other franchised businesses operated in accordance with the business system.

The franchisee and/or his or her employees are obliged to undergo training by the franchisor in the business system. The franchisee may not induce employees of fellow franchisees to leave their employment and take up employment with him. It is not in the interest of the development of a franchise network to allow franchisees to lure trained employees away from fellow franchisees.

The franchised business is usually conducted from premises that have been approved by the franchisor. The premises must be maintained in a good and clean condition. The franchisor may require the franchisee to redecorate or refurbish the premises to ensure that the premises

Van Schaik Publishers

are in the same condition as those of other franchisees. Also, the franchisee is required to observe minimum business hours.

The franchisee is not allowed to advertise or conduct promotional marketing activities without the prior written approval of the franchisor, but is obliged to use and display the franchisor's point-of-sale, advertising or promotional material.

The franchisee is also obliged to allow the franchisor at all reasonable times to carry out such inspections or investigations that may be considered necessary for the purposes of ascertaining whether the provisions of the agreement are being complied with. The franchisee must ensure that he or she and all employees cooperate fully in such inspections.

11.10.3 The protection of the franchisor's intellectual property

We have seen that franchisees obtain a right or licence to use the intellectual property of the franchisor. They do not, however, become the owners thereof and are obliged to protect it. The franchisees may not do, cause or permit anything that may adversely affect the intellectual property licences to them, or the franchisor's rights to the intellectual property. The franchisees usually acknowledge that the franchisor owns the intellectual property and undertake not to attack or challenge its existence or validity.

The franchisee not only obtains the right to use the franchisor's trademarks but is obliged to do so. The franchisee does not, however, become the owner of the trademarks. The use of a well-known and distinctive trademark obviously benefits the franchisee. To maintain the distinctiveness of the trademark, the franchisee is obliged, when using the trademark, to reproduce it exactly and accurately and in accordance with the specifications and directions laid down by the franchisor from time to time. All use of the trademarks will be to the franchisor's benefit.

The franchisee may not divulge, or allow to be divulged, to any person any aspect of the business system, the know-how or the trade secrets other than for the purposes of the franchise agreement. In this regard, the franchisee and his or her employees may be required to sign a confidentiality undertaking.

The franchisee undertakes to protect and promote the goodwill associated with the franchised business. All goodwill generated by the conduct of the franchised business will be to the benefit of the franchisor.

11.10.4 Restraints of trade on the franchisee and the franchisor

The maintenance of standards and the quest for uniformity also require that franchise agreements contain terms that place restraints of trade on the franchisee. Territorial restraints may restrict the operation of the business to certain premises or territories. There may also be price restraints in terms of which the franchisee is obliged to supply the franchise products or services at a prescribed price to the public.

The franchisor may also place restraints on the franchisee with regard to products and sales. The franchisee may, for example, be obliged to buy products or other necessities from the franchisor or another supplier designated by the franchisor. The franchisee may be obliged to carry on business only in certain products and services. There may also be a provision in terms of which the franchisee is not allowed to change the nature of the commodities or services supplied, or the nature of the business system. Also, a so-called tying agreement may be concluded in terms of which the franchisor will supply a particularly necessary product or service to the franchisee on condition that a certain requirement has been met, such as that the franchisee also buys another product from the franchisor.

Other restraints may relate to the franchisee's right to advertise, or to competition (e.g. the franchisee is not allowed to have an interest in a business that competes with the franchised business) during the term of the franchise agreement or for a certain period of time after its termination.

Restraints of trade are also placed on the franchisor. The purpose of these restraints is usually to offer the franchisee protection against competition by the franchisor or third parties. If the franchisee is granted an exclusive territory, the franchisor may be obliged not to operate, or grant any other person the right to operate, the same franchise within that territory. The franchisor may also be obliged not to sell products to the franchisee's competitors at a price lower than that at which products are sold to the franchisee. He may even be obliged to provide and supply products only to the franchisee.

11.10.5 Payment obligations

In addition to the financial obligations incurred at the establishment of the franchise (such as the buying of equipment and products, and obtaining premises), the payment obligations of the franchisee usually include an initial lump sum payment to the franchisor at the conclusion of the contract and royalties payable periodically during the term of the agreement.

The lump sum payment is usually an initial payment for the rights agreed to in terms of the agreement and for the equipment, advice, assistance and training provided by the franchisor to enable the franchisee to establish the business.

The royalties may be fixed amounts that are payable periodically (weekly or monthly). The royalties may also be calculated as a percentage of the franchisee's turnover or net sales within a certain period. The royalties are amounts that are payable for the continuing support provided by the franchisor and the continuing use of the rights granted in terms of the agreement.

In addition to the royalties, the franchise agreement may also provide for additional levies related to specific services of the franchisor. The franchisee may, for example, be obliged to pay the franchisor an amount for marketing or advertising campaigns, which are also calculated as a percentage of the net sales.

11.10.6 Termination of the agreement

Franchise agreements may provide for the termination of the contract after a time period or on the death, insolvency or incapacity of the franchisee.

The contract may also provide that on the death of the franchisee, the franchisor may approve the transfer of the franchised business to any of the beneficiaries of the deceased franchisee. They will be required to assume the management of the franchised business as soon as they have bound themselves to observe the terms and conditions of the franchise agreement. Before such transfer takes place, the franchisor will be entitled to assume control and management of the franchised business and to operate it for the benefit and account of the franchisee's deceased estate. The franchisor will also be entitled to charge the usual fee for the conduct and management of the franchised business. If the franchisor does not approve of the transfer of the franchised business to a beneficiary, the franchise may be disposed of at an agreed price to another person approved by the franchisor.

The franchisor usually strengthens his or her remedies against the franchisee by including provisions in the franchise contract in terms of which the franchisor may divert from the contract on the grounds of certain defined forms of breach of contract. Upon termination of the agreement, the franchisee must immediately cease any further use of the trademarks and other intellectual property that were licensed to him. The franchisee must hand over all dies, blocks, labels, advertising material, and printed matter featuring the trademarks that were obtained from, or which he was authorised to use by, the franchisor.

Franchise contracts often oblige franchisees upon termination of the contract to participate directly or indirectly in the management or control of a business that conducts business in the nature of, or similar to, the franchised business for a certain period of time. The former franchisee is also obliged not to disclose confidential information or other trade secrets of the franchisor.

11.11 The potential of franchises within the emerging entrepreneurial sector

Economic empowerment, upliftment and the increase in employment opportunities, followed by improvements in the standard of living amongst previously disadvantaged communities, must surely rank among the most discussed topics at various national and regional governmental forums (FASA 2002). Consensus exists that the micro- and small business sector holds the key to achieving these goals. This begs the question: How does one incorporate this macroeconomic strategy into actual operations? Is there a system or a formula available that makes it possible to apply all components of upliftment through economic empowerment towards creating a self-sufficient, economically viable and sustainable model? The answer is – a very conditional – "yes".

No single role-player can hope to achieve this in isolation. It has to be an end product of joint ventures between the government in its capacity as legislator, the Department of Trade and Industry, the banking fraternity, FASA, service providers and franchisors. The definition of such a model and its successful implementation could well become the best example of public/private partnership our country has ever experienced.

From the franchisor's viewpoint, franchising is already a demanding, multidisciplinary business format. To tailor it for use by emerging entrepreneurs adds an important new dimension to the equation. One could argue that to set up an emerging entrepreneur as a franchisee should be no different from any standard application of franchising. This is true, but it demands the application of franchising at maximum capacity, simply because most emerging entrepreneurs are unable to make a meaningful equity contribution and lack general business experience. These problems, caused by the virtual non-existence of opportunities available under the previous dispensation, are elements that a good franchise system should be able to accommodate, but tolerance levels will be substantially lower. Much as partners in a marriage are rarely "perfect", it is widely accepted that the "perfect franchisee" does not exist. Traditionally, however, to be considered as franchisees, individuals have had to possess a certain mix of attributes, including the ability to make a substantial investment. Accepting emerging entrepreneurs as franchisees will force franchise systems to lower the barrier to entry.

Some of the major advantages for developing franchises within the emerging entrepreneurial sector can be summarised as follows:

- Emerging entrepreneurs, especially in rural areas, enjoy far greater consumer loyalty than can be found in traditional trading areas. This is especially the case if the fran-

chisee originates from the area in which the business is set up.

- Although the process of transferring the necessary skills is a much more intense and costly affair, the system's standards and adherence thereto are seldom questioned. Indeed, the franchisee that boasts the smallest operational variances has been drawn from the ranks of emerging entrepreneurs.

- The selection of management and operational staff in the operations of emerging franchisees is a more efficient process because of the virtual absence of cultural and communication gaps.

- The aspirations and expectations of emerging entrepreneurs are generally modest, thus reducing pressure on the profitability of the business during the early days. Moreover, emerging entrepreneurs tend to focus on the operation of a single outlet – not for them the "multiple operation syndrome" traditional franchisees frequently develop.

11.12 Conclusion

Whether one looks at it from the point of view of the franchisor or the franchisee, franchising is one of the ideal routes to business success in South Africa. FASA has done much to disseminate information and ensure ethical conduct, and these efforts continue. The value of a pilot franchising operation cannot be overemphasised. It is essential that the business concept be fully developed and tested before the first franchise is sold. A comprehensive franchise package must also be prepared and made available to prospective franchisees.

Prospective franchisors have to take note of the ethical requirements associated with franchising. These are basically the Consumer Code for Franchising (issued by the Business Practice Committee), the Disclosure Document of the Franchise Association of Southern Africa (FASA), and membership of FASA.

At the end of the day, however, it is up to each individual to do the necessary homework before parting with hard-earned cash. In this way, franchising will continue to grow to the benefit of all concerned.

Looking back

1. Explain the key elements of the "franchising concept".
   - A franchise operation is a contractual relationship between the franchisor and the franchisee.
   - The franchisor offers or is obliged to maintain a continuing interest in the business of the franchisee in such areas as know-how and training.
   - The franchisee operates under a common trade name, format and/or procedure owned or controlled by the franchisor.
   - The franchisee has made, or will make, a substantial capital investment in the business from his own resources.
2. Identify the three types of franchising.
   - The first type is the dealership, a form commonly found in the car industry. The manufacturers use franchises to distribute their product lines.
   - The second (and most common type of franchise) is referred to as business format franchising. This is the type that offers a name, image and method of doing business, such as McDonald's, KFC, Nando's, Spec-Savers and Supa Quick.
   - The third type of franchise offers services.
3. Identify the key elements of the franchise contract.
   - The duties of the franchisor
   - The duties of the franchisee
   - The protection of the franchisor's intellectual property
   - Restraints of trade on the franchisee and the franchisor
   - Payment obligations
   - Termination of the agreement
4. What are some of the major advantages of developing franchises within the emerging entrepreneurial sector?
   - Emerging entrepreneurs enjoy far greater consumer loyalty than can be found in traditional trading areas.
   - Although the process of transferring the necessary skills is a much more intense and costly affair, standards and adherence thereto are seldom questioned.
   - The selection of management and operational staff in the operations of emerging franchisees is a more efficient process because of the virtual absence of cultural and communication gaps.
   - The aspirations and expectations of emerging entrepreneurs are generally modest, thus reducing pressure on the profitability of the business during the early days.

Key terms

Advertising
Franchise agreement
Franchise fee
Franchisee

Franchisor
Franchisor/franchisee relationship
Royalties

Discussion questions

1. What makes franchising different from other types of business?
2. Identify and describe the parties in the franchising system.
3. Identify and discuss the pros and cons of franchising from the franchisor's and the franchisee's point of view.

4. What types of limitations on franchise independence might be included in a typical franchise contract?
5. Give a brief overview of the drivers of the franchise system in the emerging markets in South Africa.

Case studies

Case study 1: Franchising a preferred vehicle

Franchising has proved to be a popular vehicle for the growth of convenience stores in South Africa as many employees forsake the corporate world to embark on new careers as entrepreneurs.

Tom Voges, marketing manager of the OK franchise division, says the greatest attraction for franchisees is the reasonable entry level and the enormous benefits of being part of a professional group. He says franchisees must be given scope to operate as entrepreneurs, as well as the opportunity and guidance to run successful and profitable businesses. The chain of 8 Till Late neighbourhood convenience superettes is one of the brands in the OK franchise division portfolio, which is part of the Shoprite-Checkers group. The brand was launched in October 1998 and operates in the Western Cape and Gauteng.

Voges says an important aspect in running an 8 Till Late franchise is that members are given the opportunity to share ideas and provide input into the structure and management style of the division. "We provide the tools, but the members have to make them work. This ensures that it is more than a we-you relationship but an us relationship, which is beneficial to both franchisee and franchisor."

George Hadjidakis, founder and MD of the 7-Eleven Corporation SA, says the franchising of convenience stores has probably succeeded better in South Africa than in most countries

because it took off at time when many people in this country were taking retrenchment packages. Retrenchment packages were used in many instances to upgrade outlets such as coffee shops into convenience stores, with owners perhaps later selling the business and moving on to another industry.

Franchising minimises the business risk, Hadjidakis says, in that the franchisor is able to provide franchisees with the training and guidance to be successful. He says statistics indicate that over the past decade, up to 70 per cent of all new start-up businesses have failed. The failure rate with 7-Eleven has been 16 per cent. "My advice to first-time franchisees is to have a close look at the history and future potential of the company they intend going into business with," Hadjidakis says. "There have been a number of fly-by-night operators in franchising and some people have lost their money. Franchisees need to find a franchisor with the muscle, infrastructure and years of experience to back them up," he says.

Source: Franchising a preferred vehicle, David Jackson, *Business Day,* 3 December 2001.

Questions

1. Do you think that the 7-Eleven franchise would satisfy the evaluation and selection criteria of a preferred franchise? Explain in detail.
2. Why do you think that the failure rate of the convenience stores in South Africa is relatively low?

Case study 2: House of Health complements South Africa's burgeoning drug industry

In 1990 Gordon Wilson bought his company for R1 500, using three post-dated cheques. Today, the House of Health has a monthly turnover in excess of R1,5 million. The business was hailed in KwaZulu-Natal this week for marketing excellence as one of the Institute of Marketing Management marketing organisations of the year.

The province's first nutritional supplement network marketing company sells a range of locally manufactured products, including African ginger, African potato and spirulina, in South Africa, Uganda, Tanzania and Mauritius. According to Wilson, the local market for complementary medicines is worth about R1,74 billion, of which direct sales make up R522 million.

Based in Durban, the company directly employs six people but has 40 000 agents in the four countries who use the products and earn money by selling to other consumers.

Wilson says government policies towards natural health products are becoming positive and he plans to expand the business by setting up franchise outlets across the country.

The company owns a store at Windermere Centre in Durban and has opened franchises at Sanlam Centre in Pinetown and Fields Mall in Kloof. It is negotiating for space at La Lucia Mall and the Pavilion. He would like 20 more stores by the end of 2003.

A major banking group has indicated it would give financial support to successful franchise applicants. Wilson says he has drawn from the model used by the master licence holder in Uganda, where there are 28 franchise stores and 24 000 members who buy from these outlets. Tanzania is looking at 22 outlets by 2004 and Mauritius has plans for six.

In much of Africa, people have poor nutrition and the company's products have helped many HIV-positive people to improve their immune systems sufficiently for them to leave their sick beds and return to work.

Many people have become entrepreneurs by selling House of Health products.

Born in Durban, Wilson (48) developed an interest in complementary medicines and natural healing from his parents, who in 1969 founded Attwells Health Foods, one of the country's oldest and most respected health food companies.

After matriculating at Marist Brothers College, Wilson studied homeopathy but ended his studies when the government refused to recognise the discipline. He worked for his parents for a year and started freelancing, selling products to chemists and health shops. Offered a shipload of vitamin E, he was able to sell the consignment and, having created a demand, he set out to satisfy the need.

In 1974 he created the Vitality brand of vitamins and health supplements. In 1980 he was the first person to import aloe vera and spirulina, which are now recognised health products. In 1996, after experiencing management problems, Wilson sold Vitality, which is now part of Aspen Pharmacare.

At that stage he already owned the House of Health registration and trademarks, which had started out as a party-plan business that he bought when the owner decided to close it down. From 1996 he gave this business his full attention.

In his previous business Wilson had focused on the retail trade, but found a suitable business plan for the House of Health range in Australia from Don Fayler, a multilevel marketing guru.

Source: Deon Delport. *Business Report*, 13 October 2002.

Questions

1. What are the competitive advantages of House of Health?

2. House of Health developed different sales and distribution strategies for different types of clients. Do you think this makes good business sense, or should the company focus on one distribution channel?

Experiential exercises

1. Interview the local owner-manager of a popular franchise, such as the Spur or the Spar. Ask him to explain the process through which he went in obtaining the franchise, and what he thinks are the major pros and cons of owning and managing the franchise.

2. Make a list of criteria which you think are crucial when evaluating and selecting a potential franchise. Rate these criteria from 10 (as an excellent opportunity) to 1 (meaning "not an option").

Exploring the Web

You will find additional information on franchising at the following websites:

- Franchise Advice and Information Network (FRAIN): http://www.frain.org.za

- Franchise Association of Southern Africa (FASA): http://www.fasa.co.za
- International Franchise Association (IFA): http://www.franchise.org

References and recommended reading

Franchise Advice and Information Network (FRAIN). 2002. *Selecting and evaluating a franchise opportunity.* Available at http://www.frain.org.za. Accessed August 2002.

Franchising Association of South Africa (FASA). 2002. *The franchising handbook of southern Africa.* Johannesburg: FASA.

Hisrich, R.D. & Peters, M.P. 2002. *Entrepreneurship.* 5th ed. New York: McGraw-Hill.

Longenecker, J.G., Moore, C.W. & Petty, J.W. 2003. *Small business management,* 12th ed. Cincinnati: South-Western.

Mendelsohn, M. & Bynoe, R. 1992. *Franchising.* London: FT Law and Tax.

Nieman, G. 1998. *The franchise option: how to franchise your business.* Kenwyn: Juta.

Unisa. 1999. *The South African business world.* African Management Programme. Pretoria: Centre for Business Management.

12

The business buyout

Kobus Lazenby

Learning outcomes

After completion of this chapter, you should be able to:

- Evaluate the option of buying an existing business
- Conduct a self-audit as a requirement for finding a business to buy
- Identify the steps in finding a business to buy
- Evaluate available businesses before buying one
- Implement methods for determining the value of a business
- Identify important issues in the negotiation process
- Identify the traps to avoid when buying an existing business

12.1 Introduction

It is not always necessary, or essential, for would-be entrepreneurs to start their new business from scratch or join a family business to be regarded as a true entrepreneur or to become the owner of a business. The alternative option is to buy an existing business or a franchise – this is known as a buyout. In the late 1990s it became a hot trend in the United States to purchase an existing business as a result of the ongoing boom in entrepreneurship (Zimmerer & Scarborough 1998).

The reasons and evaluation criteria for a buyout might not necessarily differ from those for a totally new start-up or for joining the family business. The urge of "doing one's own thing" is still there; the means, however, differ. There are different routes to a start-up and the buying of an existing business, despite the fact that both have the same goal, namely to own a business. It is important to stress that this is not something to be done hastily. The buying of an existing business is often a disappointing experience. That is why the entrepreneur has to make sure that his or her decision to buy an existing business, instead of starting one from scratch, is a sound one. Do not rush into the deal without doing your homework properly.

In this chapter we will explore the whole process of buying a business. We will start with an evaluation of the advantages and disadvantages of buying an existing business; how to find a business to buy; how to evaluate the existing business; methods for determining the value and/or price of a business; and the negotiating process. We shall conclude with some traps to avoid in the process of buying a business.

12.2 Evaluating the option of buying an existing business

The option of buying a business is best evaluated by considering the reasons for the decision to buy a business. Evaluating the advantages and disadvantages of buying an existing business can be a fruitful exercise and will ensure that one does not rush into things.

12.2.1 The advantages of buying a business

There are a number of advantages in buying an established business. There is less risk involved in buying an existing business, it is in many ways easier and there is a chance to get a business at a bargain price (Lambing & Kuehl 1997). Zimmerer and Scarborough (1998: 100-101) add the following advantages:

- The business is an ongoing concern. This will save the new owner the time, money and energy that are usually required when someone planning and launching a new business.

- A successful existing business may have a better chance to continue to be successful. A successful business usually has an established customer base that will carry the new owner while he or she is learning the business. It is a common fact that the early days of a new business are devoted to intensive efforts to expand the customer base. It is, however, a challenge to learn how to keep these customers happy.

- Location is of the utmost importance and critical to the success of a business. An existing business may have the advantage of already having an excellent location. A second-best location will not draw the attention of customers.

- Experienced and reliable employees are already on the payroll of the business, and can continue their services. Finding such employees in the labour market takes a great deal of effort and energy, and may not be worthwhile in the end.

- The suppliers are also established, and the owner is spared the effort of building new relationships with suppliers. Trade credit may also have been established, because suppliers would not want to lose a good customer.

- The inventory is in place. The previous owner's knowledge of striking the right balance between too little inventory (i.e. one may not be able to meet the needs of customers) and too much inventory (tying up excessive capital) is invaluable to the new owner.

- The equipment is installed and the production capacity is known. When buying an existing business, the new owner can determine the condition of the equipment and its capacity. He or she may be able to buy these facilities and equipment at a price below replacement costs. This is of tremendous benefit to the entrepreneur's financial resources.

- It is possible to buy an existing business at a bargain price. The current owner may be forced to sell at short notice due to personal or health reasons. If an entrepreneur is able to pay cash for the business, or to make a substantial down payment if buying on credit, it is possible to negotiate a good deal.

12.2.2 The disadvantages of buying a business

In the previous section several good reasons were discussed that favoured the buying of a new business. Unfortunately, there are also some problems or disadvantages that should be considered. Zimmerer and Scarborough (1998: 102-103) list the following external and internal problems or limitations that the entrepreneur should take into account:

- The business was never profitable, but the owner has disguised it by employing a creative accounting technique. Be aware that a business owner may have more than one income statement. There may be the true one (only for the eyes of the owner), one for the Receiver of Revenue (stating a loss in order to save on income tax) and one for the potential buyer (stating a favourable income and profit).

- A business can have an inadequate sales volume. Despite a well-run operation, the profit level to support the owner may be too low due to the low sales volume (Lambing & Kuehl 1997: 91). This may perhaps be because there are not enough customers to support the business.

- A business may have a poor reputation or image. Poor business behaviour in terms of unethical and socially irresponsible business dealings creates ill will for a business. The business may seemingly be sound, but some customers, suppliers, employees and creditors may be negative about it. Usually such negativity has a long-term effect on the business, and it might happen that these effects are not yet reflected in the financial statements.

- Some of the employees inherited with the business may not be suitable for the job. Also, a history of internal conflict and politics will not be erased by a change in ownership. There may be many unsettled grievances that will now be dumped on the new owner. The previous owner could also have employed marginal employees, and it is now the unpleasant task of the new owner to terminate their contracts with the business.

- The business location may be not that favourable. The location could have been satisfactory in the past, but as a result of new developments like shopping malls and new competitors, this once favourable location spells disaster for the business area in which the enterprise is located. It may also have developed a bad reputation. The prospective buyer therefore needs to do a thorough evaluation of the market in the immediate environment.

- The equipment, facilities and inventory may be obsolete. It is common knowledge that inventory is only valuable if it can be sold. Obsolete inventory is worthless – it may look good and valuable, but it may be outdated. Equipment and facilities that are no longer useful may entail excessively high costs for the new owner.

- The business may be overpriced, i.e. the price of the business is higher than its value in terms of its assets on the balance sheet. Sometimes the price of the business is not the most crucial aspect, but the terms on which the deal is negotiated.

- According to Lambing and Kuehl (1997), it is also important to consider the disadvantage of operating in the shadow of the previous owner. This is especially true of a service-rendering business where a great deal of trust and confidence was established between the previous owner and his or her clients. These elements are not that easily transferred to the new owner.

When looking at all these disadvantages, it is important to realise that it can be very risky to buy an existing business. Thorough evaluation and the scrutinising of every relevant detail are vital.

12.3 Finding a business to buy

After having considered all the advantages and disadvantages of buying an existing business, the next logical step is to find a business to buy. Before engaging in the actual process of searching for one, it is important to analyse one's own skills, abilities and interests thoroughly. It is important that there is a fit between the entrepreneur and the business. A "self-audit" helps one to identify the type of business one will be happy in and thus make a success of.

Zimmerer and Scarborough (1998: 105) state that it is important to answer the following questions:

- What business activities do you enjoy the most and/or least? Why?
- What kind of business do you want to buy/avoid?
- How much time, energy and money are you willing to put into the business?
- How many risks are you willing to take?
- What size business do you want to buy?
- What business skills and experience do you have or are you lacking?
- What do you expect to get out of the business?
- What industries interest you the most or the least? Why?

The answers to these questions may help the prospective buyer to draw up a list of criteria that an existing business must meet before it becomes an option for a buyout. As said earlier, this will also help to create and ensure a fit between the business and the new owner. Without this fit, the owner will already be at a distinct disadvantage.

With a clear mind about the self-audit, it is time to start the search for a suitable business. When opening a newspaper at the section "Businesses for sale", one is overwhelmed by the number of available concerns for sale.

Sometimes one will hear about a business for sale by word of mouth. Other sources of information include suppliers, trade organisations like the South African Business Chamber, and even financial institutions. The obvious place to start will be to prepare a list of potential businesses to buy. It is important to remember to look for businesses on the market, as well as those on the so-called hidden market.

12.3.1 Businesses on the market

These are known businesses for sale. They are advertised in the newspaper and through property or business brokers. In the majority of cases, the owner tries to sell the business on his or her own.

Finding a business in this way is not a problem, but finding a good one may be. Ask yourself: Why is the business being advertised? Why does the owner want to get rid of it? There may be a number of reasons for the owner wanting to sell, but the most common one may be that the business is struggling (Lambing & Kuehl 1997). Is this the type of business you want? If you have a solution to remedy this problem, it should be in place and well developed before you proceed too far with the purchase of the business.

12.3.2 Businesses not on the market

Zimmerer and Scarborough (1998: 105) regard the so-called hidden market as one of the richest sources of top-quality businesses. A very high percentage of buyout opportunities can be found in the unadvertised market. Usually these types of available businesses are those that may represent an attractive opportunity. The typical sources that can be used to uncover this hidden market include:

- Property agents
- Financial institutions
- Accountants and auditors
- Suppliers
- Friends and relatives
- Knocking on the doors of businesses one is interested in
- The Business Chambers

The one advantage of finding a business in this manner is that they are not necessarily in trouble or struggling. They remain in the hands of the owner because there is no real intention or need to sell. There is, however, a saying that "if the price is right, everything is for sale". The real task is, therefore, to find such businesses.

Table 12.1 gives a few guidelines that will help potential buyers find the right business for them.

Table 12.1 Hints to ensure that a prospective buyer will find the right business

- Find the answers for the self-audit. Be honest with yourself.
- Determine what you really want from the business. Is it money or freedom or flexibility?
- Reconsider your lifestyle. Think about having a business and that you will own it for a very long time – is this really what you want; will you really enjoy it?
- Be critical and sceptical. Do not look at reasons why you want to buy the business, rather try to find reasons why you should not buy the business.
- Answer honestly the question whether it would not be better to start the business from scratch.
- Do you really like the seller, the employees and the type of customers of the business? You are buying the business with all its stakeholders.
- Do you like the location of the business?

Source: Adapted from Zimmerer and Scarborough (1998: 107).

12.4 Evaluating available businesses

Now that the prospective buyer has a list of available businesses, it is time to start evaluating and investigating the businesses. No matter what the source of the business opportunities, careful analysis and homework are fundamental requirements. The following questions should be addressed.

12.4.1 Why is the business for sale?

It is very important to establish the real reason why a business is for sale. It is sometimes not found in the financial statements, nor on the spreadsheets used to analyse the financial position of the business.

Only through proper research can surprises pop up as real reasons why a business is for sale. A new, strong competitor may be about to move into the market. Perhaps the traffic planning of the local authority will make the location of the business inconvenient to customers. The lease agreement for the business may be about to change in the near future. There may also be a decline in the customer base of the business.

12.4.2 Is the business profitable?

What is the general financial situation or condition of the business? Does the business generate a positive cash flow?

As mentioned earlier, it is possible that the figures on the financial statements may be inflated. When evaluating the financial statements, bear in mind that you must earn a salary from the business. If no provision was made for a salary for the owner in the earlier financial records, a high profit might be very misleading. Be aware of such a situation.

The financial history of the business is very important because it is an indication of the future prospects of the business. The future will be a reflection of the past. The comparison of past with current records is therefore of the utmost importance. Do not rely on financial statements only, but also ask for VAT records, income tax records and bank account statements. With the consent of the owner, banks are willing to provide you with a summary of all deposits and withdrawals during a year. This can also be compared with the cash flow statement of the business. If it is a sound business, the owner will supply this information, given that you are a trustworthy person who will treat the information with confidentiality.

12.4.3 What skills and competencies do I need for managing the business?

Businesses in different industries need different skills and competencies. A manufacturing business will definitely require different competencies than those for a service-rendering or retail business. Make sure that you are skilled

to meet the demands of the specific type of business.

12.4.4 What is the history of the business in terms of its previous owners, its reputation and public image?

What was the original name of the business and when was it founded and by whom? Get names and contact information so you will be able to establish why the business might perhaps have been sold quite often. This will reveal some hidden information not identifiable in the financial records.

12.4.5 What is the physical condition of the business, its facilities and all other assets?

These aspects are important because they will help the prospective owner to determine the value of the business. Close inspection of the equipment and inventory will reveal important information about the condition and efficiency of the business. Experts sometimes need to be called in to examine the plumbing, electrical and other specialised systems. If one has to repair something one has not budgeted for, it can cause cash flow problems.

A close inspection of the various items on the balance sheet is very important. The following items must be scrutinised very carefully:

- Fixed assets and their condition
- Accounts receivable
- Inventory
- Intangible assets, like goodwill, patents, etc.
- Liabilities, like lease agreements, loans, etc.

12.4.6 What are the degree and scope of competition?

Who are the major competitors? The identification of the direct competitors is important. This is one of the strongest forces in the business environment that will determine the success and, for that matter, the profitability of the business.

Trend analysis in terms of the competitors is also important because it will give an indication of what is happening in the industry. What causes competitors to start up or to close down? It will also help you to determine the key success factors in the industry, because there may be some competitors who are successful and others who are less successful. What are the reasons for this?

12.4.7 What is the existing and the potential market size?

This links up with the previous point. Important and valuable information that may come to the fore will include the demographic profile of the customers, the reasons why customers will buy the product, what needs they have that must still be met, how loyal they are, what can be done to attract new customers, and whether there are perhaps any seasonal trends. This information is very important in terms of developing a sound marketing plan.

12.4.8 What important legal aspects must be considered?

Make sure that all the legal aspects are in place in order to avoid severe pitfalls and to ensure the smooth transition of the sale. Clarity about ongoing liabilities and contracts is of the utmost importance to prevent bitter tears and financial losses later. Apart from other important legal aspects, one thing that also plays an important role is the restraint of trade agreement. The rationale for this agreement is to restrict the seller of the business from starting a similar enterprise and taking away the customer base from his or her former business.

It is especially important to hire a professional legal consultant to make sure that all the legal aspects are spelled out clearly and there is no uncertainty or loophole that could cause problems.

12.4.9 Further questions

Other important questions that can be asked when investigating an available business include the following:

- What is the situation regarding the marketing strategy of the business? What are the present product, promotion, distribution and pricing policies?
- What is the situation regarding the employees? Will they stay? What are their skills and

what will be the effect of a management change? Analyse the current policies with regard to the employees.

- What is the type of ownership of the business you want to buy? It is important to know who the right person is to start talking to. Are there any relatives of the owner working in the business? This may later create a difficult situation to manage.

The process of buying an existing business is fraught with many traps and pitfalls. Rather walk away from a deal if there is any uncertainty about the soundness of the business. If the owner of the business is hesitant to reveal any knowledge or information, something may be less sound than it appears on the face of it. Let the phrase "be aware" always be fresh in your actions and mind. Table 12.2 summarises the information you need before entering into the deal.

Table 12.2 Information to be studied before purchasing a business

- Income statements of at least the past three years
- Balance sheets of at least the past three years
- Cash flow statements of at least the past three years
- Records of any accounts payable
- Records of accounts receivable, preferably presented in aged format
- All contracts with suppliers, e.g. leases on property and any equipment and vehicles
- Service (labour) contracts with employees
- Bank account information regarding deposits and withdrawals
- Income tax returns for at least the past three years
- Value-added tax statements for at least the past three years
- All records of maintenance on fixed assets
- Short-term and employee insurance policies
- Proof of all payments of LBS (employees' salaries) to the Receiver of Revenue

One important point that must be stressed again is to rely on professionals if you are not capable of doing a thorough investigation or evaluation of the business. Longenecker et al. (2003: 130) say in this regard: "The time and money spent on securing professional help in investigating a business can pay big dividends, especially when the buyer is inexperienced." An important piece of advice is, however, not to leave the decision only to the experts. It must be your decision also, because you are going to take all the risks, do the hard work, etc.

12.5 Methods for determining the value of a business

After having investigated the business carefully, it is important to determine the value of the concern. This is necessary before putting in a bid for the business. By "value" we mean the monetary worth of the business, i.e. the marketable price that can be asked for it.

Several methods can be applied to determine the value of a business. Different people will perhaps give you different suggestions. Valuing a business is a complex process, but in the end it is worth the effort and expense. It is not the intention of this chapter to go into too much detail with regard to each method, but only to stimulate the interest and stress the importance of these methods. It is, however, necessary to mention a few guidelines that will help you choose a specific method.

- The most suitable method should be used for a specific transaction. Each business transaction is unique. Sometimes it is better to use every possible method, compare them and then choose the one that makes the most sense.

- It is important that both the buyer and the seller are satisfied with the transaction. Buyers have to make sure that they will be able to pay for the business from realised profits, while sellers must be satisfied that they will receive a fair price for the value they have created.

- Honesty always pays off. This is a golden rule that both seller and buyer must understand and apply.

The question may be asked why one has to do a business valuation. When the process is com-pleted, you will be at the higher end of the continuum of making rock-solid decisions! The benefits of such a valuation can be summarised as follows:

- A business loan is more easily secured with a quality business valuation.

- Understanding the true value of the business spares one financial loss and perhaps also a deflated ego.

- Costs to be incurred later to rectify a situation may be prohibited.

The most well-known methods for determining the value of a business will be discussed in the next section (Zimmerer & Scarborough 1998; Longenecker et al. 2003).

12.5.1 The asset-based method

This method can also be referred to as the balance sheet method. This is where the worth or value of the business is determined by equity – total assets minus the liabilities. It is important to determine which assets are included in the deal. This is, therefore, the first important step, because some owners sometimes want to exclude some of the assets. When looking at the balance sheet values of Quick Shoe Repairs (Table 12.3), the value of the business will be R384 300 (total assets of R452 000 minus total liabilities of R67 700).

A variation on this method is to use the replacement value of the assets rather than the book value. This means that one has to look at the replacement value of the buildings, machinery and vehicles. This can, for example, increase the value of the assets by R100 000. One could also take the real value of the assets into account. Then it is necessary to adjust the values of debtors and the inventory, for example. It might happen that the value of debtors on the books is R54 000, but in practice we know it will be impossible to collect all this outstanding debt. An adjustment should be made, taking the age structure of debtors into consideration. (See Table 12.4 where the total value of debtors is actually only R40 900.) The buildings, machinery, vehicles and inventory are also re-evaluated. It remains important for the buyer to investigate the inventory to make sure that it is at least worth the book value.

It is thus important that the buyer and the

Table 12.3 Balance sheet of Quick Shoe Repairs on 31 December

Fixed assets			Equity		
Buildings	180 000		Capital	287 045	
Machinery	150 000		Accumulated profits	97 255	
Vehicles	37 500				384 300
		367 500	Long-term loan		30 000
Current assets			**Current liabilities**		
Prepaid expenses	5 000		Creditors	27 700	
Debtors	54 000		Bank overdraft	10 000	37 700
Inventory	25 500				
		84 500			
		452 000			452 000

Table 12.4 Value of debtors according to age structure

Age of account	Amount	Chance of getting money	Amount
0–30 days	29 000	90%	26 100
31–60 days	18 000	70%	12 600
61–90 days	5 000	40%	2 000
> 90 days	2 000	10%	200
	54 000		40 900

seller agree on how to evaluate these assets, as this will determine which variation of the asset-based method will be used. After all these considerations, a new adjusted balance sheet can be presented. (Table 12.5). The value of the business will now be R350 900 (R418 600 minus R67 700).

12.5.2 The market-based method

This valuation technique relies on the financial markets to estimate the value of the business. The actual market prices of similar businesses

Table 12.5 Adjusted balance sheet of Quick Shoe Repairs on 31 December

Fixed assets			Equity		
Buildings	195 000		Capital	253 645	
Machinery	127 700		Accumulated profits	97 255	
Vehicles	27 500				350 900
		350 200	Long-term loan		30 000
Current assets			**Current liabilities**		
Prepaid expenses	5 000		Creditors	27 700	
Debtors	40 900		Bank overdraft	10 000	37 700
Inventory	22 500				
		68 400			
		418 600			418 600

that have been sold recently can be taken as an indication. This is, however, difficult because no two businesses are the same. They not only differ with regard to location, but also in terms of image, customer profiles, quality of services rendered, etc. The list can be endless. The market-based method can only give a fair idea of the value of the business.

A more sophisticated approach using the market-based valuation is to determine the price-to-earnings ratio:

Price-to-earnings ratio = Market price / Aftertax earnings

To determine the market price one still has to compare the prices of similar businesses that were sold recently. Say, for example, the prices of three recently sold businesses are R260 000, R280 000 and R300 000 respectively. The average market price will thus be R280 000. Let us also assume that the average aftertax earnings of these three businesses is R83 000. The price-to-earnings ratio will then be:

Price-to-earnings ratio = Market price / Aftertax earnings

= R280 000 / R83 000

= 3,4

To determine the value of Quick Shoe Repairs (net profit aftertax of R97 255 in Table 12.6):

Price-to-earnings ratio = Market price / Aftertax earnings

3,4 = Market price / R97 255

Therefore: Market price = 3,4(R97 255)

= R330 667

When using the expected net earnings for the coming year (see Step 3 under "The excess earning method" below), the market price for Quick Shoe Repairs will be R404 736 (3,4 × R119 040).

When working with businesses of which the stock trades publicly, it is easier to find the price-to-earnings ratio. Despite the advantage of simplicity, this method also has important disadvantages, one of which is the fact that owners try to minimise profits in order to save on taxes. The aftertax earnings may therefore not be a true reflection of the potential of the business. Despite this drawback, it remains a useful general guideline for establishing the value of a business.

12.5.3 The earnings-based approach

When one buys a business, one is actually buying future income. This is, in fact, what one is interested in. The earnings approach meets this requirement of taking into consideration the income potential of the business. Here are also some variations, which will be discussed in the next sections.

■ The excess earnings method

In this method, a combination of the value of the existing assets of the business and an estimation of future earnings is used. This actually leads to an estimate of goodwill. Sometimes in a business sale transaction an arbitrary adjustment is made for goodwill – that intangible asset that is based on the business's reputation and its ability to attract customers. The deter-

Table 12.6 Condensed income statement for Quick Shoe Repairs for the year ending on 31 December

	1999	2000	2001
Turnover	276 500	334 890	376 500
Cost of sales	165 900	200 934	225 900
Gross profit	110 600	133 956	150 600
Operating expenses and tax	45 678	48 975	53 345
Net profit	64 922	84 981	97 255

mination of goodwill creates problems in the assessment of the value of a business.

This method is, however, an attempt to provide a more realistic calculation of the value of goodwill. It also assumes that the owner is entitled to a reasonable return on the firm's net worth. We will now go through this approach step by step. The calculations are based on the information in Tables 12.5 and 12.6.

Step 1: Determine the **adjusted tangible net worth** of the business. In Table 12.5, the values of Quick Shoe Repairs have been adjusted to real market value. The net tangible worth of the business is R350 900.

Step 2: Calculate the **opportunity costs** of investing in the business. The concept of opportunity cost is known as the cost of forgoing another choice. In buying a business, the opportunity cost will be the interest a person would have received if he or she invested the money in an investment of similar risk. The greater the risk, the higher the rate of return will be.

The opportunity cost (i.e. return on investment – we decide on 20 per cent for a risky investment) is R70 180, i.e. 20 per cent of R350 900. It is also very important to remember that the person who is buying the business is forgoing a salary. Provision must therefore be made, in this example, for a salary of R40 000 (this is also an opportunity cost). The total opportunity cost of the choice of buying the business will be R110 180 (R70 180 + R40 000).

Step 3: The next step involves the estimation of the **net earnings** of the business for the coming year. To do this, the growth rate in the net profit of the business can be determined by looking at the performance of the business over the past three to five years. If there is no information available for this period because the business is still relatively young, an accountant can help determine the projected net earnings. When looking at Table 12.6, the growth rate of the turnover over the past three years is 16,7 per cent and for the net profit the growth rate is 22,4 per cent. When calculating the net earnings for the coming year, this 22,4 per cent can be used. The net earnings will be R119 040. The growth rate is calculated by means of the following formula:

$$
\begin{aligned}
\text{Growth rate} &= \text{Turnover of last period/} \\
&\quad \text{Turnover of beginning} \\
&\quad \text{period:}^{1/\text{time periods}} - 1 \times 100 \\
&= [(376\,500\,/\,276\,500)^{0,5} - 1] \times 100 \\
&= 16,69\%
\end{aligned}
$$

Step 4: Compute the **extra earning power**. The difference between the estimated net earnings for the coming year (Step 3) and the total opportunity costs (Step 2) can be regarded as the extra earning power of the business. For Quick Shoe Repairs, the extra earning power is R8 860.

Step 5: Determine the **value of goodwill**. The value of the intangible asset of goodwill can be determined by using the extra earning power. Many small businesses do not have this marginal earning power. If one expects a return of at least 25 per cent on goodwill, the value of goodwill is then R35 440 (8 860 / 25 per cent). This actually means you can invest R35 440 in goodwill and can expect a return of R8 860 (the extra earning power) on your investment.

Step 6: Determine the **value of the business**. All the figures to be used are now calculated. The buyer can simply add the values of tangible net worth (Step 1) and goodwill (Step 5). The value of Quick Shoe Repairs is thus R350 900 + R35 440 = R386 340.

The success of using this method depends on the ability to determine the future net earnings of the business, as well as deciding on the appropriate return on investment and goodwill (risk of the investment).

▪ The capitalised earnings approach

This is another variation of the earnings approach. Again, it is important to determine the net earnings for the coming year by using the income statements of previous years. It is also important to determine the rate of return the buyer requires from making the investment when buying the business. Remember, the more risky the business, the higher the expected return on investment. If the buyer requires a return on his or her investment of 20 per cent when buying Quick Shoe Repairs, the following calculation can be made after deciding on a reasonable salary for the owner:

Value of business = Net earnings (after deducting owner's salary) / Rate of return

= (R119 040 – R40 000) / 20%

= R395 200

The higher the risk, the lower the value of the business. It is important to determine the appropriate risk when determining the value of the business. The lowest risk that buyers will accept for investing in any business will range from 15 to 20 per cent

■ **The discounted future earnings approach**

Although this approach is beyond the scope of this textbook, and is therefore not explained in detail, the basics will be discussed. This variation of the earnings approach makes the assumption that a rand earned in the future will be worth less than a rand today. By using historical income statements, the average growth rate in the net earnings can be calculated (see Step 3 above) and then, using this rate, the future net earnings for the next five years can be determined. According to Zimmerer and Scarborough (1998), a better approach will be to determine three forecasts: an optimistic, a pessimistic and a most likely forecast for each year.

The second step in this approach is to discount these future earnings at the appropriate present value rate. Say, for example, the future net earnings are R119 040 (after one year), then the present value of this amount at a discounted rate of 20 per cent will be R99 200 [R119 040 / (1 + 20%)]. This rate of 20 per cent is again the rate that a buyer could have earned on a similar risk investment. The third step involves the estimation of the income stream beyond five years and then discounting this income stream again, using the present value factor. The last step involves the adding up of all these discounted values. This total will then be the value of the business.

12.5.4 Non-quantitative factors in valuing a business

Although the above methods of valuing a business are important, there are also other more qualitative factors that need consideration when evaluating an existing business. These factors will, obviously, affect the future cash flows and financial position of the business. According to Longenecker et al. (2003: 136), they are the following:

- *Competition:* Market share is important for every business. The prospective buyer should therefore look into the extent, intensity and also the location of competing businesses. It is also important to determine whether the market will be able to carry all the competing business units.

- *Future community developments:* It is important to research future developments in the community. Some of these developments may include, for example, a change in land-use zoning that may have an influence on traffic flow – changing it from a two-way to a one-way flow. This may have serious implications for the business.

- *Legal commitments:* It is important that the prospective buyer makes sure that there are no contingent liabilities, unsettled lawsuits, delinquent tax payments, missed payrolls and overdue rent or instalment payments against any of the assets that are to be acquired.

- *Employee contracts:* It is important to determine what the employee contracts entail, as well as the quality of the business's relations with the employees.

These are but a few of the factors to consider. The specific nature of the business for sale may also bring other factors to the fore that need attention.

12.6 The negotiation process

The final purchase price of the business is determined through negotiation between the buyer and the seller. It is important to understand that the calculated price (value) the seller arrived at by implementing one of the above-mentioned methods, may not be the price eventually paid for the business. This calculated value does, however, give the buyer an estimated value to use when negotiating the price he or she is willing to pay for the business.

The complete negotiation process will include the following steps (Zimmerer & Scarborough 1998: 116):

- The identification and approach of the business for sale. The buyer and seller each do preliminary research about the credentials of the other party.

- After the buyer and the seller are satisfied with their preliminary research, they are ready to begin serious negotiations. They sign a non-disclosure document that ensures the secrecy of their negotiations.

- Before the buyer makes a legal offer to buy the business, he or she will sign a letter of intent. This is a non-binding document (i.e. it gives either party the right to walk away from the deal) and addresses terms such as price, payment, the categories of assets to be sold and a deadline for closing the final deal.

- The next step in the negotiation process is the buyer's due diligence investigation – the buyer is doing his or her "homework" to make sure that the business is good value for money.

- After the buyer's "homework" has been done and within the time agreed upon in the letter of intent, the parties draw up the purchase agreement. This agreement spells out the final deal in terms of all the details and is the final product of the negotiation process.

- After the drafting of the purchase agreement, the buyer and the seller close the deal by signing the necessary documents. They must agree on the attorney to draw up these documents. The buyer delivers the required money and the seller turns the business over to the buyer.

- The real challenge now begins for the buyer, who has to make the transition to being a successful business owner.

12.6.1 Price vs value

According to Lambing and Kuehl (1997: 99), the value of a business is set in the marketplace and is what someone is willing to pay for it. It is ultimately set by the buyer. The seller determines a price for the business by using a computational method. When the buyer agrees that the business is worth as much, or perhaps more, the sale is made. Setting the price for the business does not make the business worth that

amount – price and value are therefore two different things.

What factors contribute to the difference between price and value? The determined value does not reflect the full potential of the business. Although the business may have been profitable over the past few years, the possible potential of an entirely new business at that specific site may be significantly higher. The calculated price is then below the actual value of the business. It is also possible that the business is situated in a less desirable location, in which case the calculated price might be an overestimation of the value of the business.

Finally, it is important to remember that price is only one of the factors that make up the total sale package. Other factors include the rate of payment and non-financial arrangements.

12.6.2 Sources of power in negotiations

During the negotiation process, it is obvious that there are different sources of power that may come into play. One of the most important sources of power during negotiations is information. As stated, the real value of the business is determined by a number of different factors. These factors include all the elements of the external environment, like the market, competition and the social, economic, political and technological environments. If the buyer does not have complete and reliable information about these factors, he or she is at a serious disadvantage. The worst mistake that a buyer can make is to rely completely on the seller for this type of information. This will imply a lack of information power on the buyer's side.

Timing will also influence negotiations. If the seller is in desperate need of money because he or she is already involved in another business, the buyer is in a favourable situation if he or she is the only interested buyer. The party with the most time available to strike the deal has the advantage in terms of timing as a negotiation power.

There may also be pressure from other persons when striking the deal. In the case of a business having more than one owner, there may be pressure from some of the owners or partners to make it a quick sale while others may want to maximise the final agreement. These opposing demands from the sellers create a powerful advantage on the side of the buyer. However, similar distractions on the buyer's side may create an advantage for the seller.

There are also other factors that can create power for one of the sides. It is always important not to be too eager to strike the deal, because it will create more power for the other party.

12.7 Traps to avoid when buying an existing business

According to Timmons (1999), there are a few sandtraps to avoid when buying a business. These include:

- *Legal circumference:* People tend to believe that when they pay their attorneys a sizeable professional fee, their advisers should and will pay enough attention to the details of the transaction. Buyers should know that "the devil is in the details". It is important for any buyer to make sure that he or she understands everything in the final purchasing documents.

- *Attraction to status and size:* It seems that there is an attraction to higher status and larger size. It is dangerous for a potential buyer to be attracted to the largest or the best-known businesses or the most prestigious firms just because of size or status. These businesses may not necessarily be good investments.

- *Unknown territory:* To enter an unknown terrain is another trap. As a potential buyer, it is important to know the detail of the specific industry and the specific type of business. One cannot venture into a manufacturing business if one does not know anything about manufacturing.

- *Opportunity cost:* A prospective buyer of a business may tend to think that there is a lot

of money out there with his or her name on it. It is, however, not all that easy to make money. This optimism may lead him or her to forget about the opportunity costs of forgoing a monthly salary, the opportunity cost of working 18 hours per day, the opportunity costs of other market options that he or she could have pursued, etc.

- *Underestimation of other costs:* There are many other costs involved when buying a business and people tend to underestimate these out-of-pocket costs. The payment of auditors, insurance premiums and legal fees can add up to quite a substantial amount.

- *Greed:* It is a trap to let greed guide one's decisions. It is important that one's actions be guided by fundamental and sound decisions.

- *Being too anxious and impatient:* After months of searching for and negotiating the right deal, it is a trap to believe that the deal is now done, and therefore terminating discussions with one's advisers too soon. Also, make sure that as the prospective new owner of the business, you know everything about the new business.

12.8 Conclusion

In this chapter we considered the business buy-out as an alternative to starting a new business venture. From the advantages and disadvantages it is clear that the legal caveat *"Let the buyer beware"* also applies to buying a business. It is clearly an easier and quicker way to get into business, but it can have many pitfalls.

The decision to purchase an existing business should be made only after careful investigation and consideration of all the facts. It is critical that the entrepreneur uses skilled accountants and other professional people in collecting data, deciding and negotiating the deal, and clinching the deal.

Looking back

1. Mention five reasons for buying an existing business rather than starting a new one.
   - It is an ongoing concern.
   - A successful existing business may have a better chance of continuing to be successful.
   - An existing business may have the advantage of already having the best location.
   - Experienced and reliable employees are already on the payroll of the business.
   - Suppliers are also established.

2. Mention five reasons for starting a new business rather than buying an existing one.
   - The business was never profitable, but the owner has disguised it by employing a creative accounting technique.
   - The business may have a poor reputation or image.
   - Some employees inherited with the business may not be suitable.
   - The business location may be not that favourable.
   - The equipment, facilities and inventory may be obsolete.

3. Where will you start when looking for a business to buy?
   - Identify businesses for sale.
   - Identify businesses for sale not on the market (that may be for sale if the price is right).

4. What questions should be addressed when evaluating a business to buy?
   - Why is the business for sale?
   - Is the business profitable?
   - What skills and competencies do I need to be able to manage the business?
   - What is the history of the business in terms of previous owners, its reputation and public image?
   - What is the physical condition of the business, its facilities and all other assets?
   - What is the degree and scope of competition?

   - What is the situation regarding the existing and potential market size?
   - What important legal aspects must be considered?

5. Identify the basic quantitative methods to use for determining a fair value for a business, and indicate the essence of each method.
   - *Asset-based method:* The value of the business is determined by subtracting total liabilities from total assets.
   - *Market-based methods:* This valuation technique relies on the financial markets to estimate the value of the business.
   - *Excess earnings method:* This method uses a combination of the value of the business's existing assets and an estimation of the future earnings.
   - *Capitalised earnings method:* This is another variation of the earnings approach. The basis for this method is to determine the net earnings for the coming year by using the income statements of previous years.
   - *Discounted future earnings method:* The value of a business is based on the present value of its future earnings.

6. Mention a few non-quantitative factors that can be used in valuing a business.
   - Competition
   - Future community developments
   - Legal commitments
   - Employee contracts

7. What are the steps to follow in the negotiation process?
   - The identification and approach of the business for sale.
   - The signing of a non-disclosure document that ensures the secrecy of the parties' negotiations.
   - The signing of a letter of intent by the buyer before making a legal offer.
   - The buyer's due diligence investigation.
   - Drafting of the purchase agreement.

- Closing of the deal by signing the necessary documents.
- The buyer has to make the transition to be a successful business owner.

8. What is the difference between price and value?
   - The value of a business is set in the marketplace and is what someone is willing to pay for it. It is ultimately set by the buyer.
   - The seller determines a price for the business by using a computational method.

9. What are the different sources of power that may play a role during the negotiation process?
   - Information about elements in the external environment, like the market, competition and the social, economic, political and technological environments
   - Timing
   - Pressure from other persons
   - Eagerness to strike the deal

10. Mention the traps to avoid when buying a business.
   - Legal circumference
   - Attraction to status and size
   - Unknown territory
   - Opportunity cost
   - Underestimation of other costs
   - Greed
   - Being too anxious and impatient

Key terms

Asset-based method
Buyout
Capitalised earnings approach
Discounted future earnings approach
Earnings-based approach
Excess earnings method
Extra earning power

Goodwill
Market-based method
Negotiation
Opportunity costs
Price-to-earnings ratio
Price versus value
Rate of return

Discussion questions

1. Why might an entrepreneur prefer to buy an existing business?

2. What may be the reasons why a business can be sold without advertising it?

3. Explain to a friend of yours how he or she must go about deciding which business to buy.

4. Contrast the asset-based method with the market-based method in determining the value of a business. Which method is easier to apply? Which method will be the more appropriate of the two, and why?

5. Explain why the excess earnings approach might be the best method to use in determining the value of a business.

6. Use the market-based method, the excess earnings method and the capitalised earnings method to determine the value of the following business:
   - The adjusted tangible net worth is R280 500.
   - The required rate of return is 25 per cent.
   - The price-to-earnings ratio is 2,9.
   - The average growth rate in net income is 28,5 per cent.

© Van Schaik Publishers

- The previous year's net income was R104 550.
- The prospective entrepreneur is currently earning a salary of R60 000 per year.

7. You are appointed as a consultant for an entrepreneur who is interested in buying a business. How will you go about in structuring the deal?

Case studies

Case study 1

James and his wife Mary started their business, a supermarket, five years ago. They worked very hard to make the business a success. Long hours and no vacations were their way of life the past five years. Unfortunately, James fell ill and they had to take some decisions about their future. One of these decisions was to sell the business. They gave the following information to a real estate agency to market their business. The value of the net assets is R375 000. The average growth in their turnover and net profit the past five years is 40 and 25 per cent respectively. Last year's net profit was R120 500.

Questions

1. What methods can a prospective buyer use to calculate the value of the business with the information given? What will be a reasonable value of the business?
2. What non-quantitative factors can be considered when determining the value of the business?

Case study 2

Susan and Martha are two housewives who discovered that they had the same dream. Three years ago, they met at a restaurant while waiting for their orders to be carried out and started to talk about service delivery and being a business owner. They soon realised that they had a common talent and interest, namely that of baking cakes and biscuits. They decided to meet again and to discuss the possibility of going into business.

They started their business in the garage of Susan's house, which they transformed into a small bakery. They had a few breaks that helped them to get where they are today. All of these breaks came in the form of people who were prepared to get involved and walk that extra mile to assist them. A consultant of Business Partners was prepared to listen to their dream and helped them draft a business plan in order to get their first loan. "It took hard work and dedication," Susan remembers of those early days. They now have five people working for them and they supply their products to various coffee shops and home industry shops.

They have now reached a crossroads. Either they expand or decide to stay small. "We can't afford it any longer to work in this small setting – we need space," says Martha. An estate agent let them know about an existing bakery for sale, and they have to take a decision. Do they have to buy this existing bakery or not?

Questions

1. What will be the advantages and disadvantages for Susan and Martha when buying this bakery?
2. You are appointed as their business consultant. Explain to them the negotiation process if they decide to buy this bakery.
3. What quantitative technique will you recommend they use in the valuation of the business?

Experiential exercises

1. Visit a few business owners and determine the following:
   - What method did they use to determine the value of the business when they bought it?
   - Did they adjust the balance sheet, or did they accept the balance sheet as correct when buying the business?

2. Some estate agents specialise in the selling of businesses. Visit them and determine the following:
   - How do they see their role in the facilitation of the deal?
   - How do they make sure that the price asked for the business is not too high?

Exploring the Web

1. At http://www.bodbusiness.co.za there is valuable information about valuation methods and related topics. You will find:
   - A discussion of the different valuation methods
   - An article about valuable advice for business buyers
   - How to buy and sell a business

2. There are critical reasons why it is important to valuate a business. Visit http://www.micro-course.com/bval/reasons.html and find some of these reasons.

3. A business with the name of CCS IT Computer Training in Stellenbosch has its budget on its website. Visit http://www.geocities.com/ccsit2001/incstat.htm and determine the value of this business by using some of the methods you have studied in this chapter.

4. Go to any search engine, e.g. Google or Yahoo, and type in the words "business valuation". Report on some of the articles that you find there.

References and recommended reading

AlNajjar, F.A. & Riahi-Belkaoui, A. 1999. Multinationality, profitability and firm value. *Managerial Finance,* 25(12): 31-41.

French, N. 1997. Market information management for better valuations. Part I: Concepts and definitions of price and worth. *Journal of Property Valuation and Investment,* 15(5): 403-410.

Kroon, J. (red.). 1998. *Entrepreneurskap: begin jou eie onderneming.* Kaapstad: Kagiso.

Lambing, P. & Kuehl, C. 1997. *Entrepreneurship.* Upper Saddle River, NJ: Prentice Hall.

Longenecker, J.G., Moore, C.W. & Petty, J.W. 2003. *Small business management: an entrepreneurial emphasis,* 12th ed. Cincinnati: South-Western College Publishing.

Peto, R. 1997. Market information management for better valuations. Part II: Data availability and application. *Journal of Property Valuation and Investment,* 15(5): 411-422.

Timmons, J.A. 1999. *New venture creation: entrepreneurship for the 21st century,* 5th ed. Boston: Irwin McGraw-Hill.

Zimmerer, T.W. & Scarborough, N.M. 1998. *Essentials of entrepreneurship and small business management,* 2nd ed. Upper Saddle River, NJ: Prentice Hall.

PART **D**

Post-start-up
challenges

Managing growth

Gideon Nieman

13.1 Introduction

Growth is written into the culture of a business enterprise as the hallmark of its success. Growth brings with it the promise of expansion, new premises, greater profitability, an increase in personnel, greater influence in the labour market, pulling power to attract more highly developed people, or a general increase in resources. These, in turn, promise further growth and even higher status in the business community for the owners (Murphy 1996: 172).

In this chapter, the dimensions and measurement of growth will be expanded upon. The significance of the direct contribution made to employment levels and the economy by rapidly growing small firms can be easily demonstrated. Storey (1994: 158) found that rapidly growing firms constitute a tiny proportion of the small firm population but that, over a ten-year period, they make a major contribution to job creation.

Large corporations are not the creators of jobs. In fact, they are the ones where most job losses occur due to re-engineering, reorganisation or downsizing. "Concentrating on core business" is a phrase that trade unions and people working in large firms have come to dread.

13.2 Why South Africa needs businesses that grow

Small, medium and micro-enterprise (SMME) development was identified by the new government as a priority in creating jobs to solve the high unemployment rate in South Africa. The country's unemployment figure currently stands at 37 per cent. In other words, 6,9 million people out of a possible economically active population of 18,8 million are unemployed (SSA 2001: x). The growth of the labour force in South Africa is about 2,8 per cent per annum. An average annual real economic growth rate of approximately 6 per cent per annum will be required to keep pace with labour force growth.

Learning outcomes

After completion of this chapter, you should be able to:

- Explain why South Africa needs businesses that grow
- Set growth objectives for a business member
- Explain the dimensions of business growth
- Discuss the characteristics of growing firms
- Describe the stages of growth in the business life cycle
- Explain the management problems in the growth life cycle

The promotion of entrepreneurship and small business development was seen by the new South African government in 1994 as a way of addressing the following generic development goals in the country (RSA 1995):

- Job creation
- Poverty alleviation
- Equity and participation
- Wealth creation
- Social stability

In 1994, Sunter (1994: 4) identified the need for large numbers of entrepreneurs to build up a successful economy in South Africa. Four years later, Sunter (1998: 2) was still calling for entrepreneurial development by highlighting its importance: "It is only through the creation of millions of enterprises that millions of jobs will be created."

The government recognises the importance of developing a strong small, medium and micro-enterprise sector. Today it is internationally accepted and acknowledged that the SMME sector is an essential factor in promoting and achieving economic growth and development, and in the widespread creation of wealth and employment. To further this, a National Small Business Act was promulgated in 1996 (RSA 1996).

It is a feather in the cap of the new government to have done this in such a short space of time. In our history of more than 300 years, successive governments failed to give this particular impetus and status to SMMEs. The focus of the government's strategy is, however, primarily on the development of SMMEs in the previously disadvantaged communities. Such communities are those sections of the population that have been disadvantaged by apartheid and the segregationist development policies of the past.

13.3 The desire to grow

The lack of an entrepreneurial mindset or desire to grow might subconsciously be the major barrier to growth experienced by many business owners. Growth and the desire to grow should be embedded in the mindset of the person starting or creating a new business venture. An entrepreneurial mindset constantly seeks growth and innovation, and has certain strategic objectives. A small business is an

organisation that has reached its full potential given its existing resources. Normally, the owners have no intention of growing the business beyond normal inflation and economic growth.

This mindset is supported by research in the United Kingdom, as reported by Storey (1994). The proportion of small firms stating that they are seeking growth is much higher than the proportion of those that appear to achieve growth (Storey 1994: 120). There may be several reasons for this:

- Some firms that do not seek growth are reluctant to admit this.

- The definitions of growth may differ between those asked in advance by researchers, compared with the actual measures used after the fact finding.

- While firms might seek growth, there could be certain barriers preventing them from achieving such growth.

- Firms might feel that growth is risky; that faster growth leads to a greater risk of failure. Research in the United States has supported this view.

For many business owners, growth is not an objective. *Trundlers* are those businesses that survive but do not add significantly to job creation (Storey 1994: 117). *Failures* are those businesses that cease to trade. *Flyers* are growing firms: they are the only group that constantly contributes to job creation. Storey (1994) reports on research that found typical no-growth firms to be unincorporated businesses that are home based and employ only one or two people, including the owner-manager. Another study demonstrated that micro-enterprises were more likely to report that their objectives were either to stay as they are or to become even smaller.

These are important findings that public policy makers should take note of. Quite often one gains the impression that policy makers in South Africa seem to favour the creation of micro-enterprises as a solution to unemployment or the need for job creation. The establishment of survivalist micro-enterprises in the informal sector is not a solution to unemployment. It does engage a large number of unemployed people with little or no entrepreneurial or business skills, but this is not a substitute for a decent job. These people demonstrate some entrepreneurial characteristics such as risk taking and hard work, because it is a rather brave person who takes his or her last R100 to buy goods and then sit in the hot sun, trying to sell the goods at a profit. Few of them ever get out of this survivalist mode despite many barriers being removed.

The wish to take advantage of the growth potential of a venture mostly relates to the need for achievement. It might also be due to a desire to increase personal wealth and control. The need to grow the venture can therefore quite often be attributed to the following needs of an entrepreneur:

• Achievement
• Personal wealth
• Power

13.4 Growth as an object for the business venture

From the preceding section it is clear that there must be a desire to grow. The potential for growth distinguishes an entrepreneurial venture from a small business. A small business operates *within* a given market while the entrepreneurial venture creates its *own* market (Wickham 1998: 19).

The entrepreneurial venture still needs to be managed proficiently and compete effectively. This implies that it will need to set growth objectives. Setting growth targets, however, creates challenges with regard to the venture's strategy and resources and the risk to which it is exposed. (Wickham 1998: 269).

13.4.1 Growth and strategy

Growth must be achieved. This implies that there must a long-term plan (strategy) and objectives for achieving growth. Strategies can focus on internal or external growth, or a combination of both. Growth targets need to be set and the expansion strategy must be consistent with the capabilities of the firm. These strategies are devised when developing the strategic plan and direction (see Chapter 14). Growth targets must take account of the resources that the venture is able to attract. Growth must be clearly defined in terms of increased sales, increased income or another quantifiable goal.

Such targets must be feasible, and consistent with a strategy for achieving that growth.

13.4.2 Growth and resources

All the strategies of the venture must have action plans to achieve these goals. Each action plan must clearly set out the resources (capital, people and assets) that will be required to achieve the goals. Growth is dependent on the venture's ability to attract new resources (Wickham 1998: 269). Capital might be the main source but is not useful in itself. It must be converted into productive assets, such as people and operating resources. The ability of the venture to attract these resources required for growth is, therefore, a major consideration. If the ability is lacking, it will limit the growth of the firm and the strategies will need to be amended.

13.4.3 Growth and risk

The entrepreneur must know that growth carries a degree of risk. Growth will intensify the demands made on the resources, which can only be countered by an ability to attract resources. Should the firm not be able to attract resources, it could easily end up in a situation of overtrading. Overtrading occurs when a firm is trading at certain volumes without a proper base of assets to support these volumes.

Another risk lies in the growth itself. Growth implies developing new business, which means venturing into the unknown. New markets, new ventures and new products carry an underlying risk factor. Expansion also requires new knowledge of the products and markets, and this adds to the demand on resources. Wickham (1998: 270) believes that growth must be treated like any investment decision. It must be judged in the light of the risk it presents, the returns it offers and the opportunity costs it impairs.

13.5 Controlling and planning for growth

Growth presents strategic, resources and investment decision making and is therefore a process that must be planned for, and controlled. The following key factors are required.

13.5.1 Desire

The desire to grow must be reflected in the entrepreneurial vision. The vision statement of the strategic plan of any venture is its shining light, the star by which to steer, the illuminator of the path (Pettinger 1996: 3). The desire and the passion to grow are often reflected in a firm's vision statement.

13.5.2 Potential

The potential for growth must be reflected in the mission of the enterprise. The mission statement tells the stakeholders how the venture plans to accomplish the mission. The mission should stretch the venture into making maximum use of its capabilities and exploiting its competitive potential.

13.5.3 Direction

The direction of growth must be indicated in the business strategy. There must be strategic objectives and these need to be quantified. Strategic objectives relate to growth targets, market development, market share and market position. The firm's direction is also indicated by its products, the particular markets in which it will operate and the competitive advantages it will develop.

13.5.4 Management of growth

Growth must be managed. It requires planning, organisation, direction and control activities. It is especially important to manage the resource flows in the organisation. Appropriate functions for acquiring resources must be in place (Wickham 1998: 270).

There are a number of challenges facing growing entrepreneurial ventures:

- *Finding capital:* Finding capital for pursuing growth is much like the gains acquired through the initial financing of the venture. Hopefully the established firm will have developed a successful track record with which to back up new financing proposals. Part of planning for growth is about how growth will be financed.

- *Finding people:* Opening additional outlets, increasing sales of products, and innovating and selling new products will require additional employees to do the work. Finding talented, competent and capable people is a challenge in itself. Quite often in the fast-growing venture this challenge is intensified because of the time constraints involved.

- *Reinforcing organisational controls:* It is important to reinforce controls over cash flow, inventory, debtors, customer data, sales order creditors and costs when the venture is expanding.

13.5.5 Achievement

The achievement of growth is a result of the decision-making processes that go with a venture. The entrepreneur must control these through his or her power and leadership strategies (Wickham 1998: 271). It is important to create a positive, growth-oriented culture in the organisation. This enhances the opportunities for achieving success, both organisationally and individually.

13.6 What is business growth?

Growth is critical to entrepreneurial success and is one of the factors that distinguishes the entrepreneurial venture from a small business venture. Although growth is a defining feature of the entrepreneurial venture, this does not mean that an entrepreneurial business has the right to grow. It merely means that, if managed the right way, it has the potential to grow (Wickham 1998: 225). Growth must be an *objective* and a strategy for the venture, and it must be *managed*.

What do we mean when we speak of business growth? Growth and performance are generally seen as substitutes for, or surrogates of, each other. A growing firm is usually considered to be a successful business that performs well (Crijns & Ooghe 1997: 53).

In the literature there are a variety of means of measuring growth, mostly quantifiable from an accounting or marketing viewpoint. It is our point of departure that the term "growth" refers to the increase in a specific parameter during a specific term or time period.

13.7 Characteristics of growing firms

In a review of successful business enterprises, a number of strategic characteristics emerge (Crijns & Ooghe 1997: 56):
- Market domination
- Differentiation
- Product leadership
- Flexibility
- Innovation
- Future orientated
- Export
- Related growth

13.7.1 Market domination

Market domination occurs in certain niche markets and is measured in terms of the relative market share in the niche market. Market and product domination seems to be the main differentiator between good and bad performers in an industry. Successful firms appear to have clearly demarcated market segments.

13.7.2 Differentiation

The firms are unique through a strategy of differentiation from their competitors in product, geography and distribution.

13.7.3 Product leadership

Successful growing firms are product oriented in their emphasis on quality, branding and value for customers. They are characterised by superior performance and a competitive edge through the introduction of new products and customer service.

13.7.4 Flexibility

Flexibility indicates the speed and ability to change direction to gain advantage from new opportunities and to counter and/or reduce threats. Growing firms are characterised by their ability to change their market position or competitive strategy to meet the demands of the market and macroenvironment.

13.7.5 Innovation

Innovation is a way of life for growing firms. The introduction of innovation (i.e. doing things differently and better) happens faster and more quickly in growing firms. Technology is introduced sooner.

13.7.6 Future orientated

Growing firms are inclined to invest in the future. Examples of these investments are: marketing, development and expansion of distribution channels, product development and capacity building.

13.7.7 Export

The development of an export market constitutes a considerable part of growing firms' turnover and most are successful exploiters of the global market.

13.7.8 Related growth

Most are seeking growth in related segments or niche markets to supplement possible growth limits in their original segments or niches. Successful growth firms strive for active, cognizant growth as opposed to uncontrolled growth. They avoid a "growing to grow" attitude, but rather grow in order to utilise opportunities and to realise their goals. The combination of market choices and selection and the maintaining of competitive advantages seems to result in continuous growth.

Vinturella (1999: 248) refers to the critical success factors for growth as the following:
- *Market intelligence:* The ability to perceive and adapt to changes in the marketplace, including future industry trends, a competitive environment and customer feedback
- *Strategic leadership:* The ability to provide clear direction, delegation, decision making and long-term planning
- *Clarity of purpose and direction:* A detailed picture vision of the firm in the future; a shared understanding of its uniqueness and identity
- *Strategic planning:* Specific action steps to achieve future goals
- *Internal infrastructure:* The ability to support the business strategies through its internal operations, systems and organisational structures.

13.8 The process of growth

Wickham (1998: 223) believes that due to the multifaceted nature of organisations, the entrepreneur must constantly view the growth and development of a venture from four major perspectives: the financial, the strategic, the structural and the organisational. These four types of growth are not independent of each other (Figure 13.1). They are different facets, but an entrepreneur has to consider all of them when planning for growth. Failure to attend to one while favouring another could result in failure or a managerial crisis.

13.8.1 Financial growth

Financial growth relates to the development of the venture as a commercial entity. Quantita-

tive measures are generally used as norms in the financial world to determine growth. Financial growth measures the additional value that the organisation is creating and is an important measurement of the success of the venture. Stakeholders will use these financial measurements as an assessment of how well the business is doing.

Measurement of financial growth can be expressed in a number of ways:
- Increase in turnover (sales)
- Increase in total assets
- Increase in profit
- Increase in return on investment
- Increase in any other performance measure

The firm's performance must, however, also be considered relative to its particular business

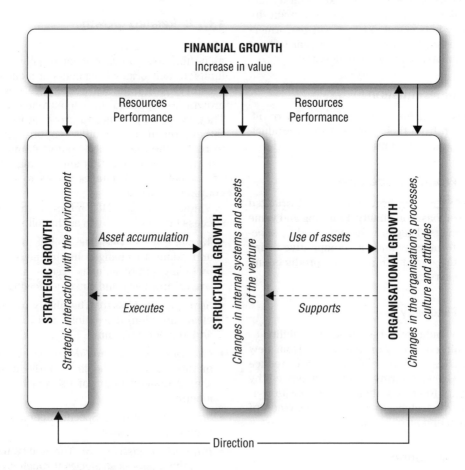

Figure 13.1 Dynamics of growth
Source: Adapted from Wickham (1998: 224).

sector and the overall trends in the firm's performance. There are no absolute measures of performance.

It must be emphasised that financial growth should not occur without a proportional growth in the other three supporting pillars, namely strategic, structural and organisational growth. Financial growth without structural growth quite often leads to overtrading, where the turnover is too high for the supporting asset base. This, in turn, will require a strategy for acquiring more capital to increase the asset base. A larger asset base will require more control systems and a change in organisation.

13.8.2 Strategic growth

Strategic growth refers to the changes that take place in the way the venture interacts with its environment. It is concerned with the manner in which the firm develops its capabilities to exploit a presence in the marketplace. It is necessary that the firm adapts and changes its strategy as it develops and grows. Crijns and Ooghe (1997: 63) stress that strategic objectives change as the organisation moves through the stages of the life cycle. In the start-up and early growth stages, the strategy is mainly aimed at survival, whereas in the next stage the focus is on developing a customer base, maintaining a profit and obtaining resources.

13.8.3 Structural growth

Structure follows strategy. Structural growth relates to the changes taking place in the way the venture organises its internal systems, managerial roles and responsibilities, reporting relationships, communication links and resource control systems. The organisation needs to develop and change its structure to meet the demands of change and growth. Each strategic phase requires an adaptation of the structure and processes of the organisation.

The structure of the organisation represents a response to the contingencies of size, technology, strategy and environment:

- *Size:* The larger the organisation, the more complex its structure will be.

- *Operational technology:* This is the way the firm goes about performing its tasks. Some of these may be straightforward while others

might be complex (e.g. Kentucky Fried Chicken vs South African Airways).

- *Strategy:* This refers to the way the organisation goes about competing for its customers' attention.

- *Environment:* The environment impacts on strategy and structure. It offers both resources and also challenges their availability.

13.8.4 Organisational growth

Organisational growth relates to changes that take place in the organisation's processes, culture and attitudes as it grows and develops. There are, therefore, changes in the entrepreneur's role and leadership style as the organisation moves from being a "small" to a "large" firm (Wickham 1998: 224).

It is important to develop or design an organisation that can manage the resource requirements (assets, capital, information and people) of the venture. The role of the entrepreneur changes as the organisation develops. There are certain structures an organisation needs to adopt given the particular situation with which it is faced.

As the business grows and more staff is appointed, the entrepreneur is freer to undertake the decision making and to delegate general activities. The appointment of a management team in the later stages may act as the basis for more formal department or business functions. The entrepreneur's role then becomes that of chief executive and the organisation settles down to maturity (Wickham 1998: 248).

13.9 Stages of growth

To understand and manage growth, it is essential to understand the concept of venture life cycle (VLC) and its underlying characteristics.

The life cycle follows the evolution of a new business venture from its pre-start-up (incubation) stage until its decline or rejuvenation. Knowing what can be expected at the different stages of growth helps the entrepreneur to anticipate what may lie ahead so that he or she can plan to meet these challenges.

The new business venture will go through a number of stages of growth. These stages are determined by the size of the firm – as the business grows, so its size increases. The size of a business can be measured in terms of volume of turnover (sales), total assets, net profit or number of employees or even a combination of these measures. Figure 13.2 is a simple illustration of the concept of the five stages of a firm's life cycle.

Venture life cycle models must be used as a guide. Although these models provide an indication of what *can* happen at a certain stage, they have little power to predict what *will* happen. The defining line and time frames of each stage are not clear and have not been researched. It is difficult to say at a particular time exactly what stage a venture has reached or when it can be expected to move on to the next one. Individual firms will move through different stages at different rates and may miss out some stages altogether (Wickham 1998: 248).

There are more limitations to the stage models (Storey 1994: 122):

• Not all firms begin at Stage 1 and move to Stage 5. This is because a significant proportion of small businesses cease to trade (see Chapter 15) fairly early in their lifetime and never progress beyond the first or second stage.

• Some firms may achieve a particular stage (survival) but never advance beyond that stage.

The life cycle models depict the levels of development of a growing firm as a smooth curve with rapidly ascending sales and profits and a levelling-off towards the peak, and then dipping towards decline. In truth, however, very few new and growing firms experience such smooth and linear stages of growth. By and large, the growth curves of new firms look more like the ups and downs of a roller coaster ride than the smooth progression depicted (Timmons 2000: 576). During each of the stages of a firm's growth there will be entrepreneurial crises, or hurdles.

The following discussion will consider some indications of such crises. These are signals that a crisis is imminent. While the list is long, they are not the only indicators but the most common ones (Timmons 2000: 577).

13.9.1 Stage 1: Pre-start-up (incubation)

Incubation, or the pre-birth process, means taking all the steps necessary to reach start-up.

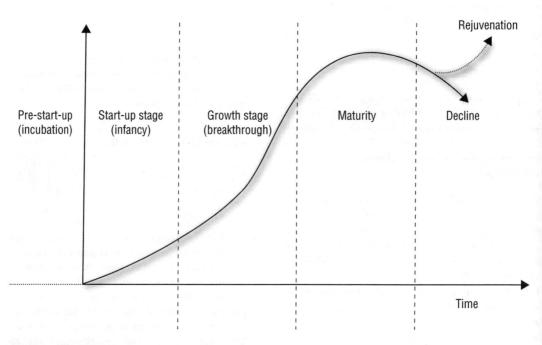

Figure 13.2 The stages of venture growth

This is really the entrepreneurial process. It is, however, critical that the entrepreneur should take note of factors influencing growth in this pre-birth stage, as many decisions will be critical at a later stage.

The following three components have been identified by researchers as dimensions or components that contribute to growth in the small firm. These are the starting resources of the entrepreneur, the firm, and the strategy (Storey 1994: 123).

Each of these components has a variety of elements. The elements within the entrepreneur's resources component refer to the characteristics of the individual who provides the prime managerial resources of the business. These elements are:

- Motivation
- Education
- Management experience
- Number of founders
- Prior self-employment
- Family history
- Social marginality
- Functional skills
- Training
- Age
- Prior business failure
- Prior experience of sector
- Prior experience of firm size
- Gender

It is important to identify the entrepreneur's position with regard to these components before the business is established. Each element can be measured or assessed, and relates to the entrepreneur and his or her access to resources, not to the business that is being established.

The characteristics of the firm itself, when it begins, is another component. They reflect the decisions made by the entrepreneur upon starting the business. These are not operational decisions that are made once the business starts, since they would then be included in the strategy component. These elements are factors that are generally held constant when examining the growth performance, namely:

- Age
- Location
- Sector
- Size
- Legal form
- Ownership

Strategy actually refers to the managerial actions that are required to make the firm grow once it has started. These actions are likely to be associated with more rapid rates of growth (Storey 1994: 124-125) and are:

- Workforce training
- Management training
- External equity
- Technological sophistication
- Market positioning
- Market adjustments
- Planning
- New products
- Management recruitment
- State support
- Customer concentration
- Competition
- Information and advice
- Exporting

13.9.2 Stage 2: Start-up (infancy)

In the infancy or start-up stage, entrepreneurs may struggle to break even as they introduce their new product. In this stage they are close to their ventures, and can spot obstacles and act quickly to remove them. Growth is slow.

There are some key factors to consider in this stage:

- *Timing:* The exact time of start-up is crucial as it affects the financing of the operation. It differs slightly between manufacturing, retail and service businesses.

- *Flow of funds:* To mark the beginning of the start-up phase there should be some flow of funds into the venture or out of the venture, whether it is expenditure to create infrastructure or the first sale that is made. Creation of infrastructure is therefore associated with the early start-up phase.

- *Start of business:* The real business operations start when the first trading transaction is finalised. It varies for different types of businesses. A manufacturing venture will require a longer time frame from start of production to the sale than, for example, the fast-food take-away store on the corner. This time frame requires planning for resources.

13.9.3 Stage 3: Breakthrough or growth stage

In the breakthrough stage, the rate of growth accelerates and resources are under major pressure. Growth is quite often so fast that the entrepreneur cannot keep up with it. At the same time, competition may become stronger. Problems begin to surface in the following areas:

- Cash flow
- Production
- Delivery
- Appointment of personnel

This is the most dangerous stage in the life cycle of the new enterprise. This is when most business failures occur, mostly due to the pressure on resources. Overtrading (i.e. one's turnover is too high for the asset base) is often the most quoted reason in liquidators' reports.

13.9.4 Stage 4: Maturity

In this stage, the entrepreneur must learn to manage time and to delegate. The number of decisions and activities outstrips the time available, and the entrepreneur must rely increasingly on other persons to perform major functions. Key issues are those of expense control, productivity, and entry into niche markets to offset any potential decline in the firm's traditional management. By this stage the firm should be enjoying retained profits, as well as the benefits of secured long-term loans. Its products are likely to be established by now and sold through multiple distribution channels.

13.9.5 Stage 5: Decline/rejuvenation

One of the criticisms against the life cycle approach is that it (falsely) suggests that organisational decline is inevitable. It does, however, serve to warn the entrepreneur against complacency as the venture becomes successful.

Some ventures can stay in the maturity stage for extended periods of time. Pick 'n Pay and Edgars stores, for example, have been in existence for a long time and have spent most of their life cycle in the maturity stage. Although Edgars has experienced stages of decline it, it

has been able to change and come in line with maturity again.

Decline is not inevitable in the life cycle of a business. It will only occur if the business does not constantly develop new and innovative ideas to prevent the entrepreneur from becoming complacent as the venture becomes successful. Quite often the "I have arrived" factor can lead to decline. In other instances, the original entrepreneur is either dead or has left the business, and his or her vision for the enterprise has been lost.

We believe that the entrepreneur needs to be aware of the signs of decline in order to rejuvenate the business as the final stage of the venture life cycle.

By creating an environment conducive to creativity and innovation during the maturity stage, decline can be prevented. Creativity and innovation will rejuvenate the venture on an ongoing basis. Rejuvenation of the firm means that it virtually goes through the various stages of the venture life cycle *again*.

13.10 Key factors during the growth stages

Kuratko and Hodgetts (2001: 506) suggest that entrepreneurs must understand the key factors of the specific managerial actions necessary during the growth stages, namely control, responsibility, tolerance of failure, and change.

- *Control:* Growth creates problems of command and control. There needs to be a blend of control and trust in the firm.
- *Responsibility:* As the firm grows, the distinction between authority and responsibility becomes more apparent. Authority can be delegated with the control. Delegation without control amounts to abdication. A sense of responsibility needs to be created.
- *Tolerance of failure:* Even though one has avoided the initial start-up pitfalls, it is important to remain tolerant of failure. Three forms of failure can be distinguished:
  - *Moral failure:* Violation of internal trust can have negative consequences.
  - *Personal failure:* Failure due to a lack of skills or application is normally shared by the firm and the individual.
  - *Uncontrollable failure:* This is caused by

external factors and is most difficult to deal with. Resource limitations, strategic direction and market changes are examples. The manager must work to prevent recurrence.

- *Change:* Planning, operations and implementation need to be subject to continual changes as the venture moves through the growth stage and beyond. Innovation and change are required. Change holds many implications in terms of resources, people and structure.

Many entrepreneurs are unable to deal with the challenge that growth brings about. A six-step programme is required:

1. Get the facts.
2. Create a growth task force.
3. Plan for growth.
4. Staff for growth.
5. Maintain a growth culture.
6. Use an advisory board.

Crijns and Ooghe (1997: 65-69) summarise all the actions and changes taking place in the dif-ferent stages of the growth process. They refer to these as the "professionalisation" of the entrepreneur. In managing the process of growth it is essential for the entrepreneur to take note of what could be expected in respect of a number of variables in the firm. These are summarised in Table 13.1 below.

13.11 Conclusion

Businesses that grow are crucial for economic growth and other socio-economic objectives that need to be achieved in southern Africa. Growth is critical to entrepreneurial success and distinguishes the entrepreneurial venture from the small business.

The growth of the venture must be approached from a number of perspectives, of which financial, structural, strategic and organi-sational growth are key ones. Understanding the dynamics of the venture and how they change and interact during the stages of growth (the venture's life cycle) is important. To ensure success, the entrepreneur can plan accordingly and organise strategies with regard to resources.

Table 13.1 Changes during the venture life cycle

Aspect	Start-up	Early growth	Later growth (expansion)	Maturity
Strategic objectives	Survival	Maintenance of profitability and acquiring resources	Growth via expansion	Return on investment and market value
Structure	Informal	Functional	Decentralised	Matrix or product groups
Control systems	Direct market feedback	Standards and cost centres	Profit centres and formal reporting	Planning and investment centres
Management style	Creative	Leading	Delegating	Coordinating
Role of the entrepreneur	Owner-worker	Owner-manager	General manager	Controller
Function of the entrepreneur	Direct supervision	Overall supervision	Indirect control	Controlling interest
Focus of the entrepreneur	Make and sell	Efficient operations	Market expansion	Consolidation and innovation

Looking back

1. List the development goals of South Africa.
    - Job creation
    - Poverty alleviation
    - Equity and participation
    - Wealth creation
    - Social stability

2. Briefly discuss the three critical components when considering growth as an objective.
    - Growth must be achieved and requires a strategy.
    - Growth is dependent on the venture's ability to attract new resources.
    - Growth carries with it an element of risk.

3. List the key factors in controlling and planning for growth.
    - Desire
    - Potential
    - Direction
    - Management
    - Achievement

4. List the characteristics of growing firms.
    - Market domination
    - Differentiation
    - Product leadership
    - Flexibility

    - Innovation
    - Future oriented
    - Export
    - Related growth

5. List the four types of growth that a firm must achieve.
    - Financial
    - Strategic
    - Structural
    - Organisational

6. What stages (phases) of growth can be identified in the life cycle of the venture?
    - Pre-start-up
    - Start-up
    - Growth
    - Maturity
    - Decline

7. Briefly discuss the key factors to consider during the growth stages of a business.
    - Growth creates problems of command and control.
    - The distinction between authority and responsibility becomes more apparent.
    - It is important to remain tolerant of failure.
    - Planning, operations and implementation need continual change.
    - A programme is required for confronting the growth wall.

Key terms

Decline
Financial growth
Growth
Growth stages
Incubation
Maturity

Organisational growth
Rejuvenation
Strategic growth
Structural growth
Venture life cycle

Discussion questions

1. Why do South African companies need to grow?
2. Discuss the entrepreneurial mindset with regard to growth.
3. Why is it necessary to set growth objectives for a firm?
4. How does one plan for and control growth?
5. Can a firm grow in financial terms without considering structure or strategy? If not, why?
6. What pressure is there on resources at the different stages of the firm's growth?

242   © Van Schaik Publishers

Case studies

Case study 1: "Beauty R Us" (fictitious example)

Jaconet Brunette opened her beauty salon in Menlyn shopping centre in Pretoria in April 1992. She grew up in an entrepreneurial home and, except for a short period in training, had always had her own business. By October 1995 she had four employees and her turnover had trebled. In March 1996 she opened a second salon in Hatfield in Pretoria some 5 km away from the Menlyn salon. She appointed her best employee to run the business, hoping to convert it into a franchise eventually. In June 1996 she went to a major exhibition in London and managed to identify a range of products to import exclusively for the franchise system. A few containers were imported and most of the products were sold. It did, however, require additional financing from the bank and time to arrange for clearing of the goods at Customs and Excise in Kempton Park.

The Hatfield branch never seemed to take off and only managed to break even. Jaconet spent a lot of time at the Hatfield branch trying to develop a client base and to control activities. The good employee turned out not to be such a good manager and eventually resigned. By the end of 1999, Jaconet decided to sell the Hatfield branch as it did not seem to grow at all. She believed that the attention Hatfield required was impacting negatively on her Menlyn salon which, after a few years, had shown a decline in turnover. She downsized this salon from five to four employees and the business is back on track again. When asked about further expansion her comment was: "I don't want the hassle of another branch. I'm quite happy with the present business. I did not make any more money having two outlets."

Questions

1. Discuss whether this is a small business or an entrepreneurial venture.
2. Does the desire to grow make a venture more entrepreneurial? Discuss.
3. Discuss the pressure on resources in this case.

Case study 2: Chrysler Corporation

In 1990 Chrysler Corporation in the United States was short of money, offered a limited range of products, had a poor reputation and was moving into a major recession from which few believed it could possibly emerge. In 1994, however, the company broke retail sales records and generated more income than in any previous year. Dealers experienced their most profitable year ever, and Chrysler became the lowest-cost car manufacturer in the world. How did it accomplish this turnaround?

Chrysler woke up and realised that, to survive, it had to recreate itself. The company started communicating openly and regularly with key audiences, and simultaneously developed new products to meet market demands and solidify its market position. Management formed "platform teams" to improve the design and accelerate production of Chrysler's vehicles – particularly its pioneering mini-vans.

Source: Adapted from Grates (1995).

Questions

1. Can you identify the stage of the venture life cycle in which Chrysler found itself in 1990? Motivate your answer.
2. What did the management of Chrysler do to avoid decline?

Experiential exercises

1. Interview an entrepreneur about the growth in his or her firm. Identify the pressure on the various resources at each growth stage. Also find out whether the entrepreneur was aware of, or could identify, the different growth stages.

2. Obtain the annual reports of any listed company on the Johannesburg Securities Exchange for the past five years and determine the financial growth in turnover, total assets and employees.

3. Using the same data as in the exercise above, compare and contrast the financial, strategic, structural and organisational aspects of growth of this particular firm.

4. Find a recent newspaper report on the growth of a specific firm. Prepare a report on the types of growth in this particular firm.

Exploring the Web

1. Go to http://www.economist.com/ – *The Economist* is a business journal with regular relevant articles on the growth of firms.

2. Visit the following websites of South African companies and read about their growth: www.sasol.com

   www.bidvest.com
   www.implats.co.za
   www.picknpay.co.za

3. Visit www.benlore.com/index2.html, a website with real-life stories of entrepreneurs and how they grew their businesses.

References and recommended reading

Crijns, H. & Ooghe, H. 1997. *Groeimanagement: lessen van dynamische ondernemers.* Tielt: Lannoo.

Grates, G.F. 1995. Chrysler: a paradigm for growth. *Public Relations Quarterly,* 40(3): 46-47.

Kuratko, D.F. & Hodgetts, R.M. 2001. *Entrepreneurship: a contemporary approach,* 5th ed. Ford Worth: Harcourt College.

Murphy, M. 1996. *Small business management.* London: *Financial Times*/Prentice Hall.

Nieman, G. 2001. The entrepreneurial process. In: Nieman, G. & Bennett, A. (Eds), *Business management: a value chain approach.* Pretoria: Van Schaik.

Pettinger, R. 1996. *Introduction to corporate strategy.* London: Macmillan.

Republic of South Africa (RSA). 1995. *White Paper on national strategy for the development and promotion of small business in South Africa.* Cape Town: Government Printer.

Republic of South Africa (RSA). 1996. *National Small Business Act No. 102 of 1996.* Cape Town: Government Printer.

Statistics South Africa (SSA). 2001. *Labour force survey: February 2001.* Statistical release P0210. Pretoria: SSA.

Storey, D.J. 1994. *Understanding the small business sector.* London: Routledge.

Sunter, C. 1994. *The casino model.* Cape Town. Tafelberg.

Sunter, C. 1998. We need to focus on creating an entrepreneurial class. *Entrepreneurial Update,* November, 2.

Timmons, J. 2000. *New venture creation,* 5th ed. Boston: McGraw-Hill/Irwin.

Vinturella, J.B. 1999. *The entrepreneur's fieldbook.* Upper Saddle River, NJ: Prentice Hall.

Wickham, P.A. 1998. *Strategic entrepreneurship: a decision-making approach to new venture creation and management.* London: Pitman.

14

Growth strategies and options

Gideon Nieman

14.1 Introduction

In the previous chapter on the management of growth, the word "strategy" was used on numerous occasions. It was also emphasised that growth must be achieved and that there must be a long-term plan (strategy) and objectives for achieving this growth. A growth strategy must be devised when developing a strategic plan and direction.

This chapter focuses on the various growth strategies and methods of putting them into effect. We also investigate the financing of growth, as it is one of the most important resources required in the growth process.

14.2 What is a strategy?

Bateman and Snell (1999: 127) define strategy as a pattern of action and resource allocation to achieve the goals of the organisation. A strategy is normally the result of a strategic planning session. Strategic planning involves making decisions about the firm's long-term goals and strategies. This is a process, which normally involves the following steps (Oosthuizen 2002: 103):

1. Develop the firm's vision ("dream") and mission (i.e. the reason for its existence).
2. Analyse the business environment (macro, market and micro).
3. Set long-term objectives.
4. Develop strategies (corporate, business and functional).
5. Develop action plans for the attainment of each strategy, with a resource and time allocation for each.
6. Implement and control the most appropriate strategies selected.

The strategic planning process is used throughout to reassess the organisational system in order to determine any contradictions to organisational goals and objectives involving internal resources, capabilities or systems.

Learning outcomes

After completion of this chapter, you should be able to:

- Understand that a growth strategy is necessary for a business venture
- Explain internal and external growth strategies
- Distinguish between growth strategies and the methods to exploit them
- Discuss the various methods of internal or organic growth
- Explain the various integration strategies
- Discuss the various methods of external growth
- Explain how to obtain growth financing
- Discuss issues relating to raising growth capital

14.3 Growth strategies and methods

Growth or expansion of the business means expanding the amount of trade it undertakes. It also means that the resources, systems and structures of the business venture will need some expansion, although not proportionately.

Pettinger's (1996: 1) definition of corporate strategy states that it "is concerned with directing and guiding the inception and growth of an organisation, and the changes that occur as they conduct their activities". In this section, the aim is to give direction to the growth strategies. The methods for implementing and achieving these strategies are set out in a next section.

The basic growth strategies are aimed at either internal or external growth, or a combination of these.

14.3.1 Internal growth

Internal growth is also known as organic, generic, internal base or core growth. With organic growth the entrepreneur brings new resources together in an innovative combination to create new value. This means growing the business through an increase in market share, developing new products and/or entering new markets.

The internal expansion and growth strategies can take one or more of the following forms:

- Increase of market share – this is either related to expansion of the total market size, or takes place at the expense of other operators in the sector.

- Expansion and growth of turnover, volume, income or profit – this may relate to market share also; to a drive for efficiencies within the organisation; or to the seeking of greater levels and volumes of business with the existing customer base.

- The achievement of economies of scale and command of technology and distribution.

- The command of the means of gaining and maintaining customer and consumer confidence.

- Expansion into new market areas and niches – this is where the existing product ranges are priced or differentiated in ways designed to appeal to different niches. Additionally, in

a highly competitive sector the requirement is to broaden the appeal of the offering in question in relation to those of the other players. Related to this is often the extension and expansion of the offering range (real or differentiated).

- Expansion into new locations, both indigenous and international.

For internal or organic growth, a distinctive strategic position must first be identified. The venture has to decide which parts of the market it wants to serve and then establish a distinctive basis for this to be achieved.

- *Cost leadership:* The gaining of advantage through being the most efficient operator and competing in the market on the price advantage that is available as the result of this

- *Focus or specialisation:* The offering of a distinctive and often narrow range of products in a particular niche

- *Differentiation:* The basis of business success is founded on marketing, advertising and image-building activities, the purpose of which is to set the product apart from others in the sector and maintain the ability to sell at a premium price.

14.3.2 External growth

The external growth strategies deal with factors outside the micro- and market business environment. External growth is beyond the boundaries of the existing business. External growth strategies must position the firm in relation to the industry value chain. Figure 14.1 shows the firm's position within the value chain and the various options it has to expand within the value chain.

■ Vertical integration

This happens when the venture acquires a firm that is positioned either above or below it in the value addition chain, i.e. it acquires a business that is either a customer or a supplier. The acquisition of customers is referred to as forward integration and that of a supplier as backward integration. *Backward integration* has the objective to control the supply of materials or components. It may also serve the purpose

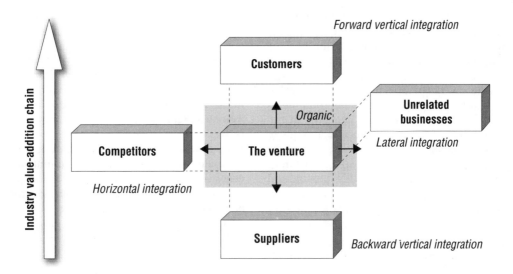

Figure 14.1 External growth strategies in the industry value chain
Source: Adapted from Wickham (2001: 262).

of limiting the volume or quantity of a component or material to competitors. Backward integration can also occur when the firm purchases the makers of its own production or information technology, or the means of transport of raw materials and supplies.

Forward vertical integration is where the firm buys up its customers. This can be extended to means of distribution, transport fleets, retail outlets and any agencies that provide aftersales as repair activities. It may also be apparent where component firms require the means of setting up assembly points; and where assembly points set up the means of finishing and packaging (Pettinger 1996: 250).

■ Horizontal integration

This happens when the venture integrates a business that is on the same level of value addition as itself, i.e. a business that is in essence a competitor. Horizontal integration can take the form of a merger or joint venture between two or more competitors in the sector or industry in order to create a dominant or more influential organisation. Quite often the reason for this integration is to create synergy with regard to the technology, customer base, location, distribution and outlets at each of the firms contemplating the merger.

■ Lateral integration

This occurs when the integrated business is neither a supplier, customer nor competitor. Lateral integration is usually pursued when a business wishes to diversify to another industry or product in order to reduce the risk or the seasonality of its existing business.

Another approach to the strategic concepts of integration is Porter's five-force model of competition (cited in Pettinger 1996: 252). In this model, competition is nested in competitors, suppliers, distribution rivals and substitutes. From this model Porter developed two additional integration strategies:

- *Northern integration:* This is where a firm buys up those seeking to enter the particular sector in order to prevent this from happening. It is used as a drive towards some form of market domination.

- *Southern integration:* The firm buys up the means of production of critical substitute products. This is done to dominate the sector, to increase the firm's influence, or to preserve and maintain the original product.

14.4 External growth methods

A strategy gives direction. To implement a strategy the firm needs to develop strategic objectives and action plans. To execute the plans requires certain methods. The external growth strategies give direction to the venture in respect of its positioning in the industry value chain.

Moving up, down or sideways in the value chain will require the firm to use certain methods. It must be stressed here that most of the literature does not distinguish between strategy and the methods of executing it. A firm might develop a specific strategy in respect of each of these "methods" discussed in this section and refer to it as a "strategy".

To pursue any one of these strategies, a firm can use a number of methods: joint ventures, acquisitions, mergers, franchising, etc. This is illustrated in Figure 14.2. These methods of growth strategy implementation will be discussed separately under their respective headings.

14.5 Mergers and acquisitions

Acquisitions refers to the purchase of an existing business or firm or part thereof such that it is completely absorbed and no longer exists. Acquisitions or takeovers are attractive for rapid growth because the only limitations to the growth rate are the availability of targets (i.e. firms to acquire) and the funds with which to buy them.

Mergers, like acquisitions, are transactions involving two or more firms in which only one survives or a new corporate name and firm emerges. The reasons for mergers range from survival to protection, from diversification to growth. Mergers differ from acquisitions purely in the way in which the relationship is entered into. A merger is normally much more collaborative, voluntary and mutually entered into than an acquisition. In an acquisition, the firm responsible for the merger dominates the other.

In some instances firms are taken over or acquired and then merged. An example is the Volkskas group that took over Trust Bank, United Bank and Allied Bank in the 1990s and then merged Volkskas and these other banks to form Absa Bank Ltd.

Mergers and acquisitions may be contemplated for the purpose of gaining access to, and control of, the following (Pettinger 1994: 251):

- Customer bases and portfolios
- Specialised technology and expertise
- High-profile brand names
- High-value firms
- Prime sites
- Footholds in new markets, sectors, locations and markets
- Control of capacity, output, price and value in the sector

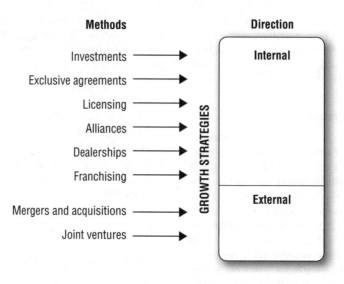

Figure 14.2 Growth strategies and methods of implementation

Acquisitions or takeovers may be either friendly or hostile, and the firm being taken over can enter the relationship willingly or unwillingly. South Africa witnessed a hostile takeover bid in the first half of 2002 when DataMirror Corporation of the United States obtained 16,5 per cent of the shares in Idion Technologies, a company listed on the Johannesburg Securities Exchange. Idion had to fight this hostile takeover attempt at the cost of millions of rands but managed to avert it by the end of June 2002.

14.5.1 Challenges to the success of mergers and acquisitions

Much can be gained from mergers and acquisitions, but there are a number of challenges or important matters that need to be considered in these processes (Weston & Weaver 2001: 90):

• Evaluation of the business
• Cultural factors
• Implementation difficulties

■ Evaluation of the business

All aspects of the targeted firm or firms must be examined. This requires an investigation of the financial statements for a number of years, as well as all legal aspects. Broader business aspects also need to be taken into account, such as management relationships.

It is similar to the investigation required in a business buyout, except that in this more formal setting, it should be a due diligence investigation performed by a team consisting of chartered accountants, marketing specialists and legal experts. Due diligence investigations are costly but cannot be neglected.

■ Cultural factors

Corporate culture refers to an organisation's values, traditions, norms, beliefs and behavioural patterns. Cultural differences are almost certain to be involved when firms are combined, and have caused mergers to fail as they prevented the firms from achieving their potential.

In takeovers, the new owners quite often impose their culture on the targeted firm. This dominance often leads to loss in productivity and motivation. It is important for the acquiring firm to recognise differences in corporate culture and to respect them.

■ Implementation

Implementation should start when mergers or acquisitions are contemplated as a strategy or method of growth. It does not start when the agreement is signed. The key is to formulate implementation and integration plans to accomplish effectively the goals of the takeover process (Weston & Weaver 2001: 93).

14.5.2 Requirements of the Competition Act

The Competition Act No. 89 of 1998 (as amended) provides for the establishment of a Competition Commission. This Commission is responsible for the investigation, control and evaluation of restrictive practices, abuse of dominant position, and mergers (Competition Commission, c2001: 2). Section 12 of the Act states that a merger occurs when one or more firms directly or indirectly acquire, or establish direct or indirect control over, the whole or part of the business of another firm.

In terms of the Act, the Competition Commission must be notified of mergers. Parties to a "small" merger (Section 13) need not notify the Commission. General Notice No. 254 of 2001 sets the lower threshold of the merger at R200 million combined annual turnover and/or assets, and the higher threshold at R3,5 billion. The Competition Commission can order the reversal of mergers within six months of their occurrence.

Fees are payable to the Competition Board to consider the approval of mergers. Intermediate mergers (falling between the lower and higher thresholds) will pay between R5 000 and R350 000 for the application, while large mergers (above the R3,5 billion threshold) will pay R500 000. These fees are amended from time to time and are only given here as an indication of the possible cost.

14.6 Joint ventures

Joint ventures, or strategic alliances, are separate entities involving two or more active participants as partners. For example, Boeing, Mitsubishi, Fuji and Kawasaki entered into a joint venture for the production of small aircraft in order to share technology and cut costs (Hisrich & Peters 1998). The participants in a joint venture continue as separate firms, and usually only a fraction of their activities is involved.

The entrepreneur needs to assess this method of growth carefully to understand the factors that help ensure success, as well as the problems involved. The requirements for successful joint ventures can be summarised as follows:

- Each participant must have something to offer.
- Careful pre-planning must be done; key executives must be assigned to implement it.
- There must be a written agreement in which matters such as profit sharing, management, termination or buyout by one party are set out.
- The objectives of the former venture must be clear.
- Expectations of the results of the joint venture must be reasonable and realistic.

Joint ventures can be an excellent tool for promoting the interests of the parties concerned. The participating firms get the opportunity to share risks, while working with other firms reduces the investment costs of entering potentially risky new markets. Joint ventures also allow firms to gain knowledge and to share managerial skills and technology. A joint venture also presents an opportunity to combine certain assets without violating the regulations governing mergers and acquisitions.

14.7 Franchising

Franchising provides an opportunity for an entrepreneur to expand his or her business by expanding the distribution channel of the venture. It can be used in a number of ways:

- Expand the business by having others pay for the use of the name, process, product, service, etc.
- Convert a product or trade name into business format franchising.
- Convert a branch network into a franchise network.

- Convert independent operators into an infrastructure for cooperative buying and to eliminate competition.

There are several types of franchises, but this section deals solely with the concept of business format franchising. Business format franchising is an arrangement whereby the person or firm (the franchisor) grants an independent party (the franchisee) the right to sell the firm's products or services according to the guidelines set by the franchisor.

14.7.1 Advantages and disadvantages of a franchise chain

■ Advantages for the franchisor

- The distribution network can be expanded without having to borrow funds or raise additional equity finance. Some capital will be required to prepare for franchising but, in general, the franchisees will supply the capital as they fund their own outlets.
- Franchisors can spread the unavoidable risk that arises in any major expansion programme. Some of the risk is shifted to the franchisees.
- Franchisees are usually much more motivated than hired managers, because they own their outlets and are at risk.
- The network can be expanded rapidly and thereby shut out or pre-empt competitors.
- The franchisor can compete with larger rival firms, as franchising allows wider geographical coverage and exposure of the product and service.
- The franchisor can also reap the benefits of greater negotiating strength because of bulk buying on behalf of many franchisees.
- Through cooperative advertising both franchisor and franchisee can share the costs of advertising.

■ Disadvantages for the franchisor

- It is difficult to ensure that all franchisees will adhere to standard operating methods in order to achieve uniformity in all outlets. The franchisee is not an employee and therefore cannot simply be ordered to follow instructions. The franchisee owns the business and has the final say as long as he or she complies with the operations manual and the franchise agreement.

- The objectives of the franchisor and franchisee may differ in respect of profit, turnover, corporate image, etc. This could lead to disputes and a lack of cooperation between the two parties.

- The franchise contract will allow the franchisor to terminate the agreement only under certain circumstances. This may make it difficult to dispose of an unsuitable franchisee.

- The franchisor may find that franchised outlets are in some cases less profitable than company-owned operations.

- A franchisee may try to undertake turnover (sales), thereby avoiding or reducing the management fee payable to the franchisor.

- A successful franchisee may want to start his or her own independent operation in direct competition with the franchisor.

14.7.2 Criteria for identifying and developing a business suitable for franchising

Certain criteria must be considered before embarking on a franchise operation. These are set out in Figure 14.3 and are discussed below.

- *Standardisation in products or services:* There must be a high degree of standardisation in the products or services, the way they are sold, and in the overall image and appearance of the franchised outlets. For example, the products, image and appearance of all outlets in the Kentucky Fried Chicken franchise group are the same.

- *Reproducibility:* Business concepts must be developed that can easily be reproduced in any location. Again, one can look at any successful franchise chain, such as Kentucky Fried Chicken, to see that the same business concept has been reproduced at a number of locations.

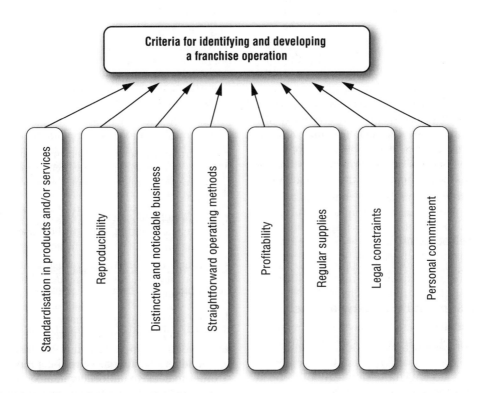

Figure 14.3 Criteria for identifying and developing a franchise operation
Source: Adapted from Nieman (1998: 18).

- *Distinctive and noticeable business:* The business must be distinctive and noticeable in order to distinguish it from its competitors. It should have some sort of unique selling point that cannot easily be copied by others. Trademarks and service marks should be used to protect business names, logos, etc. wherever possible.

- *Straightforward operating methods:* The operating methods of the business must be reasonably straightforward so that franchisees can quickly learn the operating system. They must be able to develop the required skills within weeks so that they can open their outlet and have it operational as soon as possible.

- *Profitability:* The business must have a history of profitability, and the market for the service or product must be large enough to support a sizeable franchise network. The breakeven point in a franchised outlet should also be reached relatively quickly.

- *Regular supplies:* There should be sufficient stock or suppliers available of a specific product if the business depends on the supply of that product. For example, if you are going to sell shirts made from a unique cloth, there should be a sufficient supply of that type of fabric available.

- *Legal constraints:* Determine what legal constraints there are (if any) in respect of the type of business. It is also important to study the requirements of the Business Practices Committee and the Competition Board.

- *Personal commitment:* One must be willing to make a substantial investment in systems development and support infrastructure. One must also accept a moral responsibility for the well-being of the franchisees. Commitment from spouses, family members and business partners is equally essential.

14.7.3 Steps in developing a franchise system

There are certain basic steps in creating and developing a franchise system. It is important that all, or most, of these steps are followed in setting up the system to ensure efficient and effective operation. Figure 14.4 shows the steps, which are briefly discussed here.

■ **Step 1: Establish whether the business is suitable for franchising**

To do this, you need to evaluate your business or business idea against the criteria listed in section 14.7.2. You will have to set out the concept and weigh it up against each criterion.

■ **Step 2: Draw up a business plan or feasibility study**

The next step is to determine the feasibility of developing a potential or existing business into a franchise operation. A business plan or feasibility study is drawn up to assess the overall viability of the business concept.

It must be determined whether the firm will:

- Be able to administer the franchising system properly
- Be able to support franchisees with administrative functions
- Benefit more through franchising than by operating a separate, independent business.

■ **Step 3: Establish a pilot operation**

The next step in the development of a franchise operation deals with the setting up of a pilot operation. It is essential that the business concept has been fully developed before the first franchise is sold. Hall and Dixon (1998: 115) believe it is unethical to use the franchisees as guinea pigs, and their business will soon suffer if operating methods are constantly changed simply because the system was not fully thought out and tested beforehand. Therefore, at least one franchisor-owned pilot outlet should be set up. These outlets should be operated for at least one year in order to test the proposed franchise system rigorously under actual working conditions.

■ **Step 4: Develop the franchise package**

Developing the franchise package involves bringing together the elements of the business, thus reflecting the accumulation of the franchisor's total operational experience in a transmittable form (Mendelsohn 1992: 60). This comprehensive package must be prepared in advance and the experience obtained in setting up and running the pilot operation will provide the basis upon which the elements in the package are structured.

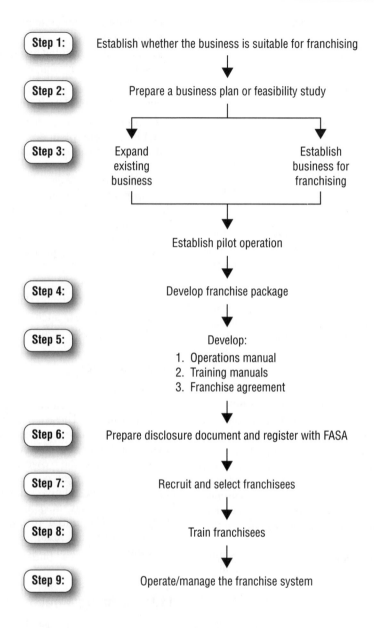

Step 1: Establish whether the business is suitable for franchising

Step 2: Prepare a business plan or feasibility study

Step 3: Expand existing business   Establish business for franchising

Establish pilot operation

Step 4: Develop franchise package

Step 5: Develop:
1. Operations manual
2. Training manuals
3. Franchise agreement

Step 6: Prepare disclosure document and register with FASA

Step 7: Recruit and select franchisees

Step 8: Train franchisees

Step 9: Operate/manage the franchise system

Figure 14.4 Steps in developing a franchise system

Source: Adapted from Nieman (1998).

The franchise package will cover the following aspects:
- Franchise marketing kit
- Training programme and facilities
- Operations and procedures manual
- Start-up assistance

■ Step 5: Develop the manuals and agreement

The operations and procedures manual, training manual and franchise agreement must be developed. It is recommended that the agreement be drawn up by a legal firm specialising in franchise agreements.

▪ Step 6: Meet all ethical requirements

The offer and sale of franchises are not strictly regulated in South Africa as is the case in most other countries. Many unscrupulous business-people and confidence tricksters have used the word "franchise" in advertisements in recent years to add some credibility to their business proposals. Many unsuspecting consumers (or would-be franchisees) have lost their life savings as a result of falling for these scams. It is therefore imperative that any prospective franchisor should take note of the ethical requirements associated with franchising. These are basically the Consumer Code for franchising (issued by the Business Practices Committee), the disclosure document of the Franchise Association of Southern Africa (FASA) and membership of FASA.

There is nothing to be gained, and much that can be lost, from a negative attitude towards the Consumer Code and disclosure requirements emanating from the Code. One should rather regard compliance with these regulations as marketing tools.

▪ Step 7: Recruit and select franchisees

The South African franchise market has grown considerably in the past few years and can be regarded as a buyer's market. Franchisors are therefore competing for quality applicants who can become successful franchisees. Marketing the franchise requires considerable patience. Very few of the mass of initial enquiries end up as suitable franchisees with the capital to invest in the franchise.

To attract these applicants, franchisors must promote their franchises and handle enquiries promptly and in a professional manner. Franchisees are seen by many as entrepreneurs "not by themselves but for themselves". Some others talk of cooperative entrepreneurship. In selecting franchisees one would look for many, or most, of the characteristics of the entrepreneur.

▪ Step 8: Train the franchisees

The franchisor is responsible for providing suitable training so that each franchisee is capable of running a franchise outlet competently. Developing the training component of a franchise system will require three major actions by a franchisor:

- Designing and implementing a training unit or function
- Establishing a training location
- Developing the training programme

▪ Step 9: Manage the franchise system

The normal management actions apply to the franchise system: plan, organise, lead and control. It is only the relationships of the participants that are different. The constructive support of franchisees is essential for efficient operation and the ultimate success of a franchise system. The franchisor must therefore develop and maintain a support structure that will meet the needs of each franchisee.

Franchisees normally require the following support:

- Initial training to instil confidence
- Assistance in setting up the business
- Ongoing support, such as market information, product development and procedures

14.8 Alliances

Alliances are less formal than joint ventures and offer flexibility. Alliances may involve multiple partners. These partner firms pool resources, expertise and ideas so that they will have a continuing need for one another.

Alliances have their own distinctive characteristics. There might not be a formal written contract and the relative sizes of participating firms may be highly unequal (Weston & Weaver 2001: 125). The initial resource commitment may be quite small. Alliances create the ability to initiate and disband projects with a minimum of paperwork.

14.9 Exclusive agreements

Exclusive agreements usually involve rights for manufacturing or marketing. It means that the venture can expand without having to invest in a manufacturing plant or a marketing team. Contractual arrangements ensure that a formal alliance is established.

14.10 Licensing

A licence agreement confers on the licensee the right to manufacture, sell or use something that is the exclusive property of the licensor. The licence agreement normally stipulates an exclusive territory in which the licensee can exercise this right.

The licensee pays the licensor a royalty (commission) on sales in exchange for the licence. The licensor usually has little or no control over the licensee beyond the terms of the agreement. Motor car manufacturers are a good example. The company in South Africa would manufacture Nissan motor cars under the licence in southern Africa and pay a royalty to Nissan in Japan. Nissan in Japan has no control over the South African manufacturer apart from the terms of the agreement.

Licensing is the granting of know-how and sometimes also the physical equipment required to produce specified products. It speeds up entry into new markets and helps build broader market recognition and acceptance. Licensing can also include the right to exploit a trademark commercially. For example, a company in South Africa may obtain the right to use a trademark, such as Sanyo, in South Africa for its products. Normally there would be certain conditions in respect of quality, etc.

14.11 Dealerships

In a dealership, the manufacturer grants a second party, the dealer, the right to sell the manufacturer's products within a given area. The dealer gets the exclusive rights to a specific territory and the right to operate under the manufacturer's trademark. The dealer is required to maintain the standards and corporate image demanded by the manufacturer.

A dealership constitutes a sales entity that undertakes to sell a line of products for a manufacturer or a wholesaler. This is the customary form of business licensing in the motor industry. In reality there is little difference between a dealership and a distributor, except that dealers usually sell directly to the public. An example is Toit's Nissan, which has the right (a dealership) granted by Nissan South Africa to sell Nissan motor cars in a certain area of Pretoria.

14.12 Financing growth

Growth puts a tremendous strain on the resources of the business at a time when it most needs them. Growth requires capital, and often the financial resources that saw the business through start-up and early growth are not sufficient to feed the demands of rapid growth (Allen 1999: 493).

Growth capital consists of those funds needed to take the firm out of the start-up phase and into becoming a significant contender in the marketplace.

Raising growth capital is a time-consuming and costly process. Most of the extended growth strategies and methods would not be available or accessible to small, medium and micro-enterprises (SMMEs). Mergers, acquisitions, joint ventures and franchising will require capital injection. These funds will normally be acquired through the corporate banking division of commercial banks or even merchant bankers.

The most common sources of finance for growth would be the venture capital market or even private placement or listing of shares on the Johannesburg Securities Exchange. These sources of capital and how to access them are discussed in Chapter 8.

14.13 Conclusion

Growth in a business must be achieved and there must be a strategy for achieving it. Growth strategies must be part of the strategic plan, and they are normally aimed at internal or external growth or a combination thereof.

External growth strategies must position the firm in relation to its place in the industry value chain. This involves a strategy of integration, which can be vertical, horizontal or lateral.

Internal growth strategies focus on an increase in market share, developing new products and services and/or entering new markets.

To implement external growth strategies certain methods or substrategies can be used, such as mergers and acquisitions, joint ventures, franchising, licensing, dealerships and exclusive agreements. Each situation might call for a different method. Most of these strategies and methods will require resources – in particular, capital. The sources of financing the venture will need to be revisited in order to raise capital for growth.

Looking back

1. List the process of strategic planning.
   - Develop a vision.
   - Analyse the environment.
   - Set objectives.
   - Develop strategies.
   - Develop action plans.
   - Implement and control.

2. List the basic growth strategies.
   - Internal growth
   - External growth
   - A combination of the two

3. Briefly discuss internal growth.
   - Increase in market share
   - Growth of turnover, volume, income and/or profit
   - New market areas and niches
   - New locations

4. Briefly discuss the external growth strategies.
   - Vertical integration – backwards and forwards
   - Horizontal integration
   - Lateral integration
   - Northern integration
   - Southern integration

5. List and discuss the various growth methods.
   - Mergers and acquisitions
   - Joint ventures
   - Franchising
   - Alliances
   - Exclusive agreements
   - Licensing
   - Dealerships

Key terms

Acquisitions
Alliances
Dealerships
Exclusive agreements
External growth
Financial growth
Franchising

Horizontal integration
Internal growth
Joint ventures
Lateral integration
Licensing
Mergers
Northern integration

Organisational growth
Southern integration
Strategic growth
Strategy
Structural growth
Vertical integration

Discussion questions

1. What is meant by growth strategy? Does it need to be formal or informal?

2. Discuss internal growth strategies. Can any of the growth methods be used to achieve some of these strategies?

3. Give some examples of the different integration strategies.

4. Explain the advantages of mergers and acquisitions.

5. Explain how franchising can be used to expand the distribution channel of the venture.

6. Is franchising a form of licensing? Discuss the different forms of licensing (including dealerships).

7. Consider the various growth methods, and explain which are easier and less costly to use.

Case studies

Case study 1: Lean Impala seeks new growth pastures

Impala Platinum (Implats) produces 25 per cent of the world's platinum, its share price has increased over 1 000 per cent in five years and market capitalisation stands at over R40 million – yet the platinum giant's head office is manned by only ten executives.

Says Keith Rumble, Chief Executive of Implats: "It makes things very entrepreneurial. You don't have in-house support groups, so you either do it yourself or make use of outside agencies." The business is now a far cry from the one that was "left behind" in the Gencor stable when Billiton listed offshore. "The assets weren't delivering, we had to identify growth opportunities," says Rumble. It would be easy to attribute the success of Implats to rising metal prices and a declining rand. These have certainly played a role, but looking further one finds a vibrant company that has done much to secure its own destiny.

A few years ago the business embarked on a long-term growth strategy. The first aspect was to improve efficiencies via a process-re-engineering programme, which helped Implats become the highest-efficiency producer in the industry. Headcount dropped from 58 000 to 27 000. The second aspect was to consider new revenue opportunities. The trouble was that mining rights limited output to one million ounces a year, which also meant that surface assets, such as the processing plants, were underutilised. Implats' growth strategy has elegantly dealt with these issues. Partnerships and joint ventures have been agreed on with a number of companies, including Aquarius, Mimosa and Zimplats.

These equity agreements not only give Implats greater volumes for its refinement facilities, but also ensure access to additional reserves on a "life of mine" basis. In time they could also lead to further shareholding. Greenfield projects are also part of the Implats strategy. Marula Platinum is an example where the ore reserves have been acquired, and commissioning will begin next year.

Implats' value growth strategy will mean that production will move from one million ounces in 1998 to 2,2 million ounces this year: International exploration, which is carried out through partnerships to keep expenditure down, continues as a "long-term insurance policy". Implats aims to remain lean and mean. The chain of command is kept short, and transparency is maintained at all levels in the business. The company recently signed a two-year wage agreement. "Good union relations are enabled through active engagement," says Rumble, who adds that "unions are encouraged to have a voice in the workplace".

Implats led the industry in implementing "self-directed" work teams. Rumble explains that Implats does not use traditional mining structures; each team has a crew captain plus ten members. Furthermore, the crew captain is often rotated within the ranks of the team. Implats does not take bets on the currency or hedge metal prices. Explains Rumble: "We don't cover sales; treasury repatriates sales as and when they occur."

Asked if Implats' results and share price have reached a plateau, Rumble remains bullish. He contends that demand for platinum remains strong both in industrial markets (auto-catalysts and electronics), as well as jewellery markets.

Source: The Growth Awards 2002. A special projects supplement to *Business Report,* 9 May 2002, p. 5.

Questions

1. Identify the growth strategies and methods followed by Impala.
2. How did Impala benefit from each of these strategies?

Case study 2: CS Holdings aims to grow organically

A busy period of acquisitions for technology group CS Holdings has come to an end, with the company closing its chequebook and saying its future growth will be organic.

In the past year the group has made several large investments, acquiring Getronics SA, Agril Intellect and the JD Edwards software division of PriceWaterhouseCoopers. Since the books closed, it has bought the software integration business of Idion Technology.

CEO Annette van der Laan said all the acquisitions were successfully integrated, but the next phase had to focus on organic growth to capitalise on the skills the company had amassed and to increase its market share. One division of the group that shrank last year was its technology training arm, which reported slow growth and added far less than expected to the overall turnover. Four branches were closed as the group focused more on e-learning technologies that did not require a physical national presence.

Van der Laan said no other closures were expected, even though the division accounted for only 10 per cent of group revenue. "We are still the biggest technology training company for corporations in South Africa." She said other divisions had performed well in the year ending June 2002, due to a clear long-term strategy and tight financial controls.

CS Holdings' revenue of R403 million was up 99 per cent from R202 million. Gross profit of R139 million was up from R70 million, but was diminished by operating costs, depreciation, amortisation and a R6 million loss on discontinued operations, leaving a net profit of R22 million, up 34 per cent from last year. Profit was partly subdued compared with the enormous growth in turnover, because the operating margins in the business it acquired were lower than those of its existing operations.

However, the running costs have been reduced and the overall operating margin before exceptional items now stands at 11,5 per cent, which the company says is sustainable. Van der Laan said CS Holdings now claimed about 5 per cent of South Africa's market for technology consulting, infrastructure and outsourcing, and aimed to grow that to 8 per cent within three years. The group was competing head-on with first-tier information technology players in South Africa and would work hard to gain ground on its rivals. What should score it points locally was the empowerment deal with Worldwide African Investment Holdings, giving it a better profile to penetrate the parastatals and public sector markets.

The company has identified Africa as a key market for its software and hardware. In the past year it has won contracts in Angola, Ethiopia, Mozambique and Botswana, and is bidding for business in Uganda, Namibia and Nigeria. Van der Laan said the group's R12 million cash reserves and strong cash flow were sufficient to keep the business going forward. CS Holdings shares closed 4,82 per cent higher at 87c yesterday after the results were published. No dividend was paid as the earnings are being retained to fund further growth.

Source: CS Holdings aims to grow organically, Lesley Stones, *Business Day,* 4 September 2002, p. 19.

Questions

1. Identify the growth strategies and methods followed by CS Holdings.
2. Can (and should) a business venture pursue external growth before growing first internally?

Experiential exercises

1. Interview the entrepreneur (or chief executive officer) of a growing firm on the strategies the firm developed for growth. Then determine how these strategies were implemented.

2. Find a recent newspaper article on a merger, acquisition or joint venture. Prepare a report on the reasons and the strategy for this action.

3. Interview the owner of a major franchise system. Ask him or her to explain the process of developing and managing the system.

4. Interview the chief executive officer (CEO) of a recently listed company. Determine whether the listing is used to finance expansion or not. Write a report on the expansion resulting from this listing.

© Van Schaik Publishers

Exploring the Web

1. Go to www.compcom.co.za for more information on the Competition Commission and the Competition Act.

2. Go to http://www.financehum.com/ for a database of American investors and venture capital firms.

3. Visit http://www.economist.com/ The Economist – an excellent business journal with many reports on growth companies, mergers, acquisitions, etc.

References and recommended reading

Allen, K.R. 1999. *Growing and managing an entrepreneurial business.* Boston: Houghton Mifflin.

Bateman, T.S. & Snell, S.A. 1999. *Management: building competitive advantage,* 4th ed. Boston: Irwin/McGraw-Hill.

Competition Commission. c2001. *Competition Act No. 89 of 1998.* Pretoria: Competition Commission.

Crijns, H. & Ooghe, H. 1997. *Groeimanagement: lessen van dynamische ondernemers.* Tielt: Lannoo.

Hall, P. & Dixon, R. 1988. *Franchising.* London: Pitman.

Hisrich, R.D. & Peters, M.P. 1998. *Entrepreneurship,* 4th ed. Boston: Irwin/McGraw-Hill.

Mendelsohn, M. 1992. *The guide to franchising,* 5th ed. London: Cassell.

Nieman, G. 1998. *The franchise option: how to franchise your business.* Cape Town: Juta.

Oosthuizen, T.F.J. 2002. General management and leadership. In Nieman, G. & Bennett, A. (Eds), *Business management: a value chain approach.* Pretoria: Van Schaik.

Pettinger, R. 1996. *Introduction to corporate strategy.* London: Machullan Business.

Weston, J.F. & Weaver, S.C. 2001. *Mergers and acquisitions.* New York: McGraw-Hill.

Wickham, P. 2001. *Strategic entrepreneurship: a decision-making approach to new venture creation and management,* 2nd ed. Harlow: *Financial Times*/Prentice Hall.

15

Business failure and turnaround measures

Marius Pretorius

Learning outcomes

After completion of this chapter, you should be able to:

▸ Distinguish between "trouble" and levels of failure

▸ Gain insight into the reasons why ventures have difficulties and fail

▸ Identify the core factors driving failure in a venture

▸ Understand the interrelationships between elements responsible for success and failure

▸ Recognise the levels of failure in a venture and how they might arise

▸ Identify early warning signs of pending trouble

▸ Understand the causes of failure

▸ Identify potential management actions available to the entrepreneur to manage trouble

▸ Understand the action necessary to turn a venture from a troubled performance towards a good one

15.1 Introduction

Following on the discussion in an earlier chapter of the venture life cycle (VLC) and its impact on the venture, it is clear that "trouble" can loom everywhere. Often, trouble in a venture forces one to refocus one's thinking on success activities.

Reports about venture failure vary and range between 30 and 80 per cent of all new ventures within the first two years after establishment, depending on how failure is defined (DTI, 2000). The odds against the entrepreneur achieving success seem to be enormous. The 33 per cent success rate for small businesses is indeed alarming.

Previous chapters have indicated how things change over the life cycle of the venture. This is also true for the potential troubles that may face a venture. If one knows what can be expected and where to look, early signs of trouble should be detected and acted on early before trouble turns into crisis. Failure is not exclusive to new start-up ventures and may also strike mature ventures. Micro- and small ventures are especially vulnerable to possible failure – the environmental threats may become too severe because these ventures simply do not have the "back-up" of extra finances and resources that larger companies have. Moreover, they normally are less able to source finance from banking institutions.

Bearing possible failure in mind – when one wants to be successful – serves two purposes:

• It makes you aware of what to look out for to ensure that things do not go wrong and warn you when they do.

• It also helps to warn you of pending trouble in the ventures of those with whom you do business. These include your suppliers and customers, who may buy on credit from you. If there is looming trouble, you may be the one coming off second best.

To understand failure in a venture requires a thorough understanding of the intricacies of business operations and the business environment. To be able to turn around from a failing position, one needs to understand motivation, strategy, finance, marketing, operations and all the other functions within a business venture.

This chapter deals primarily with failure in a business venture and the signs of pending trouble. Secondly, it explains how one should act, depending on the level of failure that exists in the business.

15.2 Failure in perspective

Success seems to be well understood in the area of sports and life in general and is normally defined as the achievement of realistic goals. Thus, if someone sets out to achieve some or other goal and then eventually does so, he or she is perceived to be successful.

If failure is the opposite of success, one may deduce that non-achievement of realistic goals will be regarded as failure. Unfortunately, this only solves part of the problem, as the question arises as to whether it is possible to be partly successful or to fail partly. If someone achieves seven out of ten goals, he or she may be regarded as successful or partly successful, and if three out of ten goals are achieved, they would probably be perceived as partially failed or marginally successful. Business ventures normally do not have a single goal whereby success or failure can be determined.

For the purpose of this chapter, success will be measured on a continuum between success and failure. To evaluate whether entrepreneurial ventures fail or succeed, therefore, would require assessing the goals of the venture. Thus, what are realistic goals for a venture? Are these goals also the goals of the entrepreneur?

15.3 Typical goals for the entrepreneurial venture

Venture goals vary significantly, depending on the type of business, industry, entrepreneur, life cycle stage, original reason for establishment, etc. Overall, venture goals can be categorised into personal, financial and strategic goals. Each of these is briefly explored below.

15.3.1 Personal goals of the entrepreneur

The initial motivation for starting a venture varies broadly from the need just to survive (survivalist or necessity entrepreneurs) to the drive to develop a new product and achieve financial independence (opportunity entrepreneurs). Often, it would be a combination of several motives that prompts the entrepreneur to start the venture. In developing countries, many "survivalist" entrepreneurs are forced to pursue venture establishment in order to provide for their basic needs of survival on a day-to-day basis.

Frequently, an entrepreneur would start a venture with the idea of becoming his own boss and having the freedom to do whatever he wants. After a while and when faced with long hours of tedious work that is often not related to the original perception of what he thought he would do, he feels dejected and disappointed. The ideal picture that he had in his mind did not materialise. He then has to re-evaluate his goals.

Although he is not a failure yet, the entrepreneur may lose motivation and determination, as he is not really doing what he wants to do. Not achieving one's personal goals may then result in lower effort and input, thus leading to the next level of non-achievement of the financial goals of the venture.

Control over the resources of the venture may also be an important goal to some entrepreneurs and can serve as one of their personal goals. According to Timmons (1999), ownership of resources should not be paramount. However, many entrepreneurs have a control mindset. When a venture fails, the entrepreneur normally also loses control over the assets of the venture.

15.3.2 Financial goals of the venture

Depending on the type of the business venture, the financial goals of the entrepreneur may differ. A "survivalist" venture refers to a business activity which a person enters into to earn an income for physical survival on a day-to-day basis. Such income is normally irregular in amount and timing. The micro-enterprise, on the other hand, may be able to generate regular profits over a more sustainable period of time. The venture may not have the potential to grow, but can sustain the entrepreneur's financial requirements. This is sometimes referred to as a "lifestyle" venture, and the entrepreneur becomes a manager of his or her small enterprise that supplies the required income levels to satisfy the lifestyle goals.

Financial goals for small and medium-sized ventures require an understanding why people put their funds into a business venture. Firstly, entrepreneurs normally want their own funds to grow and generate more funds, so part of the decision is an investment decision. These people are, in fact, shareholders who take the risk of investing their money in the venture. External investors may also seek growth in the venture's assets through sales and market share. The financial goals of shareholders that are relevant here typically include:

• Return on investment (ROI) for shareholders
• Increased sales and revenue
• Increased market share
• Continued growth in profits and size

It is also important to realise that there are different stakeholders with financial interests in the venture. They include the entrepreneur with his or her own equity, other equity holders (external shareholders like family or partners), lenders and suppliers of credit to the venture. All the financial goals serve these stakeholders in some or other way. Employees (not necessarily shareholders) are beneficiaries of the venture and have no rights with regard to the determination of the financial goals. The financial goals of the venture are driven by the shareholders' requirement for return on investment as they take the risk of investing their funds in the business. ROI is, therefore, the key financial goal while the others complement it.

15.3.3 Strategic goals of the venture

Strategic goals of the venture refer to the utilisation of the opportunity and the achievement of a fit between the venture and its environment to ensure long-term profitability. Underlying the strategic goals are the financial and personal goals.

Firstly, the opportunity of the venture is based on the original idea that is converted into an entrepreneurial opportunity, which brings value to a target market and which they will pay for. The venture thus presents the target market with a concept offering that will meet their needs. Strategically seen, the objective of the venture is to develop the ability to adapt its offerings to the changes that may occur in the

target market's needs and requirements. If there is a change in the needs, the venture must respond to it or, even better, anticipate it to keep on serving the target market successfully.

The second strategic goal of the venture is to ensure long-term profitability by meeting the needs of customers. Decisions should therefore be of such a nature that they focus on the long-term rather than short-term profits. Strategic goals have to do with the continuous, long-term existence of the venture.

15.4 Levels of failure in ventures

Failure has different levels when evaluated in the business environment. Figure 15.1 shows the levels of venture performance ranging between a venture that is performing well and one that fails completely. Each level in between is characterised by a different set of circumstances. The levels are explained in the rest of the chapter.

15.4.1 The venture that is performing well

The venture gets a green light at this level and there are no obvious problems. All the goals are being achieved, including personal, financial and strategic goals. This is also the level that all ventures aspire to.

At this level of performance, the shareholders are (at least fairly) satisfied with their investment. The entrepreneur, who is a shareholder, is motivated by the venture's performance and external shareholders want to make more funds available to share in the prosperity.

15.4.2 The underperforming venture

Underperformance in the venture means that some goals are not achieved but, overall, there are no visible differences between the well-performing and the underperforming venture. One has to start digging into the figures and make comparisons to identify relevant issues. Underperformance is usually seen when comparing the financial statements over a period of time. The venture that is underperforming gets a yellow light, serving as a warning that something bad may be coming and that the entrepreneur should rectify what is wrong.

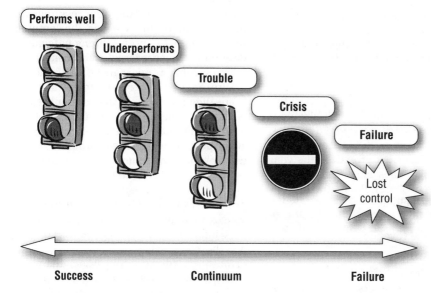

Figure 15.1 The venture failure slide

Figure 15.2 shows the first and main signs associated with each level of failure. As the venture moves in the direction of complete failure, more and more signs become visible, provided that the necessary records are properly kept to be able to identify these signs. Financial statements should be made available as soon after the end of the month as possible. The signs of trouble are discussed later in this chapter.

15.4.3 Trouble or difficulty in the venture

Trouble in the venture gets a red light, requiring the entrepreneur to stop and evaluate the situation immediately before taking corrective actions.

At this point, the signs of trouble are fairly clear but often the entrepreneur does not want to acknowledge that something is wrong. He

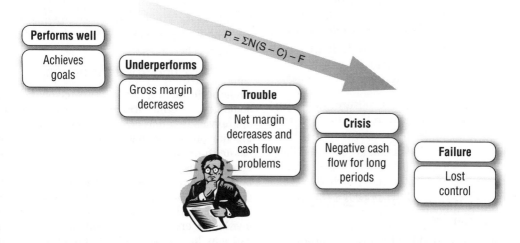

Figure 15.2 Performance indicator levels associated with venture failure

works harder and hopes that the problems will have gone when he wakes up tomorrow. This usually never happens and things only get worse. Before he knows it, the venture is in crisis.

> The key signs are decreasing net margins and early irregular cash flow patterns.

This phase is characterised by a venture that has come close to being insolvent when its liabilities are greater than its assets, and if it proceeds in the same way as before, it will encounter legal and financial problems. Full insolvency would be the next phase.

It is important to realise that there is hope for the venture to turn the situation around when it is in trouble, but it becomes very difficult once the trouble turns into a crisis.

15.4.4 The venture in crisis

During a crisis the irregular cash flows associated with trouble in the previous phase become worse and are constantly negative for long periods. The same reasons could be cited, but they are affecting the venture more severely. This is evident through rapidly declining sales and market share to confirm the trends of the trouble phase.

Equally serious as the cash flow problem at this point is the loss of confidence by the stakeholders and even employees, as they want to abandon ship and may even do so. It is only a matter of time before creditors apply for bankruptcy to be filed against the venture.

15.4.5 The venture that failed

Once under bankruptcy or closure, the entrepreneur finally loses control of the venture. Depending on the specific situation, a plan is prepared for salvaging what is left. It is rarely possible to save a venture at this stage.

15.5 Key issues of business success or failure

This chapter started by describing venture failure as the opposite of success that is achieved

in a business venture. Success means the achievement of the venture's different goals. Many authors report different factors that determine the success of a business. It is thus fair to say that a lack of these success factors in a venture will contribute to its failure. The more they are lacking, the further the venture will slide down the failure scale.

This section looks at five keys that lead to successful business ventures. These factors are interrelated and impact on each other in different ways. It is crucial to consider how they fit in and affect the venture's profitability and growth. Each one has to do with the signs and causes of failure. Figure 15.3 shows the complex interrelationships between venture failure and these key issues.

Mastering the concepts associated with each of these keys will help the entrepreneur to make a success and halt the failure slide. Understanding these keys will lead to more questions and answers, which will eventually distinguish you from the average person in business.

15.5.1 Attitude and motivation

The first of the five keys to business success is to have an attitude of success and be motivated to achieve.

An attitude of success means that you must have a positive outlook and feeling about being successful in business. This goes hand in hand with a high "locus of control" exhibited by successful entrepreneurs. It is your choice to have a positive outlook. If you are a negative person who is always complaining, it is better to not try business. The longer an attitude is held, the stronger it becomes.

With the correct attitude, one can achieve almost anything, while a negative attitude is a definite recipe for failure. Focus on how to make things work rather than on why they cannot work. This will give you a new perspective on the problems that come your way. Think about the proverbial glass that is half-full rather than half-empty.

An attitude of success refers to the frame of mind with which individuals approach tasks and problems. The way you think and how you approach life and work will determine your success. Think positively about everything and the negatives will stop following you.

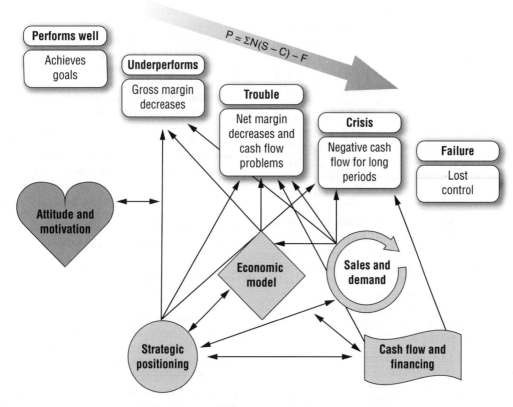

Figure 15.3 Core issues and their relationship to venture failure

Perseverance refers to refusing to give up or let go of your objectives, especially in the face of obstacles and discouragement. Perseverance means that you are energetic and positive about your plan and the goals you pursue. You are driven to achieve them. Accept that giving up is not an option. Perseverance, however, does not mean that you should be stubborn, bull-headed or plain stupid about things that cannot work.

Answer the following questions to get an indication of whether you have what it takes:

- Have you recently blamed someone or something for what happened to you?
- How often have you given up on something important to you? Why?
- Are you willing to work 18 hours per day for six days a week to achieve your goals?

If there are low levels of attitude and achievement motivation, the chances of failure are higher, both at the personal and the venture level.

15.5.2 Positioning

As very few people seem to grasp the notion of positioning, one should perhaps start by looking at an example. Three well-known food franchises in South Africa all sell chicken as part of their main line, namely KFC, Nando's and Chicken Licken. How do they "position" their concept offerings? Studying their advertisements, set-ups, pricing strategies, apparent target groups and what their managers say will teach one a lot about each one's positioning.

The concept of KFC seems to be positioned as a "convenience" product, which is also fun while being priced for the average family or individual with medium income. There are even drive-through facilities for greater convenience. The chicken pieces make it ideal for the families of busy parents. KFC focuses on take-aways but occasionally there are some very basic sit-down facilities. KFC's marketing often involves promotions with toys and user coupons focused on children.

Nando's, on the other hand, focuses on giving people a "memorable experience" for which they will come back time after time. Their products are more highly priced, have larger portions (quarter, half and full) and are prepared more "healthily" for the higher-income groups. The "taste of Portugal" and open-fire preparation bring an added experience component. Nando's has better sit-down facilities as part of the experience.

Chicken Licken, on the other hand, positions its product as basically good food that makes up a fair-sized meal at a low price. The outlets normally have no sit-down but only take-away facilities. Nothing that can increase costs is tolerated. Chicken Licken focuses on the lower-income group and combines its products with traditional cheaper foods, such pap (stiff porridge) and bread.

As you may by now realise, positioning largely takes place in the minds of the consumers. It is how they see your product (their perception); it is also what you believe the customers will value and what you can provide. Think how differently a normal loaf of bread and garlic bread are positioned. Ordinary bread is widely distributed, low priced, never advertised (basic food), while garlic bread is highly priced, exclusively distributed and promoted (upper-class party item). Obviously these products are aimed at different target markets.

The needs of the target market therefore determine what "value" the concept can bring to them and therefore the entrepreneur has to understand their needs well. Positioning has a lot to do with the target market one selects to serve. It is an important concept that has strategic impact.

15.5.3 Economic model

The economic model describes the relationship between selling price, cost, volume and fixed expenses. If the economic model is not sound, there is no basis for the business venture to exist. To test the venture's economic viability, three key questions should be asked.

■ Is the business model economically sound?

To answer this question one should know what the margin is for the concept offering (or product). The margin is the difference between the selling price [S] and variable cost [C] of one unit of a product or service. Remember, the margin is always calculated **per unit**. For example, if you sell one can of soft drink for R2,50 and it costs you R2,00, the margin is 50c. If you make a chair to sell, the variable cost consists of all the material you require to make the chair, namely wood, nails, paint and glue. Normally it is fairly easy to find a selling price, but it is more difficult to know the exact variable cost per unit. This is especially so for manufacturing enterprises, and is also true for services.

■ How many concept offerings (products) can be sold in the market?

For the economic model to be sound, one has to know whether there are enough people who need the concept offering and are willing to pay for it. One needs to know how many items can be sold [N]. For example, one knows that some left-handed people want special left-handed scissors and are willing to pay for them – even at a premium price – and therefore the offering seems feasible. Manufacturing these scissors for the South African market alone is, however, not viable because the local market is too small. The number of products that one can sell is too small to create a viable business. One should then combine this product with other products in a different business model.

■ How many fixed expenses are required to produce the required number of products?

Fixed expenses [F] involve facilities, equipment, salaries, overhead costs such as telephone, rent and repayments. This is not part of the cost of sales [N × C] and must be considered separately.

From answering these questions, one can calculate the sales income [N × S] and the sales cost [N × C], which are both important values for one's planning. Combining these into one formula gives the contribution margin = $\sum N[S - C]$, which must be positive. A positive contribution margin can then be used to cover the fixed costs [F]. Combining all of the above gives the profit formula: $P = \sum N[S - C] - F$. From this formula it is clear that the number of products [N] is vital to the profit.

Economic viability therefore indicates that the venture can be profitable and can be pursued meaningfully. So, if the concept is feasible and viable, one can seriously plan to implement it. The relationship between the variables P, N, S, C and F will be explored further below, as its importance demands a more detailed discussion.

15.5.4 Sales and market share

If the profit of the venture is calculated as $P = \sum N[S - C] - F$, it is clear that profit can be improved in four ways only:

- Increase the sales volume [N].
- Increase the margin, which can be done by:
  - Increasing the selling price [S]
  - Decreasing the cost price [C]
- Decrease the fixed costs [F].

The relationship between the variables makes it difficult to change any one variable independently without affecting some of the others. For example, if the selling price [S] is increased (to make more profit), the number of products [N] demanded by customers will probably decrease accordingly, which again leads to reduced profit. Similarly, if fuel costs increase [C], the margin drops; and if labour cost [F] increases, the profit drops if there is no improvement in sales [N] or the selling price [S]. To improve profits, one should therefore find ways to increase N and S, or decrease C and F, without affecting the other variables.

As a practical example, try to follow this case in point. McDonald's opens a franchise near an existing and established KFC outlet. Regular customers of KFC now may spend a portion of their disposable income at McDonald's, even if only to experiment with the new product. KFC therefore experiences a lower N, especially over the initial period. KFC starts to do some expensive marketing to improve sales and counter the impact of McDonald's, which leads to higher F and may reduce the profit further. There is a decrease in the market share of KFC due to the activities of McDonald's.

One should understand that many factors could affect the demand for one's concept negatively and influence the sales volume [N]. Competitor actions and products, changes in customer tastes and disposable income, economic changes in interest rates and inflation that affect disposable incomes, and many other factors can influence the profit.

What is clear is that, for every concept, different events and actions have different effects. One should, therefore, not make generalisations but research the specific concept offering and relevant factors well. The basic issues of demand and supply are very relevant when studying the relationship between N and S that is responsible for the income part of the venture. The C and F factors are expense issues that indirectly influence the income and margin issues.

The economic model and the sales forecast require an understanding of the relationships between the various factors – this is crucial to business success. The importance of knowing how these factors interact cannot be stressed enough. One should then move on to study each factor individually. A later section will explain how the selling price [S] is determined. Determining the selling price requires consideration of several of the factors referred to above.

Incorrect sales forecasting that does not materialise after start-up is reported to be the second most important reason for business failure.

When prospective entrepreneurs forecast the number of product concepts [N] that they will sell, they tend to overestimate because this makes the venture look more viable. The higher the forecasted N, the higher the profit will be. During the forecasting stage, one should rather err on the conservative side than overestimate. However, it is best to be as accurate as possible – for one's own sake, that of the external shareholders and that of the financier who will do his own research on the potential N.

The question is, therefore, how one can accurately determine the number of products that will be sold. One can never be 100 per cent accurate, although one should strive to be without spending too much money. For example, a fellow who wanted to buy a fuel station visited the filling stations in the vicinity (12 o'clock at night in the winter over a couple of weeks) to read the pump meters. This gave him a good idea of how many litres of fuel had been sold in the area and he made some fairly accurate projections.

Market research should not necessarily be highly sophisticated and expensive. Try to keep it simple. You could start by drawing up a simple questionnaire to assist you. You could observe and count customers at a specific point. For retail business the number of potential customers is very important and "feet" can be counted at low cost.

You can also do some desk research. Phone the local chamber of business office and find out who the specialists in your type of business are. Ask them some questions.

Another method that is often used is to meet with mentors – a few businessmen who are trusted and respected for their business acumen and experience. Visit them one at a time and explain your idea and research needs. Ask their advice on how to obtain information or whom to speak to. It is important to have such people one can turn to for general ideas and suggestions.

You can also use the telephone directory to identify similar types of businesses in order to form an idea of the apparent size of the industry. Remember, the more businesses in your type of industry, the less they will react when a new business enters the market. It also means that the customers are not as loyal to a specific competitor and that they care more about the price. The *Yellow Pages*, in particular, can give you meaningful information regarding the industry you are in.

All of this research is done to ensure that you can project your future sales as accurately as possible *before* you start. The financiers will probably also want to be assured that your projections are correct. The more you are certain about the sales you can make, the fewer problems you should have in future.

These guidelines are also true if you want to increase your sales when you are already in business. Remember, one of the four ways to increase profit is to increase volume [N].

15.5.5 Cash flow

Many entrepreneurs cannot understand why their banks want to foreclose their loans while their accountants indicate that they must pay tax because they are making a profit. The answer is often hidden in the cash flow statement. Some important concepts about the cash flow of a business are briefly explained below. One has to understand the venture's cash flow situation very well, as it is the final key to success.

The two important issues about cash flow are "flow" and "timing". There are two kinds of flow, namely inflow and outflow. Inflows into the enterprise primarily come from payments received from customers. Other inflows can be capital from different sources, as discussed earlier, and normally occur at the start (= timing) of the enterprise. Customer payments take place regularly during and mostly at the end of the month (= timing).

Outflows, on the other hand, are monies paid for stock and fixed expenses. Typically, an enterprise must buy the inventory before it can sell it. It means that the money must be paid before selling can take place and therefore the inflow follows long after the outflow. If this time gap is too wide, a cash flow problem may arise unless provision is made for it by obtaining bridging finance.

Another illustration can explain the effect of the timing and the flow.

Joe's Carpentry produces expensive wooden furniture for the higher-income groups. He buys wood on 7 January to the value of R17 000 (N × C) and for which he must pay cash before delivery. After payment it takes a week (14 January) before delivery. On average, the wood is transformed into four saleable furniture sets of R9 000 [S] each within three weeks (5 February), after which it takes another week (14 February) to reach the different shop floors. A set normally sells within two weeks (28 February) after it arrives on the floor. All sales of the month are paid for on the 27th of the specific or following month, thus Joe will receive his money on 28 March. Inflow therefore takes place almost three months after outflow. During the three months, some other expenses of R5 000 per month are incurred. With the formula, the profit for the three months is calculated as:

$P = \Sigma N(S - C) - F$, or $P = \Sigma NS - \Sigma NC - F$

$P = (4 \times 9\ 000) - 17\ 000 - 15\ 000$

$P = R4\ 000$ for three months

The profit is therefore approximately R1 333 per month.

Look at the same case from a cash flow perspective:

	January	February	March	April
Cash balance	0	(22 000)	(27 000)	4 000
Income	0	0	36 000	
Cost of goods				
Wood	17 000			
Fixed expenses	5 000	5 000	5 000	
Cash level	(22 000)	(27 000)	4 000	

Think what happens to the cash flow if Joe buys some more wood in early February for selling in April.

Joe requires a loan or capital from another source to flow in at the beginning of January to ensure that he can pay all his commitments for January and February. The calculation also does not consider interest on the money if borrowed. So, although the enterprise seems profitable over the three-month period, there is no cash to pay for the goods and expenses. The timing is therefore as important as the inflow or outflow.

Negative cash flows make financiers jittery and the entrepreneur must show a proper plan for a smooth cash level. No financier will support a venture unless proper cash flow projections are provided.

Now that we understand these issues, we can look at business failure and its signs from a different perspective.

15.6 Signs of trouble

As the venture moves between the levels of trouble as shown in Figure 15.1, the different signs appear and serve to warn the entrepreneur of impending trouble and its severity. These signs, however, do not follow a set sequence, which makes it difficult to follow the pattern of trouble. The signs are explained in the general pattern, but can appear at any stage because they are interrelated and are affected by many external issues.

15.6.1 Decline in gross margin

The first sign to look for is a decrease in the gross margin. This requires a comparison of the current gross margins to those of previous periods. Here one looks for trends that appear after three consecutive periods (normally months).

Gross margin = $\Sigma NS - \Sigma NC$, or (Sales – Cost of goods sold)

If there is a decrease over three consecutive periods (months), it signals the start of a trend. Reasons for this should be investigated through a more detailed analysis of the factors determining the margin.

15.6.2 Decrease in net margin

After identifying a decrease in gross margin, the second sign to look for is a decrease in the net margin. The net margin considers the fixed expenses that are related to the operation of the venture. This also requires a comparison of the current net margins to those of previous periods, and one should look for trends that appear after three consecutive periods.

Net margin = $\Sigma NS - \Sigma NC - F$, or (Sales – Cost of goods sold) – Fixed expenses

Again, if there is a decrease over three consecutive periods (months), it is the start of a trend and reasons for this should be investigated.

15.6.3 Irregular cash flows

A second sign, which is difficult to notice and follows the decrease in net margin during the early stages of failure is erratic cash flow at this point (see cash flow issues are discussed later in the chapter).

15.6.4 Faltering value proposition and sustainable competitive advantage

Value proposition, like beauty, is in the eyes of the beholder (customer) and is all about concept positioning. It is necessary for the venture to have a certain competitive advantage (CA) in its concept offering. Competitive advantage means that the venture has some advantage over its competitors that is difficult to copy or follow, and which distinguishes it from the others. Typical examples include a brand name or patent, access to a distribution channel, access to a supplier network or raw material, unique production facilities, special technical know-how and new technologies. A competitive advantage becomes sustainable (SCA) only if it can be sustained for a long period of time and is virtually impossible for the competition to follow.

It is, therefore, clear that competing at a low price cannot be a competitive advantage, as it never is sustainable. Often new entrepreneurs think that they can position their business on a lower price, only to find out too late that it does not give them a competitive advantage.

This is exactly what is referred to when SCA falters. It means that the competition has caught up with you or even improved their concept offering, and now the customers value their offerings more than yours. Immediately, the sales volume [N] comes under pressure and one would probably have to lower one's selling prices [S] to generate more sales, with a resulting drop in margin. The whole economic model comes under pressure and the venture slides down the failure scale.

15.6.5 Sales decrease and drops in market share

Sales volume and its impact have been discussed in detail. However, sales volume has such an impact on all the other factors in the economic model and cash flow that the entrepreneur should monitor it constantly and be able to give reasons for any deviations from the projected sales figures.

When market share starts to drop, it means that a lower percentage of the total number of customers supports your venture. Therefore, more of them probably support your competition or have found a different concept to meet

their needs. This may have several detrimental effects on the venture, for example:

- You buy less from your suppliers and therefore lose discounts based on volume, which increases the average variable cost [C].
- You transport fewer products and therefore the variable cost [C] increases due to the higher transport cost per item.
- Advertising cost per unit increases.
- Complementary buying of impulse products decreases as customers do not patronise your venture as frequently as before.

15.6.6 Cash flow issues

A further sign on the continuum of failure is a problem with irregular cash flow, which indicates underperformance. Most flows are out of the venture and the entrepreneur has difficulty in creating a constant stream of inflows. There could be several reasons for negative cash levels that are persistent, and only the most common are mentioned here:

- Fixed expenses that are out of proportion and often labour related
- Sales levels that are too low due to changing demand
- Higher costs for delivery, etc. that were not calculated at the beginning
- Slow payments by credit customers
- More debtors
- Slow stock turnover
- Overextension of debt, and interest rates changing for the worse
- Change in demand for the current concept positioning

When irregular cash flow turns into regular negative cash flow, the problem is more pronounced and the venture moves into the trouble stage. When the negative cash flow continues for prolonged periods, the problem forces the venture from the trouble into the crisis stage where turnaround is very difficult, if at all possible. Major refinancing is required to effect a turnaround successfully.

Cash flow problems are cited as the most important reason for venture failure. However, part of the problem is that the signs are not easy to observe, as shown in Figure 15.4, which uses the well-known iceberg metaphor to

270

explain cash flow visibility. All that is visible is the tip of the iceberg that protrudes above the water. Below the water there are several (non-visible) factors that contribute to either a healthy or a problematic cash flow.

The underlying factors that determine the cash flow are as follows:

- *Credit days*: These refer to the time that it takes to collect the money owed to the venture for credit sales. Creditor days that are longer than one month are bad for the venture and could lead to a cash flow shortage. This is because the products received by the creditor are already paid for by the supplier but the money has not yet been received. (See also the discussion on cash flow earlier in the chapter.) There are three reasons for slow credit days:
  - Poor collection mechanisms, referring to the venture's own inability and lack of drive to collect its income
  - Slack credit policy, referring to the giving of credit to customers without a proper credit screening and who are eventually poor payers
  - Bad debts, referring to monies that cannot be collected as those who owe it to the business are unable to pay
- *Inventory turnover (stock turnover)*: This refers to inventory that stays on the shelves for long periods. The inventory is paid for, but it sells slowly and therefore the cash of the venture is "locked" in the inventory.

- *Debtor days:* These refer to the time it takes for the venture to pay its suppliers (creditors). Normally, most small ventures are forced to pay cash and sell on credit, which makes the gap between creditor and debtor days too long. This leads to a negative cash flow problem.

Most financial books contain formulas that can be used to calculate these values and assist the entrepreneur in monitoring their status, provided that the venture has a proper bookkeeping system.

15.6.7 Confidence levels drop

Confidence in the venture and the entrepreneur is crucial for handling financial trouble when it comes. Unfortunately, when confidence is lost, the trouble has normally reached crisis level and is very difficult to rectify.

The core people's confidence that should be looked after are the shareholders and thereafter the financiers, whether they are banks or suppliers who give credit.

When external shareholders of a small venture lose confidence, they want to take their funds out to reinvest in a safer option. This pressurises the entrepreneur to find alternative sources of finance, such as loans, which makes the financial pressure even worse.

Once the external shareholders want their investment back, the financiers become aware of the situation. They tighten control and access to further funds to ensure that they do

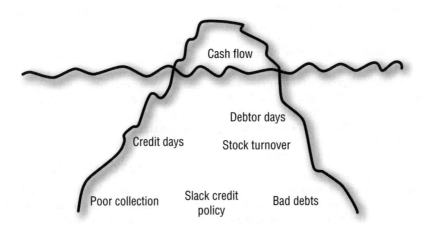

Figure 15.4 Cash flow visibility and related elements

not lose their investment. The overall pressure mounts.

Finally, the suppliers who sell to the venture on credit become aware of the trouble and they put the venture on cash terms to ensure that their income is safe. For the venture, this is the last straw as it widens the cash outflow-inflow gap even more.

15.6.8 Core employees leave

By now, the employees have picked up on the problem and, as they are not fools, they are aware of the extent of the crisis. The good ones find other jobs and leave as soon as they can, and you are left with the weaker employees. The customers start to pose questions and look for new suppliers, as they realise your reliability and service are below their requirements.

Normally, once employees start to leave, the trouble has become irreversible.

15.6.9 Non-measurable signs

Non-measurable signs can be used to identify looming trouble without having access to the facts and figures of the venture. These signs are particularly relevant for picking up trouble in the ventures of your suppliers and especially your credit customers. It is always better to be the first to identify the signs, as a few days may determine how severely you will be affected by the impending trouble. These signs are especially relevant for the person in charge of finance and/or creditors. Typical signs include:

- When the person who normally signs your cheque or payment is replaced by an unknown person, it may indicate that an external body now controls the payments and that severe control measures have been instituted to curb expenditure. The same goes for an absence of the signatory for long periods, or messages that are not returned. This is especially so when the customer suddenly cannot be contacted by telephone while it never was a problem in the past.

- If a creditor cannot meet your regular payment period of 30 days, it may indicate that he is having cash flow problems. This may lead to bad debt. Such a creditor should be put on cash terms or alternative arrangements should be made.

- An unexplained change in financier or in creditors or suppliers will raise suspicion.

- A change in the order patterns of customers from monthly to weekly and smaller quantities may also indicate cash shortages, especially when they are on a cash basis. The same goes for sudden increases in order size when they want to maximise discounts.

- A change in payment patterns from one regular payment to several smaller and irregular payments can indicate cash manoeuvring. Requests for extensions must also be noted.

- A sudden change in director or key financial officer may indicate that institutional or financial controls have been instituted to ward off their own cash flow problems.

- An irregular supply of certain products may indicate that the supplier moves between providers to optimise his own volume discounts and special prices.

- Low stock levels and disarray in the yard or premises of the supplier or customer may be a sign of trouble.

- Empty shelves are proof of low buying levels, which already is a serious problem.

- A change in payment beneficiary may indicate that the supplier wants to channel funds out of an ailing business. Even a change in address must be noted and questioned.

- Customers are not willing to accept a reasonable resolve of queries as in the past.

- Suppliers request urgent payments.

- There are rumours in the industry from sales representatives, other creditors and even staff.

When any of these signs are observed, it is necessary to investigate. Often it is best to ask directly and to act immediately. A later section in this chapter explores the turnaround strategies and the actions to take.

15.7 Causes of trouble

Trouble normally develops over time and typically results from an accumulation of fundamental errors. It is one thing to know the different levels of failure and recognise the signs associated with each level that serve as a warning system, but it is also necessary to understand the possible causes responsible for the failure.

Many causes underlie the signs of trouble discussed above. Although some have been touched upon, it is necessary to explore and categorise these causes for greater understanding. The causes are also fundamental in guiding the strategies and action plans of the entrepreneur.

15.7.1 Strategic issues

Strategic issues are typically concerned with the effectiveness of the venture within its environment. Selecting the correct positioning for the target market and satisfying the opportunity that has been identified are important aspects. Timmons (1999: 536) suggests several issues that should be considered:

- Misunderstood positioning (market niche) refers to pursuing the needs of a target market that is insufficient in size and growth potential. Typically, this happens when an entrepreneur has access to equipment that can produce certain products while the customers need something else. The venture then operates in a low margin market instead of identifying the correct strategy or a new market.

- Mismanaged relationships with suppliers and customers as far as payment terms and delivery agreements are concerned can hamper growth opportunities due to one-sided decisions.

- Diversification into an unrelated business area is mentioned as the most important reason for strategic mismatches. It happens when ventures lose focus and want to grow for the sake of growth. They then invest their profits and cash in unrelated ventures that make no sense for the current operation. Often this simply leads to more overheads without increased profits. Diversifying into unrelated business where no synergies can be generated is a sign of focus that is lost.

- Being idea driven instead of opportunity driven means that the entrepreneur has an idea that is excellent but that cannot be converted into an opportunity (i.e. a large enough demand at a sufficient margin).

- Focusing on the big project without considering the cash flow impacts of the development may lead to the appointment of personnel and the creation of capacity before the associated sales materialise. The result is higher outflow and lower inflow, with subsequent cash flow problems.

- Having no contingency planning indicates that there is a lack of analysis of the things that determine the venture's success, its environment and what could go wrong and force the venture down the failure slide.

- Lack of specific sectoral experience can also cause the entrepreneur to be "punished" through the learning cycle before he masters the industry's key success factors.

- Unreal and unfounded expectations were held of the market potential.

15.7.2 Management issues

Management issues such as the following contribute to the venture's slide into failure:

- If the owner has lost interest in the business, it means that he does not give it the necessary time and effort it requires. This could be the result of being disillusioned or occasionally because he has found other things he wants to pursue.

- Underestimating the importance of the financial aspects of the venture may lead to slow financial feedback and control. Often this function is the responsibility of a bookkeeper only. The financial manager (the entrepreneur in the micro- and very small business) must also monitor the margins, cash flow and overall economic model. It is the one position in the venture that should consider quality instead of cost when the appointment is done.

- Turnover in key management personnel can set the venture back a great deal, especially when they have to do with the core of the business, like operations and finance.

- Wrong management focus – aiming for asset accrual rather than cash can be a mistake for the small business. Focusing on cash generation is important.

- Having no proper management structure to control the business can also be detrimental to the management of the venture.

15.7.3 Poor planning and financial systems, practices and controls

The systems, practices and controls referred to have to do with the decision making and governing of the venture. Several factors are relevant:

- Pricing is all about setting the correct price as part of the concept offering. If the pricing is wrong (too low or too high), the target market may not be interested and demand will drop.
- Credit-granting policies are poor.
- There is poor use of leverage (debt). When debt is too high it places unnecessary strain on the venture. During start-up the entrepreneur should go for equity rather than loans.
- The lack of cash budgets and projections was discussed under cash flow earlier. It is necessary for the planning of expansions and growth plans.
- Poor management reporting refers to a focus on financial reporting instead of management reporting that could be used by the entrepreneur to make decisions. Reports that are useful include inventory analysis, creditor age analysis and sales reports.
- Lack of standard costing refers to the inability to cost items correctly, especially for manufacturing ventures.

- Poorly understood cost behaviour refers to a poor understanding of the economic model of the venture.

Figure 15.5 illustrates the level of risk for each of the causes of failure that a venture is exposed to, and the different causes of trouble associated with its VLC. It is clear from the diagram that strategic issues are more likely to affect failure during the early and later VLC stages, while management and system issues are more relevant during the middle and later stages. Of course, this is not a hard and fast rule, but should serve as a guideline as to where to start the process of analysing failure.

15.7.4 Environmental issues

Environmental issues include customers, suppliers, competitors and intermediaries from the venture's market environment. On top of these are the political, economic, social, technological, globalisation and physical factors from the macro-environment that govern the market environment. A change in one factor alone is hardly sufficient to lead to total venture failure, but due to the interactions of these factors with one another, a change in a few interrelated factors may influence the venture quite severely.

Several of these factors have already been discussed, as they relate especially to strategic issues that cause venture failure.

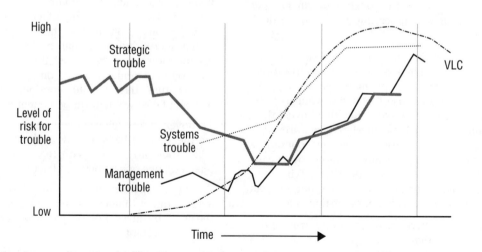

Figure 15.5 Directional and typical times when trouble could be expected during the venture life cycle

Figure 15.6 illustrates how the factors from the environment impact on the consumer demand for the concept offerings of the venture. All these factors affect the economic model, mainly through the influence on sales volume [N] and selling prices [S]. Economic factors such as interest rates and exchange rates may also impact on the economic model, but through fixed expenses [F], variable costs [C], etc.

15.8 When growth leads to trouble (overtrading)

Most entrepreneurs are delighted when their ventures grow faster than anticipated, especially during the start-up and growth phases. This could, however, land them in difficulties as well. The question is how fast growth can be bad for the business.

The construction industry is a typical sector where overtrading can take place. An example is given below.

ABC Builders is a microconstruction venture with an owner entrepreneur and six workers. The owner does not have an overdraft or significant cash reserves. A large customer he gets work from wants him to start another job in a

few days (a larger job than usual) to run alongside the job he is currently doing for them. This is the break the owner has been waiting for and he accepts the challenge immediately.

The new contract needs ten extra workers. The owner has to hire an excavator, a small concrete mixer, transport for the workers, etc. As he has to deal with the needs of the second job, he needs someone to run the first job. For the first time he has to leave one of his workers in charge.

In the past when he wanted an excavator, he hired one for the day and made good use of it all day long. He will now need an excavator on site for six days a week, which will probably only be in use for three to four days during the week at different times. The same scenario can be assumed for the mixer, which in the past he could plan for accurately when he wanted to use it.

The entrepreneur manages to get the ten extra workers and hopes that they will all turn up on the first day. He has arranged with a minibus to collect them.

On the first day only seven workers turn up. To maintain credibility, the owner has to take three of the six workers off the first job to make up the numbers. Taking workers off the first job means less work is being completed. He is paid

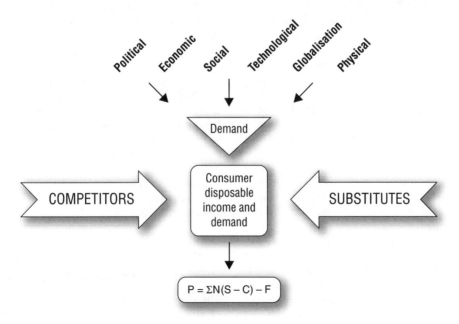

Figure 15.6 Environmental factors (PESTGP) impacting on profit

on a "piece work" basis for both jobs, i.e. he gets paid on certificates when he completes certain portions of the job and he is limited to the time period.

The excavator and mixer are not used during the first day due to a hold-up in work being carried out by another contractor, who is behind on schedule (this happens more often than the owner has planned for).

The owner has to provide all the materials and supplies for the job. He has to increase his credit account with his suppliers to uncomfortable levels.

For the rest of the first week he has to split his time between the two jobs, finding workers, sorting out problems that are stopping his machines from working, organising supplies and reporting progress to site management (larger jobs mean schedules, constraints and more paperwork). By the end of the first week he has lost many days' work on the first job due to prioritising his work force on the second job. He thinks of appointing a supervisor to assist him, as he feels "too thinly spread".

On the second job he has had ten workers there all week, but due to circumstances beyond his control, on average only seven workers have been working during the week. The excavator and the mixer have each been in use for less than three days of the week. The owner is under pressure on the first job due to the slow progress. He promises to rectify this by the following week.

He decides to raise his worker teams from 16 to 20 to ensure a full workforce. There is nothing he can do about the equipment standing idle. For the first time since he started the venture, he has spent the week without actually working on any job. He decides that he will have to employ someone to share the administration of the business. He still does not know the names of most of his workforce. He will have to wait up to six weeks before the certificate for payments comes through for the work he has completed.

Much of what happened in the first week is repeated in the second week. The owner feels like a juggler with too many balls in the air. During the third week the site developers call him to a meeting, saying that they are confident about his ability to maintain his workforce and apply his equipment. As such, they want him to tender for a new job next week!

This calls for important decisions and, on top of it all, he does not have much time as he is already doing the administration work till late at night.

If he does not take this new tender, future work with this company would probably revert to small jobs, if at all. If he takes the job, he is unlikely to survive because the increase in business is out of his control and not based on a sound financial plan.

If a large customer wanted an increase in sales or service, the owner would have to consider not only whether or not he wants to be a bigger company, but also whether he wants to expose his business to increased borrowing in order to finance the means of meeting the customer's needs. He may need bigger, better and more equipment, bulk stock, more staff, bigger premises, increased administration, etc. He would probably also lose his close contact at the coalface where quality counts.

If he had a customer who represented 70 per cent of his sales income, he would further be susceptible to price, product, delivery, service and payment demands. If such a customer stated that a similar supplier could provide the same quality, etc. for 10 per cent less, could he react without severely impacting on his cash flow requirements?

What is the status for ABC at this point? The owner has work, lots of it or even too much. He does not have the capacity although he could hire and subcontract certain parts of the job. In a nutshell, he is faced with overtrading.

When one gets a larger response for one's goods or services than anticipated, the natural action is to accommodate what is being asked for because one's economic model requires that sales volume [N] must be as high as possible. It is important to realise that the higher sales [N] have a severe cost [C] and fixed expense [F] effect. One has to calculate the additional sales and consider the additional costs that will be associated with it.

15.9 The size of the venture and signs or causes of trouble

The size of a venture is relevant to the visibility of the signs, as well as to establishing their causes. The survivalist entrepreneur often keeps no records, so the determination of gross and net margins is already difficult while such ventures have constant cash flow problems. Micro- and very small ventures have only basic record keeping.

The signs of failure are probably the same for all sizes of business, although their measurement and visibility may be impaired due to a lack of records. Similarly, the causes are also universal and expected to have a more pronounced effect on the smaller venture. The remedies available for turnaround will also be limited for the smaller enterprise. (This aspect will be explored when turnaround is discussed.)

15.10 Franchising and failure

Franchisors mostly claim that by getting involved in a franchise organisation as a franchisee, the chances of failure are decreased. What, then, does the franchise system bring to reduce failure?

Within the many benefits of franchising, it is clear that the monitoring systems that franchisors implement to control their franchise operations help them to detect the signs of failure early. Early detection, of course, is very beneficial for action, as the potential slide into failure has no time to gain momentum.

Being part of a franchise organisation also contributes to early warning through the problems that are observed with other members, thereby sensitising the rest of the group to be aware.

The franchisor is normally a relatively bigger organisation with the means to assist on the strategic front, which benefits the smaller franchisee who gains through the "group effect".

15.11 Success signs that oppose failure

In business the aim is to perform well, and the following signs will point to a successful venture:

- A sensible financing structure that incorporates the utilisation of debt and equity
- A strong cash position
- Above-average profitability measured as return on assets
- Rapid growth in sales revenue

- Attractive market segment with expansion possibilities
- Seeks to lead the industry from a specialist vantage point
- A strong brand name or franchise
- A significant research budget
- A competitive advantage that is not price based
- Operates in close relationship with its customers
- Well managed with good expertise

All these factors act as a mix, with some being more visible than others.

15.12 Conclusions about failure

Failure is not merely the non-achievement of goals, as suggested in the introduction of this chapter. To really understand failure, an integrated model is proposed in Figure 15.7, which indicates all the relevant constructs that influence failure.

The usefulness of the model lies in its core components of signs, levels, causes and action to be taken.

Each of these constructs is influenced by several other factors to present the whole picture of failure within the business environment. There are signs that indicate the severity of the trouble and relate to the cause of trouble. Everything cannot be measured in financial terms, and some issues, such as positioning and strategic matters, require a great deal of insight into the operations of a venture under normal and abnormal conditions. Sound judgement is required all the time, while gut feeling and intuition may be as important a rational decision-making ability.

15.13 Turnaround

To turn around an ailing (sick) venture and put it back on the road to good performance and growth is no small task. This is even more so for micro- and very small business, as defined in the South African context. The smaller the business, the more the owner or shareholder of the business is involved, and often the entrepreneur is part of the problem responsible for the slip along the failure slide.

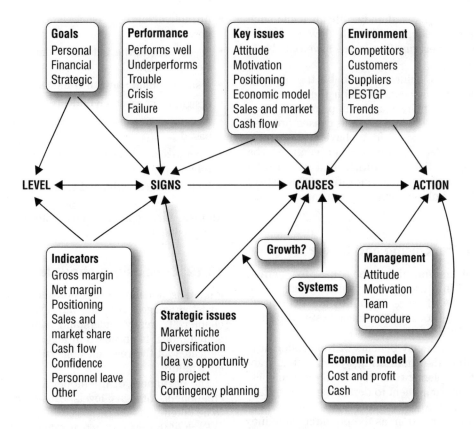

Figure 15.7 Integrated model for understanding failure in ventures

However, it is possible to put the business back on track to performing well. The earlier the signs of failure are observed, the easier it is for the turnaround process to be effective. Figure 15.8 shows the steps of the basic turnaround procedure. The procedure essentially requires a decision to engage in the process of turning around. This decision requires some diagnoses that must be done rather quickly, as time is a valuable asset and one which the venture does not really have. Quick action is required.

The process steps are explained in more detail in the next section.

15.13.1 Core principles or focuses of the turnaround

Figure 15.9 depicts the integrated turnaround model and shows that the turnaround process requires the consideration of most of the factors that are pertinent to failure and have been discussed already.

15.13.2 Diagnoses

During this phase a quick (sometimes superficial) evaluation is made to establish the status quo. One needs to gain an understanding of the level of the failure and whether it is still possible to reverse the slide and inch back towards success.

Figures 15.8 and 15.9 also show the difficulty gradient for the turnaround process, which indicates how far down the scale of failure the venture has slipped. Turnarounds become more difficult during the trouble stage and very difficult once in a crisis. For complete failure, there is almost no chance of turning around. One cannot say that it is impossible, but the result of such a turnaround will mostly be second prize because the venture will usually not proceed in its current form. Rather, it is a case of saving what can be saved, or of minimising the damage. So, the further down the slide, the higher the difficulty gradient becomes.

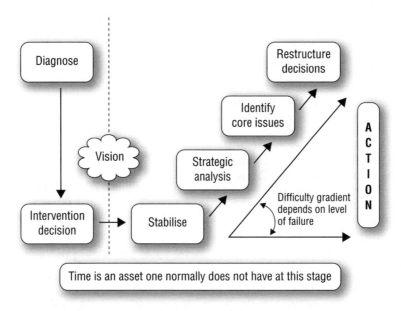

Figure 15.8 The basic turnaround procedure

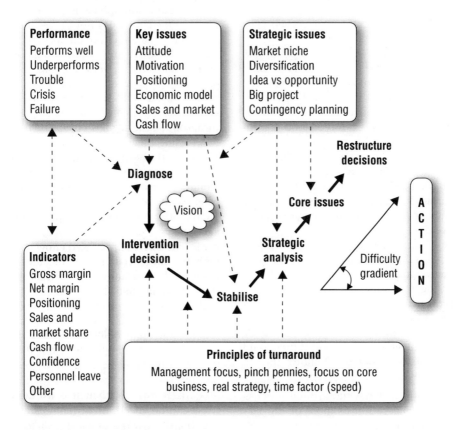

Figure 15.9 Integrated model for the turnaround of a venture

15.13.3 Intervention decision

Following the diagnosis of the level of failure, a decision has to be taken. This decision is based on the outcome of the diagnosis, which determines the level of failure, as well as gives an indication of the possible causes of the status quo. This is normally when it comes to the crunch.

It is always better to get an outsider in the form of a turnaround specialist or at least a mentor to assist with the decision. The entrepreneur, when left alone, may not want to acknowledge the seriousness of the situation because it may reflect on him personally.

The inability to acknowledge that the business is in trouble has been the reason for many unsuccessful turnaround attempts. Often there have been sufficient grounds for a turnaround, were it not that the entrepreneur could not acknowledge that he had a problem. Time is a crucial asset and action should be taken.

There are also other options to pursue if turnaround is not viable. These are aimed at minimising the damage and are discussed later in the chapter.

Part of the decision is the vision that the entrepreneur has for the enterprise. The vision normally reflects the goals of the entrepreneur and the venture, as discussed earlier. An entrepreneur who does not have the motivation for the business should not be forced into a turnaround process.

It stands to reason that the entrepreneur will require a serious attitudinal change when the decision is for turnaround. This is so because further decisions during the process are mostly very painful and absolute commitment is therefore required.

The best is for the entrepreneur to accept the blame for the status quo and commit to the plan of the turnaround specialist. There should be a close working relationship between entrepreneur and specialist.

Key to answering the turnaround question is whether the opportunity is still a good one or not. A quick analysis of the opportunity should therefore be done. Figure 15.10 shows the six elements that should be considered:

- Market demand (consumer)
- Concept offering
- Economic model
- Team and resource fit
- Competitive environment
- Financing required to give a positive cash flow

The analysis is similar to that which is done before starting a new business and would form part of the business plan. A detailed analysis of the same issues is required for the strategic analysis phase of the turnaround process. The elements of the opportunity analysis are shown in Figure 15.10.

At this point, the decision is partly based on gut feeling and partly on analysis, although the analysis is very basic at this stage.

15.13.4 Stabilising the venture

Once the decision has been taken to embark on a turnaround, quick actions should be taken to stabilise the business. Figure 15.11 shows that the management, finance and systems are key components of stabilisation.

The stabilisation phase is generally driven by a cost-and-cash focus after the establishment of a proper management team, as depicted in Figure 15.11. Stabilising requires that one should accept that cost is enemy number one. Thus, one has to go back to the basic economic model discussed earlier. Serious cost cuts should be implemented as fast as possible. Any turnaround strategy has cost as its base.

An ailing business is like a festering wound. There is no use in trying to heal it with a band-aid strip and a few tablets or ointments. The wound needs to be cut open to remove the cause of the rot.

To reduce costs means to "pinch and scrape", i.e. to be very careful about every cent spent, be it variable costs [C] or fixed expenses [F]. Start with the large cost items first and cut down relentlessly. Normally a priority list will contain the following cuts:

- **Fixed expenses**
  - Management salaries should be reduced through selecting only the core staff and without creating an "overtrading" situation.

  - Wages and unproductive workers – set up an outsourcing strategy.

  - Rent – are the current premises the best there is and can one negotiate with the

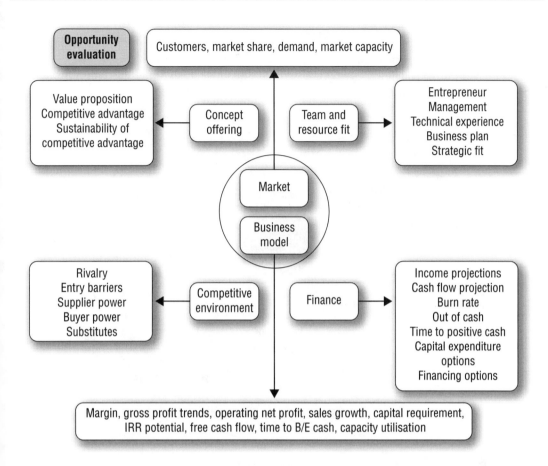

Figure 15.10 Elements to consider for an opportunity analysis

landlord? If you go under, the landlord loses in any case.

- Reduce interest on debt by reducing debt.
- Inefficient marketing costs.
- Consulting fees.
- Unnecessary overhead costs, like fuel and entertainment benefits that are unrelated.
- Uncontrolled pocketing from the cash registers – remove the fingers from the till.

• **Variable costs**
  - Cost price of items – this may require an investigation into the supplier currently used and whether the supply relationship is a long-standing one. See whether supplies cannot be sourced more cheaply and, if necessary, terminate the current relationship if they do not give discounts, rebates and/or commissions (kickbacks).

- Inventory levels should be reduced to minimum level where "out of stock" is tested occasionally but not to the point where the shelves appear empty.
- Leverage volume rebates optimally.
- Improving economic quantities and delivery times should reduce distribution costs.
- Discontinue low margin lines unless they contribute through spare capacity.
- Investigate the current cost recovery system to ensure that all costs are passed on to the customer.

Secondly, and to be done simultaneously with cost cutting, is to improve the cash flow situation as quickly as possible. This can be achieved by:

• Lowering creditor days through:

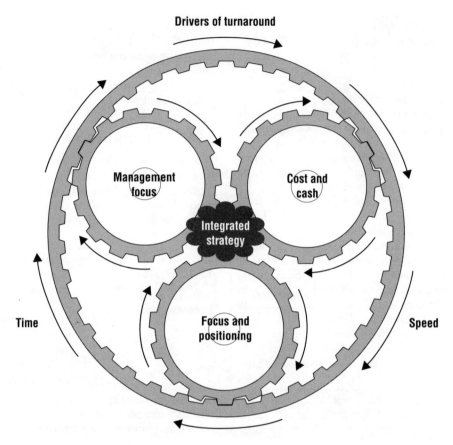

Figure 15.11 Factors driving the turnaround process

- Improved collection and billing to optimise cost recovery
- Stricter policy for credit advancements
• Stretching debtor days by negotiating better terms
• Increasing cash sales
• Negotiating better payment terms with vendors and suppliers
• Reducing debt and its associated interest by:
  - Selling old inventory
  - Selling unproductive assets and equipment
  - Sell non-core business units (this may follow the strategic analysis phase)

Stabilising the venture focuses on straightening out the management team, controlling the costs and improving the cash flow. These are urgent matters and no time should be wasted

to effect as many of these measures as possible.

It is clear that many of the proposed actions will contribute only marginally, but if all are pooled it can make a significant difference to the economic model of the venture. Once cost and cash are under control, the strategic analysis can be undertaken.

At this stage, time is still a most important factor. Do not try to phase in cost reductions, thinking you will lay off some personnel later. The rule is to cut immediately, to cut deep and cut finally. The sooner the people leave, the sooner others can see that the situation is serious and that everyone must either contribute or leave. Morale is also better once this part of the process has been completed. Remember, confidence is important for everyone and a sword over one's head diminishes confidence.

Stabilising therefore focuses on the expenses side of the profit equation. The strategic analysis has to do with the income side of the equation.

15.13.5 Strategic analysis

The strategic analysis focuses on the sales (income side) and positioning aspects of the venture. Some serious questions need to be asked concerning the business fit with the environment, the market and demand, the core business of the venture, and so on.

Figure 15.11 also shows the other drivers of a successful turnaround process, namely focus and repositioning, time and speed.

The main outcome of the strategic analysis is to determine the core business (focus and positioning) of the venture and what it should focus on. Anything that is revealed by the analysis to be non-core business should be outsourced as quickly as possible.

An extensive opportunity analysis (as referred to in Figure 15.10) should be undertaken for the core business. Such an analysis considers the market, concept offering and competitive environment that will determine the potential sales of the venture. The team and resource fit, the economic model and the financing required for the venture will also indicate whether the opportunity should be pursued any further.

Figure 15.12 shows a detailed opportunity analysis diagram that was used to evaluate a pipe factory before the turnaround strategy was determined. While the opportunity analysis is normally done during the pre-start-up stage of a new business, it is necessary to repeat it for the turnaround phase.

When the strategic analysis is completed, it must spell out how the income side of the venture will be approached. How is sales volume [N] to be increased based on the selected positioning?

15.13.6 Identification of the core issues

The core issues that should be focused on will emerge from the strategic opportunity analysis. The core issues have to do with positioning and sustainable competitive advantage.

The question that should be answered at this point is whether the venture serves an opportunity or not. If the answer is yes, the turnaround is well supported and could be refined only by restructuring. If the answer is no, a new focus should be selected based on the correct business strategy. The analysis should indicate where the turnaround should take the business in the next five years.

15.13.7 Restructure decisions

The decisions on the core issues help the venture to focus and direct the application of funds, whether these are own or borrowed funds. Priorities are set and listed for immediate implementation. Remember, time is still crucial at this point.

15.13.8 Action

Action should be taken through action plans so as to keep a record of the intervention. Action plans help everyone to focus on the new end goals of the venture.

Figure 15.9 shows the integrated model for turnaround, indicating the procedure as well as the relevant factors to consider in the process of decision making. It shows many of the factors that are relevant for the integrated failure model and proves the close relation between failure and turnaround principles.

15.14 Principles of a turnaround process

From the above it is clear that there are five restructuring principles, which are also shown in Figure 15.9 and specifically in Figure 15.11. They are discussed below.

15.14.1 Management focus

The management team is crucial, as the microbusiness will normally consist of the entrepreneur only and sometimes also the financial controller. The turnaround strategist can play only a supportive role. Key decision making lies with the entrepreneur. In larger businesses the persons responsible for marketing or operation can be added.

The motivation and attitude of the entrepreneur are absolutely crucial, a point which cannot be emphasised enough. The entrepreneur

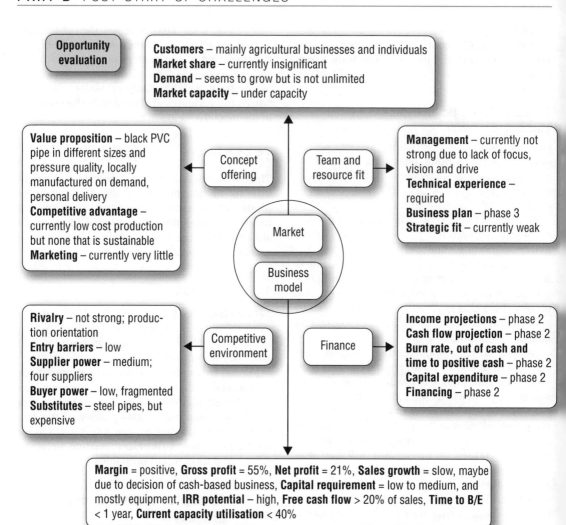

Figure 15.12 An example of an extensive opportunity analysis applied to a pipe factory

should focus on the turnaround and a viable economic model. The attitude and motivation of the entrepreneur were identified before as critical to the decision as to whether or not to attempt the turnaround strategy.

15.14.2 Cost and cash

Cost has to do with the expenses of the venture and include all control issues. Every possible attempt must be made to reduce costs at all levels, starting with the important cost elements first and working down the list.

A turnaround strategy is always cost driven, no matter what strategy is pursued later.

15.14.3 Focusing on the core business

Keeping one's eye on the ball is vital to a successful venture. Determine the core business and focus on it. Differentiation should not be pursued at all. Once cost is controlled, the core business will determine what strategy can be employed.

Differentiation can sometimes be regarded as clutching at a last straw. The entrepreneur may hope that by diversifying he can raise the income, but he forgets and underestimates the expenses associated with the move. Rather, differentiation is a trap for the business in trouble and should be avoided.

15.14.4 Strategy

Once the core business has been established, there should be a clear strategy. Strategy determines the application of funds, manpower, and the time and energy of everyone within the venture.

15.14.5 Time factor

Time is vital and time is money, and both time and money are crucial for a successful turnaround process. The faster the process can be completed, the better for the venture, shareholders, stakeholders and personnel. The cost reduction measures, in particular, should be implemented immediately. Quick implementation also indicates to the personnel that there is a definite plan and contributes to the confidence of all involved, including creditors and suppliers.

Also relevant is the timing of actions that are taken. Each element has its specific place within the overall procedure.

15.15 Options other than a turnaround

15.15.1 Harvesting alternatives

Harvesting alternatives cannot be contemplated for a venture that has slipped down the failure slide too far, as it will drive the selling price down.

Growth could be achieved by taking a new direction after a successful turnaround and with the new strategy in place. (Different growth strategies are covered in other chapters of this book.) Suffice to mention here the ways that the entrepreneur could consider to move or let go of the venture. These include:

- Outright sale of the business venture:
  - To another entrepreneur
  - To a firm looking for acquisitions
  - To a competitor (strategic sale)
- Forming an alliance with another venture

- Merging with another venture (offensive merger)
- Going public through shares on the stock exchange

Of course, if the harvest route is contemplated, the entrepreneur should start planning it as early as possible. Waiting for the failure to progress will mean that the venture is left to the mercy of the buyer, if such a potential buyer could be identified. The harvesting potential of a venture in trouble is very low. It may be better to think about divestment alternatives.

Also affecting the decision of what route to follow is the question as to whether the entrepreneur is willing to stay on or wants to leave the venture. (Harvesting is discussed in more detail in the next chapter.)

15.15.2 Divestment alternatives

Divestment alternatives are pursued when the option to harvest or turn the venture around is no longer possible, as is typical at the crisis level. The options that exist for the entrepreneur can help to recover as much as possible at that stage only. This is a choice of last resort but should still be considered, as there are not many alternatives. The available alternatives include:

- Closing the business and selling the assets
- Entering into a defensive merger, which leaves no bargaining power
- Splitting the business into functional/workable units and selling to interested parties, such as employees that could proceed as outsourced ventures to bigger clients

As seen from the above, the venture that is in crisis mode does not have many options.

15.16 Conclusion

This chapter has as its main aim to assist the entrepreneur in being receptive to the signs of failure that may face the venture. Understanding failure and its integrated model brings insights that could be used to counter the effects associated with regressive movement along the success/failure continuum.

Understanding the dynamics of the failure slide and how the signs and causes change and interact helps the entrepreneur to meaningfully anticipate, identify and correct problems as they arise.

The entrepreneur can then also monitor his suppliers and customers for signs of failure, to best manage the anticipated changes and pressures that their problems may bring to the venture. This is also true for the franchisor and the franchisees to be forewarned about pending trouble. It also helps the entrepreneur to apply entrepreneurial and managerial thinking as and when it is required.

Cash flow difficulties have been identified as the key problem that a venture must overcome. This chapter has confirmed this as the salient theme underlying financial trouble in a venture. Cash shortages are normally experienced dur-ing all levels of failure and as the business moves down the failure slide, these shortages become more severe.

Each level of failure may also bring different opportunities and threats to the venture. Anticipating the threats may help the entrepreneur to eliminate them and use the opportunities.

Turning a business in trouble around depends on the level of failure and the strategic opportunity that exists for the business at that specific time in its venture life cycle.

The drivers of a turnaround process are cost and cash, management team, focus and positioning and how they are integrated. Successful integration depends also on the time and speed of implementation.

Looking back

1. List the core elements of the integrated failure model.
   - Level of failure
   - Signs of failure
   - Causes of failure
   - Action to handle failure
   - Turnaround

2. List the levels of failure.
   - Performs well
   - Underperforms
   - Trouble
   - Crisis
   - Failure

3. What are the goals that can be used to evaluate failure?
   - Personal goals
   - Financial goals
   - Strategic goals

4. Name the indicators that determine the different levels of failure.
   - Gross margin declines
   - Net margin declines
   - Positioning falters
   - Sales and market share drop
   - Confidence disappears
   - Personnel leave
   - Other

5. What are the causes of failure in a venture?
   - Strategic issues
   - Management issues
   - Systems issues
   - Growth problems

6. What are the actions available to the venture in trouble?
   - Turnaround
   - Harvesting
   - Divesting

7. What are the environmental factors to consider during business failure?
   - Macroenvironmental factors such as political, economic, sociocultural, technological, globalisation and physical environments
   - Competitors
   - Customers
   - Suppliers
   - Intermediaries

8. What are the core elements of the turnaround process?
   - Diagnosis
   - Intervention decision
   - Stabilisation
   - Strategic analysis
   - Core issues
   - Restructuring decisions

9. What are the core issues that should be considered for an opportunity analysis?
   - Market demand
   - Economic model
   - Concept offering
   - Competitive environment
   - Team and resource fit
   - Financing

10. What are the directional movements of trouble over the venture life cycle?
   - Strategic trouble would be more relevant during start-up and early growth stages.
   - Management trouble is more prevalent during later growth and maturity stages.
   - Systems trouble is more prevalent during the growth and maturity stages.

Key terms

Capital
Cash flow
Cash level
Communication
Competitive advantage
Competitors
Concept offering
Consumer
Consumer demand
Creditor days
Creditors
Crisis
Debtor
Debtor days
Disposable income
External shareholder
Failure
Financier

Flow of funds
Gap
Inflows
Interest
Lender
Loan
Opportunity analysis
Outflows
Overtrading
Positioning
Shareholders
Strategic plan
Supplier
Target market
Trouble
Turnaround
Underperformance
Working capital

Discussion questions

1. What is the core factor that contributes to failure?
2. How do the levels of failure relate to the turnaround strategy?
3. What factors drive any turnaround strategy?
4. Can a venture that slid to failure be turned around?
5. Why are strategic issues so important in determining whether a venture should be turned around?

Case studies

Case study 1

DBC is a training college that asked for assistance from a turnaround specialist when it was perceived to be experiencing some trouble. On investigation, the turnaround specialist found the following relevant signs and conditions:

- The college offered short courses at different levels on a full-time and part-time basis.
- They subcontracted qualified lecturers when needed for different courses and paid them per hour of lecturing.
- The staff component consisted of two family member owners, a further family member in a sales management position, three administrative staff, three sales consultants and two cleaners.
- The college recently moved to new premises with lots of parking for their clients.
- The franchise group that DBC belongs to was performing relatively well.
- They had difficulty in keeping up with the rental payments of the new premises.
- The two owners took regular expensive holidays as the management was the responsibility of the family member as manager.
- DBC was experiencing a decrease in student numbers that was contrary to what it had projected prior to the move.
- Their accountant warned them of a pending cash shortage.
- They could not pay their franchise fee due to the low turnover.
- The lecturers complained that they had a hard time in getting their payment for work done and that the rates were below those offered by other institutions.
- The owners started selling off equipment (computers, chairs, etc.) to generate cash.
- They started stretching their suppliers (mainly the franchisor).

Questions

1. Thinking about the signs and levels of failure in ventures, what is your call on the situation?
2. What level of failure is the college experiencing and what are the causes thereof?

Case study 2

Mr Ex Plorer recently lost his job due to a retrenchment programme at his work. Being entrepreneurial, he decided to market an idea that he had been working on over the past years.

He started production of the "conserver" stove, a heating device for cooking food. Its unique feature was that it used less than half the wood and coal than the well-known "konka" stove.

He bought some equipment and tools with his pension money. At first, he did all the production himself but as demand grew, he employed some workers to assist with this. Many people in his village bought the "conserver", as it was more efficient than other similar products. They collected it from his little shop and occasionally he delivered some stoves to the elderly.

After about eight months, the demand for his product seemed to drop sharply as most people in and around his village now used the stove. He spoke to the people but there were no apparent problems with the stoves and they were all happy.

Questions

1. Thinking about failure in ventures, what is your call on the situation?
2. What level of failure is he experiencing and what are the causes thereof?

Experiential exercises

1. Go to an old-age home near you. Identify an entrepreneur from the past and ask him or her about failure and what value the person gained from it.

2. Ask the person what had helped him or her to turn from failure back to success.

Exploring the Web

You will find additional information at the following websites:

- www.businessfailure.ez.nl
- www.cascadebusnews.co.uk
- www.credit-to-cash.com/small-business/avoiding.htm
- www.insolvencyhelpline.co.uk
- www.istart.co.nz
- www.smalltownmarketing.com

References and recommended reading

Bekker, F. & Staude, G. 1984. *Starting and managing a small business*, 2nd ed. Cape Town: Juta.

Department of Trade and Industry (DTI). 2000. *National strategy for fostering entrepreneurship study*. Code A.1.005. Pretoria: DTI.

Hisrich, R.D. & Peters, M.P. 1998. *Entrepreneurship*, 5th ed. London: McGraw-Hill.

IT World. 2002. *Failure factors in E-commerce*. Available at www.itworld.com. Accessed 17 September.

Legace, M. 2001. *Confessions of a venture capitalist*. HBS Working Knowledge, HBS special reports.

Pretorius, M. 1999. *Successoneur business decision simulator: experience the success of being an entrepreneur*. Management Transfer cc.

Timmons, J.A. 1999. *New venture creation: entrepreneurship for the 21st century*. Burr Ridge: Irwin.

Wickam, P.A. 1998. *Strategic entrepreneurship: a decision-making approach to new venture creation and management,* 2nd ed. London: Prentice Hall.

16

Harvesting and exiting the venture

Marius Pretorius

Learning outcomes

After completion of this chapter, you should be able to:

▶ Distinguish between the different methods of harvesting

▶ Gain insight into the reasons why harvesting is important

▶ Identify the core factors driving the harvesting process

▶ Understand the interrelationships between elements impacting on the harvesting strategy

▶ Appreciate the principles that drive the harvesting process

▶ Identify potential management actions to be taken for a successful harvest

▶ Understand the role of strategic thinking in the process of harvesting.

16.1 Introduction

For many entrepreneurs, the primary source of returns occurs at the end of their relationship with the venture, when they want to "cash out" and harvest the profit.

Why would one discuss harvesting issues in a book dealing with entrepreneurship and venture start-up? Why is it important to know about harvesting when one wants to start or buy an existing venture? It serves two purposes:

• It makes one aware of the things to look out for in the longer term, and thus forces long-term planning. It is also relevant to general entrepreneurial thinking.

• It governs management decision making and may even impact on the business form that is selected at the start of the venture.

A harvest goal is not just a goal of selling and leaving the company. Rather, it is a long-term goal to create real value added to the business and to gain from it. The best-known harvesting method is to sell the venture, but even when selling there are several potential avenues to pursue.

This chapter focuses on the micro- and small business entrepreneur rather than the large business, although there are many similarities. The idea is to give relevant information to the entrepreneur who does not necessarily have access to a large organisation that can assist him or her with the research that needs to be done before harvesting.

16.2 Harvesting in perspective

Retiring from a regular job seems to be well understood in the field of normal employment and life in general, and can generally be defined as leaving one's employment at the end of one's working career. Thus, if someone terminates his or her working career, it ends a stage or phase in that person's life.

Likewise, a farmer sows seeds with the aim of harvesting a crop at a later stage. The harvest is sold (or used) at the end of the process to make a profit. The harvest is therefore the end goal of the farming process and if not achieved successfully, the whole object is defeated. There is also the possibility of a good or a poor harvest.

This chapter discusses harvesting as a process to achieve some or other end goal that will repay the entrepreneur for the hard work and inputs. The end goal is important for the decision making that is done during the life cycle of the venture. One should understand that harvesting is part of the strategy for the venture; it cannot happen overnight. Strategy considers the context (environment), as well as the venture and its performance within that context.

16.3 Reasons for harvesting

Reasons for harvesting in business vary widely, but can be categorised into four broad categories: personal reasons, financial reasons, failure and outside forces. Each of these is briefly explored.

16.3.1 Personal goals of the entrepreneur

The initial reason for starting a venture varies widely from the need just to survive (survivalist or necessity entrepreneurs), to the drive to develop a new product and achieve financial independence (opportunity entrepreneurs). Usually, it is a combination of several motives that prompts the entrepreneur to start the venture. In developing countries, many "survivalist" entrepreneurs are forced to establish a small venture to provide for their basic needs of survival on a day-to-day basis.

At this early stage of start-up in a venture's life cycle, harvesting is probably the last thing on the entrepreneur's mind and only becomes important when he or she starts thinking about exiting the business. On exiting, the entrepreneur wants to profit from all the inputs he made over time and hence the concept of harvesting.

Often the entrepreneur starts a venture in order to become his own boss and be free to do whatever he wants. After a while, and when faced with long hours of tedious work that is frequently unrelated to the original perception

he had of what he would do, he may feel dejected and disappointed. The picture that he had did not materialise, and he has to re-evaluate his goals. Harvesting suddenly becomes a relevant issue.

16.3.2 Retirement

Normally, when entrepreneurs have been in business for a long time and have reached the age of 50 to 60 years, they think of retiring from the business. They have put everything (money, time and energy) into the business and now they want to reap the harvest. Of course, they want maximum returns at this point. They may also feel that they have made enough money and that it is time to leave before they are too old.

16.3.3 Succession

Succession is normally associated with family businesses, but is not limited to it. When a child has to be taken up in a business with the aim to take over leadership later, the situation could become very awkward. Most of the time there is some kind of conflict between the old and the new generations, especially if there is no proper succession plan in place. Role definition is very important.

Succession is not limited to one's own family but includes in-laws that may be taken up in the business. One normally cannot choose one's new family members and it often requires finding some or other position for them. Kuratko and Welsch (2001: 305) describe the problems of family businesses extensively and the interested reader is referred to their writings.

Succession could be both a reason for the harvest, as well as a harvest option.

16.3.4 Wanting to make a change

Another reason for wanting to harvest is when the entrepreneur wants to pursue another opportunity that he or she has identified. This is typical of the real entrepreneurial mind, which regularly seeks opportunities, and of the entrepreneur who has achieved his or her goals within the current business operation. Normally they would need the capital from the existing business to pursue the new challenge.

Also, within the process of harvesting, the seeds of renewal and reinvestment are sown. Such a recycling of entrepreneurial talent and capital is at the very heart of the entrepreneurial process.

16.3.5 Other forces

Other factors or situations that may arise and force a harvesting decision are normally associated with external forces that are beyond the entrepreneur's control. These include:

- Death of the entrepreneur or spouse
- Ill health
- Mental or psychological breakdown
- Loss of key expertise from the venture
- Negative external environmental conditions

16.4 Severity of the situation

This refers to pressure placed on the entrepreneur to "harvest". If the harvest is required to be quick, the situation changes and the number of options decreases. It is always better to harvest when the time is right or beneficial for harvesting, and not when the entrepreneur is forced to make the best of a poor situation.

Factors that contribute to the severity of the situation are discussed below.

16.4.1 Strategic pressure

Strategic pressure refers to the loss of a venture's strategic positioning within the marketplace. This could be due to market conditions no longer being conducive to the venture or its products. It is simply not a good opportunity anymore. This concept is better explained by an example.

Within the meat industry the face of meat retailing is changing. There is a definite move from smaller, local butchers who serve their immediate community towards large general retailers with local franchise shops that also sell meat. The customer therefore does her general shopping and while she is doing so, she buys her meat because it is convenient, despite being offered at a higher price. As a result, smaller community butcheries observe dwindling customer numbers due to the changing purchasing patterns.

The positioning that smaller private butchers

hold therefore no longer matches the changing environment and they come under strategic pressure. The opportunity is not a good one anymore and there are no new entrants into the meat industry at this end of the market. This situation may soon drive the venture down the failure slide due to lower margins and negative cash flow. Unless these butchers change their strategic positioning, more and more of them will go out of business.

Strategic pressure is often not clearly outlined nor is it visible, yet it has a greater impact on the harvesting options than other problems do. As seen in the chapter on failure, strategic pressure is more serious than other issues.

16.4.2 Urgency

Urgency has to do with how quickly the entrepreneur needs to harvest. A rule of thumb is that the more urgently a harvest is required, the poorer the harvest will be and vice versa. Time is an asset for the harvest goal.

Urgency is closely related to timing and patience, which are principles of the harvesting process that is elaborated on later.

16.4.3 Other

Other factors may have to do with issues such as the performance level of the venture at the point where harvesting is contemplated.

Several issues can complicate one's choice of harvest strategy. These factors cannot be anticipated but experience has shown that anything could become an issue, depending on the people involved and the perceptions that they hold.

16.5 A broad strategy

The existing strategy of the venture may influence the options available to the entrepreneur at harvest time.

16.5.1 Growth strategy

If the entrepreneur embarked on a growth strategy, he has two basic options: to grow the business internally in size (organic growth) or to grow it externally through acquiring more ventures.

■ Organic growth

Organic growth requires the expansion of the business through increased market share. This could be done by enlarging the existing business or by adding market share and sales through new market development and even more outlets, to serve the existing customer base better. Normally, the growth is achieved by becoming more efficient within the existing business.

If the growth has been achieved or the potential result of the growth strategy is clear, it would probably improve the size of the potential harvest. It is always a good thing if a buyer can pay for potential sales in future.

■ Growth by acquisition

Growth by acquisition refers to the buying of additional related or unrelated ventures to enlarge the business operations, and is referred to as external growth in an earlier chapter.

Under acquisition circumstances and depending on the extent and time after embarking on the strategy, it becomes difficult to consider harvesting. The potential buyer may wonder why the entrepreneur wants to harvest at that particular time. The first question in his mind is whether the chosen strategy was an incorrect one and the entrepreneur now wants to get rid of his "problems". The acquisition must, therefore, be in a fairly advanced or completed stage, otherwise it may hamper the harvest.

16.5.2 Retrenchment

It may be that the entrepreneur embarked on a retrenchment strategy, which is the opposite of a growth strategy. This strategy requires that some of the operations be scaled down or eliminated completely. The net impact of such a strategy is that the future sales and costs are limited. The elimination of fixed costs, of which the main contributor is labour expense (payroll) and therefore people, is part and parcel of such a process. The potential buyer of the venture will be concerned about the negative growth and the reasons for selecting a retrenchment strategy. Unfortunately, such a strategy is often related to trouble within the venture. At least it will create some questions in the mind

of the potential buyer. This situation is explored in Chapter 15.

16.5.3 Stability

When the entrepreneur does not want to grow or retrench the total operation, his strategy is one of stability. Naturally, most entrepreneurs want to grow but sometimes they may be satisfied with the size of the venture and wish to keep it that way. Another reason may be that further growth would require significant capital investment and they choose not to take that route.

Stability may not necessarily influence the harvest decision significantly. However, if it has been going on for too long, it may be perceived by the buyer as stagnant market demand, and he or she will be unwilling to pay a higher price.

16.5.4 Combination strategy

A combination strategy could be any combination of the growth, retrenchment and stability strategies. It may happen that an entrepreneur decides to grow in one part of the business while simultaneously wanting to retrench another part of the business. Such choices have to do with the positioning of the different business units. Depending on the age of the strategy, they may affect the harvest decision.

The existing strategy in a venture may be an important factor in determining the intensity of, as well as the choice available for, the harvest. It is possible that the potential buyer sees an opportunity to replace the existing strategy with a "better" one.

16.6 Environmental issues

Environmental issues include customers, suppliers, competitors and intermediaries from the venture's market environment. On top of these are the political, economic, social, technological, globalisation and physical factors from the macro-environment that govern the market environment. Environmental issues may influence the strategy that has been chosen, as well as the severity of the situation when the harvest option is selected.

It is questionable whether a change in one factor alone is sufficient to determine the harvest choice, but it is not impossible. Normally, the factors interact with each other and a change in a few complementary factors may influence the options significantly.

16.7 Performance level

As the venture moves between the levels of trouble, as shown in Chapter 15, it may influence both the intensity and the choice of harvest. Lower performance is associated with a less beneficial harvest. The different levels of trouble have been explained extensively in the previous chapter and their impacts on the harvest strategy and process will be described only briefly below.

16.7.1 Good performance

The best opportunity to harvest is when the venture is performing well in sales revenue and profits. If the market share is projected to improve, it is the ideal time to harvest. The problem is usually that the entrepreneur is so busy making profits in the short term that harvesting is last thing on his or her mind.

16.7.2 Underperformance

Underperformance is really hard to differentiate without proper analysis and comparison. At this level the harvest options are still many, provided that the opportunity is still a good one for the successor.

16.7.3 Trouble

When the business enters the trouble stage, options to harvest decrease unless the buyer is not knowledgeable about the industry and business. Of course, the reason for the trouble is also relevant. Strategic positioning that is lost may have a greater effect on the harvest options than when the trouble emanates from an additional competitor who recently entered the market.

The potential buyer must see an opportunity to gain through a change in strategy, through synergy or by applying economies of scale.

16.7.4 Crisis

There are not many options available at this level, except for selling to a competitor or someone looking for an acquisition. The harvest will, however, be significantly less than for the levels mentioned above.

16.7.5 Failure

Once the business has entered the failure level, there are almost no options left for harvesting without making a significant loss.

16.8 The venture life cycle stage

The life cycle stage of the venture is crucially important for the harvest decision. General guidelines for the different stages are given below.

16.8.1 Incubation stage (pre-start-up)

During this stage there are few options for harvesting. Because the venture is conceptual there is not much to harvest. Investors are sought, with the promise of a potential future harvest.

The only way that an entrepreneur could harvest at this stage is when the concept is potentially threatening to another business or competitive industry, and they decide to eliminate the threat by buying the patent to protect their own business. This, however, is the exception to the rule.

16.8.2 Start-up stage

During the start-up stage, harvesting is normally the last thing on the entrepreneur's mind. This stage is associated with greater risk and potential for failure. The uncertainties of the market demand make the ability to harvest less attractive.

16.8.3 Growth stage

The growth stage is a good time to think about harvesting, although it is still not an important consideration for the average entrepreneur. During this stage there is visible growth in demand and associated sales. Potential competitors are on the prowl to gain access to the apparently lucrative market.

During this stage it is possible to sell the venture, based on its recent performance as well as its projected potential in the immediate future

The impact of the potential competition is not clear yet and a premium price could be asked for the venture.

16.8.4 Maturity stage

The maturity stage is characterised by more and tougher competition, with pressure on the price and distribution elements of the concept offering. Sales start to decline and so do profits. During the early maturity stage some of the growth stage principles are still relevant but during the later maturity stage, the plain selling option becomes less desirable. Other options such as mergers and alliances become more relevant.

16.8.5 Decline stage

During the decline stage, sales may decrease rapidly, and so too do profitability and future potential. The options to harvest decrease drastically and only through creative application could a harvest be constructed.

Entrepreneurs frequently do not see this stage approaching until it is too late. Declining business prospects are often the result of a venture that has lost its strategic positioning anyway, and there is little interest in taking over such a business. The typical harvest options associated with the different life cycle stages are shown in Figure 16.1.

16.9 Harvest options

Harvesting alternatives cannot be contemplated for a venture that has slipped down the failure slide too far, as it will drive the selling price down. Similarly, harvesting becomes difficult for a venture that has moved to the maturity and especially the decline stages of its life cycle.

Each of the harvest options is explained shortly and the typical circumstances that are associated with each are given.

16.9.1 Outright sale of the business venture

Selling the business is the most obvious route to follow and it can take many forms. Each option requires different measures and plan-

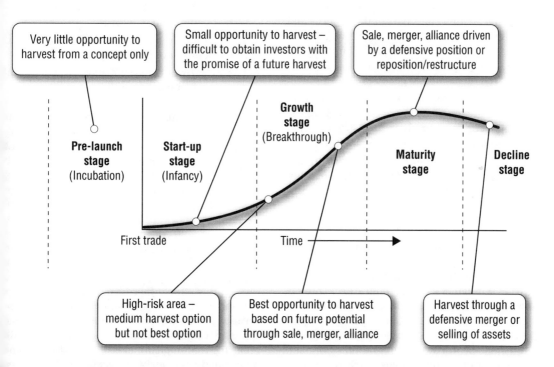

Figure 16.1 Typical harvest options over the venture life cycle

ning, and takes place under different circumstances.

■ Outright sale

The outright sale of a business requires that the owner take a decision to sell the venture to any willing buyer. Normally, a broker will be approached or an advertisement will be placed. If there is agreement about the price, a deal is signed. It is the responsibility of the buyer to ensure that he buys what is for sale relative to the assets, sales, consumers, etc.

The market is full of prospective entrepreneurs of which some may be interested in buying an existing business rather than starting from scratch. It appears that they might be more successful that way, as they eliminate the dangers of the start-up phase. It is important to seek potential buyers in this market segment. This is done by:

- Scanning newspaper advertisements.
- Enquiring from professional people such as accountants, lawyers and management consultants.
- Enquiring from business brokers and even estate agents. Business brokering has become an important part of the process and, despite commissions, is a "safer" way for the uninformed entrepreneur. It is important to find a reputable broker and to do some research on his or her past deals.
- Contacting trade sources. Suppliers, distributors or clients may know about a business that is for sale in their industry or when someone is interested in an acquisition.
- Checking out potential deals and brokers through business organisations like a chamber of business.

■ Selling to a firm looking for acquisitions

Often there are other businesses in an industry that want to expand their operations and grow through acquisition. Buying an existing business in a related industry could be beneficial and involves less risk.

The entrepreneur should quietly enquire from his or her suppliers whether they might be interested in forward integration. Suppliers may sometimes contemplate such a move to ensure that an opposition supplier cannot

"steal" their market share, or to give them entry to a new area.

Another potential buyer may be a larger customer who is interested in backward integration. This customer may contemplate buying the business if it could lead to better profitability or give him or her control over the raw materials or other resources.

Both suppliers and customers may not think of the possibility of buying but if it is presented to them as an opportunity, they could develop the necessary interest in such a deal, especially if the venture for sale is healthy and performing well. The owner should, therefore, "plant" the idea in their minds. This would require doing proper research and having a strategy for getting the message across.

Advantages:

- The potential client has information about the potential of the business.
- The owner can negotiate a reasonably quick exit.

Disadvantages:

- The owner is sometimes required to stay on for a period to train the new management – so he becomes an employee.
- There could be rumours in the marketplace if the deal does not go through.
- The new owner may not have a conceptual grasp of the business until he is in it.

A variation of this option is to look for an international business that wants to enter this country and requires an agent, with the idea of taking over the business at a later stage. Such buyers may be willing to pay a premium as they have a longer-term goal of accessing the foreign market. They would probably require the entrepreneur to stay on until they have learnt the ropes of the business and become knowledgeable about local market conditions.

■ Selling to a competitor

If a sale to a supplier or larger customer is not possible, one can consider selling to a competitor. This option (a strategic sale) is more difficult to accomplish practically than those mentioned previously, especially as it requires the owner to give the competitor access to con fidential information. There are, however, several ways to overcome that problem.

This option requires one to do some homework on the competitor's strategy and problems. There is always a possibility that he or she wants to gain market share through this avenue. Several issues such as industry size, number and pricing strategies may influence such a deal.

Once, in a real case, the following happened. Person A worked for Person B and later left to start a competitive operation. The market grew and there was business enough for both firms as well as other similar firms. Eventually Person B decided to retire and through a consultant offered the business to Person A. Person A was specifically interested in the sale, as it has been his life-long dream (for personal and non-financial reasons) to take Person B out. He really wanted to have that specific business. Person B suspected that this would be person A's attitude, but the consultant exploited these personal reasons to close the deal.

Advantages:

- The prospective client has information about the potential of the business.
- The owner can make a reasonably quick exit.

Disadvantages:

- There could be rumours in the marketplace.
- With a structured payment, the owner is at risk and therefore a complete deal is required.

16.9.2 Management buyout

Selling the business to the existing management is sometimes an option. The existing management obtains capital (normally a loan) and pays the owner, who leaves.

Advantages:

- The management already knows the business.
- The owner can make a quick exit.
- Payment could be structured over a time period (but this could be dangerous).

Disadvantages:

- Management normally works for a salary and access to capital is a problem.

- With a structured payment the owner is at risk.
- Managers are often not entrepreneurial and there is a strong possibility that the business may stagnate.

16.9.3 Employee share option plan

This plan is similar to the management buyout except that a structure is formed through which the employees can take ownership of the venture through shareholding. This is possible only for ventures with a fair number of employees. Such a deal sometimes requires specialised financing, which can be obtained through land restitution claim funds, or donor bodies that have a political agenda.

Advantages:

- The employees gain ownership, which may be positive for job motivation.
- The owner can be phased out.
- Management can stay on and participate in the plan.

Disadvantages:

- The entrepreneurial drive may be lost, which can be detrimental to the venture in the long term.
- It is only for relatively large businesses.
- Structuring the deal can be complex.

16.9.4 Forming an alliance with another venture

Alliances (partnerships) are different in that no one takes up equity in the other business, as with a merger or a joint venture. There are joint benefits to both partners. For example, one gains from the distribution systems of the other while he does the manufacturing from which the other party benefits.

This option is often an interim step that leads to a complete takeover and the owner's withdrawal after a period of time. The owner will identify a potential candidate and enter into an alliance agreement with that business. Agreements can be about distribution, purchasing or production. As soon as benefits are visible, more and more integration takes place, the administration and systems cannot keep up and the next logical step is a complete takeover or buyout.

Alliances are helpful during the growth process when "other people's resources" are used to expand operations. An example is to use another business for distribution or to combine promotion efforts in order to reduce costs.

Advantages:
- There is a long-term relationship that develops.
- Several additional doors may open for an improved relationship.
- If the alliance does not work out, it is easy to end the relationship.
- Opportunities may arise to pursue some of the other harvest alternatives.

Disadvantages:
- The timing is crucial.
- There is often no legal agreement.
- Time is required for the development process to reach a stage where the owner could offer his operation.
- If the alliance does not work out, it could have a negative impact on the business.
- Management styles may be different, which may lead to conflict

16.9.5 Merging with another venture (offensive merger)

The merger is a quicker route than the alliance but is very similar. In this case a formal combination of the two enterprises takes place, either through forming a new enterprise or through taking up shares in each other's venture.

This option is available when the venture is performing well and is probably in the late growth stage with lots of market potential.

Advantages:
- The relationship is much stronger.
- The merger is much more formal and cannot be reversed easily.

Disadvantages:
- Both businesses must be valued to determine shareholding (this may also be advantageous).
- A minority owner is somewhat exposed.

- There is no harvesting until one party leaves and it may even postpone the harvesting point.
- Management styles may be different, which could lead to conflict.

16.9.6 Proceed with a professional manager

Another option is to employ a manager to operate the business while the owner withdraws his involvement.

Advantage:
- The option works well when the entrepreneur has health or similar problems.

Disadvantages:
- Management style clashes can occur.
- The owner may feel he is losing control.
- There is no "big" harvest.

16.9.7 Capital cow

The capital cow option refers to the entrepreneur proceeding with the enterprise, but he uses the cash that it generates as capital for the establishment of an alternative venture. The cash generated in this way could also be used for investment other than direct business.

Advantages:
- It serves as a source of capital.
- It offers a different route to harvesting despite being slow.
- It enables the entrepreneur to exploit other windows of opportunity that come along.

Disadvantages:
- Harvesting takes longer.
- It could drive the business down the failure slide due to the cash withdrawals that may lead to cash flow problems.
- There is no big harvest.
- The owner cannot leave easily.
- Growth is normally not possible within the existing venture, which may lead to a lower selling price at a later stage. Obviously, the withdrawal of the cash reflects poorer performance and eventually will be seen as poor performance.

16.9.8 Public offering

The public offering is well described under growth strategies in Chapter 14 of this book. As the harvesting potential of a venture in trouble is very low, this option is not possible unless the business has been performing well for several years. It may be better to think about divestment alternatives where failure is relevant.

Advantages:

• Harvest is quick and normally good.
• It serves as a valuing mechanism.
• Prestige is gained.

Disadvantages:

• It is mostly for big business only.
• It depends on the general economic environment and cycles.
• It is expensive upfront.
• Full disclosure of personal and venture information is needed.
• There is loss of control.
• It requires specialist advice and experience.
• Much more formal management systems are involved than are found in small business.

Also influencing the decision of what route to follow is the question of whether the entrepreneur is willing to stay on or wants to leave the venture after the deal has been closed.

16.9.9 Divestment alternatives

Divestment alternatives are pursued when the option to harvest or turn the venture around is not possible anymore, as is typical at the crisis or failure levels. The alternatives that exist for the entrepreneur can help him to recover as much as possible at that stage only. This is a choice of last resort but still one to be considered, as there are not many alternatives. The available alternatives include:

• Filing for bankruptcy
• Closing the business and selling assets that are exempt from collateral agreements
• Entering a defensive merger, which leaves no bargaining power
• Splitting the business into functional/workable units and selling to interested parties such as employees, who could let the units proceed as outsourced ventures to bigger clients

The venture that is in crisis mode does not have many options for harvesting successfully.

16.10 Principles of a harvest strategy

Figure 16.2 indicates the principles that govern the harvest strategy. Each of these elements can contribute to a better harvest.

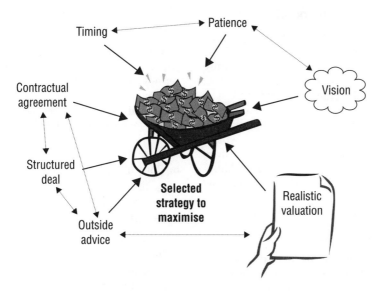

Figure 16.2 Principles of the harvest strategy

16.10.1 Timing

Each action to be taken by the entrepreneur during the harvesting process should consider timing. Each harvesting option demands different preparation. In Chapter 4 the concept of a "window of opportunity" is explained. Harvesting at the right time, willingly, involves entering a strategic window, one of many or few that the entrepreneur will face. It is wiser to sell when the window is opening than when it is closing. Harvesting early mostly means that the deal is based on future potential for which some buyers are willing to pay handsomely. On the other end, when the growth cycle has passed, there are not many options or interested buyers. Timing is closely related to patience.

16.10.2 Patience

When harvesting is forced on the entrepreneur or when it must be done urgently, it eliminates some of the options available. Patience is closely related to the enterprise's vision and planning. It has been shown that to build a successful business can take as long as seven to ten years. A harvest strategy requires patience for the window to open but quick action when it does. Quick action is only possible if the entrepreneur has a contingency plan in place.

16.10.3 Vision to plan ahead

Harvesting demands careful planning, which requires a vision by the entrepreneur of the selected harvest option. If a sale of the venture to a supplier or competitor is contemplated, particularly careful planning is required. The entrepreneur should consider the contingency of being faced with a harvesting opportunity and the possibility of selling his "life's work". Sometimes the entrepreneur can be so involved that the thought of letting go of his "baby" may not cross his mind when the window opens.

16.10.4 Realistic evaluation

Valuation is probably one of the more difficult requirements for most of the harvesting options. Every entrepreneur should be able to calculate the value of his or her business and also that of another business. Valuation is valuable in these cases:

- Buying or selling a business, division or major asset
- Raising capital through selling shares
- For a management buyout or employee stock option plan, or even for profit-sharing plans
- Selling to a partner or buying out a partner
- Taxation issues
- Going public

Incorrect valuations could lead to any one or more of the following:

- A lower harvest for the entrepreneur if the valuation is too low
- Scaring off the potential buyer if it is too high
- Eliminating prospective buyers
- Scaring off potential shareholders or financiers

Care should be taken not to divulge details to a buyer that is apparently not serious about buying. The industry suggests that the buyer must be willing to show the "colour of his money" before one opens the books. Valuation is discussed in Chapter 12 but it is important to get a lawyer involved from the beginning. Rather pay the lawyer a fee than lose your business on a technical point.

16.10.5 Contractual agreement

Having an agreement is good but putting it on paper is better. You may be honest but it is better not to assume that the other person is trustworthy. A proper legal agreement is always beneficial to both parties, as it anticipates most contingencies based on years of previous experience.

Typical contractual agreements that should be done in writing include:

- Confidential agreements with a prospective agent or buyer
- Valuations
- A buying agreement stating all the assets and specifications
- Evaluation of the current entrepreneur for the management training
- Role definitions of the parties after the sale

- Mentoring agreement
- Restraint of trade

The above contractual agreements form part of the next principle, namely that the deal should be structured. One of the agreements is, however, highlighted.

16.10.6 Mentoring agreement

It is important to elaborate on the mentoring agreement, as it has become an integral part of most of the harvesting options described in this chapter.

While the entrepreneur may be replaced as the head of the venture, he or she may sometimes be required to make certain inputs, especially that of training the new management, successor or owner. The previous owner is often bound to the business for a period of one to three years after the deal to ensure a smooth transition and not to upset any suppliers or customers. It could be a very precarious situation for him, as his authority to make decisions may already have been transferred to the new boss.

The mentoring agreement offers a means of clarifying the exact role distribution of the new and the old. Things that should be covered in this agreement include:

- Powers of decision making, such as:
  - Signing powers
  - Making deals and sales
  - Negotiation
- Freedom and access to information
- Authority that changes from a line to a staff function
- Working hours
- Responsibilities
- Reporting to the new boss

At this point, these issues may seem frivolous but they can become very important and can even make a deal go down if not correctly structured.

The mentoring agreement is also important to the new successor in the family business as it should govern the powers of the previous owner, who should not keep control but let the new management take charge. This is a very sensitive issue and the source of several family break-ups.

16.10.7 Structured deal

Structuring the deal is very specific for every situation. Care should be taken to note in writing everything that is agreed. A knowledgeable business broker should be used to ensure that everything is considered and included in the contract. Especially relevant are issues of liability for debtors, payments and previous agreements.

16.11 Questions about harvesting

The issues surrounding harvesting are complex and it is difficult to lay down rules to follow. However, Figure 16.3 depicts the integrated harvesting process and highlights all the elements that should be considered to benefit from it.

When crafting a harvesting strategy, there are several factors that influence the eventual choice. The questions one should ask when planning a harvesting strategy are:

- What is the reason for the harvest?
- At what level of performance does one need to harvest?
- At what level is the venture performing now?
- At what stage of the venture life cycle is the venture now?
- Which level of performance will improve the harvest decision?
- How severely is the harvest required and what are the reasons for the intensity of the choice?
- Which environmental factors are affecting the venture and how will they change at the harvest point?
- How does harvesting fit in with the current broad strategy?
- Does one know exactly what the venture is worth?
- Are there any complicating factors that should be considered?
- Given the opportunity that exists, how does it influence the valuation?

16.12 Conclusion

This chapter has as its main aim to assist the entrepreneur in considering every alternative possible for harvesting. Harvesting is a strategic goal and requires a strategy for achieving it.

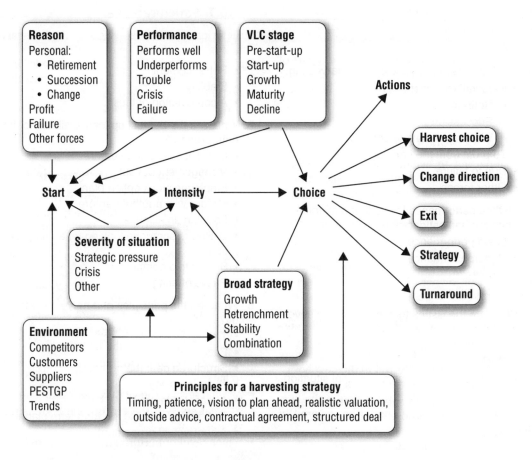

Figure 16.3 The integrated harvesting process model

Understanding the dynamics of the harvesting process brings insight to the entrepreneur in order to meaningfully anticipate, plan and execute a harvest successfully. Remember that the size of the harvest is very important.

The entrepreneur can then also monitor the process and adapt it according to the changing environment. A strategy, even a broad one, will help the entrepreneur to be alert to any windows that may open to optimise a potential harvest.

Many of the issues relevant to failure and turnaround as described in the previous chapter are also relevant to the harvesting process.

There are principles that govern the harvesting process. Timing is crucial and requires patience. Harvesting should be part of the vision of the entrepreneur and should be planned for. One should use outside advice to establish a realistic valuation, else the size of the harvest could be significantly reduced. Once the deal is properly structured it should be formalised through a contractual agreement.

Harvesting from a business in trouble is always much more difficult than when it is planned properly with enough time. Asking the right questions could lead to crafting a workable harvest strategy.

Looking back

1. List the reasons associated with harvesting.
   - Personal reasons:
     - Retirement
     - Succession
     - Wanting to make a change
   - To profit from the harvest
   - Due to failure
   - Other forces

2. List the performance levels that may influence the harvest decision.
   - Good performance
   - Underperformance
   - Trouble
   - Crisis failure

3. What are the issues that influence the severity of the harvest situation?
   - Strategic pressure
   - Crisis
   - Other issues, such as a personal situation

4. Name the broad strategies that can impact on the harvest decision.
   - Growth

   - Retrenchment
   - Stability
   - A combination of these

5. What are the harvest options available to the entrepreneur?
   - Outright sale of the venture
   - Management buyout
   - Employee stock option plan
   - Merger with another venture
   - Forming an alliance
   - Selling to someone looking for an acquisition
   - Selling to a competitor
   - Public offering

6. What are the principles of a harvest strategy?
   - Timing
   - Patience
   - Structured deal (beforehand)
   - Outside advice
   - A realistic valuation
   - The vision for doing the long-term planning
   - A contractual agreement

Key terms

Acquisition
Alliance
Buyout
Capital cow
Creditor days
Creditors
Crisis
Growth
Harvesting process
Harvest reasons
Merger

Organic growth
Patience
Retirement
Retrenchment
Severity
Stability
Strategic pressure
Succession
Urgency
Valuation

Discussion questions

1. What, in your mind, is the core factor that governs the business harvest?

2. Which is the best harvest alternative to pursue? Explain.

Case study

Case study

NRLT is a community newspaper in a town in the Limpopo province. It has been doing business for more than 35 years and has had three owners during that time, of which the current owner has been involved as an employee for seven years and as an owner for 19 years. His wife was also involved in the business.

His only daughter married an excellent salesman and about ten years ago, he was asked to join *NRLT* as sales manager. The thinking at the time was to train him, as the children would eventually take over the business in any case.

His joining the venture led to some good growth and development of different revenue streams, and he was offered additional shares above the original 15 per cent that he started with. A process was designed to allow him to buy shares with his profit sharing. Unfortunately, the valuation was very poorly executed and within two years he had bought the maximum shares to the level of 44 per cent. The share distribution was:

- Owners (parents) 51 per cent
- Children 44 per cent
- Administration manager 5 per cent

Apparently the children latched onto the idea of an early harvest and bought the 5 per cent from the administration manager who did not want to become involved in the family in-fighting, as the owners perceived the move to be threatening

and greedy. However, the owners were quite safe holding the majority share.

The children started making life difficult for their parents. They went so far as to prevent the grandchildren from visiting their grandparents. The whole thing became an ugly situation.

The children pressed for a sale of the business so they could harvest early and buy some property they were very interested in. However, they did not realise that the business supplied a massive cash stream of which they did not know the extent. During this time the atmosphere turned so sour that the mother left the business, as did some key staff members.

At that stage, the national newspapers started to consolidate their operations and wanted to make inroads into the community newspaper market. They were planning to start several of their own community papers.

A complicating factor was that *NRLT* printed its newspaper at the plant of the official opposition local newspaper, as it had no printing press of its own.

Questions

1. Thinking about the options of harvesting, what is your call on the situation? Suggest some harvesting options. What are the complicating factors described in this example? What business questions should one ask?

2. Can you relate any of the comments to the principles governing the harvesting process?

Experiential exercise

- Visit a business owner and discuss the harvesting options that he or she is contemplating, if any.
- Ask about his or her plans to maximise the harvest.
- Find out whether there are any complicating factors, such as in the example above.

References and recommended reading

Bekker, F. & Staude, G. 1984. *Starting and managing a small business*, 2nd ed. Cape Town: Juta.

Hisrich, R.D. & Peters, M.P. 1998. *Entrepreneurship.* 5th ed. London: McGraw-Hill.

Hitt, M.A., Ireland, R.D., Camp, S.M. & Sexton, D.L. 2002. *Strategic entrepreneurship.* Oxford: Blackwell.

Kuratko, D.F. & Hodgetts, R.M. 2001. *Entrepreneurship: a contemporary approach,* 5th ed. London: Harcourt College.

Kuratko, D.F. & Welsch, H.P. 2001. *Strategic entrepreneurial growth.* London: Harcourt College.

Pearce, J.A. & Robinson, R.B. Jr. 2000. *Strategic management: formulation, implementation and control,* 7th ed. Chicago, IL: R.D. Irwin

Pretorius, M. 1999. *Successoneur business decision simulator: experience the success of being an entrepreneur.* Pietersburg: Management Transfer cc.

Timmons, J.A. 1999. *New venture creation: entrepreneurship for the 21st century.* Burr Ridge: Irwin.

Wickam, P.A. 1998. *Strategic entrepreneurship: a decision-making approach to new venture creation and management,* 2nd ed. London: Prentice Hall.

17

International business opportunities

Johan Hough

Learning outcomes

After completion of this chapter, you should be able to:

- Appreciate the importance of international opportunities for business in South Africa
- Know the factors that have contributed significantly to the positive growth in international business
- Identify the various strategies for entry into the international business arena
- Map South Africa's road to globalisation and the factors affecting our trading patterns
- Appreciate the complexity involved and strategic issues to consider when going "global"
- Explain the factors to be considered when entering into strategic alliances

17.1 Introduction

In the past, doing business overseas was an option available only to major corporations. But, as the marketplace becomes increasingly global and through an increase in assistance programmes and efforts by the South African government and businesses, it is easier and sometimes even necessary for small and medium enterprises to enter the global marketplace. The international opportunities for small business will increase, as the export of goods and services is no longer the complicated undertaking it used to be. Rapid technological change and the increasingly global nature of competition are also forcing South African firms to distribute their products more widely and quickly, to cope with environmental change and to reduce costs.

Successful businesses of the future will treat the entire world as their domain in terms of meeting their supply and demand requirements. In such a globalised market, the domestic firm will not be sustainably competitive. Globalisation is not a new concept, but there are relatively new factors that have contributed to its recent prominence, such as the opening up of new markets for (South African) businesses and new communication and transport technology, which have resulted in a major expansion of international trade and investment.

The 2001 and 2002 World Competitiveness Reports by the World Economic Forum in Switzerland show a decline in South Africa's competitive position (relative to other newly industrialised nations), especially in the area of internationalisation. Internationalisation is measured in terms of trade, exports, imports, cross-border investment flows, international alliances and partnerships with foreign firms, protectionism and export/import diversification. South Africa's level of internationalisation declined from 1995, while our partnerships with foreign firms currently put us in the penultimate competitive position among newly industrialised nations. We will now focus on the importance of global opportunities for businesses in southern Africa.

17.2 The importance of international opportunities for business in South Africa

Research on the retail financial services sector (Figure 17.1) shows the relative importance of globalisation for South Africa's financial institutions over the next five years. About 90 per cent of executives based in South Africa have planned for international expansion over the next five years, while 87 per cent of the firms in the United States and Canada anticipated the same, compared with European firms, of which only 27 per cent planned for international expansion.

It is therefore becoming increasingly important for South African enterprises to be aware of the significance of international business issues, the reasons for international relations, environments and factors influencing international business and foreign investment, and events that affect trade and investment patterns.

17.3 Growth in global business activities

The reasons for the internationalisation of an enterprise's business include expansion of sales, resource acquisition, diversification, minimisation of competitive risk, saturated markets and depreciating currencies. Other objectives are to achieve low costs in order to strengthen the enterprise's competitive position and to gain access to natural resources. The political stability of countries that are business partners is another important reason for doing business beyond one's national borders.

Besides the tendency to pursue greater sales and profits, the following factors have contributed significantly to the positive growth in international business:

- Modern communication media have made it possible to exchange scientific, technical and commercial information rapidly and efficiently. This has facilitated the creation of new markets, as well as increased competition. Modern communication has also accelerated and facilitated purchasing activities, especially in countries like South Africa, Zimbabwe and Botswana, which are remote from the major international purchasing markets.

- Rapid means of international travel and transport without corresponding price hikes have made it possible to control subsidiaries in different parts of the world and to visit suppliers in other countries. The lifting of

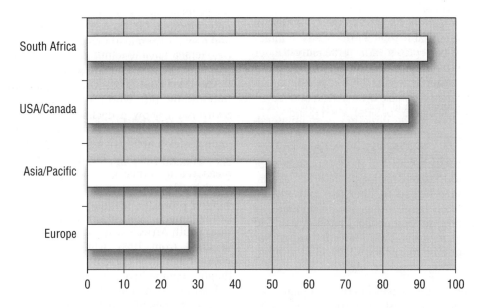

Figure 17.1 Percentage of firms most committed to global expansion

economic sanctions in the early 1990s has, for example, reopened international air routes to South African businesspeople and facilitated access to international selling and purchasing markets.

- Modern management techniques used by multinational enterprises have channelled new ideas, technology and production processes, and also resources and capital to wherever they are needed on the world market. The presence in South and southern Africa of numerous multinational enterprises from countries such as Germany, France, the United Kingdom, the United States, Japan, Malaysia and Singapore has therefore contributed significantly to the growth of the southern African economy, especially since the early 1990s.

- Private firms have shown that they can adapt to changing circumstances and still efficiently exploit overseas markets and function under foreign governments with their diverse political policies.

- An understanding of the principle of economic expediency has enabled managers to develop foreign markets before their competitors could enter the field. Southern African enterprises are now well placed to expand their business operations on the North African market. The world's capital markets have developed to the point where they are now able to meet the needs of multinational enterprises more efficiently. Under its new political dispensation, South Africa has far easier access to these markets.

- International trade has moved away from bilateralism in the direction of multilateralism. Various rounds of the General Agreement on Tariffs and Trade (GATT) negotiations resulted in the establishment of the World Trade Organisation. These negotiations have helped to liberalise and expand world trade. Large foreign aid programmes of the European Union, the United States and the former Soviet Union have helped recipient countries to expand their share in international trade considerably.

- The diplomatic tension between communist and non-communist countries resulted in greater political and economic cooperation

between the non-communist countries, and served as an incentive for the operations of multinational countries. The downfall of the communist regimes has opened the door for South Africa to establish commercial ties with countries like Russia, Poland, Hungary and Romania.

- Sustained growth in the world's gross product has resulted in the creation of new markets and the expansion of existing ones. South African enterprises should be on the lookout for new markets to develop (including in southern Africa). Botswana is one of the countries where there is a liberal foreign exchange and payments system and no exchange control restrictions on current remittances.

17.4 Entrepreneurial entry into international business

There are various ways in which an entrepreneur can become a player in international business and market products internationally. The method of entry into a market and the mode of operating overseas are dependent on the goals of the entrepreneur and the firm's strengths and weaknesses. Figure 17.2 shows the risks and rewards of these global strategies.

The modes of entering or engaging in international business can be divided into three broad categories: exporting, non-equity arrangements, and direct foreign investment, mainly by means of overseas manufacturing. The following section is partly based on Hisrich and Peters (2002: 97-100) and Phatak (1997).

17.4.1 Exporting (selling goods made in one country to another country)

As a general rule, an entrepreneur starts doing international business through exporting. Exporting normally involves the sale and shipping of products manufactured in one country to a customer located in another country. This process might happen through the following three phases.

■ Phase 1

Phase 1 begins when a firm receives an enquiry about one of its products directly from a for-

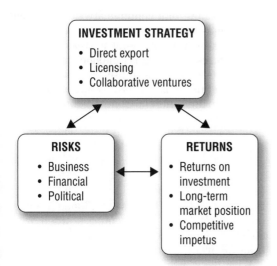

Figure 17.2 Risks and rewards of global strategies

Source: Kirconnell (1988).

eign businessperson or from an independent domestic exporter and importer. The firm may ignore the enquiry, in which case there is no further development. However, if the firm responds positively and its product sells at a profit on the foreign market, then the stage is set for more sales of its products abroad, and the firm's executives are likely to become favourably disposed to the idea. Other enquiries from the foreign buyers are received more enthusiastically and the firm sells its products abroad through a domestic export intermediate. The latter could be an export merchant, an export commission house, a resident buyer (i.e. a buyer who is domiciled in the exporting firm's home market and represents all types of private or government buyers from abroad), a broker or a combination export manager (i.e. an exporter who serves as the exclusive export department of several non-competing manufacturers).

■ **Phase 2**

The second phase starts when a firm's exports continue to expand and the executives decide that the time is ripe to take export management into their own hands and no longer rely on unsolicited enquiries from abroad. They may decide to assume a proactive rather than a

reactive position on exports. An export manager with a small staff is appointed to actively search for foreign markets for the firm's products.

■ **Phase 3**

The third phase develops when export sales continue their upward surge. The firm has difficulty operating with only an export manager and his or her small staff. A fully fledged export department or division is established at the same level as the domestic sales department. The firm then drops the domestic export intermediate and starts to sell directly to importers or buyers located in foreign markets.

17.4.2 Licensing (allowing someone else to use something of the firm's)

Licensing involves an entrepreneur who is a manufacturer (licensee) giving a foreign manufacturer (licensor) the right to use a patent, trademark, technology, production process or product in return for the payment of a royalty. The licensing arrangement is most appropriate when the entrepreneur has no intention of entering a particular market through exporting or direct investment. Since the process is low risk, yet provides a way to generate incremental income, a licensing arrangement can be a good method for the entrepreneur to engage in international business. Unfortunately, some entrepreneurs have entered into these arrangements without careful analysis and have later found that they have allowed their largest competitor licensor to adopt the technology or know-how being licensed.

17.4.3 Turnkey projects (developing and operationalising projects in a foreign country)

Another method by which the entrepreneur can gain some international business experience without much risk is via turnkey projects. The underdeveloped or lesser-developed countries of the world have recognised their need for manufacturing technology and infrastructure and yet do not want to turn over substantial portions of their economy to foreign ownership. One solution to this dilemma has been to have a foreign entrepreneur build a factory or other facility, train the workers to operate the equipment, train the management to run the installation, and then turn it over to local owners once the operation is going, hence the name turnkey operation.

Entrepreneurs have found the turnkey project an attractive alternative. Initial profits can be made from this method, and follow-up export sales can result. The local firm or the government often provides financing, with periodic payments being made over the life of the project.

17.4.4 Management contracts (a method for performing a specific international task)

Another non-equity method the entrepreneur can use in international business is the management contract. Several entrepreneurs have successfully entered the international business arena by contracting their management techniques and managerial skills. These contracts sometimes follow a turnkey project, where the foreign owner wants to use the management of the turnkey supplier.

The management contract allows the purchasing country to gain foreign expertise without giving ownership of its resources to a foreigner. For the entrepreneur, the management contract is another way of entering markets that would otherwise be closed, and of obtaining a profit without a large equity investment.

17.4.5 Joint ventures (two firms forming a third firm)

Another method of direct foreign investment used by entrepreneurs to enter foreign markets is the joint venture. Although a joint venture can take on many forms, in its most traditional form two firms (e.g. one American and one German firm) get together and form a third firm in which they share the equity. Entrepreneurs have used joint ventures most often in two situations: when the entrepreneur wants to purchase local knowledge, as well as an already established marketing or manufacturing facility, and when rapid entry into a market is need-

ed. Sometimes joint ventures are dissolved and the entrepreneur takes total ownership.

Even though using a joint venture to enter a foreign market is a major strategic decision, the keys to its success have not been well understood, and the reasons for forming a joint venture today are different from those of the past. Previously, joint ventures were viewed as partnerships and often involved firms whose stock was owned by several other firms. Originally, joint ventures were used for trading purposes. Merchants of ancient Babylon, Egypt and Phoenicia used joint ventures to conduct large trading operations. This use continued throughout the 15th and 16th centuries when merchants in Great Britain used joint ventures to trade all over the world.

What has caused the present increase in the use of joint ventures, particularly when many have failed? Studies of the success or failure of joint ventures have indicated many different motives for their formation:

- One of the most frequent reasons for a joint venture is to share the costs and risks of a project. Projects where new, very costly technology is involved frequently need resource sharing. This can be particularly important when an entrepreneur does not have the financial resources necessary to engage in capital-intensive activities.

- Synergy between firms is another reason why an entrepreneur may form a joint venture. Synergy is the qualitative impact on the acquiring firm brought about by complementary factors inherent in the firm being acquired. Synergy in the form of people, customers, inventory, plant or equipment provides leverage for the joint venture. The degree of synergy determines how beneficial the joint venture will be for the companies involved.

- Another reason for forming a joint venture is to obtain a competitive advantage. A joint venture can pre-empt competitors, allowing an entrepreneur to access new customers and to expand the market base. It can also result in an entity that is more competitive than the original firm, since hybrids of companies tend to possess the strength of each of the joint venture partners.

- Joint ventures are frequently used by entrepreneurs to enter markets and economies that pose entrance difficulties or to compensate for a firm's lack of foreign experience.

17.4.6 Overseas investment and manufacturing

At this stage, the firm has a well-developed export programme supported by country market studies, promotion and distribution programmes tailored to the needs of each country market, and research aimed at identifying new foreign markets. The firm's executives may now begin to experience difficulties in increasing the total sales volume and profits in foreign markets in which they currently have a foothold, or they may find it impossible to enter other potentially lucrative markets via exports. These difficulties often occur when local governments impose high tariffs or quotas on the import of certain products, or when they ban the import totally if the products are also being produced locally by a domestic firm. In such cases, the firm's executives may decide to penetrate the foreign market by producing the product right in the foreign market itself.

17.5 South Africa's road to globalisation

In this section, we briefly discuss South Africa's road to globalisation and the factors affecting the country's trading patterns. (This section is based on Gouws and Bothma, 2000.)

17.5.1 A brief overview of South Africa's globalisation

South Africa has always been heavily dependent on international trade. In the years up to 1925, economic growth depended almost entirely on the exports of gold, diamonds and agricultural products. Thereafter, during the period leading up to World War II, there was a strong move towards the development of domestic industry as a substitute for imports and, as a result, South Africa's manufacturing industry grew rapidly.

This policy of import substitution was to continue into the 1960s. Import substitution is the policy of promoting locally manufactured products instead of imports in order to meet domestic market needs. In the process, extensive use is made of trade barriers, such as high import duties and quotas, as well as subsidisation to protect local industries against foreign competition. The main arguments used in favour of import substitution are that it creates employment; that the local industries will eventually be able to benefit from larger-scale production and lower unit costs; and that the balance of payments will improve as fewer consumer goods are imported.

In the years following World War II, South Africa began to show an ongoing deficit in the current account of its balance of payments. The country relied on the inflow of foreign investment to maintain the equilibrium in the overall balance of payments. Towards the end of the 1960s, the deficit in the balance of payments increased to such an extent that import controls and a devaluation of the rand became necessary to correct the situation. Moreover, it became clear that the main sources of foreign currency (gold and agricultural products) could no longer be relied on to the extent that they had been in the past. The country's ore reserves were becoming depleted and agricultural products were often affected by poor weather and volatile international supply and demand patterns.

It was therefore felt that greater attention would have to be given to developing the export potential of the manufacturing industry. In the 1980s, the need for a shift in South Africa's protectionist policy became apparent. A commission of enquiry into South Africa's industrial development strategy was initiated in the early 1980s. In the report on the findings of the investigation, it was stated that import substitution had to be accompanied by export development and that the encouragement of local industry had to take place within a competitive, free enterprise system, i.e. protectionism had to be curtailed. This view was in line with the findings of studies conducted by the World Bank and the International Monetary Fund, namely that countries that largely pursued an import substitution path had achieved far lower economic growth rates than countries following an export development policy.

The South African government is now committed to making the economy more competitive. International competitiveness is the only way in which South Africa will be able to provide sustainable and high-value employment. The government therefore does not see exporting as being mutually exclusive from producing for the domestic market. The ability to export is essentially the same as being in business in the first place.

Globalisation makes it possible to produce anywhere in the world and, as a result, the world market is the market firms participate in, not just the domestic market. Within the current global environment, we have witnessed the strengthening of the systems of global governance to manage the process of globalisation and liberalisation. The United Nations Conference on Trade and Development (UNCTAD) and the World Trade Organisation (WTO) are the two intergovernmental institutions involved in these processes.

South Africa has played a prominent role in both, especially UNCTAD, where our Minister of Trade and Industry was the president. South Africa has also actively negotiated with trading blocs such as the European Union (EU) and the Southern African Development Community (SADC). Today, the South African government is fully committed to a competitive, free enterprise system. This shift in policy was to some extent prompted by the growing pressure on the country to conform to GATT requirements – particularly from the early 1990s when sanctions against the country began to subside. South Africa was an active participant in the Uruguay Round of GATT negotiations and, in terms of the agreements concluded, it undertook to eliminate quantitative restrictions and to lower tariffs substantially.

A closer adherence to the principles of the WTO – GATT's successor – has presented new challenges to marketers domestically and abroad as they are faced with greater direct competition from abroad. The advantages of South Africa's membership of the WTO have sometimes been questioned on two counts. It has been argued that South Africa, a founder-member of GATT, is prevented through its membership of the WTO from providing adequate protection to the local industry. It has also been argued that membership would only really be beneficial if South Africa were regarded in the WTO as a developing country (i.e. the country's classification was changed from "developed country" to a more concessionary

"economy in transition"), so that South Africa could qualify for certain concessions granted only to developing countries (e.g. the ability to use quantitative restrictions – such as quotas – to protect growing industries).

Nonetheless, the benefits of South Africa's membership of the WTO are as follows: South Africa benefits from tariff concessions made by any WTO member through the most favoured nation or non-discrimination principle; i.e. South African exports enter WTO member countries at tariffs lower than would be the case were South Africa not a WTO member. Tariff reductions afford great advantages to South African exporters and can lead to new and larger markets, as well as to significant increases in foreign exchange earnings.

Tariff concessions facilitate the marketing of South African products abroad. South Africa benefits from the flexibility of many of the WTO rules. For example, although one of the articles of the Agreement prohibits quantitative restrictions between member countries, another article makes provision for countries experiencing balance of payments difficulties to impose import quotas so as to prevent a serious decline in foreign currency reserves. South Africa has occasionally made use of this concession. This country retains a secure position in an international organisation that determines future global trading relationships.

The South African government's attitude towards the country's position in the WTO is that the advantages of membership outweigh the disadvantages, and that non-membership would actually introduce serious risks for South Africa, given the volume and nature of the country's trade and its status as an important trading nation. Export development (particularly with regard to manufactured goods) is being given serious attention at both public and private sector levels in South Africa. For example, the South African government offers exporters a variety of export marketing incentives, is negotiating an increasing number of trade agreements with other countries, and is heavily involved in trade promotion activities, such as the organisation of trade missions abroad, international trade fairs, etc. In the private sector, a number of organisations offer a wide range of services to equip the exporting community with the information and expertise needed to tackle export markets.

17.5.2 Factors affecting South Africa's foreign trade patterns

South Africa's foreign trade patterns are affected by a number of factors, as set out below.

■ Abundance of natural resources

A large percentage of South Africa's exports is made up of unprocessed raw materials reflecting the abundance of natural resources in this country. Gold, in particular, has historically contributed significantly to South Africa's export earnings. Over the past decade, however, export revenues from gold have steadily declined. This is attributable mainly to the fall in the gold price and the increase in manufactured exports.

■ Degree of sophistication

Highly industrialised countries have tended to import raw materials and export manufactured goods and services. Developing countries, on the other hand, have tended to export commodities and import nearly all their other requirements (consumer goods and services), with the resultant trade deficit usually being offset by the inflow of capital investment.

South Africa, although relatively industrialised within the African context, is clearly still a developing country in comparison with the major industrialised countries of the world (South Africa is commonly classified as an emerging market). Manufactured goods such as chemicals, processed steel, machinery and spares, pharmaceuticals and food products represent a relatively small percentage of South Africa's total exports, and are exported primarily to other African countries. Although exports of manufactured goods have been showing a steady increase in the last few years, the majority of South Africa's exports still consists of raw and beneficiated materials that are sold to Japan, the United Kingdom, Germany and the United States. Beneficiated goods are items that have undergone a transformation as a result of some process – like the process of transforming cotton into thread.

Most of South Africa's imports, on the other hand, consist of processed and finished goods. Relatively few raw materials are imported apart from oil and petroleum products, because the country is so rich in natural resources. It is essential that South Africa continues to export greater varieties and volumes of manufactured goods, as this will enable the country to develop a strong and varied industrial base and, in so doing, reduce its susceptibility to changes in the price of gold and other commodities.

■ Emergence of service-oriented economies

A recent trend has been the economic restructuring of many developed nations from an industrial manufacturing base towards a service-oriented one in the areas of, for example, banking, insurance, and information and communications technologies. This has long-term implications for South Africa's trade patterns, primarily because these sophisticated economies are moving away from imports of raw materials to imports of manufactured goods.

The newly industrialised countries such as South Korea, Singapore, Taiwan and Hong Kong have become the centres of light industry and heavy engineering, the products of which are to an increasing extent being supplied to the developed economies. Given this changing nature of global trade, South African exporters of both finished goods and raw materials need to be aware of new sources of supply and demand, and they should avail themselves of the opportunities arising from shifting international trade relations.

■ Economic conditions in foreign markets

The economic conditions in foreign markets will have a significant influence on the types of products required, their consumption patterns, and so on. The Far East, for example, has always been a major market for South Africa's primary and beneficiated goods, because countries such as Japan, Taiwan, South Korea and Hong Kong are poor in natural resources. In addition, the rapidly growing economies of many of the countries in this region have led to an even greater need for raw materials. Our manufactured goods have also been gaining increasing acceptance; for example, South African processed foods have been well received in many Far East markets.

■ Size of foreign markets

The size of the foreign market (whether the

term "market" is taken to mean a whole country or a specific region within a country) will often impact on the volume and variety of goods required from South Africa. The United States, for example, still represents the world's largest market for raw materials (which has important implications for South Africa) and it is also the largest single consumer market. At the other end of the scale are the much smaller and less sophisticated markets of Africa, which require imports of manufactured products, not raw materials. While exports to Africa account for only about 10 per cent of South Africa's non-gold exports, they account for about 30 per cent of the country's manufactured exports.

■ **Traditional markets and new market opportunities**

South Africa's foreign trade patterns, although continuously evolving and changing, originated as a result of the country's trade with Western Europe. This is still our most important market for primary products. However, the importance of other traditional trading partners, such as the United States and Japan, should not be overlooked.

In addition, the economic integration of Europe, combined with the opening up of markets in Central Europe, the former Soviet Union and China, has presented new challenges to South African international firms. Furthermore, the potential of Latin America and the Gulf remains still largely unexplored for South African companies. Newer regional groupings, such as the North American Free Trade Area (NAFTA) and the emergence of stronger trading relations amongst the countries of the Indian Ocean Rim, will have a substantial impact on the way business is conducted in a particular region.

■ **Political factors**

Over the years, political factors have had a noticeable effect on the pattern of South Africa's trade. Sanctions placed restraints on many South African products in several of the country's traditional export markets. At the same time, trade union action and consumer resistance disrupted trade. Times have changed, however, and today South Africa faces few, if any, political barriers to trade and,

indeed, is viewed rather favourably in this regard. Nevertheless, there are other countries with which South Africa trades that face political sanctions, such as Libya. South Africa is therefore affected indirectly by the trade sanctions placed on these countries.

17.6 Opportunities and problems facing South African exporters

South Africa has a number of strengths that makes it an attractive trading partner. These strengths will be briefly discussed below.

- *Infrastructure:* South Africa has excellent infrastructure in the form of ports, rail and road systems and readily available air transport. The control of port and rail facilities by Portnet and Spoornet respectively ensures the efficient movement and transfer of freight using multimodal transport. Road transport is provided either by private haulers or Autonet. Approximately 50 international air services link South Africa with international destinations.

- *Business sector:* South Africa has a sophisticated business sector. Because the South African business community has experienced a high degree of exposure to international business and management practices over the years, it is able to perform well in the international arena.

- *Trade expertise:* South Africa's trade expertise is extensive. The country's links with Europe are strong due to excellent communications; close commercial, trade and financial ties; and well-established technical and cultural exchanges.

- *Trading links:* South Africa's links with the Far East are quite substantial and are expanding rapidly. Important trading partners in the region include Japan, Singapore, Hong Kong, South Korea and China. South Africa also conducts a growing volume of trade with less developed countries such as Argentina, Brazil, Chile, India, Malawi, Mauritius, Pakistan, Sri Lanka, Turkey, Zaire, Zambia and Zimbabwe, and the list of such countries is growing rapidly.

- *Banking system:* The South African banking system is highly sophisticated and, indeed, its level of automation outranks that of North America and many Western European countries.

- *Natural resources:* South Africa is a world supplier of natural resources – metals and minerals, in particular. The country's position as a world supplier in this area is likely to be strengthened, given the parlous state of the economy of the former Soviet Union, which was a major competitor for South Africa in the field of minerals.

- *Geographical position:* South Africa occupies a strategic geographical position. Historically, the Cape of Good Hope represented an important halfway point in the sea route from Europe to the East. Since the Gulf War, the Cape sea route has been used with increasing frequency.

- *African identity:* South Africa's competitive advantage as a manufacturing centre, export base and regional head office for sub-Saharan Africa is particularly important for companies that are considering trading with countries in this region. South Africa has a similar climate and can therefore advise on the technological modifications necessary to withstand harsh African conditions, and on design modifications appropriate to a labour force different from that of the more developed regions of the world. Proximity and sound infrastructure facilitate comparatively easy access to African countries. Furthermore, South Africa has an African identity that is important for establishing the personal relationships necessary for doing business in the region.

- *Regional expertise and international aid:* Despite the fact that Africa is often seen as a difficult market, particularly with its poor payment record, South Africa has developed expertise in the region and is conducting successful and growing business with many countries in Africa. As part of their policy of stimulating economic and social development in Third World countries, a number of international aid agencies have emerged as major sources of funding for development projects and programmes, giving rise to millions of rands worth of goods and services. This has gone a long way towards solving some of the problems related to payment in Africa.

- *Relationship with sub-Saharan Africa:* As South Africa's strong relations with other African countries could influence potential trading partners, one should be aware of the aims and activities of the various regional groupings in sub-Saharan Africa – particularly as South Africa is now a member of a number of them and is already playing an active role in the functioning of these blocs. (Some of these are discussed in more detail later in this chapter.)

While it is important to stress the benefits of doing business with South Africa, some of the problems that might to some extent frustrate the country's export efforts include the following:

- *High cost of raw materials:* The high costs of imported and domestic raw materials, coupled with the anomalous pricing of locally produced commodities in accordance with world market prices (e.g. London Metal Exchange prices) and artificial price differentials, have an adverse effect on the international competitiveness of many South African products.

- *High cost of capital goods:* The current weak state of the rand, relatively high import tariffs and high interest rates mean that the importation of essential capital goods is expensive.

- *High transport costs:* Since South Africa's major export production facilities are situated in Gauteng, a large percentage of export products has to be railed over considerable distances to the various ports (primarily to Durban). High rail transport costs to these ports present exporters with a cost disadvantage. Inland rail costs can be as much as 75 per cent of the total export transport cost. High harbour costs also pose a problem. Furthermore, exporters have to incur additional costs to transport goods beyond South Africa's borders to the major world markets. This situation places them at a disadvantage in relation to the European countries, for instance, where a number of South Africa's competitors have relatively low transport costs with which to contend, because of their close proximity to the market(s) concerned.

- *Low productivity:* Productivity in South Africa is low compared with international standards. This is exacerbated by labour disputes (e.g. strikes and stay-aways lead to delays in the production and shipment of goods, thereby disrupting quality controls and impairing long-term relationships with overseas customers). However, low productivity of both labour and capital is essentially a management problem.

- *Lack of production capacity:* Some South African firms lack the capacity to meet large overseas orders, while the expansion of plants is normally very costly.

- *Tax structures:* Tax structures in other countries are often more favourable than in South Africa, enabling competitors' products to be more price advantageous.

- *Financial constraints in foreign markets:* While South Africa's proximity to other countries in Africa offers a number of advantages in respect of trade, these are often offset by foreign exchange shortages experienced in these countries.

- *Inadequate and costly trade finance schemes:* The cost and availability of export financing schemes for first-time exporters in South Africa do not compare favourably with facilities available to competitors abroad.

17.7 Principles for going international

The following seven principles have assisted companies in developing and implementing global strategies. These principles provide a framework for applying the market entry approaches to individual markets in such a way as to create a coherent global strategy (Kirconnell 1988).

17.7.1 Clarify the international business mission

The international business mission is a clear and concise statement of the firm's purpose in "going international". By defining, within the context of the overall corporation, the aim, geographical/product focus, unique strengths and management culture of the international enterprise, the mission predetermines the acceptable levels of investment, return and risk for international ventures.

Most importantly, to understand the competitive requirements in the international arena, companies must understand the existing patterns of competition in their industry to determine whether it is multidomestic or global in nature. To use Michael Porter's definition, in a multidomestic industry, a firm's competitive position in a given country is essentially independent of the competition in other countries. In a global industry, a firm's competitive position in one country is significantly influenced by its position in other countries (Porter 1998).

This is a critical distinction. If an industry is global, or in the process of becoming global, firms must develop a mission that integrates their worldwide activities while simultaneously balancing the political needs of the various host countries. On the other hand, an enterprise operating in a multidomestic industry can be managed as a portfolio of domestic businesses, with the channel to market (joint ventures, representatives, etc.) being decided on a discrete, investment/return vs risk basis.

Although a critical distinction, it is often a difficult one to make. A key trend in many traditionally multidomestic industries is to become global in nature. Successful companies are discovering that short product life cycles and steep learning curves mean that products must be of high quality and low cost by world standards in order to enjoy a sustained competitive advantage against foreign competition. In many instances, even products that have traditionally been highly differentiated, such as computers, are developing market characteristics that resemble those of commodity products.

Therefore, in the next decade, for an increasing number of businesses, success or failure will depend more on global strategy than on the design, technology, price or quality of particular products.

To manage this transition and ensure a strategic orientation to international business decision making, companies should follow the examples of such successful Canadian companies as Bata, Northern Telecom Limited and Connaught Laboratories. They should centralise their international strategy decision-making activities within their corporate strategy process, while decentralising the formulation of competitive strategies to regional management teams.

17.7.2 Challenge assumptions about "closed" markets

The extent to which a firm can be open-minded is primarily a function of the resources it has available for market investigation and analysis. Rudimentary "rules of thumb" should not be allowed to ruin management thinking. For instance, management should not rule out an opportunity simply because a market is perceived at the outset as "closed". Although there is considerable virtue in keeping things simple by avoiding apparently closed markets, seldom is any market so closed that business cannot be carried out under any circumstances. Perhaps short-term opportunities will materialise or be developed, which will position a firm for long-term benefits should the regulatory environment change.

It is most likely, however, that opportunities, either short or long term, will materialise for those firms that have a good grasp of their international mission in general, and of local conditions, in particular.

For years, key telecommunications markets such as the United Kingdom, Germany and Japan have been considered "closed" to foreign competition. During the 1980s, the United Kingdom substantially "opened" its markets, and current trends indicate that some form of liberalisation can be expected in Germany and Japan. Global "winners" will be companies that position themselves today to capture a significant market share in these key markets.

17.7.3 Host country contacts are critical for successful market assessment

Each country, each market and each customer is distinct. These distinctions take the form of economic, nationalistic, cultural and financial differences, to name but a few. To negotiate successfully in the international marketplace, management must have a clear understanding of the balance of bargaining power among four main stakeholder groups in the host nation – the ruling authorities, business interests, managerial groups and labour groups.

The specific terms of reference for the market assessment, i.e. the questions requiring answers, will be defined by the business mission. The analysis must, however, provide management with the following:

- Understanding of the national imperative (e.g. employment, balance of payments)
- Understanding of the business environment (e.g. politics, languages, market system)
- Market accessibility (is it open or closed, and under what terms?)
- Market potential (is there sufficient potential return to offset the risks and levels of investment?)

As noted above, changing market circumstances may, over time, create opportunities where none previously existed. It is critical, therefore, for management to develop a network of contacts within those markets where it might have an immediate or future interest.

Japanese automakers are among the best at preparing for market entry. "Exhaustive" and "exhausting" is how one individual described his work of assisting Japanese automakers prepare assessments and analysis prior to their investing in North American facilities. As another industry observer noted, "North Americans make decisions in six months that take the Japanese 18 months. However, it takes the Japanese only six months to implement a plan vs the North American's 18 months, and the Japanese do not need a ready supply of 'band aids' available during the implementation stage".

17.7.4 Fit market entry strategies with the host country's needs and the firm's capabilities

As outlined earlier, market entry strategies are many and various. In considering such entry strategies, management must be flexible.

Where management is convinced – either because of industry economics or corporate culture – that it must conduct business in a certain way (e.g. direct investment), it should choose only those markets where that entry strategy will work. To force a market entry approach on an inappropriate business environment substantially increases risk.

As a corollary, if a firm decides to conduct business in many different business environments, then it must be flexible in its choice of market entry strategies.

Bata Limited, the Canadian shoe manufacturer, is composed of more than 100 companies, almost all of which required direct investment and operate as indigenous, "national" companies. In contrast, Connaught Laboratories, a world leader in human vaccines based in Canada, exports, licenses technology, enters into joint ventures and invests directly in host countries, thereby generating over 50 per cent of its revenue from international markets.

17.7.5 Successful partnerships require a clear understanding of the partners' goals

The process of forging international business partnerships is often hampered because prospective collaborators do not know each other and are unable to negotiate in an atmosphere of mutual trust. Hence, time must be invested in researching and understanding the needs of prospective partners in order to negotiate profitable arrangements.

"Partners", in this sense, include not only joint venture partners or licensees, but also representatives and distributors. If representatives or distributors are one's "eyes and ears" in the host countries, it is foolish to negotiate as if they are easily replaceable.

Particularly difficult partners to identify are potential licensees or joint venture collaborators. A potential licensee should be chosen from among the available strong, national companies with good management and the right financial, technological and personnel resources. If such a local firm does not exist at all, it may be a situation that requires a joint venture. In this case, or if a joint venture partner is required for political reasons, the most attractive partners are those that will be the joint venture's main customer.

In 1967, Northern Telecom Limited, the Canadian telecommunications manufacturer, established a joint venture with a Turkish telephone firm to manufacture telephone switching equipment in Turkey. The joint venture currently employs 2 000 people, fewer than five of whom are expatriates. During the past 20 years, Northern Telecom's equity participation has declined from 51 to 30 per cent. Total export sales of subcomponents from Canada to the joint venture during this period are measured in billions of dollars.

17.7.6 Feasibility analyses must test "competitiveness" and "fairness"

An appropriate entry strategy may have been identified, but the detailed implementation plan must also be established, tested and negotiated. At this stage, where levels of investment, risk and return are being considered, a detailed feasibility study is invaluable. Such a study must include the following:

- Market assessment
- Revenue potential
- Operating costs
- Financing costs
- Tax implications
- Foreign exchange controls
- Risk and sensitivity analyses

A key test of feasibility is to understand clearly how the foreign participant will make its local partner superior to local competitors. For instance, Northern Telecom Limited provides its European licensees with technology superior to their own, thereby making them more competitive in their local business environments. It is the value of the foreign firm's contribution to the local firm's competitive position that must be evaluated. This is true no matter which entry strategy is being considered.

Upon completion of the feasibility study, it is important to negotiate a fair deal with prospective partners. If foreign partners do not make an adequate return on investment, then there is little motivation to make the venture successful. Many companies "win" international negotiations only to subsequently lose money.

An important consideration is the participants' motives for entering into joint ventures. For instance, European and North American companies usually prefer to negotiate rights to products. Developing nations such as China, however, will also insist on assistance with implementation through the transfer of process technology and management training. A Western firm that "wins" a negotiation with the Chinese by avoiding the implementation issues of process technology and training is almost certainly doomed to failure.

17.7.7 Let local executives manage once the strategy is set

Rigorous upfront analysis is a corporate invest-ment. Only when the deal is made and imple-mented does a firm even have the potential to earn a return on its investment. Oddly, this is also the stage at which there is the greatest ten-dency for corporate management to lose inter-est.

17.8 Strategic partnerships and alliances

A strategic alliance is defined as a cooperative arrangement between two or more local and/or global firms that can affect the competitive positioning of either participant in the market segment in which they set out to compete (Hough 1997).

A strategic alliance can also be described as a particular mode of interorganisational rela-tions in which the partners make substantial investments in developing a long-term collabo-rative effort and a common orientation towards their individual and mutual goals. These alliances are partnerships in which more inti-mate connections evolve between separate organisations. In many cases, the linkages between the two companies are so strong that the boundaries blur and it is difficult to discern where one organisation ends and the other begins.

Strategic alliances embody a future-oriented relationship forged between two or more inde-pendent companies, in which each attempts to leverage the strengths of the other to achieve mutually beneficial goals. The alliance need not be based on a singular superordinate goal that drives the relationship. However, there must be perceptual congruity with, or consensus on, the goals of each member. In other words, domain consensus is more important than a shared uni-fying focus. Hennart (1987) suggests that firms typically engage in joint ventures to achieve objectives such as:

- Taking advantage of economies of scale and diversifying risk
- Overcoming entry barriers to new markets
- Pooling complementary knowledge

Companies are forming international strategic alliances in response to these demands. Many South African companies, especially research and development-intensive companies, have already formed alliances with foreign partners and companies for the following reasons:

- To seek out new markets as a way of sustain-ing or increasing growth in sales and profits
- To achieve lower development, research and marketing costs
- To share resources
- To access natural resource deposits in other countries
- To do business in a more stable political environment
- To learn new skills from competitors

There is a whole range of strategic alliances, including purchasing agreements, marketing/distribution agreements, shared research and development efforts, cross-licensing, coopera-tive agreements and equity-based relationships.

17.8.1 The importance of strategic alliances in South Africa

Hough (1997) conducted extensive research into the formation of strategic alliances by South African companies. Companies listed in the importers and exporters registers of the Bureau of Market Research at Unisa were used as the population for this study. A randomised, stratified sample of 1 800 companies was drawn proportionally from two of the nine Standard Industrial Classification (SIC) sections, namely the manufacturing and the wholesale and retail sections. The remainder of this chapter is large-ly based on this empirical research.

South African companies involved in strate-gic alliances, or that are considering such alliances, are analysed in Figure 17.3.

Some 39 per cent of South African companies that responded are involved in a local or for-eign alliance (the strategic alliance group), while 9 per cent are considering forming a local or foreign strategic alliance. Some 52 per cent are not linked to any local or overseas alliance. From an analysis of the strategic alliance group, it becomes clear that more than 50 per cent of these alliances are with South African companies. More than 40 per cent of these alliances are with overseas companies, while 73 per cent of the strategic alliance group are involved with local and overseas alliances.

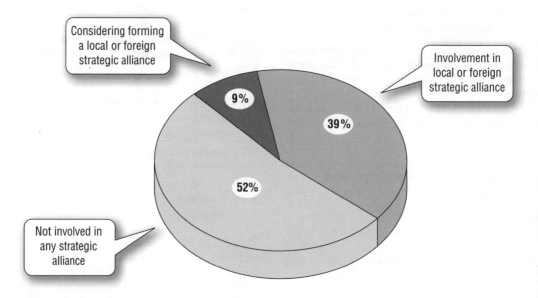

Figure 17.3 Strategic alliances by South African companies

Table 17.1 Strategic alliances by South African companies based on turnover and number of employees

Strategic alliance group	Percentage
Turnover of less than R2 million	18,6
Turnover of less than R10 million	50,3
Turnover of more than R10 million	49,7
Less than 100 employees	65,4
Less than 600 employees	85,4
More than 1 000 employees	12,4

Table 17.1 illustrates the percentages of companies involved in strategic alliances, based on categories of turnover/employees.

Some 50,3 per cent of the companies have turnovers of less than R10 million. In the majority of cases, companies have less than 100 employees.

17.8.2 Strategic alliances profile of South African companies

Table 17.2 provides details concerning types of alliances being formed with local and overseas partners (details of companies involved in alliances or considering forming alliances were put together).

The choice of strategic alliances is influenced by a variety of factors, such as legal requirements, access to technology, fixed costs, experience, competition, risks, control aspects, product complexity, international expansion of the enterprise, and the degree of similarity between countries in respect of language and culture.

It is clear from Table 17.2 that South African businesses overwhelmingly choose marketing and/or distribution agreements when doing business with partners. Joint ventures and informal alliances are also popular, while they shrink from forming cross-licensing and equity alliances. Research and development partnerships are responsible for only 24 per cent of the alliances formed.

Most alliances are based on marketing and/or distribution agreements with local and overseas partners. More than 50 per cent of all alliance business with overseas partners is being done through marketing and/or distribu-

Table 17.2 Strategic alliance profile of South African companies

Types of alliances formed (South Africa and overseas)	Total	South African alliance	Overseas alliance
Joint ventures	36%	19%	25%
Marketing/distribution agreements	76%	41%	56%
Cooperative agreements	30%	16%	19%
Research and development agreements	24%	10%	17%
Informal alliances	34%	20%	19%
Cross-licensing	14%	4%	12%
Equity alliances	7%	4%	4%

tion agreements, followed by joint ventures, cooperative agreements and informal alliances. Businesses are also more open to becoming involved in research and development agreements with overseas partners than with local organisations. Alliances with local partners follow very much the same pattern with marketing and/or distribution agreements in first place, followed by informal alliances, joint ventures and cooperative agreements.

17.8.3 Factors to be considered when entering strategic alliances

Various factors must be considered when planning to form relationships or alliances with any business partner. The maintenance of these relationships also plays a decisive role in the success of the partnership. Japan's Toshiba Corporation is one of the world's most successful companies when it comes to forming and maintaining strategic relationships. Despite its own technological and manufacturing expertise, Toshiba knows that it cannot rely solely on itself in the global world of digital electronics. Toshiba is currently engaged in more than two dozen major partnerships and joint ventures, and has yet to experience an ugly falling out. Its success is attributed mainly to the following factors (Schlender 1993):

• Construction of alliances so that the roles and rights of each partner are clearly defined from the very beginning
• The active participation of senior management in each relationship

• Total openness about all Toshiba's different relationships
• Streamlining and accelerating every aspect of relationships
• Carefully chosen partners

Figure 17.4 gives an analysis of factors that South African managers regard as crucial when considering forming strategic alliances with local or overseas partners.

Checking the partner's credibility is seen as the most important factor when forming relationships, followed by analysing the benefits and advantages of the prospective partner. Retaining the management responsibility, focusing on the overall value added and the possibility of developing new products in the partnership are also seen as crucial when considering alliances. Discussing performance standards, checking the tax, financial and legal issues, holding periodic meetings to monitor progress, and avoiding complete dependency on the alliance partner are high on the agenda of companies considering alliances with local or overseas partners.

17.9 Conclusion

Successful businesses of the future will treat the entire world as their domain in terms of meeting their supply and demand requirements. In such a globalised market, the domestic firm will not be sustainably competitive. Globalisation is not a new concept, but relatively new factors have contributed to its recent promi-

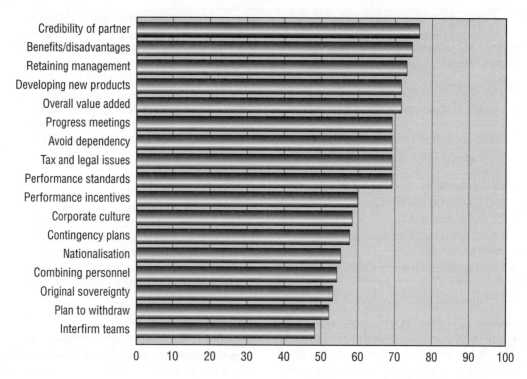

Figure 17.4 Factors to be considered when entering strategic alliances

nence, such as the opening up of new markets for (South African) businesses and new communication and transport technology, which have resulted in a major expansion of international trade and investment.

Small and medium enterprises in South Africa are uniquely positioned to take advantage of these favourable conditions and should exploit the many opportunities for entering new markets. However, they should be aware of the various entry strategies and the pros and cons of "going international".

Looking back

1. Explain the importance of international opportunities for doing business in South Africa.

   International opportunities are important for South African companies, for the following reasons:
   - To seek out new markets as a way of sustaining or increasing growth in sales and profits
   - To achieve lower development, research and marketing costs
   - To share resources
   - To access natural resource deposits in other countries
   - To do business in a more stable political environment
   - To learn new skills from competitors

2. Discuss the factors that have contributed significantly to the positive growth in international business for South African businesses.
   - Modern communication media have made it possible to exchange scientific, technical and commercial information rapidly and efficiently.
   - Rapid means of international travel and transport without corresponding price hikes have made it possible to control subsidiaries in different parts of the world and to visit suppliers in other countries.
   - Modern management techniques used by multinational enterprises have channelled new ideas, technology and production processes, and also resources and capital to other countries.
   - Private firms have shown that they can adapt to changing circumstances and still efficiently exploit overseas markets and function under foreign governments with their diverse political policies.
   - An understanding of the principle of economic expediency has enabled managers to develop foreign markets before their competitors could enter the field.
   - International trade has moved away from bilateralism in the direction of multilateralism. Various rounds of GATT negotiations

   resulted in the establishment of the WTO. These negotiations have helped to liberalise and expand world trade.
   - The downfall of the communist regimes has opened the door for South Africa to establish commercial ties with countries like Russia, Poland, Hungary and Romania.

3. Identify the various entry strategies into the international business arena.

   There is a whole range of strategies, including exporting, purchasing agreements, marketing/distribution agreements, shared research and development efforts, cross-licensing, franchising, cooperative agreements and other equity-based relationships.

4. Identify seven strategic issues to be considered when going "global".
   - Clarify the international business mission.
   - Challenge the assumptions about "closed" markets.
   - Host country contacts are critical for successful market assessment.
   - Fit the market entry strategies to the host country's needs and the firm's capabilities.
   - International business partners require a clear understanding of each other's goals.
   - Feasibility analyses must test "competitiveness" and "fairness".
   - Let local executives manage once the strategy is set.

5. Name the factors to be considered when entering into strategic alliances.
   - Check the potential partner's credibility.
   - Analyse the benefits and advantages of the prospective partner.
   - Retain the management responsibility.
   - Focus on the overall value added and the possibility of developing new products in the partnership.
   - Set performance standards.
   - Check the tax, financial and legal issues.
   - Avoid complete dependency on the alliance partner.

Key terms

Entry strategies
Exporting
Globalisation
Joint ventures
Licensing

Management contracts
Overseas investment and manufacturing
Strategic alliances
Turnkey projects

Discussion questions

1. What makes international business issues different from local business aspects?

2. Give a brief overview of the opportunities for, and problems facing, South African exporters.

3. Give a brief overview of strategic alliances in South Africa.

Case studies

Case study 1: Global gourmet coffees – growth in spite of expensive lessons

"If there had been something like site science, we would all have been millionaires." This insight comes from Seattle Coffee Co. MD Barry Parker after his firm lost R1 million because one shop opened in the wrong location. The firm's 16 other shops in South Africa are doing well. Seattle, which turned over roughly R16 million last year, grew by 22 per cent and plans similar growth for the next four years, which includes expanding the concept through the sale of franchises from 1 June 2002.

"Our big failure was the shop at the Johannesburg airport, a location no one would ever have thought wouldn't work. Part of the problem is that the airport is a hive of activity early in the morning but is so quiet between noon and 3 p.m. that you could run through there naked without anyone noticing. To benefit from busy periods, you need a large shop that will

inevitably stand empty for long periods. At a rental of R1 000/sq. m., this just cannot work," says Parker.

He and a school friend, Pete Howie, who decided to enter the business world together, opened the first Seattle shop in South Africa. "Pete went to London, where he worked at the Seattle Coffee Co. and eventually managed a shop. He liked the concept and persuaded me we should start it in South Africa."

The two friends and their fathers formed the firm Howie Parker Investments and, with about R420 000, started the first outlet in 1997 – in Exclusive Books, Cavendish Square, Claremont, a southern suburb of Cape Town.

Last year, they acquired the rights to run the firm in southern Africa and Mauritius for US$100 000 (then about R1 million). Five of the Seattle outlets are run by Star Mart, Caltex's convenience stores.

According to Parker, Seattle is a new concept in South Africa. "Our country has an established wine culture, but the same doesn't apply to coffee – though there are similarities between the two. Just as good wine depends on where the grapes grow, the place where the coffee beans are grown and the soil, for example, are important. But an increasing number of South Africans are gradually becoming coffee connoisseurs who appreciate gourmet coffee."

The idea of service station outlets is to get the market for coffee takeaways to grow. "People here have not yet developed the habit of taking coffee away in their cars; overseas this makes up 85 per cent of the industry," says Parker. Seattle's other outlets are in Exclusive Books stores because they provide a relaxing environment where people can sit and read.

A new development is Andersen's outsourcing of coffee for staff at its head office in Melrose Arch, north of Johannesburg's central business district. "This concept, where we run a shop that is subsidised by the employer, is a definite growth area," says Parker.

He is also a great believer in franchising. "We tested our business model thoroughly with the firm-owned stores over the past five years. We have already made the mistakes, such as the shop at the airport and the opening of a second outlet in Cavendish. The second shop went from bad to worse and the old one kept getting better. Franchisees will be able to benefit from these, and other, positive experiences." It costs between R300 000 and R650 000 to equip a Seattle shop. Unlike many starry-eyed entrepreneurs who think listing the firm is "the next big step", Parker plans to ensure Seattle remains a private firm.

"You see all too often how a dynamic firm loses its focus after listing. The concentration on results becomes so overpowering that, ironically, the share price often suffers. I think that is what happened at Starbucks. The American firm was initially focused, especially on its employees, but after listing lost some of its entrepreneurial oomph and became more of a corporate institution. Even though, according to its latest statements, the firm's sales are up by 25 per cent, the share price is under pressure."

Parker is not worried about greater health consciousness being bad for business. To cater for the trend, choices include full cream or low-fat milk and decaffeinated coffee (the so-called "harmless" coffee, known in the United States as "why bother?").

Source: Growth in spite of expensive lessons, Colleen Naudé, *Finance Week,* 23 April 2002.

Questions

1. Do you think that the Seattle Coffee Co. will be successful in South Africa? Motivate your answer.
2. What were the main reasons for the failure of the Seattle coffee shop at the Johannesburg International Airport?
3. Advise Barry Parker and Pete Howie in respect of "staying private" or listing on the stock exchange. What are the pros and cons of each option, especially for exposure to international investors?

Case study 2: Technology alliance between Denel and Zeiss Optronik

South Africa's high-technology sector received a boost with the R62 million agreement between Zeiss Optronik GmbH of Germany and Eloptro, the electro-optical division of Denel, to jointly build at least ten advanced submarine periscopes in Kempton Park. The periscopes, which cost millions of rands each, are destined for submarines under construction for the South African, Greek and South Korean navies. Zeiss Optronik is pursuing further contracts internationally, which would bring additional work to Eloptro.

What is interesting is that South Africa's defence industry is taking another step into the top end of international defence development and manufacture. This also means the industry will gain access to new technologies and markets, and the South African National Defence Force will benefit from more focused research, development and the industry's strategic independence.

These developments are mainly an outcome of the defence packages. Before the process began, our defence industry was able to develop and produce interesting and effective equipment, even in demanding fields such as guided missiles. But there was always doubt as to whether it was not like other smaller industries that look good but whose equipment does not really work, or is not as advanced as it looks, or is a copy of something else.

That changed when some of the major European defence companies came to South Africa to investigate defence industrial participation demanded by the government under the packages. Many European executives and engineers were surprised by an industry that was as capable as it looked from outside, and that had breadth and depth of technology. It was an industry with which companies not only could work with on the South African projects, but could also draw into their own research, development, design and manufacturing programmes.

The outcome of that quick education has been a number of alliances between South African and European defence companies, including some such as EADS, which did not benefit greatly from the packages. Denel, this country's largest defence company, is the main beneficiary, with several divisions winning valuable export work. While these contracts are valuable, their real importance lies in South African equipment being incorporated into systems used by major armed forces. That brings business and access to new technologies, and cachet that will stand the industry well in other export and joint ventures.

The importance of the defence industrial participation contracts goes even further. The defence industry is a very effective incubator of engineers, scientists and technicians. The industry offers challenges, demands precision and rewards innovation, and many people who now run small and medium engineering and electronics firms in South Africa cut their teeth on defence projects.

The defence industrial participation project under the umbrella of the German Submarine Consortium (GSC), which is building three class U-209/1400 boats for the South African Navy "is the beginning of a long-term technology partnership between Eloptro and Zeiss Optronik," said Zeiss Optronik Submarine Periscope Unit head Manfred Kriese. "We were very pleasantly surprised to find a partner able to be much more than just an extended workbench. We have found design and manufacturing skills we can link straight into our German operations," said Kriese.

The decision to integrate this crucial piece of equipment into the Greek and South Korean boats is "an international seal of approval for Eloptro and a powerful indication that the South African government's offset strategy is working," said Hans-Dieter Mühlenbeck, MD of Ferrostaal's defence division. "Without the industrial participation programme connected to the German Submarine Consortium, our subcon-

tractor Zeiss Optronik and Eloptro would not have developed this strategic relationship. Now they are developing an important strategic cooperation that already extends well beyond the South African Navy."

Ferrostaal is the member of the German Submarine Consortium responsible for the industrial participation agreements. Eloptro has, together with Zeiss Optronik, completed the design phase on the periscopes. Manufacture of the optical and mechanical components is proceeding on schedule for delivery in 2003 of the first set of the South African Navy's mast and ocular box, crucial components of the periscope. Zeiss Optronik will then integrate these components into the rest of the periscope for delivery to the shipyard where the submarines are being built. Eloptro and Zeiss Optronik have agreed to produce two of the very complex periscopes a year for five years. Eloptro has been active in the upgrading of periscopes since 1989, initially concentrating on the South African Navy's Daphne-class submarines. Its world-class capacity is now being further enhanced by the industrial participation programme linked to the South African government's order for three submarines.

Modern electro-optical periscopes are essential to a submarine's ability to observe and record for judicial purposes maritime breaches of a nation's economic security such as piracy, drug smuggling, and illegal trawling while themselves remaining undetected. Together with a submarine's electronic listening equipment, periscopes are also essential to its primary military capability.

The collaboration with Zeiss Optronik has positioned Eloptro's Maritime Engineering unit strategically for the future. "The partnership with Zeiss Optronik has given added impetus to Eloptro's periscope capabilities and we are operating at full capacity as a result of this work," said Eloptro general manager Knox Msebenzi. "In fact, we are considering expanding our facilities and staff numbers to enable us to take on more work through this alliance." According to Msebenzi, the company has gained substantially in terms of human resource development and capital investment from the partnership. "Nine of our employees – five engineers and four draughtsmen – have already received advanced training for the project, and our German partner also made a substantial investment in equipment," said Msebenzi.

Zeiss Optronik has not only brought work to South Africa, but has agreed to a skills and technology transfer programme worth several million rand. The value placed on the industrial participation is broken down into components reflecting work for the South African submarines, obligations to integrate South African-made defence equipment into other contracts, as well as technology transfer. Thus far, the German Submarine Consortium and its subcontractor Zeiss Optronik have met 97 per cent of their obligations directly connected to the South African periscopes due for fulfilment by 2005, by placing contracts with Eloptro worth R61,7 million at current exchange rates. Further technology transfer plans, which form part of the industrial participation programme and are part of the long-term strategic relationship between Zeiss Optronik and Eloptro, are expected to be signed within the next few months. They are to be completed by 2006 and are valued at almost R46 million.

Source: SA defence industry is aiming for the top, Helmoed Römer-Heitmann, *Business Day,* 22 April 2002; www.mbendi.co.za/18 April 2002

Questions

1. Define the joint venture between Zeiss Optronik and Denel's Eloptro in your own words.
2. Identify the main benefits of this alliance for South Africa and for Denel.
3. Indicate the factors that influence the working relationship between the companies.
4. Do you think this relationship will last very long? Why?

Experiential exercises

1. Interview the manager of any Seattle coffee Shop or Mugg & Bean in your area and determine the following:
   - The reason for their existence
   - The market share in their area
   - Main competitors in their area
   - Their views on the health aspect of coffee
2. Read the latest edition of *Business Report, Financial Mail, Finance Week* or *Business Day* and identify the South African and global (strategic) alliances that are quoted or described in these financial publications. In addition, describe the following:
   - Products, services or technologies that are involved
   - Industries that are suitable for alliance formation
   - The competitive advantages these alliances should bring to the individual alliance partners

Exploring the Web

You will find additional information on international business issues at the following websites:

- www.btimes.co.za
  www.dti.org.za
  www.economist.com
- www.globaledge.msu.edu
- www.worldtrademag.com

References and recommended reading

Bureau of Market Research. 2000. Unpublished research report. Pretoria: University of South Africa.

Daniels, J.D. & Radebaugh, L.H. 2000. *International business: environments and operations*, 9th ed. Reading, MA: Addison Wesley.

Gouws, A.R. & Bothma, C.H. 2000. *Export marketing handbook: export now.* Self-published.

Hennart, J.F. 1987. A transaction costs theory of equity joint ventures. *Strategic Management Journal,* 9.

Hill, C.W.L. 2003. *International business: competing in the global marketplace,* 4th ed. Washington: Irwin/McGraw-Hill.

Hisrich, R.D. & Peters, M.P. 2002. *Entrepreneurship,* 5th ed. New York: McGraw-Hill.

Hough, J. 1997. *Creating strategic alliances in the global village: the South African case.* Paper read at the Academy of International Business Conference, Monterrey, Mexico.

Hough, J., Neuland, E.W. & Bothma, N. 2003. *Global business: environments and strategies,* 2nd ed. Cape Town: Oxford University Press.

Kirconnell, P.A. 1988. Practical thinking about going international. *Business Quarterly,* Autumn edition.

Longenecker, J.G., Moore, C.W. & Petty, J.W. 2003. *Small business management,* 12th ed. Cincinnati: South-Western.

Lorange, P. & Roos, J. 1993. *Strategic alliances: formation, implementation and evolution.* London: Blackwell.

Phatak, A.V. 1992. *International dimensions of management,* 3rd ed. Boston: PWS-Kent.

Pilafidis, E.J. 1994. *Effective structuring and managing of interrelationships: case studies in domestic strategic alliances.* Unpublished doctoral dissertation. Claremont, USA: Claremont Graduate School.

Porter, M.E. 1998. *On competition.* Boston: Harvard Business School Press.

Schlender, B.R. 1993. How Toshiba makes alliances work. *Fortune International,* 4 October.

Spekman, R.E. & Sawhney, K. 1990. *Toward a conceptual understanding of the antecedents of strategic alliances.* Working Paper. Cambridge, MA: Marketing Science Institute.

Wray, Q. 2002. Public opinion poll reveals mixed messages on globalisation. *World Economic Forum research.* Available at www.WEForum.gov. Accessed 2 February 2002.

18

E-commerce opportunities

Jacques Nel

"It is either e-business or no business!"

– Advertising slogan of an e-commerce solutions provider

Learning outcomes

After completion of this chapter, you should be able to:

- ◗ Understand the benefits of e-commerce for a small business
- ◗ Identify the size of an e-commerce opportunity by analysing the Internet community in South Africa
- ◗ Explain the link between product characteristics and the possibility of selling a product over the Internet
- ◗ Explain the most common business models on the Internet
- ◗ Explain which elements could be included in a website
- ◗ Formulate an online promotional strategy for a business

18.1 Introduction

The dawn of the "new economy" not only opened new opportunities for major companies in South Africa, but also for potential or existing entrepreneurs. The Internet provides many new opportunities for entrepreneurs, such as a cost-effective channel for marketing products and services to potential clients in new markets. South African entrepreneurs can now (with marginal additional costs) market their products and services to untapped markets in Europe, the United States and other countries. For the potential entrepreneur the opportunity also exists to start a profitable business online, eliminating high start-up costs and minimising other costs associated with launching a new venture.

Starting a profitable business on the Internet is not only for adults. Anyone that has an entrepreneurial spirit can do it. Edward Odendal, a Grade 8 student from Welgemoed, established his own Harry Potter website (www.harrypotternews.cjb.net) and made hundreds of US dollars through an affiliate programme with Amazon.com. His website sells Harry Potter books, videos and DVDs through the Internet. For each item that is sold through his website, Amazon.com pays him commission.

The above is a good example of a new economy business opportunity. The business was started with a minimum of resources and only exists online. Many such and other opportunities exist online for entrepreneurs. In order to assist potential and existing entrepreneurs in capitalising on online opportunities, this chapter aims at demystifying e-commerce. We will start this process by discussing the history of the Internet in the next section. This chapter will also deal with important related topics for the entrepreneur, such as the Internet market in South Africa, business models, and designing a website.

18.2 The history of the Internet

The most basic definition of the Internet is that it is a network of computers. The computers in a single network are each attached to a server, which is a large computer that manages the communication for a network. These servers are connected with each other and communication is accomplished between them by fibre-optic cables, satellite transmissions, phone lines, microwave, and Ethernet lines. The history of the Internet dates back to 1957 and the following time line depicts its growth:

- *1957:* The USSR launches Sputnik, the first artificial earth satellite. In response, the United States forms the Advanced Research Projects Agency (ARPA) within the Department of Defence to establish America's lead in science and technology applicable to the military.

- *1962:* Paul Baran, of the RAND Corporation (a government agency), was commissioned by the United States Air Force to do a study on how the Air Force could maintain its command and control over its missiles and bombers after a nuclear attack. This was to be a military research network that could survive a nuclear strike, decentralised so that if any locations in America were attacked, the military could still have control of nuclear arms for a counter-attack. Baran's finished document described several ways to accomplish this. His final proposal was a packet-switched network. "Packet switching is the breaking down of data into datagrams or packets that are labelled to indicate the origin and the destination of the information and the forwarding of these packets from one computer to another computer until the information arrives at its final destination computer. This was crucial to the realization of a computer network. If packets are lost at any given point, the message can be resent by the originator."

- *1968:* ARPA awarded the ARPANET contract to BBN. BBN had selected a Honeywell minicomputer as the base on which it would build the switch. The physical network was constructed in 1969, linking four nodes: the University of California at Los Angeles, SRI (in Stanford), the University of California at Santa Barbara, and the University of Utah.

The network was wired together via 50 Kbps circuits.

- *1972:* The first email program was created by Ray Tomlinson of BBN. ARPA was renamed the Defence Advanced Research Projects Agency (or DARPA). ARPANET was currently using the network control protocol (NCP) to transfer data. This allowed communications between hosts running on the same network.

- *1973:* Development began on the protocol later to be called Transmission Control Protocol/Internet Protocol (TCP/IP). It was developed by a group headed by Vinton Cerf from Stanford and Bob Kahn from DARPA. This new protocol was to allow diverse computer networks to interconnect and communicate with each other.

- *1974:* The first use of the term Internet by Vinton Cerf and Bob Kahn in a paper on transmission control protocol.

- *1976:* Dr Robert M. Metcalfe developed the Ethernet, which allowed coaxial cable to move data extremely fast. This was a crucial component in the development of local-area networks. The packet satellite project went into practical use. SATNET, the Atlantic packet satellite network, was born and linked the United States with Europe. Surprisingly, it used INTELSAT satellites that were owned by a consortium of countries and not exclusively the United States government. Unix-to-Unix CoPy (UUCP) was developed at AT&T Bell Labs and distributed with UNIX one year later. The Department of Defence began to experiment with the TCP/IP protocol and soon decided to require it for use on ARPANET.

- *1979:* USENET (the decentralised news group network) was created by Steve Bellovin, a graduate student at the University of North Carolina, and programmers Tom Truscott and Jim Ellis. It was based on UUCP. The creation of BITNET ("Because it's Time Network") by IBM introduced the "store and forward" network. It was used for email and listservs.

- *1981:* The National Science Foundation created the backbone called CSNET 56 Kbps network for institutions without access to

© Van Schaik Publishers

ARPANET. Vinton Cerf proposed a plan for an inter-network connection between CSNET and ARPANET.

- *1983:* The Internet Activities Board (IAB) was created in 1983. On 1 January, every machine connected to ARPANET had to use TCP/IP. TCP/IP became the core Internet protocol and replaced NCP entirely. The University of Wisconsin created the Domain Name System (DNS). This allowed packets to be directed to a domain name, which would be translated by the server database into the corresponding IP number. This made it much easier for people to access other servers, because they no longer had to remember numbers.

- *1984:* ARPANET was divided into two networks: MILNET and ARPANET. MILNET was to serve the needs of the military and ARPANET to support the advanced research component. The Department of Defence continued to support both networks. The upgrade to CSNET was contracted to MCI. New circuits would be T1 lines, 1,5 Mbps, which are 25 times faster than the old 56 Kbps lines. IBM would provide advanced routers and Merit would manage the network. The new network was to be called NSFNET (National Science Foundation Network), and the old lines were to remain CSNET.

- *1985:* The National Science Foundation began deploying its new T1 lines, which would be finished by 1988.

- *1986:* The Internet Engineering Task Force (IETF) was created to serve as a forum for technical coordination by contractors for DARPA working on ARPANET, US Defence Data Network (DDN), and the Internet core gateway system.

- *1987:* BITNET and CSNET merged to form the Corporation for Research and Educational Networking (CREN), another work of the National Science Foundation.

- *1988:* Soon after the completion of the T1 NSFNET backbone, traffic increased so quickly that plans immediately began for upgrading the network again.

- *1990:* Merit, IBM and MCI formed a not-for-profit corporation called ANS (Advanced Network and Services), which was to conduct research into high-speed networking. It soon came up with the concept of the T3, a 45 Mbps line. The National Science Foundation quickly adopted the new network and at the end of 1991 connected all of its sites by this new backbone. While the T3 lines were being constructed, the Department of Defence disbanded ARPANET and it was replaced by the NSFNET backbone. The original 50 Kbps lines of ARPANET were taken out of service. Tim Berners-Lee and CERN in Geneva implemented a hypertext system to provide efficient information access to the members of the international high-energy physics community.

- *1991:* CSNET (which consisted of 56 Kbps lines) was discontinued, having fulfilled its important early role in the provision of an academic networking service. A key feature of CREN is that its operational costs are fully met through dues paid by its member organisations. The National Science Foundation established a new network, named NREN (the National Research and Education Network). The purpose of this network was to conduct high-speed networking research. It was not to be used as a commercial network, nor was it to be used to send much of the data that the Internet now transfers.

- *1992:* The Internet Society was chartered. The World Wide Web (WWW) was released by CERN.

- *1993:* InterNIC was created by the National Science Foundation to provide specific Internet services: directory and database services (by AT&T), registration services (by Network Solutions Inc.) and information services (by General Atomics/CERFnet). Marc Andreessen, NCSA and the University of Illinois develop a graphical user interface to the WWW, called "Mosaic for X".

- *1994:* No major changes were made to the physical network. The most significant thing that happened was the growth. Many new networks were added to the NSF backbone. Hundreds of thousands of new hosts were added to the Internet during this time period. Pizza Hut offered pizza ordering on its web page. First Virtual, the first cyberbank, opened ATM.

- *1995:* The National Science Foundation announced that as of 30 April 1995 it would no longer allow direct access to the NSF backbone. It contracted with four companies that would be providers of access to the NSF backbone (Merit). These companies would then sell connections to groups, organisations and companies. An annual fee of US$50 is imposed on domains, excluding .edu and .gov domains, which are still funded by the National Science Foundation.

- *1996 to date:* Most Internet traffic is carried by backbones of independent Internet service providers, including MCI, AT&T, Sprint, UUnet, BBN planet, ANS, and more. Currently the Internet Society, the group that controls the Internet, is trying to figure out a new TCP/IP to be able to have billions of addresses, rather than the limited system of today. The problem that has arisen is that it is not known how both the old and the new addressing systems will be able to work at the same time during a transition period.

18.3 Benefits of e-commerce for a business

E-commerce has benefits not only for businesses, but also for consumers and society. The main benefits for businesses are as follows:

- The electronic marketplace expands the local marketplace to national and international markets. With a minimal capital outlay, a company can easily and quickly locate more customers, the best suppliers, and the most suitable business partners worldwide.

- Electronic commerce decreases the cost of creating, processing, distributing, and retrieving paper-based information.

- Supply chain inefficiencies, such as excessive inventories and delivery delays, can be minimised by e-commerce.

- The pull-type processing allows for inexpensive customisation of products and services, and provides a competitive advantage for companies that implement these strategies. An example of a South African company that uses this is Incredible Connection. Potential clients can "build" their own computer online before ordering it.

- E-commerce reduces the time between the outlay of capital and the receipt of products and services. Starting an online business can sometimes be much faster than off-line. For instance, you do not have to build offices or search for premises. You only have to design the website, host it on a server of an Internet service provider, and you can be in business.

- E-commerce supports business process re-engineering. By changing processes, the productivity of people, knowledge workers and administrators can increase by 100 per cent.

- E-commerce lowers the cost of telecommunications. It is definitely cheaper to email to a person in Europe than phoning or even sending a fax.

Other benefits of e-commerce may include an improved corporate image, improved customer service, new business partners, simplified processes, compressed time to the market, increased productivity, reduced paper and paperwork, increased access to information, reduced transportation costs, and increased flexibility.

18.4 The Internet market in South Africa

Any business aims at satisfying the unmet needs or wants of its customers, whether these customers are businesses or consumers. For the entrepreneur who wishes to meet these needs or wants online, the "Internet connectivity" of the potential market is a critical factor to consider. What's more, the identified target market(s) on the Internet must be significant enough to be profitable, as well as increasing in size.

Awareness of the "fit" between the potential target market(s) of a business and the online community is one of the fundamental success factors to online marketing. Hence, it is of value for the South African entrepreneur who wants to use the Internet for marketing products and/or services to other South Africans, to firstly ascertain this "fit". One possible way of doing this is to analyse the demographic information of the South African Internet community.

A number of websites report statistics on the South African Internet community. *The e-business handbook for South Africa* (2001) reports that various sources, measuring different time periods, estimate the number of people with Web access via work or home in South Africa at between 1,2 and 3 million. Therefore, a number of 2 million might be considered a useful average to work from.

The South African Internet User Survey conducted by South Africa Online in 1998 revealed the following regarding the South African user profile:

- The average age of respondents was 35. The age distribution of the respondents is illustrated in Figure 18.1.
- The South African Web user is highly educated, with an average level of one year of post-matriculation education, and the educational level is rising.
- Some 43 per cent of the Web users have already made a purchase online in the past. According to the survey, the future looks even better. Altogether 89 per cent of the users who participated in the survey indicated that they intend to use the Web for making purchases in the future.

- The average income is extremely high, at more than R11 000,00 per month. Some 56 per cent of the respondents were married or living together. A high proportion of the respondents owned their own homes.

The 1999 survey by South Africa Online showed the following emerging trends:

- Some 30 per cent of the respondents in the survey were female. This was an increase of 19 per cent from the previous year.
- The number of Afrikaans-speaking people also increased by 3 per cent to 27 per cent.

These statistics already paint a clearer picture of who the potential online clients are. Businesses whose customer profile overlaps with this "picture" could consider the Internet as a possible marketing vehicle. When planning to sell products or services over the Internet, the "fit" between the potential market(s) and the Internet community in South Africa is just one of the issues to consider. Another important issue that is worth discussing is product characteristics. Given the nature of the Internet, some products or services are better suited than others to be sold over the Internet.

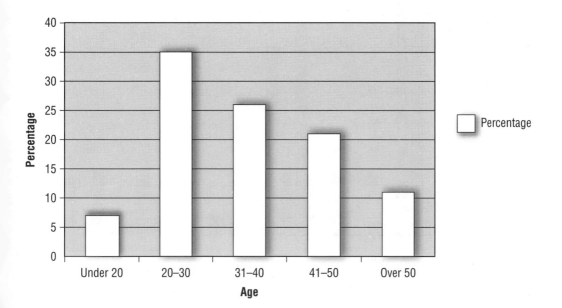

Figure 18.1 Age of respondents in the South African Internet User Survey, 1998

Source: Adapted from www.southafrica.co.za/survey_two/key_findings.html

18.5 Products that sell vs products that do not sell

The tenth WWW User Survey provides entrepreneurs with a better understanding of what products sell on the Internet and what products do not. The survey was conducted in 1998 and 5 000 Internet users from all over the world participated. The results of the survey on products bought by respondents online are illustrated in Figure 18.2.

The survey revealed that the respondents predominantly bought hardware, software, books and music. Tom Vassos, the author of *Strategic Internet marketing* (1996), listed criteria that could predict the potential of a product to sell on the Internet. Studying these criteria will aid one's understanding of the results of the survey. The following criteria put forward by Vassos (1996) should be taken note of:

- Is the product or service computer related? If yes, the likelihood is better. One of the reasons for this is that sufficient information can

be provided through the Internet to make the purchase decision. Furthermore, software cannot only be sold over the Internet, but the delivery can also take place through the Internet. Internet users can also download demo versions of software for trial purposes. If they like it, then they can buy it through the Internet. This explains why software sells well, as indicated by the survey.

- Does the offering need to be physically seen, "tried on" and/or touched before a purchase decision is made? If so, the possibility of successfully selling this product over the Internet is low. This criterion identified by Vassos is well illustrated by the Graphic, Visualization and Usability Center (GVU) survey, which indicates that very few respondents have bought apparel or jewellery online. These are items that typically need to be "tried on" and/or handled.

- Is the offering simple or complex to understand, configure and order – and can this

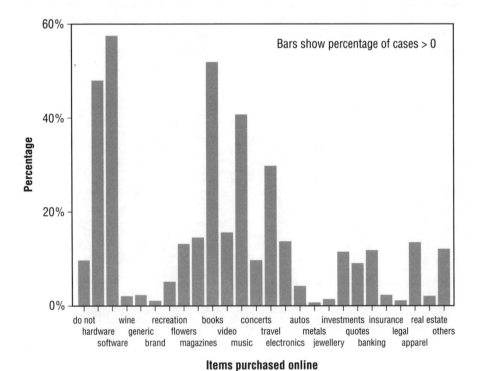

Items purchased online

Figure 18.2 Items purchased online

Source: GVU's tenth WWW User Survey, October 1998. Printed with permission of Georgia Tech Research Corporation, copyright 1996–1999, Atlanta GA 30332.

process be automated? If the process of configuring and ordering the offer can be simplified and automated, then it may be possible to sell this offering on the Internet. Complex goods that need an expert to configure them have little chance of achieving sales on the Internet.

- What is the nature of the offering? Is it a physical product, physical service, virtual service or intellectual property? The general guideline is that the more the product can be digitised, the greater is the possibility that it can be sold over the Internet. This also explains why music, software and travel bookings are some of the items that are regularly bought online.

- High-tech offerings are more likely to sell online than low-tech offerings. The reason for this is that Internet users are technology innovators or early adopters. In the future, when the late adopters also start using the Internet, the likelihood of selling low-tech offerings online will increase.

- Currently, commodity offerings (i.e. offerings that can be standardised) are more likely to achieve sales on the Internet because the purchasers know exactly what to expect if they decide to make a purchase.

- Is it an offering with global reference or appeal? The Internet is a global medium. Products and services with a global relevance and appeal are more likely to succeed than offerings limited to specific countries or regions.

- Are competitive offerings readily available from traditional channel members (such as retailers) locally? An Internet offering competing in an environment with well-established retailers may have difficulty succeeding.

- Is the distribution channel of the company limited to a local or national market? The less the company is able to offer the product globally, the less it will be able to capitalise on the advantages of the Internet.

- Very expensive and inexpensive items may have difficulty in achieving success with Internet sales. High-priced items may not sell easily on the Internet because buyers are more likely to want to talk to the sales repre-

sentatives personally, or to test-drive the car, for example. Inexpensive products may also be difficult to sell on the Internet. For example, selling a product for less than R30,00 could be difficult, because the transportation costs to deliver such a product could be R50,00 or more.

Entrepreneurs can use these criteria, combined with an analysis of the Internet community, to determine whether an opportunity exists and what its potential is. Also, conventional principles that were used in the "old economy" to screen an opportunity still apply. For example, the entrepreneur still has to establish which other businesses offer the same products or services online, and what will differentiate his or her business from theirs. Once the entrepreneur has established that an opportunity does exist, and that he or she can compete in the market, one of the next steps is to develop an e-commerce business model to bring the opportunity to life. In the following section, the main generic business models will be discussed.

18.6 E-commerce business models

A business model can be defined as a method of doing business by which a company can generate revenue to sustain itself. The model spells out how the company is positioned in the value chain (Turban et al. 2002: 6). There are many types of business models that the entrepreneur can choose from. In this section, the most common and visible business models will be discussed and examples provided.

18.6.1 Business-to-consumer (B2C)

Most electronic retailers, also known as e-tailers, use this business model, where the product or service is sold to the end customer through a website. Kalahari.net (www.kalahari.net) is an example of a South African e-tailer. The home page of another e-tailer, Amazon.com®, is shown in Figure 18.1.

The B2C business model is not only used by pure-play business (i.e. businesses that only exist on the Internet). Manufacturers that sell directly to the end consumer can also use this model. This is termed direct marketing. As a result, disintermediation takes place – intermediaries are eliminated from the value chain.

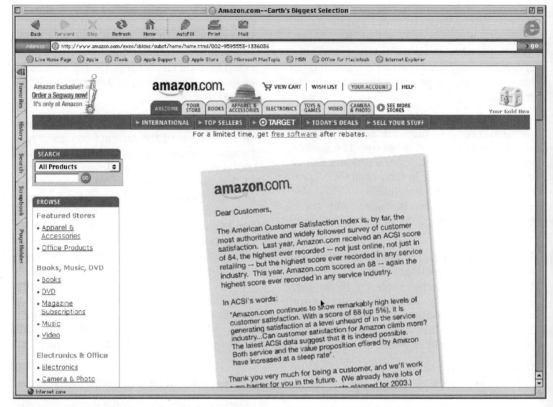

Figure 18.3 The home page of Amazon.com

Amazon.com is the registered trademark of Amazon.com, Inc.

Also, traditional retailers can establish websites and sell their products and services to customers through the Internet. These traditional retailers are called "click-and-mortar" retailers.

Another way to classify B2C business models is to categorise them by the way revenues are generated, e.g. subscription models, transaction fee models, advertising-supported models or various sponsorship models:

- *Subscription models:* Charge a monthly or annual subscription fee for the service.
- *Transaction fee models:* Charge a service fee based on the level of transactions offered.
- *Advertising-supported models:* Instead of charging to users, charge to advertising companies.
- *Sponsorship models:* The companies who can benefit or who are willing to donate beyond financial reasons, may sponsor the business. This model is usually a supplementary source of income.

Depending on the business situation, each of these business models operates on a set of success factors. While developing the business model, the e-tailer also needs to consider the role of the customer's decision-making process. The means whereby the site deals with the customer's decision-making process is possibly one of the criteria that greatly affects the success of the B2C site. This process is depicted in Figure 18.4.

The ideal is that the B2C business model moves the customer through the different phases of the decision-making process. We now look at each of the phases in the process and how the business model could facilitate the step:

- *Phase 1 – Need recognition:* Consider the example of a business selling flowers over the Internet. The customer's need for flowers may be due to an upcoming birthday of a friend or family member, or an anniversary. A

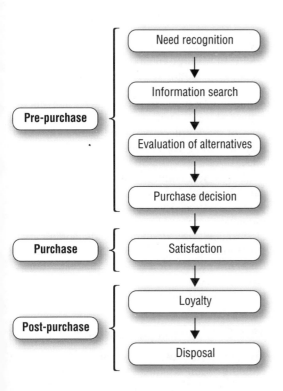

Figure 18.4 The customer's decision-making process

typical business model for such an online business would include a database where a person can enter important dates and receive reminders a week or two before the birthday or anniversary. These reminders could then include floral suggestions that could be bought through the site. This will attract the visitor to the site.

- *Phase 2 – Information search:* After a customer recognises the need for a specific product or service, he or she will begin to search and collect information on the different available alternatives. On the website the customer must be able to find the information needed to make a purchase decision. In the case of the online flower shop, information could include pictures of the different bouquets available for birthdays, their price and availability or delivery time. Other interactive functions, such a virtual adviser, could also provide valuable information to the customer.

- *Phase 3 – Evaluation of alternatives:* In the next step, the customer will evaluate the alternatives for specific criteria that are important to him or her. Some Internet sites provide customers with site features that enable them to compare items on specific criteria.

- *Phase 4 – Purchase decision:* Once the customer has reviewed all the different alternatives, the purchase decision can be made. With the online flower shop, the customer must be able to select the bouquet of flowers, enter a secure connection and provide credit card details, enter a delivery address and a date/time for delivery, and be able to add a personal note to the flowers. All these are elements that could be included on the website.

- *Phase 5 – Satisfaction:* Creating satisfaction after the sales can include generic strategies such as order tracking or customer service function. It would also include correct billing.

- *Phase 6 – Loyalty:* Developing customer loyalty is an important feature to consider in any e-commerce business model. In the beginning of the e-commerce revolution, it was adequate for a business to only attract customers to the website. Online competition was scarce and alternatives were limited. In the past few years, however, the number of online shops has increased exponentially and customer retention has become vital. The emphasis has shifted towards creating customer loyalty through the website. To do this, businesses develop loyalty programme(s) or even tiered loyalty programmes. In the case of the flower shop, the customer could collect points when purchasing flowers through the online shop. The customer could then use these points to get discounts at other sites.

- *Phase 7 – Disposal:* Some sites provide the consumer with an opportunity to resell an item. A good example in this regard is the Amazon.com site. On the site customers can resell used books to other customers.

One of the major limitations of B2C e-commerce is the problem of security. The tenth GVU User Survey (1998) revealed that almost 25 per cent of the respondents had their credit card information stolen. To overcome the paranoia of providing credit card information on the Internet, site owners can place cues to increase customer confidence. These cues could include slogans like "secure online shopping", or even "your credit card info is safe". The site could also provide alternative methods for paying for goods purchased on the site.

18.6.2 Business-to-business (B2B)

In contrast to the B2C e-commerce model, the B2B sales or service is between two businesses. Turban et al. (2002: 217) define B2B e-commerce as a transaction conducted electronically between businesses over the Internet, Extranets, Intranets, or private networks. Such transactions may be conducted between the business and its supply chain members, as well as between a business and any other business. Furthermore, B2B commerce can be conducted directly between a buyer and seller or via an online intermediary. The intermediary can be an organisation, a person or an electronic system. The common B2B activities are usually conducted along the supply chain of a manufacturing or assembling company. There are a number of B2B models that could be used by entrepreneurs. Each of these business models is briefly discussed below.

The most common model used by entrepreneurs is the company-centric business model. This model has two variations, the first being where one company uses the Internet to sell products and services to other companies. These sites operate on the same principles as the B2C model discussed earlier. The only difference is that the customer is another business. The other variation is where one company uses the Internet site for procurement activities. Managing procurement through the Internet could provide a company with a number of benefits, such as increasing the productivity of the procurement department, streamlining the purchasing process, making it simple and fast, improving the payment process or lowering purchase prices through product standardisation and consolidation of buys.

In contrast to the company-centric business model, which is either one-to-many or many-to-one, another B2B business model is a many-to-many marketplace. This business model connects many buyers with many sellers for the purpose of trading electronically with each other. These are usually the typical intermediary sites. These many-to-many marketplaces could focus on an industry (e.g. brokering steel), or it could focus on products and services that are required by many industries. An example of a many-to-many marketplace is the selling of paper stationery. The revenue for this type of marketplace could be transaction fees, membership fees, service fees or advertising fees.

B2B models could also be classified as vertical or horizontal marketplaces. Vertical marketplaces are those that deal with one industry or industry segment. Examples of these include electronics, cars, steel, chemicals, and so forth. Horizontal marketplaces are those that concentrate on a service or a product that is used in all types of industries. Examples are office supplies, PCs or travel services.

18.6.3 Consumer-to-consumer (C2C)

According to Lawrence et al. (2000: 44), the online auction business has become the most lucrative commerce strategy on the Web. What is more, the online auction business has been the biggest growth sector by far in the already booming American e-commerce industry. Online auctions are mainly categorised as C2C e-commerce, but a number of sites also facilitate auctions between businesses. The best-known auction site on the Internet is eBay (www.ebay.com). In addition to providing the platform to facilitate the bidding and buying process between customers, businesses can also participate in auctions on the site.

A number of auction models exist on the Internet. The most common are the English auction, the Dutch auction, the first-price sealed-bid auction and the reverse first-price sealed-bid auction (Mohammed et al. 2002: 333-338).

■ English auction

English auctions are open auctions in which buyers successively raise their bids until only one buyer remains. The term "open auction" means that all the bidders know the amount of the highest bid all the time. In many instances, the product seller can maintain a reserve price – if the bid does not equal or exceed the reserve price, the item is not sold. Depending on the auction structure, the reserve bid is either known or unknown.

Many auction sites – B2B sites, in particular – use reverse-price auctions to help firms save on supply costs. On these sites, firms often submit a request for proposals (RFPs) or a request for quotations (RFQs) to initiate the supply auctions. The auction winner is the firm that provides the lowest bid to supply the requested goods or service.

▪ Dutch auction

In this type of auction, sellers list several items so that bidders may bid for the entire lot or choose any quantity (Lawrence 2000: 44). At eBay, a Dutch auction refers to a special auction format in which sellers sell multiple identical items. The seller specifies the minimum price (the starting bid) and the number of items available. Buyers bid at or above the minimum price for the quantity they are interested in purchasing. At the close of the auction, the highest bidders purchase the items at the price offered by the lowest winning bidder.

▪ First-price sealed-bid auction

This is a very straightforward type of auction. Sellers offer an item for buyers to evaluate and consider bidding on. Before a specific time, potential buyers have the option to submit one sealed bid for the product. One of the implications of this auction is that since the bidding is sealed, buyers do not know the bid amount of competing bidders. After the bidding deadline, the product is sold to the highest bidder.

▪ Reverse first-price sealed-bid auction

In a similar fashion, firms can use reverse first-price sealed-bid auctions to purchase goods. As in the case of the auction type discussed above, the bids are sealed. The auction also operates on the same principles as the reverse auction.

One of the major problems to be overcome in C2C auctions is the trust factor. How do the buyers know that the product shown in the photo will be exactly what they get? EBay has found an interesting solution to this problem: buyers on eBay can rate suppliers on past purchases. EBay has introduced the eBay ID card (Figure 18.5) that provides past information on the seller. Interested bidders can also read through comments posted on the website by other bidders.

18.7 The design of a website

The website plays a major role in the success of an online venture. Although this may seem an easy task, anyone surfing the Web has came across some dreadfully designed websites. The following is a list of items that could be included in a website. The entrepreneur should review this list and decide which elements will be incorporated in his or her site. More importantly, the entrepreneur should also consider how these elements will be used in the website. Most of these elements are mandatory and must be present. Optional elements have been labelled as such.

- *Home page:* This is the first screen that visitors will encounter when they visit the site. The home page should contain links to the other main sections of the site. The entrepreneur also has to consider how much information will be displayed on the home page. Some site owners prefer an "uncluttered" approach, while others prefer having a great deal of information displayed on this page.

- *Additional pages:* These additional screens contain all the information that the entrepreneur wants to display on the website. Any additional page may contain any or all of the remaining elements discussed hereafter.

- *Banner with title:* In this section on the home page, the name of the company appears, usually with a graphic design as a background and the name of the website superimposed on the graphic. The use of graphic images should be done with care. Although these images make the site more attractive, large images can lead to slow downloading times.

- *Subtitle:* This element is often used to further define the purpose and content of the website. The use of a subtitle is optional and, if included, is normally found only on the home page.

- *Main and submenus:* These elements are used to inform visitors about the content of the website. They are also used as a means of navigation through various additional pages

ebaY ID card **Pleaseratemegood** ☆ **power** *seller* **me**

Member since: Monday, July 01, 1998
Location: United States

Summary of most recent comments

	Past 7 days	Past month	Past 6 months
Positive	5	31	215
Neutral	0	0	1
Negative	0	0	3
Total	5	31	219
Bid retractions	0	0	0

Figure 18.5 An eBay ID card of a seller

that comprise the website. The main menus and submenus assist in organising the website into a convenient and meaningful hierarchical system.

- *Customer service:* This element includes titles, such as Service, About us, Who we are, etc. It should be displayed prominently on the home page, and when selected, a new additional page should come up containing the information.
- *Help:* This element takes the visitor to a different additional page, where information is displayed explaining how to complete the task that the visitor encountered on the screen containing the Help element.
- *Hypertext links:* Hypertext links are words and graphics that are linked to related information located somewhere else on the website. When this element is selected, visitors are immediately taken to another page on the website where the related information may be viewed. Information could also be located on another site, which can be linked to this website.

- *Text on screen:* This element is to display printed information on the screen.
- *Graphics:* These elements provide a colourful look or design to the site and additional pages to improve the overall appearance. From a marketing perspective, graphics provide additional information that assists the customer in the decision-making process.
- *Searchable database:* A searchable database is a special computer software program that can store an unlimited amount of information about a particular subject, and which can then be queried by users in search of information.
- *Downloadable files:* On the website, files can be made available for visitors to download at their discretion. These files could be screen savers, photos, sound clips, text information or even video clips.
- *Fill-in-the-blank form:* This element is included to collect information needed to process a customer's purchase. The order form may collect information such as the customer's name, mailing address, phone

number, fax number, email address, credit card preference, credit card number, credit card expiry date, quantity and name of products and/or services wanted, preferred method of shipping, date of order, and other information.

18.8 Promoting a website

The objectives of promoting a website are to attract potential clients to the site or to retain the attention of existing customers. Website promotion is a critical factor for success, since the Internet is a pull medium and not a push medium. When doing searches with search engines, one becomes aware of the huge number of businesses on the Internet that deliver similar services. This fact further emphasises the importance for entrepreneurs to plan creative promotion campaigns to create awareness and remind customers of the site, and the products or services offered on the site.

A promotion campaign should follow a combination of online and off-line promotional strategies. Since this chapter focuses on the use of the Internet in business, the remainder of the discussion will be on general online promotional strategies. Entrepreneurs can use the following online tools to either attract or retain customers:

- *Banner ads:* This is probably the most common form of advertising on the Internet. Banner ads are the flashing boxes situated at the top of a screen or down the side. Most banners are hyperlinked to a site where the Internet user can find more on the information presented in the banner. Banners are purchased in cost-per-thousand (CPM) impressions. An impression is defined as an exposure to the banner advertisement. The negative side to this model of buying banners is that an impression does not necessarily lead to the client clicking on the banner and visiting the site.

- *Search engine:* Another approach that can be used by entrepreneurs is to register with a search engine. The only problem with this approach is how to get the site listed among the top hits.

- *Affiliate programmes:* In an affiliate programme, the partner site independently advertises the products of the other site. When the Internet user purchases a product through the partner site, commission is paid to the owners of the site.

- *Sponsorships:* Sites and emails can be sponsored by a business. This will create more awareness of the business.

- *Chat rooms/Internet communities:* Many businesses establish their own chat rooms or Internet communities on their sites. One of the characteristics of chat rooms or Internet communities is that the users who participate in these chat rooms have a common interest. This makes it easier for a business to target a specific group of people and therefore the advertising should be more effective. Entrepreneurs can use these chat rooms or Internet communities to inform users of their products. But, beware! Before doing this, first find out whether advertising is allowed. In some cases it is not, and you may receive a lot of spam if you break the rules.

- *E-mail:* Email is a cost-effective and fast way to communicate with customers and keep them returning to the site. Many sites ask customers if they want to receive emails regarding products or just general information that may be of interest. The information that is sent to the user must be valuable to them.

- *Viral marketing:* Whom do you trust most – someone you know or some one you do not know? Of course, someone you know. This is the principle on which viral marketing works. Some sites provide a function where customers can inform their friends and acquaintances about something on the website. This is the easiest way to facilitate viral marketing.

18.9 Conclusion

The Internet has created many new opportunities for entrepreneurs. In this chapter, some of the different uses of the Internet in business and Internet business models were discussed. Depending on the business opportunity, entrepreneurs can apply these models either to start a new business online or as an extension of a business already existing off-line. For entrepreneurs to capitalise on Internet opportunities, the basics of starting a new business still apply. Even in the "new economy" the entrepreneur must do market research, develop a business plan and negotiate with business partners.

The networked economy is a totally different economy to operate a business in. The environment changes faster than it does off-line and sometimes the entrepreneur must let go of "old economy" principles to be successful in the "new economy". Entrepreneurs need to prepare themselves for the new challenges brought about by the Internet. In this economy, is it sometimes the rabbit that wins the race and not the tortoise?

Looking back

1. List the benefits of e-commerce for a small business.
   - E-commerce can increase the market size of a business.
   - E-commerce can create cost savings for a business, such as saving on paper and telecommunications costs.
   - E-commerce can improve inefficient business processes.

2. Identify the size of an e-commerce opportunity by analysing the Internet community in South Africa.
   - The average age of Internet users appears to be 35 years.
   - More males than females are currently using the Internet.
   - The South African user is generally highly educated.

3. Explain the link between product characteristics and the possibility of selling a product over the Internet.
   - There must be a "fit" between the target market of the business and the Internet community.
   - Products that are computer related sell well over the Internet.
   - Products that do not have to be physically seen, "tried on" or touched also have potential to sell over the Internet.
   - Products that are standardised also sell well over the Internet.

4. Explain the most common business models on the Internet.
   - The B2C business model links sellers (manufacturers, wholesalers or retailers) directly with customers.

   - Revenue can be created in B2C models through advertising, transaction fees, membership fees and sponsorships.
   - B2B business models facilitate sales and/or service between businesses.
   - The company-centric business model is used to sell products and services to other businesses.
   - Many-to-many marketplaces connect many buyers with many sellers.
   - B2B models could also be classified as vertical or horizontal marketplaces.
   - Online auctions facilitate C2C e-commerce most.
   - English auctions are open auctions in which buyers successively raise their bids until only one buyer remains.
   - In Dutch auctions, sellers list several items so that bidders may bid for the entire lot or choose any quantity.
   - In a first-price sealed-bid auction, buyers place sealed bids and the highest bidder wins.

5. Explain which elements could be included on a website.
   - Every site starts with a home page.
   - Additional pages are linked to the home page and other pages by means of hyperlinks.
   - Entrepreneurs should also consider which downloadable files or searchable database could be included on the site.
   - Images must also be included on a website. This must be carefully planned, since large images can slow down the loading speed of the site. The site owner should

also consider the value of the image to the visitor.

6. Formulate an online promotional strategy for a business.
   - Businesses should consider a combination of online and off-line communication methods in developing a promotional strategy.

- Banner ads are a general tool used to advertise on the Internet.
- In an affiliate programme, a partner site independently advertises the products of the other site.
- Viral marketing uses personal references to market products or services.

Key terms

Affiliate programmes
Banner ads
Banners with title
Business process re-engineering
Business-to-business business model
Business-to-consumer business model
Clicks-and-mortar businesses
Company-centric business model
Customer's decision-making process
Customer-to-customer business model
Downloadable files
Dutch auction
English auction

E-tailer
First-price sealed-bid auction
Home page
Horizontal marketplace
Hypertext links
Main and submenus
Many-to-many marketplace
Pure-play businesses
Reverse first-price sealed-bid auction
Searchable database
Supply chain inefficiencies
Vertical marketplace
Viral marketing

Discussion questions

1. Did the Internet change the basic principles of starting a business?
2. Would movie tickets be a good product to sell over the Internet? Why?
3. In your opinion, what product or service is currently bought or used the most by South African Internet users?

4. Can any small business use the Internet to manage procurement? Defend your answer.
5. Rate the promotional tools discussed in the chapter in sequence of most effective to least effective in creating awareness of a site.

Case study

Case study

A knife maker in Cape Town is considering using the Internet to sell his knives to potential buyers over the world. The knives are handmade and are mostly bought by collectors in South Africa. Sometimes, these knives are also bought as gifts. The going price per knife is usually between R2 000,00 and R3 000,00.

Questions

1. What is the possibility of these speciality products being sold over the Internet?
2. Design a site on paper for the business. Provide as much detail as possible.
3. Develop an online promotional strategy, firstly to attract collectors to the site, and secondly, to retain the attention of these collectors.

Experiential exercises

1. Visit a website designer in your city or town. Ask the designer to show you the process he or she uses when designing a website and how it is put on the Internet.

2. Visit a local business owner who has a website (preferably selling over the Internet). Ask the owner how the business got online, what problems he experienced, what he would do differently if he could do it over again, and what advice he can give you.

Exploring the Web

1. Search on the Internet for other information on the profile of South African Internet users. Also, try to find more information on what is currently being bought online by South African Internet users.

2. Visit any business online that is listed in the MWeb online mall (www.mweb.co.za).

When visiting the site, do the following:

- Assess the design of the site. Does the outlay of the site address the customer's decision-making process? What would you change in the design?

- Try to identify the different website elements that were discussed in the chapter.

References and recommended reading

Bayne, K.M. 1997. *The Internet marketing plan.* London: John Wiley.

Emery, V. 1996. *How to grow your business on the Internet,* 2nd ed. Scottsdale: Coriolis Group Books.

Gonyea, J.C. & Gonyea, W.M. 2001. *Selling on the Internet.* New York: McGraw-Hill.

Graphic, Visualization and Usability Center's tenth WWW User Survey. Available at http://www.gvu.gatech.edu/user_surveys/survey-1998-10/.

Lawrence, E., Corbitt, B., Fisher, J., Lawrence, J. & Tidwell, A. 2000. *Internet commerce.* Brisbane: John Wiley.

Mohammed, R.A., Fisher, R.J., Jaworski, B.J. &

Cahill, A.M. 2002. *Internet marketing: building advantage in a networked economy.* New York: McGraw-Hill Higher Education.

Smith, P.R. & Chaffey, D. 2002. *eMarketing eXcellence.* Oxford: Butterworth Heinemann.

South Africa Internet User Survey. Available online at http://www.southafrica.co.za.

The E-Business Handbook. 2001. Trialogue.

Turban, E., King, D., Lee, J., Warkentin, M. & Chung, H.M. 2002. *Electronic commerce: a managerial perspective.* New Jersey: Pearson Education, Inc.

Vassos, T. 1996. *Strategic Internet marketing.* Indianapolis: QueCorp.

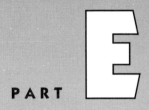

PART

Corporate venturing

19

Intrapreneurship

Miemie Struwig

19.1 Introduction

In Part D of this textbook, attention was paid to post-start-up challenges and, in particular, to the growth of the venture. Once the venture has grown into a large concern, it still needs to be competitive but entrepreneurship may not be found to the same extent as in the newly established business. There is now a shift, where entrepreneurs are sought inside the venture to ensure innovation and to stay globally competitive. This chapter will outline entrepreneurship as found inside the venture – also referred to as intrapreneurship, corporate entrepreneurship or corporate venturing.

19.2 Definition of intrapreneurship

In today's changing climate, large businesses should find ways of harnessing the drive, creativity, vision and ambition of entrepreneurship within their businesses. Pinchot (2000: viii) invented the concept "intrapreneurship" to describe the practice of entrepreneurship within the large business and refers to the intrapreneur, who practises intrapreneurship, as:

> ... Any of the dreamers who do. Those who take hands-on responsibility for creating innovation of any kind, within a business. The intrapreneur may be the creator or inventor but is always the dreamer who figures out how to turn an idea into a profitable reality.

Intrapreneurs are therefore people who put new ideas into action within established businesses. Although employed in a corporate position, intrapreneurs are nevertheless given the freedom and incentives to create and market their own ideas.

Hisrich (1990: 209) states that the intrapreneur is a corporate entrepreneur who takes new ideas and develops them into profitable businesses.

Although many authors discuss entrepreneurs inside the business, they do not refer to them as intrapreneurs, but rather prefer to call

Learning outcomes

After completion of this chapter, you should be able to:

- Define intrapreneurship
- Differentiate between entrepreneurs and intrapreneurs
- Explain how creativity and innovation are related
- List the characteristics of creative people
- List the characteristics of a creative climate in a business
- Distinguish between innovation, creativity and entrepreneurship
- Mention the actions that are necessary to create the ability to innovate in a business
- Outline the sources of innovation in a business
- Discuss the intrapreneurial process
- Identify the factors that hamper intrapreneurship
- Discuss the intrapreneurial way of leadership
- Briefly outline how to manage intrapreneurship in a business
- Discuss how intrapreneurship is implemented in the South African business

them corporate entrepreneurs. Both terms refer to a person executing the same activity of corporate entrepreneurship, intrapreneurship or corporate venturing.

19.3 Differences between entrepreneurs and intrapreneurs

To understand who the intrapreneur is, Pinchot (2000: 54) distinguishes between certain aspects of the entrepreneur and the intrapreneur. Hisrich (1990: 218) also makes this distinction to clarify intrapreneurship. Morris and Kuratko (2002: 63) distinguish between start-up entrepreneurs and corporate entrepreneurs (intrapreneurs). Table 19.1 outlines this distinction.

In many ways, intrapreneurs are just like entrepreneurs, but due to the nature of their activities they need some special characteristics. These characteristics include patience and compromise to deal with the existing structures in a business, the ability to solve problems within the existing system, the courage to disagree, and the ability to develop support for their ideas.

There are, of course, a few differences between intrapreneurship and entrepreneurship. For example, the intrapreneur acts within the confines of an existing business. The dictates of most businesses would be that the intrapreneur should ask for permission before attempting to create a desired future. In practice, however, the intrapreneur is more inclined to act first and then ask for forgiveness (if needed) than to ask for permission before acting.

The intrapreneur is also typically the intra-organisational revolutionary – challenging the status quo and fighting to change the system from within. This ordinarily creates a certain amount of organisational friction. A healthy dose of mutual respect is required to ensure that such friction can be positively channelled.

Intrapreneurship may seem to include the phenomenon that produces innovation in a business. It is, however, not a single phenomenon, but can take on a variety of different forms. Each of these forms further distinguishes the corporate setting from the start-up venture. There are seven different forms taken by intrapreneurship (Morris & Kuratko 2002: 69):

- *Traditional research and development:* Many businesses have a department staffed by people who work on improving existing products and developing new ones, making it easy for everyone else in the company to escape the responsibility for innovation.

- *Ad hoc venture team:* Management commits to an opportunity or responds to a threat. It puts together a team of employees and charges them to come up with a specific innovation. They are set up outside the corporate mainstream.

- *New venture divisions:* Here a permanent unit is established with the objectives of creating breakthrough innovation and entirely new markets. It is a kind of incubator where new ventures can be formulated and brought to life.

- *Champions and sponsors:* Employees recognise opportunities and develop innovative concepts, and then attempt to sell them to senior management. They become champions and they seek out higher-level sponsors.

- *Acquisitions:* Some businesses prefer to achieve entrepreneurial growth through acquisitions or purchasing other businesses. The key here is strategic fit – to make an acquisition that is related to the core competencies of the business.

- *Outsourcing:* Rather than acquiring another business, a growing number of businesses are buying some of the intellectual capital of other businesses and individuals.

- *Hybrid forms:* Within the six forms described above, there is considerable variance across firms. An example of a hybrid form is champions within the mainstream who are empowered to outsource some of the new product development work as they move a project through to completion.

Entrepreneurship can happen anytime and anywhere in a business. The managerial challenge is how to make it sustainable and how to maintain it on a sustainable basis.

19.4 Roles in intrapreneurship

Achieving constant entrepreneurship requires that the firm recognises the specific roles that must be performed for an entrepreneurial event to occur successfully. These key roles are the following:

Table 19.1 A distinction between start-up entrepreneurs and intrapreneurs

Start-up entrepreneur	Intrapreneur
Takes the risk	Business assumes the risks, other than career-related risk
"Owns" the concept and business	Business owns the concept, and typically the intellectual rights surrounding the concept
Owns all or much of the business	Intrapreneur may have no equity in the business, or a very small percentage
Potential rewards are theoretically unlimited	Clear limits are placed on the rewards
One misstep can mean failure	More room for errors; business can absorb failure
Vulnerable to outside influence	More insulated from outside influence
Independence (although the successful entrepreneur is usually backed by a strong team)	Interdependence of champion with many others; may also have to share credit with several people
Flexibility in changing course, experimenting, or trying new directions	Rules, procedures and bureaucracy hinder the intrapreneur's ability to manoeuvre
High speed of decision making	Longer approval cycles
Little security	Job security
No safety net	Dependable benefits package
Few people with whom to talk	Extensive network for bouncing around ideas
Limited scale and scope, at least initially	Potential for sizeable scale and scope is achieved fairly quickly
Severe resource limitations	Access to finances, research and development, production facilities for trial runs, an established sales force, an existing brand, existing distribution channels, existing databases and market research resources, and an established customer base

Source: Adapted from Pinchot (2000: 54-56).

- *Initiator:* Triggers the new entrepreneurial event – this role could be filled by a champion or someone else.
- *Sponsor/facilitator:* Pushes for acceptance and completion, and plays a major advising or mentoring role – must be a high-level person.
- *Champion/manager:* Takes the lead in directing the project and bringing it to the implementation phase.

- *Team supporter:* Augments the team by providing expertise.
- *Reactor:* Plays devil's advocate – serves to pinpoint weaknesses and possible ways in which the idea can be refined.

While all these roles need to be filled, the two most critical ones are those of the champion and the sponsor. There are, however, 15 more specific jobs that must be accomplished in order to bring an entrepreneurial concept to fruition:

- *Researcher/analyser:* Gathers intelligence, assesses potential and evaluates key factors in the market.
- *Interpreter/strategist:* Identifies patterns, trends and future development, and draws implications for project development.
- *Visionary/inventory:* Provides creativity, intuition and judgement in recognising opportunities and ways to capitalise on them.
- *Catalyst or leader:* Provides motivation and impetus for getting projects off the ground.
- *Endorser:* Endorses the entrepreneurial concept and lends credibility to the pursuit of the concept by the project champion.
- *Team player:* Plays a collaborative role with people from other specialty areas.
- *Resource provider:* Assists with information – human, financial and other inputs – to exploit opportunities.
- *Problem solver:* Responds to a particular question or challenge that the innovation team encounters along the way.
- *Coordinator:* Helps to bring together and integrate key inputs and resources over time.
- *Negotiator:* Helps bridge differences among various involved parties regarding what the project or concept should consist of, its scope, resources, commitment levels and timetable.
- *Politician:* Helps overcome internal resistance and gains top management support.
- *Change manager:* Oversees any strategic redirection, modification of infrastructure, and employee training or reorientation necessary to implement a new initiative.
- *Missionary:* Motivates and inspires management and all relevant interest groups regarding the ongoing need for innovation.
- *Opportunist:* Reacts quickly to emerging developments and provides new direction if necessary.
- *Critic/judge:* Identifies key flaws, downside risks and likely impact on other parts of the business.

Creativity is the soul of entrepreneurship. It is required in spotting the patterns and trends that define an opportunity. It is needed to develop innovative business concepts.

19.5 Creativity and innovation

Creativity and innovation are two major components for both entrepreneurs and intrapreneurs. Figure 19.1 illustrates how the creative process fits into the innovation process.

From Figure 19.1 it can be seen that the creative process is part of the innovation process, as it forms the link between the first two steps of the innovation process. Creative people also exhibit certain characteristics.

19.5.1 Characteristics of creative people

Creative people are:

- Bright but not necessarily brilliant. Creativity is not directly related to extraordinarily high intelligence.
- Good at generating a high degree of different ideas in a short period of time.
- People with a positive image of themselves – they like who they are.
- Sensitive to the world around them and the feelings of others.
- Motivated by challenging problems.
- Able to withhold a decision on a problem until sufficient facts have been collected.
- People who value their independence and do not have strong needs for group approval.
- Capable of a rich, almost bizarre, fantasy life.
- Flexible as opposed to rigid or dogmatic.
- More concerned with the meanings and implications of a problem than with small details.

From the above it is clear that intrapreneurs possess certain personality traits. In addition, however, creativity is most likely to occur when the organisational climate is right. No

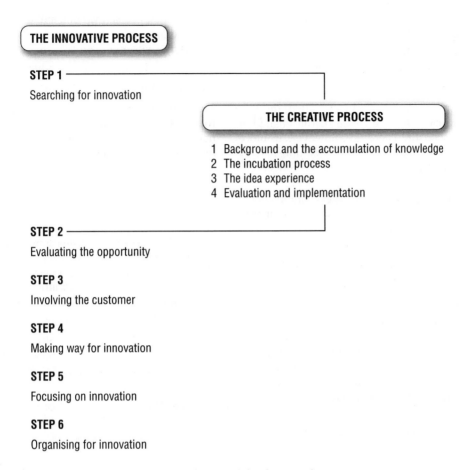

Figure 19.1 The creative process as part of the innovation process

business will have creative employees if a conducive climate is not established and nurtured.

19.5.2 The creative climate

The characteristics of a creative climate in a business include the following:

- A trusting management that does not over-control personnel
- Open channels of communication among all employees in the business
- Considerable contact and communication with outsiders
- A large variety of personality types among the employees in the business
- Willingness to accept change
- Experimentation with new ideas in the business

- No fear of the negative consequences of making a mistake
- Selection and promotion of employees on the basis of merit
- Use of techniques that encourage ideas, including suggestion systems and brainstorming
- Sufficient financial, managerial, human and time resources to accomplish goals

19.5.3 Distinctions between innovation, creativity and entrepreneurship

Creativity deals with getting an idea, while innovation relates to implementing the idea. Entrepreneurship requires innovation. The distinctions between these concepts are shown in Figure 19.2.

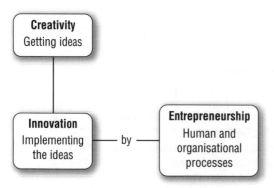

Figure 19.2 Distinctions between innovation, creativity and entrepreneurship

From Figure 19.2 it can be seen that without creativity there can be no innovation, because creativity initiates innovation. It is also clear that without entrepreneurship (the act of the entrepreneur), no innovation can occur, as entrepreneurship is the means by which innovation can take place. Entrepreneurship and creativity are thus prerequisites for innovation. We have also learned that intrapreneurs are entrepreneurs inside the business.

19.5.4 Stimulating innovation in the business

The climate and structures that encourage the flow of ideas usually describe how innovation is stimulated in a business. The individual is responsible for innovation and innovative people exhibit certain characteristics. In analysing these characteristics, some actions are necessary to create the ability to innovate in a business. These include:

- Focusing the intelligence of the employees in a business on the product and the customer

- Enhancing the subject matter expertise of the employees by hands-on learning in the business

- Encouraging unconventional ideas of the employees, as these ideas might provide solutions to problems or potential problems

- Encouraging employees not to fear ambiguity or uncertainty

- Avoiding forcing employees to explain and justify themselves – performance appraisals should be limited to feedback needs

- Motivating employees in a suitable manner – do not use fair treatment of employees, for example, as a motivating factor

19.5.5 Sources of innovation

Although there are innovations that are birthed from creative thought, most innovations result from a purposeful search for innovation opportunities. Areas of opportunities exist both within and outside a business. Figure 19.3 illustrates the areas of opportunities that may lead to innovation.

Sources outside the business	Sources within the business
• Demographic changes	• Unexpected occurrences
• Changes in perception	• Incongruities
• New knowledge	• Process needs
	• Industry and market changes

Figure 19.3 Sources of opportunities to the business

Source: Adapted from Drucker (1985: 68).

The sources indicated in the figure may overlap, as potential for innovation can be present in more than one area at a time.

19.6 The intrapreneurial process

The intrapreneurial process as discussed by Pinchot (2000: 119-162) consists of three stages, as discussed below.

19.6.1 Stage 1: Choosing an idea

After a number of ideas have been developed, idea selection can begin. Three kinds of needs – customer needs, the needs of the business and the needs of the intrapreneur – should be considered to evaluate an intrapreneurial idea. A meaningful intrapreneurial idea should include the following:

- Intrapreneurial ideas meet strongly felt customer needs which existing products and services do not meet well.

- An idea should fit in with the corporate strategy for meeting the needs of the business itself.
- An idea should fit in with whom the intrapreneurs are, what their skills and experience are, and what their values seem to be.

19.6.2 Stage 2: Planning the business

The basic task of the intrapreneur is to conceive business visions and turn them into business realities. Vision has two parts: intuitive discovery of a potential business pattern, and building a vision through business planning. Business planning involves documenting what is important to the business, such as:

- The destination of the business
- Strategies for getting there
- Where the business should be at specified times
- Obstacles that may be encountered
- Approaches to help overcome these obstacles

Some important aspects to remember in business planning are:

- Firstly, decide when and with whom to share the business plan. As intrapreneurial plans are often misunderstood, they should not be revealed to people who do not need to see them.
- Secondly, the length of a business plan is important. On average, the intrapreneurial plan is far shorter than entrepreneurial ones, because in all probability management already understands many aspects of the business.
- Thirdly, by the time an intrapreneurial business plan is formally presented, the decision whether or not to proceed has already been made. Thus, the informal pre-selling of the idea is usually the key to gaining approval.

19.6.3 Stage 3: Identifying sponsors – the protectors of new ideas

Intrapreneurs almost always need active sponsors who ensure that they receive the required resources. Sponsors also temper the grievances of those who feel threatened by the innovation. Many intrapreneurs have several sponsors: lower-level sponsors to take care of the day-to-day support needs, and higher-level sponsors to fend off major strategic attacks that might threaten them.

Sponsorship solves three of the most basic barriers to intrapreneurship. Firstly, most intrapreneurs cannot authorise their own activities, budgets and personnel. A sponsor who believes in them and their vision can either give or get these approvals.

Secondly, intrapreneurs need quality investors to fund their venture. Unprofessional investors who are unsure of their own judgement might remove the funding when faced with setbacks, which could be harmful to the intrapreneur.

Lastly, the support of sponsors deters those who would attack. Their position allows them to defend activities of the intrapreneur at levels where the intrapreneurs cannot speak for themselves.

The discussion of the intrapreneurial process above views the process as the activities necessary to establish a new business inside a large business. The intrapreneurial process emphasises the innovative aspects involved in the process of intrapreneurship. Instead of concentrating on the innovation aspects involved in intrapreneurship, another viewpoint is to emphasise the human aspects of intrapreneurship.

19.7 Factors hampering intrapreneurship

The primary factors that hamper intrapreneurship are set out below:

19.7.1 Costs and rewards

The costs of failure are too high and the rewards of success are too low. Intrapreneurs need to be given the space in which to fail, since failure is an unavoidable aspect of the intrapreneurial process. This is not to say that businesses should simply condone failure, but rather that businesses need to begin to measure and attribute failure to either a fault of the intrapreneur, or to circumstances beyond the intrapreneur's control – and punish and reward accordingly. Moreover, the rewards for success are usually inadequate. Few businesses provide rewards for intrapreneurs that even closely approximate the rewards available to their entrepreneurial counterparts. Most incentive systems need to be upgraded accordingly.

19.7.2 Inertia

Established systems, which no one is willing to change, cause inertia. Most businesses are governed by implicit and explicit systems, and in many cases people are reluctant to change them. Intrapreneurs are often met with "this is the way we've always done it around here", "if it ain't broken, don't fix it" and "changing it now would just take too much effort …". Many businesses use their existing systems to prove they already have the "right answer", effectively dousing creativity.

19.7.3 Hierarchy

Organisational hierarchies are what create the need to ask for permission – the deeper the hierarchy, the harder it is to get permission for anything new. Hierarchies also tend to create narrow career paths and myopic thinking, further stifling creativity and innovation. People lower down in the hierarchy tend to become disempowered through having to ask permis-

sion, eventually developing the "victim mentality" that causes reactivity.

Morris and Kuratko (2002: 173) identified a framework for understanding the obstacles to intrapreneurship. This is provided in Table 19.2.

As seen from the table, all the obstacles can be divided into six groups: systems, structures, strategic direction, procedures, people and culture. The specific constraints found in each group are listed, but this set of items is not exhaustive.

19.8 The intrapreneurial way of leadership

Leadership is an inherent part of the intrapreneur's task. While it is not different from other kinds of leadership, it is quite different from management (Pinchot 2000: 174). Managers taking on a new assignment inherit a working business where their job is to expand and improve it. Intrapreneurs, on the other hand, must create a new order by selecting from apparently unrelated potential parts to fit the pieces into a new pattern. Intrapreneurs thus face a broader array of options than most managers do.

Table 19.2 A framework for understanding the obstacles to intrapreneurship

Systems	Structures	Direction	Procedures	People	Culture
• Misdirected reward and evaluation systems • Oppressive control systems • Inflexible budgeting systems • Arbitrary cost allocation systems • Overly rigid, formal planning system	• Too many hierarchical levels • Overly narrow span of control • Responsibility without authority • Top-down management • Restricted communication channels • Lack of accountability	• Absence of innovation goals • No formal strategy for entrepreneurship • No vision from the top • Lack of commitment from senior executives • No entrepreneurial role models at the top	• Long, complex approval cycles • Extensive documentation requirements • Overreliance on established rules • Unrealistic performance criteria	• Fear of failure • Resistance to change • Parochial bias • Protection of "turf" • Complacency • Short-term orientation • Inappropriate skills/talents	• Ill-defined values • Lack of consensus on priorities • Lack of fit • Values that conflict with entrepreneurial requirements

Source: From *Corporate entrepreneurship.* Michael H. Morris & Donald F. Kuratko. Copyright © 2002. Reproduced with permission of Greenwood Publishing Group, Inc. Westport, CT.

The basic paradox of intrapreneurial leadership is as follows (Pinchot 2000: 175):

- There is a strong need for decisive, centralised direction setting in the early phases of a new business. Contrary to general intrapreneurial principles, group decision making will not work. What is needed at first is a clear entrepreneurial statement, not a committee-designed compromise.

- The age of domineering leaders and subservient team members is over. An important part of the task of the team members is not just to execute the leader's vision, but also to question, clarify and upgrade it. Successful intrapreneurial leaders resolve this paradox by using participatory management.

Some important components of intrapreneurial leadership include the following (Pinchot 2000: 176):

- *Freedom, democracy and trade-offs:* Instead of letting people gain control of their work lives by seeking consensus, intrapreneurs do so by allowing them freedom in their own areas.

- *Making others feel good:* The job of an intrapreneurial leader is to make the team members feel good about their own contribution. Dedication and competitiveness should be shared by the group and the competition is addressed to those outside it.

- *No need for power:* Intrapreneurs are almost never power hungry. They are driven by a need to achieve their objectives, not by a desire to hold power over others.

- *Avoiding conflict:* Conflict among team members is avoided by focusing on the product and its effect on the customer, and not on personalities.

- *Sharing the visionary task:* One of the most powerful incentives for getting the enthusiastic cooperation of others is allowing them the freedom to help create the new vision. They will thus strive to make it work, whatever the decision was.

Leadership of an established business (intrapreneurial leadership) can be a focal point for change and for inculcating entrepreneurial values. As the source of corporate authority, the leader can recreate or protect a great deal of the informality and flexibility that often disappear as the business matures. The role the intrapreneurial leader plays in coping with the changes in the business is invaluable.

19.9 The management of intrapreneurship in a business

For intrapreneurship attempts to be of benefit to the business, intrapreneurial energy and drive need to be managed effectively. This includes:

- From the outset, intrapreneurial efforts must be grounded in, guided by and directed towards the aims, purposes, values and strategies of the business. They must also use the underlying strengths of the business.

- The intrapreneurial activity should be focused on those aspects that matter most to business. It should not be confined only to new products and services, but should also make a significant impact on other areas, such as improved efficiency, new operating methods and secondary marketing approaches.

- All stages of the intrapreneurial process must be understood, well-managed and effectively linked together.

- Sponsors, team members and intrapreneurs need to play their parts at the right time and in the right combination if they are to have maximum effect.

The management of intrapreneurship indicates the importance of intrapreneurial leaders in the management process. Cooperation and communication are vital.

19.10 Implementation of intrapreneurship in the South African business

In a study conducted by Struwig (1991), it was concluded that the implementation of intrapreneurship in the South African business required a special programme. It was not the intention of Struwig's study to establish how South African businesses could implement intrapreneurship; rather, it set out to establish whether South African businesses could embrace intrapreneurship at all. The study proved that intrapreneurship can indeed be implemented in South

African businesses, and recommended further research on how to do so.

However, there are general guidelines for businesses that wish to implement intrapreneurship. There are a number of approaches that they can follow:

- *The individual intrapreneur:* This approach focuses particularly on identifying, developing and training the individual intrapreneur. The business needs to understand the intrapreneur as well as the incentives that will motivate him or her. A programme to be used will include a definition of a framework for action, and the identification, selection and training of intrapreneurs.

- *The intrapreneurial team:* This involves group approaches to innovation effort. The programme will include the selection of members of the team, their training, roles and team structures, and maintaining commitment.

- *The intrapreneurial organisation:* This approach focuses on organisations whose central aim is innovation, new products and new businesses. The programme should emphasise the organisational structure as well as the organisational culture of the business.

- *Intrapreneurial outposts:* This approach focuses on businesses that have established business units outside the confines of the main business. Although such business units (outposts) can be regarded as independent businesses, they can enhance the innovative abilities of the organisation.

19.11 Conclusion

The concept of intrapreneurship was clarified in this chapter. The intrapreneur, who is an entrepreneur inside the business, differs from an entrepreneur due to the nature of his or her activities.

As the intrapreneur is an entrepreneur who operates within the business, it would be expected that intrapreneurs exhibit the same characteristics as entrepreneurs. However, besides being entrepreneurial, the intrapreneur should also understand his or her environment, be experienced in business exploitation, have the freedom to disagree, be open to employees in order to develop supporters, be more patient and willing to compromise, and be able to handle problems within the system.

Creativity and innovation are two major components of both entrepreneurship and intrapreneurship. The relationship between the creative process and the innovative process was outlined. The characteristics of creative people, the creative climate and the distinctions between innovation, creativity and entrepreneurship were dealt with, as well as how to stimulate innovation and the sources of innovation.

It was seen that the intrapreneurial process starts with generating an idea through to the full exploitation of the idea. The factors hampering intrapreneurship were discussed, as well as how to develop intrapreneurs. The intrapreneurial way of leadership and the management of intrapreneurs in a business were also discussed. The chapter concludes with a brief note on the implementation of intrapreneurship in South African business.

Looking back

1. Define intrapreneurship.
   Intrapreneurs are people who put new ideas into action within an established business.

2. List the differences between start-up entrepreneurs and intrapreneurs.

Entrepreneur	Intrapreneur
Takes the risk	Business assumes the risks, other than career-related risk
"Owns" the concept and business	Business owns the concept, and typically the intellectual rights surrounding the concept
Owns all or much of the business	Intrapreneur may have no equity in the business, or a very small percentage
Potential rewards are theoretically unlimited	Clear limits are placed on the rewards
One misstep can mean failure	More room for errors; business can absorb failure
Vulnerable to outside influence	More insulated from outside influence
Independence (although the successful entrepreneur is usually backed by a strong team)	Interdependence of champion with many others; may also have to share credit with several people
Flexibility in changing course, experimenting, or trying new directions	Rules, procedures and bureaucracy hinder the intrapreneur's ability to manoeuvre
High speed of decision making	Longer approval cycles
Little security	Job security
No safety net	Dependable benefits package
Few people with whom to talk	Extensive network for bouncing around ideas
Limited scale and scope, at least initially	Potential for sizeable scale and scope is achieved fairly quickly
Severe resource limitations	Access to finances, research and development, production facilities for trial runs, an established sales force, an existing brand, existing distribution channels, existing databases and market research resources, and an established customer base

3. Distinguish between innovation, creativity and entrepreneurship.

Creativity = getting ideas

Innovation = implementing the ideas

Entrepreneurship = ideas are implemented by means of human and organisational processes

4. List the steps in the intrapreneurial process.

Step 1: Choose an idea

Step 2: Plan the business

Step 3: Identify sponsors and protectors of the new ideas

5. Briefly discuss the intrapreneurial way of leadership.

- Leadership is an inherent part of the intrapreneur's task. Intrapreneurs must create a new order by selecting from apparently unrelated potential parts to fit the pieces into a new pattern. Intrapreneurs thus face a broader array of options than most managers do.
- There is a strong need for decisive, centralised direction setting in the early phases of a new business – group decision making will not work.
- The age of domineering leaders and subservient team members is over.
- Some important components of intrapreneurial leadership include:
  - Freedom, democracy and trade-offs
  - Making others feel good
  - No need for power
  - Avoiding conflict
  - Sharing the visionary task
- The role the intrapreneurial leader plays in coping with the changes in the business is invaluable.

6. Explain how to manage intrapreneurship in a business.

For intrapreneurship attempts to be of benefit to the business, intrapreneurial energy and drive need to be managed effectively. This includes:

- From the outset, intrapreneurial efforts must be grounded in, guided by and directed towards the aims, purposes, values and strategies of the business.
- The intrapreneurial activity should be focused on those aspects that matter most to business.

All stages of the intrapreneurial process must be understood, managed well and effectively linked together.

- Sponsors, team members and intrapreneurs need to play their parts at the right time and in the right combination if they are to have maximum effect.
- The management of intrapreneurship indicates the importance of intrapreneurial leaders in the management process, as cooperation and communication are vital.

Key terms

Change agent
Creativity
Entrepreneur

Innovation
Intrapreneur
Sponsors

Discussion questions

1. Define intrapreneurship.
2. Differentiate between entrepreneurs and intrapreneurs.
3. Explain how creativity and innovation are related, and how this fits in with intrapreneurs.
4. Distinguish between innovation, creativity and entrepreneurship.
5. Briefly outline how you would stimulate innovation and list the sources of innovation.
6. Discuss the intrapreneurial process.
7. Outline the factors that hamper intrapreneurship.
8. Explain the intrapreneurial way of leadership.
9. Explain how the intrapreneurial leader is important to the management of intrapreneurship.
10. Indicate how intrapreneurship is implemented in the South African business.

Case study

Case study: Intrapreneuring in the service industry

From a position of relative obscurity at the SA Bank, Bongani Khosa launched a string of major banking innovations, including consumer certificates of deposit, simplified current accounts and master charge, which he played a major role in establishing. How he was able to do this is the result of a "loophole" that makes intrapreneuring in service organisations simpler than intrapreneuring new manufactured products. As the cost of developing a new service can be relatively low, Bongani was able to launch many of his innovations before management found out about them. When they did, he was able to show them successes rather than ideas, and thus it was too late for them to object.

As the director of market research, Bongani was not satisfied just to find customer needs and then tell others about them, hoping someone would then develop the new services to meet the needs he had identified. A true intrapreneur, he took responsibility for the entire effort, from beginning to end, working to invent the services *and* to make them happen. To do so, he worked with a team in marketing, including his boss, Bob Klaas, and the director of advertising, Sam Mti.

Part of what made Bongani so successful in this and other intrapreneurial ventures, were his political skills, stemming perhaps from his experience as SASCO president and his work as a campaign manager for the local government. Whether by luck or design, he seems to have encountered little resistance in introducing major innovations.

For all his efforts at helpfulness and his basic political skills, Bongani still was an irritant at the SA Bank. He survived only because of the constant guidance and protection of Bob Klaas and the overall umbrella Paul Dewey provided. "Bob Klaas understood and could explain what I was trying to do in terms other bankers could comprehend," Bongani said. Bob Klaas recalls, "Sometimes it was quite necessary to tone Bongani down." When Bongani designed the simplified current account plan, later called the "3-2-1 current account plan", he wanted to call it the "honest current account". He came to this name because he believed there was a dishonest motive behind the complexity of the bank's existing current account service charges. It is true that, in his market research, Bongani found that some customers believed that current account plans were a conscious attempt to confuse and exploit the ordinary individual customer, but it was highly impolitic to suggest that he believed they were right. This line of reasoning was hardly flattering to the bank's officers, and it would not have been an effective way to introduce the concept of simplified current accounts to them. Bob talked Bongani out of the name by pointing out that only pawn shops and used-car salesmen use the word "honest" in their advertisements or names. By doing so, he saved Bongani from his own idealism.

Towards the end of his stay at the SA Bank, Bob Klaas sued his friend Dewey in an internal battle. Bob Klaas left the bank and went into operation in another bank. Within three months,

without the guidance and protection of his sponsors, Bongani was fired.

Source: Please note that the information used in this case study is for illustration purposes only and is not factually correct. The main story line was adapted from Pinchot (2000).

Questions

1. Explain whether you would regard Bongani as an intrapreneur or not. Motivate your answer.
2. Why was Bongani fired when his sponsor left the bank?

Experiential exercises

1. Identify an intrapreneur who operates in an existing business. Conduct an interview with this person to investigate whether he or she differs from an entrepreneur.

2. Interview the same person again in two months' time, but this time focus on creativity and innovation as implemented and practised by this intrapreneur.

Exploring the Web

1. Go to www.Bplans.com for, amongst other things, articles on intrapreneurship (such as the case study by Pinchot).

2. Visit www.businessplans.org for a library of useful information on intrapreneurship. A history of the development of the concept of intrapreneurship can also be found at this address.

3. Go to www.morebusiness.com for an online copy of *INC*, a magazine for growing companies.

4. Go to www.Bpiplans.com for resources for intrapreneurship, articles on intrapreneurship, books on the topic, and so on.

References and recommended reading

Drucker, P.F. 1985. The discipline of innovation. *Harvard Business Review,* 3: 67-72.

Hisrich, R.D. 1990. Entrepreneurship/intrapreneurship. *American Psychologist,* 45(2): 209-222.

Morris, M.H. & Kuratko, D.F. 2002. *Corporate entrepreneurship: entrepreneurial development within organisations.* London: Greenwood Publishing.

Pinchot III, G. 2000. *Intrapreneuring: why you don't have to leave the corporation to become an entrepreneur.* New York: Harper & Row. (Original work published 1985.)

Struwig, F.W. 1991. *Intrapreneurship: a strategy for managing change and innovation.* Unpublished Ph.D. thesis. Port Elizabeth: Vista University.

PART **F**

Case studies

1: Chicken Licken

PAUL MAYHEW & GIDEON NIEMAN

Chicken Licken, one of our home-grown and more successful food outlet franchise operations, is an unusual company. It defies conventional business wisdom, is run from modest headquarters in Booysens and has grown to become the largest non-American-owned fried chicken chain in the world.

After setting up the first branch in 1981, the group now has just over 300 branches, two-thirds of which are black owned and situated in the townships. All executives, except George Sombonos, are women and most of them are black. Women manage all nine stores owned by the company, with the kitchen staff consisting mainly of men.

"Women are more efficient than men," Sombonos says. "They don't expect big expense accounts, they aren't continually disappearing for a few hours to deal with some private matter, they're harder working and don't always think they know better."

Background

After attending Potchefstroom Boys High School, George Sombonos completed his mandatory two-year military service at the Air Force Gym. Three months into his training he qualified as a radio operator but realised that the rigid structure of the military was not his forte. Upon completing his military service, he attempted to enter the marketing industry. However, at that stage marketing was extremely difficult to get into and only a fortunate few with personal connections managed to land a marketing job.

With no job prospects available at that time, his father, who owned a roadhouse in Johannesburg – called the Dairy Den – asked George to mind the business while he went away. His father had bought the roadhouse late in his life, as he did not have enough money to retire on. The roadhouse was not changed much by his father, as he was content to keep his income constant.

Sombonos used to work there on Sundays while still at school, selling ice creams, and so was familiar with the workings of the Dairy Den. He accepted his father's offer and ended up working there until the end of the year. He was determined to leave and find other employment after that year, but he never managed to get away as he was given odd jobs such as printing docket books and so forth.

In return for his hard work, his father rewarded George by giving him a plane ticket to America to learn about the different types of food found there. His mission was to sample fast foods in different parts of the United States and see what was new and what might be successful in South Africa. "If you find one you like, go back the next day and eat some more, if you still like it, go back again and if you like it for three days in a row, get the recipe."

There was no direct flight to America in those days and so Sombonos had to stop over in Brazil. He usually spent two weeks there before moving on to America. His experiences abroad taught him the injustice of racial discrimination. While in America he met up with the editor of a fast food magazine he subscribed to. Intrigued by the fact that a South African was reading his magazine, the editor took Sombonos out to lunch in New York. He gave Sombonos the definition of fast food he still uses today – "fast food is the West's answer to feeding the masses". The editor organised for Sombonos to visit Chicago and see all the major fast food chains such as McDonald's and Wendy's. Those experiences resulted in Sombonos becoming very interested in the whole fast food industry and eager to learn more about it. He began eating at all the different fast food outlets and taking note of how the food was prepared and presented – on some days he would eat as many as ten hamburgers! Every year after that he would be given another plane ticket to the United States from his father and again he would sample all the different types of food. He specifically looked at chicken and burgers as that was what was sold at the Dairy Den, and he was interested in improving it.

Motivating factors

In 1972 his father had a heart attack, which put George in charge of the Dairy Den. He would manage and run the place, and his father would count and collect the money at the end of the day. "That was where I really cut my teeth and learned how to run a business."

In 1975, the Dairy Den was having difficulty dealing with its black customers. At that stage black customers were prohibited from being served in the same area as whites and could only get service from a small counter at the back. They argued that their money was just as good as any white person's. Sombonos saw their point and while his father was overseas, he split the Dairy Den in two, one side serving whites and the other serving blacks. The response he received from the black people was overwhelming and sales reflected this. When Sombonos' father returned, he was furious with what had happened to his shop. It was not allowed by law and could lead to the Dairy Den having its licence revoked. There was little his father could do as sales were at an all-time high and Sombonos had come to an agreement with the health inspector to turn a blind eye.

Around the same time, George again went over to America. Each time he would visit a different state and this time he found himself in the little town of Waco, Texas. Here he stumbled across a small fried chicken outlet – the "holy grail" of Chicken Licken, so to speak. From the first bite Sombonos knew he had a winner, but figuring out how to get hold of the recipe was another matter. After returning another three times to make sure he was confident about its special qualities, he approached the owner for the recipe. The man offered to sell him the recipe for US$5 000. Sombonos could only afford US$1 000 at the time and so offered to take the owner out to dinner to discuss the matter. He plied him with copious amounts of wine and managed to get him to agree on US$1 000 for the recipe on which his empire was to be built. Sombonos returned to

South Africa cash strapped and with a recipe he did not even know would work. He secretly mixed the recipe and substituted it for the one in the Dairy Den. He knew his father would not be happy with his tampering and tried to keep it under wraps. However, his father eventually did find out but the vast increase in sales prompted them to take the recipe to Robertson's and have the firm premix it for them. As a result, Robertson's started up an entire food services division which today supplies all the major food chains with their spice mixes.

By 1978, sales had grown from R25 000 before the recipe was introduced and was being served, to R200 000 a year. Sombonos was not seeing any of that money as his father still owned the shop and kept all the profits. Sombonos then approached his father for a 5 per cent share in the business, as he had built up the enterprise into a major organisation. His father was not very accommodating and replied, "You and I are not equal – we don't share – if you don't like it, leave!" Although disheartened, Sombonos continued, as the business had become his passion and he did not want to give up all he had built up. There was a stigma attached to the fast food industry at that time, namely that only "stupid people" worked behind a counter serving food. Sombonos laughed away the criticism and was determined to prove his worth and the value of the industry.

He had developed a passion for the business and realised he needed to gain ownership of his own business and run it the way he wanted.

The influence of role models

Sombonos cites the entire fast food industry in general as his role model. He learnt many principles from it, which he still applies in his stores today, such as not to have any telephones, cigarette machines, dogs, and other brand names present.

Sombonos had outside help from his accountant and his equipment supplier. They gave him the confidence to proceed and gave him a few ideas he could use to keep his venture growing. The decision to serve chicken wings was from his friend who supplied him with all his kitchen equipment. He also helped Sombonos work out what the essence of the Chicken Licken brand was about, as well as encouraging him to sell whole chickens and rice.

Beginning and establishment of the business

By some twist of fate, one of his customers one evening was a representative of the company that leased out the property to Sombonos' father. Sombonos told him about his dilemma and showed him how much business he brought to the area. A few days later the representative brought his boss to the shop to have a look at what Sombonos had done. The man sympathised with George and gave him the lease. On 1 January 1979, the business became his – unbeknown to his father. Eventually when Sombonos' father went to renew the lease and found out that his son had taken it, he was furious and did not speak to him for three months. Eventually when he did, he told Sombonos: "Now I know you will look after that business because you have fought for it." Sombonos promised to pay him for the lease but before he could, his father passed away and he never did. Before his father passed away, George also managed to borrow R30 000 from him without his knowledge. It was taken from his account he used for betting on horses, so it took him quite a while to realise that the money had been taken. Sombonos was determined to repay it once he got on his feet, but his father passed away before he had the chance. This caused many family dilemmas but such was Sombonos' desire to get his business going that he weathered the family turbulence. He now had a starting point for his new venture.

Sombonos needed a name, a logo and an entire concept on which to base his fried chicken venture. He had very little money at the time and could not pay his accountant the R800 to register his companies Golden Fried Chicken (the franchise company) and Burger King (the company that controlled the stores). Sombonos gave 10 per cent of his still-to-be-formed business in return for his services, which the accountant still owns today. A signwriter that painted the outside of the shop designed the chicken head for which he was paid R75. A name for the business was still eluding Sombonos and he knew it was important for him to have one in order to build a proper product image. One of his workers in the shop saw his stress and suggested he call it "Chicken Licken". When asked how he came up with the name, he showed Sombonos the book about

Chicken Licken that he read to his daughter. He was given a R300 thank you gift and Sombonos had a name for his business. In 1981, Chicken Licken started trading officially in Ridgeway, Johannesburg. His goals at that stage were typical of Sombonos' passion to succeed. He wanted his own franchise, to buy a house for his family, to buy the property at Booysens where the head office was, and to own a Porsche.

The first Chicken Licken fast food store was opened in Lenasia later that year. It was set up in the typical fast food model of today with no waiters or waitresses. It differed from the way the Dairy Den was structured because he worked there until one o'clock in the morning serving customers, and the Kentucky Fried Chicken next to him that closed at nine o'clock was far more profitable than he was. The store in Lenasia streamlined the production of chicken and formed the basis for the Chicken Licken stores today.

Once the store opened, sales went through the roof and within two weeks, Chicken Licken had taken half of Kentucky Fried Chicken's (KFC) customers opposite them in Lenasia. This caused quite a stir in the KFC hierarchy, which accused Chicken Licken of confusing the public with its name, as it was similar to KFC's slogan "Finger lickin' good". Sombonos was threatened with court action if he did not change the name of his business. After ignoring those threats, he was issued with a summons to appear in the Supreme Court. He borrowed R10 000 from his mother to secure an attorney and went to court. He won the first case but was later taken to the Appeals Court. At the Appeals Court, the Chicken Licken story book was submitted as evidence, after which the judge remarked: "It's been a long time since I've read that book." This, along with other important arguments, led to the appeal being turned down. It was a major victory and something that gave George a lot of confidence.

Growth

It took Sombonos five years from when he got the recipe from America to opening his first Chicken Licken store. It was a long process, but he had to wait until he had enough money and a shop to trade in. In the first year of operation, Chicken Licken had reached a positive cash flow with sales topping R500 000 – the profit was promptly reinvested in the business.

While the lengthy KFC legal process dragged on, Sombonos began expanding and managed to get a few franchises going. When he began looking for franchisees, very little interest was shown and so he gave the first eight franchises away for free, with a royalty holiday for the first six months. In three years, these eight stores turned into 25 and Sombonos hired a British domestic science teacher to oversee the franchising.

Sombonos had no marketing experience and he feels that if he had some, it would have hindered him more than anything else. It would have made him do things by the book and not by what his instincts told him. He did all the marketing, advertising, etc. during this time, but eventually the workload became too much and he hired someone to take charge of all the promotion.

At that stage, Chicken Licken had R160 000 to spend on advertising and began doing a few television advertisements on Bop TV. The advertisements showed mainly black people enjoying chicken. Sombonos targeted black people in his advertisements because of what he had seen at his Ridgeway store. At the time there were no restaurants for black people and so by serving blacks at his Dairy Den, Sombonos had identified a huge potential market. He opened franchises in all the major black areas and in so doing he subconsciously flanked KFC and entered a market that KFC had not even considered yet.

Sombonos then invested all his money in developing more stores. He opened three shops in Soweto and one in Johannesburg Central in Commissioner Street. This was around 1986 – the time when there were large-scale uprisings by the United Democratic Movement. All trucks that entered Soweto were stoned, which made it extremely difficult for deliveries to get through. As a result of these riots, people also did not want to leave their homes and risk being hurt. Chicken Licken suffered drastically and Sombonos found himself in huge debt because of all the money he had put into his own eight stores. Sombonos was determined not to sell any of his stores, however, and tried his best to weather the storm.

The year 1989 was a turning point for Chicken Licken. The advertising agency for Chicken Licken, Joubert-Graham-Scott, did a few focus group studies to get an indication of what customers would respond to in an advertisement. An idea came to use a comedian to do the advertisements. A television programme called *s'good s'nice* was highlighted as a good tool that could be used in advertising. It was the most popular black programme around – even Nelson Mandela watched it from prison. It was decided to buy the rights to the television show from the SABC at a cost of R500 000. It was a hefty sum, but such was Sombonos' passion for the brand that he paid it in three instalments and never looked back. Three commercials were made with the star of the show, Joe Mafela, and sales rocketed. It was a huge hit in the townships and did wonders for Chicken Licken's brand awareness. Later on, a deal was made between the actor and Sombonos, as he was vital to Chicken Licken's continued success. As Chicken Licken began to grow very rapidly, Sombonos had problems expanding his business to meet the demand. In 1992, 11 years after starting the business, Chicken Licken did not have proper offices yet. All accounts and administration were done in a 50 m² office above a store in Booysens. A proper telephone exchange was also not in place yet. This presented problems as buyers and suppliers could not always get through. (Some sales and staff information could not be obtained by the researcher as it is rather sensitive information and can be used by competitors.)

Position in the industry

According to the *Sunday Times* Markinor 2000 Brand Survey, Chicken Licken is the second biggest food brand in South Africa. According to the Henny Penny Corporation, which is the largest supplier of equipment to the fried chicken industry worldwide, Chicken Licken is the largest non-American fried chicken franchise in the world.

In 1992 Sombonos heard a rumour that at a KFC convention they were preparing to launch chicken wings called "Hot Wings" onto their menus. Sombonos phoned his lawyer and asked him to quickly register the name "Hot Wings". Surprisingly, KFC had not done it yet and so the name became Chicken Licken's. Sombonos then went to Rainbow Chickens and drew them a rough sketch of how he wanted the wings cut off the chicken. During this time he also paid

R750 to a shop in Cape Town that had registered the name "Hot Wings" but was not using it. The shop was obliged to sell the name or have it expunged. "Hot Wings" became the property of Chicken Licken and when KFC went to register the name two weeks later, they were shocked to find their idea had been taken. KFC tried to buy the rights from Sombonos but no amount of money would persuade him. Today, Chicken Licken controls the chicken wing market with 10 per cent of its sales being made up from "Hot Wings" sales – KFC never managed to make a serious challenge ever again.

Preceding this, Sombonos had never actually disclosed how many stores he had, but during the court battle it emerged that he had built up an empire of 100 stores. This made KFC sit up and take note of him – KFC realised that it had a serious competitor to contend with.

Competition

Sombonos never really evaluated the opportunity of the fried chicken market; he just wanted to sell good quality food to people who did not have access to restaurants, and so on. KFC was his main competitor but he used its structured and uniform way of doing things to his advantage. He would never copy KFC and knew that if he wanted to beat them, he would have to become almost the opposite of them. He aimed at giving better value and used the fact that KFC could not change to his advantage. In trying to use opposite strategies to KFC, Sombonos went for the black market – something KFC had neglected. Black people were also allowed to buy franchises on their own without the aid of a white partner, something KFC did not allow.

Future prospects

Chicken Licken has grown at a rapid pace and is now perched at just over 300 stores in and around Africa. Plans are in place to expand into the whole of Africa and perhaps also into the Middle East. Sombonos has a desire to stretch Chicken Licken from Cape to Cairo in the next five years. Looking at his previous track record there is a good probability that his vision will become a reality.

Chicken Licken is facing a few problems, however, the main one being the Aids epidemic.

It is estimated that in the year 2010 the economically active population will have to support approximately 2 million orphans – not to mention the number of those economically active people who will suffer from Aids themselves. This presents a concern for Sombonos, as Aids has affected Africa the worst and thus his potential market is rapidly being eroded.

Black people of today, who form most of Chicken Licken's market, have also changed. For example, they prefer to use English. Sombonos has had to keep abreast of these changes and adapt some of his strategies to suit them.

Characteristics and driving force

Sombonos does not have any partners in the true sense of the word, as he likes to remain self-determining. He does surround himself with good people and aims to look after them. He sees his partners as all the franchise owners. Sombonos sets new goals all the time and constantly sets his sights on new levels of success.

When looking for franchisees, Sombonos is very careful about whom he chooses. First of all, they must have the drive and motivation to run a franchise. They must also share the same passion and commitment that Sombonos does in his business.

Running the Chicken Licken enterprise has become more predictable for Sombonos, but he still puts in a 12-hour day, just as he always has. He takes a more managerial role now than he did when he started Chicken Licken, although he says the entrepreneur in him will always be there and it still influences his decision making.

In an ideal world, Sombonos would only want to work six months of the year and holiday the rest. There are no plans at the moment to retire just yet. There is still a lot that Sombonos wants to accomplish before he throws in the towel.

Sombonos' most valuable asset is his determination to see projects through to the end. He is a fighter and never says die. If he had the chance to do it over again, he would do most things in the same way – if he had traditional business knowledge he feels it would have hindered his ability to be flexible and capitalise on opportunities. Sombonos' most critical skills and attitudes he used to make his business a success, are his clear vision of where he wanted Chicken Licken to be and his ability to remain headstrong and focused on his goals.

Stress did not become a stumbling block for Sombonos, as his philosophy of having fun in whatever one does has overshadowed any stresses. A managing director of a company has more stress than he does, as George does not have to answer to anyone and can do things as he wishes.

Sombonos cites the fact that he trusts the wrong people too easily as one of his major weaknesses. His strengths are that he does not change his mind when it is made up and he sticks to a decision, no matter what. He also likes to take pleasure in whatever he does and always sees projects he starts right through to the end.

The most triumphant moment for Sombonos was beating KFC twice in court and taking control of the chicken wing market. His worst moment while building up his empire was losing in court to McDonald's in a costly and widely publicised court case over the rights to the name and trademark. After winning the first court case, Sombonos lost the appeal after some behind-the-scenes interference. Even today in most South African universities' law faculties, it is thought that the first judgement is the correct one.

Meeting a host of different people is one of Sombonos' main rewards he gets from being an entrepreneur. His job has allowed him to meet people he normally would never have, and to experience a vast range of different things.

The main risks Sombonos has had to face were all the court cases he was involved in, as well as his recent decision to change the store designs of all the franchises, which requires a huge amount of capital. The three most important lessons that Sombonos has learned is to stick to your beliefs, get good people around you and keep setting new goals all the time.

According to Sombonos, people who are suited to an entrepreneurial lifestyle are those people who are willing to take risks and believe in themselves enough to risk everything they own. People who are very conservative and not prepared to take any risks would not find it easy becoming an entrepreneur – these people are content with what they have and see no need to change.

In closing

Sombonos has proved himself over the years to be an entrepreneur in the true sense of the word. He has taken many risks that could have crippled him, he sticks to his vision and makes sure he finishes anything he starts. He is constantly adapting to a changing environment and is always attuned to possible opportunities. Chicken Licken bears testimony to a man who saw things differently to most people and created an opportunity from it.

Fieldwork done by Paul Mayhew BCom(Hons) student, University of Pretoria. Edited by Gideon Nieman.

2: Black Tie

GIDEON NIEMAN

Growth and diversification

Mr Jannie de Villiers started Black Tie in 1952/53 in Pretoria Central. At that stage, he was the only member of his family in the business, and the company assumed the status of a public company. It started as a wedding business and focused primarily on the female market. This was the first formal business in South Africa specialising in wedding apparel.

By 1960, the size of the business had doubled, resulting in a need for more hands. To cope with this, Mr de Villiers hired his wife, Isie, to help out with the accounting. For the first time the business could be described as a family business.

Three years later, in 1963, their sons, Laddier and Pierre, joined the business and played an active role in the organisation. Approximately two years later, Laddier left the family business to pursue his own interests. It should, however, be noted that he did not leave due to business-related family conflict.

In 1969 the business was still growing and it was decided to move to premises in the Old Chapel in Church Street, Pretoria. At the same time, two additional branches were opened in Johannesburg.

One year later, in 1970, the two daughters also joined the business to run the Johannesburg branches. This brought the number of family members involved to five. It is interesting to note that up to this stage only direct family members had been involved in the business and no in-laws were included.

In 1970 this changed when Pierre's wife Alice joined the business. One of the primary reasons for this move was that Pierre and Alice were to buy the business from his father later in the same year. This was the first change in ownership in 19 years and naturally resulted in certain changes. Due to the marriage of one daughter and the immigration to Canada of the other, the Johannesburg branches were closed down. The only two family members left were Pierre and Alice.

In 1975 another branch was opened in Johannesburg, with Pierre and Alice running the Johannesburg and Pretoria branches together. This went on for another five years. In 1980 they decided to sell the Johannesburg branch and open a second one in Pretoria.

In 1984 the company moved to larger premises in Van Erkoms Arcade near Church Square. These were hired premises and not owned by the company. In the period from 1984 to 1992 the following changes took place. Initially operations were consolidated and only one shop, De Villiers Bridals, was opened in the arcade. Growth allowed for the enlargement of the same premises in the mall. Yet, there was still room for more growth based on a different market need – the male market. De Villiers Formals was duly opened in the shop next door. A few years later a third shop was opened in the same mall, namely Black Tie. Little did they know that this name would be the one on the lips of so many people nearly 15 years later. In 1988 Pierre and Alice's son, Jean and daughter, Lené, started working part-time while still at school.

By 1992, business was still growing and a fourth shop, Rent-A-Tux, was also opened in the mall. In 1994, after acquiring his commercial pilot's licence, Jean started working on a full-time basis for the business. Due to the growth of Black Tie, this sector of the business was separated from Bride-to-Be at this stage, and each was housed in its own premises.

In 1995 a fifth family member joined the business. Jean's sister Lené agreed to join on a part-time basis to assist with the graphic design and development of advertising material.

In 1998, for the first time in 15 years, Black Tie returned to the Johannesburg market with premises in Midrand and Boksburg. At the same time Black Tie was franchised in Boksburg.

Future prospects for Black Tie are bright, with planned (and almost implemented) moves to open branches in the West Rand, Cape Town and Australia.

This description of the progression of one of South Africa's most successful family businesses leaves one with the impression that nothing ever went wrong and that there was constant growth. However, reality dictates that this can almost never be the case. What is not indicated in the discussion is that at one stage the De Villiers family had lost everything and owned only one asset, a Venter trailer. What is encouraging to note is the perseverance of, and dedication to the business by all the family members, and how they weathered the difficult times. The need for change and diversification is also noteworthy.

Family involvement

Black Tie currently employs five family members, with four members being permanent and one on a part-time basis.

Pierre de Villiers owns 100 per cent of the business after buying it from his father, the founding member. Mr de Villiers has grown the venture from a small family business to the multibranded close corporation that it is today. Mr de Villiers began as a designer for the business, and 37 years later is now the managing director.

Alice de Villiers, wife of Pierre de Villiers, has been employed by Black Tie for 30 years, starting when she and her husband bought the business from Pierre's father. She began her career as the bookkeeper and fashion designer, and is now the administrator. Mrs de Villiers is quite influential in running the business and in plans for the future business.

Jean de Villiers, their son, grew up in the business and joined the company officially five years ago in the position of salesperson. During his five years in the business he has been promoted to the position of director and is being groomed for the position of managing director.

Shireen de Villiers is married to Jean de Villiers. The two met at Black Tie and Shireen has been working for the business for ten years, three years longer than Jean. She started as a salesperson and has moved up the ranks to the position of sales director.

Pierre and Alice have another daughter who works part-time as a graphic designer for the business. She created the logos for Black Tie and Bride-to-Be, as well as all the business cards and brochures.

For the family, the priority is business first, and then family, which they admit does cause some conflict amongst the family members. They are, however, in the process of reverting this mindset to set the family before business. They see loyalty, dedication and mutual respect as being the main advantages of working together as a family. The family members claim that there are no real disadvantages to working together; they do not see the occasional conflict as a disadvantage.

Originally Black Tie consisted of a husband and wife team; this trend continues throughout the history of the business, with the founding members, current owners and future owners consisting of husband and wife teams. Husband and wife teams are able to manage a business successfully because of their deeper understanding of each other's strengths and weaknesses and long-term goals and vision. The disadvantage is that the business may place incredible strain on the relationship, which may affect the business negatively.

In the case of Black Tie, both children were given the opportunity to develop themselves in the business. The son decided to work on a full-time basis and is being groomed for the position of managing director after being a salesperson for a few years and getting to know every aspect of the business. The daughter chose another career as a graphic designer and is opening her own business. She does add some input into the family business, but in her own capacity as a graphic designer. Sibling rivalry does not create a problem in this case, as the children are involved in separate areas of the business and do not intrude on each other's "territories" or capabilities.

Structure

Black Tie has a poorly defined structure of authority amongst the family members, but the father has the final say when it comes to decision making. The atmosphere is relaxed and casual, but a sense of teamwork prevails. The family behaves how one would expect a family to behave and interact. They even live in the same security complex, with the parents, daughter, and the son and his wife all having their own house. Meetings can therefore be held informally and after hours if need be. There seems to be no succession plan in place and promotions are done on the basis of merit and ability.

Organisational structure

The organisation of Black Tie is remarkably similar to that of a family. At the head of the business is Pierre, the father, who has assumed the title of managing director. Alice, the mother, has taken up the role of administrator and her authority is evident in all aspects of the business. Hers is more of a staff relationship where she has authority over all aspects of the business due to her wide-ranging skills, whereas Pierre, Jean and Shireen assume line authority. In this case, authority flows directly down and responsibility up. Jean has the title of public relations director and Shireen that of sales director. Although they do not necessarily assume the roles of directors, they have been given these titles.

Below the management structure are 20 salespeople and shop attendants who have more or less the same responsibilities, and they all answer directly to management.

Culture and values

Black Tie believes its core value is that of honesty. Current management had no difficulty in identifying this as the core value passed down through the hierarchy over the years, initiated by the founder, Mr Jannie de Villiers.

Management identifies the business culture to be formal in nature. They attribute this largely to the core business in which they are involved – namely formal wear, and its effect on the general atmosphere in which the employees are required to work. They do, however, see this as an appropriate culture in that it supports such values as respect, honesty and integrity.

The business pattern is seen by management to be "participative" in nature. This is attributed to the way in which all-important decisions to be made are bounced off the middle management before being finalised. The managing director does, however, have the final say in all decision making. It is interesting to note that the business pattern chosen was not paternalistic in nature, especially since the top four members in management are all members of the De Villiers family.

The family pattern is "collaborative" in nature. Collaborative, meaning to work jointly, even with one's enemies, is very similar to the word "participative", which refers to the action of involving all staff in the decision making of an organisation. Management mentioned that there is little distinction between family and business at present. Almost all of the time the family members spend together is specifically business orientated. With this in mind, it is understandable that they chose both the family and the business pattern to be collaborative. It must also be mentioned, however, that the family members wish to increase the distinction between family and business. They feel that the current emphasis on business as taking priority over family matters must change.

Conclusion

At a glance it would seem that a family business cannot fail and that it undoubtedly is a good form of business ownership. This is definitely the case with Black Tie, which has prospered in this form; however, in many other family businesses, conflict and differing family opinions and roles have ended businesses prematurely.

Why, then, has Black Tie done so well? Firstly, the key role played by the fathers, both in the past and present eras, is noteworthy. This ensured that conflicts were more rapidly resolved, even if they were not in the interests of all family members. Another factor contributing to their success is the formal culture maintained within the family business, which ensures that matters are dealt with professionally rather than emotionally. Lastly, the structure at Black Tie ensures that there will be future opportunities for husband and wife combinations within the business, and progressive routes to the top for family members.

Source: Original research and fieldwork by Gwyneth Bevan, Russell Wordsworth, Jonny de Villiers and Lawrence Bowen – BCom (Hons) students, University of Pretoria, 2001.

3: Nando's

GIDEON NIEMAN

Nando's is a quick service restaurant chain that specialises in grilled peri-peri chicken. Nando's has a combination of franchise- and company-owned stores situated nation- and worldwide, with its head office located in Johannesburg.

The founder

Robert Brozin was born in December 1959, in Middelburg. He attended King David High School where he matriculated. Robert did his compulsory military service in the Signal Corps. He then attended Wits University and graduated with a BCom. While at university, Robert used to "smous" clothing to earn extra income. After graduating, he worked for Teltron, the Sanyo agents as the marketing manager.

Robert's role model and mentor is his father, who is "a wealth of knowledge" for Robert. To this day, they still discuss everything. At the time that Robert started Nando's, his father owned his own business. He was the Sanyo agent for South Africa and his company was Teltron.

His father's knowledge, advice and assistance, as well as Robert's own marketing experience with the Sanyo products, gave him a grounding and a basis from which to work when he spotted the opportunity for Nando's.

The venture

Nando's was Robert's first venture. He was motivated to take this risky step into entrepreneurship because he was bored with the role he played as marketing manager for Sanyo video products. Also, once Robert had tasted the product, he knew that this was the direction he would take. This knowledge sprung from the experience he had on his honeymoon in Portugal, where he fell in love with the food as well as the people. A combination of these factors provided Robert with the motivation to take the step to start his own business.

Robert's friend and partner, Fernando Duarte, spotted the original store, Chickenland. In 1987, Fernando invited Robert to lunch. They ate at Chickenland, tasted the "great" chicken and decided to "market this fantastic product to the world". Eventually, Robert and Fernando bought the shop, cleaned it up, and standardised the recipes and procedures.

Planning was not as scientific as it is today. Although there was no start-up business plan to speak of, research was conducted on specific areas before opening new stores there. They concentrated first on the shop that they bought, before thinking of expansion.

The company had very little finance and the joint venture system helped them to get up and running. Robert and Fernando took over the Chickenland store, spending 18 hours a day, seven days a week, cleaning and redecorating. They opened the first store in Rosettenville, Johannesburg within a month of taking over the original store.

For Robert, cash flows and break-even sales volumes were not considerations at that stage. Since the second store was opened 18 months after the first one, it was assumed that they had reached break-even and started making a profit within the first 18 months of business. The Nando's outlets were run very leanly.

One of the greatest pressures in the early days was identifying a banker and suppliers that had some faith in them. Robert and Fernando eventually developed relationships with their suppliers and started a network by making them partners. The early stores were joint ventures, not franchises, with Nando's holding 51 per cent and the operators holding 49 per cent. This procedure identified quality partners, many of whom are still around today.

Robert Brozin knew nothing about the food business at the time, and considered – and still does – anyone selling food to be the opposition. Robert's idea still is that Nando's competes for "share of stomach". With no knowledge of the food industry, they took advice from various avenues, including their auditor at the time – who is now managing director of Nando's SA. They would always bounce ideas off Robert's father. They also had a patent attorney who worked on the various registrations for Nando's.

Robert's goal has always been to take their product global. Robert and Fernando wanted the product and experience to be of a high quality and inspirational for those only able to afford it occasionally, as well as for those people fortunate enough to eat it regularly.

Robert's view is seeing to it that his family is well cared for, as well as finding a healthy balance between family and work.

Robert's strength lies in marketing and the vision he has. He therefore views networking as important. For Nando's, a network is still being built – it continues to be an ongoing process due to the steady growth of Nando's.

The strength of Robert's venture is "the product, the experience, and the provocative; irreverent marketing and advertising". The venture's weaknesses include the number of other "food people" in the market, i.e. competition, and a lack of capital in the early days.

For Robert, with a venture like Nando's it is all about people; it is not something he would consider doing solo. Fernando is a great help and partner, and to this day he is still active in running Nando's.

Once Nando's got going

For Nando's, the most difficult gaps to fill were, and are still are, good people. Nando's was listed on the JSE on 25 April 1997 for relevant reasons:

- *Cash management:* All of the stores opened were individual (Pty) Ltds, and they therefore could not transfer funds from stores with a positive cash flow to stores in the red.

- *Taxation:* They could not offset losses against profits and therefore "landed up paying far too much tax".

- *People:* They were unable to utilise good people in group roles, as they each owned a store and thus concentrated only on that store.

Nando's only started franchising about two years ago; to date they have 73 co-owned stores

and 93 franchised. Many franchisees and co-owners were personal referrals and introductions from friends, existing staff members and management, as well as suppliers. Robert looks for people who are of "like thinking" and "have similar values". It is also important for future franchisees to be committed to a long-term relationship with Nando's. Another prerequisite to becoming a partner or franchisee is experience in the quick service restaurant business or, alternatively, the ability to procure such management. The "partners to be" must also be able to make a substantial investment in both people and finance requirements.

Nando's is at the beginning of its journey; it is continually expanding both locally and internationally. There are approximately 380 stores in 25 countries. Expansion occurs yearly at a rate of approximately 20 stores in South Africa and double that internationally. For Robert, nothing becomes predictable; each day brings new challenges that have to be considered and responded to independently. For example, in the red meat industry, no one could have predicted the foot-and-mouth disease epidemic.

As an entrepreneurial venture grows, so does the need for control and the management skills necessary to enable growth to take place. It is important that the entrepreneurial skills should not be minimised in any way, thereby ensuring the maintenance of the competitive advantage.

In an ideal world, Robert Brozin would take off at least the Sabbath to spend with his family, as well as the school holidays to spend time with his children. He is not considering retirement at this stage and certainly will not be considering it as long as he is still enjoying what he is doing.

Robert Brozin started Nando's when his eldest son was a few days old – the child is now almost 16 years old. Robert now has three children, which highlights the challenge of maintaining a healthy balance between work and family. Travel becomes more and more difficult now with a wife and children, as it is never fun to leave them at home. Ideally, Robert would like to take them with him, but he needs to travel to keep abreast of international developments and up-and-coming competition.

Robert spends approximately the same amount of time on his venture now as when Nando's was in its infancy. The only difference is that now he has people around him on whom he can rely and trust to help him. This allows Robert the flexibility to be able to fetch his children from school and watch them play sport.

As a company grows, so do its goals. Nando's goals are never fully attained, since they are dynamic and are constantly changing as the company grows. Once Nando's was up and running, and expanding steadily, the company developed Ten Basic Beliefs that have helped standardise all stores:

1. When other companies say they cannot, Nando's says we can, and do!

2. There is no limit to what ordinary people can achieve, if fired up by extraordinary aspirations.

3. Our frontline people are the real heroes of Nando's. To our customers, they are Nando's.

4. At Nando's quality is not a word, but a way of life. Nando's sets standards, then raises them.

5. There are no short cuts. Nando's demands solid foundations ahead of growth.

6. Nando's is about sharing, ownership and total involvement. We give with our heads, hands and hearts.

7. Nando's dares to go where the competition is afraid to follow. Our pioneering spirit is fuelled by our success.

8. Nando's never competes for price. We compete for value. Customers understand value above price.

9. However big we get, we'll never be just another chain. Each store retains Nando's unique character and touch.

10. Justice and good luck come our way if we always do the right thing, even if it's the hardest thing to do.

For Nando's, customer care is a fundamental philosophy: In a business in which people, not machines, make things happen, the odd "cluck-up" is to be expected. But that does not mean it is accepted. Nando's has a dedicated customer care unit that sees to all complaints, queries and suggestions.

Growth

The following section sets out the growth Nando's experienced from 1997 to 2000.

1997

- Milestones reached:
  - The company was listed on the JSE on 25 April 1997, following the issue of 25 million ordinary shares of one cent each at an issue price of 100 cents per share.[1]
  - Nando's was recognised by the World Economic Forum as an emerging global brand.
- Turnover increased by 15 per cent.
- Operating profits increased by 27 per cent.
- Financing costs decreased; this was attributed to funds raised pursuant to the listing of Nando's on the JSE.
- Earnings per share increased by 31 per cent.
- The company opened 13 new stores.
- Capital expenditure derived primarily from the store-opening programme. Total capital expenditure amounted to R16,5 million.
- A maiden dividend of one cent per share was declared.
- International operations participated via a 30 per cent profit. The number of stores increased from 37 to 45.
- A prospectus forecast of 6,25 cents per share for the year ending 28 February 1998.

1998

- Turnover rose by 15 per cent.
- The group operating income had increased by 30 per cent.
- Earnings per share rose by 33 per cent to 6,85 cents per share, exceeding the prospectus forecast of 6,25 cents per share.
- Cash flow from operating activities increased to R27,9 million.
- Operating margins improved from 11,3 per cent to 12,5 per cent.
- A reduction in finance costs was attributed to the stronger cash flow and funds raised due to listing on the JSE.
- The gearing ratio was reduced to 21,3 per cent from 59,1 per cent.

---

1 As a result of international restructuring, it was decided to delist the company and operate as a private company once more. Nando's was delisted on 15 April 2003.

- Capital expenditure amounted to R30,4 million.
- Capital commitments for the next year were expected to be R25 million.
- Nando's International achieved remarkable growth, increasing from 37 stores in eight countries to 52 stores in 12 countries.
- Directors declared a dividend of 1,5 cents per share.
- Management was confident that their strong market position would enable the group to achieve double-digit growth.

1999

- There was a 12,8 per cent increase in revenue.
- Headline earnings declined by 2,5 per cent due to a flat consumer market.
- The operating profit was R25,2 million before depreciation and interest.
- The net finance cost increased from R3 million to R6,1 million due to higher levels of interest and increased borrowings.
- A further 12 stores were opened. The group now had 137 company-owned stores.
- The capital expenditure was R36,5 million.
- The group's business model was reviewed and the board resolved that the core of the company-owned stores would be best enhanced and supported by a franchising element.
- No final dividend was declared.

2000

- Nando's maintained its growth path.
- Revenue increased by 49,7 per cent.
- Operating profit before finance costs increased by 40,5 per cent.
- Finance costs increased by 139,3 per cent.
- Net finance costs were: interest paid R11,3 million and interest received R1,8 million.
- Headline earnings increased by 17,4 per cent.
- Strong cash flows generated by the group were used to reduce interest-bearing debt by R34,7 million.
- Franchising continued: South Africa opened six franchise units, Australia opened 19 franchise stores and the Middle East hub had a successful signing of master franchises.

- The group's presence expanded from London to Manchester and Birmingham.
- No dividend was declared.
- The earnings forecast was 2,83 cents per share.
- October 2000: Nando's ranked 11th as South Africa's most global company. It is also one of the top ten South African companies for three of four major globalisation criteria. This is a clear recognition of the stature and presence that the Nando's brand has achieved.

Since Nando's started, there has been a strong and steady growth, which continues to this day. Its combination of local and offshore interests has created a unified brand characterised by the orchestration of global effort. The Nando's group is only beginning to realise and extract the promise of the vast potential and synergistic benefits inherent in the group structure.

Conclusion

Robert Brozin believes that his most valuable assets were, and still are, his understanding wife and wonderful children, from whom he received the support and encouragement necessary to make it. For Nando's, its people are the most valuable and important asset: dedicated staff, good customers and reliable suppliers are what make the business a success.

Robert says the most critical element needed in starting a venture is the ability to trust and accept the opinions and advice of experts in the various fields. "Never be afraid to hire someone better than yourself."

In the next five years, emerging markets need to plan for their expansion and ensure they have the manpower and infrastructure to grow. These skills can be learned from other, more established countries in which we operate. It is also important for the success of an entrepreneurial venture to use all the skills available throughout the group.

One of his greatest rewards has been the creation of wealth and opportunity for a number of people, most of whom would have had "absolutely nothing on their horizons".

Robert believes that anyone who has a dream of becoming an entrepreneur should follow that dream and become one. "If you can dream it, you can do it!"

Source: Based on research and assignments by the 2000 MBA group, University of Pretoria. Also refer to www.nandos.co.za.

4: Garage in the eastern suburbs

GIDEON NIEMAN

Advertisement in *Pretoria News*

> **For sale:**
>
> Garage in eastern suburbs
>
> Pumps 375 000 litres a month
>
> Nett 34 000 per month
>
> Well established
>
> Asking R1 500 000 plus stock

Background of the potential buyer

I have been working in the motor trade for the last ten years, and have been a manager of a relatively small garage for the last four years. I attended the University of Pretoria and obtained a BCom accounting degree. I am currently completing an MBA degree. I have also attended the retail academy of a specific oil company and completed all of their management courses. I need to have my own business where I can create and shape my own future.

Report on the business that is for sale

The garage in question has been operating for the past 30 years. It is situated on a busy road and has become a landmark, according to the owner.

In a radius of 2 km there are ten garages serving the community. The owner (seller) pointed out that four of these were built in the last three years. As a result, his fuel sales decreased from 430 000 to 345 000 litres per month, which is a drop of 20 per cent.

However, he was quick to point out that he compensated for the loss in fuel sales by diversifying into other services. As a result, he maintained his turnover and even increased it in the last two years. His current fuel sales are growing at 8 per cent above last year's sales.

Research by the oil company revealed that the fuel industry was growing by 5,5 per cent from the previous year, so his garage was outperforming the market. Further research by the oil company revealed that the garages in the area were not growing according to the industry, therefore they were losing market share.

The owner, however, warned me. He said there are many changes to come to the motor industry, the biggest threat being "deregulation". There has been much speculation of late in the newspapers. The owner said it is a matter of time before it happens and when it does, we will be faced with new challenges.

He has assured me that the oil company in question will give me the necessary backing and support the garages under its flag during the transition period, when it occurs.

The garage in question has a fully equipped workshop. It has a spares shop, a small fitment centre and a café. The garage is due for a rebuild next year. The oil company is going to add some more features to the premises. It wants to extend the driveway, set up a convenience store, an ATM and a car wash facility.

The owner is 60 years old and wants to retire. His two children both have different careers. He would like to sell the business to one of his employees (most of them have been with him since he started), but none of them has the financial backing. He maintains the business has great potential with the rebuild, but he says age is catching up with him.

The 1998 income statement has been split into two parts: fuel, and other activities.

The reason for this is to determine what income is derived from fuel and from the other activities of the garage. A business broker indicated that the going rate for garages is R3,00 per litre, plus a 15 per cent return on the nett profit of the other activities.

The garage is currently pumping 375 000 litres per month, therefore:

375 000 × R3,00 = R1 125 000

Nett profit from other activities: $\dfrac{60\ 000}{15\%} = 400\ 000$

Therefore, the asking price of R1 500 000 is justifiable.

Table A: Income statement 28 February 1998

	Fuel	Other	Total
Gross profit	700 000	547 956	1 247 956
Less overheads			
Audit fees	6 200	6 201	12 401
Advertising	–	3 425	3 425
Bad debts	5 200	3 428	8 628
Bank charges	6 856	12 000	18 856
Collection fees	6 000	4 003	10 003
Computer costs	–	1 881	1 881
Depreciation	–	4 027	4 027
Insurance	8 500	8 367	15 867
Licences	–	1 368	1 368
Water and lights	12 400	8 116	20 516
Overhauls	1 216	–	1 216
Postbox rental	–	33	33
Printing and postage	2 000	884	2 884
Rent	72 000	52 993	124 993
Repairs and maintenance	10 000	4 235	14 235
Regional services	12 900	3 318	16 218
Salaries and wages	246 000	348 822	594 822
Staff refreshments	–	574	574
Subscriptions	–	894	894
Telephone	–	12 981	12 981
Travelling	–	12 604	12 604
Workmen's compensation	2 955	–	2 955
Nett profit	305 892	59 683	365 575

Table B: Income statement for previous years

	1997	1996	1995
Gross profit	1 145 769	1 023 991	969 363
Less overheads			
Audit fees	10 008	8 603	8 975
Advertising	9 079	1 019	1 434
Bad debts	789	3 219	4 913
Bank charges	14 781	11 595	11 350
Collection fees	17 151	4 411	—
Computer costs	—	5 900	1 501
Depreciation	1 925	2 140	1 852
Insurance	12 523	13 147	17 155
Licences	348	1 699	492
Water and lights	14 709	11 656	8 950
Overhauls	938	993	986
Postbox rental	30		15
Printing and postage	3 508	3 427	5 251
Rent	109 338	92 462	80 926
Repairs and maintenance	1 073	2 321	4 305
Regional services	16 454	14 980	14 180
Salaries and wages	550 455	530 746	466 784
Staff refreshments	83	377	1 147
Subscriptions	1 121	366	283
Telephone	10 047	8 436	9 036
Travelling	13 810	18 564	14 758
Workmen's compensation	2 660	2 562	1 493
Nett profit	354 939	285 398	313 587

Contents

1. Management summary

The mission of the Pool Doctor is to establish a service that will deliver a complete service to pool owners in Kimberley. We will definitely do more for our customers than simply scoop up the leaves, but even want to go as far as ensuring that they can relax comfortably next to the swimming pool.

The Pool Doctor is not an entirely new concept in Kimberley, but it will look at the whole idea of pool maintenance from a different perspective. A mind map can be used to portray the idea and the scope that it will initially have and what it can possibly become. This mind map summarises the services provided by the Pool Doctor.

Currently, there is one competitor, but he only concentrates on repairs. Statistics show that there are 4 500 pool owners in Kimberley, with 89 per cent of these residents being in the higher income group for whom time is of the essence. Definite marketing strategies will be employed to obtain the biggest share of the market. (Refer to paragraph 2.3).

An aggressive marketing campaign, excellent service and maintaining the competitive advantage over the competitor will help to attain the goal of a 15 per cent return on investment after 18 months.

The capital needed for the first six months will amount to R4 570 × 6 = R27 420. This amount includes all costs – equipment, chemicals, vehicle and fuel, marketing, telephone and labour. (Refer to Addendum A1.)

I have R18 000 available and the other R10 000 will be borrowed from the bank using my house, which is worth R380 000, as security. Although there will be income at the end of the first month already, it should take about three months to increase the number of customers. Once the customers have signed the contracts, the Pool Doctor will start paying back this loan.

The goal is to pay it back within six months. (Refer to Addendum A3.)

2. Current position of the enterprise

2.1 Primary activities

The Pool Doctor will render a full, absolutely comprehensive and expert service to pool owners in Kimberley, which will enable them to get optimal use from their pool without having to spend any time or effort on this very expensive facility.

The Pool Doctor will enter into 12-month contracts with its customers wherein it will undertake to:

- Visit the pool twice a week.
- Scoop up all leaves.
- Scrub the pool once a week.
- Get rid of any algae.
- Clean all filters twice a week.
- Backwash as is necessary (more often in summer than in winter).
- Test the acid and chlorine levels of the pool.
- Administer any treatment as is necessary.
- Supply all the acid and chlorine to keep the pool sparkling clean.

The Pool Doctor will also undertake the following:

- If there are problems with the pump, filters or pool-cleaning system, quotes will be obtained.
- Once the client has made the decision as to who must do the repair work, it will be further seen to by the Pool Doctor.
- Initially some repairs will be contracted to others, but after a year stocks will be carried of parts, and then repair costs will amount to material costs plus 15 per cent.
- If the client wants us to use his own nets, brushes, etc. we will repair such (if possible), with only the material being paid for, or else equipment will be sold at low cost to the client.
- Sand in filters will be replaced and only the material has to be paid for.
- The Pool Doctor will install and service safety nets.
- The extras will also be seen to (as explained below).

The Pool Doctor will have different brochures of, and contracts with, suppliers of safety nets, safety tubes and wings for youngsters, deck chairs, cushions and umbrellas, which customers will be able to order from the comfort of their homes. Orders will be handled and delivery arranged by the Pool Doctor at a service charge. Rendering the complete service will definitely make this a more sought-after service than that of the competitor in Kimberley.

To give clients further peace of mind, there will be swimming lessons at the house and lessons for making babies "drown-proof". These lessons will be slightly more expensive than those given in Kimberley at present, but there is a big advantage in having the instructor coming to the client's pool instead of the client trying to get to the municipal pool.

The Pool Doctor will offer a service that is a cut above the only other competitor in town. Pool Services only attends to minor problems and does not provide an ongoing service, which is what is needed. The Pool Doctor, on the other hand, will render a complete expert service, which includes the normal upkeep of the pool, seeing to any repairs that need to be done, seeing to the safety aspects of the pool, offering swimming lessons and selling pool furniture.

Pool owners in Kimberley fall within the category of people who lead very busy lives. There is normally more than one salaried person in these households – they leave home early and come back late during the week, setting the weekends aside for relaxation and social activities. These are the people who are prepared to pay for a good service, who want peace of mind about the safety of their children, and who do not want to spend a little here and there and then still have a problem with the swimming pool.

Initially, the Pool Doctor will operate from the owner's residence, as no need exists for separate premises. Swimming lessons and drown-proofing will be done by the owner, who has all the necessary qualifications, as well as certificates in life-saving. The four labourers needed for the primary service will commute between work and the owner's residence (relatively short distances) and any materials needed will be ordered from the owner's residence or bought from Johannesburg. The necessary contact with wholesalers of pool supplies has already been established, which would enable the Pool Doctor to pass on low prices to the consumer. Brochures for pool furniture will be readily available and the customers will use these in the comfort of their own homes.

2.2 History

Kimberley is situated in a part of the country where the winters are relatively short and the summers long and hot. Statistics show that there are approximately 4 500 swimming pools, which need regular upkeep and are subject to problems that can best be solved if attended to by an expert. A quick survey of pool owners has shown that there is a definite need for a comprehensive and reliable service and that pool owners are quite prepared to pay for it.

2.3 Positioning of the enterprise

I already know that the higher middle-income and high-income groups are those with swimming pools and will be interested in making use of this service. In Kimberley there is a definite concentration of these potential customers in the suburbs of Carters' Glen, Belgravia, Hillcrest, Hadison Park, Monument Heights and Klisserville. These are the families who spend much of their time in and around the swimming pool during summer and "hate" the upkeep. Knowing the city, I will be able to target those areas specifically when marketing the service.

The only competition in Kimberley occasionally advertises in the local newspaper and provides a much smaller service than that which the Pool Doctor intends providing. The competition might, however, at this stage be able to deliver a better service for repairs, as it has been in the market for longer and already has all the contacts. With so few players in the market, and none with exactly the same type of service, the Pool Doctor should be able to serve a large percentage of potential customers. The obvious problem is that the idea can very easily be copied. For this very reason, the initial marketing will have to be very efficient and the service will have to be outstanding. Customers have to sign a one-year contract, which will enable the Pool Doctor to continue servicing

the same people for a fairly long period. Changing to another pool service will have to become too laborious and costly for the customers so that they will want to stay with the Pool Doctor. Making use of a telephone answering service, email and the Internet should also enable the Pool Doctor to have a strategic advantage over other potential competitors.

Knowing the competitor and the type of service being provided, the Pool Doctor, with its more comprehensive service, should be able to attend to the specific needs of the potential customers. During a quick survey amongst pool owners it was found that the majority would be prepared to pay R100,00 per month for this particular service. They would also willingly pay service charges if a reliable company would see to all the other aspects of pool care. The R85,00 charged for the service will therefore not be outpricing the business.

The marketing of this service will determine its success, and various options are open:

- Advertise in the local newspaper.
- Contact estate agents and obtain the addresses of pool owners.
- Contact gardening services and obtain the addresses of pool owners.
- Have pamphlets printed to advertise the service.
- Go from door to door in the identified areas and promote the business.
- The best advertisement would be an excellent service and word-of-mouth recommendations.

2.4 Service plan

2.4.1 Infrastructure

Initially, the Pool Doctor will operate from the owner's home, as no extra floor space is needed. The necessary infrastructure of a vehicle (pickup), telephone, fax machine and computer equipment exists. As the business grows, it will be necessary to move to bigger premises so that stock for repairs and for DIY pool owners can be available.

2.4.2 Equipment and materials

These include nets, brushes and test kits. R500,00 has been budgeted to pay for the initial purchase of this equipment. The necessary chemicals, e.g. chlorine and acid, will be available from wholesalers and it will cost R3 000,00 to treat 200 pools for one month. As this is a service being rendered, the products used must be of high quality. Even though it would cut costs to obtain materials from wholesalers, it must remain a high-quality product. Initially, stock for repairs will be ordered as necessary. When sufficient capital has been accrued, this aspect will receive attention again. All other brochures will be available so as to meet the needs of the customer. The capital needed for the first six months will amount to R4 570 × 6 = R27 420. This figure includes all costs – equipment, chemicals, vehicle and fuel, marketing, telephone and labour.

I have R18 000 available and the other R10 000 will be borrowed from the bank using my house, which is worth R380 000, as security. Although there will be income at the end of the first month already, it should take about three months to increase the number of customers. Once the customers have signed a contract, the Pool Doctor will start repaying this loan. The goal is to have it paid back in full within six months.

2.4.3 Labour and staff

With the present shortage of jobs in South Africa, there should be no problem in getting the two labourers needed. Initially, there will be one full-time team consisting of two labourers, whom I will take to the customers. As the demand increases, two or more teams will be operative. No specific skills are needed and a certain amount of training will take place beforehand, but a greater amount of in-service training will be given. The wages have been calculated at R200 per person per week. Provision has been made for obtaining the necessary finances. (Refer to paragraph 2.4.2). I will perform all administrative duties and a telephone answering service will be available to take calls.

2.4.4 Costs per unit

The cost per service amount is R19,53. The R85,00 service fee charged will therefore more than cover the layout. (Refer to Addendum A1.)

3. Mission, objective and goals of the enterprise

3.1 Mission

The Pool Doctor will render a full, absolutely comprehensive and expert service to pool owners in Kimberley, which will enable them to get full use of their pool without having to spend any time or effort on this very expensive facility.

3.2 Objectives

This specific service will take care of all the menial, time-consuming jobs for pool owners in Kimberley. It will enable them to enjoy the facility for which they have paid so much money, instead of having to spend a great deal of time, money and effort on its upkeep.

The Pool Doctor will be providing this outstanding, unique service to customers and the objective is to make a satisfactory profit on the invested capital. To work towards this objective, the goal of 15 per cent return on invested capital within 18 months must not be lost sight of.

3.3 Strengths

- The Pool Doctor provides a full range of services.
- It gives clients more time to do the things they really want to do.
- It takes an extra load off clients' shoulders, thereby lowering the stress factor.
- The Pool Doctor will look after the pool during holidays, making this arrangement convenient for the customer.
- It enables customers to save money as a very efficient service will be provided, using wholesalers as suppliers and also ensuring the best (but not necessarily cheapest) repairs.
- It ensures, as far as possible, the safety of customers' children in this regard.

3.4 Weaknesses

- Initially all repairs will be contracted out – this represents a loss of income.
- Initially a very wide range of services will be provided, for which excellent administration and time management will be needed.

- The service will not be efficiently launched during winter.

3.5 Threats

The idea could be copied by new competitors.

3.6 Opportunities

- The scope for this service is vast.
- The full range of service will be worth much to potential customers.

4. Strategy for achieving goals and opportunities

4.1 Costs of the project

As stated earlier, the Pool Doctor will operate from the owner's home as no extra floor space is needed. The necessary infrastructure of a vehicle (pickup), telephone, fax machine and computer equipment exists. As the business grows, it will be necessary to move to bigger premises so that stock for repairs and for DIY pool owners can be available.

The costs required for the project will be:

- All costs for the vehicle used (fuel, wear and tear, insurance)
- Materials needed (nets, brushes, test kits, chemicals)
- Telephone, fax, computer
- Marketing

The cost per service amounts to R19,53 (refer to Addendum A1). Potential income for the first year amounts to R29 580 (refer to Addendum A2).

4.2 Capital required

The capital needed for the first six months will amount to R4 570 × 6 = R27 420. This figure includes all costs – equipment, chemicals, vehicle and fuel, marketing, telephone and labour. (Refer to Addendum A1, which reflects costs for one month.)

I have R18 000 available and the other R10 000 will be borrowed from the bank using my house, which is worth R380 000, as security. Although there will be income at the end of the first month already, it should take about three

months to increase the number of customers. Once the customers have signed a contract, then the Pool Doctor will start repaying this loan. The goal is to have it paid back in full within six months. (Refer to Addendum A3.)

4.3 Break-even point

It has been calculated that to break even, 65 clients will be needed to be serviced per month. (Refer to Addendum A4.)

4.4 Nett profit

The nett profit for a bad year, when there are 117 clients, will be R29 580 (refer to Addendum A2).

The nett profit, which will be attained when as many customers as possible are serviced with two teams, has been established at R103 860 (refer to Addendum A5).

4.5 Return on capital

While initially operating the business from home, the goal of 15 per cent return on invested capital should be attained.

5. Addenda

Addendum A1: Cost per unit

Business hours per month:
Operate from 08:00 to 17:00 = 234 hours per month

Costs (expenses) per month:	Rand
Vehicle fuel	350,00
Vehicle wear and tear	300,00
Labourers (2 × R200 per week = R400 × 4 weeks)	1 600,00
Equipment (brushes, nets, etc.)	500,00
Chemicals (new chemicals on the market at wholesale price, which will be enough to service 200 pools per month)	3 000,00
Telephone and technology	450,00
Marketing	200,00

Therefore, total cost for one service: R4 570 / 234 hours = R19,53 per service. When doing repairs later on and using own labourers to do the work, additional labour costs will come into play.

Addendum A2: Pro forma income statement for the first year (worst case scenario)

INCOME STATEMENT – FIRST 12 MONTHS

Period starting:	Month 1	Month 2	Month 3	Month 4	Month 5	Month 6	Month 7	Month 8	Month 9	Month 10	Month 11	Month 12	Totals
Sales													
Service to 117 clients @ R85	9 945	9 945	9 945	9 945	9 945	9 945	9 945	9 945	9 945	9 945	9 945	9 945	119 340
Estimated income from other services	800	800	800	800	800	800	800	800	800	800	800	800	9 600
Total sales	10 745	10 745	10 745	10 745	10 745	10 745	10 745	10 745	10 745	10 745	10 745	10 745	128 940
Less cost of goods sales													
Materials: direct	1 755	1 755	2 255	1 755	1 755	2 255	1 755	1 755	2 255	1 755	1 755	1 755	22 560
Labour	1 600	1 600	1 600	1 600	1 600	1 600	1 600	1 600	1 600	1 600	1 600	1 600	19 200
Total cost of goods sold	3 355	3 355	3 855	3 355	3 355	3 855	3 355	3 355	3 855	3 355	3 355	3 355	41 760
Gross income	7 390	7 390	6 890	7 390	7 390	6 890	7 390	7 390	6 890	7 390	7 390	7 390	87 180
Operating expenses													
Salary of owner	3 500	3 500	3 500	3 500	3 500	3 500	3 500	3 500	3 500	3 500	3 500	3 500	42 000
Fuel	350	350	350	350	350	350	350	350	350	350	350	350	4 200
Wear and tear	300	300	300	300	300	300	300	300	300	300	300	300	3 600
Telephone	450	450	450	450	450	450	450	450	450	450	450	450	5 400
Marketing/promotion	200	200	200	200	200	200	200	200	200	200	200	200	2 400
Total operating expenses	4 800	4 800	4 800	4 800	4 800	4 800	4 800	4 800	4 800	4 800	4 800	4 800	57 600
Nett profit	2 590	2 590	2 090	2 590	2 590	2 090	2 590	2 590	2 090	2 590	2 590	2 590	29 580

© Van Schaik Publishers

Addendum A3: Abridged cash flow statement (117 customers)

Income		Expenses	
Service rendered (117 × 85):	9 945	Material	1 755
Sales, repairs, etc.	800	Labour	1 600
		Fuel	350
		Wear and tear	300
		Telephone, fax	450
		Marketing	200
		Salary (owner)	3 500
		Loan repayment	1 700
	R10 745		R9 855

Nett profit per month: R890 for the first six months (to enable repayment of loan).

Addendum A4: Pro forma income statement (for break-even point)

Variable costs	Rand	49 560
Direct material	22 560	
Direct labour	19 200	
Fuel	4 200	
Wear & tear	3 600	

Fixed costs	Rand	49 800
Telephone	5 400	
Marketing	2 400	
Salary of owner	42 000	

$$\text{Break-even point} = \frac{\text{Fixed costs}}{\text{Price per unit} - \text{variable costs per unit}}$$

$$= \frac{49\ 800}{85,00 - (49\ 560 \div 2\ 400)}$$

$$= \frac{49\ 800}{85,00 - 20,65}$$

$$= 774 \text{ clients per year}$$

$$= 65 \text{ clients per month}$$

Addendum A5: Pro forma income statement (for most prosperous scenario)

INCOME STATEMENT – FIRST 12 MONTHS

Period starting:	Month 1	Month 2	Month 3	Month 4	Month 5	Month 6	Month 7	Month 8	Month 9	Month 10	Month 11	Month 12	Totals
Sales													
Service to 234 clients @ R85	19 890	19 890	19 890	19 890	19 890	19 890	19 890	19 890	19 890	19 890	19 890	19 890	238 680
Estimated income from other services	1 000	1 000	1 000	1 000	1 000	1 000	1 000	1 000	1 000	1 000	1 000	1 000	12 000
Total sales	20 890	20 890	20 890	20 890	20 890	20 890	20 890	20 890	20 890	20 890	20 890	20 890	250 680
Less **cost of goods sales**													
Materials: direct	3 510	3 510	3 510	4 010	3 510	3 510	3 510	4 010	3 510	3 510	3 510	4 010	43 620
Labour	3 200	3 200	3 200	3 200	3 200	3 200	3 200	3 200	3 200	3 200	3 200	3 200	38 400
Total cost of goods sold	6 710	6 710	6 710	7 210	6 710	6 710	6 710	7 210	6 710	6 710	6 710	7 210	82 020
Gross income	14 180	14 180	14 180	13 680	14 180	14 180	14 180	13 680	14 180	14 180	14 180	13 680	168 660
Operating expenses													
Salary of owner	3 500	3 500	3 500	3 500	3 500	3 500	3 500	3 500	3 500	3 500	3 500	3 500	42 000
Fuel	600	600	600	600	600	600	600	600	600	600	600	600	7 200
Wear and tear	500	500	500	500	500	500	500	500	500	500	500	500	6 000
Telephone	550	550	550	550	550	550	550	550	550	550	550	550	6 600
Marketing/promotion	250	250	250	250	250	250	250	250	250	250	250	250	3 000
Total operating expenses	5 400	5 400	5 400	5 400	5 400	5 400	5 400	5 400	5 400	5 400	5 400	5 400	64 800
Nett profit	8 780	8 780	8 780	8 280	8 780	8 780	8 780	8 280	8 780	8 780	8 780	8 280	103 860

It is estimated that the Pool Doctor will need 30 minutes per pool per month with two labourers per pool. One team can attend to 117 pools per month. The operating costs will be less in winter, but any chemicals not used will be used in the months thereafter, thus cutting costs in summer. Income from swimming lessons are not included, as this will be on a seasonal basis (at R30,00 per half hour).

6: Megamed (1) – Failure

MARIUS PRETORIUS

Background

During 1991, Andre Visser, a pharmacist owning a family pharmacy that had been in the family for over 20 years, completed his Master's degree in Business Leadership through correspondence study. When Merf Swart, one of 11 other pharmacists in Pietersburg, suggested to him the benefits they could obtain by pooling their buying power, he was very interested. Discussing the idea, more and more potential benefits were identified. As they shared the idea with the other players, more people became interested.

Formation and role-players

Eventually, a totally new plan evolved. The vision developed into the establishment of a megapharmacy in Pietersburg, which is the provincial capital, with fair buying power from mainly the city but also from the surrounding rural areas. This megapharmacy was planned to have at least four pharmacists behind the prescription counter, other medical services such as a nurse for family matters and advice, a doctor on the premises, a hearing aid clinic, and more.

As the plan developed, more and more of the players decided to buy in. Being qualified in business management, Andre started to put a plan together with Merf, Chris du Toit and Henk Espach. With the business plan, building plans and financial projections they convinced the bank and a local property developer to erect a retail-specific building for them at a convenient location. It would be in the central business district with ample parking. Their financial exposure in fixed assets was approximately R4,8 million on opening day.

On 15 October 1995, Megamed Pharmacy had its grand opening. It consisted of the megafacility plus four satellite pharmacies selected from the previous dispensation, which would proceed under the new management structure. The auditors calculated each director's contribution based on the nett asset value contributed to the pool to determine shareholding percentages.

Personnel

The total complement of staff grew to just below 100. The 12 directors worked as pharmacists in the main outlet and on a rotation basis at the satellites. Other personnel included the head of operations (also a pharmacist) in charge of stock control and purchasing. There were several counter assistants in charge of the divisions, cashiers and approximately 60 packers, drivers, delivery staff, cleaners, etc.

Andre was elected as the first chief executive officer (CEO) for the initial two-year period. Megamed appointed a bookkeeper, who was known to them, to take control of the finances. The best of the administrative staff from the previous dispensation were also kept as debtors and creditors clerks.

During the second year they appointed an accountant as the financial manager, after a strong disagreement between the directors about the position and ability of the existing incumbent.

Henk, who specialised in audio equipment and hearing problems, ran the hearing aid clinic, as well as taking responsibility for the human resources function of the venture. A nurse was appointed to service the mothers and babies division as an additional service.

First-year operations

Megamed's stock operating system functioned on a just-in-time basis and was controlled by Chris du Toit, who ordered directly from one of three main suppliers: South African Druggists (SAD), United Pharmaceutical Distributors and

International Health Distributors, of which SAD was the biggest. Agreements were also entered into with other smaller suppliers, especially for perfume and other non-medical products.

Several problems developed, but regular planning sessions held afterhours assisted in overcoming most of them.

Within the first three months, the cash balance was stretched far to the negative side but it was nothing serious, as this was projected and planned for. However, two of the directors left. One of these directors could not "cash strip" his original outlet (as he had done before) and decided to opt out of the whole deal. The other one was asked to leave for reasons of dishonesty. The financial burden fell back on the ten directors who stayed in the deal.

Other issues suddenly came to the fore, which were not part of the planning. One month, Henk calculated theft and pilferage of perfumes of over R80 000. On investigation of the problem, he found it to be an inside job and fired the people involved. Unfortunately the damage was done, as there was no income for the stolen goods. The end result was further capital expenditure on security equipment, as well as monthly expenses for guards, both which were not originally planned for.

Andre, Merf, Chris and Henk formed an executive committee (Exco) to speed up decision making but Andre frequently had to make decisions of an operational nature on his own. A division started to develop between the CEO and the directors who were not part of the Exco, as they blamed him for being autocratic. Later this divide also entered the Exco. It led to

Andre withdrawing more and making decisions by himself more often. There were regular fights during and after the meetings, and the members started questioning the decision-making process.

A big problem was the payment speed of the medical aid funds. The average debtor days varied between 70 and 90 days, instead of the planned 45 days' maximum. One of the pharmacists was tasked to address this problem and soon an improvement was visible.

Signs of trouble

The first measurable sign of trouble was an increase in the overdraft every month despite a steady increase in sales.

From the start of operations there was a problem with irregular cash flow. The problem is a well-known phenomenon in the industry and is ascribed to the irregular and inconsistent payment by medical aid schemes.

Disagreement in the board about management decisions grew over time. There were big differences of opinion due to weak flow of information, slow and late statements, as well as distrust. One of the key issues was the financial manager's inability to manage the finances.

A new financial manager was appointed and one of his first tasks was to solve the cash flow problem. For that he required a cash flow projection. He immediately realised that the financial decisions were made on historical data instead of current figures. There was a marked improvement once the financial information became more user-friendly and current.

7: Megamed (2) – Turnaround

MARIUS PRETORIUS

Both Andre and Henk were friends with an independent local business consultant and occasionally shared their experiences with him, seeking advice. Early in the second year, he was asked to intervene in a conflict session of the board. At this meeting, the financial manager presented the financial situation, as well as a projected cash flow showing that no improvement was expected over the next six months, but thereafter the deficit started improving significantly. Break-even was projected within another 15 months.

A quick analysis of the opportunity was done, which showed the following:

- The economic model was positive as far as margin and sales demand were concerned, but the fixed cost structure was doubtful.
- The market and consumer projections were accurate, as was clear from the beginning, being based on the known volumes of the previous dispensation.
- The team and resources were at acceptable levels, especially with the appointment of the financial manager.
- The concept offering and positioning were already proven by the performance up to that point.
- There was a definite competitive advantage to be found in the buying power and market share.
- The projected financing seemed to be becoming positive although the current cash flow was bad, as could be deduced by the empty shelves.

From the opportunity, it was clear that despite entering the crisis phase of failure, turnaround was a strong possibility, given that the proposed actions could be implemented immediately. A decision to that extent was therefore made by the board and tasks were assigned to the different directors. During the meeting several specific decisions were made:

- To play open cards with the bank
- To improve the inventory to "almost out of stock" levels
- To immediately reduce fixed expenses of personnel cost by retrenchments
- To reduce payments to directors who were all optimally indebted by personal bonds, etc.
- To obtain credit from suppliers to maximum levels
- To reduce pilferage
- To improve sales by marketing
- To focus on the core business and freeze the peripheral issues for the time being, e.g. the mobile clinic for community services
- To investigate a sale of the business or partial buy-in by a willing partner
- To sell the building to a property developer
- To involve more directors in the operations
- To improve communication
- To let one of the directors take up the lecturing position he was offered at the local university, in order to supplement his income and reduce pressure on salaries

All the way, the bank stood by them while they implemented the action steps. There was still some blaming between members, but it seemed mostly due to the financial pressure the individual members were under.

8: Megamed (3) – The real outcome

MARIUS PRETORIUS

At the end of the first 18 months it seemed that Megamed was hovering between the trouble and crisis categories, with signs that the slide had been stopped and an expectation that a turnaround would be possible. Even the bank supported the process and actions taken.

Finally, while being at the point of selling Megamed to an unknown buyer through an agent, one of Megamed's suppliers (referred to as Company A hereafter) filed for bankruptcy so that it would be able to take over the sales of Megamed to ensure that its credit to Megamed was recovered.

With hindsight, it became clear that Company A had purposely extended credit to Megamed earlier to boost sales and to gain a financial grip on them. The aim was seemingly to take over Megamed and by doing so, report an additional R25 million to Company A's sales revenue. Approximately another 18 months after this episode, SAD was also divested, as it was perceived to be a "dog" by its parent company.

Immediately after filing for bankruptcy, Company A removed all the stock from the Megamed shop, as this was the only thing it had claim to.

The unknown buyer turned out to be Pharmarama, a company with branches in several of the big cities. It negotiated with the bank to buy the shelves and computer equipment. A developer was identified who bought the property and leased it to Pharmarama, requiring only a five-year lease agreement. Pharmarama was more interested in the main facility and was not even bothered about the satellites – it sold these.

Within 60 days Pharmarama reopened the same operation, reappointed most of the original key personnel and has proceeded successfully to this day. It has brought down the debtor days to under 40 days.

Some of the directors left for greener pastures and through selective buyouts, bought some of the satellite pharmacies for themselves from the bank. Henk is in charge of Pharmarama, while Andre bought back his old family shop and has opened another pharmacy in a recently developed shopping centre.

We proceed with a discussion of this case.

What role did the debt at start-up play?

Using nett asset value to determine the contribution of each participant meant that all directors could also contribute their debt to the new organisation. Fundamentally, and with hindsight, this could have been one of the contributing factors to the cash problem as debt also comes with interest payments. On paper, financing a venture seems the same whether done by equity or by debt, but it is better to finance with equity because of the impact of interest. However, the inclusion of individual debts was one of the negotiation tools to get everyone on board. Without the option of debt consolidation, half the members would probably not have participated and thereby rendered the project not viable in the first place. This should also have served as a warning sign of the risk involved. Further investigation later showed that a significant portion of the debt taken over on start-up turned out to be bad debt that could not be recovered. This is not a good way to start a venture where trust between director shareholders is paramount, is it?

Should a finger be pointed at the CEO for the failure?

Pharmarama, as it operates today, is almost exactly what was envisioned during start-up, showing that strategically the opportunity was a good one. The turnaround of Megamed was about to work when Company A pulled the plug. No one can be blamed for not realising the plan that Company A had for the hostile takeover. This plan was the ace in the deck that nobody knew about and it upset all the plans. Here is, however, a lesson to be learned – study the situation and strategies of your suppliers (and customers) for it can forewarn you to looming trouble that may eventually affect you.

A core mistake that was made was to start a venture of this magnitude with a bookkeeper in charge of the finances. Especially where everyone was weak in financial knowledge and background, this was a crucial position. This mistake is typical, and often occurs when appointments are made with a micro-mindset (cost saving) instead of a macro-mindset (the big picture). Looking back, this was probably the main reason for Megamed getting into trouble in the first place. The saying "penny wise and pound foolish" comes to mind. This is especially so when a financial manager must be appointed.

Should CEOs be allowed to take autocratic decisions?

Once a CEO is appointed, he must be given the authority, responsibility and accountability to make decisions. At the board meeting he then has to defend his actions based on the strategy that the board has accepted. The board can therefore question the strategy, but should not question the way he does things. Typically, there was a breakdown in communication that led to some distrust, and distrust has the ability to escalate quickly.

Is disagreement between directors good or bad?

Disagreement is never a bad thing – the problem is how one manages it. There should be differences of opinion but once these have been discussed and agreement has been reached, both parties should stick to the decision.

The difference between technical skills and management skills was obvious during this case. Several of the not-so-involved pharmacists were very unhappy that Andre, while being elected CEO, did not dispense medicine,

as this is what pharmacists do. This put additional pressure on him and probably distracted his focus from the daunting management issues. Apart from being qualified, experience in management is most valuable.

Further to this, it is not easy for a pharmacist to suddenly become a purchasing manager, stock controller, human resources manager and operations manager. The challenges are many, and are significantly different to those associated with running a smaller operation where the key focus is on professional client service. A venture of this magnitude of retailing requires a new attitude and motivation.

To ask for increased credit from one's suppliers is an option to improve cash flow. However, one must realise that it is for a short period only and can be detrimental to the venture's health. This is what Company A did. It seems to have been in trouble too and therefore wanted to increase sales. It gave more credit, reporting the sales to the parent company. When it pulled the plug on Megamed, there were very few options left. Timing was bad.

Having independent board members could have been beneficial to Megamed. For a small fee, it could have obtained good advice from properly selected non-executive members.

The question remains: could Megamed have been turned around at that point? The general consensus suggests that considering the following points could give a clear answer:

- Most ventures of this magnitude are cash negative after 18 months.

- They had their problems but the turnaround was just beginning.

- Inexperience about management almost landed them in trouble before they obtained professional advice.

- They ran out of time with negotiation of the sale.

- The impact of Company A's decision (for their own benefit) and their unwillingness to negotiate did not leave any options. Once the doors closed, everyone that owed Megamed money stopped paying, which aggravated the negative cash flow situation.

- The fact that Pharmarama is operating almost exactly as originally intended is proof of the probability that the plan could have worked.

- The opportunity analysis pointed to a great opportunity.

What could be learned from this case?

There are several valuable lessons to be learnt. Unfortunately, one can only do so with hindsight. Some of these lessons include:

- Bookkeepers are not financial managers. This is such a key function that one should appoint the best and not the cheapest.
- Management skills are crucial and differ between levels of operation.
- Taking over the debt of the individual directors was a mistake. Debt and equity are very different, even if they appear the same on the balance sheet.

- Clear decision-making structures are crucial for communication and trust.
- Trust is hard to earn and easy to squander.
- As so often happens, a good concept, opportunity, competitive advantage, strategy and business model were almost sunk by bad attitudes and definitely by cash flow problems.

Did the directors consider any of the harvesting options?

At the early stage of Megamed's life cycle, no one even thought of harvesting until they were presented with the option to sell to the unknown buyer. The management was pressured so much that no one was able to think about approaching one of the bigger suppliers to offer them an opportunity for forward integration.

9: Habakuk, the Cane King

WATSON LADZANI

The saying that *fortune favours the brave* seems to be so true for an intrepid entrepreneur who rose from rags to riches. This is the story of Habakuk Makgabutlane Shikoane, the man who was not only able to give birth to his entrepreneurial venture, but also grew it successfully over the years. Habakuk Cane Furniture (Pty) Limited had humble beginnings. Having started in the backyard of his aunt's home with only three employees, this cane furniture manufacturing venture grew to an extent where the factory once employed over 500 staff. This factory is continuing to contribute greatly to the rural and national economy of South Africa. The import of raw materials to such an insignificant rural community of the Limpopo province equally benefits the international community. Habakuk proved that success is not confined to any particular environment for an entrepreneur.

Who is Habakuk Shikoane?

Mr Habakuk Makgabutlane Shikoane is the founder-owner and director of Habakuk Cane Furniture (Pty) Limited. He is also known as the *Cane King of the North*.[1] He was born in 1928 in Sekhukhuneland, part of the former Lebowa homeland government. He attended school at a Lutheran missionary school in this area. He managed to pass Standard 6, which was a great achievement at that stage. As was the trend, he left for Johannesburg at an early age to seek employment. He was employed as a "tea boy" and later joined a cane manufacturing business. His cane basket weaving skills were self-taught from an early age. He used to make

baskets at school as part of his arts and crafts lessons. These baskets were made of *moretloa*, a certain type of tree that grows mainly in the Limpopo and North West provinces. At this stage he never thought of cane weaving as a career that would bring him fame and fortune. Habakuk later started his own cane manufacturing business in Soweto in 1958. He was forced by the laws of the country at that time to move to Hammanskraal. After 16 years of operation in Hammanskraal, Habakuk was again forced to move, this time to his home township, Lebowakgomo.

A few highlights of Habakuk's illustrious career include:

- The Institute of Marketing Management named him Man of the Year in 1978.
- The National Federated Chamber of Commerce (Nafcoc) honoured him as the Black Businessman of the Year in 1981.
- The Business Initiative Directions (BID), for renowned international recognition of companies committed to quality, technology and innovation, awarded Habakuk Cane Furniture the International World Quality Commitment award in year 2000. His products were the most amazing, durable and modern cane furniture ever made in South Africa.

Habakuk helped improve South Africa's image in the United States. His photograph was generously displayed in a large advertisement in the *Christian Science Monitor* and other American newspapers, along with details of how he rose to become a "black capitalist". At the age of 43 he owned the largest cane furniture plant in Africa.[2]

Habakuk lives in Lebowakgomo with his wife, Nellie, and five children – two sons and three daughters. Habakuk speaks proudly of his children who studied in the United States and England.

---

1 Mashabela, H. 1977. Lebowa cane king: village school task brought him success. *Africa Star Newspaper*, 21 November.
2 *The Star*, 1971. America told of SA's "black capitalist". 20 October.

How Habakuk spotted and acted on the opportunity

One day, when Habakuk was working as a tea boy he saw a big truck passing by, carrying a load of cane chairs and baskets. "Transvaal Wicker Works" was written on it, which attracted his attention. He followed the truck and went where it stopped. He told the men that he was looking for a job, and they asked him if he could make baskets. He asked them what kind of basket they wanted him to make. The first basket he made was a bread basket, which he finished in one hour. He then made an egg basket with a handle and later a flower basket. His expertise in making these baskets landed him a job. He was told to come to work the following day. Habakuk devised a way to free himself from his current job as a tea boy. When he reached his work station he started crying. When his employer asked what was wrong, his answer was that his mother was very sick and he needed to go home. His employer gave him five shillings towards his trip. This amount was enough to pay for his transport to and from home. He never came back.

Habakuk started working at the Transvaal Wicker Works factory the following day. His passion for making baskets was rejuvenated. Habakuk told his new employers that he wanted to show them one or two things about baskets. He was given raw materials and a small chair to sit on and started to make baskets – one after another. The more baskets he made, the more his employers were impressed with his work. The factory also made grass chairs. When they started with piecework, Habakuk could make more products than all of his fellow workers at the factory. Even though he had been working at the factory for only few months, he could show all his colleagues at the factory how to make baskets. He was promoted to supervisor of the whole factory within only six months. It was at this stage, young as he was, that he could afford to buy trousers and a pair of shoes. His bosses liked Habakuk because of his hard work, his skill and the fact that he could speak better English than most of his colleagues. He was the one who would speak with customers whenever they visited the factory. Habakuk also learnt a number of things at the factory, and improved and excelled in his career. Habakuk started a side

job – he manufactured cane products at home, indirectly being in competition with his boss.[3]

Starting and growing on his own

Habakuk's motivation to go on his own

Habakuk started to attend a night school offered by the African National Congress (ANC), while he was still working for the basket factory. Habakuk was put in the second grade, then third grade and soon he was in the fourth grade as a student. He came to understand, among other things, the French Revolution, the Spanish Revolution and the Russian revolution, and knew about Stalin, the Treaty of Versailles and World War II. Habakuk, together with other ANC members, started selling the paper written by the ANC called *Inkululeko*, meaning "freedom". Although they were not paid for doing this, they were very happy because they were given free education. Attending the night school contributed to Habakuk's career in a number of ways. He could, amongst other things, understand why certain things were happening and how he could help his own people. Over and above this enlightenment, Habakuk was not a complacent person. He believed that nothing can be achieved if a person is satisfied. Habakuk firmly believed that a person should be dissatisfied with what he is, then something will start happening.

Operating in Soweto

In 1958 Habakuk told his employers that he was going to start out on his own. They were very disappointed and tried to convince him to stay, even promising to increase his salary. But Habakuk had made up his mind to be on his own. He started with three people in the backyard of his aunt's home in Orlando East. He later bought his own house in the Dube township and started working from home. He worked very hard, sometimes until ten o'clock at night, until he built a factory in Orlando West. By 1960, his £6 000 factory was fully paid for, he had stock of cane furniture valued at £2 000 and a further £2 500's worth of materials,

3 Raboroko, J. 1989. A millionaire who started in his own backyard. *Sowetan*, 2 November.

all paid for. The business was booming. He bought brand new cars for cash – an Opel Kadett and a four-ton Chevrolet. His wife, Nellie, was in charge of the bookkeeping and clerical work. Habakuk's business had an annual turnover of about £30 000. An agency firm in each province marketed his products.[4]

It was in 1960 that the government told him that he could no longer run a manufacturing factory there. He was ordered either to go to the homelands or they would close him down. He was promised help on condition that he moved to the homelands. Habakuk chose to move to Hammanskraal in 1961 rather than face closure. He had already employed 50 people in only three years of working in Soweto. Most of his employees were, however, recruited from his home village in Sekhukhuneland.

The move to Hammanskraal

In 1961 Habakuk established his business in Hammanskraal, an all-African town about 20 kilometres north of Pretoria. The Bantu Investment Corporation (BIC) put up a factory for him and gave him a loan. Habakuk started operating from these premises. He had 180 employees by 1970. His business grew from strength to strength. His monthly turnover was around R100 000, from a 2 500 square metre factory, employing 300 people by the year 1976.

Habakuk turned his attention to the retail trade. He built the Afrisport Shopping Centre in 1970. In this shopping centre he had a ladies' boutique, a shoe shop and a men's boutique. He did not want to sell food, lest he should drive the small food shops out of business. The shopping centre was built with his own capital derived from the cane furniture factory.

In the late 1970s, Habakuk had a clash with Mr Lucas Mangope, then president of Bophuthatswana. The clash was on political grounds. This led Habakuk to move back to his roots, Lebowakgomo, 40 km southeast of Pietersburg (now Polokwane), in 1978.

Business in Lebowakgomo

Habakuk started erecting a R900 000, 8 000 square metre cane factory at Lebowakgomo in

1977, the capital of the former Lebowa government. He established his own building company to do the work in order to save on building costs. He had his own cement brickyard to manufacture bricks for the project.

Habakuk finally started operating from his homeground, working with and among his own people. His desire has always been to contribute to one of the most important things in life: *bread on the table of my people*. This makes him feel good, as the Limpopo province is characterised by starvation and hunger.

Habakuk had big dreams at Lebowakgomo. He planned to diversify into other fields, including erecting a R2 000 000 shopping centre comprising a restaurant, furniture store, supermarket, butchery and bottle store. He further planned for a cinema and commercial school for training typists, secretaries and bookkeepers. Included in his plans were also to erect houses for his married employees and a hostel for other workers. His motivation was that the residential area of Lebowakgomo was too far from his factory. Most of Habakuk's dreams came true.

Habakuk continued to expand into other exciting ventures over and above all the enterprises he established. The following are some of the businesses he started: Kgabong Construction and Window Frames; Gateway Chips, which makes corn chips; and Northern Feed Manufacturers (Pty) Ltd, which produces cattle feed and has a feedlot to fatten cattle of farmers in the region. This business employed 455 people at one stage and had a turnover of about R13 million a year. Some of these businesses have, however, closed down. Habakuk needed to have only enough work that he could manage. He felt that adding more ventures would impede him from focusing on his cane furniture business.

Habakuk currently owns the following businesses: Habakuk Cane Furniture factory; an HCF outlet in Polokwane; Kgabong Constructions; Shakes Bottle Store, Bar Lounge, Restaurant and Motors (Winners Service Station – Toyota Dealership); and Afrisport General Dealer and Butchery. He also owns 50 houses that are rented out to his employees.

The move to Lebowakgomo affected his cane manufacturing business to a certain extent. He reckons that "transport costs are high and I no longer have direct access to my main markets

4 The Staff Reporter. 1970. Hard work puts him at top. Now he's worth R250 000. *The Star*, 7 August.

on the Reef, Pretoria and the Vaal Triangle".[5] In spite of the challenges of having moved, his cane furniture business is doing reasonably well. His factory once employed 550 people had a turnover of R250 000 a month.

Due to sanctions, scarcity of raw materials and the high cost of transport, Habakuk has downsized. His staff complement currently stands at 150. However, he hopes to start exporting to international markets, aiming to export 10 to 15 containers of Habakuk Cane Furniture per month. More people in the area should get employment as the business expands.

Although HCF never had a formal organisational structure with fully fledged departmental heads, Habakuk managed to take the factory to higher levels. The factory has supervisors and administrative clerks that help him to run the business. Bookkeeping functions are outsourced to a consulting firm that checks the books on a weekly basis.

The products

Habakuk became a household name from as early as the 1970s. Designs from his factory were seen in houses and hotels. Habakuk Cane Furniture (Pty) Ltd manufactures furniture ranging from dining room tables and chairs, kitchen chairs, lounge couches and chairs, television stands, coffee tables, headboards and dressing tables, to bar counters with bar chairs.

The main raw material, cane, is imported mainly from Indonesia, Malaysia, Hong Kong and the Philippines. These materials are called *rattan* in such countries. Other materials like nails, sealant and varnish are South African products.

There was a time when business was very good – he had nine trucks and every day a truck would be loading and delivering.

The secret of success

Habakuk is proud to say that he trained his staff to manufacture quality products. He indicates that quality is the standard he has lived by for many years. Apart from training his staff, he does quality checks on the products as he does not want to compromise in this area. He values quality so much that even when he starts

exporting, he reckons that he will keep himself more involved in the factory and get a marketing organisation to do the sales. "I must be on the production side so that my products can be of top quality all the time". Habakuk says that the biggest strategy in manufacturing is quality. He pointed out that if one can produce a quality product, that product is half-sold.

Habakuk is on record sharing the secret of his success to BBC radio listeners: "I feel I owe it all to hard work, courage, determination and, occasionally, a little luck," he said on the "World Tonight" programme.[6] A few days before this broadcast, the same paper indicated that hard work had put him on top.[7]

Cane furniture market

Habakuk believes in the power of marketing his products. He started by visiting several stores throughout the country to introduce himself and the products that he manufactures. He supplies mainly furniture stores and private individuals that visit his factory. He has big stores, departmental stores and furniture stores buying from him. Furniture stores like Lubners, Geen & Richards, Bradlows, Ellerines Furnishers and the Beares Brothers groups are still buying regularly.

Secret for sustaining suppliers

Habakuk has learnt over the years that one of the most important things that big retailers will always look at is the supply that one gives them. He indicated that if one is able to give them a good supply and one's deliveries are good, they will always be a customer.

The export market

Habakuk is seriously contemplating penetrating the international market. His goal is to travel extensively into Europe and the United States in order to sell his products there. He reckons

5 Cohen, M. 1981. The Shikwana story – backyard to success. *The Citizen*, 8 October.
6 *The Star* Bureau. 1970. African Mr Success tells all. *The Star*, 12 August.
7 The Staff Reporter. 1960. He's Rand native "tycoon": "Country boy" now has £30 000-a-year factory. *The Star*, 29 June.

that South Africa is closer to Western Europe and the United States than Asia is. He is also aware of the effect on price and delivery that this move will have. He desires to compete with the Asian manufacturers, confident of the quality of his products.

Conclusion

Habakuk is continuing to contribute greatly to the local, national and international economy. He has helped curb unemployment and brought businesses and modern facilities to that rural community. Habakuk planned to start exporting in 2003.

Habakuk is an entrepreneur par excellence, a true star of black economic empowerment. However, he had a long and difficult road to walk to get to where he is today. Government restrictions on black people's movement were his major drawback to reaching greater heights. When he moved from Hammanskraal to Lebowakgomo, he was never compensated for the huge investments he made in that area.

Habakuk has only one constraint which he cannot do anything about – his age. He is over 70 now. Although he hopes to continue to be strong until the age of 85, he is doing something about the succession of his business. His children are not into rural business. Habakuk plans to sell a 50 per cent shareholding to his employees, based on their wages and skills. This move is hoped not only to make his employees proud co-owners, but also to motivate them to produce even more furniture for the export market.

10: How open is this window?

WATSON LADZANI

Rural entrepreneurs – who are they?

Who said opportunities present themselves only in urban areas? Is it not a misconception that rural communities cannot offer anything of economic value? Is it not unfortunate that those who believe these myths migrate to urban areas where they subject themselves to appalling conditions, including being hobos? There are some rural entrepreneurs who are breaking the rules: providing a better life for rural people, curbing unemployment and reducing levels of poverty in these areas.

These are the people who go beyond the ordinary – they are creative and innovative, with ideas that make a difference in their communities. They identify gaps in the market and fill them. With all the odds facing these communities, these entrepreneurs forge ahead to success whether or not they have access to credit, markets, information or appropriate training – not even poor infrastructure can stop these vision-minded entrepreneurs. One example of a rural entrepreneur is Mr John Ramaano Sigidi, who runs a very promising funeral undertaking enterprise in the rural area of Venda (Zwavhavhili, Tshifulanani, Lwamondo), in the Limpopo province.

How rural is the Limpopo province?

The Limpopo province is one of the nine provinces of South Africa and has a population of about 4,9 million. Almost 4,7 million (i.e. 97 per cent) of these people are Africans. This province has the largest rural population (89 per cent) compared with the other eight provinces. Unemployment is the second highest in all the provinces (46 per cent).[1] This province is one of the poorest and is the worst affected by the divisions of the past.

The Human Development Index and the household income (55,8 per cent of the workforce earn less than R6 500 per annum) are the lowest of all provinces in South Africa. The public sector is the single most important provider of employment opportunities. In 1993, the most important sectors for employment were provincial government (36,7 per cent), agriculture (21 per cent) and mining (9 per cent). Some 32 per cent of the population still live in traditional dwellings, as opposed to 18 per cent nationally. While 23 per cent of the national population still use wood for cooking, Limpopo's statistics are 64 per cent. Only 18 per cent of households have water in their dwellings, as opposed to 45 per cent nationally.[2]

Is it not amazing that this bleak picture does not tarnish the verve, vigour and zeal of a real entrepreneur? These are the people who should be nourished, developed and get all the support they need because they are helping to turn the poor rural communities into a haven for the unemployed, poor and destitute. Mr John Sigidi is one such entrepreneur who spotted an opportunity in the rural Far North region of the Limpopo province.

Who is John Sigidi?

Mr John Ramaano Sigidi was born in Lwamondo in Venda, Limpopo province. He started school at Maphuphe Primary School. He proceeded to Lwamondo Secondary School, where he passed Standard 8 (called the Junior Certificate then). John grew up doing odd jobs in his rural community. He used to be hired to dig pit

1 Statistics South Africa (SSA). 2000. *Statistics in brief.* Pretoria: SSA.
2 Ladzani, M.W. 2001. *Small business development in South Africa under the majority rule.* Paper presented at the 14th Conference of the Small Enterprise Association of Australia and New Zealand, Wellington, New Zealand, 13-15 September.

toilets, build places for storing mealies (*dulu* in Venda) and thatch roofs of mostly huts in the local community. This led him to study building and construction at Finyazwanda Technical College (currently known as Techniven). Upon completion of his vocational training in 1972, he started his own building construction business. He won tenders to build community schools and residential houses. John did his work with excellence. The government officials from the Department of Works were impressed with his work when they inspected it.

John was finally recruited to work for the Department of Works. The government officials were happy to work with someone who could express himself well in English and Afrikaans. John even understood the building industry well – he could read and interpret building plans and measurements. John worked as a foreman, supervising people who were employed long before he joined the government service. His competitive advantage was his skill in reading measurements, building, and speaking English and Afrikaans better than his colleagues. He was involved with a number of government building projects in Venda at the time.

While working for the government service, John was saddened by the fact that some people he was working with lost their jobs when he joined the service. He tried to create something that could earn these people a living. He started a musical band in 1986, with the aim of assisting talented unemployed youth. Prosperity Band became so popular that it was invited to perform in many places and at many functions, including weddings. Its focus was gospel music.

When his mother passed away in 1990, John had a dream. The details of how he should build a last home for her were thoroughly explained to him in the dream. Although this dream was strange both to him and his relatives, he decided to follow it. John built a wall inside and right around the grave. When people came to bury his mother, they marvelled at his skill and creativity. Some people criticised this approach, but many admired it. Moreover, his Prosperity Band also sang at the funeral service – something that was unheard of at the time. After the funeral service, there was talk both for and against what had happened at the service throughout the neighbouring villages.

A window of opportunity opening for John

The idea that was conceived in a dream gave birth to a highly successful funeral undertaking business. People who were at his mother's funeral desired the same for their loved ones. From the very first week, the orders started pouring in. The requests were for John to come and build a "last home" for their loved ones as he did for his mother. People wanted their loved ones to be laid to rest in a decent and dignified manner. By the third week, more people were coming with similar requests. They even demanded that they should be charged for the services he was rendering. Although John never wanted to make a business out of his services, he was compelled to do so, due to the high demand. His initial fees were R750 per customer. The market pressurised him to increase his fees but he managed to overcome this temptation for some time.

John could not cope with the demand for the funeral services required. He started hiring and training staff to help him build the last homes for his customers. He managed to convince his staff that the business of building graves is unusual, and that they should not be ashamed but must feel proud about it. In 1993 he decided to add to his existing business another component – erecting tombstones – and therefore he partnered with a local tombstone manufacturer. While John was building a wall inside the grave, his partner would be manufacturing a tombstone. John soon learnt how to erect tombstones. His staff was trained to erect tombstones immediately after the burial. His motivation for learning this was to render a good service. The partnership, however, did not last long enough. John had to get his supplies via a number of middlemen that made him pay higher prices. The business was run informally until 1995, when John succumbed to the pressure to start a funeral undertaking business.

Growth of the business

John started conducting a thorough market research of the funeral undertaking industry. He wanted to find out what the people's real needs in this respect were, and how he could meet those needs. A number of gaps were identified and John used these to position his business. Chief amongst these gaps was the shortage of hearses and equipment to lower the coffin into the grave, as well as the waiting time at the graveyard for the burial service to be completed. The belief among Africans is that all the burial rights must be completed in their presence. These findings propelled John to think big: he would have a fleet of cars and enough equipment in order to reduce the waiting period and render an excellent and speedy service. He honestly desired to provide an excellent service to all his customers. Meeting these goals would not be easy in terms of the huge capital outlay needed for this venture. John realised the enormity of the challenge awaiting him and was determined to make his way to success.

John started to research how to set up and run a mortuary. This information included the legal implications of his move, as well as greater financial requirements. Fortunately, he could raise the required capital from his savings from working in the government service and the informal funeral services he was rendering.

The building project started in 1997, after John received the news that his application had been successful. The business was registered as a close corporation, Tshitshite Funeral Undertakers. John launched an official opening of the mortuary at the end of October 1998.

He was able to buy three hearses and equipment for lowering coffins at the time of opening business. Since the business started, there has not been a single weekend that they have not been conducting a funeral. The other popular trend amongst Africans is to bury their dead on weekends, as most people who should attend are working during the week. Africans lead a communal life – they believe in sharing their joys and sorrows. Funeral services are therefore highly regarded in many African communities. Masses of people gather together before and on the burial day to pay their last respects to the deceased. This function has huge economic implications. There are, however, contingency plans in place for such sad events, and food is served, whether or not the family is poor.

Quality services

Tshitshite Funeral Undertakers renders a full range of services to the bereaved family. The package includes erection of the grave, provision of a coffin or casket, a tombstone, transport of the corpse and the bereaved family, and burial. The money generated is used for buying more cars and equipment in order to improve on the services. John does not believe in buying on credit. All the capital goods in the business were bought for cash; some of the equipment was bought through a lay-bye system. The business currently has a fleet of over 60 cars. There are 48 hearse vehicles, trucks and vans that are used in the running of the business. Five of these vehicles are limousines, costing in excess of R350 000 each. Some of these vehicles are on stand-by for emergencies so that no service should be compromised due to shortage of transport. There is a workshop or the premises that services the fleet of cars.

The infrastructure of many rural areas is very poor. Many of the roads are gravel, and are slippery and muddy during rainy seasons. John also bought 4×4 vehicles that are used in such weather conditions.

Tshitshite Funeral Undertakers conducts 30 funeral services on average per week. With such equipment, vehicles and manpower, the business always manages to deliver quality service.

Staff complement

When the business officially and formally started in November 1998, there were 13 staff members. John prefers to call them "service providers" rather than workers. His understanding is that there is dignity in such a description.

In 2000, when the tombstone factory was started, the business had about 30 staff members. This number grew with the business and in 2001, 65 employees were registered. The employees have, amongst other things, a pension fund, provident fund and Unemployment Insurance Fund benefits. There was a huge celebration in April 2001 over this achievement. Apart from many other people who attended, there were up to 30 chiefs from different villages. The attendance of these chiefs is a milestone for the business, as they represent their constituencies. In April 2002, the business had registered 80 employees. There are currently 85 full-time employees and 90 casual labourers. John runs his business along acceptable management principles. His current organisational structure is as follows:

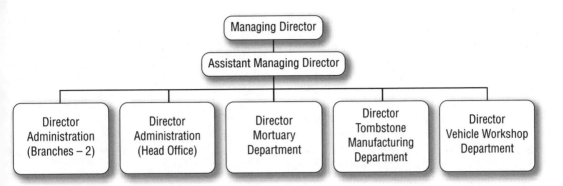

John is the founder and managing director of this enterprise. His staff consists of an assistant managing director, five directors, several supervisors, a bookkeeper, typist, frontline staff (receptionists), mortuary controllers, chapel designers and pastors, tombstone manufacturers, drivers, mechanics and panelbeaters. The business has two branches – at Madombidzha and Tshilwavhusiku villages – and are managed by a director.

Operations

The whole chain of funeral operations takes a great deal of effort and time. Once the bereaved family has decided on what needs to be done and how much they can afford, Tshitshite Funeral Undertakers takes over. The staff is sent to the graveside during the week, sometimes as early as Tuesday or Wednesday, to start preparing the grave. This is where the built-in wall is erected and plastered right around the grave. At the same time, the chosen tombstone is being manufactured.

Clients are encouraged to choose the type of service they can afford from a range of services. Standard funeral services cost between R6 000 and R7 000, and medium-range services are between R12 000 and R15 000. There are also high-class services for those who can afford them. These are classified as follows: Class one costs between R15 000 and R20 000, class two between R20 000 and R30 000, and class three between R30 000 and R50 000. Tshitshite Funeral Undertakers prides itself in the type of quality services it offers.

Fridays are very busy days for the staff of Tshitshite Funeral Undertakers. They hardly get any sleep due to a number of activities that are being organised for the "big day" – Satur-

day, the day on which most of the customers conduct the burial. The building staff will be finalising the grave and erecting the tombstone, at times even into the early hours of Saturday morning. The frontline staff will be preparing for the evening service with the bereaved families and their relatives. There are a series of services where the bereaved come and pay their last respects the night before. This is done in order to avoid wasting time and the "drama" on the day of the burial that some emotional people display. There is a chapel specifically arranged for this purpose. For those who desire a video recording, arrangements are also made for the occasion.

When people come for burial say, on Saturday morning, they find everything ready. Tshitshite staff are ready with all the required equipment and materials. Their work is very minimal at this stage. After the minister of religion has conducted the burial service, the funeral service workers spend only 10 to 15 minutes to lower the coffin and close the opening at the side of the grave. This speedy service is a record that many competitors will have difficulty in matching. Other funeral undertakers take up to three hours to conduct their funeral services and erect the tombstone. This is the gap that competitors are still battling to fill. John realised that it is difficult and tiring for customers to wait this long in the graveyard.

Strategies for growth

John held an official opening ceremony for his business in October 1998 and celebrated its first anniversary in 1999. This function attracted many local people, including chiefs and headmen. While people were wining and dining, celebrating the opening of the mortuary (something people usually associate with fear), John was busy with research. To him the gathering was yet another opportunity to find out what further needs the potential customers have. The motive was to win the people's hearts and confidence, and to implement the finding in order to improve on the service.

The idea of developing a product related to the services they were rendering was born from the research findings. There was a great need for establishing a tombstone manufacturing plant on the premises. Relevant information in this regard was sought. The tombstone manufacturing plant started operating in January 2000. Granite stones are ordered from Brits. The bereaved come in and either choose a tombstone from the existing ones or have it manufactured according to their choice of design. This is the business's competitive edge, and unique designs are possible.

Over and above these services rendered and products manufactured, Tshitshite Funeral Undertakers also provides coffins and caskets of all kinds. This enterprise has become a "one-stop shop" for bereaved families. The moment a case arises, John and his service providers are only a phone call away. They collect corpses from anywhere in the country and have their mortuary available when the family arranges for a burial service. There are a variety of coffins and caskets on display on the premises. John can order the type of casket required if the desired choice is not in stock.

John is not threatened by competition. His competitive advantage is the high-quality service that Tshitshite Funeral Undertakers provides. John also boasts of ever-changing styles and approaches in rendering the services.

Tshitshite Funeral Undertakers even goes as far to provide free services to selected desperate and needy families. These are people who have lost loved ones through tragedies like fire and motor accidents. After thorough investigation and assessment of the situation, some of these people receive free services. Even in such cases, the services are still of a high quality.

On other occasions, John provides his services on credit. This facility is not used indiscriminately. All the required information about the family is gathered in order to minimise bad debts and doubtful payments.

For how long will this window stay open?

Many entrepreneurship scholars allude to the fact that a "window of opportunity" must be opening and remain open long enough for one to make it in business. An entrepreneur must seize this opportunity while the window is opening.[3]

John seized his opportunity at the right time. This window is open for Tshitshite Funeral Undertakers and is continuing to open even wider. With the necessary nurturing, this business has the potential for further growth, as John's services are sought after also outside Venda.

Apart from establishing branches at selected areas, John is seriously thinking of franchising his services. Like any other industry, Tshitshite Funeral Undertakers will reach a maturity stage. The challenge is for John to develop entrepreneurial and managerial skills among his staff to keep the window of opportunity open long enough.

3 Timmons, J.A. 1999. *New venture creations: entrepreneurship for the 21st century*, 4th revised ed. Chicago: Irwin.

Index

A

acceptance credits 150
achievement 30
acquisition (*see also* takeover) 100, 248, 296
advertising fee, franchise 197
advertising practice, franchise 202
advisory board, family business 187
age, entrepreneur 29
agreements, exclusive 254
alliances 254, 297, 319, 320, 321, 322
asset-based evaluation 218
attitude, entrepreneur 16, 264
auctions
    Dutch 339
    English 338
    first-price sealed-bid 339
    reverse first-price sealed-bid 339

B

balance sheet evaluation 218
bank credit 149
banking system (*see also* commercial banks)
    314
Basic Conditions of Employment Act 126
behaviourists 6
bill of exchange 150
break-even analysis 94
business
    failure (*see also* failure) 260–289
    growth 234
    incubation 169
    legal forms of 114
    opportunity (*see also* opportunities) 20,
      47–74
    support 165, 166
business, buyout 212
    advantages of 213
    determining the value of 218
    disadvantages of 213
    evaluating available businesses 215, 217
    finding a business to buy 214
    negotiation process 222
    traps to avoid 224
Business Partners 173
business plan 20, 56, 90–110, 353
    definition of 90
    format and layout of 91

    franchise 252
    Internet as a tool for 101
    problems when drawing up 101, 102
    reasons for drawing up 90
    selecting the most appropriate 96
    start-up 134–146
    types of 97
Business Practices Committee 201
buyout 212–228, 297

C

capital cow 298
capital goods, cost of 315
capitalised earnings method, of evaluation 221
cash flow 268, 270
    irregular 269, 270
    visibility of 271
client service 18
climatic conditions 137
close corporation 115, 116, 153
commercial banks 173
    ABSA 174
    First National Bank 174
    NedEnterprise 174
    Standard Bank 173
commitment, entrepreneur 17
companies 154
Compensation Fund 123
competition 18, 59, 128, 216, 296
Competition Act 128, 249
Competition Board 202
Competition Commission 128
competitive advantage 85, 270, 318
Consumer Code for Franchising 201
consumer protection 128
contracts 124, 300
control, internal 142
copyright 59, 118
core business 284
cost
    and cash 284
    leadership 246
    structure 79
costs
    establishment 93
    transport 315
    variable 281